BY THE EDITORS OF CONSUMER GUIDE®

WHOLE HOUSE CATALOG

REVISED AND UPDATED

FIRESIDE

A Fireside Book
Published by Simon and Schuster
New York

Contents

Copyright © 1981 by Publications International, Ltd.
All rights reserved
including the right of reproduction
in whole or in part in any form
without written permission from:
Louis Weber, President
Publications International, Ltd.
3841 W. Oakton Street
Skokie, Illinois 60076
Permission is never granted for commercial purposes.
A Fireside Book
Published by Simon and Schuster
A Division of Gulf & Western Corporation
Simon & Schuster Building
Rockefeller Center
1230 Avenue of the Americas
New York, New York 10020
SIMON and SCHUSTER and colophon are trademarks
of Simon & Schuster
Manufactured in the United States of America
1 2 3 4 5 6 7 8 9 10 Pbk.

Library of Congress Cataloging in Publication Data
Main entry under title: Whole house catalog.

(A Fireside book)
Includes index.
1. Dwellings—Maintenance and repair—Amateurs'
manuals.   2. Dwellings—Remodeling—Amateurs'
manuals.   I. Consumer guide.
TH4817.3.W5   1981   643'.7   81-82238
                                    AACR2
ISBN 0-671-43640-6 Pbk.

COVER PHOTOS: Brooks & VanKirk ILLUSTRATIONS: C. A. Moberg

The Editors of CONSUMER GUIDE® and PUBLICATIONS
INTERNATIONAL, LTD., have made every effort to ensure the
accuracy and reliability of the information, instructions, and
directions in this book; however, this is in no way to be
construed as a guarantee, and The Editors of CONSUMER
GUIDE® and PUBLICATIONS INTERNATIONAL, LTD., are not
liable in case of misinterpretations of the directions, human
error, or typographical mistakes.

Contents

Contents

The Whole House Catalog

Are you troubled by a clogged toilet, a damp basement, a defective light switch, a leaky roof? Would you like to install an outdoor electrical outlet, a wood parquet floor, a roof ventilator, or wall-to-wall carpeting? Do you want to insulate your attic or basement, weatherstrip your windows, or paint, panel, or paper a room? You'll find out how to do all of these tasks—and many, many more—in the WHOLE HOUSE CATALOG, a new, updated guide to curing the ailments, large and small, that can afflict your home.

Even if you've never done anything more difficult than changing a light bulb, the WHOLE HOUSE CATALOG will show you how to fix, maintain, and improve just about everything in and around your home. Simple, step-by-step instructions, a list of tools and materials required for each job, and clear illustrations carry you from start to finish—whether your project is a simple repair or a new installation, a quick fix-it task, or a from-the-ground-up job.

Whatever your home needs, the WHOLE HOUSE CATALOG can help you, with easy-to-follow information on plumbing, electrical work, appliances, heating and cooling, saving energy, painting, brick and masonry work, floors, walls, ceilings, doors, windows, and much more besides. The basic information is all here—and there's a lot more here than the basics, too. In a special chapter on saving energy, for example, the WHOLE HOUSE CATALOG tells you how to install storm windows and doors, insulation, and weatherstripping. It also shows you how to caulk and how to apply sun control film on windows. There's important safety information and cleaning instructions on wood- and coal-burning stoves as well.

But what really sets the WHOLE HOUSE CATALOG apart from other repair and maintenance manuals is that it also recommends brand-name tools and materials for the projects throughout the book, and products that can make your home more comfortable and more efficient. In the chapter on appliances, for instance, you'll find innovative and exciting devices to help you save money and energy, like power factor controllers that deliver only the minimum amount of power appliances need to operate efficiently. Elsewhere, you'll discover a master control system that lets you control lights and appliances from a central location; a programmable light/dimmer switch; an electronic air cleaner for forced-air heating and cooling systems that filters air throughout your home; set-back thermostats that select the proper temperatures at the times you have programmed into them—and more of the best and latest products the new technology has to offer.

The products and tools listed in the WHOLE HOUSE CATALOG are all good ones, chosen for reliability, efficiency, all-around usefulness, and wide availability. You can find most of them, or products of comparable quality, at your nearby hardware store, lumberyard, or home center. In case you can't track down a tool or product, the WHOLE HOUSE CATALOG gives you a complete directory of manufacturers or distributors—a combination that makes this the one do-it-yourself book no homeowner should be without. Start working with it today, and take the first step toward putting your whole house in top condition.

Your Home's Plumbing System

THE PLUMBING system in your house or apartment is not as complicated as it might seem. Plumbing depends on three basic things: gravity, water pressure, and the fact that water seeks its own level to work. And, there are only three things that can go wrong with plumbing: Pipes or connections can spring a leak; pipes or drains can become clogged; or valves or fixtures can leak. Sinks, lavatories, tubs, showers, and toilets are *fixtures*.

Your home has two separate but interdependent plumbing subsystems. The plumbing supply system supplies water under pressure through relatively small pipes—usually no larger than ¾ inch in diameter. The other is the drainage subsystem, which drains water and debris. The drainage subsystem, however, is not under pressure; it operates by means of gravity. These drainpipes are larger than water supply pipes—usually 1½ to 4 inches in diameter.

The Water Supply Subsystem

Your home's water supply is delivered from a public utility or deep well under pressure through a water main; if your water supply is a deep well, a pump provides the pressure. If your water is supplied by a utility company, there will be a water meter located

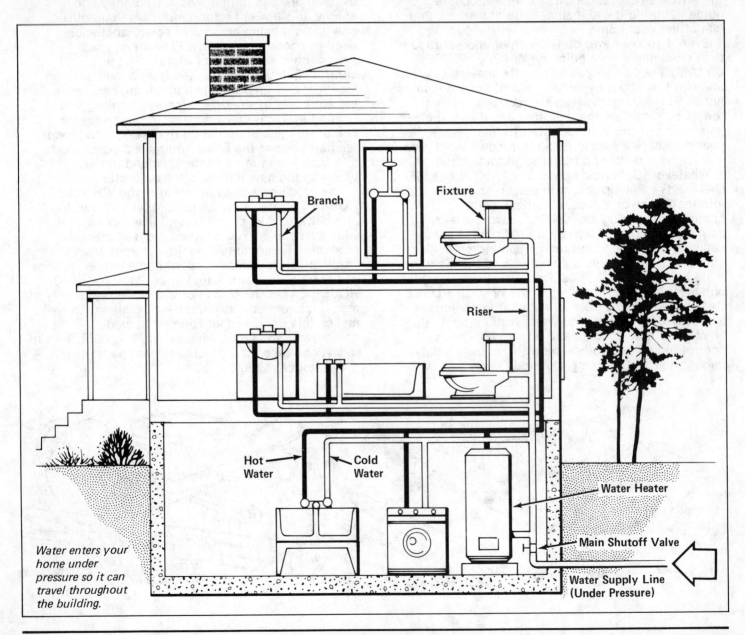

Water enters your home under pressure so it can travel throughout the building.

near the point where the water supply line enters your property. The meter may be inside or outside the house, or it may be underground and reached by means of a metal access cover. The meter records the amount of water supplied. If your water supply is a well, there will be no meter.

Somewhere near the point the water supply line enters your home—usually near the water meter—is a main shutoff valve, which can completely shut off the water supply for the entire house. If you haven't already done so, locate this valve and tag it to indicate which way it should be turned to shut it; this will help anyone who needs to stop the water flow quickly during a plumbing emergency.

The water supply is cold water. It's piped directly to all faucets and other devices that use unheated water through the cold water main. One part of the cold water system carries water to the heater. From the water heater, a hot water main carries heated water to fixtures and appliances that use hot water. Generally, there's a hot water main shutoff valve at the water heater so the hot water supply for the entire house can be turned off.

Water supply pipes to individual fixtures are called *branches*. Pipes that run vertically, to upper floors for example, are called *risers*.

The Drainage Subsystem

Drains operate by gravity. These pipes pitch, or angle, downward so that waste can flow into a sewer. To function properly, the drainage subsystem needs air vents, traps, and clean-outs.

Vents are vertical pipes that stick out of the roof of the house and allow air to enter the drainage subsystem. Usually, a vent is an extension of the soil stack, or main drainpipe. The introduction of air pressure through the vent and into the drain helps the waste to flow. It also prevents a syphoning action at traps located under sinks, bathtubs, toilets, and other fixtures.

For example, the curved pipe under a kitchen sink is a trap. When the sink basin is emptied, the water flows out with enough force to push through the trap and into the drainpipe, but enough water is left in the trap to provide a seal that prevents

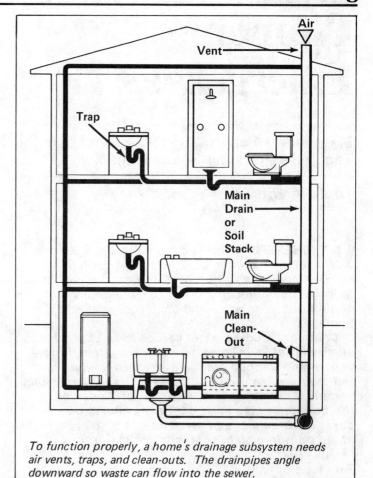

To function properly, a home's drainage subsystem needs air vents, traps, and clean-outs. The drainpipes angle downward so waste can flow into the sewer.

dangerous sewer gas from backing up into the house. Each fixture drain must have a trap. Toilets have built-in traps.

A clean-out is an opening in a drainpipe or trap that is installed at points of directional change to allow access for cleaning out blockages. The clean-out opening is closed by a threaded or locking plug or cap.

These are the basics of plumbing. Because most plumbing is hidden in the walls, under floors, and beneath the ground, plumbing may seem mysterious, but it's a simple and logical system.

Use Foam Insulation to Seal Pipe Runs

Often when running pipes through dissimilar building materials such as concrete blocks, poured concrete, brick, paneling, and framing members, the hole drilled for the pipe should be sealed. Great Stuff, a urethane insulating foam, is ideal for this purpose. It not only seals the hole but helps cushion the pipe through the material in which the hole has been drilled. Great Stuff dispenses from an aerosol container as a foam, and solidifies to form an airtight seal. Great Stuff also can be used to seal windows, doors, and other sources of air infiltration, according to the manu-facturer, Insta-Foam Products, Inc.

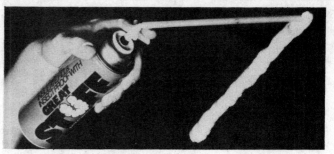

Plumbing Emergencies

Materials • Penetrating Oil • Cardboard Tag • Self-Tapping Screw Plugs

Tools • Wrench • Screwdriver

WHENEVER THERE is a plumbing emergency, such as a broken pipe, you and your family should know how to turn off the water supply quickly. In minutes, hundreds of gallons of water could flood your home and cause considerable damage.

Caution: Flooding water can come in contact with some part of your home's electrical system. Before you enter a flooded area, always make certain that the main switch or circuit breaker to your household electrical current is turned to the "off" position. If the floor under the main entrance panel is damp, cover it with a piece of plywood or a plank and stand on it to isolate yourself from the ground.

Be Prepared

Now, while there is no plumbing emergency, is the time to learn what to do. Follow these steps:

1. Know where to turn off the water supply at fixtures when a leak is located *between* the fixture's shutoff valve and the fixture. Every sink, tub, and appliance that uses water should have its own shutoff valve or valves; fixtures that use hot water will have a valve for the hot water supply and one for the cold. Usually, they are located directly under the fixture. To close such valves, turn them clockwise.

2. Know where to turn off the water supply at the main shutoff valve, which shuts off the water supply to the entire house. Usually, the main shutoff is located near the point where the water supply enters your home. It may be a gate valve or it may be an L-shaped rod. In some cases, a wrench may be needed to turn this valve.

   Note: If there's a problem in the hot water supply line, you can stop the flow of water in these pipes only, by turning off the water inlet valve at the water heater. This cuts the pressure in the hot water pipes and the water flow will stop as soon as the pipes drain. The main shutoff valve, meanwhile, will cut the pressure throughout the plumbing system.

3. Test all water supply shutoff valves to see if they operate properly. Turn each valve off and go to the nearest faucet and turn it on. If the water flows out and then stops, you can assume that the water supply at the fixture has been turned off. If the water continues to flow—even at a trickle—the shutoff valve has not been closed tightly enough.

   Note: Little-used valves tend to corrode. If

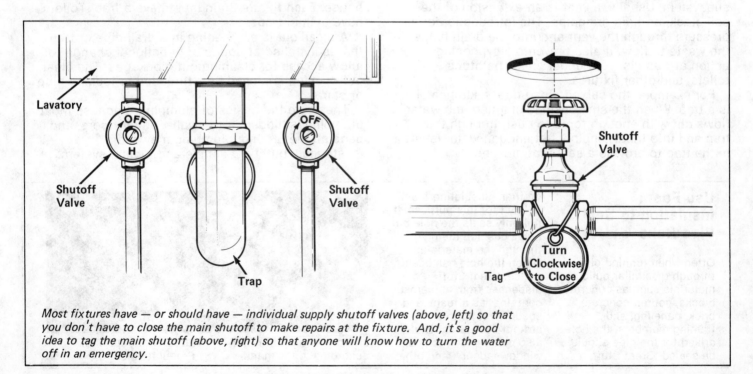

Most fixtures have — or should have — individual supply shutoff valves (above, left) so that you don't have to close the main shutoff to make repairs at the fixture. And, it's a good idea to tag the main shutoff (above, right) so that anyone will know how to turn the water off in an emergency.

the valve is difficult to turn or cannot be turned at all, apply several drops of penetrating oil to the valve stem and allow the lubricant to work for 30 minutes or so.

4. Tag the main shutoff valve to clearly identify it; also indicate which way it must be turned to close it so that anyone can shut off the water supply in an emergency. Test the valve every six months or so to keep it in working order.

Solving Emergencies

Various types of leaks are treated differently. Here are several common plumbing emergencies and what you can do about them:

LEAKS CAUSED BY FROZEN PIPES. Turn off the water supply at the main shutoff valve. Although you may find the main source of the leak, freezing can cause damage to the pipes and fixtures elsewhere in your plumbing system. After thawing the pipe, repair the damage.

TANK LEAKS. Turn off the water supply at the main shutoff valve. Then you can plug the leaking tank with a self-tapping screw plug. When tightened, the screw applies enough pressure to a rubberlike gasket under the screw head to stop the leak. If, however, the tank is rusted through, you will have to replace the tank. Such holes in tanks can never be satisfactorily repaired.

Sometimes, self-tapping screw plugs can be used to stop leaks in pipes temporarily, although the damaged pipe must be replaced as soon as possible.

DRAIN LEAKS. Because drains are not under pressure, a leak will stop flowing as soon as the level of the water drops below the leak. Often, you can stop the leak by simply tightening a joint or connection. If, however, there is a hole in the drainpipe or trap, it must be replaced. Self-tapping screw plugs or waterproof pipe tape will not stop such a leak for long.

FIXTURE LEAKS. Cracked or broken toilet flush tanks and bowls and lavatories and sinks can't be repaired. Turn off the water supply at the fixture and replace the damaged fixture immediately.

Bending and Cutting Tubing Takes Care

If you cut flexible copper tubing with a hacksaw, you must be careful because it's much more prone to bending and kinking than rigid copper pipe. Use a fine-tooth hacksaw blade and a miter box for square cut ends. The best tool, however, is a tubing cutter. Bending flexible copper tubing demands care too. You can place it over your knee and gently form the bend with your hands; but if you kink the tubing, you'll have to start again. It's virtually impossible to remove a kink. A safer way is to use a spring-type tubing bender that slips over the tubing.

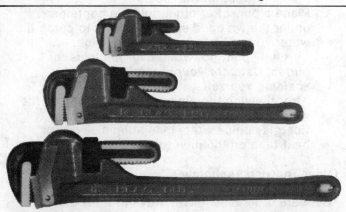

Pipe Wrenches for Most Jobs

Heavy-duty pipe wrenches, made by Disston, are available in nine sizes ranging from 8 inches to 48 inches. All have hardened steel jaws and pre-marked jaw opening measurements to make almost any plumbing job go faster. For most plumbing jobs, you will need two wrenches. Same-size wrenches are best, although you can select one that is slightly smaller or larger than the other.

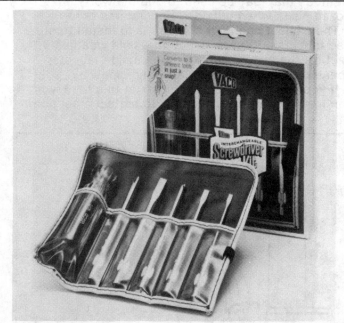

A Selection of Screwdrivers Speeds Faucet Repairs

Similar faucets often have different screw slots, requiring several different screwdrivers for repair. The Interchangeable Screwdriver Kit, No. 90050, from Vaco Products Co. contains a popular assortment of the most frequently used Phillips and slotted blade styles. All of the blades are interchangeable, and fit into one full-size handle. The blade sizes include ⅛-inch, ³⁄₁₆-inch, and ¼-inch slotted and Nos. 1 and 2 Phillips. All five blades snap in and out of the handle quickly for easy conversion. The kit has a vinyl pouch designed for workbench or toolbox storage.

Thawing Frozen Pipes

Materials • Heavy Towel or Burlap Bag • Twine • Bucket • Pot or Pan • Rags • Pipe Insulation or Heat Tape • Patio Block

Tools • Propane Torch With Flame-Spreader Nozzle • Pipe Wrench • Garden Hose • Funnel

PREVENTIVE MAINTENANCE is the key to frost-free water pipes, and there are several methods that may be used to end the worry of frozen pipes when outside temperatures drop.

The easiest and best solution is to install frost-free faucets outdoors, and during cold weather, shut off the water supply to the outside faucets, opening them to drain the exposed pipes.

If you can't afford such faucets at this time, you can install heat tape, or cable, to protect a section

A messy but safe way to thaw a frozen pipe, including those made of plastic, is to pour hot water over rags wrapped around the pipe.

of pipe that is vulnerable to freezing. Some tapes have an automatic thermostat to start the heating whenever the outside temperature drops to about 35° F.

A less expensive method, although not quite as effective, is to cover pipes exposed to cold with a fiberglass insulation wrapping designed for pipes. Or, you can use lengths of molded insulating sleeves that closely fit around the pipe. These sleeves are more expensive than fiberglass wrap, but are easy to install.

All of these products come with installation instructions.

Thawing With Hot Water

Freeze-fighting tips, however, are of little value when you are confronted with a pipe that is frozen solid. A messy but safe way to thaw a frozen pipe, including those made of plastic, is with hot water. Here's what to do:

1. Open the faucet on the pipe; this allows the steam and water produced by your thawing activities to escape.
2. Wrap the pipe, beginning at the faucet, with a heavy towel or burlap bag; secure the material with twine. The material will concentrate and hold the heat against the pipe. **Note:** Always start any heat application at the faucet and work toward the other end of the frozen section so as the ice melts, the water and steam will flow out the faucet. If you were to start thawing in the middle of the frozen pipe, the steam produced could build up enough pressure to burst the pipe.
3. Place a bucket or other suitable container under the wrapped section of pipe to catch the water you will be pouring on the pipe.
4. Carefully pour hot water over the towel or burlap. *Caution: Pour carefully to avoid scalding yourself.*
5. After thawing the pipe completely, remove the wrapping, wipe the pipe dry, and install fiberglass pipe wrap, insulating sleeves, or heat tape on the pipe to prevent a recurrence.

Other Thawing Techniques

There are other less messy ways to thaw metal pipes, although some methods may take longer than using hot water. The fastest way is to use a propane torch equipped with a flame-spreader nozzle. Other items that can be used include a heat lamp or a hair dryer.

Caution: When using a propane torch or a heat lamp, be extremely careful that the device does not ignite or scorch wall or ceiling materials near the pipe. Never use a torch or other direct high-heat source on plastic pipe.

To thaw a frozen pipe using a propane torch, follow these steps:

1. Open the faucet on the pipe; this allows the steam and water produced by your thawing activities to escape.
2. Using a propane torch with a flame-spreader nozzle, apply the flame to the frozen pipe, beginning at the faucet end. Keep the flame moving back and forth; never leave it in one spot long. Be especially careful if you are near any soldered pipe joints; pass over them quickly or they may melt and cause leaks. *Caution: Be extremely careful not to ignite or scorch wall or ceiling materials near the pipe.* Have someone hold a thin patio block or some other suitable fireproof material between the pipe and the wall or ceiling.

Frozen Drainpipes

Hot water is the best way to thaw a frozen drainpipe, but if the blockage is some distance away from the opening, a special technique may be necessary. Follow these steps:

1. Carefully pour hot water down the drain to melt the blockage. If this fails to do the trick, place a bucket under the trap and remove the trap from the drain; use a pipe wrench to loosen the trap's slip nuts.
2. Insert a length of garden hose into the drainpipe until it reaches the frozen section.
3. Using a funnel on the end of the hose, pour

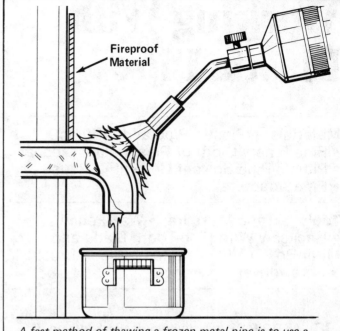

A fast method of thawing a frozen metal pipe is to use a propane torch with a flame-spreader nozzle. Be careful not to ignite materials near the pipe.

hot water into the hose. *Caution: Until the ice melts and drains down the pipe, the hot water you pour in will back up the hose toward you; have the bucket ready to catch the overflow, and be careful so you don't scald yourself.*

4. After the drainpipe has been thawed, remove the hose and replace the trap.

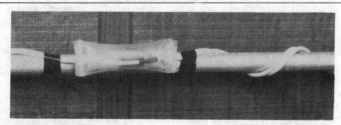

Heating Cable Prevents Frozen Pipes

Add-On heat tapes from Easy Heat-Wirekraft, a division of Bristol Corp., are what you need if freezing water pipes are a big problem in your household. The add-on system uses a heated base unit and power cord to which a number of 12-foot heat tape sections may be connected with weatherproof couplings. It's then wrapped around water pipes that are prone to freeze. Easy Heat-Wirekraft reports that a 12-foot section of tape uses about 60 watts and 0.6 amps of electrical power per hour. A thermostat turns the tape on automatically when the temperature drops below 38° F. The complete system consists of either a 6-foot or a 12-foot base unit with up to ten 12-foot heating tape sections.

Vacuum Cleaner Can Thaw Pipe

A slow but safe method of thawing a frozen pipe is to attach a vacuum cleaner's hose and crevice nozzle to the machine's blower end. Direct the air flow at the frozen pipe. The vacuum cleaner doesn't furnish a lot of heat, but there should be enough to thaw the pipe.

Tubular Insulation for Hot, Cold Pipes

Tubular pipe insulating weather seal, made by Stanley Hardware, a division of The Stanley Works, is designed to insulate hot water pipes as well as prevent sweating of cold water pipes. There is no danger from heat; the insulation's thick wall of closed-cell polyethylene foam contains flame-retardant material. Stanley tubular pipe insulating

weather seal comes in four sizes: ½ inch, ¾ inch, 1 inch, and 1¼ inches; all packages contain 12 feet of insulation.

Working With Plastic Pipe

Materials • Plastic Pipe and Fittings
• Fine Emery Cloth or Plastic-Pipe Cleaner
• Plastic-Pipe Solvent Cement • Rags
• Pipe Adapters

Tools • Tape Measure • Wax Pencil
• Hacksaw With Fine-Tooth Blade and
Miter Box • Utility Knife or File • Brush
• Screwdriver • Wrench

PLASTIC PIPE is a do-it-yourselfer's dream if your community's plumbing code allows its use. It is light; virtually self-cleaning; not subject to corrosion, scaling, or rust; and easy to use.

There are several types of plastic pipe in common use for various home applications. CPVC (chlorinated polyvinyl chloride) pipe is rigid and used for hot and cold water supply systems. PB (polybutylene) pipe is a new, heat-resistant, highly flexible tubing used for the same purpose as CPVC pipe. One form of PVC (polyvinyl chloride) pipe is made for outdoor cold water supply lines, another for drain-waste-vent systems, and a third for sewer lines and underground drainage systems. Rigid ABS (acrylonitrile butadiene styrene) pipe is made for the same applications as PVC, except for water supply or distribution uses. Perhaps the most popular plastic pipe for cold water supply lines, lawn sprinkling, and irrigation purposes is PE (polyethylene), which is flexible and available in several grades. SR (styrene rubber) is used primarily for underground drainage systems, while PP (polypropylene) is available in plumbing fixture traps, tailpieces, trap extensions, and their associated parts, and is by far the best choice for new or replacement use. Both SR and PP are rigid types of pipe.

Where permitted, all of these types of plastic pipe can be used in new installations, additions to existing systems made of metal pipe, or for repair work, because adapters are available to allow you to connect just about any type of pipe to just about any other type.

Flexible plastic pipe is the simplest to install because little cutting and joining is required. Rigid plastic pipe requires more careful measuring, cutting, and assembling, but it, too, is easy to work with. To install rigid plastic pipe, follow these steps:

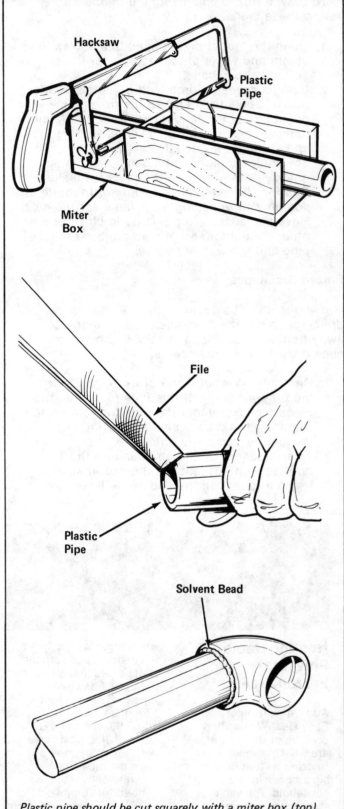

Plastic pipe should be cut squarely with a miter box (top). Burrs can be removed with a sharp knife or a file (center). After removing oil and wax from the pipe, apply the chemical solvent. A properly cemented joint will have a small, even bead of solvent around the joint (bottom).

1. Carefully measure, mark, and cut the lengths of plastic pipe to fit. When cutting, use a miter box and a hacksaw with a fine-tooth blade to make each cut square; the hacksaw blade should be mounted so that it cuts on the forward stroke.
2. Use a sharp utility knife or file to remove the burrs from the inside and outside of each cut end carefully. Don't damage the plastic; if you do, it won't fit properly.
3. Use fine emery cloth to lightly buff the end of the pipe to remove oil and wax; don't remove any plastic—the object is to clean and degloss the end. You also may use a special cleaner to remove oil and wax.
4. Temporarily assemble the run of plastic pipe with the fittings, but without using any chemical solvent; make sure the pipe lengths and fittings join properly. Seat the end of the pipe tightly against the slight shoulder inside the fitting.
5. When the run of pipe is satisfactory, mark each pipe and fitting across the joint for matching later; use a wax pencil.
6. Begin assembling the run of pipe by applying the chemical solvent to the end of the pipe—not to the fitting—and slip the pipe end into the fitting with a quarter turn; this distributes the solvent more evenly. Do this, however, quickly and without hesitation, because the solvent begins fusing the parts together immediately. Align the pipe and fitting with your mark. Clean off any excess solvent.

    Note: Make sure you use the proper solvent. It is a good idea to purchase the correct plastic-pipe cleaner and solvent when you buy the plastic pipe. Also, avoid using a brush with synthetic bristles to apply the solvent; it will dissolve the bristles.
7. Examine the joint. A properly cemented joint has a small, even bead of solvent around the joint. If it isn't present, the connection may leak. In such a case, you'll have to remove the pipe from the fitting immediately and wipe off all the solvent you can and rejoin the parts. Once the solvent sets, you cannot separate the joint; the pipe and fitting will have to be discarded, or you will have to cut the fitting off the pipe and use a new fitting.
8. Allow the assembled and cemented run of pipe to set and cure according to the solvent manufacturer's instructions before turning the water back on. It can take 12 to 48 hours for the solvent to cure.

If you are connecting a run of plastic pipe to copper or galvanized steel pipe, you can use special pipe adapters. For measuring purposes, however, be sure to install the adapter to the copper or steel pipe run before connecting the plastic pipe, and don't forget to turn off the water before starting the job.

Some types of plastic pipe, meanwhile, are not joined with solvent at all. With PE pipe, for example, ringed insertion fittings are slipped into the pipe and secured with stainless steel clamps around the outside of the pipe. PB pipe lengths can be joined in the same manner, but special mechanically gripping transition adapter fittings are most commonly used.

Plumbing System Makes 'Perfect' Connections

The Failsafe plumbing system, according to the Marshall Brass Co., makes a perfect leakproof connection in four simple steps. You cut the system's tubing to the desired length; slide a crimping ring on the tubing; insert the appropriate fitting into the end of the tubing; and crimp the clamping ring into place with a special Failsafe hand tool. The system, designed for new installations or for modernizing old systems, includes a variety of fittings including reducers, couplings, sweat adapters, elbows, line plugs, female tees, and flares. The Failsafe crimping hand tool is universal; it crimps ⅜-inch, ½-inch, and ¾-inch ring sizes. Also available are hand crimpers for ½-inch and ¾-inch tubing. The Failsafe tubing is polybutylene for hot or cold water plumbing installations. Complete instructions are included with the system.

Plastic Laundry Tubs Are Easy to Install

Designed especially for the do-it-yourselfer, these laundry and utility tubs by Plaskolite, Inc., feature a molded-in-drain strainer, molded leg slots, and knock-outs for faucets. The tubs have a drain stopper, leveling-leg kit, and preformed legs that may be anchored to the floor. For easy connections, a compression nut and tubing are furnished with the tub, along with complete installation instructions. Tub capacity is 22 gallons of water. Tubs measure 23 inches wide by 25½ inches from front to back; they are 12 inches deep and 33 inches high. Made of high-impact-strength polypropylene, the tubs are said to be resistant to stains and chemicals, and are available in single or double tub models.

Sink and Toilet Kits for Easy Connections

These three plumbing installation kits by Keystone Brass & Rubber Co. feature "no-tool" fittings and tubing to connect water lines without soldering or cementing. The Wall Mount Sink or Vanity Installation Kit has a PVC trap, a reducing adaptor to accommodate outlets with an outside diameter of 1½ or 1¼ inches, and the fittings. The Floor Mount Sink or Vanity Installation Kit has a PVC trap and a reducing adaptor to complete the drainage system, and the no-tool fittings and tubing. The Toilet Installation Kit contains a wax ring, toilet bolts and screws, and the no-tool fittings and tubings. A feature of the kits is the 1½-inch and 1¼-inch fittings that adapt to most standard hookups. Complete installation instructions are furnished.

Tubing—Easy-to-Use for Fixture Hookups

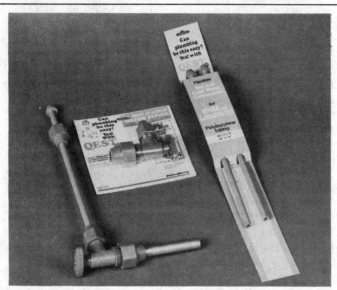

Flexible polybutylene tubing makes plumbing installations easier to perform. Flexible tubing can be "fished" into hard-to-reach places, doesn't require precise measurements, and eliminates the need for fittings and elbows—just curve the tubing. The Qest plumbing system, from U.S. Brass, is a complete system of tubing, fittings, and valves for do-it-yourself applications. The polybutylene system connects to nearly any existing plumbing system—copper, galvanized pipe, CPVC, or polybutylene—with an end compression-type connection. The connection is made with a sealing cone, retaining ring, and a special Qest nut. The nut is hand-tightened, then given a turn or two with a pliers or wrench. Shown here are Qest risers and valves that can be combined for sink or toilet shutoffs. All necessary parts are included, and, according to the manufacturer, no special tools are needed. The Qest system includes tubing from ⅛-inch through ¾-inch interior diameter for hot water, and up to 2-inch for cold water. There are more than 100 fittings available.

Plastic Compression Fittings Are Available

Although much plastic pipe is joined together with special solvent, you can buy special compression fittings that simply snap into place. This kind of fitting has a nut, locking ring, and washer that provides a watertight connection. Once the fitting is in place, it can't be removed, except by cutting the plastic pipe behind the fitting.

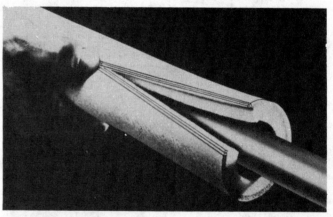

Insulation Sleeves Install Quickly

A tubular insulation for hot and cold water pipes that needs no clips, tape, adhesive, or string to install is Plasti-Zip, made by the Frelan Corp. Plasti-Zip insulation sleeves, made of cross-linked cellular polyethylene, are slit down the side; their zipper-like closure is similar to that used on food storage bags. The sleeves may be reopened without damage. To use, simply slip a sleeve around the pipe with light hand pressure and close it. It may be cut and shaped with a utility knife; it may also be painted. Frelan engineers set the insulation's R-value at 1.6; various diameters are available for the different pipe sizes found in standard home plumbing systems. According to the manufacturer, the insulation qualifies for the federal energy tax credit. One package of Plasti-Zip holds four 3-foot lengths of insulation sleeves.

Working With Copper Pipe

Materials • Copper Pipe and Fittings • Fine Steel Wool, Emery Cloth, or Sandpaper • Non-Acid Soldering Flux • 50/50 Lead-Tin, Solid-Core Solder • Patio Block • Coarse Towel • Copper Pipe Hangers

Tools • Tape Measure • Pencil • Tubing Cutter or Hacksaw With Fine-Tooth Blade and Miter Box • Half-Round Metal File • Toothbrush • Propane Torch

COPPER PIPE can be joined in several ways. Sweat-soldering, however, is the most popular and least expensive method of joining rigid copper pipe, while flare and compression fittings are used mainly for flexible copper tubing.

Rigid copper pipe is available in 10-foot and 20-foot lengths and three wall thicknesses: Type K (thick), Type L (medium), and Type M (thin). Type K is for underground use; Types L and M are for interior use. Type M, however, may be unacceptable to your local plumbing code, so it's best to check.

Unlike conventional soldering with an iron or gun, sweat-soldering is done with a torch. Most people use a propane torch, which is easier and safer to use than a blowtorch. In addition to the heat source, you need a good non-acid, or rosin-type, paste flux; emery cloth or steel wool; and 50/50 lead-tin solid-core solder.

At least as important as having the right materials is properly preparing the pipe and fittings to be sweat-soldered. There are three key factors for good sweat-soldered joints: clean copper, totally dry pipes, and proper heat.

Caution: One of the most crucial factors in sweat-soldering is making sure that all the pipes and fittings are completely dry. If there is any residual moisture, it will turn to steam when the pipes are heated and the result will be a weak or even a leaking joint. The buildup of trapped steam in a pipe could also cause an explosion. Therefore, make absolutely certain that no moisture is present. If you are soldering on part of your existing plumbing system, drain the pipes and leave the faucets open so steam can escape.

To sweat-solder rigid copper pipe, follow these steps:

1. Measure, mark, and cut the lengths of pipe to fit. Use a tubing cutter; it leaves a clean, square end. Turn the cutter around the pipe, tightening the cutter adjustment screw as the tool slices through the metal. A hacksaw may be used, but use the finest-tooth blade you can find. Saw as straight as possible—using a miter box will help you obtain a square cut.
2. Use a half-round metal file to remove any cutting burrs from the ends of the pipe—inside and out.
3. Buff all metal surfaces that you plan to join so that they are clean and shiny. You can use fine sandpaper or emery cloth, but fine steel wool does an excellent job. You want the metal to shine, but be careful not to remove so much metal that you lose a snug fit. **Note:** Avoid touching the buffed surfaces; oils from your fingers can cause poor solder joints.
4. Apply non-acid soldering flux to the cleaned metal surfaces. Spread the flux evenly on both the pipe and the fitting surfaces to be joined; an old toothbrush makes a good spreading tool.
5. Temporarily assemble the pipe and fitting to

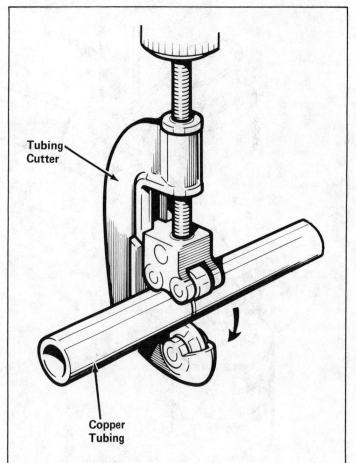

Tubing Cutter

Copper Tubing

To avoid damaging the ends of copper pipe, a tubing cutter should be used; it makes a clean, square end.

see if they fit properly. The end of the pipe should butt tightly against the shoulder in the fitting.

6. When you are ready to begin soldering, reassemble the pipe and fitting.
7. Light the propane torch, and get the solder ready in your other hand. **Note:** Protect the surface behind the pipe and fitting with a patio block or some other fireproof material.
8. Apply the tip of the flame to the fitting—not the pipe or the solder. You will have to heat the copper to about 400° F.
9. When the copper is hot enough, touch the solder to the joint. The solder should melt on contact, and capillary action will cause the melting solder to be drawn up into the joint under the fitting; this action occurs even if the pipe runs vertically up into the fitting. When the solder begins to flow, remove the flame and keep applying solder until the entire joint is filled. You'll know that point is reached when you see a continuous bead of solder form completely around the lip of the fitting. Be careful not to overheat the pipe and fitting.
10. For neater joints, you can wipe away any

excess solder by taking a quick swipe around the fitting lip with a piece of coarse toweling when the joint has cooled slightly but before the solder has hardened. *Caution: Be careful not to touch the hot metal with your hand and don't disturb the soldered joint until the solder has solidified; it could dislodge the solder and cause leaks.*

Many amateur plumbers are so proud of their first sweat-soldered joints that they immediately turn on the water. That, however, is a big mistake! Be sure to allow the soldered joints to cool naturally; the sudden cooling effect of rushing water can weaken the joint or cause it to crack.

If, when you finally do turn the water on, you discover a leak in the sweat-soldered joint, you'll have to start over: shut off the water supply, drain the pipes thoroughly, melt the soldered joint, remove the fitting, dry and reclean the pipe and fitting surfaces, reflux, and finally resolder.

Copper pipe must be supported every 3 feet with copper pipe hangers. A pipe run that sags will put stress on soldered joints, and in time this can cause leaks.

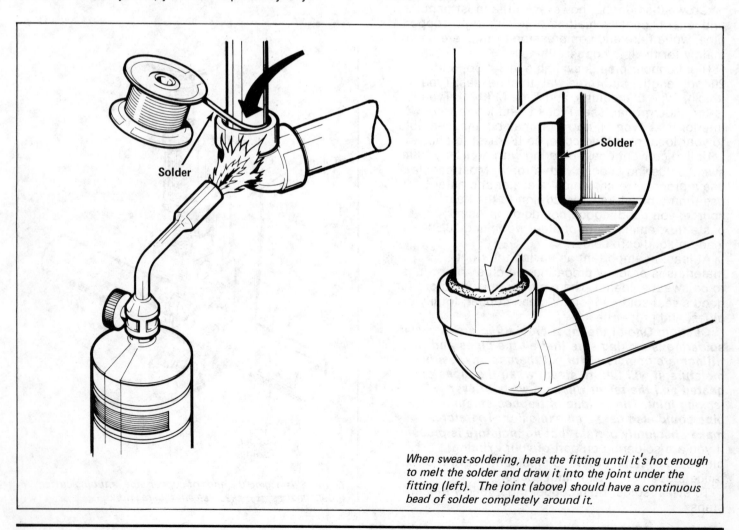

Solder

Solder

When sweat-soldering, heat the fitting until it's hot enough to melt the solder and draw it into the joint under the fitting (left). The joint (above) should have a continuous bead of solder completely around it.

Two Are Better Than One

Almost always, two pipe wrenches are needed to assemble or disassemble galvanized steel pipe and fittings. For multi-purpose use, buy a 10-inch and a 16-inch-size pipe wrench. They'll let you handle virtually any project.

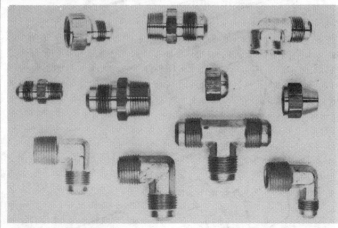

Fittings Used With Copper or Aluminum Tubing

A wide range of flare and compression fittings for use with copper and aluminum tubing is available from Chicago Specialty Manufacturing Co. The fittings, packaged individually, include male and female connectors, tees, elbows, caps, nuts, unions, and reducing unions in all standard sizes. Also available are gas connector and water heater supply lines; faucet, drain, sink, and toilet repair parts; aerators; shower accessories; and plumbing tools.

For the Best Results Replace the Pipe

Pipe tape, epoxy paste, and other patching materials are excellent for repairing leaking pipes. However in most cases, galvanized steel pipe that is leaking must be replaced or leaks will drip through the patch. To replace a length of galvanized steel pipe that is leaking, first turn off the water. Then brace the pipe and use a hacksaw to cut the pipe through at an angle. Remove the pipe from its connection at both ends, using a pipe wrench to hold the connection and another pipe wrench to turn out the severed pipe. Measure for two lengths of replacement pipe, threaded on both ends, that will be joined by a union fitting. Use pipe compound on all the male threads. Insert the new pipe in one connection and tighten it. Attach the union on the other end. Screw the other section of pipe first into the other connection and then into the union. Tighten both connections; use two pipe wrenches for this—one wrench on the connection, the other to turn the pipe. Then tighten the nut on the union fitting. Two pieces of pipe are required for the replacement, along with the union. You cannot install a single length of pipe into the connections because the threads at the ends of the pipe turn in opposite directions.

Fittings for Flexible Copper Tubing

Some plumbing jobs may require you to use flexible copper tubing. Flare or compression fittings are mainly used to connect such tubing. To make a flare connection, you need a flaring tool and a special fitting that includes a flare nut. You slip the nut over the cut end of the tubing. Then, you insert the tubing into the proper-size hole in the flaring tool's vise. The tool's flaring cone is turned down to flare the end of the tubing. Finally, you put the fitting on the flared end of the tubing, pull the nut up to it, and tighten the nut. Compression fittings are much like flare fittings but without the flare. A compression fitting includes a flange nut and a compression ring, or ferrule. You slip the flange nut onto the tubing followed by the ring. Then, you insert the tubing into the fitting and tighten the nut.

Use the Right Tool to Cut Metal Tubing

Most plumbing tools aren't specialized, but there are a couple of special tools that you should have on hand when plumbing or remodeling jobs arise. One of these is a tubing cutter, such as this one from Waxman Industries, Inc. The cutter cuts metal tubing (not galvanized steel pipe) with outside diameters from $\frac{3}{16}$ to $1\frac{1}{8}$ inches. It has a double roller with a high carbon alloy steel cutting wheel and a snap-out reamer. To use this tool, you hook it around the tubing to be cut, turn the handle to set the blade, and turn the cutter around the pipe. For best results, turn the handle as the cutter is turned to keep the cutter firmly against the metal.

Solder Eraser for Metal Mistakes

Solder Off is a solder-removing aid made by Kester Solder, a division of Litton Industries. It allows you to remove solder from badly soldered copper pipe joints so that you can re-solder the joint immediately. Solder Off is made of pure copper braid. You touch the end of the braid to the solder you want to remove and apply a heated soldering iron to the braid. The melted solder under the braid is absorbed. You then cut off the solder-filled portion of the braid with scissors. Solder Off is sold in a 5-foot spool.

Pipe Leaks

Materials • Rags • Leak-Stopping Compound or Waterproof Tape • Epoxy Paste • Pipe-Patching Kit or Inner Tube and Hose Clamps • Self-Tapping Screw Plugs • Pipe Joint Compound or Tape

Tools • Screwdriver • Pipe Wrenches

W HEN A PIPE leaks, it can cause considerable damage. You must act quickly; small leaks grow into large leaks rapidly. The first thing you should do is to stop the flow of water in the leaking pipe. This can be done at the fixture's shutoff valve or, if necessary, at the main shutoff valve. Because the source of a leak can be difficult to locate, you can start at the main shutoff valve and trace the water supply line to find the leak, unless you know it is between a fixture and its shutoff.

Waterproof Tape

Small leaks in a length of copper, galvanized steel, or plastic pipe between fittings may be temporarily stopped by rubbing the hole with a stick of special leak-stopping compound or with waterproof tape. To use waterproof tape, follow these steps:

1. Turn off the water.
2. Clean and dry the exterior of the pipe with a rag.
3. Wrap waterproof tape in a spiral around the pipe so the tape overlaps about half its width; apply the tape so it covers 2 to 3 inches of pipe on both sides of the leak.

Epoxy Paste

Specially compounded epoxy paste for stopping leaks in metal pipe can be used anywhere along a length of pipe or at pipe fittings. The leaking pipe or fitting should be replaced as soon as possible. To use epoxy paste, follow these steps:

1. Turn off the water.
2. Clean and dry the exterior of the pipe thoroughly with a rag.
3. Apply the epoxy to the leaking pipe or fitting, and allow it to dry according to the manufacturer's instructions before turning the water on.

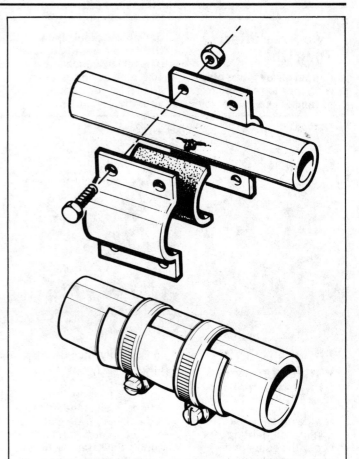

There are several ways to stop a leak in a pipe, including a patching kit (top), which consists of a rubber pad and two plates that are bolted together. You also can make a patch (bottom) with a piece of heavy rubber and hose clamps.

Pipe-Patching Kits

A pipe-patching kit that consists of a rubber pad and two metal plates that are bolted together is a good way to stop larger leaks in a length of galvanized steel or copper pipe. To use such a kit, follow these steps:

1. Turn off the water.
2. Clean and dry the exterior of the pipe with a rag.
3. Position the rubber pad over the leak and clamp it in place with the metal plates by tightening the bolts with a screwdriver or wrench.

You can make your own patching kit with a piece of rubber inner tube and two hose clamps, such as those used for auto radiator hoses. After the clamps have been installed loosely on the pipe, wrap the inner tube tightly around the leaking pipe. Move the clamps over the ends of the inner tube patch and tighten the clamps with a screwdriver. Replace the pipe as soon as possible.

Leak-Stopping Screws

Some minor leaks in metal pipe—and tanks—can be stopped with special self-tapping screw plugs that feature rubber washers under their heads. **Note:** The screw tip will slow the flow of water, especially in small-diameter pipes. This is only a temporary repair; replace the pipe immediately.

To use a leak-stopping screw, follow these steps:

1. Turn off the water.
2. Clean and dry the exterior of the pipe with a rag.
3. Start turning the screw clockwise in the hole by hand; then drive it in with a screwdriver or wrench—depending on the type of screw head—until the rubber washer seals itself against the pipe. Various sizes of such screws are available.

Leaking Fittings

A leak in a pipe fitting is more common than a hole in a length of pipe. Different types of pipe materials are treated differently; however, in all cases, turn off the water before making any repairs.

For galvanized pipe fittings, try tightening the connection with pipe wrenches. If this fails to stop the leak, loosen the fitting, apply pipe joint compound or tape to the threads, and retighten the joint.

For copper pipe fittings, the joint will have to be disassembled, refitted, and sweat-soldered.

For plastic pipe fittings that have been cemented with solvent, the only solution is to cut out the fitting and replace it. You may have to replace a length of plastic pipe next to the fitting as well; the pipe section can be joined to the run of pipe by a plastic coupling.

Stopping That Pounding Noise

Water hammer isn't a tool; it's a noise that sounds like someone is gently rapping on your water pipes. It occurs when you shut off the water suddenly, and the force of the fast-moving water rushing through the pipe is brought to an abrupt halt—creating a sort of shock wave and a hammering noise. There are several possible solutions. You can replace the faucet causing the noise—if it's a spring-loaded model—with a manually closed faucet; a manually closed faucet turns the water off more slowly. You also might try closing the main shutoff valve slightly to reduce the water pressure in the system. If the problem is in a hot water pipe, lower the temperature setting of your water heater. If the noisy pipe or pipes are equipped with air chambers to absorb the force of the rushing water, they may be waterlogged. Or, if there are no air chambers, you can have a plumber install them.

Emergency Solder Melts With a Match

Emergency Solder is a self-fluxing, tin/lead solder tape that can be melted with a match for on-the-spot soldering repairs almost anywhere. The solder, made by Multicore Solders, may be used on plumbing or electrical connections, and it works on almost any metal—except aluminum—that can be soldered. Multicore's Emergency Solder comes in a shirt-pocket package that can be easily stored or carried anywhere.

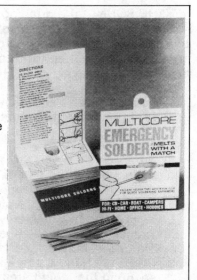

You Knead This to Stop Leaky Pipes

Permabond Epoxy Strips, an adhesive sealant that is handled much like modeling clay, may be used to stop plumbing leaks fast. Cut off a length of the black and white strip, and knead it until the mixture is a solid gray color; this indicates that the epoxy is ready to use. Epoxy Strips, made by Permabond International Corp., can then be molded around leaking pipe joints. Once it hardens, it can be drilled, sanded, filed, and finished. The product also has other uses; it works underwater for repairs around swimming pools, and can be used to anchor fixtures to metal, wood, brick, concrete, and tile. It is not affected by water, gasoline, or oil.

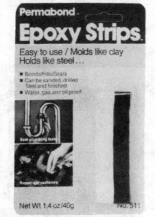

The Right Way to Use Pipe Wrenches

When assembling plumbing runs with galvanized steel pipe, two pipe wrenches are almost always needed. The pipe wrenches are used in opposite directions, the jaw openings of one wrench face the jaw openings of the other wrench. It also is important to have a slight gap between the back of the wrench's jaw and the pipe. This applies the pressure at two points, and provides the best gripping and rotating action. You should never use a pipe wrench to bend, lift, or raise a pipe. Never, under any circumstances, use an extension on the handle of a pipe wrench to gain more turning power.

Solder By the Numbers

Numbers, such as 50/50 and 40/60, on rolls of solder indicate percentages of tin and lead of which the solder is composed. For copper pipe, the most common solder used is 50/50 solid-core wire solder, but 40/60 is acceptable.

Dripping Stem Faucets

Materials • Adhesive Tape • Washers and Screws • Packing Material • Petroleum Jelly • Replacement Faucet Valve Seat • Pipe Joint Compound

Tools • Screwdriver • Allen Wrench • Adjustable Wrench or Slip-Joint Pliers • Valve Seat Grinder • Seat Wrench

THE SOUND of a dripping faucet can be torture; paying for the water wasted can be unpleasant too. The good news is that a dripping faucet can be repaired easily—often for less than a dollar. To fix a dripping stem faucet, follow these steps:

1. Turn off the water supply to the dripping faucet at the fixture shutoff valve below the sink or lavatory, or, if necessary, at the main shutoff valve.
2. With a screwdriver, remove the screw securing the handle to the faucet. Some faucets have a decorative cap that conceals the screw; pry up or unscrew this cap. **Note:** Some handles may be secured by a setscrew; use an Allen wrench, sometimes called a hex-key wrench, to remove a setscrew.
3. Under the handle, there is a packing nut securing the faucet stem. Wrap the packing nut with a piece of adhesive tape to avoid scarring it.
4. With an adjustable wrench or slip-joint pliers, remove the packing nut by turning it counterclockwise.
5. Twist out the stem of the faucet by turning it counterclockwise—in the direction in which the faucet is turned on. If it's difficult to remove, slip on the handle temporarily and use it to turn the stem out.
6. Remove the brass screw holding the washer at the base of the stem.
   Note: Instead of washers, some faucets use rubber diaphragms to control the flow of water. If you have this type, you may have to remove the stem with pliers. The rubber diaphragm covers the base of the stem, and you may have to pry it off with a screwdriver.
   Another type uses a rubber seat ring that acts like a washer. To remove it, use pliers to hold the end of the stem while you unscrew

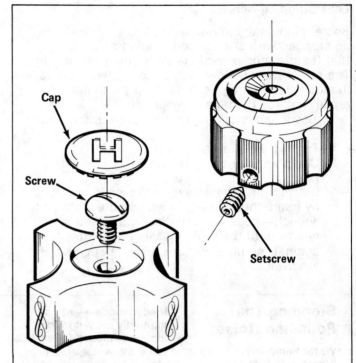

Some faucets are secured by a screw on top, which may be concealed behind a snap-out or threaded cap (left); others (right) are secured by a setscrew.

the threaded centerpiece that holds the seat ring. Remove the sleeve to insert the new seat ring, but be sure that the ring's lettering faces the threaded part of the stem.

There also are faucets with washers that

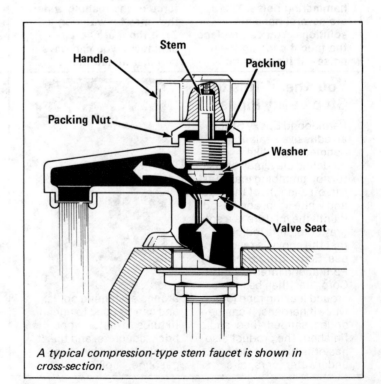

A typical compression-type stem faucet is shown in cross-section.

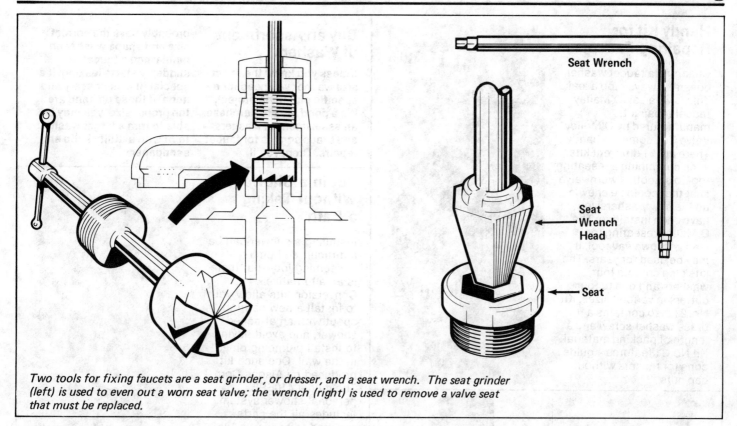

Two tools for fixing faucets are a seat grinder, or dresser, and a seat wrench. The seat grinder (left) is used to even out a worn seat valve; the wrench (right) is used to remove a valve seat that must be replaced.

have the faucet seat built into the stem itself. This type lifts from the base in a removable sleeve, which contains the valve seat. Unscrew the nut from the base of the stem, and remove the metal washer and metal retainer, which contains a rubber washer. The new washer can be inserted—bevel-side-up—into the retainer.

7. Remove and examine the washer. It is essential that you install a replacement that is exactly the right size, shape, and type. For example, note if the washer is beveled or flat. Washer assortment packages usually contain just about every size and shape you'll need; find an exact replacement.

8. Fit the new washer to the end of the stem and be sure that it is seated properly. Secure it in place with the brass screw. **Note:** Washer assortments often have replacement screws; if possible, use a new screw.

9. Check to see if the stem has any O-ring washers along its length. If so, replace them too.

10. Replace the stem in the faucet body by turning it clockwise.

11. Examine the packing nut. It may have a washer or packing material. Replace the washer or the packing.

12. Coat the packing nut threads with petroleum jelly, and replace the packing nut on the faucet body by turning it clockwise.

13. Replace the handle and decorative cap.

14. Turn the water on and test the faucet. If it still leaks, turn the water off and proceed to the next step.

15. Remove the cap, handle, packing nut, and stem.

16. Insert a valve seat grinder into the faucet body and adjust the tool's guide nut to align the grinder in the faucet body.

17. Turn the grinder carefully; the metal of the faucet seat is soft and doesn't need much grinding to smooth it.

18. Remove the valve seat grinder and reassemble the faucet.

19. Turn the water on and test the faucet again by turning the faucet on all the way to wash out the metal debris left by grinding. If the faucet continues to leak, the valve seat is probably damaged and must be replaced. Turn the water off and proceed to the next step.

20. Remove the cap, handle, packing nut, and stem.

21. Insert a seat wrench into the faucet body, turn it counterclockwise to unscrew the seat, and lift the seat out.

22. Take the seat to a store that sells plumbing supplies and buy an exact replacement.

23. Lubricate the new seat with pipe joint compound and install it with the seat wrench by turning the wrench clockwise.

24. Reassemble the faucet and turn the water back on.

Plumbing

Handy Kit for Repairing Faucets

Changing a faucet washer doesn't always stop a leak. This is when an O'Malley faucet repair kit, manufactured by O'Malley Valve Co., comes in handy. There are 11 different kits, each containing a reseating tool to smooth a worn valve seat that could be chewing up the new washers you have been installing. The O'Malley reseating tool isn't a throwaway tool; it may be used for years. The kits also contain four washers and one to four cutters in various sizes. Kit No. 21 also contains a brass washer screw and a length of packing material. Kit No. 31 features a guide cone for faucets without cap nuts.

Screw Tool Works Faster

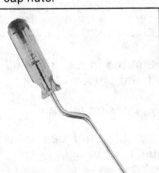

Screws are usually the first obstacle you face when attempting faucet repairs. A Rapidriv screwdriver can remove screws much faster than a conventional screwdriver, according to the Vaco Products Company. Instead of turning the handle, you simply rotate your wrist with a crank-like motion a few times, and the screws come free. Rapidriv screwdrivers are available in the most popular slotted and Phillips sizes. They can be used in all situations where a screwdriver is required.

Shower Head Saves You Water

The flow rate of the Con-Serv Deluxe Fuel Saver shower head is just 2.45 gallons of water per minute at 60 pounds per square inch, normal city water pressure. This means that you can save up to 70 percent in hot water fuel, water, and sewer costs, according to Con-Serv, Inc. The chrome-plated, solid-brass shower head may be installed quickly on any ½-inch shower arm with an adjustable wrench. The product is designed to meet all new federal energy codes.

Buy an Assortment of Washers

Unless you know the exact size washer you need for a specific plumbing project, it's a good idea to purchase an assortment of washers and brass screws for faucet repairs. Then, you'll probably have the correct size and shape washer on hand when a faucet suddenly starts leaking. If a special fit is necessary and none of those on hand are the proper size, you may be able to trim a larger washer to fit with a utility knife and sandpaper.

Put in a Shower Without Taking a Bath

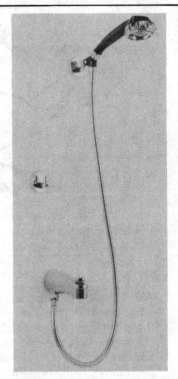

Installing a shower can be a difficult and time-consuming job—but there is an alternative. Conversion kits allow you to install a new bathtub spout with an attached shower, and avoid having to install plumbing pipes in the wall. One such kit is produced by Alsons Corp. The model 410SPB personal shower system includes all the parts required to convert a tub to a shower: diverter tub spout, white hand-held shower with push-button on/off, swivel shower mount, 59-inch nonmetallic hose, and two wall brackets. Three other kits from Alsons offer shower heads with both regular flow and a massage action: in black, the model 415S; in chrome, the model 415SC; and ivory-colored, the model 415SV.

Faucet Attachment Filters Drinking Water

The Peerless Home Water Filter screws onto the spout of any faucet where normally an aerator is attached. Once in place and twisted hand-tight, the filter helps to eliminate the taste and odors found in tap water. It removes rust, sediment, and other suspended particles. The filter's disposable cartridge is easy to replace; the cost of the filtered water can be as little as six cents per gallon, the manufacturer says. The five-stage disposable cartridge in the Peerless filter features a membrane developed for use in hospitals; it traps chemicals and bacteria that charcoal granule filters are not able to, according to the Peerless Faucet Co.

Repairing a Cartridge Faucet

Materials • O-Rings • Faucet Cartridge

Tools • Screwdriver • Allen Wrench

MANY MODERN single-handle faucets on sinks, lavatories, tubs, and showers use a cartridge-type valve assembly that is moved by the faucet handle to turn the water on and off and to control the mix of hot and cold water. To cure a leak in this type of faucet, follow these steps:

1. Turn off the water to the faucet at the fixture shutoff valve or, if necessary, at the main shutoff valve.
2. With a screwdriver, remove the screw securing the handle to the faucet. Some faucets have a decorative cap that conceals the screw; pry up or unscrew this cap. **Note:** Some handles may be secured by a setscrew; use an Allen wrench to remove a setscrew.
3. Remove the handle. **Note:** Tub and shower faucets with metal sleeve cartridges will have an escutcheon and stop tube behind the handle; remove them.
4. On some sink and lavatory faucets, the spout must be removed to reach the cartridge. In this case, unscrew the retaining nut and remove

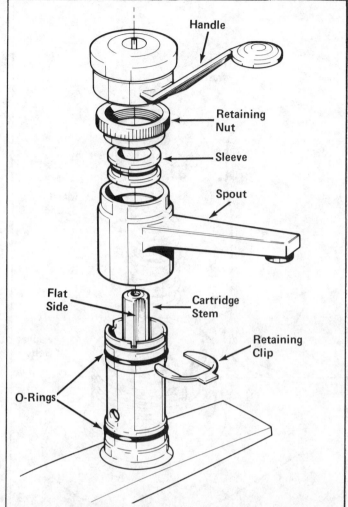

The cartridge-type valve assembly has a single handle to turn water on and off and to control the mix of hot and cold water.

A Bar/Utility Sink for All Occasions

The Midcor bar/utility sink, made by Middlefield Corp., will fit almost anywhere—recreation room, summer cottage, van, boat, greenhouse, garage, or workshop. The durable sink is 14 inches wide and 13½ inches deep, and has a 6-inch-deep basin. It's crack-proof, chip-proof, and craze-proof, according to the manufacturer who offers a 10-year limited warranty. It has a non-corrosive, drip-free, washerless faucet, which features a 10-inch-high gooseneck spout and strainer in a chrome finish. Molded from a high-strength plastic resin, the sink's material discourages stains and dirt or grease buildup; it wipes clean with a damp cloth. The sink is said not to be harmed by household cleaners, caustic drain cleaners, lotions, nail polish, or solvents. The Midcor bar/utility sink kit, model 0701, contains sink, countertop template, chromed drain assembly, hold-down clips, and faucet with all attachment fittings. It's available in three colors—red, beige, or chocolate. The model 7901 comes without the faucet.

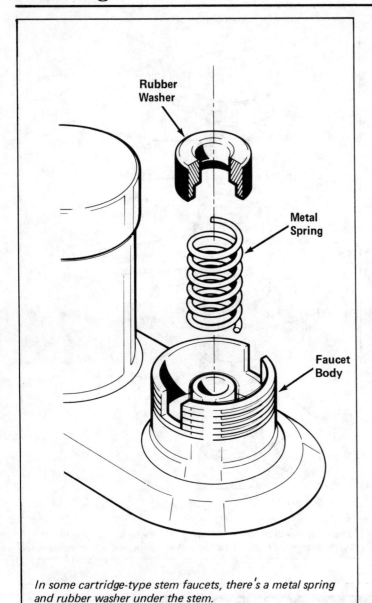

In some cartridge-type stem faucets, there's a metal spring and rubber washer under the stem.

(Rubber Washer, Metal Spring, Faucet Body)

the metal sleeve in the faucet.

5. Remove the spout body by twisting it off the faucet housing.
6. Replace any O-rings on the faucet housing.
7. Use a screwdriver to pull out the copper retaining clip or clips that hold the cartridge in the faucet housing.
8. Lift out the cartridge and replace it with a new one. **Note:** One flat area on the cartridge stem will be coded in some way; make sure this area is facing the sink or lavatory when it is installed or, in the case of a tub or shower, the coded area is facing up.
9. Replace the retaining clip or clips to secure the cartridge.
10. Replace the metal sleeve, the spout, the retaining nut, the stop tube and escutcheon, handle, and decorative cap.

Watch Those Pliers When Sweating Copper Pipe.

Locking-jaw pliers are excellent tools to hold copper pipe while sweating the joints with a propane torch and solder. However, do not position the pliers too close to the heat. Too much heat can affect the hardness of the metal and ruin the pliers. To prevent this, keep the pliers about 6 inches from the tip of the propane torch flame.

Replacement Faucet Has European Design

The Europa Water-Guard lavatory faucet from Kohler Co. features continental styling, water-saving flow control, and a selection of five finishes to match other faucets and accessories in a bath or powder room. The assembly has clear acrylic handles and an escutcheon plate with an attached chain and stopper. The escutcheon plate covers two of three faucet holes usually found on conventional lavatories so installation with an adjustable wrench is often possible. You simply unhook the old faucet and

install the Europa. The faucet is available in chrome or 24-carat gold finish either brushed or polished; it also comes in a burnished brass finish.

A Special Wrench Simplifies Repairs

A basin wrench is designed to reach up under a sink or basin to turn the connections holding pipes to faucet assemblies. Without such a tool, faucet repairs can be difficult, and sometimes impossible. This basin wrench produced by Waxman Industries, Inc., fits in tight places and turns 180 degrees. The jaw of the wrench is designed to reposition and grip the connection after each turn, so you don't have to remove the wrench and reset the jaw.

Don't Damage the Washers

Whenever you sweat-solder copper pipe to a faucet, remove the stem or valve. Otherwise, heat from a propane torch may damage the washers.

Fixing Tipping-Valve and Disc Faucets

Materials • Adhesive Tape • O-Ring(s)
• Tipping-Valve Faucet Repair Kit • Inlet
Seals • Faucet Cartridge

Tools • Adjustable Wrench • Screwdriver
• Seat Wrench • Toothbrush • Allen
Wrench

TIPPING-VALVE and disc faucets are among the most common single-lever faucets. They use a single handle to control the flow and mix of water.

Tipping-Valve Faucets

There are no washers in tipping-valve faucets, but they have valve assemblies that sometimes leak. Lime deposits can also block tiny strainers so that the flow of water is restricted. If the problem is merely a reduced water flow, there's no need to replace components. You just need to remove the strainer plugs on each side of the faucet. Then remove the gaskets and strainers, and clean the parts with soapy water and an old toothbrush. If the faucet is leaking, however, you'll have to go to a store that sells plumbing supplies, and buy a kit to replace the faucet's valve assemblies, except for the strainers and plugs, which can be cleaned and reused.

To repair a leaking tipping-valve faucet, follow these steps:

1. Turn off the water to the faucet at the fixture shutoff valve or, if necessary, at the main shutoff valve.
2. Wrap adhesive tape around the spout ring to avoid scarring it.
3. With an adjustable wrench, remove the spout ring by turning it counterclockwise. Lift the spout off. **Note:** If necessary, pry up the faucet body cover to gain access to the faucet strainer plugs.
4. Pry the O-ring off the base of the spout; replace it with a new one of the same size.
5. With an adjustable wrench, unscrew the strainer plugs on each side of the faucet, and remove the gaskets, strainers, and springs.
6. Use a seat wrench to remove the valve seats. **Note:** If you are merely cleaning the strainers, there's no need to remove the springs and valve seats; just clean the strainers and reassemble the faucet.
7. Install the new valve seats, new springs, cleaned strainers, and new gaskets. Secure the valve assemblies with the strainer plugs.
8. Replace the faucet body cover—if it was removed—the spout, and the spout ring.

Strainer Plug
Gasket
Strainer
Spring
Stem
Valve Seat

The valve assembly in a tipping-valve faucet has no washers, but it can still leak.

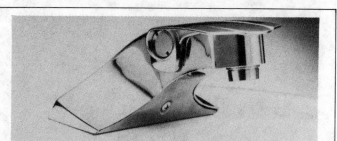

Washerless Faucet Is Top-Mounted

The Endura Faucet by Fillpro, a division of JH Industries, is said to be the only top-mount faucet that eliminates under-the-sink installation. Endura's Pinch Flo system is said to eliminate repair parts: no washers, stems, cartridges, O-rings, or seals are ever necessary to repair the faucet, which has a five-year warranty. The moving parts are not in contact with water. The faucet, according to Fillpro engineers, has a unique lever location that eliminates dripping around the sink deck; it also eliminates hot water waste and offers precise hot and cold flow control. Both bathroom and lavatory faucets are available in two sizes.

Disc Faucets

A disc faucet seldom causes problems, but when it does, the trouble often can be traced to the inlet seals at the bottom of the assembly or to dirt lodged between two ceramic discs. You can troubleshoot a disc faucet by following these steps:

1. Turn off the water to the faucet at the fixture shutoff valve or, if necessary, at the main shutoff valve.
2. Remove the handle. To do this, raise the handle to reveal a setscrew. Loosen the setscrew with an Allen wrench and remove the handle.
3. To remove the faucet body cover, first disconnect any linkage to a pop-up drain under the sink, and then unscrew the screws under the faucet. The body cover lifts off. **Note:** Other types of disc faucets have a screw in the handle and a ring that unscrews to gain access to the round cartridge.
4. With a screwdriver, remove the screws that hold the round cartridge in place and withdraw the cartridge.
5. Examine the ceramic discs and clean any dirt or grit that may be between them.
6. Remove the inlet seals at the bottom of the cartridge; you may have to pry them out with a screwdriver.
7. Install new inlet seals and reassemble the faucet, making sure the screw holes are properly aligned.

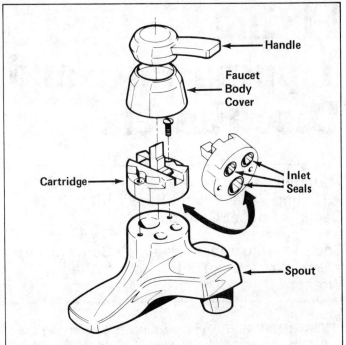

Trouble with a disc faucet often can be traced to the inlet seals at the bottom of the round cartridge assembly or to dirt trapped between its ceramic discs.

8. Turn on the water and test the faucet. If the faucet leaks around the handle, remove it once again and tighten the screws that hold the disc assembly together. If the leak persists, install a new cartridge.

All That Glitters May Be Faucets

New lavatory faucets from the Bradley Corp. feature cast brass bodies with hand-polished finishes for the elegant look of gold. The faucets are available in a number of styles. The faucet cartridges inside the faucet housing carry the company's free-replacement warranty, which insures against leaks or drips for 1,000 months. Complete installation instructions are included with each faucet.

Filter Unit Cleans Water at Every Tap

No expensive or gimmick plumbing runs are needed to hook up the Omni clean water system in your home. The Omni cartridge filter, which is installed in your main water supply line, cleans water at every tap—not just at one. It removes rust, silt, sludge, scale, and other sediments, according to the Omni Corp., which offers a one-year warranty and a 30-day, unconditional, money-back guarantee. Most installations take less than 30 minutes, and complete instructions are included with the Omni kit. The system may be attached to existing copper or plastic water lines; all materials are included. If, however, your plumbing

system is galvanized steel pipe, a 2-inch nipple and ¾-inch union are also required for installation.

Clogged Drains

Materials • Rags • Petroleum Jelly • Container • Adhesive Tape • Wire Coat Hanger • Pipe Joint Compound or Tape • Chemical Drain Cleaner

Tools • Plunger • Screwdriver • Hammer • Long-Nose Pliers • Adjustable Wrench • Pipe Wrench • Drain-and-Trap Auger

GREASE, hair, detergent, and other debris can quickly clog a sink, lavatory, or bathtub drain. To prevent this, put a dose of chemical drain cleaner in all household drains once a week to keep them clean; carefully follow product directions and warnings.

If, however, a drain becomes partially clogged, the trouble is usually easy to correct; add some chemical drain cleaner and give it time to work—at least 30 minutes or more.

Sink and Lavatory Drains

Caution: If the drain is completely stopped, don't use a chemical drain cleaner. It wouldn't effectively reach the clog, and you may have to remove the fixture's trap or clean-out plug to free the blockage. This would expose you to caustic agents in the cleaner. Instead, follow these steps:

1. Locate the fixture's overflow vent opening and block it with a wet rag to seal the opening as tightly as possible.
   Note: Most kitchen sinks don't have a vent, but if you are working on one of two side-by-side basins, you'll have to plug the other basin's drain opening with a wet cloth too. In addition, there may yet be another drain outlet connected to the drain line you are working on that must be blocked as well.
2. Fill the clogged basin with enough water to cover the head of a plunger, or rubber force cup. It also is a good idea to coat the rim of the plunger's cup with petroleum jelly; this creates a tighter seal between the cup and fixture surface.
3. Slide the plunger cup over the drain opening.
4. Rapidly pump the plunger up and down about 15 to 30 times; feel the water move in and out of the drain. It is this alternating water pressure and vacuum that can eventually build up enough force to dislodge whatever is blocking the drain. After vigorously stroking, jerk the plunger up quickly; the water should swirl down the drain.
5. If the drain is still clogged, repeat Step 4 two or three more times before proceeding.
6. If the plunger doesn't unclog the drain, remove the stopper and strainer, if present, in the drain.
   Note: In some sinks, the stopper is removed by twisting and lifting it out. In others, the stopper may be removed by loosening a knurled cap that holds the stopper lever into the drainpipe below the basin; twist the lever to disengage it from the bottom of the stopper. In kitchen sinks, the strainer can be removed by unscrewing a large locknut directly below the strainer under the basin. Use a screwdriver and hammer to tap the locknut loose so that it can be unscrewed. Long-nose pliers can be used as a wrench to unscrew the locknut; spread the handles of the pliers, insert them into the strainer holes, and turn the strainer.
7. Place a container large enough to collect the water in the basin under the fixture's trap. The trap is a U-shaped pipe directly below the fixture.
   Note: If the trap has a clean-out plug, remove it with an adjustable wrench to drain the water, and proceed to Step 12.
8. Apply adhesive tape to the jaws of a large pipe

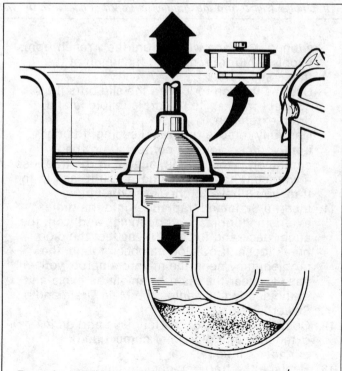

To unclog a sink or lavatory drain, cover the plunger's rubber cup with water and plug the vent opening with wet rags.

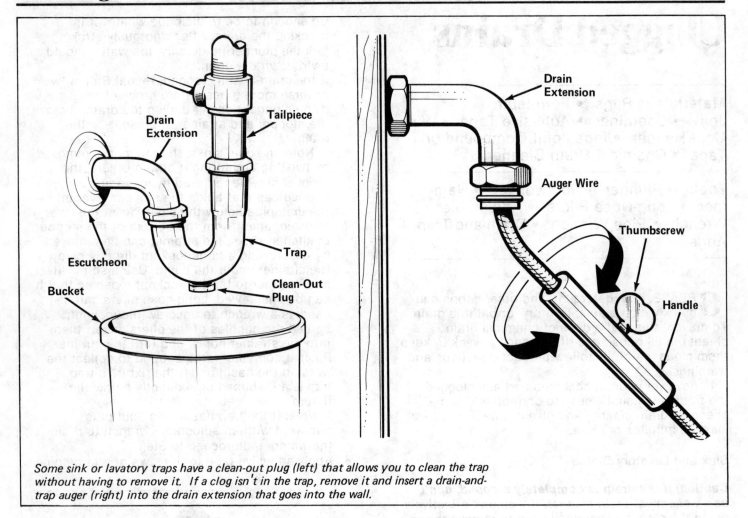

Some sink or lavatory traps have a clean-out plug (left) that allows you to clean the trap without having to remove it. If a clog isn't in the trap, remove it and insert a drain-and-trap auger (right) into the drain extension that goes into the wall.

wrench; the tape will prevent the wrench from slipping and from marring the finish of the trap's slip nuts.

9. Use the wrench to loosen the slip nuts that connect the trap to the drain tailpiece and drain extension.
10. Carefully remove the trap, keeping it upright until you can pour its contents into the container. If the clog is located in the trap, use a wire coat hanger to remove it. If it isn't in the trap, you'll have to check the drainpipe.
11. Insert a drain-and-trap auger into the drain extension (or clean-out opening), and work the auger back and forth until you feel the clog break loose. If no clog has been found, the problem may be in the main drainpipe; you will have to clear the main clean-out as explained in the section "Opening the Main Drain and Sewer" in this chapter.
12. Coat the threads of the tailpiece and drain extension with pipe joint compound or plumber's tape.
13. Replace the trap or clean-out plug.
14. Run water through the drain until it is thoroughly flushed.

Bathtub Drain

A bathtub drain is more difficult to unclog because you can't reach the trap as easily as you can reach sink and lavatory traps. Follow this procedure:

1. Remove the stopper and strainer from the bathtub drain.
2. Block the tub's overflow vent opening with a wet rag.
3. Use a plunger as described in Steps 2 through 5 in the procedure for unclogging a sink or lavatory drain.
4. If the plunger doesn't unclog the drain, remove the metal escutcheon plate that aligns the stopper lever on the front of the tub over the drain; two screws usually hold this plate to the tub.
5. Remove the lever assembly.
6. Insert a drain-and-trap auger through the escutcheon opening until it is threaded through the drainpipe underneath the tub; you will have to push hard so the auger turns the corners in the pipe. Move the auger back and forth until you feel it penetrate the clog.

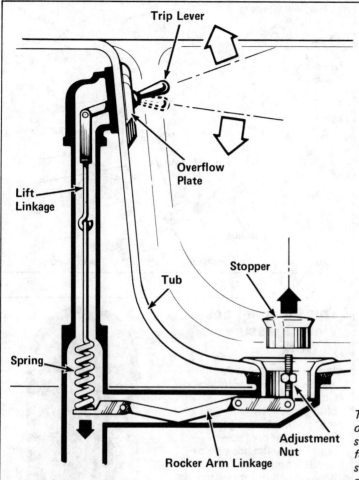

Trip Lever

Overflow Plate

Lift Linkage

Spring

Tub

Stopper

Rocker Arm Linkage

Adjustment Nut

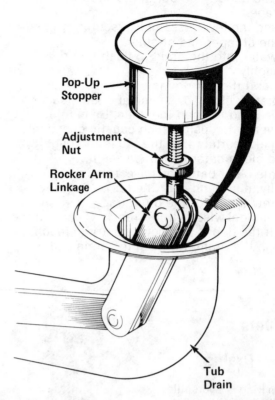

Pop-Up Stopper

Adjustment Nut

Rocker Arm Linkage

Tub Drain

This tub pop-up stopper (left) has a spring that rests on one end of a rocker arm; the other end of the arm is attached to the stopper itself. When the trip lever is raised, the spring is depressed, forcing one end of the rocker arm down; the other end raises the stopper in the tub. Usually, there's a nut at the stopper for height adjustment (right).

Drain Parts Designed for Do-It-Yourselfer

Because they're made of chrome-plated brass, drain components produced by Chicago Specialty Manufacturing Co. won't rust and cause leaks. The tubular parts, especially designed for do-it-yourself installation, include a 5-inch lavatory plug assembly; 6-inch threaded extension tube; 15-inch waste arm; 7½-inch wall tube; and slip-joint extension tubes in 6-inch and 12-inch lengths. The parts will work with 1¼-inch and 1½-inch drains in the kitchen, laundry, or bathroom. The only tools needed for installation are a slip-joint pliers, adjustable wrench,

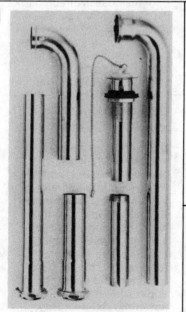

or pipe wrench. Complete installation instructions are included with each part.

Keep Drains Clean When You Shampoo

Shampooing can cause sink and lavatory drains to clog with hair. Hair-Snare, a simple, plastic strainer from the O'Malley Valve Co., keeps hair out of drains yet retains water for rinsing. The device can be used on almost any drain in your home; it snaps over the drain opening.

Types of Pipe Vises and How to Use Them

There are two types of vises used for plumbing—the yoke vise and the chain vise. They are available in several capacities and will hold pipe up to about 8 inches in diameter. The chain vise is for irregular work. For most plumbing jobs, the yoke type vise is probably your best buy. This vise is bolted to a workbench. It has a hinge at one end and a hook at the other so the pipe can be locked into the unit.

7. With the auger, pull out or break up the blockage.
8. Replace the lever assembly, escutcheon plate, and the stopper and strainer.
9. Run water into the drain to flush it out thoroughly.

Note: If the tub drains slowly, but is not completely blocked, chemical drain cleaner can be used to open the drain. Be careful, however, when using such caustic chemicals, and make certain that the tub is thoroughly rinsed clean before anyone uses it.

Some older bathtubs have a drum trap. Usually, it's found near the tub at floor level. Unscrew the lid of the drum trap counterclockwise with a wrench. Clean out the trap. If the debris is elsewhere, try to reach it through the drum trap with the drain-and-trap auger.

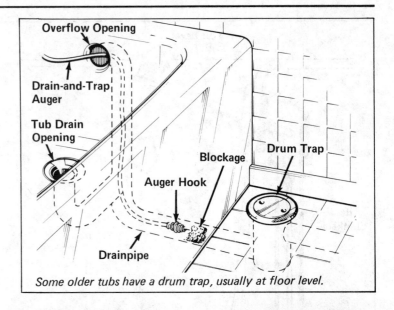

Some older tubs have a drum trap, usually at floor level.

Pulsed Water Jets Attack Clogged Drains

The Drain King is a versatile bladder-like device that uses ordinary household water to unclog sinks, tubs, showers, and main drains. You connect the Drain King to a garden hose and insert the device into the clogged drainpipe. After you turn on the water, the Drain King automatically expands to form a seal in the pipe above the clog; a surge valve then sends pulses of water through the pipe to loosen and clear the blockage. An automatic lock-in valve locks the device in place so that negative back-pressure will not cause it to slip out of the pipe while it's working. And, a check valve protects the water supply by preventing any backflow from occurring. The product, manufactured by G. T. Water Products, Inc., is recommended for use with cold water pressure from 40 to 80 pounds per square inch. Several Drain King models are available for 1-inch to 6-inch drains. The product comes with instructions for use.

This Plunger Uses Water Pressure to Work

The Splunger from Pacific Hardware Manufacturing Co., is a suction-type plunger with two handles that connects to a garden hose. Water pressure supplied by the hose helps the Splunger dislodge and break up obstructions in drains, tubs, toilets, and garbage disposers. Water from the hose is directed to the clog and then backs up when the water has no return. This pressure is then forced to the blockage to release it. The device carries a one-year warranty.

Use an Auger to Clear Clogs

Drain-and-trap augers, sometimes called plumber's snakes, come in various lengths. When you buy an auger, look for one that comes encased in a metal housing—it's easier and less messy to use. If the clog is in the trap, remove the stopper from the drain and insert the auger wire. If the clog is not in the fixture's trap, remove the trap, and insert the auger into the drain extension that goes into the wall. Feed in the flexible wire while you crank the auger handle clockwise. Loosen and then tighten the thumbscrew on the handle as you feed the wire down the drain. When you hit the blockage—you'll feel the difference in the tension on the auger—crank the handle while you slowly withdraw the auger. If a bathtub drain is clogged, first use the auger through the drain. If that doesn't work, insert it into the overflow pipe and down the drain.

Clogged Toilets

Materials • Heavy Plastic Garbage Bag • Twine • Container • Bucket

Tools • Toilet Plunger • Toilet Auger

WHEN A foreign object clogs a toilet, the obstruction usually isn't noticed until the tank has been flushed several times and the bowl is overflowing with water and debris. To clear the toilet, follow these steps:

1. Place your arm in a heavy plastic garbage bag and tie it loosely around your wrist and upper arm. It will protect you from the mess in the bowl.
2. With a container, bail out the excess water in the bowl, leaving enough to cover the head of a toilet plunger. Don't flush the toilet!
3. Place a bulb-type plunger into the bowl. This type of plunger is designed for toilets. You can use a standard plunger, but it won't be as effective. If you discover that the water in the bowl doesn't cover the plunger head, don't flush the toilet; bring a container of water from the lavatory to supply enough to cover the head of the plunger.
4. Rapidly pump the plunger up and down about 15 to 30 times; feel the water move in and out of the bowl. It's this alternating water pressure and vacuum that can eventually build up enough force to dislodge whatever is blocking the toilet. After vigorously stroking, jerk the plunger up quickly; the water should swirl down the toilet. If it's still clogged, repeat the process two or three more times.

    Note: If the plunger has dislodged any objects, such as a washcloth, diaper, small bottle, or toy, don't try to flush them down the toilet; remove the object. And, if the bowl appears to be open, don't flush it yet; pour a bucket of water into the bowl. If the water runs out, you can assume that the clog has been removed. But if the toilet is still clogged, you'll have to use a closet, or toilet, auger.
5. Insert the end of the auger into the toilet trap; this tool has a long sleeve or tube to guide the snake and auger hook on the end into the trap. A crank on the other end enables you to turn the hook. Turn the crank until it feels tight. This means that the snake has twisted its way to and into the blockage. Reverse the direction of the crank every few turns; this will prevent compacting whatever is causing the clog.
6. Once the auger has worked through the clog, pull in the auger and you should be able to remove whatever is clogging the toilet. If you're not successful at first, try the auger several more times. **Note:** If the clog is caused by some solid foreign object, the object must be removed; forcing it down the toilet will only create further problems.
7. When the drain is open, flush the toilet about 10 times; the water will flood the pipe and wash away any small chunks of debris before they can reblock the drain. If all your efforts fail, call a professional plumber.

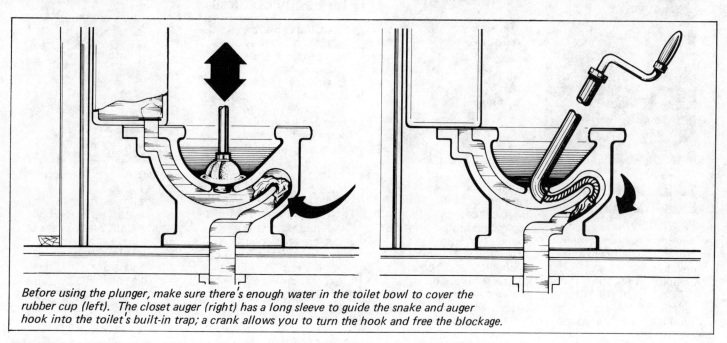

Before using the plunger, make sure there's enough water in the toilet bowl to cover the rubber cup (left). The closet auger (right) has a long sleeve to guide the snake and auger hook into the toilet's built-in trap; a crank allows you to turn the hook and free the blockage.

You Can Buy Just What You Need

You don't have to buy an entire kit of replacement parts to make minor flush tank repairs; the components can be purchased separately. If you are uncertain about sizes or shapes when buying a new part, remove the old part and take it with you to the store. This way you can be sure of getting the exact replacement part, and eliminate the need for exchanges or refunds.

Biological Toilet Uses Hot Water

The Biolet composting toilet from Biolet Corp. doesn't need flushing, chemicals, or a septic tank, and uses little or no electricity to operate. Heat to decompose waste comes from hot water that is circulated through stainless steel tubing inside the toilet. The hot water for the toilet can be provided by your solar heater, a water heater, or other hot water source. Gravity causes the hot water to continuously flow through the coils and air is exhausted by a wind-driven ventilator on the roof. On electrical models, air is pulled through the unit by a small fan. By maintaining tropical humidity and temperatures of about 86° F within the Biolet, and by adding

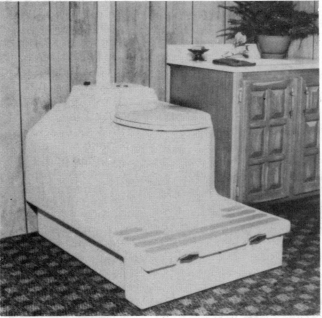

outside air, organic solids are biologically decomposed; liquid is exhausted in the form of water vapor. Except for roof flashing and 2-inch-diameter PVC circulation pipe, ventilation parts are supplied with the Biolet. Application and installation instructions are included.

Emergency Packing for Faucet Leaks

In an emergency, you can soak heavy twine in ordinary motor oil and use it as string packing around a faucet's leaking packing nut. The string, however, should be replaced with regular packing material as soon as possible.

Flush Tank Device Reduces Water Use

One way to reduce water consumption is to limit the amount of water used for flushing. The Toilet Tank Water Saver, produced by Con-Serv., Inc., holds back up to 3 gallons of unnecessary water with every flush. This action, according to the company, can reduce water bills by as much as 20 percent. The water-saving unit is made of stainless steel and thermo-plastic rubber; it reportedly won't break, rust, or move out of position. The product fits most flush tanks, and comes packaged with complete installation instructions.

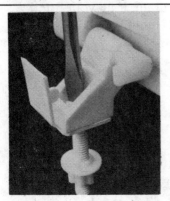

Toilet Seat Offers Easy-Cleaning Feature

A hinge design that permits quick, easy removal of the cover and seat for thorough cleaning is a feature of the E-Z On/E-Z Off solid-plastic toilet seat from Magnolia Products. Both the cover and the seat have a sanitary, contoured lift. Semi-concealed Hi-Rise top-mount hinges offer fast installation with just a screwdriver. The toilet seat, available in solid colors or a marbleized version, in white, pink, blue, parchment, gold, and green, fits standard toilet bowls.

Flusher Flapper Fixer for Faulty Fixtures

Flush tank balls can be a problem when they don't seat properly. The water runs constantly and costs you money. The Flusher Fixer Kit from Fluidmaster, Inc., solves this problem because the flapper ball comes with its own stainless steel replacement seat. This eliminates misalignment that so often is the problem with hook-on flappers. The Flusher Fixer also eliminates lift wires and guides and the problems they cause. No tools are needed for installation. The Flusher Fixer is bonded to the existing brass or plastic flush valve seat with a ready-to-apply epoxy

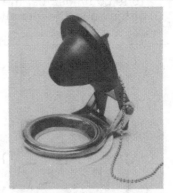

sealant. A special adapter ring is provided for installation on most flush valve seats. The assembly fits standard 2-inch brass or plastic flush valve seats. Complete installation instructions are provided. Once installed, Fluidmaster claims that you should never have to replace the part.

Flush Tank Repairs

Materials • Float Ball • Lift Wire • Emery Cloth or Steel Wool • Tank Ball • Water-Resistant Lubricant • Handle • Trip Lever • Ballcock Washers • Sponge • Penetrating Oil • Ballcock Assembly • Pipe Joint Compound • Spud Pipe • Flush Tank Mounting Washers

Tools • Utility Knife • Adjustable Wrench • Screwdriver • Locking-Jaw Pliers • Spudwrench

THE TOILET is one of the most important fixtures in your home. Although it's a sturdy and reliable component of the plumbing system, it's a rare homeowner or apartment-dweller who never has problems with a toilet. Fortunately, most troubles can be fixed by the do-it-yourselfer.

Silencing a Noisy Toilet

Toilet noises are not only disturbing, they also can be costly. Usually, such noises can be easy to stop.

For example, splashing sounds may be caused by the water flow from the flush tank's refill tube spilling—or partially spilling—into the flush tank instead of the overflow tube. To cure this, bend the refill tube to align it properly. If the tube's plastic, make sure the clip at the end slips over the lip of the overflow tube.

A high-pitched water noise can often be corrected by simply adjusting the water flow into the flush tank at the fixture's shutoff valve; turn the valve slightly one way or the other. If this doesn't solve the problem, the noise may be caused by a worn washer in the ballcock assembly. The replacement procedure is covered in ''Repairing a Ballcock Assembly,'' later in this section.

A toilet that runs continuously is especially annoying. Almost always the trouble can be isolated to one of three areas: the tank ball and the flush valve seat, the lift wire and its guide, or the ballcock assembly. To determine the cause, follow these steps:

1. Remove the top of the flush tank and slowly lift the float arm and ball. If the water stops running, carefully bend the arm slightly downward so there's a gentle curve in the arm; don't kink it. If the ball is rubbing against the side of the tank, bend the arm slightly to move the ball away. It's also possible that there is water in the ball. In this case, hold the arm up and unscrew the ball counterclockwise from the arm, and drain the ball. If the ball is leaking, replace it; if not, screw it back on the arm. If the arm and float ball are not the problem, you'll have to check the tank ball's alignment.
2. Flush the toilet several times and observe the tank ball dropping onto the flush valve seat at the bottom of the tank. If the ball doesn't seat properly, check the lift wire; it may be bent. Bend the wire back into position or replace it. Be sure the lift wire is connected to the proper hole in the trip lever. You also may have to rotate the guide so that it directs the lift wire and tank ball correctly onto the valve seat. If this adjustment doesn't correct the problem, you'll have to inspect the tank ball and flush valve seat.
3. Turn off the water to the toilet at the fixture shutoff valve or, if necessary, at the main

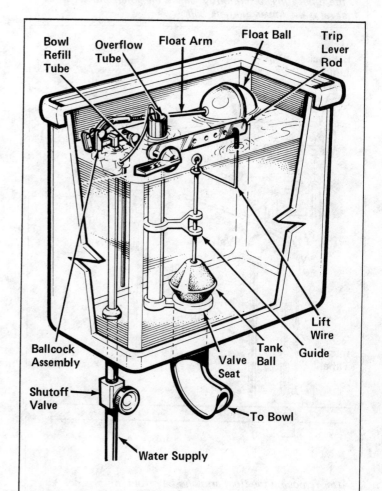

Most toilet flush tank troubles can be fixed quickly and easily. Shown is a cross-section of a typical flush tank and its components.

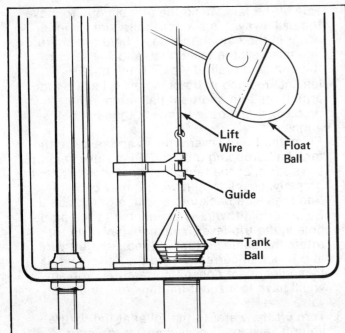

If the toilet runs continuously, check the guide and lift wires that raise and lower the tank ball.

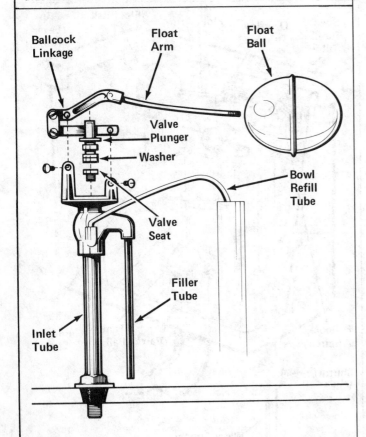

After removing the float arm and ball from the ballcock assembly, remove the screws at the top of the assembly. Then pry out the valve plunger to gain access to the washer or washers at the base of the valve.

shutoff valve, and flush the toilet to drain the tank.

4. Inspect the flush valve seat for signs of corrosion. Use emery cloth, steel wool, or a utility knife to clean any debris around the seat.
5. Examine the tank ball for signs of wear or damage and, if necessary, replace it. If the tank ball operates properly and is in good condition, you'll have to check the handle-to-tank ball linkage.
6. Examine the trip lever; it should be aligned with the tank ball linkage, although it may be, by design, slightly offset. If the trip lever is not aligned, bend it into proper alignment gently.
7. Apply water-resistant lubricant to the threads of the handle assembly inside the flush tank and tighten the handle nuts with an adjustable wrench. If tightening doesn't solve the problem, you'll have to replace the handle.
8. Remove the nut that holds the handle and then disconnect the lift wire, which is usually held to the trip lever by a clip or chain. Remove the assembly from the tank.
   Note: In some tanks, the handle is held by a setscrew. Loosen it with a screwdriver and slip it off. Also remove the nut directly in back of the front of the handle. Remove the handle and trip lever.
9. Install a new handle and trip lever assembly.
10. If the toilet continues to run, you've narrowed the problem down to the ballcock assembly.

Repairing a Ballcock Assembly

If water flowing into the flush tank will not shut off or if the flushing mechanism operates sluggishly or not at all, the ballcock assembly may be the cause. This component is a simple valve that is opened and closed on most flush tanks by the up-and-down movement of the float ball on the water in the tank. Here's how to troubleshoot this problem:

1. Remove the float arm and ball from the ballcock assembly by unscrewing the arm counterclockwise.
2. Remove the thumbscrews at the top of the ballcock assembly. **Note:** If your unit has a different linkage arrangement, you still should be able to determine how to remove the assembly's valve plunger. Some assemblies have washers under a top cap held by two screws that are threaded into the ballcock housing; remove these screws and the cap to expose and replace the washers. Some ballcock assemblies, however, are completely sealed, and there's no way to get inside the units. In such a case, you'll have to purchase a replacement ballcock assembly.
3. With the tip of a screwdriver, pry out the valve

plunger; lightly buff it with emery cloth or steel wool to remove any corrosion.

4. After removing the valve plunger, you'll see one or two washers; replace them. **Note:** The washer at the base of the valve may be held by a screw or it may be a push-fit washer that goes into a round recess. If the valve has a split washer—usually made of leather—along its stem, remove it with a screwdriver or your fingers, and snap a new one into the groove.

5. Replace the valve plunger and reassemble the ballcock linkage.

6. Turn on the water at the fixture shutoff valve and test the flushing action. You may have to bend the float arm slightly or turn an adjustment screw at the base of the arm to obtain the proper water level in the flush tank. **Note:** For adequate flushing, the water level should be about ½ inch below the top of the overflow tube.

Replacing a Ballcock Valve

If your ballcock valve cannot be adjusted or repaired, you'll have to replace it. There are about four basic ballcock valve designs and all of them have the same function: regulating the water flow into the flush tank or toilet bowl. For installing a typical ballcock valve, use the following procedure:

1. Remove the flush tank cover, turn off the water at the fixture shutoff valve, and flush the toilet to drain the water out of the flush tank.

2. With a sponge, soak up the water remaining in the flush tank.

3. Unscrew the float arm and ball from the ballcock assembly by turning the arm counterclockwise, and remove the end of the refill tube from the overflow tube; it may be clipped on or bent into position.

4. Under the flush tank, use an adjustable wrench to disconnect the coupling nut on the water inlet pipe where it enters the tank.

5. Use an adjustable wrench to grip the retaining nut or locknut immediately above the coupling nut under the tank, and a locking-jaw pliers to grip the base of the ballcock assembly shaft inside the tank. Unscrew the nut under the tank to remove the ballcock assembly. If the nut is stubborn, try using some penetrating oil to loosen it.

6. Lift the ballcock assembly out of the tank. Save all washers, gaskets, and other parts until you install the new unit; these parts should be included with the new unit, but it's smart to keep them handy just in case.

7. Insert the new ballcock assembly in the hole in the bottom of the tank with the inside washer in place, and hand-tighten the retaining nut. With an adjustable wrench tighten this nut

sufficiently to make the inside washer fit watertight against the hole, but don't overtighten it or you may crack the tank.

8. Reconnect the water inlet pipe's coupling nut, replace the float arm and ball, and insert the end of the refill tube in the overflow tube.

9. Turn the water on at the shutoff valve, and check for leaks at all connections. Retighten any connections if necessary. **Note:** A leak may be around the water inlet pipe—not the ballcock assembly retaining nut. Try tightening the water supply nut at the ballcock base.

Fixing Flush Tank Leaks

On older fixtures, a wall-mounted flush tank may be connected to the toilet bowl by a spud pipe. There sometimes can be leakage at the spud pipe connections. If this is the case, try tightening the slip nuts at the pipe connections with a spudwrench. If this doesn't stop the leak, remove the spud pipe and apply pipe joint compound to the male threads of the spud pipe, and reconnect it. If the pipe continues to leak, replace it.

On newer, two-piece toilets, the flush tank is bolted to the bowl, and leaks are usually caused by loose bolts or worn washers and gaskets between the tank and bowl. To treat such leaks, follow these steps:

1. Remove the flush tank cover, turn off the water at the fixture shutoff valve, and flush the toilet to drain the water out of the flush tank.

2. With a sponge, soak up the water remaining in the flush tank.

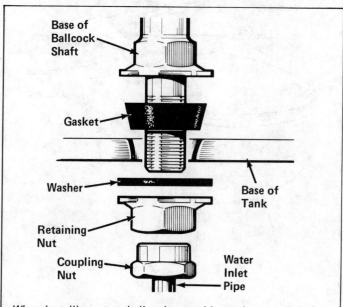

When installing a new ballcock assembly, make sure that the gasket and washer at the base of the tank are properly seated and firmly secured by the shaft's retaining nut.

3. Use an adjustable wrench and screwdriver to tighten the hold-down bolts that connect the flush tank to the toilet bowl. *Caution: Don't apply too much pressure on the bolts; this can crack the fixture.* If this doesn't stop the leakage, you will have to replace the washers between the flush tank and bowl.

4. With an adjustable wrench, disconnect the coupling nut on the water inlet pipe from the bottom of the flush tank.

5. With an adjustable wrench and screwdriver, remove the hold-down bolts connecting the flush tank to the toilet bowl.

6. Lift the tank off the bowl, being careful not to drop rubber washers, locking nuts, or other parts into the bowl.

7. Install new washers and reassemble the fixture. Tighten the hold-down bolts snugly but not too tightly or you might damage the fixture.

8. Connect the water inlet pipe to the flush tank.

9. Turn the water on at the shutoff valve and check for leaks at all connections.

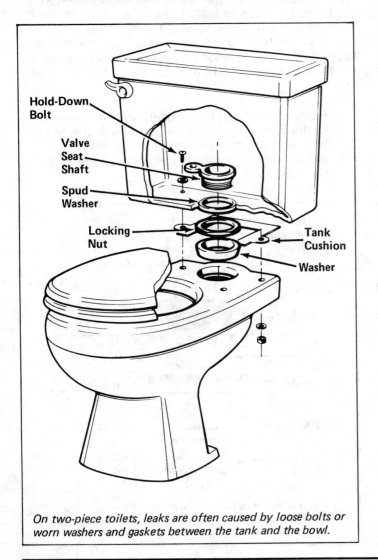

Hold-Down Bolt

Valve Seat Shaft

Spud Washer

Locking Nut

Tank Cushion

Washer

On two-piece toilets, leaks are often caused by loose bolts or worn washers and gaskets between the tank and the bowl.

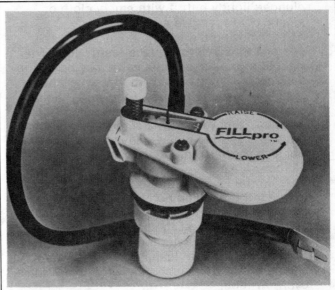

Low-Profile Ballcock Eliminates the Float

The Fillpro toilet tank fill valve is a replacement for the old-style float ball, which is often the cause of tank overflow and noisy operation problems. The Fillpro valve, according to the manufacturer JH Industries, operates on hydrostatic principles that measure and control the water level in the flush tank. The water level may be set to the minimum amount—about 3 gallons—by turning a screw on top of the valve. The valve connects to the water supply pipe; all hardware to make the connections is included. Complete installation instructions are furnished with the valve, which is guaranteed for five years.

Ballcock Fits Any Standard Flush Tank

It's adjustable, which means that this plastic ballcock made by the Chicago Specialty Manufacturing Co. will fit all standard toilet flush tanks and regulate the amount of water used. The ballcock shaft telescopes to nine different adjustments—between 9 and 13 inches—eliminating the need for an exact-size replacement. The ballcock float arm is also adjustable so you can control and save water—down to 3½ gallons per flush. Approved for use by all plumbing codes, the non-corrosive ballcock can be installed easily. Complete instructions are included.

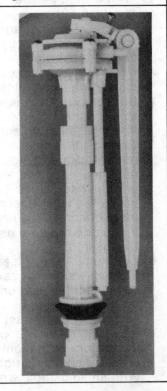

Opening the Main Drain and Sewer

Materials • Bucket • Newspapers and Rags • Penetrating Oil

Tools • Pipe Wrench • Drain-and-Trap Auger • Power Rooter • Garden Hose

---

WHENEVER A clog is not found in a fixture's trap or drainpipe, most likely it's farther down the drainage system—in the main drain or sewer.

The Main Drain

If you suspect a clog may be in the main drainpipe, locate the main clean-out; it's a Y-shaped fitting near the bottom of your home's soil stack or where the drain leaves your building. Follow these steps:

1. Place a large bucket beneath the clean-out and prepare plenty of newspapers and rags around the site to soak up backed-up water.
2. Using a pipe wrench, unscrew the clean-out plug counterclockwise slowly, trying to control the flow of water that will seep from the opening. If the plug is difficult to open, apply penetrating oil and wait about 30 minutes before attempting to remove the plug.
3. Once the flow of water has stopped and you have cleaned up the flooded site, insert a drain-and-trap auger in the pipe going toward your home's fixtures. When you reach the obstruction, twist the auger and use short, back-and-forth strokes until you can feel the blockage break up. Then, withdraw the auger and replace the clean-out plug. If you have not located the blockage, you may have to try a house trap—if there is one—or an outside clean-out. A house trap is a U-shaped fitting installed underground. You can locate it by finding two adjacent clean-out plugs in the floor, if the main drain runs under the floor.
   Note: Sometimes, a clog can collect in the soil stack—the vertical drainpipe that leads from the main drain and ends at the roof vent. If you have an auger long enough to reach the bottom of this pipe from the roof vent opening, you can try to free the blockage from the roof.

This, however, can be risky work especially on steeply pitched roofs, and it may be better to call in a professional.

4. At the house trap, place plenty of newspapers and rags around the trap to soak up water.
5. Use a wrench to unscrew the clean-out plug nearest the sewer outside. Turn the plug counterclockwise slowly. If water starts flowing out of the trap as you unscrew it, you'll have to work fast to try to remove the clog toward the sewer outside with the auger; otherwise, replace the plug and call in a professional. If the clog, however, is in the direction of the main clean-out, you should be able to remove it with little trouble.
6. Insert the auger into the trap and remove the blockage. If the trap is not blocked, remove the other clean-out plug.
7. Insert the auger in the clean-out opening closest to the main clean-out to remove the blockage.
8. After the blockage has been removed, replace the clean-out plugs.

Clearing the Sewer

In older homes—sometimes newer ones too—sewer clogging can be a problem because tree roots grow through the joints of clay sewer pipe. Even cast-iron pipe can become clogged. This type of blockage needs more than a plunger or drain-and-trap auger can provide. The most effective solution is to use an electric rooter that is inserted into the pipe and cuts away roots from the pipe walls as it is moved along. You can rent one of these power rooters at a tool-rental firm. Follow these steps:

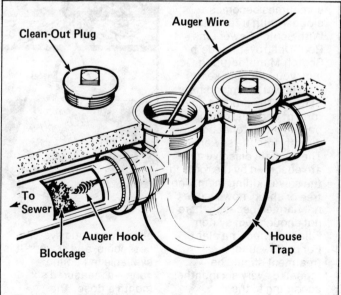

The house trap is a U-shaped fitting. You can locate it by finding two adjacent clean-out plugs in the floor.

Plumbing

1. Locate the clean-out that is closest to the blockage. This may be the main clean-out, a house trap, or an outside sewer clean-out.
2. Place plenty of newspapers and rags around the site to soak up backed-up water.
3. Remove the clean-out plug by turning it counterclockwise.
4. Insert the flexible blades of the power rooter into the opening and turn on the device. When the machine's cutting blades encounter roots, you should be able to feel the cable strain. Give the machine time to chew away any roots and keep feeding in the cable slowly until you feel a breakthrough; then go over the area again.
5. Turn off and remove the power rooter.
6. Insert a garden hose into the clean-out and flood the pipe for at least 10 minutes to wash away root cuttings and other debris.
7. Before returning the power rooter to the rental firm, replace the clean-out plug and flush a toilet several times. When you are convinced that the pipe is free of tree roots, clean the power rooter and return it.

   Note: If you cannot rent a power rooter or dislodge the blockage with a garden hose or drain-and-trap auger, call a professional. Delaying the cleaning job will only pack the pipe tighter and may cause trouble elsewhere in your drainage system.

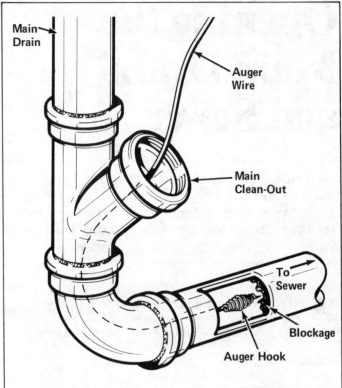

A clog in the main drain may be reached from the main clean-out; it's a Y-shaped fitting near the bottom of your home's soil stack or where the drain leaves the building.

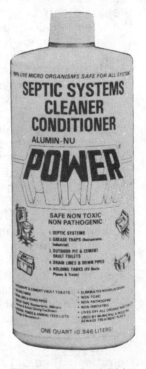

Your Home's Electrical System

ELECTRICITY ENTERS your home by means of three wires (older homes may have two) that supply 220-240 volts AC (alternating current) to a main entrance panel. There, the power is split into a series of 110-120-volt circuits that furnish electricity for lighting, outlets, and appliances. One or two circuits may remain at 220-240 volts to power a clothes dryer, an air conditioner, or other appliances that require higher voltage to operate.

The main entrance panel may be equipped with circuit breakers, a combination of circuit breakers and plug or cartridge fuses, or just plug or cartridge fuses. In some older homes, there may be more than one panel; one or more additional panels may have been added to meet a demand for more power.

No matter what type of main entrance panel you have, it should have a main disconnect that shuts off *all* power to *all* circuits. The main disconnect could be a set of pull-out fuses, a circuit breaker, or a large switch. There will also be separate circuit breakers or fuses to shut off power to individual circuits.

Individual circuits should be labeled at the main entrance panel so you'll know what rooms they supply. If they're not labeled, do so now, so when there is a power failure you will know which circuit to check.

Circuit breakers and fuses are safety devices built into your electrical system. They are there to prevent overloading of a particular circuit. They are designed to trip or blow, stopping the flow of current to the overloaded cable. A blown fuse or a tripped circuit breaker is the signal to look for trouble. *Caution: Never attempt to defeat this safety system. Heat generated by an electrical overload could start a fire.*

When the power in a circuit fails, follow these steps:

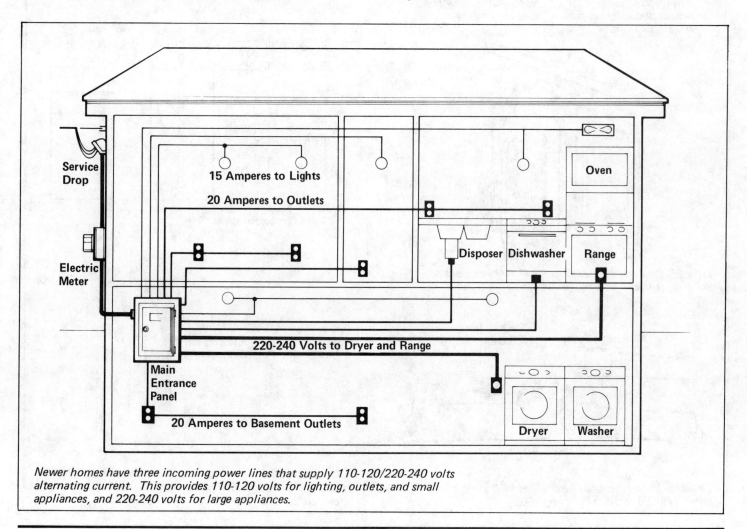

Newer homes have three incoming power lines that supply 110-120/220-240 volts alternating current. This provides 110-120 volts for lighting, outlets, and small appliances, and 220-240 volts for large appliances.

Fuse Panel

Circuit Breaker Panel

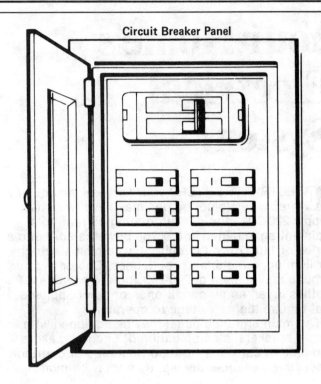

In addition to screw-in fuses, a typical main fuse panel has a main disconnect and other pull-out blocks with cartridge-type fuses.

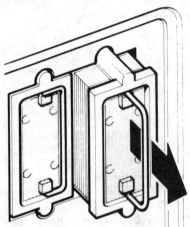

To reach the cartridge fuses, you pull the blocks out of the main entrance panel.

Cartridge Fuses

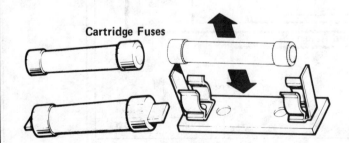

Cartridge fuses, which can be checked with a continuity tester, are held in place by spring clips.

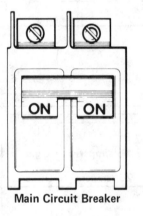

Main Circuit Breaker

Single Circuit Breaker

Double Circuit Breaker

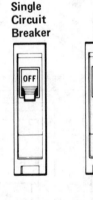

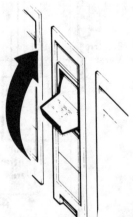

Push Tripped Circuit Breaker to "On" to Restore Power

Circuit breakers do not blow like fuses; they are switches that automatically trip open to interrupt the flow of electrical current when it overloads the circuit.

1. Reactivate a tripped circuit breaker by flipping the toggle of the switch to its "on" position. Repower a fused circuit by removing the burned-out fuse; unscrew it counterclockwise, and replace it with a new fuse of the same current-carrying capacity, or amperage. The amperage is stamped on the base of the fuse.

   Caution: When working in a main entrance panel located over a dirt or concrete surface, or any other surface that might be damp, always lay down a scrap of plywood or a plank to stand on to isolate yourself from the ground. Keep one hand behind you or in a pocket. Use a fuse-puller when changing cartridge fuses.

2. If the circuit breaker trips or the fuse blows again, this is a signal that something is wrong along the circuit. Turn off or disconnect every appliance and light on the circuit.

3. Reactivate the circuit breaker or install a new fuse in the circuit. If the circuit breaker trips or the fuse blows immediately, there is a short circuit in the wiring because you have disconnected all lights and appliances.

4. With the power to the circuit off, check behind light fixtures, outlets, and wall switches for shorts. Look for loose connections or a frayed, burnt, or bare wire. Tighten the connections; repair the damaged wiring; or replace the switch, outlet, or fixture. If this isn't the problem, call a professional; the trouble probably is behind a wall where you can't see it.

5. If the circuit breaker didn't trip or the fuse didn't blow, connect and then disconnect each appliance and light on the circuit—one at a time. When the circuit breaker trips or the fuse blows again, either the appliance, the outlet, or the switch is faulty. If none of the lights or appliances causes the circuit to blow, connect everything that was on at the time of the power failure. If the circuit blows, it is overloaded. Disconnect some of the devices and connect them to another circuit that isn't overloaded.

Note: If a circuit tends to blow often, check to see if the failure occurs whenever a motor comes on. If so, the circuit has a temporary overload. One solution for a fused main entrance panel is to install a time-delay fuse in the panel. Such a fuse will withstand a short-term overload without blowing yet gives the circuit the protection it needs.

Caution: Whenever you make any electrical repairs to a circuit, make sure that the power has been disconnected at the main service panel. If you have any doubt, disconnect all power to the house by pulling the main fuses or tripping the main circuit breakers.

When Power Goes Off, the Light Goes On

There are few things more frustrating than a power failure in the middle of the night. The refrigerator and freezer stop, maybe the heat goes off, and if you depend on an electric alarm clock to get you up, you're late for work. The Emhart Emergency Alarm Light, sold by Notifier Co., a division of Emhart Industries, Inc., can help prevent such occurrences. The unit plugs into a wall outlet, and a neon night-light lets you know it is working. When the power goes off, the unit switches to rechargeable nickel-cadmium batteries, which power a bright, portable emergency light. At the same time, a low-level alarm sounds to warn of the power failure. With the alarm turned off, the unit serves as a powerful flashlight, with an hour's worth of bright light. The unit is said to be fully

charged in 24 hours, and the manufacturer claims the batteries can be recharged 1,000 times.

Use a Puller for Safe Fuse Removals

Cartridge fuses can be difficult to reach and pull out with your fingers—that's when an inexpensive fuse puller is the answer. Leave one in your toolbox, or hang one on a string next to the fuse box. Made of non-conducting material, fuse pullers come in several sizes to match different size cartridge fuses. The fuse puller shown here, No. PFP-21 from Electripak Inc., a subsidiary of Perfect-Line Mfg. Corp., is a pocket-size fuse puller suitable for fuse sizes to 100 amps, 600 volts; and to 200 amps,

250 volts. The fuse puller is constructed of five laminated sections of dielectric-strength phenolic fiber to provide maximum insulation.

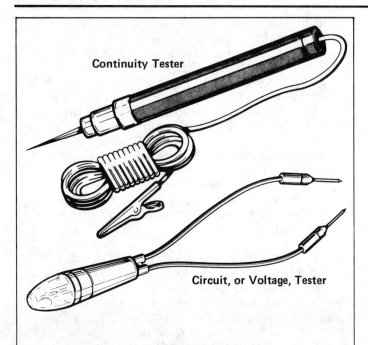

Continuity Tester

Circuit, or Voltage, Tester

Two helpful test instruments for electrical repairs are a continuity tester and a circuit, or voltage, tester.

Tools for Electrical Testing

Test instruments can be very helpful in performing electrical work, such as checking various wiring devices and for accurately diagnosing problems in your home's electrical system and appliances. One such instrument is the circuit, or voltage, tester. It is an inexpensive device that consists of a small neon bulb in a housing with two insulated wires attached; each wire ends in a metal test probe. The circuit tester is used with the power turned on to determine whether electricity is flowing through a wire or connection and to test for proper grounding.

Caution: Be extremely careful when using a circuit tester because you must make such tests with the circuit's power on.

To use a circuit tester, touch one probe to one wire or connection and the other probe to the opposite wire or connection. If the component is receiving electricity, the light in the housing will glow; if it doesn't glow, the trouble is at this point.

For example, to test an ordinary wall outlet, insert one tester probe into one of the two slots of an outlet and the other probe into the other slot; the tester will glow if the outlet is carrying power.

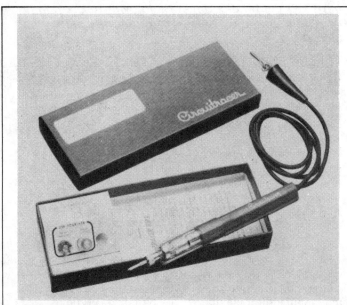

Continuity/Voltage Tester Has an Easy-to-See Test Light

Originally designed for commercial use, the Circuitracer from Desco Industries, Inc., is a testing device available to homeowners. It can be used to test for a dead circuit, or to measure the voltage in live circuits from 0 to 500 volts. The signal light of the Circuitracer is positioned at the working tip so you can keep your eye on the work while testing a series of points. This can save you time, and help eliminate test errors. The Circuitracer kit comes with all necessary test accessories and instructions for use.

Alarm System Signals That Power Is Off

When electrical current is interrupted anyplace in your house or apartment, the Snapit Electronic Power Alarm sounds a loud warning signal, and a red indicator light blinks. The alarm and the light will continue signaling for up to five days, or until the reset button is pushed. The alarm can be used as a warning when the power is off to important appliances—a refrigerator or sump pump—or it can be used to monitor time-sensitive appliances. The unit plugs into any 110-volt receptacle; it operates on a 9-volt alkaline battery, which is not included in the package. The flashing light and the alarm warn when the battery needs replacing. Manufactured by Cable Electric Products, Inc., the alarm has a one-year limited warranty.

Stick With the Right Size Fuse

Never replace a fuse or circuit breaker with a larger fuse or circuit breaker than is specified for the circuit. The fuse or circuit breaker capacity should equal, or be less than, the current-carrying capacity or amperage of the wiring in that circuit. For general household circuits, use 15-amp fuses or circuit breakers; for kitchen and laundry circuits, use 20-amp ones; for special circuits handling large electrical loads, use fuses or circuit breakers with a 25- or 30-amp capacity.

The continuity tester is another extremely useful instrument. It consists of a battery in a housing that has a metal probe at one end; the other end of the housing has a wire with an alligator clip. The continuity tester determines whether a wire or a particular component is capable of carrying electricity, and to pinpoint the cause of a malfunction. Unlike the circuit tester, the continuity tester is always used with the power turned off.

To use a continuity tester, turn off the power to the component to be tested. Fasten the clip of the tester to one wire or connection and touch the tester's probe to the other wire or connection. If the wire or component is capable of carrying electricity, the tester will light or buzz; the circuit is continuous. If it doesn't light or buzz, or if it reacts only slightly, the component is faulty.

For example, to test a simple, single-pole wall switch, shut off the power to the switch circuit. Attach the clip to one switch terminal. While touching the other switch terminal with the tester's probe, operate the switch. If it's operating properly, the tester will light or buzz when the switch is in the "on" position. If the tester doesn't light or buzz, or if it reacts only slightly, the switch is faulty.

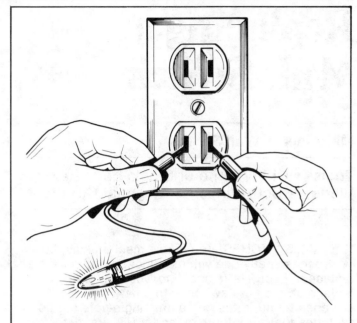

To test an outlet, insert one probe into one slot and the other probe into the other slot; the tester will glow if the outlet is carrying power.

Shockproof Your Tools

By slipping a length of small diameter rubber hose on each handle and wrapping other metal parts with electrical tape, you can add insulation to pliers used for electrical repairs. The shank of a screwdriver can be insulated by slipping a section of rubber tubing over it. Cut the tubing so that it extends from the handle down to just above the blade.

One Unit Controls Both Lights and Appliances

A remote control push-button device that allows you to operate up to 16 household lights and appliances from the comfort of your bed or easy chair is the System X-10 made by BSR (USA) Ltd. The system's Command Console and lamp and appliance modules are simply plugged into any 110-120-volt outlets; no special wiring is required. A lamp module turns on a lamp, dims and brightens it, or turns it off. Similarly, an appliance module is designed to control appliances such as stereo systems, air conditioners, TV sets, fans, and humidifiers. There is also a wall switch module designed to replace a standard wall switch; it controls incandescent lights or lamps normally operated by that switch. An ultrasonic Command Console that works with a cordless controller is also available. Its keyboard matches the one on the Command Console, allowing you to activate the console from up to 30 feet away. The Controller Starter Kit includes the Command Console, one appliance module, and two lamp modules. Modules can be purchased separately as your budget permits.

Don't Be Shocked— Be Protected Instead

Circuit devices such as load centers, safety switches, and circuit breakers offer good protection. They can be installed by a professional, or as a do-it-yourself project. A variety of these products are made by the General Electric Company. All are UL Listed. Amperage and voltage ratings are stamped on each item. Installation instructions are provided on the package.

Replacing a Wall Switch

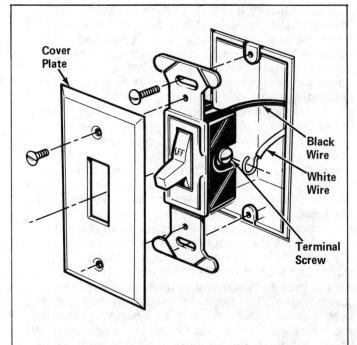

A single-pole wall switch is very easy to install. Connect the circuit wires to the terminal screws, secure the switch, and replace the cover plate.

Materials • Wall Switch

Tools • Utility Knife or Single-Edge Razor Blade • Screwdriver • Diagonal Cutters

WALL SWITCHES are reliable mechanisms, but occasionally one will malfunction and must be replaced. If you are remodeling, you may want to replace an old light switch with a new one. Most switches found in the home are single-pole toggle switches that turn lights on and off. A dimmer switch controls the brightness of the light, from bright to dim to off. A dimmer can replace almost any existing single-pole switch. But, there are also three-way and four-way switches, which are more complex. A three-way switch allows you to turn a light on and off from two different locations. The four-way switch is used with a pair of three-way switches so the light can be controlled from more than two locations. When a switch malfunctions, replace it with a new one of the same type.

Note: Some switches in older homes may have larger toggles that require special cover plates; standard plates will not fit over these switches.

To replace a wall switch, follow these steps:

1. Turn off the power to the circuit with the faulty switch by removing the proper fuse or by tripping the proper circuit breaker to the "off" position.
2. If the switch cover plate is painted, use a

Pilot Switch Reminds You the Light Is On

When you can't see the light that a switch controls, there may be a tendency to leave the light on accidently. This can happen with outdoor lights, garage lights, or closet lights. The answer is to install a pilot light switch; the pilot light glows to let you know that the switch is on. Sylvania switches with neon pilot lights, from GTE Lighting Products, can be used to replace any 15-amp single-pole switch on 120-volt circuits. The pilot light is reported to have a 25,000-hour life span; the light

has an unbreakable red lens. To install, just remove the wires from your old switch, and attach the new switch exactly the same way. The UL Listed pilot light switches are available in brown, white, or ivory.

Touch-Sensitive Dimmer Switch Has a Memory

A new touch-sensitive dimmer control switch that installs as easily as an ordinary light switch is the Dawn electronic light level control, made by Leviton Manufacturing Co., Inc. The solid-state device fits any standard wall box for incandescent lighting up to 600 watts. To turn on the light, you touch the control plate; you touch and hold the plate until the desired light level is reached. To turn off the light, touch the plate again. Touching the plate once more will turn on the light—exactly at the level

you left it before; the control remembers your previous setting. The Dawn light control is available in four colors: brown with gold touch plate and trim, ivory with gold plate and trim, white with silver plate and trim, and black with silver plate and trim. The product is UL Listed.

utility knife to carefully cut the paint film around the edge of the plate.

3. With a screwdriver, remove the screws securing the cover plate. If paint covers a screw slot, remove it with the tip of a utility knife.

4. Remove the mounting screws that secure the switch to the switch box.

5. Carefully pull the switch out of the box as far as the wires allow.

6. Use the screwdriver to loosen the terminal screws; the screws turn counterclockwise. Then, disconnect the wires from their terminals. If the switch has push-in clamp-type terminals, insert the tip of a small blade screwdriver into the slot near the terminal; this releases the clamp that holds the end of the wire in the switch.

   Note: If a bare or green wire is connected to a green hexhead screw on the old switch, it is a ground wire; connect it to the same type of screw on the new switch. If there is no screw for a grounding wire on the switch, the ground wire must be fastened securely to the metal switch box or metal switch mounting bracket.

7. Bend the end of each wire into a clockwise loop and place it around the proper terminal screw of the new switch. Then tighten the screws. Make sure all uninsulated wire is under the screw heads; trim any excess bare wire off with diagonal cutters. If the new switch has clamp-type terminals, push the ends of the wires into the proper terminal holes; the clamps inside will automatically grip them.

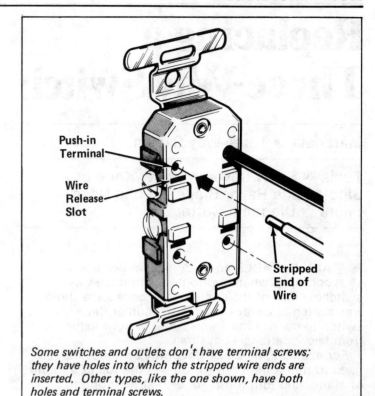

Some switches and outlets don't have terminal screws; they have holes into which the stripped wire ends are inserted. Other types, like the one shown, have both holes and terminal screws.

8. After all the wires have been connected to the new switch, carefully fold in the wires, and position the switch in the switch box.

9. Use the mounting screws provided with the new switch to secure it to the box.

10. Replace the switch cover plate and turn on the power in the circuit.

Here's an Alternative to Full-Range Dimmers

A two-level dimmer switch made by General Electric Co. offers an inexpensive alternative to more sophisticated full-range rotary dimmers. The GE dimmer is a toggle switch that offers the choice of high, low, or no lighting at all. The dimmer replaces any standard wall switch that controls 120-volt, AC, 300-watt maximum incandescent lighting. The switch is available in brown or ivory colors, and is packaged with complete installation instructions.

Change Fuses the Safe Way

Fuse boxes and circuit breakers often are located in a basement or crawl space where the floor can be damp or even wet. If your main entrance panel is located in such an area, when you change a fuse or trip a circuit breaker, it's a good idea to stand on a piece of dry plywood or a wooden platform. The wood serves as an insulator to prevent electrical shock. Also, when you change the fuse or trip the circuit breaker toggle, keep one hand in a hip pocket or behind you to avoid touching a metallic surface and inadvertently completing a circuit.

Replacing a Three-Way Switch

Materials • Three-Way Switch

Tools • Screwdriver • Utility Knife or Single-Edge Razor Blade • Long-Nose Pliers • Diagonal Cutters

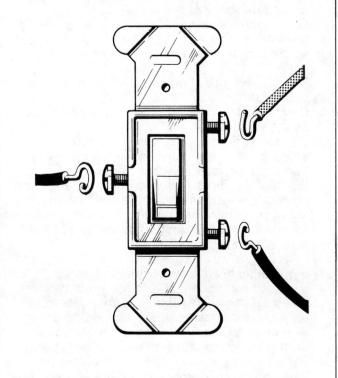

Three-way switches allow you to turn a light on and off from two different locations — such as at the top or at the bottom of a stairway.

MANY CAPABLE do-it-yourselfers become confused when confronted with three-way switches. Part of the confusion is because a three-way switch is always used with another three-way switch to control the same outlet or light fixture from two locations—not three.

For example, a pair of three-way switches can be used to turn a light on—or off—at the top of a flight of stairs, and turn if off—or on—at the bottom. Replacing a three-way switch needn't be confusing at all; to replace one, follow these steps:

1. Turn off the power to the circuit with the faulty three-way switch by removing the proper fuse or by tripping the proper circuit breaker to the "off" position.
2. If the switch cover plate is painted, use a utility knife to carefully cut the paint film around the edge of the plate.
3. With a screwdriver, remove the screws securing the cover plate. If paint covers a screw slot, remove it with a utility knife.
4. Remove the mounting screws that secure the switch to the switch box, and carefully pull out the switch as far as the wires allow.
5. Examine the terminal screws on the switch. Locate the wire that's connected to the switch's common terminal—its terminal may be marked "common" or it will have a screw that is a different color than the other two screws.
6. Use the screwdriver to loosen the common

terminal screw; all the screws turn counterclockwise.
7. Connect the common wire from the old switch to the common terminal screw on the new three-way switch. Use a long-nose pliers to bend the end of the wire into a clockwise loop. Place the loop under the terminal screw and tighten it. Make sure all uninsulated wire is under the screw head; trim away any excess bare wire with diagonal cutters. **Note:** If the new switch has clamp-type terminals, push the ends of the wires into the proper terminal holes; the clamps will automatically grip them.
8. Disconnect the other two wires and connect them to the corresponding terminals on the new switch. **Note:** If there is a bare or green wire connected to a green hexhead screw on the old switch, it's a ground wire; connect it to the same type of screw on the new switch. If there's no screw for a grounding wire on the switch, the ground wire must be fastened securely to the metal switch box or metal switch bracket.
9. After all the wires have been connected to the new switch, carefully fold in the wires, position the new switch in the box, and secure it with the mounting screws provided.
10. Replace the switch cover plate and restore power to the circuit.

Make Connections Correctly for Safety's Sake

The bare wire that you loop around a terminal screw on an outlet, switch, motor, or other device should always go from two-thirds to three-fourths of the distance around the terminal screw. The bare wire should be connected to the terminal screw in a clockwise direction, and the terminal screw should be tightened securely against the bare wire.

Toggle Dimmers Look Like Ordinary Switches

Full Range Toggle Dimmers from Aladdin Products Div., Hybrinetics, Inc., are designed to look like ordinary light switches. They provide full-range dimming control from no light to full intensity. The dimmers employ solid-state circuits, which the manufacturer claims reduce electrical consumption and prolong bulb life. Two models are available: the 810 replaces single-pole switches; the 830 replaces three-way switches. Both units are UL Listed and are available with ivory, brown, or clear lighted toggles.

Decorating Made Easy—Change a Wall Plate

No matter what room decor you have, you're likely to find a switch or outlet cover plate to complement it in the Designer Collection from the General Electric Co. The GE collection is composed of a wide variety of metal and plastic wall cover plates in eight groups: Mediterranean, Artistry, Americana, Provincial, WoodGrain, Contemporary, Nursery, and Turn-Ons. Each group, except for Nursery, includes plates for a single switch, a duplex outlet, and dual switches. The Nursery group only has plates for single switches, and a few groups feature wall plates for combinations of a single switch and a duplex outlet.

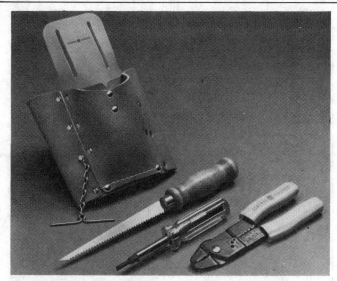

Holster and Tools for Do-It-Yourselfer

Electrical projects around the home are easier when the tools you need are kept handy on your belt. The heavy-duty belt holster from the General Electric Co., does just that. The holster has five tool compartments that will accommodate a number of other GE tools including a four-way screwdriver, multipurpose terminal crimper, and 6-inch wallboard saw. The screwdriver has two interchangeable bits—Phillips head and standard slot. The crimping tool is also a wire cutter, wire stripper, and bolt cutter. Designed for pocket cuts, the pointed blade saw is used for cutting electrical outlet and switch box openings. The holster also features an electrical tape holder at the end of a short length of chain.

A Dimmer Reduces Big Power Demands

The Power Control toggle dimmer switch by Power Controls Corp. lets you tune in the exact amount of light needed from full-on to full-off with full control of mid-range light levels. The dimmer's solid-state circuitry regulates the amount of power required so the switch uses only enough electricity to attain the desired light level. Other features include a design that allows the use of decorator or conventional wall plates, noise suppression that reduces buzzing in radios, and a device that checks the initial power surge so bulbs don't burn out too quickly. Several models are available: the Power Control 600, a 600-watt dimmer available in single-pole or three-way versions; the Power Control 1000, a

heavy-duty, 1000-watt dimmer ideal for track, recessed, security, and flood lighting; and the Power control 360, designed to provide variable speed control for overhead fans, ventilator fans, exhaust fans, and fireplace blowers. The dimmers install just like any regular toggle switch. Models 600 and 1000 come in ivory, brown, or white; model 360 is available in brown or ivory.

Light Up Your Life and Save Energy Too

The Sylvania Miniarc bulb by GTE Lighting Products is said to be more efficient in light production than an incandescent bulb; it will last about five years in average residential use. The 40-watt bulb is reported by GTE engineers to produce more illumination than a standard 100-watt incandescent bulb. According to the company, the bulb can save a homeowner about $22.50 over a lifetime of 7,500 hours. The bulb is 7 inches long and 2½ inches in diameter. It may be used in table lamps and most other household lighting fixtures.

Replacing a Lamp Socket

Materials • Lamp Socket • Wire Nuts

Tools • Screwdriver • Diagonal Cutters

IF YOU HAVE an incandescent table or floor lamp that flickers or won't work at all, the trouble can often be traced to a malfunctioning socket. If you find that the socket is faulty—after checking for a burned-out bulb or a defective plug, wiring, wall switch, or outlet—you can replace the socket easily.

Table and Floor Lamp Sockets

To replace table and floor lamp sockets, follow these steps:

1. Unplug the lamp and remove the shade and light bulb.
2. Remove the old socket. A setscrew usually holds the socket cap (the base of the socket) to a metal tube; loosen the screw with a screwdriver. The socket may also be screwed onto this tube; if so, unscrew it counterclockwise to remove it.
3. Pull up on the socket to expose several inches of wire from inside the lamp to give you adequate slack for working.
4. Squeeze the socket shell near the switch to separate the shell and cardboard insulator from the socket cap. Sometimes, the word "press" is stamped into the metal of the shell.
   Note: If the cap of the shell is stubborn, you can use a screwdriver to pry off the cap, but be careful if you wish to reuse these parts because the metal is easily dented.
5. Slide the socket cap back out of the way along the wires.
6. Use a screwdriver to loosen the terminal screws under the socket, and disconnect the wires.
7. Remove the socket and socket cap. You may have to unknot the wires inside the socket cap to do this.
8. Disassemble the new lamp socket.
9. Insert the wires through the base of the new socket cap and, if necessary, retie a knot in the wires.
10. Connect the wires to the terminals on the new socket. Bend the twisted end of each wire into a clockwise loop. Place each loop under a

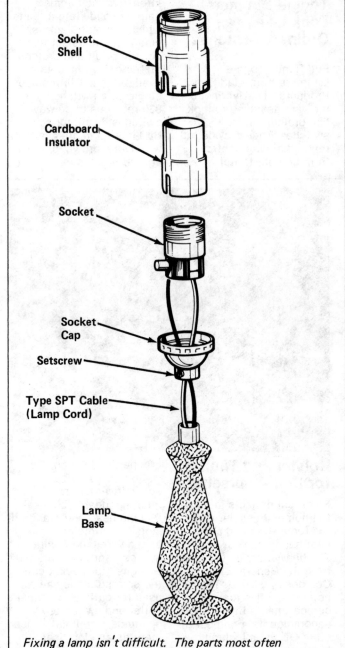

Fixing a lamp isn't difficult. The parts most often responsible for the lamp failing to work are the socket, cord, or plug.

terminal screw, with the loop curled clockwise around the screw. Then tighten the screws. Make sure all uninsulated wire is under the screw heads; trim any excess bare wire off with diagonal cutters.

11. Fasten the new cap onto the metal tube of the lamp.
12. Slide the new socket shell over the cardboard insulator, and slip shell and insulator over the socket. Then snap the shell and socket into the socket cap.

Ceiling and Wall Sockets

Some ceiling and wall fixtures use the same type of sockets found on incandescent table and floor lamps. The replacement procedure is the same, but before beginning, you must take some precautions. *Caution: Because you can't unplug a wall or ceiling fixture, you must cut the power to the circuit you'll be working on. Do this by tripping the proper circuit breaker to the "off" position or by removing the proper fuse at the main entrance panel.*

Note: Metal lamp sockets can sometimes be replaced in wall and ceiling fixtures with porcelain or high-impact plastic models. These types of sockets are wired the same way as metal ones.

And, if the socket or sockets have wires that are connected to wires from an electrical box, twist each wire end together—white wire to white wire and black wire to black wire. Screw a wire nut tightly over each pair of twisted ends.

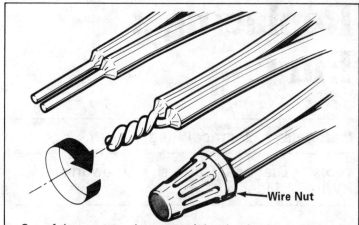

One of the most popular ways to join wires is to use wire nuts. The conductor ends are twisted together and the wire nut is screwed onto the twisted ends; make sure no bare conductor is exposed.

These Dimmers Screw Into Lamp Sockets

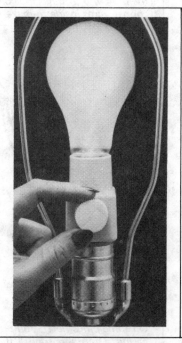

If the outlet your lamp plugs into isn't controlled by a switch—ruling out the installation of a wall-mounted dimmer—and you feel that table top dimmers are unsightly, then the Lamp Socket Dimmer by Aladdin Products Div., Hybrinetics, Inc., may be the answer. The dimmer screws right into the lamp socket—no wiring is necessary; the bulb screws into the dimmer control. The UL Listed dimmers provide full-range dimming control for bulbs up to 200 watts.

Build a Lamp or Just Repair One

If you want to build a lamp or just repair an old one, you can find what you need among lamp parts made by the General Electric Co. Items are individually packaged so you can pick and choose those you require. The parts include sockets, cord switches, lamp cord, plugs, lampshade risers, lamp harps, finials, decorative chain, swag hooks, a lighting fixture canopy kit, swag light kits, and other accessories. Each product includes easy-to-follow instructions for the do-it-yourselfer.

Turn Lights On at Dusk, Off at Dawn

Light controls automatically turn on lights at dusk and turn them off at dawn. They offer protection, convenience, and energy conservation. The light control uses a photoelectric cell to automatically turn lights on and off. You'll never have to come home to a dark house again; and you'll have the comforting knowledge that while you're away your home will look lived in, deterring burglars. The model LL-12 light control, produced by Home Equipment Manufacturing Co., a division of Kenton Industries, Inc., can be used with any lamp. Just plug your lamp into the control and plug the control into a wall outlet. The unit comes with a woodgrain-trimmed case, has a 300-watt capacity, and is UL Listed.

Replacing a Plug

Materials • Electrical Plug

Tools • Diagonal Cutters • Screwdriver
• Wire Stripper

P LUGS ON THE ends of lamp and appliance
cords are subject to stress; they're often
yanked from outlets instead of being removed at the
plug. Such abuse frequently makes it necessary to
replace the plug.

There are two basic types of plugs. One has
screw terminals. The other has a lever-and-clamp
arrangement; the end of the unstripped cord is
inserted into an opening, and a lever on the plug is
clamped down to make the connections.

To replace a plug that has screw terminals, follow
these steps:

1. Cut off the old plug. Or, on heavy-duty plugs,
   loosen the plug's clamp screw securing the
   plug to the cord. Then, pry off the insulating
   disc covering the screw terminals, loosen the
   screws by turning them counterclockwise with
   a screwdriver to release the wires, and pull off
   the plug. Other plugs may be removed
   differently; you'll have to examine a plug
   carefully to determine how this is done. If you
   can't remove it, simply cut it off.
2. Insert the end of the cord through the new
   plug.
3. If the cord has outer insulation covering two or
   more insulated wires, strip off about 3 to 4
   inches of the outer insulation from the end of
   the cord, exposing the insulated wires inside.
4. If necessary, use wire strippers to remove

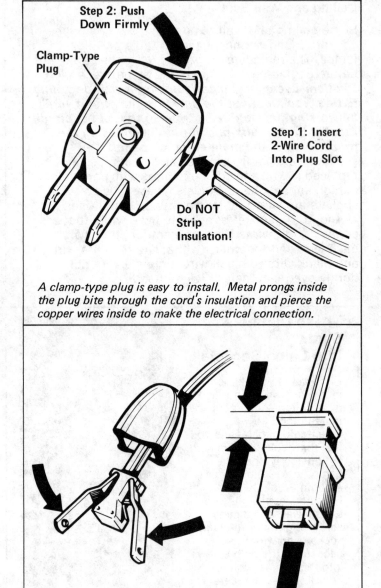

Step 2: Push Down Firmly

Clamp-Type Plug

Step 1: Insert 2-Wire Cord Into Plug Slot

Do NOT Strip Insulation!

*A clamp-type plug is easy to install. Metal prongs inside
the plug bite through the cord's insulation and pierce the
copper wires inside to make the electrical connection.*

*On some plugs (left), you pull the prongs out of the plug
casing. On others (right), the casing is pulled off an
inner section.*

Handy Tool Strips, Cuts, and Crimps

A wire stripper that also
cuts wire and small bolts
and serves as a crimping
tool, wire looper, wire
gauge, and a conduit
reamer is the Big-7 tool
made by ITT Holub. The
multipurpose tool is made
of hardened and tempered
steel. The wire-stripping
holes are precision ground;
the cutter easily cuts
through copper and
aluminum conductors,
including UF and Romex
cable. Other features
include a "Sta-Fast"
adjustable hinge bolt, hold-
open spring, and cushion-
grip handles. The Big-7
tool is 8 inches long and
weighs 7 ounces.

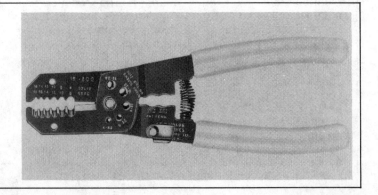

Home Timer Offers Up to 48 On/Off Operations a Day

The Super Command 48, a tabletop home timer made by AMF/Paragon Electric Co., Inc., can be programmed for up to 48 on/off operations every 24 hours, for periods as short as 15 minutes. It offers repeat accuracy within seconds, according to the manufacturer. The timer is able to control lights, appliances, television sets, and other devices. All you do is plug the unit into a wall outlet, and plug the device you want to control into the timer. The Time Commander 48 is a similar model that plugs directly into an electrical outlet.

Tabletop Unit Dims Lamps and Swags

The model TT-2 tabletop dimmer by Home Equipment Manufacturing Co., a division of Kenton Industries, Inc., offers the energy-saving and decorating advantages of dimmers that can be used with plug-in lamps. The rotary dimmer works with all plug-in and swag lamps; just plug the lamp into the dimmer control, and plug the control into a wall outlet. The dimmer features an attractive woodgrain case, has a 300-watt capacity, and comes with a one-year warranty.

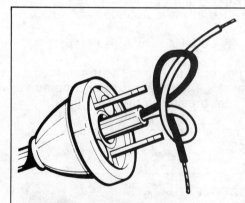

On screw-type plugs, insert the cord, tie the wires into an Underwriters' knot (left), and pull the knot down into the plug. Then, loop each wire around a prong (center) before tightening the bare end under the screw head. This helps keep the wires from touching each other accidentally (right).

about ½ inch of insulation from the end of each wire.

5. Tie the wires into an Underwriters' knot as shown in the accompanying illustrations. **Note:** On many types of plugs, it isn't necessary—or possible—to tie such a knot.

6. Pull the cord so that the knot seats itself into the recess of the plug. The knot will ease the strain on the terminal connections should the cord be yanked from an outlet.

7. Twist the strands at the end of each wire and form a clockwise loop.

8. Route the end of each wire around the outside of its prong and place the loop clockwise around its terminal screw; this will prevent the screw's movement from pushing the wire loop out from under the screw head.

9. Tighten each terminal screw.

10. Replace the insulating disc over the prongs and seat it in the plug. If there is a screw-clamp on the plug, tighten it to secure the plug to the cord.

Replacing a Wall Outlet

Materials • Electrical Outlet

Tools • Screwdriver • Utility Knife or Single-Edge Razor Blade • Wire Stripper • Long-Nose Pliers

V ERY OFTEN, people will plug in an appliance or lamp, and when nothing happens, they blame the appliance or lamp when the culprit is the wall outlet. Faulty wall outlets can be easily replaced after you determine what type is needed.

Ungrounded outlets are found on two-wire systems; they have openings, or slots, for a plug with two prongs. Grounded outlets are found on three-wire systems; they have openings for a plug with three prongs, one of which is usually U-shaped. The outlet's U-shaped opening is connected to a bare or green ground wire in the outlet box; on the outlet, the terminal for a ground wire is a green-colored hexhead screw.

A two-slot outlet can be replaced with a grounded outlet *if* the outlet box is grounded. If your outlet box isn't grounded, you can't use a grounded outlet unless extensive rewiring is done.

Newer-style outlets—ungrounded and grounded—are made with one slot slightly narrower than the other for polarization purposes. The narrower slot is connected to the black, or hot, wire in the outlet box; the larger slot is connected to the

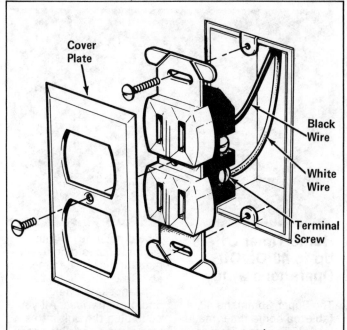

Cover Plate

Black Wire

White Wire

Terminal Screw

A replacement outlet must match the one you're removing. If you have the ungrounded type as shown, buy the same type. If you have the grounded type, you must buy an outlet that has a ground terminal screw and slots for three-prong grounded plugs.

white, or neutral, wire. Weatherproof outlets—required outdoors—usually are grounded and use a three-wire system.

To replace a faulty outlet, follow these steps:

1. Turn off the power to the circuit with the faulty outlet by removing the proper fuse or tripping the proper circuit breaker to the "off" position.
2. If the outlet cover plate is painted, use a utility knife to cut the paint film carefully around the edge of the plate.

Keep Nosy Hands Away From Unused Outlets

With small children around, an unused outlet presents an interesting curiosity; and a potential hazard. Plug up unused outlets with non-conducting safety caps, and remove the temptation. The UL Listed caps have prongs that fit into an outlet's slots to seal it off. Outlet safety caps are sold by a number of manufacturers. Sylvania safety caps, by GTE

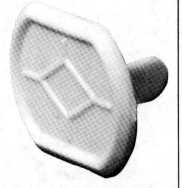

Lighting Products, come eight to a package, in a choice of brown, ivory, or clear.

Get an Air Freshener and Night Light in One Unit

Fresh 'n Lite is the name of a fan-powered air freshener and night light combined into one portable unit for use in a bathroom, bedroom, nursery, basement, or pet area. Manufactured by Emerson Environmental Products, the Fresh 'n Lite unit operates on any 120-volt AC double outlet; you just plug it in. The product uses a replaceable air freshener cartridge that

lasts up to two months. Four fragrances are available—lemon, pine, floral, and spice. Separate on/off switches let you use the freshener and the light separately or together. The product comes with a one-year limited warranty.

3. With a screwdriver, remove the screw(s) securing the outlet cover plate. If paint covers the screw slot, remove it with the tip of a utility knife.
4. Remove the mounting screws that secure the outlet to the box in the wall.
5. Carefully pull the outlet out of the box as far as the wires allow.
6. Examine the old outlet to see if the metal link between the top and bottom outlets has been broken off; if it has, break the link on the new outlet.
7. Disconnect the wires from the old outlet's terminals; the screws turn counterclockwise.
Note: Study the colors and positions of the wires connected to the old outlet before disconnecting them so you can connect the new outlet properly. If there is only one set of black and white wires in the outlet box, the outlet is at the end of a run. If a bare or green wire is present it will be connected to a green-colored screw on the outlet or to the box. In most outlets, there are two sets of black and white wires; one set brings power to the outlet and the other set carries power to another outlet in the run. In the latter case, you will connect one set of wires to the top of the outlet and the other set to the bottom of the outlet. If there are two bare or green wires, they should be connected to a green-colored screw on the outlet by means of a jumper wire.
8. If necessary, strip ½ inch of insulation off the end of each insulated wire to be connected to the outlet.
9. With a long-nose pliers, form a clockwise loop on the end of each wire.
10. Connect each wire in the outlet box to the new outlet exactly as it was connected to the old outlet; connect a white wire to a silver-colored screw, a black wire to the brass-colored screw,

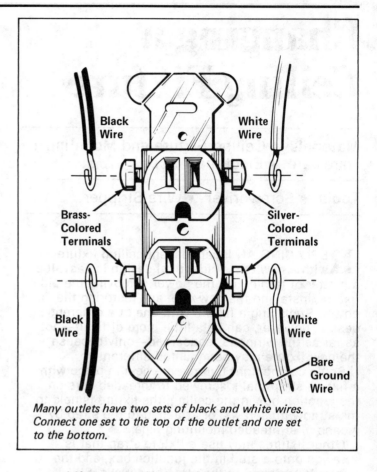

Many outlets have two sets of black and white wires. Connect one set to the top of the outlet and one set to the bottom.

and if present, the bare or green wire to the green hexhead screw. Fasten each wire by placing its loop clockwise under the screw head, and tightening the screw clockwise.
11. Carefully fold in the wires, position the outlet in the box, and secure it by tightening the mounting screws provided.
12. Replace the outlet cover plate, and restore power to the outlet.

Six-for-One Outlet Offers Grounding

You can plug this outlet adapter into any standard three-wire outlet, converting it into six grounded outlets. The device, made by the General Electric Co., may be used with two-prong or three-prong plugs. If the outlet will be temporary, simply plug the adapter in the outlet. If the adapter will be permanent, turn off the power to the circuit,

remove the outlet cover plate, plug in the adapter, secure it with a center mounting screw, and restore the power. The GE adapter, designed for indoor use only, is rated at 15 amps/125 volts, and is UL Listed.

Prevent Shocks With a GFCI Outlet

A ground fault circuit interrupter (GFCI) offers protection against current leaks; it is especially useful in moisture-producing areas. It's a good idea to install one in laundry rooms, kitchens, bathrooms, and outdoors. The Shock Detector, available from Sears Roebuck and Co., replaces standard outlets. The UL Listed unit is rated for 110- to 120-volt circuits AC, and detects current leaks

as small as 0.006 amps. If a leak is detected, the current is shut off in ½ second. It also provides protection for other outlets wired after it on the same circuit. The GFCI has a built-in test circuit and indicator.

Changing a Ceiling Fixture

Materials • Ceiling Fixture and Mounting Hardware • Electrical Tape

Tools • Screwdriver • Wire Stripper

REPLACING AN incandescent ceiling fixture with a new one of identical design is easy. It's a matter of turning off the power, removing the old fixture, installing the new one, and restoring the power. Replacing a fixture with one of a different design, however, can be a little more difficult—not as far as the wiring is concerned—only because the new fixture may be mounted differently.

Some ceiling light fixtures are held in place with a fixture strap that's screwed to threaded ears on the junction box in the ceiling; the fixture is held to the strap with screws, or attached to the strap by means of a threaded mounting pipe.

Other fixtures may use a fixture strap that is screwed onto a stud in the junction box, and the fixture is fastened to the strap by screws. Still another possibility is that the fixture has a threaded collar, and its threads fit a threaded stud in the junction box. If the stud isn't long enough or of a different size, two parts—a hickey and a nipple—may be used to connect the fixture to the stud. Usually, such parts are provided with a new fixture; if not, you can buy them separately.

In most cases, new ceiling fixtures come with complete installation instructions, or you can follow this general procedure:

1. Turn off the power to the ceiling fixture by removing the proper fuse or tripping the proper circuit breaker to the "off" position.
2. If necessary, remove the globe or translucent canopy cover from the fixture. Some are held to a bulb or bulbs by wires and simply snap off. Others are secured by a central nut or several screws—all of which can be removed or loosened counterclockwise by hand.
3. Remove the fixture bulb or bulbs, and disassemble all mounting hardware. Usually, there are screws or bolts holding the fixture to the ceiling, but if there are no visible screws or bolts, look for a decorative feature that probably doubles as a fastener and unscrew it counterclockwise.
4. Holding the fixture in one hand, disconnect the fixture's wires from the circuit wires in the

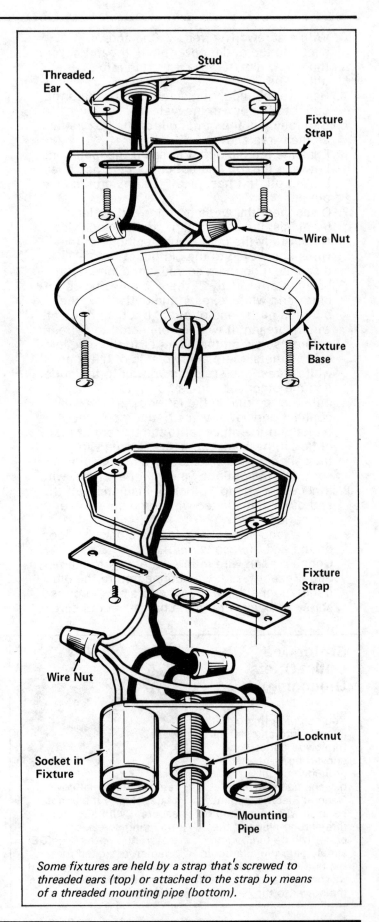

Some fixtures are held by a strap that's screwed to threaded ears (top) or attached to the strap by means of a threaded mounting pipe (bottom).

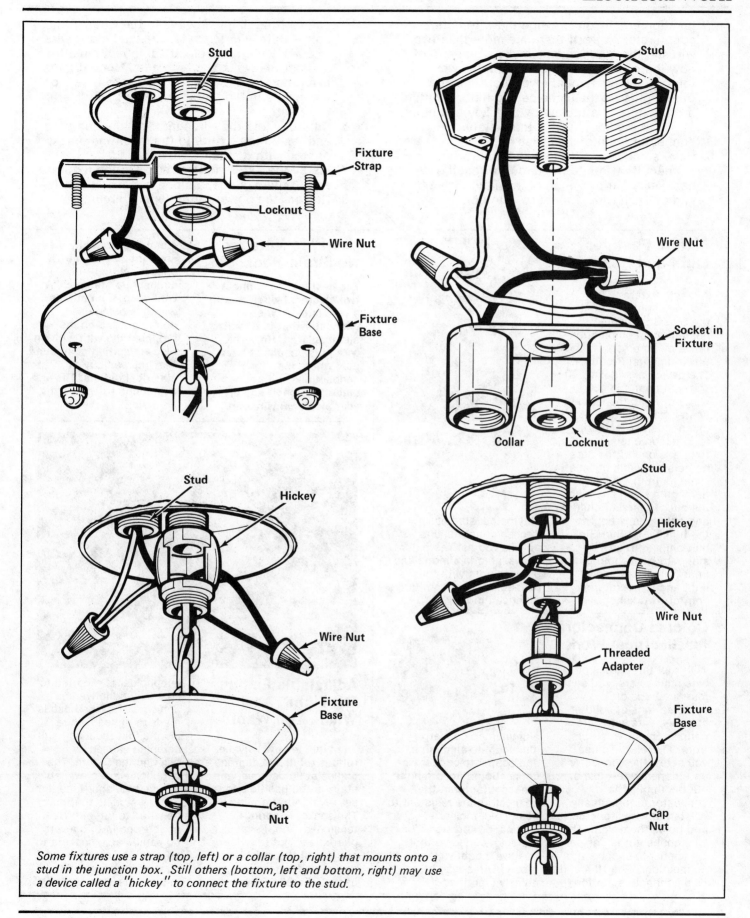

Stud

Stud

Fixture
Strap

Locknut

Wire Nut

Wire Nut

Socket in
Fixture

Fixture
Base

Collar

Locknut

Stud

Hickey

Stud

Hickey

Wire Nut

Wire Nut

Threaded
Adapter

Fixture
Base

Fixture
Base

Cap
Nut

Cap
Nut

*Some fixtures use a strap (top, left) or a collar (top, right) that mounts onto a
stud in the junction box. Still others (bottom, left and bottom, right) may use
a device called a "hickey" to connect the fixture to the stud.*

junction box by unscrewing the wire nuts counterclockwise. If there are more than two wires in the junction box, make a diagram of how the wires are connected; a three-way or four-way hookup could involve outlets and other lights on the same ceiling fixture switch. If the fixture is attached by a hickey and nipple or nut to a stud, unscrew the fastener or connector counterclockwise.

5. Have someone hold the new fixture while you connect its wires to the circuit wires. If necessary, strip ½ inch of insulation from the end of each wire. Then, use wire nuts to connect the fixture's wires to the wires in the box—white wire to white wire, and black wire to black wire. Wrap electrical tape around the ends of the wires and wire nuts. **Note:** If there is a green fixture wire, connect it to a bare or green wire in the junction box or to the metal box itself.

6. Carefully fold the wires into the junction box, and fasten the fixture to the mounting bracket or stud with the hardware provided.

7. Install the fixture bulb or bulbs in the fixture and, if there is one, a globe or canopy cover.

8. Restore the power to the fixture circuit.

Fixture Features Light and Heat

A single fixture that provides light and heat is the Sun Glo hanging heater/lamp combination made by Emerson Environmental Products. The device provides 1,200 watts of heat and 100 watts of light; the lamp or heater may be used independently. According to Emerson engineers, the fixture is one of the safest heaters available because it hangs from a ceiling hook on a swag chain so it's out of reach of children and pets, and is cool to the touch. The Sun Glo unit plugs into any standard household outlet in any area that needs light and temperature control—workshops,

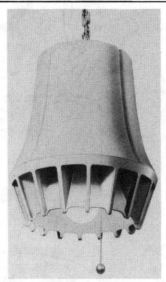

playrooms, studios, kitchen counters, and powder rooms. The fixture is available in almond and brown colors with four peel-off decals in an Early American motif.

Colored Connectors for Electrical Work

With just three sizes of wire connectors, you can join hundreds of combinations of solid or stranded wire with wire connectors, or wire nuts, from ITT Holub. To use, you screw the connector on stripped wire—like a nut on a bolt. The connector automatically twists the wires together and holds them tight. The HI 3 connector is designed for copper-to-copper wire connections. The HI 4 and HI 6 connectors are for

aluminum-to-copper, aluminum-to-aluminum, and copper-to-copper wire connections. According to the manufacturer, the connectors are resistant to heat, cold, moisture, friction, or abrasion. They are color-coded so that positive, negative, and ground wires may be quickly identified.

Use Wire Nuts for No-Strain Hookups

The best way to connect two electrical wires is with a wire nut—a twist-on connector that is threaded and insulated. However, wire nuts should be used only where the connections will not be under tension. If any of your electrical wires are aluminum—usually they are light-colored, not copper-colored—use connectors stamped "AL-CU." Also, if aluminum wiring is being used, before putting on the wire nut, coat the wire with an oxide-inhibiting compound that you can buy at electrical outlets. The compound will prevent corrosion.

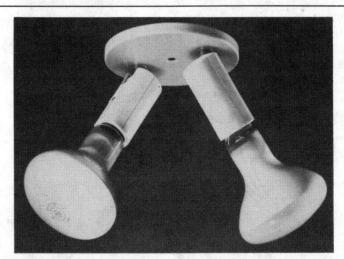

Adjustable Fixtures Put Light Where You Want It

The Lite-Flex by Swivelier rotates a full 360 degrees, angles at 90 degrees, and stays in the position you set it without drooping. The socket is spring-tensioned, and it's guaranteed not to twist or pull out of the swivel device under normal usage. The Lite-Flex lampholder is reported to be non-conductive and non-corrosive; the base is made of molded white plastic that reduces paint chipping caused by twisting the fixture. The lampholders are available in one, two, and three light canopy models that may be wired to outlet boxes, or screwed in to convert non-adjustable sockets to adjustable ones; pin-up, clamp-on, or plug-in mounts are also available.

Troubleshooting Fluorescent Fixtures

Materials • Fluorescent Tube
• Fluorescent Starter • Steel Wool
• Fluorescent Ballast

Tools • Screwdriver • Pliers

THERE ARE three basic types of fluorescent fixtures: preheat, rapid-start, and instant-start. Each type saves energy, because fluorescent tubes use less electrical current than incandescent bulbs.

The main working parts of many fluorescent fixtures are the light tube, starter, and ballast. Preheat models have a starter for each fluorescent tube in the fixture. The starter, however, has been eliminated in the rapid-start and instant-start types of fluorescent fixtures. The ballast adjusts the amount of current through the tube; it makes a surge of current arc through the tube, and then keeps the current flowing at the proper value once the tube is glowing. From external appearances, preheat and rapid-start fixtures look identical; however, you can easily tell if you have an instant-start fixture, because it has only one pin instead of two at each end of the fluorescent tube.

The ballast used in a fixture is your guide to buying all replacement parts, because a ballast— and starter in preheat models—must match the wattage, or rating, of the fluorescent tube and the type of fixture.

Fixture Won't Work at All

If your fluorescent fixture won't work at all, follow these steps:

1. Check the circuit's fuse or circuit breaker at the main entrance panel to see if the fixture is receiving power. If it is, switch off the fixture.
2. Check to see that the fluorescent tube is properly seated by turning the tube clockwise, and then counterclockwise until you hear a snap or feel the tube lock into position.
3. Turn on the switch that controls the fixture. If the tube doesn't come on, you'll have to replace it, or, if you're in doubt, test it. You can do this by trying it in another, similar fixture that works. If the tube operates in another fixture, replace the starter—if there is one—in

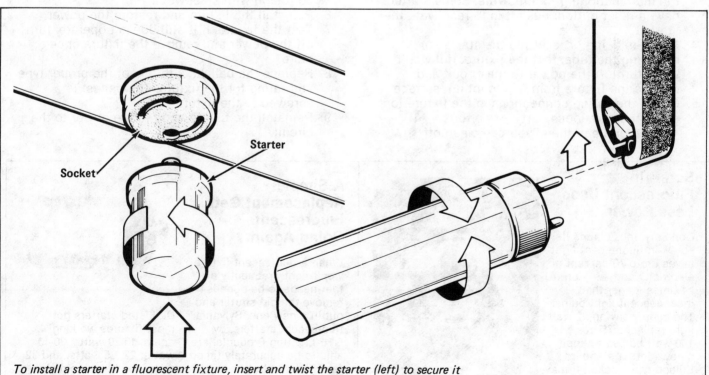

To install a starter in a fluorescent fixture, insert and twist the starter (left) to secure it in its socket. To install a fluorescent tube, insert the tube's prongs into the holder and twist the tube (right) to lock it in place.

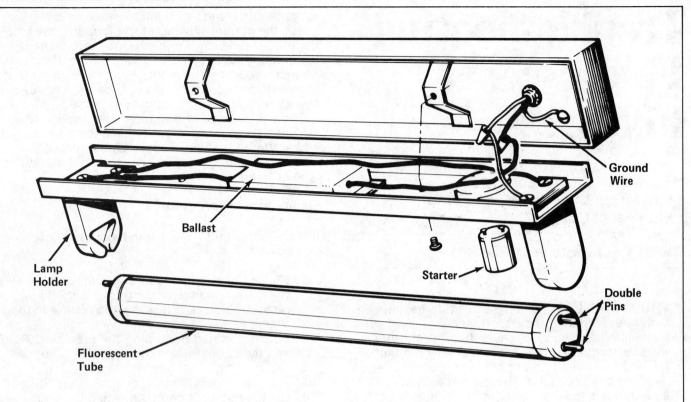

The main working parts in the preheat type of fluorescent fixture are a light tube, starter, and ballast. In the rapid-start and instant-start types of fluorescent fixtures, the starter has been eliminated.

the malfunctioning fixture. **Note:** Some starters have a reset button; push it in to reactivate the starter.

4. After replacing or resetting the starter, or replacing the tube, test the fixture. If it won't work, turn off the power to the circuit and remove the fixture from its mounting surface.
5. Check the wiring connections in the fixture to see if they are loose, dirty, or corroded. Tighten or clean them; you can clean off

corrosion with steel wool.
6. Reinstall the fixture and restore the power.
7. Test the fixture. If it still doesn't operate, turn off the power and remove the fixture once more.
8. Replace the ballast with one of the proper type and rating for the fixture. The ballast is screwed to the fixture.
9. Reinstall the fixture and restore power to the circuit.

Screw-In Fluorescent Uses Less Power

Con-Serv, Inc., claims its screw-in fluorescent light saves up to 70 percent on electricity and lasts up to 14 times longer than incandescent light bulbs. The energy-saving 22-watt light replaces 75- to 100-watt bulbs; it simply screws into a standard Edison-type socket. It may be used for table, floor, and ceiling lamps.

A Simple Replacement Gets Fluorescents Going Again

When a fluorescent fixture won't light, frequently all that needs to be done is remove the old starter and put in a new one. Sylvania fluorescent starters, by GTE Lighting Products, are said to be accurately timed for efficient starting and extended lamp life. A selection of four different

UL Listed starters get most fixtures working again: 15-20 watts; 30-40 watts; 22, 25 watts; and 32 watts for 12-inch circular fluorescent tubes. Starters come two to a package.

Light Blinks

If your fluorescent fixture blinks off and on after you switch it on, follow these steps:

1. Check the room temperature. It may be too low; most fluorescent fixtures are designed to operate properly at temperatures above 50° F.
2. If the temperature isn't the problem, switch off the fixture and remove the tube.
3. Buff the base pin or pins with steel wool, and carefully straighten any bent pins with pliers.
4. Reinstall the tube in the fixture.
5. Test the fixture. If it still blinks, replace the starter if there is one, or follow Steps 4 through 9 in "Fixture Won't Work at All."

Tube Is Discolored or Partially Lit

If the fluorescent tube is discolored or partially lit, follow these steps:

1. Check the room temperature. It may be too low; most fluorescent fixtures are designed to operate properly at temperatures above 50° F.
2. If the temperature isn't the problem, switch off the fixture.
3. Remove the tube and reverse it in the fixture.
4. Test the fixture.
5. If reversing doesn't solve the problem, replace the starter if there is one, or follow Steps 4 through 9 in "Fixture Won't Work at All."

Fixture Hums

If your fixture hums while it's on, follow these steps:

1. Turn off the power to the circuit.
2. Remove the fixture from its mounting surface.
3. Check the wiring connections in the fixture to see if they are loose, dirty, or corroded. Tighten or clean them; you can clean off corrosion with steel wool.
4. If the fixture continues to hum, turn off the power and remove the fixture again.
5. Replace the ballast with one of the proper type and rating for the fixture. The ballast is screwed to the fixture.

Light Flickers

If your fluorescent fixture flickers when it's on, follow these steps:

1. If the fluorescent tube is a new one, it may flicker only during the first hours of use. If the tube has been in operation for some time, turn the fixture on and off several times.
2. If the flickering continues, replace the starter if there is one, or follow Steps 4 through 9 in "Fixture Won't Work at All."

Fluorescent Unit Replaces Incandescent Bulb

A fluorescent conversion unit that can be screwed into a standard household incandescent lamp socket has been developed by GTE Lighting Products. The company's Sylvania fluorescent conversion unit—an 8-inch circular lamp and ballast— produces about the same illumination as a 75-watt incandescent bulb, will last up to 10 times longer, and uses about two-thirds less energy, according to GTE. The 22-watt circular fluorescent unit has a rated life of 12,000 hours, as compared to a standard household incandescent bulb's rating of 750 to

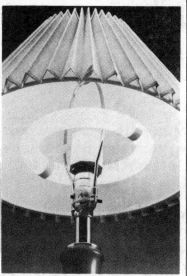

1,000 hours. To install the unit, remove the lamp's shade and harp, screw in the fluorescent unit, and replace the harp and shade.

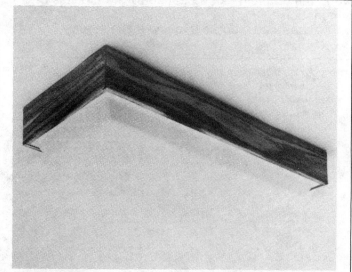

Fluorescent Fixtures Save Energy

Country Oak decorative fluorescent ceiling light fixtures have been designed by Home-Vue, a division of Lithonia Lighting, to reflect the character and texture of oak; the oak-like finish is applied to steel. The diffusers are milk-white in color to provide a soft, even light, and are made from non-yellowing acrylic plastic that is said to reduce chipping and cracking. According to Home-Vue, the fixtures feature instant-on ballasts and offer up to 75 percent savings on electricity. They are available with two 20-watt tubes (1 foot by 2 feet), two 40-watt tubes (1 foot by 4 feet), four 20-watt tubes (1½ by 4 feet), and four 40-watt tubes (2 by 2 feet). Each fixture comes with hardware, wiring, and installation instructions.

Fixing a Faulty Doorbell

Materials • Steel Wool • Doorbell Button • Petroleum-Based Solvent • Silicone Spray • Masking Tape • Bell, Buzzer, or Chimes • Transformer • Doorbell Wire

Tools • Screwdriver • Utility Knife or Single-Edge Razor Blade • Pencil • 12-Volt Circuit Tester • 110-120-Volt Circuit Tester

THERE ARE four basic doorbell components—the push button; the bell, buzzer, or chimes; the transformer; and the wiring. When a doorbell won't work, the problem can be traced by the process of elimination.

To fix a faulty doorbell, follow these steps:

1. With a screwdriver, remove the push button from its mounting surface. **Note:** Doorbells operate on 10 to 18 volts of electricity, which is provided by a transformer that steps down 110-120 volts of household power. Therefore, you can safely work on all parts of the doorbell circuit—except the transformer—without disconnecting the power supply.
2. Loosen the terminal screws on the push button with a screwdriver; turn the screws counterclockwise.
3. Disconnect the push-button wires and touch the ends of the wires together. If the doorbell sounds, the problem is the push button.
4. Scrape the ends of the wires with a utility knife to clean them, and lightly buff the terminal screws on the push button with steel wool.
5. Reconnect the wires to the terminal screws and test the doorbell. If the bell sounds, reinstall the push button; if it doesn't, install a new push button.
6. If the doorbell still doesn't work, check the bell, buzzer, or chimes to see if the wiring connections are loose, dirty, or corroded. Tighten or clean them; remove any corrosion with steel wool.
7. Check the bell clapper to see if it's close enough to the bell to strike it; clean the

If your doorbell or door chimes don't work, the fault could be in any part of the circuitry from a push button to the bell or chimes, or to the transformer. Before removing any wires at the terminal strip, tag them so you can replace them correctly.

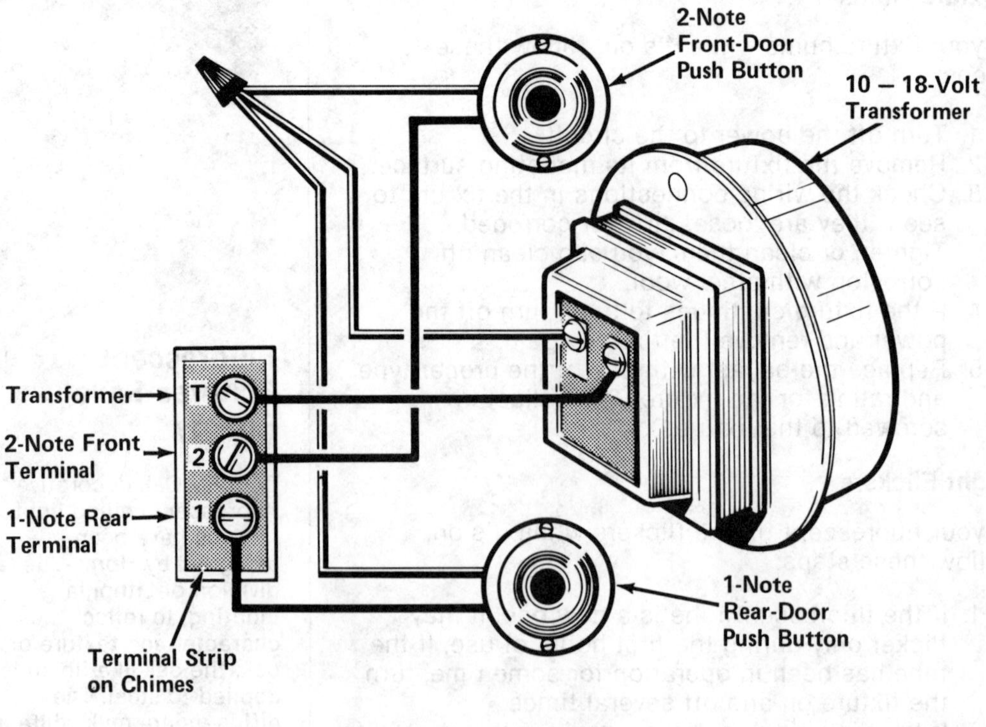

2-Note Front-Door Push Button

10 – 18-Volt Transformer

Transformer

2-Note Front Terminal

1-Note Rear Terminal

Terminal Strip on Chimes

1-Note Rear-Door Push Button

clapper. If you are working on chimes, clean the striker rods with a petroleum-based solvent, such as kerosene, so they can move properly. You also can lubricate them with a silicone spray.

8. If the doorbell still doesn't work, remove the wires from the terminals at the bell, buzzer, or chimes. **Note:** There may be two, three, or more terminals, depending on whether you have a bell or chimes, whether there are chimes for one or two entrances, and whether the chimes sound multiple notes. To help you reconnect the wires properly, tag the wires before disconnecting them. The wires at the terminal strip at the bell, buzzer, or chimes are usually marked in some manner.

9. If there are only two terminals and wires, touch the probes of a 12-volt circuit tester to the ends of the wires. Or, a 12-volt automobile lamp bulb in a socket with two wires can be used for testing purposes. If the tester lights when someone pushes the doorbell, the bell, buzzer, or chimes need to be replaced.

If there are three or more wires for chimes, connect the transformer (T) wire and the two-note front-door chime (marked "FRONT" or "2") wire to the tester. If it lights when someone pushes the front doorbell, the chime

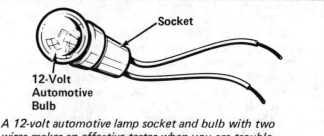

A 12-volt automotive lamp socket and bulb with two wires makes an effective tester when you are trouble-shooting a malfunctioning doorbell or door chime.

is faulty. To check this, connect the transformer (T) wire and the one-note rear-door chime (marked "REAR" or "1") wire to the tester. If it lights when someone pushes the rear doorbell, you're certain the chimes must be replaced.

10. If the light doesn't come on in either test, you'll have to check the transformer. You'll usually find the transformer mounted on an electrical junction box, a subpanel, or the main entrance panel. Generally, the transformer connections to the circuit (high-voltage) wires are hidden from view within the box. The doorbell (low-voltage) wires are attached to exposed terminal screws on the transformer.

A Familiar Tune Announces Your Guests

A guest can now push your General Electric Orchestra electronic door chime and hear one of 60 tunes that you have pre-selected. The tunes include "Silent Night," "Dixie," "Battle Hymn Of The Republic," and "Au Claire de la Lune." The door chime lets you select tunes by setting two selector slide knobs on the front of the chime base. Volume, tempo, and tone controls are built into the unit, which has a test button to check the tune selection and quality. The chime is operated by a 10-16-volt transformer or six AA batteries that are not included in the package. The only restriction on the chime is that it can't be operated with a lighted door button. Complete installation instructions are furnished

with the product; a built-in tune index is also included for reference.

Decorator Chimes Offer Custom Styling

The Williamsburg No. 67 decorator door chime, from the Trine Consumer Products Div. Square D Co., produces eight repeating loud chime notes when the doorbell button is pushed. The volume of the notes may be adjusted, and the chime can be switched to sound four different notes. Or, it can be adjusted for a single note rear, and an additional single note for a third entrance. One or two additional two-note front or one-note rear chimes also can be added. The chime is enclosed in a Westminster chime cabinet with a hand-rubbed walnut finish. The clock has an 8-inch-diameter face and a quartz movement. The chime's resonating tubes are of solid brass.

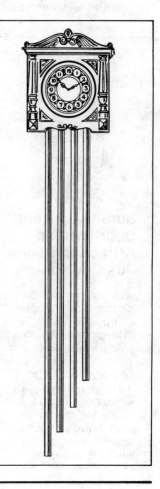

Carefully touch the probes of a 12-volt circuit tester to the doorbell (low-voltage) wires on the transformer. *Caution: Make sure you are working on the low-voltage wires!* If the light comes on, the transformer is working; if it doesn't, you have to perform another test.

11. Touch the probes of a 110-120-volt circuit tester to the high-voltage terminals of the transformer. *Caution: If you cannot reach the terminals safely, turn off the power to the circuit by removing the proper fuse or tripping the proper circuit breaker to the "off" position at the main entrance panel.* Then, disconnect the circuit wires at the transformer's high-voltage terminals. Separate the two wires so that they cannot touch each other or any other part of the electrical box. Turn the circuit back on, and carefully touch the probes of the 110-120-volt circuit tester to the ends of the wires. If the tester light comes on, the circuit is working, which means the transformer is defective.

12. If the transformer is defective, make sure the power to the circuit is turned off and remove the transformer. Buy a replacement of the same voltage and wattage (or VA—volts/amps). This information is stamped on the transformer. Installation instructions will come with the transformer.

13. If the transformer passes both tests, the problem must be in the wiring. By tracing the wiring you may be able to locate the trouble. If the trouble is in a section of low-voltage wire, replace the section with doorbell wire. If there is a visible break in the low-voltage wire and it's accessible, you can splice the broken wire; but it's better to totally replace it.

Replacing Wiring

If you've traced your doorbell problem to the low-voltage wiring and the wiring is concealed in a wall or behind a ceiling, follow these steps:

1. Disconnect the low-voltage wire at one location; for example, at the doorbell. Fasten one end of a new length of replacement wire to the end of the old one. From another location—for example, at the chimes—pull the old wire out. Usually, the new wire can be pulled into place by the old. If this isn't feasible, it may be better to simply disconnect the section of old wire at both locations and install new wire by the easiest route.

2. Connect the new doorbell wire to the terminals at both ends and test the doorbell. If this section of wire doesn't solve the problem, disconnect and replace another section of wire by using one of the methods described in Step 1.

Spruce Up Your Door With an Attractive Doorbell Push Button

A decorative doorbell push button is an attractive addition to almost any exterior door. The No. 732P custom push button from Trine Consumer Products Div., Square D. Co., features a brass plate, white push button, and a space for your name. The push button attaches with screws, and no special wiring is necessary.

Soldering Kit for Big and Little Jobs

A dual-heat control on a soldering gun lets you use low heat for small jobs and high heat for large soldering jobs. This is a feature of the Model 2410-1 soldering gun kit from Skil Corp. The Skil soldering gun kit includes three other gun tips that allow you to cut, shape, and seal metal. Other features include a built-in, pre-focused light to illuminate the work area; a compact design to make it easier to work in cramped spaces; and a high-impact plastic housing that resists breakage. The gun performs at 150 and 230 watts on 115 volts AC. The four different tips may be purchased separately—two to a package. The soldering tip (No. 84660) is designed for electrical connections and general

wiring purposes. The electronic tip (No. 84661) may be used for assembling electronic projects and other detailed work. The sealing tip (No. 84662) joins and seals plastic film and thin plastic sheeting. The cutting tip (No. 84663) is for cutting and shaping floor tile or plastic pieces.

Repairing or Replacing Appliance Cords

Materials • Appliance Cord • Electrical Plug • Terminal Connectors • Solder • Rosin Flux • Thread

Tools • Screwdriver • Pliers • Utility Knife or Single-Edge Razor Blade • Continuity Tester • Wire Stripper • Soldering Gun or Crimping Tool

SMALL APPLIANCES, such as toasters, coffeemakers, hair dryers, and clothes irons, use a variety of power cords. Many cords are permanently attached to appliances. Some, however, are detachable; they have a male plug at one end that is connected to a wall outlet, and a female plug at the other that is connected to the appliance. Faulty male plugs on both types of cords can be replaced by following the general procedure in "Replacing a Plug" elsewhere in this chapter.

On most detachable cords, meanwhile, there are two basic types of female plugs. One is the pop-out plug; it has an inner part that fits into an outer section. The other is the clamp-type plug whose two halves are fastened by screws and nuts. Some male and female plugs, which are molded, can't be disassembled at all. These plugs can't be repaired; the entire cord must be replaced.

Appliance cords are rated by amperage and voltage. When selecting a replacement, take the old one along to make sure you get the proper type and size cord.

Testing Appliance Cords

If a cord appears to be in good shape, but the appliance works intermittently, or works only when the cord is jiggled or twisted, the cord wires may be broken. To test a cord's wires, follow these steps:

1. Unplug the cord from the wall outlet and disconnect the other end from the appliance.
2. Connect the clip of a continuity tester to one prong of the male plug.
3. Touch the probe of the tester to the opposite end of this wire; on a detachable cord, touch the wire's contact in the female plug. If the tester light comes on, the wire isn't broken.

4. Test the other wire in the cord in the same manner, and if the test is negative—the tester doesn't light—replace the cord.

Pop-Out Female Plugs

To replace a damaged pop-out female plug on an appliance cord, or to install a new cord to such a plug, follow these steps:

1. Disconnect the cord from the wall outlet and the appliance.
2. With a screwdriver, pry apart the inner and outer sections of the plug; there's no need to remove the screw in the top. You may need pliers to grip the inner section, and on round plugs, twisting it may ease disassembly.
3. After separating the two sections, use a screwdriver to disconnect the two wires from the screw terminals on the inner section.
4. Untie the knot in the wires, and pull the cord out of the outer section.
5. After replacing the appliance cord or the female plug, insert the end of the cord into the base of the outer section.
6. If necessary, strip away about 2 inches of the outer insulation on the cord with a utility knife, to expose the two insulated wires. Strip about

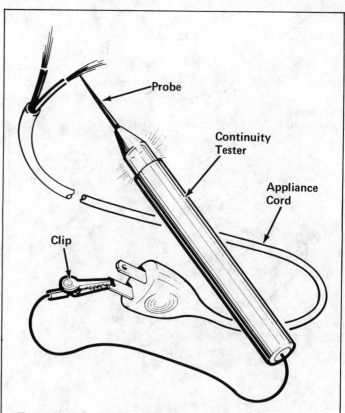

To see if a cord is broken, connect the clip of a continuity tester to one prong of the plug; touch the probe to the opposite end of this wire. If the tester light comes on, the wire isn't broken. Test the other wire the same way.

½ inch of insulation from the ends of each wire with wire strippers.

7. Tie an Underwriters' knot in the ends of the two wires, following the procedure illustrated in "Replacing a Plug" elsewhere in this chapter.
8. Insert the stripped end of one wire through the hole in one of the metal terminal strips in the inner section of the plug, and loop the end

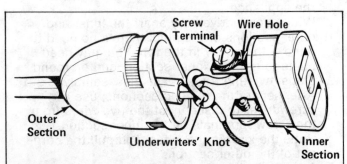

With a screwdriver, you can pry apart the inner and outer sections of a pop-out female plug.

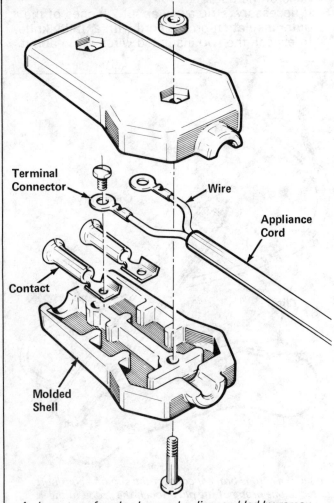

A clamp-type female plug can be disassembled by removing the screws that hold the two plug halves together.

clockwise around the screw terminal and under the screw head. Do the same with the other wire. Tighten both screws.

9. Insert the inner section of the plug into the outer section until it seats properly.

Clamp-Type Female Plugs

To replace a faulty clamp-type female plug on an appliance cord, or to install a new cord on such a plug, follow these steps:

1. Disconnect the cord from the wall outlet and the appliance.
2. With a screwdriver, remove the screws that hold the two plug halves together; don't lose the nuts.
3. With a screwdriver, remove the terminal screws securing the wires to the plug's contacts. If there is a slip-on strain-relief device, remove it.
4. If you're replacing the plug, the end of the old cord can be connected to the new plug. If you're replacing the cord, the new one will have to be prepared. First, slip the strain-relief device—if there is one—onto the new cord. Then, carefully strip about 2 inches of outer insulation from the end of the cord with a utility knife. If there is asbestos insulation between the outer insulation and the insulated wires inside, don't remove it—push it back out of your way. Also strip about ½ inch of insulation from the end of each insulated wire with wire strippers. Then, solder or crimp-on a terminal connector to the end of each wire.
5. Connect each wire to its contact with a terminal screw.
6. Make sure that the contacts, wires, cord, and any strain-relief device are correctly seated in one half of the plug. **Note:** If there is loose asbestos insulation between the end of the cord's outer insulation and the terminal connectors, wrap the asbestos around each wire and secure the asbestos with thread so that there are no bulges.
7. Position the other half of the plug on top of the half with the wire connections. Insert the plug screws and nuts, and fasten the halves together.

Permanently Attached Cords

On appliances with cords that are not detachable, often the hardest part of repairing or replacing such cords is trying to determine how the appliance comes apart, so you can reach the wire terminals inside.

If it isn't obvious how to disassemble an appliance, examine it carefully along joints or seams for some hint. Often, screws or other fasteners are concealed. Look for a tiny round plug that matches the surrounding area; a nameplate or some decorative design that can be snapped out or peeled off; a detachable covering; or rubber, cork, and other protective pads in the base that might hide fasteners.

Once you've disassembled the appliance to expose the cord's terminal connections, follow these steps to repair or replace the appliance cord:

1. Examine the terminals. Some cord wires are simply looped around and secured by terminal screws. Others may be fastened by soldered or crimped-on terminal connectors.
2. Examine the strain-relief device used to keep the cord from being pulled out of the appliance. The device may be a simple knot in the wires or cord, a spring or rubber sleeve on the cord, or even a molded section of the cord.
3. With a screwdriver, disconnect the wires from the terminal screws by turning them counter-clockwise.

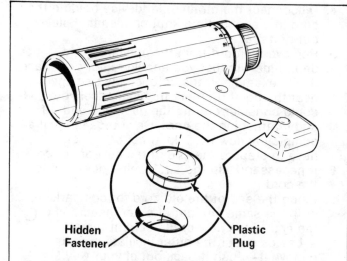

Hidden Fastener — Plastic Plug

Fasteners are often hidden beneath a scarcely visible plastic plug. To disassemble the appliance, carefully pry up the plug to expose the fastener.

Match the Cord to the Appliance

When an appliance cord has to be replaced, be sure you replace it with the correct type of cord and plug. For instance, many kitchen appliances—toasters, coffee pots, toaster ovens, and other heat-producing devices—require connectors that can withstand high temperatures. Sylvania indoor appliance cords, by GTE Lighting Products, are black Type HPN heater cords for replacing kitchen appliance cords. The standard switchless cords are 18 gauge, two-wire cords with a two-prong plug, 6-foot cord, and heat-resistant standard female appliance connector—$\frac{11}{16}$-inch terminal spacing. The miniature switchless cords come with either $2\frac{1}{2}$-foot or 6-foot cords, and miniature heat-resistant female appliance connector—$\frac{1}{2}$-inch terminal spacing. Both cords are UL Listed.

The Right Length Cord Eases Range Installations

The right length power cord can simplify replacements on a range. The No. 284 series of range cords from Leviton Manufacturing Co., Inc., are available in 3-foot, 4-foot 5-foot, and 6-foot lengths with a 50-amp rating. The three-wire cords are ready to be attached to the terminal block on the range and plugged into the circuit outlet. Gray in color, the cords also may be used for clothes dryer hookups, according to the manufacturer. The cord package is printed with all necessary rating information.

What UL Stands for

When an electrical product is stamped with the initials "UL," this indicates that the merchandise is listed by Underwriters' Laboratories Inc., an independent testing laboratory. UL tests products and materials submitted by manufacturers to see that they meet nationally-recognized safety requirements. UL Listed means that the merchandise meets the minimum standard for the purpose for which it was intended. Don't assume that if two similar products are both UL Listed that they are of equal quality. One may just meet the minimum requirement, while another may be superior. And don't assume if a product is safe for one purpose that it will be safe under a different set of circumstances. For instance, outlets approved for interior use may not be safe to install outdoors.

Kit Includes Crimping Tool and Solderless Terminals

When you repair wiring on an appliance, the correct size solderless terminal and a crimping tool to apply it is what you need to make proper electrical connections. The Vaco general-purpose solderless terminal service kit, No. 6175-63, is the answer. Made by Vaco Products Co., the kit has a crimping tool with bolt-slicer and an assortment of ten different sizes and kinds of single-

grip, insulated terminals in a handy, clear-plastic storage box. The kit comes with instructions for use.

4. Disconnect the strain-relief device holding the cord in place; untie a knot or unsnap a sleeve out of its recess.

5. Remove the cord from the appliance and determine whether you should repair or replace it. For example, if the cord is only damaged near the point it enters the appliance, you could consider cutting the damaged end off and reattaching the cord. Or, you can install a completely new cord. In either case, you'll have to prepare the end of the new or cut cord.

6. If necessary, slip the strain-relief device onto the cord.

7. Using the end of the old cord for comparison, strip the same amount of outer insulation off the end of the new or cut cord. If there's asbestos under the outer insulation, don't remove it—push it back out of your way.

8. Strip about ½ inch of insulation from the end of each wire with wire strippers.

9. Solder or crimp-on a terminal connector to the end of each wire.

10. Connect each wire to its screw terminal, and tighten each screw.

11. Reassemble the appliance.

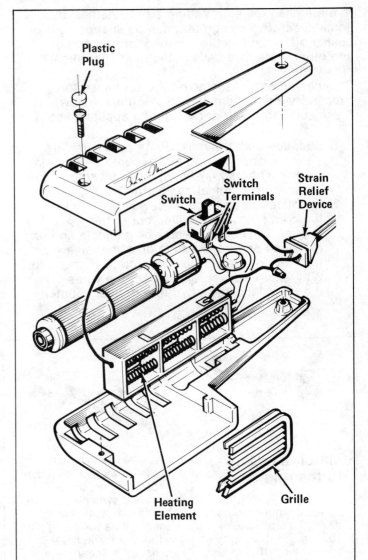

Many appliance cords are secured to the appliance by some type of strain-relief device, such as a molded section on the end of the cord.

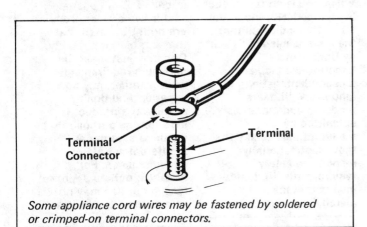

Some appliance cord wires may be fastened by soldered or crimped-on terminal connectors.

Tester Handles Most Home Circuits

The ITT Holub's No. 19-084 continuity tester is especially designed to check fuses, coils, windings, relays, switches, thermostats, and other problems in non-energized circuits having a resistance of 10 ohms or less. This includes most circuits in your home. The tester requires two penlight batteries to operate; it has a replaceable lamp, a 2-inch test probe, and a 36-inch test lead with an alligator clip. ITT also makes a voltage tester for AC-DC 120 to 600 volts. It is No. 19-087. The voltage tester features dual indicators, a round body, and an easy-to-read voltage scale.

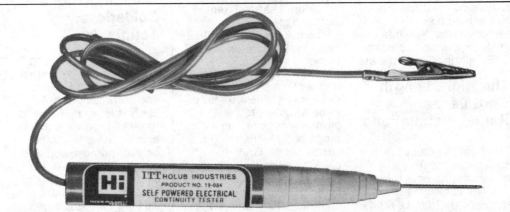

Installing Surface Wiring

Materials • Surface Wiring Kit • Electrical Tape • Twine • Type NM Cable • Small Weight • Wire Coat Hanger • Cable Connectors • Solvent Cement • Wire Nuts • Nails, Screws, or Toggle Bolts

Tools • Pencil • Tape Measure • Drill and Bits • Screwdriver • Pliers • Utility Knife or Single-Edge Razor Blade • Wire Stripper • Hammer • Hacksaw

ADDING NEW wiring to your home doesn't have to involve a lot of work; there's no need to run new wiring through the walls or ceiling, or to cut openings for switch and junction boxes. Instead, different types of multi-outlet assemblies and electrical raceways can be mounted to walls and other surfaces quickly and easily, and plugged in or connected to existing wall outlets.

Plug-In Outlet Strips

Plug-in outlet strips are lengths of metal or plastic raceway with a series of electrical outlets, usually at regular intervals. They are designed for use in a kitchen, workshop, or anywhere a number of outlets are needed for convenience, and to eliminate the use of extension cords. Usually, such strips are mounted to the wall above a countertop. Or, they may be installed—for example—to the front of kitchen base cabinets under a countertop's overhang or even along a baseboard.

To install a plug-in outlet strip, follow these steps:

1. Select a convenient location for the outlet strip, but make sure its plug will reach an existing electrical outlet.
2. Using the strip as a guide, mark the locations for mounting screws on the mounting surface.
3. Using a drill and the proper-size bit, bore pilot holes in the marked locations.
4. Fasten the outlet strip to the mounting surface with the screws provided.
5. Plug the strip into the wall outlet.

Electrical Raceways

Electrical raceways consist of one-piece or two-piece sections. One-piece raceways, made of metal, are similar to electrical conduit; wiring must be threaded through the raceway sections. With metal or plastic two-piece raceways, wiring is routed between a base piece and a cover piece; the base is mounted to the wall, and the cover snaps into place over it. The wiring connects a number of electrical outlets spaced at regular intervals or precisely where you want them, depending on the brand of raceway you use.

Raceways are often installed along the bottom of walls and fastened just above, to, or in place of a baseboard. Some may be painted to match a room's trim. The raceway wiring is connected to a circuit inside an existing electrical outlet, or to a circuit cable routed through a floor or wall.

The means of connecting the raceway to the outlet may differ. If an existing outlet box can be withdrawn from the wall, a cable inside the wall—from the raceway—can be connected to the outlet. If the outlet box can't be removed, you may have to make a hole in the wall under the box to connect the raceway cable. Or the raceway can be connected to the outlet by means of a vertical section of raceway and an adapter box assembly available from some raceway manufacturers. The adapter box allows you to remount the existing outlet, extending it from the wall to give the raceway access to the wiring in the outlet.

To install two-piece raceways, follow these general steps:

1. Locate a convenient wall outlet to serve as the power source for the raceway or route a house circuit cable into the room from some other source.
2. Turn off the power to the outlet's or branch circuit by removing the proper fuse or tripping the proper circuit breaker to the "off" position.
3. If the outlet cover plate is painted, use a utility knife to cut the paint film carefully around the edge of the plate.

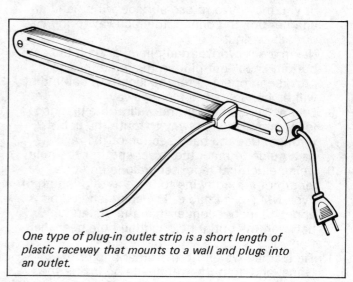

One type of plug-in outlet strip is a short length of plastic raceway that mounts to a wall and plugs into an outlet.

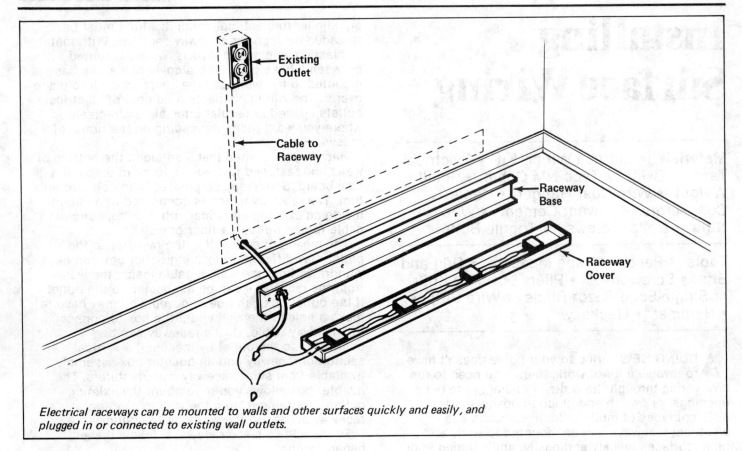

Existing Outlet

Cable to Raceway

Raceway Base

Raceway Cover

Electrical raceways can be mounted to walls and other surfaces quickly and easily, and plugged in or connected to existing wall outlets.

4. With a screwdriver, remove the screw(s) securing the outlet cover plate.
5. Remove the mounting screws that secure the outlet to the box in the wall.
6. Carefully pull the outlet out of the box as far as the wires allow.
7. Unfasten the outlet box from its mounting surface, and remove the box as far as the circuit cable(s) allow. **Note:** In some cases, this may be difficult or not feasible; the outlet box opening in the wall may have to be enlarged, or you may have to use surface wiring and an adapter box to connect the raceway to the outlet's wiring.
8. Using a screwdriver and pliers, pry out the bottom knock-out plug in the outlet box to provide an opening for the length of cable that will be connected to the raceway.
9. Drill a ¾-inch hole in the wall at the planned location for the raceway to route the cable through. Use the base section of the raceway as a guide to mark the exact spot for the hole.
10. Using electrical tape, secure one end of a length of strong twine to the end of a length of Type NM No. 14 cable. The cable should be about 12 inches longer than the distance between the outlet box and the hole near the floor.
11. Tie a small weight to the other end of the twine, and drop the weighted line inside the

wall from the box opening to the hole.
12. At the hole, use a wire coat hanger to hook the end of the weighted line and pull it out of the wall. Pull the twine to draw the cable down the wall's interior and out through the hole.
13. Use a utility knife to remove about 3 inches of outer insulation from both ends of the cable. Then, use wire strippers to remove about ½ inch of insulation from the ends of the wires at both ends of the cable.
14. At the box, fold the ground wire back over the cable and place a cable connector over the cable's outer insulation and the folded-back ground wire.
15. Secure the end of the ground wire to the cable connector by looping the end of the wire clockwise around one of the connector's screws.
16. Tighten the cable connector screws, and secure the connector to the outlet box with its locknut.
17. Reattach the outlet box to its mounting surface.
18. Connect the cable in the wall to the outlet circuit. **Note:** If there is only one set of black and white wires already connected to the outlet, connect the black and white wires from the raceway cable to the unused terminal screws on the outlet. If there are two sets of black and white wires already connected to the

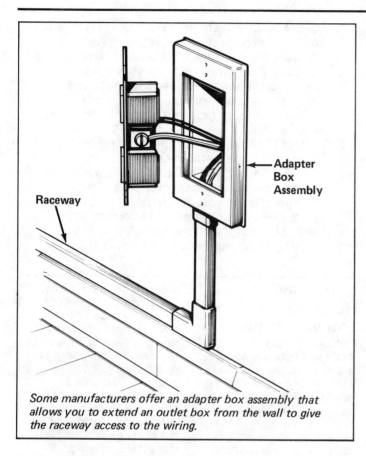

Some manufacturers offer an adapter box assembly that allows you to extend an outlet box from the wall to give the raceway access to the wiring.

outlet, disconnect one set. Then cut two short lengths of jumper wire—one black and one white—from No. 14 wire, and strip ½ inch of insulation from both ends of both wires. Connect the disconnected white wire, one end of the white jumper wire, and the white raceway cable wire with a wire nut; do the same for the disconnected black wire, the black jumper wire, and the black raceway cable wire. Then connect the other ends of the jumper wires to the terminals on the outlet.

19. Carefully fold the wires into the outlet box and position the outlet in the box.
20. Secure the outlet by replacing its mounting screws.
21. Replace the outlet cover plate.
22. Insert the other end of the cable through the back of the base piece of the metal raceway and secure it using the proper cable connector.
23. Fasten the raceway base to the wall, using nails, screws, or small toggle bolts—whatever the manufacturer recommends. If raceway sections are too long to fit the intended surface, use a hacksaw to cut them.
24. Connect the wires from the cable to the raceway wires using wire nuts; connect the black wire to the black wire and the white wire to the white wire. Snap the raceway outlets into their openings. Some outlets are mounted with screws.

Multi-Outlet Taps Put Power Where You Need It

Multi-outlet taps help eliminate the need for extension cords and provide an electrical center where it's needed most. The four-outlet and six-outlet portable taps, made by the General Electric Co., are designed with internal overload protectors; each has a 15-amp mini-circuit breaker that you trip to reset. A pilot light indicates that the tap is plugged in and the power is on. The UL Listed taps have three-prong grounding plugs on a 6-foot cord, an on/off switch, and keyhole slots for temporary hanging.

Add Outlets Without Breaking Into Your Walls

You can add electrical outlets without breaking into your walls to install new wiring by using surface-mounted electrical raceway. The Baseway electrical raceway system, made by Carlon, an Indian Head Co., may be fastened to any type of construction. Only a hammer, screwdriver, pliers, and saw are required for installation. First, you fasten a base strip to the wall. You can then install outlets where they're needed; wiring is held in the base strip with snap-in retaining clips. All 90-degree inside and outside corners also snap on. A base cover is cut to length and snapped over the base strip. Finally, the wiring is connected to a wall outlet or switch for power. Installation instructions for the UL Listed product are included. The raceway, made of PVC, will not dent or mar, and it can be covered with water-based paint to match a room's decor.

25. Attach the cover piece of the raceway to the mounted base piece.
26. After the raceway has been connected and mounted, restore the power to the circuit.

Other Types of Raceways

Other types of nonmetallic raceways are assembled much like sections of track for a toy train; raceway sections plug into each other and plug into an existing electrical outlet, or the raceway may be permanently connected to the circuit wiring. Outlets can be inserted anywhere; they twist into raceway channels and lock into place.

To install this type of surface wiring, follow these steps:

1. Locate a convenient wall outlet to serve as the power source for the raceway.
2. Connect the sections of raceway together.
3. Fasten the raceway sections to the wall following the manufacturer's instructions.
4. Insert the raceway outlets where needed; outlets twist into raceway channels and lock into place.
5. Connect the raceway to the existing outlet.
   Note: Some nonmetallic raceway systems simply plug into the existing outlet by means of a special outlet connector plug. Other systems require you to turn off the power to the outlet's circuit, remove the outlet cover plate, connect the raceway wiring to the outlet's wiring, and attach the cover plate.

Night-Light Turns Itself On and Off Automatically

A night-light that you don't have to remember to turn on can prevent accidents in the nursery, bathroom, kitchen, and other places around the home. The Sensor-Lite night-light, available at Sears, Roebuck and Company stores, can be plugged into any electrical outlet. As it gets dark, a photoelectric cells turns the light on automatically and adjusts bulb intensity; the darker it gets, the brighter the light gets—without the aid of any switches or timers. The cell also turns the

solid-state device off automatically. The product is UL Listed and the bulb is included in the price.

No-Kink Extension Cords Save Time

If you've ever spent lots of time trying to unkink an extension cord, you'll appreciate the Curly Q retractable extension cord by Carol Cable Co. The extension cord is similar to a coiled telephone cord, but is equipped with a plug and outlet. The curled design prevents kinking, and takes up less storage space. Curly Q's are available in 11 colors including white, red, yellow, blue, purple, silver, and tan. The cords extend to 12 feet, and may be used with almost any electrical

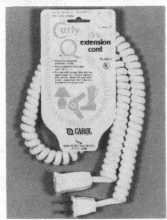

appliance. The cords are rated at 10 amps, 125 volts, and 1250 watts; they're UL Listed and polarized.

Cream Solder Holds Jobs Without Clamps

Multicore cream solder, made by Multicore Solders, is a mixture of solder and flux that can be positioned before heat is applied to the metal. Therefore, it can be accurately applied to any shape, in the desired quantity, for neater joints that follow the contours of the metal components being joined. To use the cream solder, squeeze the solder from the tube at the interface or between the metal parts to be joined. The cream is tacky so it will hold the parts in position until you apply the heat. This eliminates the need for clamps, jigs, or a helper. Each tube contains 20 grams of material. Three types of Multicore cream solder are sold; for electrical jobs buy the package labeled "for electrical soldering." A general-purpose solder for all metal joining; and a lead-free formulation for stainless steel, housewares, and jewelry are also available.

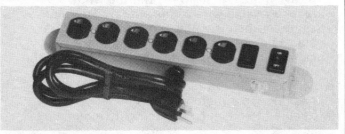

Add Outlets the Easy Way

Plug-in outlet strips provide extra outlets wherever they're needed. The model MOC-6C multiple outlet center from Electripak Inc., a subsidiary of Perfect-Line Mfg. Corp., includes six outlets, an on-off switch, and a pilot light to remind you that power to the unit is turned on. The outlet center also includes a "push-to-reset" circuit breaker; the breaker automatically shuts the power off in the event of an overload. The outlet strip features heavy-duty 15-amp, 125-volt grounded outlets; a three-wire cord almost 6 feet long; and a beige baked-enamel finish. Just plug the UL Listed outlet center into a wall outlet and it's ready to use; or it can be permanently attached to a mounting surface with two screws.

Installing an Outdoor Outlet

Materials • Weatherproof Outlet and Outlet Box • Thinwall Conduit (EMT) • Conduit Connectors • Conduit Clamps • Junction Box • Type UF Cable • Weatherproof Caulking Compound • Plastic Sheeting Material • Plastic Insulation Bushings • Conduit Ell Fitting • Concrete Block • Concrete Mix

Tools • Pencil • Tape Measure • Electric Drill and ⅞-Inch Drill Bit • Masonry Drill Bit • Safety Goggles • Keyhole or Saber Saw • Square • Screwdriver • Long-Nose Pliers • Hacksaw • Adjustable Wrench • Utility Knife • Wire Stripper • Diagonal Cutters • Caulking Gun • Spade • Conduit Bender

W HEN YOU install an outdoor outlet, it must be designed and approved for exterior use. Such electrical products are marked "weatherproof" or "weather-resistant." The circuit also must be protected by a ground fault circuit interrupter (GFCI), and the cable used for wiring the outlet must be rated for outdoor use, such as Type UF.

An outdoor outlet can be installed on the side of the house, or it may be a freestanding outlet some distance away, and connected to its power source by underground wiring.

Wall Outlet

To install an outdoor outlet on a wall, follow these steps:

1. Select a convenient location. If the outlet will be located near an interior outlet or junction box, the outdoor one can be connected to this power source. Or it can be connected to the main entrance panel by a professional electrician who can also connect a ground fault circuit interrupter (GFCI) to the circuit. A GFCI is a protective device that senses current leaks and opens the circuit, preventing a shock hazard. GFCI's are required on outdoor electrical installations. You could, however, install a duplex outlet with a built-in ground fault interrupter, and avoid the additional cost

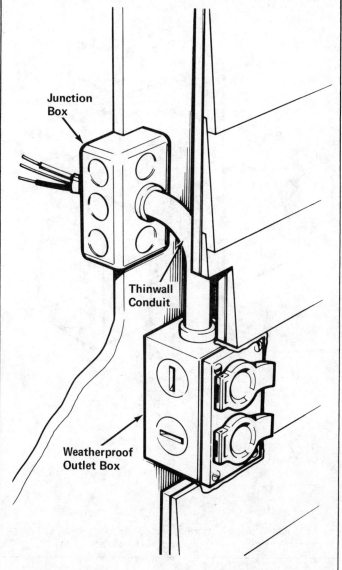

This weatherproof outlet is installed in an opening cut into the exterior wall and connected to a junction box by a length of thinwall conduit.

of having an electrician install it.

In this example, the outdoor outlet will be connected to a junction box by means of a length of thinwall conduit, or electrical metallic tubing (EMT).

2. Using a drill and keyhole saw or saber saw, cut an opening in the exterior wall to the exact size of the outlet box. If the wall is brick, concrete, stucco, or concrete block, the box can be mounted to the surface of the wall. In this case, use a suitable masonry drill to bore a ⅞-inch hole for the conduit. *Caution: Wear safety goggles when drilling through masonry.* Also, make sure that the hole will not interfere with anything inside the house.

3. Inside the house, install a junction box near

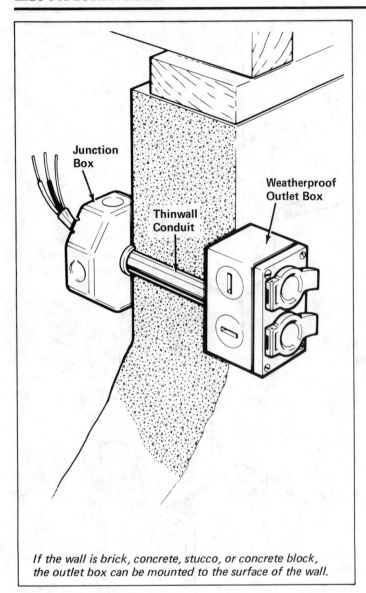

If the wall is brick, concrete, stucco, or concrete block, the outlet box can be mounted to the surface of the wall.

the location of the outdoor outlet box or use an existing junction box; with a screwdriver and a pliers, pry out a knockout disc in the back of the junction box and the back of the outlet box. *Caution: If you use an existing junction box, turn off the power to the box's circuit by removing the proper fuse or by tripping the proper circuit breaker.*

4. Use a hacksaw to cut a length of thinwall conduit long enough to connect the two boxes; you may need a conduit bender to bend the conduit so it can connect the two boxes.
5. Using connectors and locknuts, fasten the conduit to the two boxes and mount the boxes to the wall. **Note:** You may need to add some kind of spacer, like a piece of plywood, behind the inside junction box so you can fasten it solidly to the wall.
6. Use a utility knife to remove about 6 inches of outer insulation from both ends of a length of cable that's about 8 to 10 inches longer than the length of conduit. Then, use wire strippers to remove ½ inch of insulation from both ends of both wires in the cable. Run the cable through the conduit so that the stripped ends are on either side of the wall.
7. At the outlet box, form a clockwise loop on the end of each wire with a long-nose pliers.
8. Connect the white wire to a silver-colored screw on the outlet, a black wire to the brass-colored screw, and the bare or green wire to the metal box or the green hexhead screw. Fasten each wire by placing its loop clockwise under the screw head, and tightening the screws.
9. Install the outlet, the outlet gasket, and the weatherproof cover plate.
10. Use weatherproof caulking compound to seal the edges of the outlet box.

Special Covers for GFCI Outlets

When you install an outdoor outlet, it's a good idea to install one with a built-in ground fault circuit interrupter. If you do install a GFCI outlet, you need a GFCI outlet cover to protect it. This Sylvania duplex cover, from GTE Lighting Products, is designed for use with GFCI outlets. The UL Listed cover is made of die-cast aluminum with a baked-enamel finish. It comes with aluminum mounting screws, and

a rubber gasket to seal out dust and moisture.

Turn On Lights for Safety and Security

The model OLC-5 outdoor light control from Home Equipment Manufacturing Co., a division of Kenton Industries, Inc., has been designed for use with outdoor floodlights. A photoelectric cell in the unit automatically turns lights on at dusk and off at dawn. The control screws into a floodlight socket, and then the bulb—up to 300 watts—screws into the control. The device is UL Listed and reported to be weatherproof; it can be

used with ordinary bulbs or floodlights. It can be used outdoors near driveways, garages, entrances, patios, swimming pools, or anywhere you can use the convenience of automatic outdoor lighting.

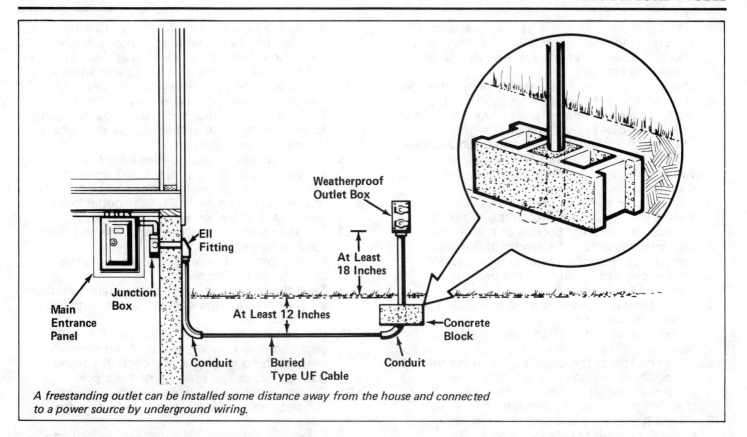

A freestanding outlet can be installed some distance away from the house and connected to a power source by underground wiring.

11. If the cable runs into an existing outlet box or junction box, you can connect the outdoor outlet to the circuit yourself as detailed earlier in this chapter. Before you start make sure that the power to the circuit has been turned off. If you have installed a new junction box, have an electrician connect the cable to the nearest power source or the main entrance panel. If you haven't already protected the outlet, have the electrician install a GFCI as well.

Freestanding Outlet

To install a freestanding outlet some distance away from the house, follow these steps:

1. Select a convenient location for a hole to be drilled through the house wall for the outlet's cable, and select a location for the free-standing outlet.
2. Drill a 7/8-inch hole through the house wall.

Grounded Duplex Outdoor Outlet, Box, and Cover Come Partially Assembled for Faster Installation

Some outdoor outlets come partially assembled making do-it-yourself installations easier. The No. DCFB-81R duplex outlet assembly made by Electripak Inc., a subsidiary of Perfect-Line Mfg. Corp., includes an outlet cover and outlet box

with a grounded duplex outlet already installed. The outlet box has a special flanged construction, which the manufacturer claims eliminates the need to locate studs. The unit installs on any exterior wall surface. The outlet assembly features die-cast aluminum construction; stainless steel springs; and a corrosion-resistant, silver-gray baked-enamel finish. The UL Listed unit fits standard outlet boxes, and comes with a weatherproof gasket for the box.

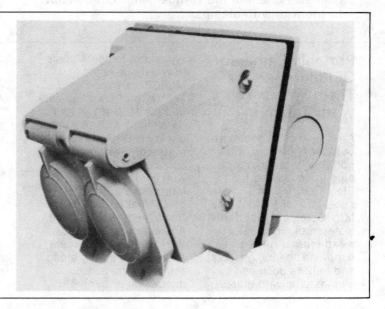

Note: If the wall is brick, concrete, stucco, or concrete block, use a suitable masonry drill. *Caution: Wear safety goggles when drilling through masonry.*

3. Dig a narrow trench at least 12 inches deep for the cable from the planned location of the outlet to a point immediately below the hole in the wall. **Note:** Spread plastic sheeting material along the edge of the trench and pile the soil on the sheeting. This will make refilling the trench easier and cause less lawn damage.

4. Lay Type UF cable in the trench, but don't bury it yet. And don't stretch the cable tight; "snake" it along the bottom of the trench.

5. Use a hacksaw to cut a length of thinwall conduit, or electrical metallic tubing (EMT) long enough to reach from the base of the trench to the hole in the wall.

6. Use a conduit bender to bend one end of the conduit 90 degrees.

7. Insert a plastic insulation bushing into the bent end of the conduit.

8. Feed the end of the cable at the house through the conduit, beginning at the bent end.

9. Fasten a conduit ell fitting with a connector to the straight end of the conduit.

10. With a hacksaw, cut a shorter length of thinwall conduit that is long enough to connect to the ell fitting, pass through the hole in the wall, and connect to a junction box inside.

11. Connect the short length of conduit to the ell fitting with a connector.

12. Thread the cable up through the ell fitting and into the short length of conduit, and insert the short length of conduit through the wall. Position the assembly so that it's vertical and its base is centered in the trench. **Note:** If necessary, fasten the vertical length of conduit to the wall with clamps.

13. Inside the house, use a connector to attach a junction box to the end of the conduit; make sure about 6 inches of cable is available inside the box. **Note:** You may need to add some kind of spacer, like a piece of plywood, behind the box so you can fasten it solidly to the wall.

14. Outside, use weatherproof caulking compound to seal the opening around the conduit where it emerges from the wall.

15. Use a hacksaw to cut another length of conduit to support the freestanding outlet. It should be long enough for one end to be bent at a 90-degree angle and for the outlet box to be at least 18 inches above ground level.

16. Use the conduit bender to bend one end of the conduit 90 degrees.

17. Insert a plastic insulation bushing into the bent end of the conduit.

18. Feed the end of the cable at the planned outlet location through the conduit, beginning at the bent end.

19. Position the conduit vertically in the trench—bent end down—and place a concrete block over the conduit so that the conduit passes through the center opening of the block.

20. Fill the support block's center opening with concrete and allow the concrete to cure for three days.

21. Fill in the trench and remove excess soil and the plastic sheeting.

22. After the concrete has cured, fasten the weatherproof outlet box to the end of the conduit with a connector.

23. Cut any excess cable but leave about 6 inches inside the box. Then, strip the cable and wires, and connect the wires to the outlet.

24. Install the outlet, the outlet gasket, and the weatherproof cover plate.

25. Have a professional electrician install a GFCI and connect the outlet circuit to the nearest power source or main entrance panel.

Portable Lights for Outdoors—Place Them Where You Want Them

An easy way to add extra outdoor lighting is with portable lights that just plug in. Moodlites from Electripak, Inc., a subsidiary of Perfect-Line Mfg. Corp., are reportedly waterproof. They have weatherproof globes, neoprene sealing gaskets, and louvers designed to eliminate upward glare.

The portable lights come in two models: the MLP-301, a three-tiered light with 75-watt capacity, and the MLP-401, a four-tiered light with 100-watt capacity. Both come with rustproof die-cast ground spikes, and 6-foot three-wire cords and plugs. The lights have a "garden green" baked-enamel finish, and are UL Listed. According to Electripak, they are ideal for accent and safety lighting along walks, stairs, and driveways; or to create

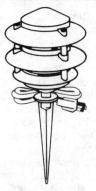 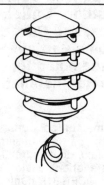

interesting lighting effects on patios, terraces, or low planted areas. Three- and four-tiered conduit-mount models—the MLC-300 and MLC-400, respectively—are available for permanent installations.

Weatherproof Cover Has a Slim Design

The No. DC-80C weatherproof outdoor switch and outlet cover from Electripak Inc., a subsidiary of Perfect-Line Mfg. Corp., offers moisture protection for switches and outlets. Stainless steel springs maintain tension in the self-closing hood to provide a weatherproof seal. The hood's construction has been designed to provide complete top and side shielding; the manufacturer claims the unit remains weathertight in the rain when the cover is up and the outlet or switch is in use. The outlet cover measures 4½ inches wide, 2⅞ inches high, and extends out only 1 inch from the mounting surface. The cover features die-cast aluminum construction; has a corrosion-resistant, silver-gray baked-enamel finish; and fits any standard outlet box. The outlet cover is UL Listed, and also meets UL requirements for covers mounted on the exterior surface of recreational vehicles. A weatherproof gasket and mounting screws are also included.

Always Work With the Right Wire

Electrical wires are identified by gauges. The larger the number or gauge, the smaller the wire. For example, No. 14 wire has a smaller diameter than No. 10 wire. The more current (electricity) you want the wire to carry, the larger the wire needs to be. Never use any wire smaller than No. 14 for household electrical hookups. A good rule of thumb is this: use 0 to 4 gauge wire for incoming power hookups; use 6 to 14 gauge wire for circuit hookups.

Control All of Your Electric Devices From One Location

A master control system that lets you control any light or appliance in your home from one central location is the Regulator 5700 by Regency Electronics, Inc. The Regulator simply plugs into a wall outlet and transmits command signals through normal house wiring to remote modules. One Regulator central command unit can control up to 100 different lights and appliances. They can be programmed to turn on and off at specified times, or can be turned on or off whenever you want by touching a button. The unit can be programmed with different times for weekdays and weekends, can dim lights, and in case of an emergency one switch will turn on all lights hooked up to the system. A number of remote modules are available. The lamp module, model LM1200, is for incandescent lamps up to 300 watts. A wall switch module, model WS1200, replaces standard switches, and controls lamps or lights normally operated by that switch. The unit dims to three different levels, and is rated up to 500 watts incandescent. A wall outlet, model WR1200, is also available. Appliance modules for appliances up to 15 amps resistance, ⅓ horsepower motors, and 500 watts are available in two versions; models AM1200 and AM1201 for two- or three-prong grounded plugs. Other modules are available for central heating and air conditioning systems and electric water heaters. Complete installation and operating instructions are furnished with the product.

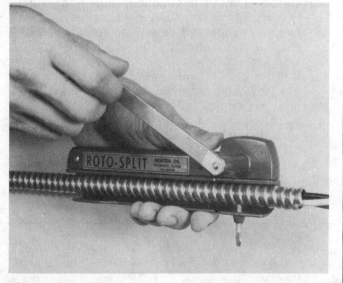

Patented Tool Cuts Armored Cable Easily and Safely

Using a hacksaw to cut armored electrical cable is a tough chore. The model RS-101 Roto-Split BX cable stripper and flexible conduit cutter, made by Seatek Co., Inc., speeds this task. The patented tool is designed to cut 14-gauge, 12-gauge, and 10-gauge BX cable and flexible conduit with two, three, or four conductors quickly, neatly, and safely. To use, you clamp the cable in the tool; a few turns of the crank produces a clean slit through the casing, which can then be separated by twisting. Seatek offers a one-year warranty and a money-back guarantee on the Roto-Split BX cable cutter.

Pilot Lights

Materials • Stick Matches • Length of Wire • Thermocouple

Tools • Stiff Brush • Adjustable Wrench • Screwdriver

WATER HEATERS, ranges, ovens, furnaces, and other appliances that use natural gas or liquid petroleum usually have constantly burning pilot lights to provide ignition to the appliance when it is turned on. When an appliance won't heat up, a burned-out pilot light is often the source of the problem.

Most new appliances don't have pilot lights; they use an electric ignition device. When an electric current is passed through the device, an element becomes hot and glows. Heat from the element lights the gas. This type of ignition system is usually sealed and can't be repaired or adjusted. When such a device fails, call a professional to replace it.

Relighting a Pilot Light

While your best guide for troubleshooting any pilot light is the owner's manual for the appliance, most pilot lights are similar in design so you can use the following general procedure for relighting one:

1. If the pilot light has gone out, check for the odor of gas. *Caution: If a strong odor of gas is present, don't try to relight the pilot light or turn on the appliance. Don't turn any lights on or off. Get out of your home immediately, leave the door open, and call the gas company or the fire department.*
2. When it's safe to do so, check the shutoff valve on the main gas supply line to the appliance and the pilot gas valve—if there is one—to see if both are turned on.
3. Unless the owner's manual or a metal servicing plate on the appliance near the pilot light says otherwise, turn the pilot gas valve off and wait about five minutes for any gas to dissipate.
4. After five minutes, turn the pilot gas valve to the "pilot" position. Then, hold a lit stick match to the pilot light orifice. If there's a pilot light reset or safety button, push it down and keep it depressed for 30 seconds or until the pilot light is burning brightly. **Note:** If there's no button or gas valve, simply hold the lit match to the pilot light orifice to light it.
5. Once the pilot light is burning brightly, release the reset button; the pilot light should keep burning. **Note:** The pilot light may ignite and then go out when the reset button is released. If this happens, try the procedure again, holding the button down again for an additional 10 to 15 seconds. If the light still fails to stay lit, the thermocouple may not be properly positioned or may be defective; the steps for correcting this are covered in the next procedure.
6. If the pilot light will not light, turn off the pilot gas valve and examine the orifice on the pilot light gas supply tube. If it's dirty, clean it with a stiff brush and a piece of wire. Don't use a wooden stick such as a match; it could break off in the orifice and block it.
7. After cleaning the orifice, repeat Steps 4 and 5.
8. If the pilot light still will not light, the problem may be a defective thermocouple.

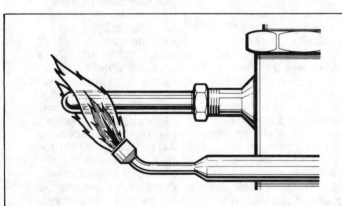

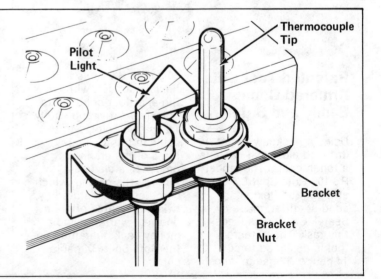

Before replacing a thermocouple, check the pilot light's flame; it should cover about 1/2 inch of the tip of the thermocouple's probe (above). If it must be replaced, use an adjustable wrench to remove the bracket nut (right).

Include These Specialized Tools in Your Appliance Kit

For many appliance repairs, you can use the hand tools and power tools commonly found in most homes. However, there are several specialized tools that can make appliance repairs easier to do. These include a continuity tester, volt-ohm meter (VOM), or both; wire strippers; nut drivers; a long-nose pliers; Allen (hexhead) wrenches; putty knife; and an adjustable wrench. Supplies should include plastic electrical tape; wire nuts; crimp-type terminals; and an assortment of nuts, bolts, and self-tapping machine screws.

Light Gas Appliances Easily With Igniter

It can often be difficult to light a gas appliance's pilot light with a match, especially in tight quarters. HandySpark, a piezoelectric gas igniter that produces up to a dozen sparks every time you squeeze its trigger, can reach into cramped areas. Marketed by Triangle Importing, Inc., the device is designed for appliances and tools that operate on propane (LP) or natural gas. The igniter never needs batteries or flints; there's nothing to replace. It has a built-in, adhesive wall hanger on its high-impact plastic and chrome-plated housing. The company offers a 10-year warranty on the HandySpark igniter.

Alarm Offers Early Warning of Gas Leaks From Appliances

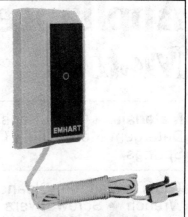

Homeowners who are concerned about the possibility of propane and natural gas leaks from a furnace, water heater, clothes dryer, space heater, or other appliance, can get early-warning protection with a gas alarm. Such a device is the model GA120 Emhart gas alarm, made by the Notifier Co., a division of Emhart Industries, Inc. It mounts to a wall with one screw and is plugged into an electrical outlet. If there's a potentially dangerous gas level caused by a leaking appliance, an 85-decibel horn sounds a warning. If the sensor fails while the power is on, the alarm automatically sounds a chirping noise every five seconds. According to the company, the UL Listed Emhart gas alarm is intended for detecting propane (LP) and natural gas only.

Don't Take Chances With a Gas Leak

If you suspect an appliance is leaking gas, extinguish all pilot lights and other open flames at once. Never use a match to locate the gas leak! And, don't use any electrical appliances. Immediately call the gas company or the fire department and leave your home.

Replacing a Thermocouple

The thermocouple is a safety device that turns the gas supply off when the pilot light's flame goes out. To troubleshoot a thermocouple, follow these steps:

1. Check the pilot light's flame. If the flame doesn't cover ½ inch of the tip of the thermocouple's steel probe, loosen the thermocouple bracket nut by turning the nut counterclockwise with an adjustable wrench, and reposition the probe's tip in the flame.
2. Tighten the nut slightly—don't apply lots of pressure—and test the thermocouple by lighting the pilot light; it should now stay lit.
3. If the pilot light still won't light, you'll have to replace the thermocouple. Turn off the gas at the shutoff valve on the supply line to the appliance or at the main gas valve.
4. Use an adjustable wrench to remove the bracket nut that holds the thermocouple assembly next to the pilot light.
5. Disconnect the thermocouple's copper lead—its other end—by turning its connection nut counterclockwise with an adjustable wrench.
6. Install the new thermocouple, but be careful not to kink its lead. Turn the connection nut finger-tight, and then tighten it one-quarter turn with an adjustable wrench.
7. Position the new thermocouple's probe so that about ½ inch of its tip will be covered by the pilot light flame, and secure it in position with the bracket nut.
8. Turn on the gas supply, and relight the pilot light following Steps 4 and 5 in the previous procedure.
9. Check the condition of the pilot light. A correctly adjusted pilot light flame will be steady and blue, and between ¼ and ½ inch high. If the flame doesn't appear as described, it may not be getting enough air. If the flame is yellow at its tip, the pilot light is getting too much air. To correct either situation, turn the pilot light adjustment screw slightly—clockwise or counterclockwise—until the flame is blue, steady, and covers the tip of the thermocouple.

Appliance Motors

Materials • Clean Rags • No. 30 Non-Detergent Motor Oil • Carbon Brushes and Springs

Tools • Vacuum Cleaner • Adjustable Wrench • Screwdrivers • Pliers • 20,000-ohm, 2-watt, Wire-Wound Resistor

AN APPLIANCE may be powered by one of several types of motors. Small appliances are often powered by a universal motor or a shaded-pole motor. Large appliances are generally powered by a split-phase or a capacitor-start motor.

Other than a few simple maintenance chores, there's little you can do in the way of repairing appliance motors, except for the universal type of motor; most motors require experience and special equipment to fix. If a motor is badly damaged, it's often cheaper and easier to replace the motor—or appliance—than to have it repaired. If you suspect little damage, consult a professional for servicing, but get a repair estimate before approving any work.

Motor Maintenance

The key to a trouble-free appliance motor is preventive maintenance. In general, follow these recommendations:

• Clean the appliance motor at least once a year. If you can't wipe the dirt and grime away with a clean, dry rag, use a vacuum cleaner. *Caution: Capacitor-start and permanent-split-capacitor motors store electricity, even after the power to the appliance is turned off. The capacitor(s) must be discharged on these types of motors before attempting cleaning.* Follow the procedure for "Discharging a Capacitor" at the end of this section.
• If a motor has oil ports on the ends where the motor shaft comes out of the motor housing, lubricate them sparingly at least once a year with No. 30 non-detergent motor oil. Don't use all-purpose oil, and don't overlubricate.
• Check motor drive belts; they shouldn't be too tight. Generally, a belt should be adjusted so that it deflects from ¼ to ½ inch when you press the belt between the motor and the nearest pulley. Adjust the belt by loosening, adjusting, and then tightening the belt adjustment bolt on the motor.
• Use the appliance for the job for which it was intended. Don't overload it by forcing it to go beyond its intended capabilities.
• If the motor won't run, runs off and on, won't shut off, or continually blows fuses or trips a circuit breaker, check the power cord or switch for the source of trouble.

Note: Some appliance motors are equipped with reset buttons, a safety device designed to protect the motor from damaging overloads. If the motor doesn't run, allow it to cool for about 30 minutes and then push the reset button firmly. If this doesn't restart the motor, try to trace the problem through the appliance power cord, its switch, the wall outlet, or at the main entrance panel before suspecting the appliance motor.

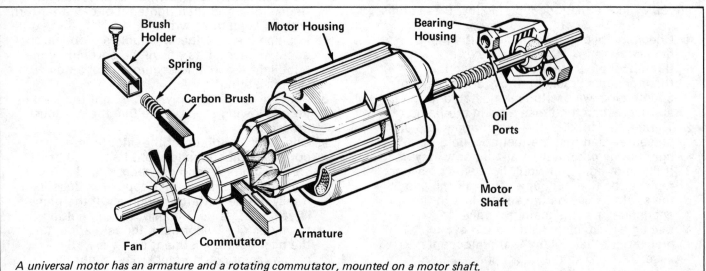

A universal motor has an armature and a rotating commutator, mounted on a motor shaft. Carbon brushes make the electrical contact; worn brushes are among the most common problems.

Universal Motors

Universal motors, which are used in many small and medium-size appliances, provide strong power at both low and high speeds.

These motors have a rotor called an "armature," with coils of wire around it, and a rotating cylinder called a "commutator," which comprises alternating strips of conducting and non-conducting materials. The armature and commutator are mounted on the motor shaft. On each side of the commutator, there is a carbon brush—a soft block of carbon—which carries current from the circuit. As the carbon brushes press against the commutator, the armature is magnetized and rotates.

Most universal motors also have a cooling fan at one end of the motor's shaft. If a motor is noisy, the fan blades may be bent. You can straighten any bent fan blades with a pliers.

A common problem with universal motors is that the carbon brushes have become worn. The ends of the brushes should be curved to fit the commutator; if they're worn down short, new brushes are needed. Another sign to look for is that worn brushes may spark where they touch the commutator. To replace worn brushes, follow these steps:

1. Turn off the power to the appliance and disassemble it to reach the motor.
2. Using a screwdriver, remove the screws that secure the carbon brush holders, springs, and carbon brushes on each side of the commutator.
3. Turn or tip the motor to remove the brush assembly.
4. Buy replacement brushes and springs. The information—number and make of the motor—you need is usually found on a metal plate on the motor itself. If the information isn't available, take the worn parts with you to an appliance parts store to make sure you get the proper parts.
5. Install the new carbon brushes and springs and secure the assembly with the screws.
6. Reassemble the appliance.

Note: New carbon brushes may have a square face, or a curved face that matches the curvature of the commutator. Until the brushes with square faces are worn to fit the shape of the commutator, the motor may tend to spark and be somewhat noisy. This is normal, but should stop once the brushes are properly seated against the commutator.

Shaded-Pole Motors

Shaded-pole motors, which provide little power, are found in many small and large appliances. Shaded-pole motors that operate at a precise, consistent

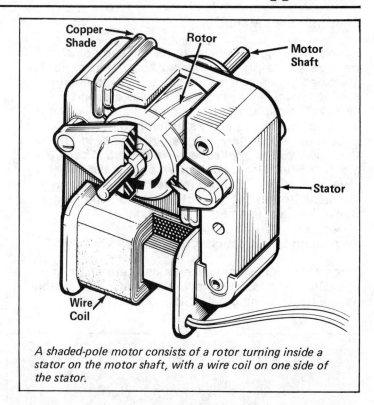

A shaded-pole motor consists of a rotor turning inside a stator on the motor shaft, with a wire coil on one side of the stator.

speed are called "synchronous" motors. In a small clock, for example, such a motor turns the dial hands. In a refrigerator, the motor starts the defrosting cycle. Most malfunctions with this type of motor are caused by a faulty starter coil, and can be corrected by replacement of the coil with a new one of the same make and model number. To replace the coil follow these steps:

1. Disconnect the power to the appliance.
2. Remove any wires connected to the motor, take out any screws that hold it in place, and remove the motor.
3. Unscrew the frame of the motor, and open the halves of the frame.
4. Disconnect the old coil and remove it.
5. Insert the new coil, and connect it the same way the old coil was connected.
6. Reinstall the motor in the appliance.

If the motor frame is riveted together—and many are—the coil is not worth the work of replacement; instead, replace the motor or the appliance.

Split-Phase Motors

Split-phase motors are fairly powerful motors used on washing machines, dryers, and dishwashers. Except for cleaning and lubrication, they require no maintenance. When such a motor malfunctions, don't attempt any repairs yourself. Buy a new one or take the faulty motor to a professional, whichever is less expensive.

Capacitor-Start Motors

Found on air conditioners, furnaces, and some freezers and refrigerators, a capacitor-start motor is a shaded-pole motor with a capacitor—an energy-storing device—that is wired into the starting circuit. The capacitor stores current and releases it in bursts to provide extra starting power.

Caution: Capacitors store electricity, even after the power to the appliance is turned off. If such a motor malfunctions, don't attempt to make any repairs yourself; call a professional. To discharge the capacitor on such a motor, see "Discharging a Capacitor" at the end of this section.

Permanent-Split-Capacitor (PSC) Motors

Large air conditioning systems use permanent-split-capacitor motors, which operate on AC. PSC motors have a large running capacitor connected to the starting circuit. The starting circuit doesn't turn off when the motor approaches its top speed. Instead, the capacitor makes a phase shift as the motor approaches top speed, causing the starting circuit to increase the efficiency of the motor.

Caution: Capacitors store electricity, even after the power to the appliance is turned off. Like capacitor-start motors, PSC motors are complex. Don't try to make repairs yourself; call a professional when such a motor malfunctions. To discharge the capacitor on such a motor, use the following procedure.

Discharging a Capacitor

The capacitors found on some motors store electricity, even after the power to the appliance is turned off, and you could receive a severe shock if this device is not discharged. When working with a capacitor-start or permanent-split-capacitor motor,

Power Controller Regulates Motors

Power factor controllers are devices that are designed to conserve power in motors of big energy-using appliances, such as refrigerators, freezers, washers, power tools, and sump pumps. The Watts Worth model PA-10 power factor controller, made by ERI and distributed by Sem-Torq, Inc., was originally developed by the National Aeronautics and Space Administration. By sensing and delivering the minimum power needed, the controller regulates the flow of electricity much in the same way that a faucet regulates water flow—automatically. To connect the device, you just plug it in to an electrical outlet, plug the appliance into the controller, and adjust it according to the manufacturer's instructions. The model PA-10 works on any AC induction motor not exceeding 10 amps or ½ horsepower. Larger models are also available.

Push the Button First

Appliances with motors frequently have built-in overload protectors or reset buttons that trip when the appliance motor overheats or is subjected to undue strain. Before you attempt to repair the appliance, or call in a professional repair person, let the appliance rest for about 30 minutes; then press the reset button. Often this will solve the problem, and save you time and money. Reset buttons are located on control panels of appliances or directly on the motor or motor housing. They are usually marked "Reset."

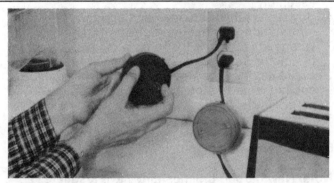

End Appliance Cord Tangles With Reel

Electrical cords on small kitchen appliances that are longer than needed can create unsightly tangles, which can be a hazard under foot or on counters. This problem can be avoided with Cord-A-Way, a 3-inch-diameter reel. Excess cord is wound onto a patented double-action reel, leaving only enough length to reach from the appliance to the nearest outlet. The device, made by Cord-A-Way Industries, attaches to any small cord in seconds, and can store up to 8 feet of lamp-size cord. The Cord-A-Way reel is available in clear plastic and four colors—white, coppertone, harvest gold, and avocado.

discharge the capacitor with a 20,000-ohm, 2-watt, wire-wound resistor—an inexpensive device available at most electrical supply stores. To discharge a capacitor, follow these steps:

1. Turn off the power to the appliance, and remove the service or control panel to gain access to the capacitor. **Note:** Some appliances, such as air conditioners, may have *two* capacitors; you must discharge both.
2. Locate the capacitor(s); a capacitor resembles a large dry-cell battery.
3. Discharge the capacitor by fastening the clips of the 20,000-ohm, 2-watt, wire-wound resistor to the terminals of the capacitor. **Note:** If the capacitor has three terminals, connect the resistor to one outer terminal and the center terminal; then to the other outer terminal and the center terminal.
4. Disconnect the resistor.

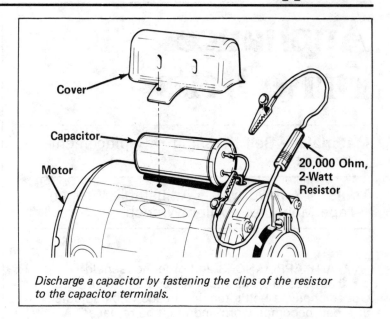

Discharge a capacitor by fastening the clips of the resistor to the capacitor terminals.

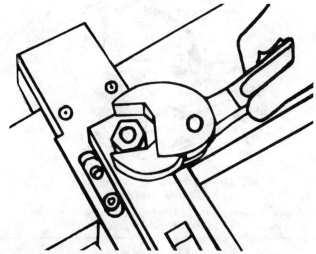

Automatic Wrench Is Self-Tightening

A wrench that is automatically self-adjusting and self-tightening is unusual. The Plattina automatic wrench, marketed by Lynnwood Distributing Co., Inc., is just that. It fits most nuts, bolts, pipes, and fittings associated with appliance repairs, and automatically adjusts to metric or standard fittings. According to the manufacturer, the wrench will grip tight on any shape—square, hex, round, or octagonal. To use, position it on the item to be tightened, turn it, and it snugs up ready for work. And, with the same ease, it disengages for successive turns. The harder the handle is pulled, the harder the jaws grip. Three sizes of Plattina automatic wrenches can replace an entire set of socket, box- or open-end wrenches. All wrench parts are made of drop-forged, chrome-vanadium steel. Model 1001 has a jaw size from 3/16 to 5/8 inch; model 1001/2 is 5/16 to 7/8 inch; model 1002 is 3/8 to 1 3/16 inches; and model 1003 is 5/8 to 1 5/8 inches. It comes with a one-year limited warranty.

Spray Lubricates and Inhibits Corrosion

A multipurpose spray that can help you loosen rusted or corroded appliance fasteners and other parts is 5-56 from CRC Chemicals, Inc. The product is also formulated to lubricate the parts and inhibit corrosion. According to the manufacturer, 5-56 spray uses no fluorocarbon propellents, and has a lower flash point (190° F) than many similar products. The multipurpose spray can also be used to start wet lawnmower and automobile engines.

When a Drop of Oil Is Plenty

When it's difficult to put just a drop of oil on an appliance's small moving part, you could use the Carbona Pin-Point Oiler. The tubelike dispenser contains quality oil that is inhibited against oxidation, rust, and foaming, which makes it ideal for appliance maintenance projects. The oiler is refillable so you don't have to buy a new one when it runs dry. The oiler, No. 552, is made by Carbona Products Co.

Appliance Drive Belts

Materials • Belt Dressing • Replacement Drive Belt

Tools • Screwdriver • Adjustable Wrench • Tape Measure • Allen Wrench

MANY APPLIANCES and other household devices use belts to drive some of their parts. Occasionally, a belt's tension needs to be adjusted or a belt becomes worn and must be replaced. A worn belt is easily diagnosed by noisy operation of the appliance. A loose belt can cause a malfunction that may seem to be caused by a faulty motor.

Adjusting Belt Tension

Belts should be inspected from time to time. They should not be too tight or too loose. Follow this procedure:

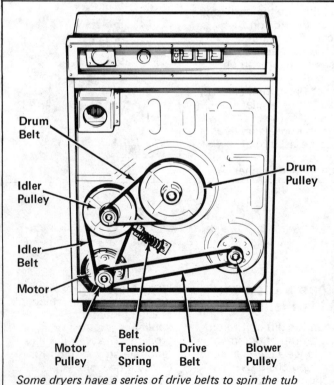

Some dryers have a series of drive belts to spin the tub instead of just one. Check to see if there's a spring tensioning adjustment.

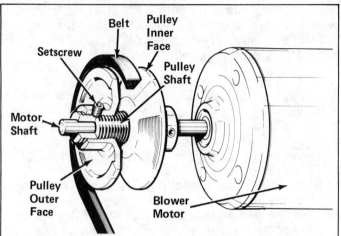

When replacing a V-belt, make sure the belt is in alignment with the pulleys.

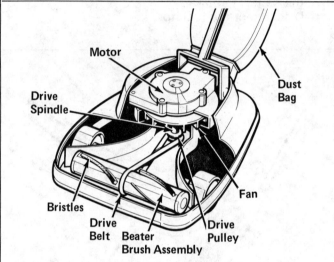

Vacuum cleaners with beater brushes — and some other appliances — use a small, flat drive belt.

1. Unplug or turn off the power to the appliance.
2. Disassemble the appliance, if necessary, to gain access to the belt.
3. Check the belt's tension; most V-belts on pulleys should have about ½ inch of deflection when you depress the belt midway between pulleys. If the belt is loose, tighten it. Follow the instructions in the owner's manual for the appliance.
4. If there are no instructions for this procedure, use an adjustable wrench to loosen the motor's mounting bolts, which are usually threaded through a base plate or bracket. The holes are slotted so the motor may be moved forward or backward.
5. Pull the motor away from the pulleys to tighten the belt. When you obtain the proper tension in the belt, tighten the bolts or nuts. If a belt is too tight, loosen the belt by moving the motor toward the pulleys.

Note: Some motor and belt systems—washing machines and dryers for example—have a spring tensioning adjustment near the motor. By turning a bolt or screw with a wrench or screwdriver, the belt may be tightened or loosened. You may have to make several attempts at adjustment before the belt is tensioned properly. Loosen the tension spring to loosen the belt; tighten the spring to tighten the belt.

Replacing a V-Belt

If you must replace a V-belt, follow these steps:

1. Measure the drive belt. Use a flexible steel tape measure and measure the belt around its top surface—not down in the pulley grooves. Also measure the width; measure the widest part of the belt. You can use these measurements to buy a replacement belt that's an exact fit. Or you can take the old belt with you when you buy a replacement.
2. Remove the old belt. Loosen the bolts or nuts holding the motor to its mounting bracket, and push the motor toward the pulley assembly. If the appliance has a spring tensioning device, loosen the screw or bolt adjustment and remove the spring to provide slack.
   Note: If you are changing the drive belt on a dryer—the flat belt that goes around the dryer drum—install the new belt next to the old belt first. Then cut off the old belt and slip the new belt into the old belt positions.
3. Slip on the new drive belt.
4. Make sure that the belt is in alignment with the pulleys. If not, you can loosen the pulleys on their shafts and move the pulleys slightly. Pulleys are fastened to the shafts with setscrews in the hubs of the pulleys or in the pulley grooves; use a screwdriver or Allen wrench to turn the setscrews.
5. Tighten the tension on the new belt so that it has about ½ inch deflection at a point midway between the motor and the first drive pulley.

Note: New belts and sometimes old belts that slip should be treated with belt dressing. If so, apply the dressing sparingly to the belt—not the pulleys.

Installing a Flat Belt

Vacuum cleaners with beater brushes and some other appliances use a small, flat drive belt. The tension is provided by the belt, which has elastic qualities. Usually, the old belt is simply slipped off its trackway and the new belt is slipped on. There are no tension springs to tighten or loosen, or pulleys to reset.

Stop Slipping Appliance Belts

Any belt-driven appliance loses its efficiency when the belt slips on its pulleys or rollers. The cure for this is a heavy-duty belt dressing such as Plasti-Kote Easy Way belt dressing and conditioner, made by Plasti-Kote, Inc. The product is formulated to increase belt life and improve belt power. The belt dressing may be used on leather, rubber, canvas, and other fabric belts that are flat, round, or V-shaped. It not only removes glazing and foreign matter, but also helps maintain belt flexibility.

Belt Dressing Stops Squeaks

Appliance belts that squeak in pulley drives should squeak no more after Duro Belt Grip has been applied, according to the manufacturer, Loctite Corp. Besides eliminating squeaks, the product also stops V-belts and fan belts from slipping, making an appliance more efficient. Duro Belt Grip comes in a 1½-ounce tube, and is applied directly from the tube. The product is approved by the Automotive Parts and Accessories Association.

Extend Life of Appliance Drive Belts

The cord fibers of V-belts eventually stretch out of shape and break with usage. With Permatex belt dressing, the belt life is extended because the dressing restores pliability and flexibility to the cord fibers, according to the manufacturer, Loctite Corp. Besides preventing belt slippage due to heat, cold, dampness, dust, and glazing, Permatex belt dressing helps eliminate squeaking and slipping. The product may be used on appliance drive belts. It may also be used on alternator/generator, timing, or fan belts on cars.

Garbage Disposers

Materials • Pipe Joint Compound or Tape • Ice and Fresh Lemon • Replacement Parts as Required

Tools • Screwdriver • Circuit Tester • Continuity Tester • Heavy Gloves • Dowel or Broom Handle • Adjustable Wrench • Pipe Wrench • Putty Knife • Drain-and-Trap Auger

G ARBAGE DISPOSERS are as breakdown- and maintenance-free as any modern household appliance can be. Almost always, a stoppage can be traced to a bone or a piece of metal, glass, or crockery stuck in the grind wheel. Even if the disposer breaks these hard objects, the pieces can clog plumbing pipes and the disposer won't work.

Because garbage disposers are fairly uncompli-cated appliances, most repairs are usually easy to make. If you can't make the repairs outlined in this section, it may be less expensive to replace the disposer. Before you make any decision to buy a new unit, check out repair costs.

No Power to Disposer

There are two kinds of garbage disposers. One is the continuous-feed model that is operated by a wall switch. The other is the batch-feed type; it has a switch built into the stopper. The stopper is inserted into the sink drain opening and turned to operate the disposer. If the disposer won't run and it appears that the unit isn't getting any power, follow these steps:

1. Check the fuse or circuit breaker for the disposer's circuit. If the fuse has blown or the circuit breaker has tripped, replace the fuse or trip the breaker to the "on" position. If the fuse continues to trip, call a professional.
2. If the circuit is on, wait 30 minutes, then press the reset button on the disposer housing under the sink and test the disposer. If the disposer has an automatic reset feature, wait for 30 minutes before testing the disposer.
3. If the disposer still doesn't operate, check the

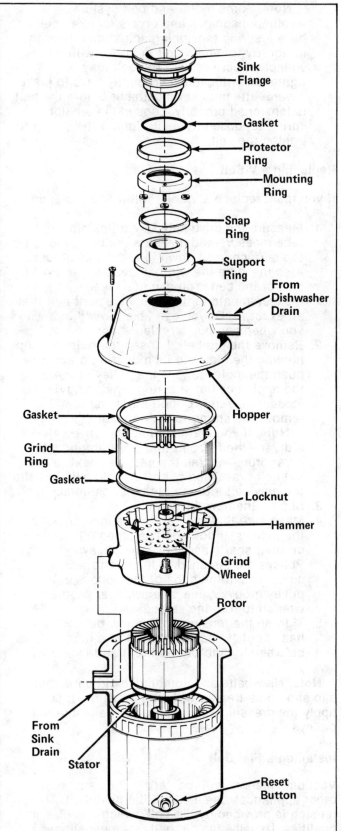

Garbage disposers use a grind wheel driven by a motor to grind up food waste. Most problems can be traced to a piece of bone or other debris stuck in the grind wheel.

power cord and wall outlet, wall switch, or disposer stopper switch, depending on the type of disposer you have and the installation.

If there's a power cord and wall outlet, check the cord for signs of damage; test the wall outlet with a circuit tester. If there's a wall switch, shut off the power to the circuit; test the switch for continuity.

If there's a disposer stopper switch, shut off the power to the circuit and disconnect at least one of the wires to the stopper switch connected to the hopper under the sink. Test the switch for continuity.

If the cord, outlet, wall switch, or stopper switch is faulty, they must be replaced. **Note:** Procedures for using a circuit tester and a continuity tester are discussed in "Your Home's Electrical System" in the chapter on Electrical Work.

4. If you still haven't found the cause of the trouble, shut off the power to the disposer's circuit at the main entrance panel and check the circuit wire connections at the disposer by removing the fasteners securing the wiring enclosure from the base of the disposer. Ordinarily, the connections simply consist of black circuit wire to black wire in the disposer, white wire to white wire, and bare or ground wire to a special grounding terminal. Make sure the wires are securely connected. Usually, they are connected by wire nuts; try tightening the wire nuts. If you have to remove the disposer to gain access to the wiring, see the procedure for "Removing the Disposer," later in this section.

Disposer Hums, Sticks, or Makes Unusual Noises

A disposer that hums and won't run probably has something jammed in its grind wheel. Usually, the machine's overload protection device will shut off the power to the unit automatically, but not always. If the disposer makes unusual noises or runs and then sticks, there is probably some foreign object in the disposer that the machine is unable to grind. To solve these problems, follow these steps:

1. Turn off the power to the disposer circuit. *Caution: Before you go ahead, test the disposer to make absolutely sure the power is off.*
2. Remove the stopper and look into the hopper. If the machine is overloaded, put on a heavy glove and remove some of the garbage. If you spot an object such as a utensil or a large bone, remove the object. If you find nothing, press the reset button, and if that doesn't work, try reversing the motor—if the disposer has such a feature.
3. Restore power to the disposer's circuit and

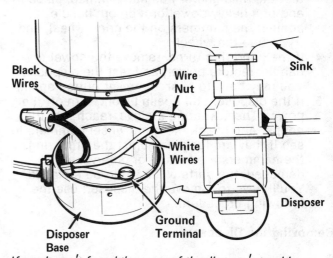

If you haven't found the cause of the disposer's trouble, shut off the power and check the connections at the base of the disposer.

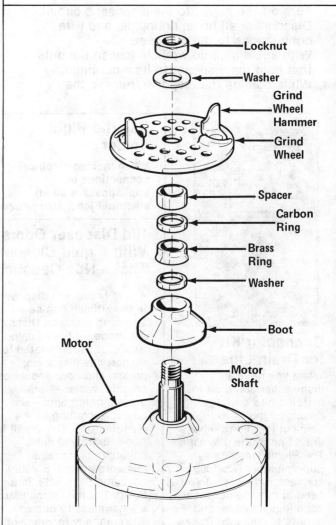

On some disposers, the hammers can be removed; on others, the hammers are part of the grind wheel, and the entire grind wheel assembly must be replaced.

test the machine. If it is still jammed, place the end of a heavy dowel or a broom handle against the hammers on the grind wheel, and try to free the wheel.

4. If the grind ring turns, remove the dowel or handle, restore power, and test the disposer. You may have to push the reset button again.
5. If the disposer still doesn't work, turn off the power. Then, wearing a glove, reach into the hopper and check the grind wheel hammers to see if they are locked against the grind ring. If the hammers are broken or otherwise damaged, the parts will have to be replaced. You'll have to remove the disposer; use the following procedure.

Removing the Disposer

If the disposer must be removed for repairs, follow these steps:

1. Turn off the power to the disposer's circuit.
2. Disconnect all hose, drainpipe, and wire connections to the disposer.
3. With an adjustable wrench, loosen the nuts that hold the disposer to its mounting ring.
4. While holding the disposer, remove the nuts and lower the disposer.
5. Remove the screws or bolts that secure the grind wheel housing to the motor assembly.
6. Open the housing so the grind wheel can be removed. As you disassemble the disposer, make a drawing of how the parts go together to ease reassembly.
7. With the grind wheel removed, check it and the hammers for sharpness. On some models, the hammers can be removed; on others they are part of the grind wheel. If either the grind wheel or hammers feel dull, and you have noticed that garbage is ground too slowly, replace the grind wheel, hammers, or both.
8. While the grind wheel is removed, clean the housing.
9. Reassemble the disposer and install it under the sink.

Water Leaks and Clogs

Because lots of water is involved in the disposal of garbage, leaks can sometimes develop in the hose connected to the disposer from a dishwasher, or the disposer drainpipe may become clogged and develop a leak. To cure these problems, follow these steps:

Connector Kit for Drain Line

When you have a dishwasher and plan to install a new garbage disposer, you need to connect the dishwasher's drain line to the disposer. The Plumb-Goodies by Superplumber No. 1009 connector kit is what you need. It has the necessary couplings, clamps, and screws for the job. The kit is made by Sinkmaster, Anaheim Manufacturing, a division of Tappan.

Use the Right Solder

When making electrical connections on appliances, or on any electrical jobs, always use rosin-core solder—never acid-core. The best solder for electrical work is 60/40 alloy (60 percent tin; 40 percent lead). "Core" solder has the flux or rosin already in it.

Rid Disposer Odors With Liquid Cleaner That's Non-Caustic

A smelly drain or disposer in the kitchen can be an annoying problem. Dispoz-All, made for the Alumin-Nu Corp., is formulated to rid garbage disposers, drains, and downspouts of organic wastes—fats, grease, detergents—and odors. According to the manufacturer, Dispoz-All is non-caustic and non-polluting; it contains microorganisms, which consume the waste, in a liquid. The microorganisms are harmless to humans. The company recommends placing 4 ounces of the product in the disposer each week or two,

depending on use. Dispoz-All comes in a 1-quart plastic bottle.

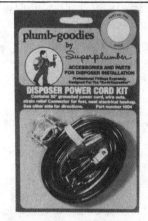

Disposer Cord Kit Fits Most Models

If you need to hook up a new garbage disposer, the Plumb-Goodies by Superplumber disposer power cord kit, No. 1004, has a 30-inch grounded power cord, wire nuts, and strain-relief connector for wiring most disposer units. The kit, manufactured by Sinkmaster, Anaheim Manufacturing, a division of Tappan, includes directions, and is designed for the do-it-yourselfer.

Appliances

1. Tighten the clamps that hold the hose from the dishwasher to the disposer. Usually, hose clamps, like those found on auto radiator hoses, are used. Turn the clamp screw clockwise with a screwdriver to tighten the clamp.
2. If the hose still leaks, the hose probably is cracked or broken. Replace the hose by unscrewing the clamps at the disposer and at the dishwasher.
3. Twist the hose at both ends to break the connections.
4. Slide hose clamps onto a new hose, and connect the hose.
5. If the disposer drainpipe is leaking, try tightening the connection with a pipe wrench.
6. Because of excessive vibration, the drainpipe may be cracked or the threads may be damaged. If so, use the wrench to remove the drainpipe, which is connected to the side of the disposer and to the drain extension with slip nuts. Apply pipe joint compound or tape to the male threads and install a new drainpipe.
7. If the drainpipe is clogged, use a pipe wrench to remove the pipe at the disposer and at the first joint beyond the trap. **Note:** Clogging is easy to spot because the garbage in the disposer hopper will not go down the drainpipe.
8. Using a drain-and-trap auger, clean out the pipe.
9. Reconnect the pipes and test the disposer.

Caution: Don't use chemical drain cleaners unless the product is specifically made to be used with disposers. If the disposer is working properly but emits foul odors, grind a hopper full of ice followed by a fresh lemon. Then, flush the system, using plenty of cold water.

To help avoid future clogs and leaks, always use cold water when you run your garbage disposer. Hot water only melts grease, which then coats both the disposer and the drainpipe. Cold water, however, lets the grease congeal into tiny globules that can be washed down the drain.

Replacing a Disposer

If a disposer can't be repaired at a price that fits your budget, you can install a brand new garbage disposer in just a few hours. Disposer manufacturers include complete installation instructions with their products, along with a list of parts required for installation.

Variety of Pliers and Wrenches for Appliance Repairs

Using the wrong tool for the job can damage a fastener or a part. You can, however, probably find the right tool to use in a selection of Handyman pliers and wrenches from Stanley Tools, a division of The Stanley Works. They include 6- and 8-inch slip-joint pliers; 7- and 8-inch linesman pliers; 5-inch, 6-inch, and 8-inch long-nose pliers; and 5-inch, 6-inch, and 7-inch diagonal cutting pliers. The pliers are made of high-carbon, drop-forged, tempered alloy steel. The long-nose, linesman, and diagonal cutting pliers are precision-machined and have finely honed cutting edges; all models have vinyl grips. The 6-inch, 8-inch, 10-inch, and 12-inch adjustable wrenches are tempered chrome-  vanadium steel with a rust-resistant, polished chrome finish. There also is a set of five open-end wrenches that have a capacity from ¼ to ¾ inch.

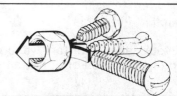

Color-Coded Nuts Fit Any Type Screw

Finding the right nut to fit bolts and screws can be a frustrating and time-consuming chore. With Homecraft Super Nuts, made by Gries Dynacast, a division of Coats & Clark, Inc., there's no need to search for hours for the right nut. Super Nuts, which are made of nylon Type 66, are color-coded as to size, and they will fit fasteners with coarse, fine, or metric threads. An assortment package contains four blue #6, four green #8, three yellow #10, and three red ¼-inch Super Nuts. According to the manufacturer, Super Nuts are corrosion-resistant, rustproof, and electrically insulating.

Vacuum Cleaners

Materials • Household Detergent
• Silicone Lubricant • Wire
Coat Hanger • Replacement Parts as
Required

Tools • Garden Hose • Pliers
• Screwdriver • Old Comb or
Nail • Diagonal Cutters or Utility
Knife • Continuity Tester • Long-Nose
Pliers

LACK OF SUCTION is the main service complaint about vacuum cleaners; the major cause is clogging. In second place is lack of power. Both problems are easy to solve on a canister, tank, or upright vacuum cleaner.

Suction Problems

If your canister or tank vacuum cleaner doesn't pick up dirt very well or not at all, look for blockage in the hose where it connects to the front of the tank. In an upright model, the blockage is usually behind the beater brush assembly or where the dust bag connects to the base. To troubleshoot a vacuum cleaner that has poor suction, follow these steps:

1. If the vacuum cleaner has a hose, disconnect it.
2. Plug in and turn on the vacuum cleaner. Place your palm across the unit's air intake port. If there's an adequate amount of suction, the problem is in the hose.
3. Turn off the vacuum cleaner and insert a garden hose into the vacuum hose; the garden hose will dislodge and push out any debris stuck inside.
4. Connect the hose and turn on the vacuum cleaner; check the hose for air leaks where it connects to the cleaning wand and the canister or tank; even small leaks will cause a significant loss of suction. The metal connection on the vacuum that the hose plugs into is usually screwed on. If it is bent out of shape or badly worn it should be replaced. If the hose is damaged and leaking air, replace the hose; most temporary repairs will be unsatisfactory.
5. Examine the sections of the cleaning wand. If there's a poor fit between the sections or where they connect to the hose, this could be causing the problem. You may be able to bend the metal wand connections slightly with pliers for a tighter fit, but if the connections are

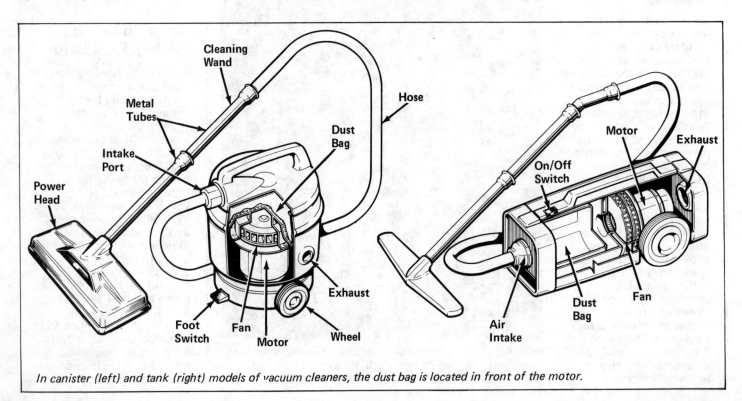

In canister (left) and tank (right) models of vacuum cleaners, the dust bag is located in front of the motor.

cracked or severely bent out of shape, replace the damaged metal cleaning wand sections.

6. If the hose and cleaning wand are clear and don't leak, check the dust bag to see if it's full. The bag should be emptied or replaced when it's half to two-thirds full; a full dust bag cuts the vacuum's air flow. Also check the bag for any rips, tears, or other damage. If necessary, replace the bag.

7. Check the gasket around the dust bag's intake port. This seal could be misaligned, worn, or broken. If so, align or replace it. This is usually a friction-fit part and may be installed without any tools.

8. Remove the dust bag and turn on the vacuum cleaner. Sometimes, this will clear any blockage.

9. If there is an air filter between the machine's fan and motor, the filter may be dirty. If it's washable, clean it with mild household detergent and water. Rinse and allow to dry. Otherwise, replace the filter with a new one.

10. If your machine is an upright model, remove the beater brush assembly. It is held by two levers, a metal plate, or spring clips. If a metal plate is used, remove the screws.

11. The beater brush assembly is usually driven by one or more drive belts. Remove the belts, and then remove the beater brush assembly.

12. Form a hook at one end of a wire coat hanger, and remove any debris caught in the air channels directly behind the beater brush assembly.

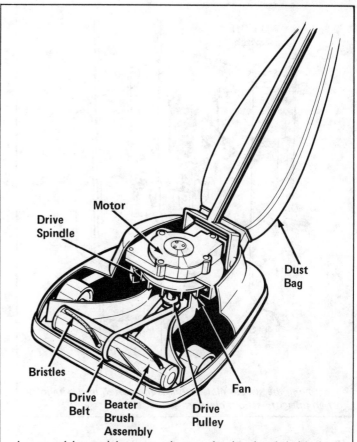

In an upright model vacuum cleaner, the dust bag is behind the motor. The bag is porous; it lets air out but keeps the dust in.

Bags to Fit Virtually Every Vacuum Cleaner

Do you have a problem locating bags to fit your vacuum cleaner? Blue Lustre vacuum cleaner bags are available in 17 styles that fit 362 different models of vacuum cleaners. Made by Blue Lustre Home Care Products, the bags, according to the manufacturer, are constructed of materials that meet or exceed the manufacturers' specifications. Instructions are printed on every package, and the company offers a money-back guarantee.

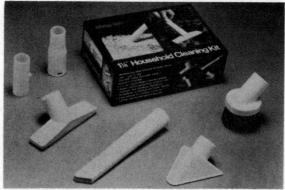

Attachment Kit for Vacuum Cleaners

If your vacuum cleaner's attachments are lost or broken, you can replace them without buying a new vacuum cleaner. The Shop-Vac Corporation, which makes a line of wet/dry vacuum cleaners, has the model 801-48 1¼-inch household cleaning kit, which consists of a set of attachments that can be used with many domestic brands of vacuum cleaners. The accessories include a round brush, crevice tool, corner nozzle, upholstery nozzle, and two universal vacuum adapters.

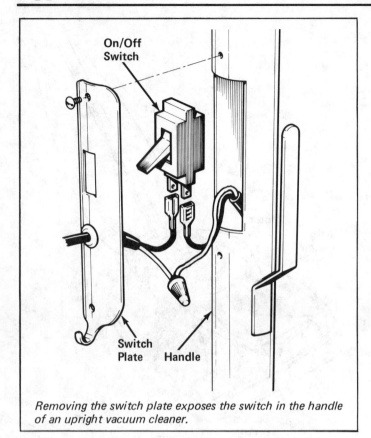

Removing the switch plate exposes the switch in the handle of an upright vacuum cleaner.

13. If the beater brush assembly itself is clogged with debris, use an old comb or a nail to remove the debris. Then wash the assembly with a solution of mild household detergent and water. Rinse the assembly and dry it.

14. Replace the beater brush assembly and belts, and lubricate the ends of the assembly lightly with a silicone lubricant.

Machine Won't Run

If the household outlet is working, the vacuum cleaner may not be receiving current because of a faulty power cord or malfunctioning on/off switch. Follow these steps:

1. Check the plug on the power cord. If it's damaged, unplug the cord and cut it about 1 inch behind the plug with diagonal cutters or a sharp utility knife. Replace the plug following the procedure outlined in "Replacing a Plug" in the Electrical Work chapter. If the power cord and plug are in good condition, you'll have to check the on/off switch.
2. Remove the screws that hold the switch in position on the vacuum cleaner's handle or housing.
3. Pry off the switch plate to expose the switch.
4. Check the operation of the switch with a continuity tester; the procedure is described in "Your Home's Electrical System" in the Electrical Work chapter.
5. If the switch is faulty, disconnect the power cord wires from the switch; they may be held by terminal screws or friction-fit terminal-end connections. If friction-fit connectors are used, pull them off carefully with a long-nose pliers to avoid bending or breaking the connectors.
6. Get a new switch made for the vacuum, and connect it the same way the old switch was.

Material Makes Appliance Plugs Safe and Shockproof

Household appliance plugs and plugs used with tools can be made safe and shockproof. Duro E-Pox-E Ribbon from Loctite Corp. seals the open ends of electrical plugs to prevent shorts. To use, you tear off 1 or 2 inches of the blue and yellow ribbon and knead it with your fingers until it's uniformly green in color. Then, insert the material into the open area of the plug so that the wires and the tops of the terminal posts are surrounded. Finally, smooth the material until it's flat with the edges of the plug. Let the plug set overnight until the material hardens. E-Pox-E Ribbon comes in a 14-inch-long strip.

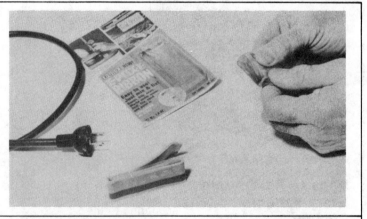

It's Easier to Replace the Part

In most cases, broken or malfunctioning appliance parts can be replaced more quickly and inexpensively than they could be repaired, by you or by a professional. Replace broken or malfunctioning parts with new parts made especially for the appliance. Appliance parts are available from appliance service centers, appliance repair dealers, and appliance parts stores. You don't always have to go to a specific brand-name appliance parts service center to obtain the parts. If you can't locate a parts service center in your area, order the part you need directly from the manufacturer; give the manufacturer all the model and parts data possible for the appliance. The name and address of the appliance manufacturer are usually printed on the appliance.

Washers

Materials • Steel Wool • Replacement Parts as Required

Tools • Long-Nose Pliers • Screwdriver • Wrench • Volt-Ohm Meter

MECHANICALLY, a washer isn't very complicated when you consider each part separately. The parts, however, are closely interrelated and controlled by a timer that triggers the machine's various cycles. Because of the timer, diagnosis of a problem is often more difficult than the repair.

Two common washing machine malfunctions that you should be able to handle include a tub that won't fill with water and a machine that won't work at all. The former is usually due to a fault at the mixing valve or at one of the solenoids that operate the valve. The latter trouble often involves the power supply to the machine or the timer. For timer problems, a test instrument like a volt-ohm meter (VOM) is very helpful.

Note: For serious appliance troubleshooting and repairs, you should consider buying a volt-ohm meter (VOM), also known as a multitester. It's a battery-powered instrument that is used to test circuit continuity and resistance, and to measure electrical current. Except when testing voltage, the VOM is always used with the current in a circuit turned off. *Caution: All VOM tests in the Appliance chapter must be made with the power to the appliance turned off.*

Before you attempt any repairs or call a professional, run through the following checklist if your washing machine isn't operating properly:

- Is the washer plugged into the outlet properly and is the outlet receiving power?
- Is the timer set properly?
- Is the lid closed securely?
- Is the lid switch latch clean and free of detergent buildup and lint?
- Is the washer overloaded?
- Are the water supply hoses free of kinks?
- Is the water-saver button fully depressed?
- Did you push the reset button on the control panel?

Washer Won't Fill

If the washing machine's tub won't fill with water, but the water is turned on and the hoses are not kinked, follow these steps:

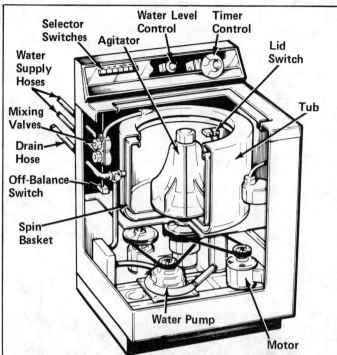

A washing machine has a tub and an agitator; various cycles operate valves and motors, turn water on, spin the tub, drain water, and control the water temperature.

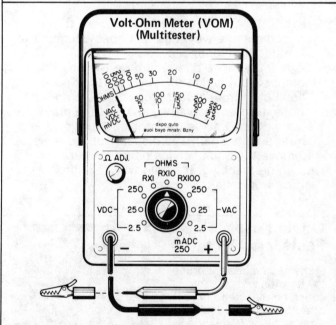

The volt-ohm meter (VOM) is a very useful instrument for troubleshooting electrical problems in appliances.

1. Turn the timer dial two or three positions. Then, push down firmly on the control start button, and push the reset button on the control panel. If this doesn't solve the problem, turn off the water supply.
2. Disconnect the water supply hoses from the water inlet ports on the mixing valve at the

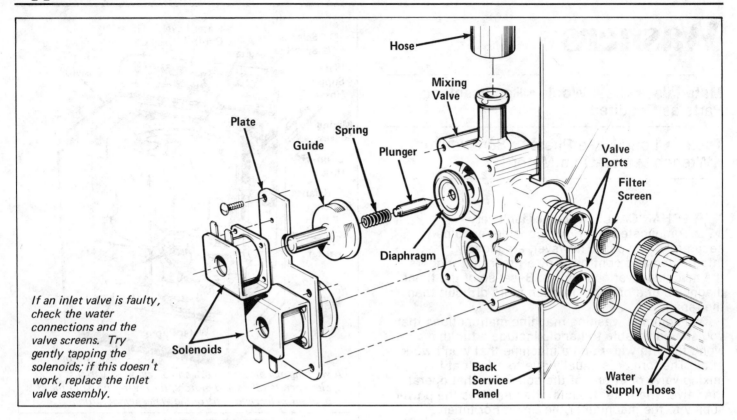

If an inlet valve is faulty, check the water connections and the valve screens. Try gently tapping the solenoids; if this doesn't work, replace the inlet valve assembly.

rear of the machine; the hoses screw to the ports the same way a garden hose connects to an outdoor sillcock.

3. With a long-nose pliers, remove the tiny filter screens from inside the valve ports or hoses.

4. Clean the filter screens, replace them and the hoses, turn on the water, and test the machine. If this doesn't solve the problem, turn off the water supply again and disconnect the hoses.

5. Remove the back service panel from the washing machine; it's held with machine screws or bolts.

6. Locate the mixing valve; usually the water supply hoses connect directly to its inlet ports.

7. With a screwdriver handle, lightly tap the front and sides of the mixing valve housing; this may jar a sticking solenoid loose.

8. Replace the back panel, replace the hoses, turn on the water, and test the machine. If the problem hasn't been solved, turn off the water, disconnect the hoses, and remove the back panel and the mixing valve. The valve may be held by a metal bracket, or it may be screwed to the washing machine housing.

Liquid Keeps Fasteners Tight

Many appliances are prone to vibration, which can cause bolts, screws, and other fasteners to loosen. Perma-Lok by Permabond International Corp. is a liquid product formulated to prevent such fasteners from loosening. To use, you apply a drop of the liquid onto the threads or shank of the fastener before tightening; neither mixing nor clamping is needed. The liquid dries in minutes, and the fastener

may be easily removed later, if necessary, with regular tools.

Five-in-One Wrench Fits in Your Pocket

A ratchet wrench that stores five drive sockets conveniently in its handle is the Pocket Socket made by New Britain Tool, a division of Litton Industries. The model No. 606 has alloy steel drive sockets for $\frac{3}{16}$-inch, $\frac{7}{32}$-inch, $\frac{1}{4}$-inch, $\frac{9}{32}$-inch, and $\frac{5}{16}$-inch nuts. The model No. 607 has metric sizes—4mm, 5mm, 6mm, 7mm, and 8mm. The Pocket Socket's handle is

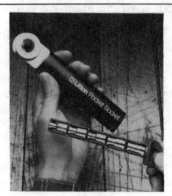

a unitized metal ratchet with a $\frac{1}{4}$-inch drive thumbwheel ratchet head that snaps out for use in confined areas.

9. Replace the mixing valve with a new one. It usually is less costly to replace the mixing valve with a new one. If you decide to have the old valve professionally repaired, be sure to get a cost estimate first.
10. Replace the back service panel, reconnect the hoses, turn on the water, and test the machine.

Troubleshooting a Timer

Washing machine timers are driven by a motor, and are extremely complicated devices. Any timer repairs should be left to a professional because special equipment is necessary. There are, however, some checks you can perform, and if the timer is defective, you may be able to replace it. Often it's less expensive to buy and install a new timer than to have the old one repaired. To troubleshoot a timer, follow these steps:

1. Unplug the washing machine.
2. Remove the knobs on the control panel; they may pull straight off or they may be held by setscrews.
3. Remove the control panel. It is held by machine screws that are usually hidden under a strip of decorative molding; the molding snaps into position. Pry the strip up and off with a screwdriver. **Note:** On some machines, access to the timer may be gained through the back service panel of the washer. If so, remove the machine screws holding the panel in place.
4. Carefully examine the wires that connect the timer to other washer components. If the wires appear burned, disconnect them and buff the ends with steel wool. Reconnect the wires. If the wires are loose or disconnected, try pushing them into their terminals; use a long-nose pliers to avoid breaking the terminal connections.

5. Reinstall the timer control knob only.
6. Plug in the washing machine and set the timer. If the machine works, reassemble the control panel. If it still doesn't operate and you don't have a volt-ohm meter, disconnect the timer but make a precise sketch of wire connections. Take the timer to a professional for testing. If the timer is faulty, you can buy a new one. Follow Steps 11 through 16 to install it.
    If you have a VOM, you can continue checking the timer.
7. Unplug the washing machine. *Caution: You'll be performing tests that require you to shut off the electrical power to the washer.*
8. Set the VOM to the R × 1 scale.
9. Disconnect one of the power wires to the timer, and connect the meter's probes to each of the timer terminals. If the timer is working, the VOM should read zero ohms.
10. Because the timer is a multiple switch, turn the control knob through its cycle to test each position in turn. The meter should read zero ohms at each of these positions. If the meter has one or more readings above zero, the timer is faulty and should be replaced.
11. Disconnect the wires to the timer, making a precise sketch of wire connections so you can reconnect the wires correctly.
12. Unscrew the timer from its mounting surface.
13. Take the timer with you and purchase an exact replacement.
14. Using the sketch you made, connect the wires to the timer.
15. Screw the timer to its mounting surface.
16. Reinstall the timer control knob, plug in the machine, and test the new timer by turning it through the washing machine cycles. If the timer operates, remove the control knob, install the control panel and back service panel, and reinstall all the control knobs.

Silicone Spray Offers Long-Lasting Lubrication

When gears or rubber-to-metal surfaces need some lubrication, a silicone spray can provide some "slip." Super Slip silicone spray, made by Cling Surface Co., is formulated with a high-grade, heavy-viscosity silicone that provides long-lasting lubrication, according to the company. The product, which also lubricates wood-to-wood surfaces, is

resistant to acids, alkalis, and moisture. Super Slip silicone spray is available in 6- and 16-ounce aerosol cans.

Contact Cleaner Will Clean Electrical Contacts

Over a period of time, electrical contacts in an appliance get dirty and can cause malfunctions. CRC contact cleaner from CRC Chemicals, Inc., is a solvent degreaser that is formulated to remove dust, lint, atmospheric oil, moisture, and carbon deposits from electrical contacts. It will clean plastic surfaces without leaving a residue.

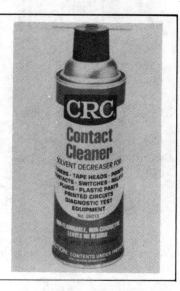

Appliances

Dryers

Materials • Wire Nuts • Replacement
Parts as Required

Tools • Brush • Screwdriver • Long-Nose
Pliers • Volt-Ohm Meter

THE TWO biggest problems encountered with
clothes dryers are no power and a faulty door
switch. If you check and find out that neither of
these is the trouble, the problem could be a
malfunctioning timer or a thermostat. Before you
attempt any repairs or call a service person, check
the following:

- Is the dryer plugged into the outlet properly and
  is the outlet receiving power? **Note:** Many
  dryers operate on separate circuits. Don't
  assume that the machine is connected to the
  main entrance panel. Look for another fused
  circuit, especially if you own an older home.
- Is the timer set properly and activated?
- Is the door closed tightly?

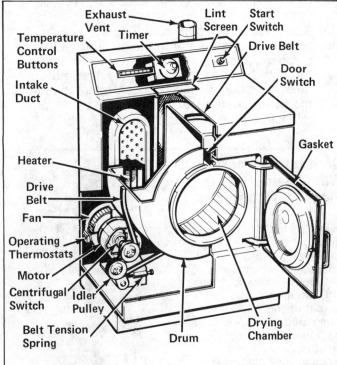

*A dryer has a large drum into which wet laundry is loaded.
A motor with pulleys, connected by a series of belts, turns
the drum.*

- Is the door switch latch clean and free of lint
  buildup?
- Is the lint-catcher clean?
- Is the dryer overloaded?
- If the dryer uses gas for a heat source, is the
  pilot light lit?
- Is the exhaust vent open and clean?
- Did you push the reset button on the
  control panel?
- Are the temperature control switches set
  properly?

Door Switch Problems

A dryer will not run unless the door switch is
operating properly. The only exception is if the dryer
is not properly grounded. If grounding is the trouble,
the dryer will run even when the door is open. Call
a professional for this repair; otherwise, follow
these steps:

1. Unplug the clothes dryer.
2. With a brush, clean the door latch of any lint
   and debris that may be preventing the door
   from closing tightly.
3. Plug in the dryer and turn it on.
4. If the problem hasn't been solved, unplug the
   dryer. Very slowly open and close the door
   noting the alignment of the switch and
   the door.
5. If the switch and door appear to be misaligned,
   loosen the setscrews that hold the switch and
   move the switch up or down to align it
   properly. This can take time to do it accurately.
   When it is aligned, tighten the setscrews.
6. Plug in the dryer and test it.
7. If this doesn't work, the switch may be faulty.
   Unplug the dryer. You'll have to test the switch
   or have it tested. You may have to remove the
   top panel of the dryer to reach the switch. If
   so, slide a putty knife under the rim of the top
   panel to locate and then release any hidden
   spring fasteners.
8. If you don't have a volt-ohm meter (VOM), you
   can have the switch tested at an appliance
   service center. And, if the switch is faulty, buy
   a new one; it's usually cheaper than having the
   old one repaired. Follow Steps 12 through 14
   to remove and replace the switch. If you have a
   VOM, proceed to the next step.
9. Set the VOM to the R × 1 scale.
10. Disconnect the power leads and connect one
    probe of the VOM to each switch terminal.
11. Press the switch to its closed position with
    your fingers. If the switch is working, the VOM
    should read zero ohms; the problem is
    elsewhere—probably the power supply or the
    timer. If the meter needle jumps or gives a
    high reading, replace the switch.
12. Disconnect the wires from the switch. If the

wires fit into terminals—like plugs—pull them straight out with a long-nose pliers to avoid damaging them. Then remove the screws that hold the switch to the door sill.

13. To install a new switch or replace the old one, wrap the ends of the wires around the switch terminals clockwise and tighten the terminal screws, or plug in the connectors with a long-nose pliers. If there are lead wires from the switch, twist them to the power wires and secure them with wire nuts.

14. Position the switch in the door sill, align the switch with the door latch, and replace the screws that hold it in place.

Testing and Changing a Timer

Electrical power, thermostats, and different drying cycles are controlled by a timer that is operated by a small motor. Some dryers have timers that can be adjusted, but this is a job for a professional with special equipment. If, however, the timer must be replaced, you can do the job yourself. Follow these steps to test and replace a faulty timer:

1. Unplug the dryer.
2. Remove the front of the dryer's control panel. Usually, it's held by machine screws that are concealed behind a decorative metal molding. The molding may be held in place by spring clips or decorative screws. If it's held by clips, pry the molding off with the tip of a screwdriver blade or putty knife. If it's secured with screws, remove the screws.
   Note: On some dryers, the timer can be reached without removing the control panel.
3. Pull the timer knob off its shaft and slip off the pointer. The pointer probably is keyed to the shaft by one or two flat surfaces to keep the pointer from slipping when it is turned, or a setscrew may hold the knob and pointer to the shaft. The setscrew should be at the base of the pointer.
4. If you don't have a volt-ohm meter (VOM), you can remove the timer and have it tested at an appliance service center. If it's faulty, buy a new one; it's usually cheaper than having the old one repaired. Remove it, and make a precise sketch of wire connections so you can reconnect the wires correctly. The timer will be mounted with bolts or screws that turn counterclockwise for removal. Follow Steps 11 and 12 to install a new timer.
   If you have a VOM, you can continue checking the timer; proceed to the next step.
5. Set the VOM to the R×1 scale.
6. Turn the timer to the "normal dry" setting; you can slip the pointer onto the timer knob shaft temporarily to find this setting.
7. Disconnect one of the power wires from the

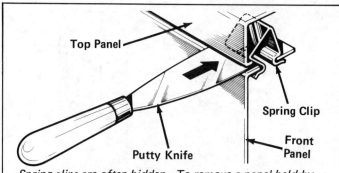

Spring clips are often hidden. To remove a panel held by such clips, use a putty knife or screwdriver to find each clip; then push in against it to release the panel.

timer. **Note:** Some timers may have several wires connected to them. You can locate the power wires—probably a white wire and a black wire—because they are usually larger than the other wires.

8. Connect one probe of the meter to each of the timer terminals. If the timer is working, the VOM should read zero ohms. If the meter shows a high reading, replace the timer.
9. Disconnect the wires to the timer, and make a precise sketch of the wire connections so you can reconnect the wires correctly.
10. Remove the screws or bolts that attach the old timer to the dryer housing.
11. To reinstall a timer, or to install a new one, connect the wires to the timer following the sketch you made earlier.
12. After all of the connections have been made to the new timer, secure it to the dryer with the same screws or bolts.
13. Replace the control panel, the timer pointer, and the timer control knob.
14. Plug in the dryer.

Thermostats

Dryers have thermostats that sometimes stick. When this occurs, the dryer may remain cool during various drying cycles, or the dryer may become too hot for too long a time.

There are several types of thermostats. Operating thermostats are usually located near the exhaust duct bulkhead or around the fan housing of the dryer. A control panel thermostat, located behind the control panel, regulates the dryer temperature. In addition, there is a safety thermostat at the base of the intake duct.

To troubleshoot thermostats, follow these steps:

1. Unplug the dryer.
2. Remove the control panel, following Steps 2 and 3 in the previous procedure.
3. Set the VOM to the R×1 scale. If you don't have a VOM, you can disconnect the dryer's

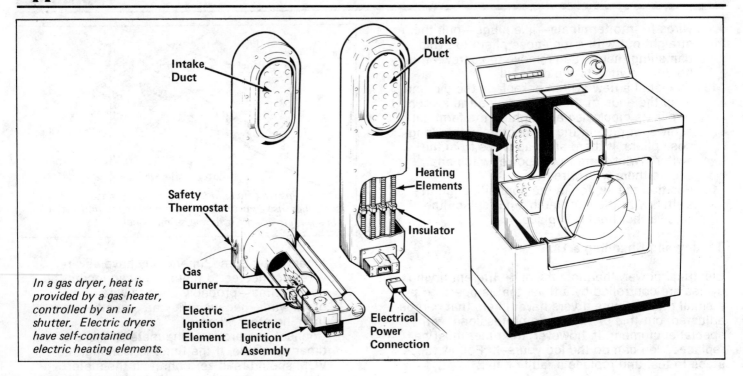

In a gas dryer, heat is provided by a gas heater, controlled by an air shutter. Electric dryers have self-contained electric heating elements.

Intake Duct

Intake Duct

Safety Thermostat

Heating Elements

Insulator

Gas Burner

Electric Ignition Element

Electric Ignition Assembly

Electrical Power Connection

thermostats and have them checked at an appliance service center. If they're faulty, buy new ones; it will be cheaper than having them repaired.

4. Disconnect the wire connected to one side of the thermostat, and connect the meter's probes to each of the thermostat terminals. If

it's working, the meter should read zero ohms. If the meter shows a high reading, replace the thermostat.

5. Connect the new thermostat the same way the old one was connected and reassemble the control panel.

6. If the control panel thermostat is working

Dryer Vent Helps Save Energy

A vent hood for clothes dryers that is designed to allow maximum exhaust flow and seal out cold air is the Supurr Vent, made by Deflect-o Corp. The vent, constructed of high-impact polystyrene, features a ½-inch trim line so it fits close to the exterior wall of a house. This, the manufacturer says, permits easier lawn mowing and trimming, and reduces the chance of accidentally damaging the vent or jamming it open. The vent's overlapping fin construction prevents rodents and insects from entering when the vent is closed. It also stops the back-up of dryer heat and the buildup of lint, which

can cause other types of vents to stick open and leak heat during cold weather. Supurr Vent is available in a brown or white color. The vent is available as a separate unit, or in kit form that includes a flexible duct. Mounting instructions are included.

Assemble Ductwork Fast With Rivets

If you have to connect appliance ductwork so that it's airtight, a riveting tool makes the job easier. The POP brand Rivetool, made by Bostik, a division of Emhart Corp., is designed to provide tighter, more secure joints than self-tapping screws or similar fasteners. To assemble ducts with the Rivetool, cut the duct to fit, overlapping joints about ½ inch. Drill ⅛-inch holes about every 4 inches around the perimeter of

the duct. Insert ¼-inch medium rivets into the holes and pull the trigger of the Rivetool. The Rivetool also may be used to fabricate aluminum gutters and downspouts, steel or aluminum garden sheds, lawn and garden equipment, and other projects where metal or leather has to be joined. POP brand rivets come in steel, aluminum, or copper with open or closed ends, threaded and unthreaded, normal and countersunk, in diameters of ⅛ inch, 5/32 inch, and 3/16 inch, and in lengths of ⅛, ¼, ½, and 5/8 inch.

properly or if you have replaced it, and the dryer still won't function, you'll have to check the operating thermostats.

7. Remove the back service panel; it is fastened with machine screws.
8. Locate the thermostats, and lightly tap their housings with a screwdriver handle; sometimes, this will jar their contact points loose.
9. Plug in the dryer and test it.
10. If this doesn't solve the problem, unplug the dryer.
11. Disconnect the wire connected to one side of one of the thermostats.
12. Set the VOM to the R × 1 scale.
13. Connect the meter's probes to each of the thermostat terminals. If it's working properly, the meter should read zero ohms. If the meter shows a high reading, replace the thermostat.
14. Connect the new thermostat the same way the old one was connected.
15. Repeat Steps 11 through 14 with the other thermostats.
16. Reinstall the back service panel and plug in the dryer.

Gas Dryers

Gas dryers are nearly identical to electric dryers except they are heated with gas instead of electricity. The gas heater is controlled by an air shutter. Look for trouble here when the dryer won't heat, or won't dry properly. To check the gas heater on a dryer follow these steps:

1. Remove the back panel on the dryer by removing a series of screws or bolts that hold the panel to the top and sides of the cabinet.
2. Locate the gas heater shutter. To adjust the shutter, turn a thumbscrew at the end of the burner, or turn two screws in a slot and bracket that positions the shutter.
3. Remove the screw(s) that holds the panel that covers the gas flame, and remove the panel.
4. Turn on the dryer so the flame is burning.
5. If the flame is a deep blue color, and the burner is whistling, the burner is receiving too much air. If the flame has a yellow tip, the mixture is not getting enough air. Turn the thumbscrew or loosen the screws slightly to cut down the air to the burner. Keep turning until the flame is a light blue color—without any yellow—and the whistling sound stops.

Note: If the gas heater won't ignite, the pilot light could be out. Follow the procedure for lighting a pilot light detailed in the "Pilot Lights" section in this chapter. If the pilot light won't light, the problem could be a faulty thermocouple. The thermocouple turns off the gas supply to the dryer when the pilot light goes out. When the thermocouple fails, the pilot light won't stay lit. To replace the thermocouple, follow the procedure detailed in the "Pilot Lights" section.

Dual Venting System Designed for Clothes Dryers

Now you can obtain a clothes dryer ducting system that not only ducts the air from the dryer but directs the heated air into nearby cold rooms. The Bede dual-venting system, No. 21, manufactured by Bede Industries, Inc., comes with a heat-saver heating vent for a gas or electric clothes dryer; a lint filter; an 8-foot length of 4-inch-diameter, flexible metal vent hose; four plastic mounting clips; an aluminum tailpipe; a louver vent; and installation instructions. The heat vent may be closed when heat and humidity from the dryer is not needed in summer. According to the manufacturer, the system

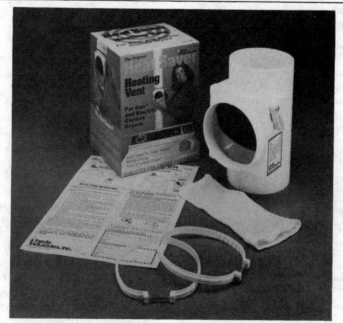

can pay for itself in heat savings in about two months. If your home is extremely dry during winter, the system is a good way to add humidity without the cost of a basement humidifier.

Duct Tape Has Many Uses

Duct tape has many uses. For example, it can be used to wrap clothes dryer ducting. It also can be used to seal blowers, storm windows, and metal and vinyl sheeting. Duct tape from Mystik Corp. features a new formulation that the company says has greater resistance to moisture, heat, and cold. The duct tape is available in two sizes—2 inches by 30 yards, and 2 inches by 60 yards.

Dishwashers

Materials • Rag • Brush • Household Detergent • Replacement Parts as Required

Tools • Screwdriver • Pliers • Putty Knife • Long-Nose Pliers • Wrenches • Volt-Ohm Meter • Wooden Pencil

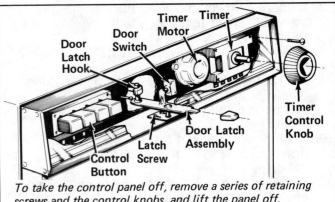

To take the control panel off, remove a series of retaining screws and the control knobs, and lift the panel off.

STUDIES SHOW that dishwasher repairs usually involve six components: door latch, heating element, timer, sprayer arm, strainer, and hoses. A breakdown of one of these components, however, is usually easy to repair. Before you attempt any repairs or call a service person, check the following:

• Is the dishwasher plugged into the outlet properly and is the outlet receiving power? **Note:** Many dishwashers are wired directly to a fused circuit. Therefore, check the circuit's fuse or circuit breaker at the main entrance panel. If you own an older home, the dishwasher could be connected to a separate circuit independent of the main panel; be sure you check this possibility.

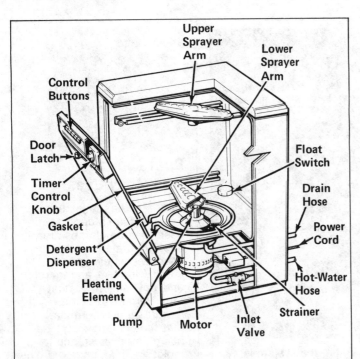

Dishwashers spray hot water into a tub stacked with dishes, then dry them with a blower or heating element. Problems often involve the water supply and drainage systems.

• Are the temperature, timer, and on/off controls set properly?
• Is the door closed tightly and latched?
• Is the strainer clean and in place?
• Are the sprayer arms clean?
• Is the drain hose free of kinks?
• Is the water turned on fully?
• Are the dishes stacked properly in their racks with plenty of space between items?
• Did you push the reset button on the control panel?

The Door Latch and Switch

If the dishwasher door is not closed tightly and the latch is not engaged properly, the dishwasher won't operate; this is a safety feature. On many dishwashers, the latch serves as a switch that activates the power. To troubleshoot the door latch, follow these steps:

1. Close the door and engage the latch, holding the latch in its locked position.
2. Turn the machine on. If the dishwasher doesn't run, try unlocking and locking the door latch several times, holding it firmly in the locked position each time. If the dishwasher runs, you know the problem is in the door latch or switch.
3. Unplug the dishwasher or turn off the power to the circuit.
4. Carefully check the latch and its alignment with the latch part inside the machine. If the latch appears to be out of alignment, loosen the screws that hold the door latch in place; slide the latch back into alignment by hand or with pliers, and tighten the screws.
   Note: If you suspect that the latch is worn, replace it. A new one is relatively inexpensive.
5. Restore power to the dishwasher and turn on the machine. If it still doesn't work, turn off the power; you'll have to test the latch switch.
6. Remove the panel covering the door latch; the panel is held by machine screws.

Note: On some dishwashers, the inside door panel must be removed to expose the latch assembly. A gasket usually covers the machine screws that hold the panel; raise the gasket with your fingers to expose the screws.

7. If you don't have a volt-ohm meter (VOM), you can remove the switch and have it tested at an appliance service center. If it's faulty, buy a new one and install it. If you have a VOM, proceed to the next step.
8. Set the volt-ohm meter to the R × 1 scale.
9. Disconnect one of the power wires to the switch, and connect one probe of the meter to each switch terminal and shut the dishwasher door. If the switch is working, the meter should read zero ohms. If the meter shows a high reading, replace the switch.
10. Remove the switch; if it has plug-in wiring connections, use a long-nose pliers to disconnect the wires to avoid breaking the connectors.
11. Install the new switch and connect the wires.
12. Restore power to the machine.

The Timer

Like other appliance timers, the one on a dishwasher is complicated. Therefore, if the timer is malfunctioning, have a professional repair it or install a new one. Usually, a new timer is less expensive than the cost of repairing an old one.

Note: Because several other dishwasher switches are controlled by the timer, check all of these switches before assuming that the timer is malfunctioning. To check the switches and the timer, follow these steps:

1. Check the float switch, which prevents the machine from overfilling; it is located under the dish rack, which lifts out of the tank. Clean any food or detergent debris around the float switch and tap it lightly with the screwdriver handle; this may loosen the float if it's stuck.
2. Although the water level in most machines is controlled by the timer, some dishwashers have a pressure switch that does this job. You can tell if your machine has one by removing the lower access panel. The switch is mounted under the tub housing, and has a small hose running to it. Make sure the hose is in good condition, and that the clip securing the hose is tight.
3. If the dishwasher won't fill with water, lightly tap the switch housing with a screwdriver handle; this may loosen a stuck switch. If the float or pressure switch seems to be working, you'll have to check the timer.
4. Turn off the power to the dishwasher's circuit.
5. Remove the screws that secure the control panel. The screws may be concealed by a

When You Make Tests, Disconnect the Power

When testing an appliance part with a continuity tester to determine whether the part is capable of carrying electricity, be sure you disconnect the appliance from the power source. A continuity tester uses batteries to supply its own power. The same rule applies when a volt-ohm meter (VOM) is used to test for continuity or resistance. The only exception is when you test to see if electricity is flowing through a wire. Either a voltage tester or a VOM can be used for this test, and the current is left on.

Appliance Paint Matches Colors of Leading Manufacturers

If an appliance needs sprucing up and you want it to match the color of other appliances in your home, Illinois Bronze Paint Co. probably makes the paint you need. The company manufactures Appliance Finish spray paint in colors to match those of leading appliance makers. It's available in appliance white, coffee, coffee shadow, almond, fresh avocado, harvest wheat, harvest wheat shadow, and gloss black. According to Illinois Bronze Paint Co., the product provides an extremely hard, porcelain-like finish, and won't chip, crack, or peel. It also resists water and most household chemicals.

A Little Help Makes Replacement Easier

Replacing a timer on a washer, dryer, dishwasher, or other appliance can be made easier with a little help from a friend. To install the new timer, have your helper hold the timer next to the old one. Disconnect the wires from the old unit, one at a time, and connect them to the corresponding terminals on the new timer. This will help you make the connections correctly, and eliminates the need for a wiring sketch. If the wires plug into the terminals, use a long-nose pliers to remove and install them to avoid breaking the terminal connections. After all the wires are connected, remove the old timer from its mounting surface, set the new timer in position, secure it the same way the old one was, and replace the control panel and knobs.

decorative molding that is held by spring clips or decorative screws. If it's held by clips, pry off the molding with the tip of a screwdriver or putty knife, or remove the setscrew that holds the molding.

6. Remove the control knobs. They pull straight off, or they may be held by setscrews.
7. If you don't have a VOM, disconnect the timer and make a sketch of the wire connections so you can reconnect the wires correctly later. Take the part to an appliance service center for testing. If it's faulty, replace it. Follow Steps 11 to 13 to install a new timer. If you have a VOM, proceed to the next step.
8. Set the VOM to the R × 1 scale.
9. Disconnect one of the timer's power wires, and connect one probe of the meter to each timer terminal. If the timer is working, the meter should read zero ohms. If the meter shows a high reading, replace the timer.

    Note: If possible, use the same procedure to test the selector and cycle switches. If the wiring is too complex to figure out, call a professional service person.
10. Disconnect the wires to the timer, making a precise sketch of wire connections so you can reconnect the wires correctly.
11. To replace the timer, follow the sketch of the wiring you made. If the wires plug in, use a long-nose pliers so you don't damage the terminal connections.
12. After the wires have been connected to the new timer, attach the timer to the dishwasher housing.
13. Replace the control knob on the timer shaft

temporarily. Turn on the power, and test the dishwasher by running it through its various cycles. If the machine functions properly, remove the control knob, replace the control panel, the control knobs, and any other parts. If the dishwasher doesn't function properly, re-check the timer wires; they may not be properly seated, or you may have mixed up the wiring sequence.

The Heating Element

A dishwasher's heating element doesn't burn out often, but when it does, the dishes won't dry properly. The element fits around the base of the tank of the machine, and resembles the heating element in an oven. To troubleshoot the heating element, follow these steps:

1. Turn off the power to the dishwasher.
2. Remove the access panel to the bottom of the machine.
3. If you don't have a VOM, disconnect the wires to the heating element and take it to an appliance service center for testing. If it's faulty, replace the part. Proceed to Step 7. If you have a VOM, proceed to the next step.
4. Disconnect one of the power wires to the element.
5. Set the VOM to the R × 1 scale.
6. Connect one probe to each element terminal. If the meter reads between 15 and 30 ohms, the element is working. If the reading is over 30-35 ohms, replace the element.
7. The element is connected to power leads or a

Screwdriver Fits Torx-Style Screws

Torx screwdrivers by Stanley Tools are the tools to use for recessed Torx-style screw heads found in some appliances, such as washers and dryers. According to the manufacturer, the screwdrivers reduce slipping, screw head distortion, and driver wear. The Torx screwdrivers, available in six sizes with chrome-plated blades and black oxide tips to resist rust, are shock-resistant and have fluted handles for better grip and added torque. The screwdrivers may also be used for servicing automobiles.

Digital Multimeter for Appliance and Other Testing Jobs

For many appliance tests, a volt-ohm meter (VOM) or multitester is what you need. The IM-2215 hand-held digital multimeter kit, from the Heath Co., has alternating high-to-low resistance test voltage for measuring semiconductors and in-circuit resistance, built-in references for calibration, and a 3½-digit liquid crystal display. Five ranges enable the unit to provide both AC and DC voltage measurement. Push-button switches allow one-hand operation, leaving the other hand free for probe placement. With

a 9-volt alkaline battery, the unit can provide up to 200 hours of operation, according to Heath. The multimeter weighs 14 ounces with the battery. The multimeter comes as a kit to be assembled, and is also available in a pre-assembled version.

terminal block with screws or nuts; loosen them to remove the heating element. Or, the element may plug into a terminal. In this case, pull the element straight out.

8. Lift out the heating element. If it's held by clips on ceramic spacing blocks in the tub, release the clips before you remove the element.
9. Install the new heating element and replace the access panel.
10. Turn on the power and test the dishwasher.

Sprayer Arms, Strainers, and Hoses

If your dishwasher isn't cleaning efficiently, or if it overfills, the problem may be caused by a buildup of food and detergent on the dishwasher's sprayer arms or strainer. Another problem may be a leaking hose. The sprayer arms and strainers can be cleaned, but a hose may have to be replaced. To fix these components, follow these steps:

1. Turn off the power to the dishwasher.
2. Remove the sprayer arms; either twist off the cap that holds them to the motor shaft, or use a wrench to remove the nut assembly that holds the arms.
3. Using mild household detergent and water, wash the sprayer arms. If the holes in the arms are clogged, open them with a wooden pencil with the lead point broken off.
4. Lift out the strainer, which is located under the lower sprayer arm. Clean it as you did the sprayer arms.
5. Replace the strainer and sprayer arms, turn on

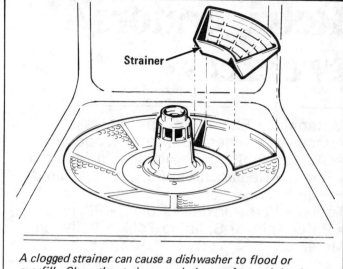

A clogged strainer can cause a dishwasher to flood or overfill. Clean the strainer regularly, or after each load of dishes is washed.

the power to the machine, and test it.

6. Many dishwashers discharge waste water through a hose that is connected to a garbage disposer under the kitchen sink. If this hose is leaking, try tightening the hose clamps at the dishwasher and disposer connection. If tightening doesn't stop the leakage, replace the hose by loosening the clamps with a screwdriver.
7. Slide the clamps down the hose toward its center.
8. Remove the hose and the clamps.
9. Place the clamps on a new hose, and install it.

Hose Clamps for Appliance Repair Jobs

For tight connection between hoses and appliance fittings, you need a stainless steel geared hose clamp of some size. Sterling, a division of Avnet, Inc., makes a wide range of clamps—from 7/32 inch up to 7 inches maximum diameter. The clamps are adjustable with arch-designed gear slots in a stainless steel band for maximum thread contact. The band and screw housing are marked as to size and clamp number for ready identification. The screw has a hex-type head with shoulders for maximum tightening power. According to the manufacturer, Sterling hose clamps will keep their circular shape for even tightening all around the hose diameter. The edges of the bands won't damage hoses.

Handy Hand Tool for Appliance Jobs

A screwdriver that can fit more than one type of fastener is a handy hand tool. Such a product is the Vaco Dual-Blade reversible screwdriver set, model DU42. It has two reversible blades and a fluted handle. Each blade has two different screwdriver styles—1/4-inch slotted and #2 Phillips, and 3/16-inch slotted and #1 Phillips. The blades insert and lock into the full-size handle. Made by Vaco Products Co., the set is packaged in a vinyl pouch for storage. Although the tool set is excellent for appliance repair work, it can also be used for almost any automotive and home maintenance project.

Refrigerators/ Freezers

Materials • Electrical Tape • Gasket Adhesive • Mineral Spirits • Wood Shims • Cardboard Shims • Household Detergent • Rags • Replacement Parts as Required

Tools • Screwdriver • Ruler • Pliers • Putty Knife • Splining Tool • Volt-Ohm Meter

MECHANICALLY, a refrigerator or freezer looks complicated, but it's not as complicated as it might seem. Many of the components—compressor, evaporator, condenser—are sealed, which makes them impossible for the do-it-yourselfer to repair without experience and special equipment. Despite this, there are many repairs that you can make, and some only involve a minor adjustment of a control knob or screw.

In a refrigerator, coolant is cooled in a condenser. From there it flows to the evaporator, where air is cooled by contact with the coil.

Before you attempt any repairs to a refrigerator or freezer or call a professional for help, run down the checklist below. Keep in mind that malfunctioning parts often can be replaced cheaper than what it would cost to have them professionally repaired—always get an estimate before having repairs made.

* Is the appliance plugged into the outlet properly and is the outlet receiving power?
* Are the controls set properly?
* Is the thermostat set properly?
* Are the condenser coils clean?
* Does the appliance have at least 2 inches of space between the evaporator coils and the wall surface?
* Are the evaporator coils clean?
* Is the appliance level?
* Is the appliance leaking cold air around the door gaskets?
* Are the door hinges tight and working properly?

The main service complaint about refrigerators or freezers is poor cooling. The problem may be caused by a malfunctioning freezer thermostat, air duct, evaporator fan, door gasket, or door hinges.

Checking the Thermostat, Air Duct, and Fan

To troubleshoot cooling problems that may be caused by a faulty freezer thermostat, air duct, or evaporator fan, follow these steps:

1. Unplug the appliance.
2. Remove the control knob from the freezer thermostat; it usually can be pulled off the control knob shaft. If not, loosen a setscrew at the base of the knob and pull the knob off.
3. Remove the plate, if any, that covers the control. If it snaps over the control, pry it out with a screwdriver. If it's held by screws, unscrew them.
4. If necessary, remove the screws holding the thermostat to reach its wires.
5. Disconnect both wires from the thermostat.
6. Twist the bare ends of the wires together and cover them with electrical tape.
7. Plug in the appliance. If the refrigerator starts and runs normally, the problem is the thermostat. Unplug the appliance, unscrew the thermostat from its mounting surface, and replace it with a new one.
   Note: If the appliance runs all the time, turn the control to "off" and unplug the appliance. Then remove either the red or the blue wire from a thermostat terminal. Plug in the appliance and if the compressor won't go on, replace the thermostat.
   If the thermostat seems to be working, the air duct near the temperature controls may be blocked.
8. Unplug the appliance.

9. Slip on the freezer control knob and turn it to "off"; turn the refrigerator temperature control knob to a mid-range position.
10. Note the position of the door on the air duct. You could use a ruler to measure its opening.
11. Close the door to the appliance, plug in the power, and wait 10 minutes.
12. After a 10-minute period, open the door and look at the air duct door. If it isn't open wider than before, the refrigerator temperature control is faulty. Unplug the appliance, unscrew the control from its mounting surface, disconnect its wiring, and replace it with a new one. If the air duct door is open wider, the control is working; a defective evaporator fan may be causing your cooling problems.
13. Locate the evaporator fan in the freezer compartment.
14. Unplug the appliance and remove the small grille that is fastened over the fan opening; it's usually held with screws.
15. Check the fan blades. If the blades are bent, try straightening them carefully with pliers. If the blades are dirty, carefully clean them.
16. Reassemble the grille and plug in the appliance. If the fan still won't run, call a professional for service.

Door Gasket

The gasket around the refrigerator or freezer door sometimes becomes stiff and cracks, allowing cold air to escape. Or, the gasket may buckle so the door won't shut tightly. Follow these steps:

1. Place a dollar bill between the gasket and the door jamb, and close the door.
2. Slowly pull the bill out. If there is some resistance, the seal is probably adequate. Test the gasket with the dollar bill at several locations around the door. If you find a gap, try adjusting the gasket or replace it, as outlined below.
3. Unplug the appliance and defrost it.
4. Buy a new gasket made specifically for your appliance.
   Note: Freezer gaskets are installed almost the same way as refrigerator door gaskets. Some freezer doors, however, are tensioned with spring devices that can be troublesome to replace if you remove the door. Don't remove the door to replace the gasket. Also, on some models, wiring in the door will have to be disassembled. Examine the job carefully; it may be better to have a professional do the work.
5. Remove the gasket. It may be held by screws, clips, adhesive, or by a retaining strip by the edge of a panel. In most cases, use a screwdriver to remove the fasteners. Use a putty knife to remove gaskets secured by

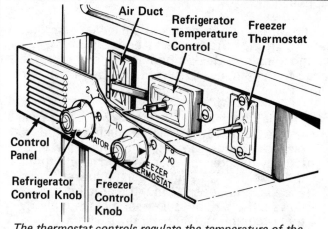

The thermostat controls regulate the temperature of the refrigerator and the freezer. Remove the control panel to reach the controls.

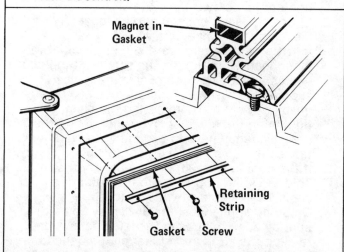

If the refrigerator or freezer door gasket is stiff and cracked, buy a new one made for your appliance. It may be held by screws, clips, adhesive, or by a retaining strip.

adhesive. **Note:** If the gasket is held by spring-steel pressure clips, don't pry hard on the clips; they are under tension and could flip out of their mountings. If the gasket is held by adhesive, clean off any old adhesive carefully with warm water and detergent, and if necessary mineral spirits.
6. Soak the new gasket in warm water to make it pliable.
7. Fit the gasket at the top of the door first; use gasket cement if specified by the manufacturer. Then work down one side, the other side, and the bottom. Smooth the gasket material so it is flat and even as it is installed, especially around corners. If you're installing a channel-mounted gasket, press it into place with a splining tool. Finally replace the retaining strip or panel and its fasteners. Remove any excess cement carefully with mineral spirits.

Appliances

Door Hinges

Worn or broken door hinges and misaligned striker plates on refrigerator and freezer doors are a common ailment. Gasket trouble sometimes can be traced to the hinges. To solve this type of problem, follow these steps:

1. Tip the appliance slightly backward, and prop up the front feet with shims such as thin pieces of wood. Or, extend the front leveling legs by unscrewing them two complete turns. If the door stays shut, doesn't allow air to escape, and doesn't bind, the problem is solved. If the door still doesn't close properly, try tightening the hinge screws with a screwdriver. **Note:** You may have to pry off a trim cap or overlay plate with a screwdriver to tighten the screws.
2. If the door sags or seems to be loose, try loosening the hinge screws slightly and inserting a thin cardboard shim in back of the hinge leaf. Then tighten the screws. If the door hinges already have been shimmed, the sagging or looseness could be caused by a misplaced shim. Try removing the shim, tightening the hinge screws, and testing the door. You may have to experiment several times before you get the door to work properly.
3. If the door is warped, tighten the screws that hold the inner door shell to the outer door shell. Then adjust the gasket to fit.
4. On some appliances, the door may be held shut by a latch. Loosen the latch screws and re-align the latch and striker plate so the latch engages the striker properly.

5. If the appliance door has a magnetic catch on the door sill, try moving the striker plate by loosening one or two setscrews. If the door still doesn't stay closed, try shimming the magnetic striker with cardboard.
6. If none of the remedies solve the problem, replace the hinges (and probably the door striker plate) with new parts. Unplug the appliance and defrost it. Remove the hinge screws and install the new hinges. You'll need someone to help hold the door in position as you remove and install the hinges.

The Defrost Timer

If the appliance compressor doesn't run and you are sure that the unit is receiving power, the problem could be caused by the defrost timer. Follow these steps:

1. Unplug the appliance.
2. Locate the defrost timer; it is located near the compressor. You may have to remove a panel to gain access to the timer.
3. Disconnect the wires from the timer and the timer motor. The wires may plug in to the terminals; pull them straight out. If the wires are connected to terminal screws, loosen the screws for removal. You may have to remove the defrost timer from its brackets to reach the wiring.
4. If you don't have a volt-ohm meter (VOM), you can take the defrost timer to an appliance service center and have it tested. If it's faulty, buy a replacement. If you have a VOM, proceed to the next step.

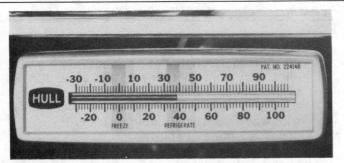

Monitor Food Storage Temperatures With Hanging Thermometer

A thermometer makes it easy to monitor food storage temperatures at a glance. The Hull No. 300 refrigerator-freezer thermometer, according to the Hull Manufacturing Co., is extremely accurate for such purposes. It hangs from a shelf so it can be easily read without stooping. The thermometer comes with a one-year factory warranty. If defective, the company will repair or replace it at no charge.

Durable Epoxy Paint for Appliances

Appliances need a tough, porcelain-like finish to resist scratches and withstand other use. According to Seymour of Sycamore, Inc., its epoxy spray paint has a durable finish that can be cleaned easily and quickly. The paint also can be used for toys, tools, furniture, sporting equipment, lamps, fixtures, and file cabinets. Appliance colors include gloss white, appliance white, gloss black, coffee (coppertone), avocado, harvest, almond, gloss red, gloss blue, gloss yellow, and gloss green. The cans contain 12.6 ounces.

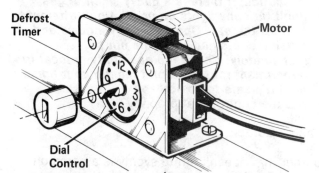

To test the defrost timer, you'll have to disconnect the wires from the timer; pull them straight out. If they are held by terminal screws, use a screwdriver to loosen the screws.

5. Set the VOM to the R × 1 scale.
6. Connect the probes of the meter to each terminal wire, and turn the timer dial control until you hear it click. The timer is working if the meter reads zero ohms. If the meter shows a high reading, replace the timer.
7. If the timer tests okay but the part still won't work properly, test the timer motor behind the timer.
8. Set the VOM to the R × 100 scale.
9. Connect one meter probe to each motor wire. If the meter reads between about 500 and 3,000 ohms, the motor is functioning properly. If the meter reads more than 3,000 ohms, replace the motor. **Note:** Because the motor and timer can be considered one component, it's a good idea to replace both parts if either one is malfunctioning, but get a cost estimate of the parts before you make a decision.

Door Light Switch

The door switch operates the light inside the refrigerator. You can get along without light inside, but you can't afford to have the light burn continually; this not only raises the temperature inside, it also raises your utility bill. To repair a faulty light, follow these steps:

1. If there's no light, check the light bulb to make sure it's not burned out. If it is, replace the bulb with one made for refrigerators.
2. If you suspect the light is on continually, depress the button on the door jamb. If the light stays on, the switch is faulty.
3. Unplug the appliance.
4. Remove the screws that hold the cover plate over the switch or the screws that hold the switch in position. Sometimes, the retaining screws are hidden by a piece of plastic trim that you must pry off to reveal the screws.
5. If you don't have a VOM, you can remove the switch and take it to an appliance repair center for testing. If it's faulty, buy a new switch and install it. If you have a VOM, proceed to the next step.
6. Set the VOM to the R × 1 scale.
7. Disconnect the wires to the switch.
8. Connect the meter's probes to each of the switch terminals, and press the push button. If the switch is working, the meter should read zero ohms. If the meter shows a high reading, replace the switch. Connect the new switch the same way the old one was connected.
9. Replace the trim and cover plate, and plug in the appliance.

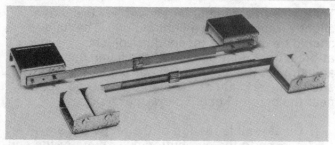

Put 'Wheels' Under Your Heavy Appliances

Wheels make it much easier to move heavy appliances for cleaning chores, but unfortunately not all appliances have wheels. The model RE-14S appliance rollers, made by Home Equipment Manu-facturing Co., a division of Kenton Industries, Inc., can be installed under appliances so you can roll them in and out quickly without straining. The appliance rollers feature an adjustable steel frame, 40 wheels, and skidproof pads. There also are four other models of rollers from which to choose.

Nut Driver Set for Appliance Jobs

For disassembling appliances, a nut driver is frequently a handy tool. A nut driver set, No. 40902, from Easco Tools, Inc., includes seven different size nut drivers for a variety of appliance repair applications. The tool handles are made of butyrate and guaranteed unbreakable. The precision ground blades are made of tempered chrome steel. The set includes the nut drivers, along with a reusable pouch. The company offers a full, no-time-limit warranty on the tools.

Gas Ranges

Materials • Household Detergent • Rags • Matches • Stiff Wire • Replacement Parts as Required

Tools • Straight Pin or Sewing Needle • Screwdriver • Volt-Ohm Meter • Cooking Thermometer

ALMOST ALWAYS, gas range breakdowns can be traced directly to dirt—usually boiled-over food that has blocked gas ports. Control knobs and switches sometimes act up, but the problem often can be solved with a very minor adjustment or two.

Before you attempt any repair job or call a professional for service, run through the following checklist:

• Is the gas valve to the range open?
• Is the range receiving electrical power? Check for a blown fuse or tripped circuit breaker at the main entrance panel or at a separate box.
• Is the pilot light on?

Gas ranges and ovens use gas burners to heat and cook food. Most malfunctions involve the support and ignition of gas in the burners.

Caution: If there is a heavy smell of gas, don't turn any lights on or off. Don't attempt to turn off the gas. Open several windows and outside doors and leave the house immediately! Phone the gas utility or local fire department for help. Don't reenter your home until it's safe to do so.

• Are the controls set properly?

Cleaning Burners

A burner that doesn't ignite evenly is a common problem. Food spilled on burners blocks the gas ports so that gas can't escape and be ignited. Follow these steps:

1. Remove the burner grate from the burner.
2. If necessary, remove the burner drip pan.
3. If your range has a top ring feature that covers the burner, unscrew it counterclockwise to expose the gas ports.
4. Wash the ring in a mild detergent solution. Then, rinse and dry it.
5. Place a rag soaked with the mild detergent solution over the burner, and allow it to soak for about 30 minutes. Remove the softened debris from the burner, rinse, and dry the burner.
6. Clean the gas ports with a straight pin or sewing needle, and wipe it clean. **Note:** Don't use a toothpick or matchstick to clear the gas ports; the wood can break off and clog the ports more seriously.
7. Reassemble the burner.
8. Turn on the burner and allow it to burn off any crust the detergent solution has missed.

Adjusting a Burner

The flame of a gas burner should be steady and slightly rounded with a light blue tip. The flame should be quiet and respond to adjustments made at the burner control knob. If the flame needs adjustment, this can be done at the air shutter/mixer plate at the end of the burner tube near the control knob. Follow these steps:

1. Disassemble the top of the range to gain access to the air shutter/mixer plate at the end of the burner tube. Remove the burner grates and then lift the top up and off the range, or back if the top is hinged.
2. Turn on the burner.
3. Release the shutter by loosening the setscrew in the shutter's slotted opening.
4. Slide the shutter and mixer plate back-and-forth to adjust the flame. If the flame is yellow, it isn't receiving enough air; open the plate slightly. If the flame is too high or makes a roaring sound, the flame is receiving too much air; close the plate slightly.

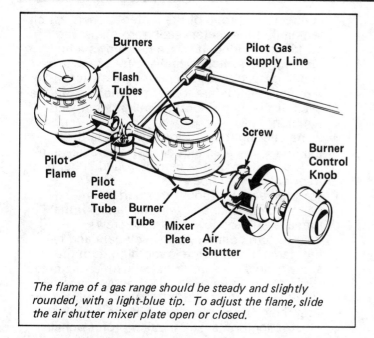

The flame of a gas range should be steady and slightly rounded, with a light-blue tip. To adjust the flame, slide the air shutter mixer plate open or closed.

Fit-All Thermocouples Install Without Tools

If your pilot light won't stay lit, you probably need a new thermocouple. Universal Thermocouples from Jade Controls are certified to 1,450° F by the American Gas Association and are available in 18-inch, 24-inch, 30-inch, and 36-inch lengths. Two versions are available. The aluminum thermocouple, shown here, comes with a limited torque nut that the manufacturer says can be tightened without tools.

This is said to eliminate damage caused by overtightening. Complete installation procedures are included on the package.

5. Tighten the setscrew, shut off the burner, and reassemble the range.

Burner Switches

The switches that control the burners are similar to an oven thermostat. On many ranges, there is a sensing bulb connected to the switch. If you suspect the switch is faulty, remove it from the range and have a professional test it. Follow these steps:

1. With a screwdriver, pry off the sensing bulb; it is generally clipped to the range cabinet. Then remove the switch. *Caution: Before doing any work on a gas range or oven, make sure it's unplugged, or turn off the electric power to the unit by removing a fuse or tripping a circuit breaker at the main entrance panel or at a separate entrance panel; if there's a grounding wire to the range, disconnect it. Close the gas supply valve to shut off the range's gas supply.*
2. Have the switch tested at an appliance service center. If the switch is faulty, buy a new one.
3. Install the new switch; connect it the same way the old one was connected.
4. If the range has a simmer adjustment and it is faulty, remove the control knob to the burner. The knob may pull straight off the control shaft, or it may be held by a setscrew at the base of the knob. Loosen the setscrew and pull the knob off.
5. Locate the screw slot inside the knob shaft.
6. Turn this screw clockwise or counterclockwise to adjust the control.
7. Test the burner. If the control doesn't work to your satisfaction, continue turning the screw until the setting is correct.

Pilot Light Failure

Often, one pilot serves all top burners of a range. On other models, there are two pilot lights, one for each side of the range. And on other ranges, there is an automatic shutoff valve in the pilot light assembly. The valve shuts off the gas to the burner any time the pilot light and the burner are both off.

A correctly adjusted pilot flame is steady, blue-tipped, and between ¼ and ½ inch high. If the flame goes out repeatedly or if it's yellow at the tip, it's getting too little air. If there's a space between the flame and the pilot feed tube, it's getting too much air. To adjust the pilot light follow these steps:

1. Disassemble the top of the range to gain access to the pilot light adjustment screw.
2. Turn the pilot adjustment screw slightly clockwise or counterclockwise on the gas line. If the flame is too high, turn the screw counterclockwise to adjust it. If the flame is too low, turn the screw clockwise.
3. If the pilot light flame goes out and there is a gas valve at the pilot, turn the valve off and wait 3 minutes.
4. Turn the valve to the pilot light position, hold a lit match to the pilot light orifice, and turn the valve on. If there is a safety or reset button at the pilot light valve, push the button and keep it depressed. Then light the pilot. When the flame is burning, release the reset button. If there is no reset button or gas valve, simply hold a lit match to the pilot orifice.

If the pilot light flame appears to be properly adjusted but the burners won't light, the trouble may be in the flash tubes.

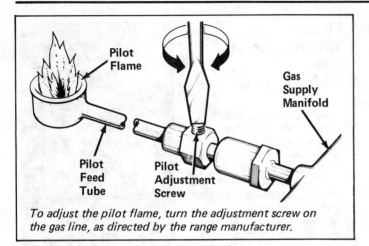

To adjust the pilot flame, turn the adjustment screw on the gas line, as directed by the range manufacturer.

5. Turn off the gas to the pilot light.
6. Using a short length of stiff wire, clear the flash tube, which runs from the pilot light to the gas burner, by working the wire back and forth through the tube. **Note:** Some flash tubes may be removed from the range by simply turning the tube and lifting them out. If you can remove the flash tube, do so and wash it in a mild detergent solution. Rinse and dry it, and replace the tube.
7. If the pilot light has a switch and you suspect it's faulty, it will have to be tested. Shut off the electrical power to the range. If you don't have a volt-ohm meter (VOM), remove the switch by disconnecting its wires and removing its retaining screws. Have it tested at an appliance service center. If it's faulty, buy a new one. If you have a VOM, set it to the $R \times 1$ scale. Disconnect the wires to the switch and connect one probe of the meter to each switch terminal. If the meter reads zero ohms, the switch is working. If the meter shows a high reading, the switch is faulty. Buy a new one.
8. Install or reconnect the pilot light switch.
9. Oven pilot lights are located at the back of the oven. If the light is out, try relighting it with a match.
10. If the pilot light is set too low, locate the ignition unit—a small box with two screws in it. The ignition unit is usually found either next to or below the pilot.
11. Turn the screws about one-quarter turn counterclockwise and test the flame. If the flame is still too low, turn the screws one-quarter turn counterclockwise again and test the flame. If the flame is too high, turn the screws clockwise until the adjustment is made.
   Note: On some oven pilot lights, you must turn the control to "off" to light the pilot. Then turn the oven dial to "broil." If the oven has an electric ignition system, call a professional.

Oven Thermostats

If your gas oven heats unevenly, or doesn't heat at all, the oven thermostat needs adjusting. You should adjust the thermostat of an oven if the temperature in the oven varies by more than 25° F from the setting on the control knob. Follow these steps:

1. Place a cooking thermometer in the center of the oven.
2. Turn on the oven, set the temperature control to a mid-range setting, close the oven door, and allow the oven temperature to stabilize for about 30 minutes.
3. Compare the thermometer reading with the control setting. If you find a difference of more than 25° F between the thermometer and the control setting, remove the oven control knob and look for an adjusting screw inside the control knob shaft housing. Insert a screwdriver into the shaft so the blade engages a screw slot. Turn the screw counterclockwise about one-eighth of a turn to raise the heat about 25° F; turn it clockwise one-eighth of a turn to decrease the heat by the same amount.
   On some ranges, you simply pull off the thermostat knob on the control panel. Behind it are two screws holding a round, notched plate. Loosen these screws but don't remove them. Use a screwdriver to change the notch setting on the plate by turning the plate counterclockwise; for every one-eighth turn, the temperature increases about 25° F. To turn the heat down, move the plate clockwise.
4. Repeat the test to check your adjustment.

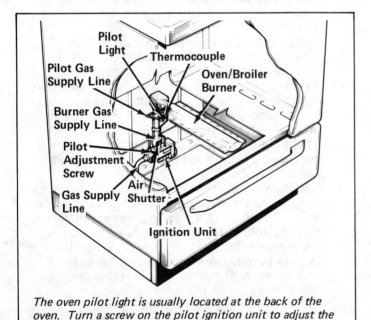

The oven pilot light is usually located at the back of the oven. Turn a screw on the pilot ignition unit to adjust the pilot light flame height.

Electric Ranges

Materials • Replacement Parts as Required

Tools • Screwdriver • Volt-Ohm Meter • Cooking Thermometer

ELECTRIC RANGES and ovens are generally easy to repair—there isn't much to go wrong. Most repairs are simple replacements, and most malfunctions can be traced to the heating elements.

Many electric ranges have a nichrome alloy heating element enclosed in a sheath that provides controlled heat to the range's cooking surface and the oven. Other ranges have thermostat controls in the center of the heating elements; the thermostat changes the resistance of power going through the element. Here, a heat sensor touches against the bottom of the cooking utensil; the device adjusts the element so it maintains an exact temperature level at the bottom of the pan or skillet. Still other ranges have flat ceramic tops over the heating elements. Heat is transferred from the element through the ceramic materials to the cooking utensils.

You can usually make repairs to ranges with the nichrome alloy elements; the other models are best left to a professional for service and repairs because specialized equipment is required. But regardless of the type of range you own, go through the following checklist before you attempt any repairs or call a service person:

- Is the range receiving power? Check the power cord, plug, and outlet. Also check for a blown fuse or a tripped circuit breaker at the main entrance panel or at a separate panel or fuse box. Check the in-range fuse system.
- Have you pressed the appliance's reset button?
- Is the timer control set properly in the manual or normal position?

The Fusing System

When an electric range fails to operate properly, chances are good that its fusing system—not a heating element or the wiring—is at fault. There are several things to check; follow these steps:

1. Check the fuses or circuit breakers at the main entrance panel.

2. In many older homes, the electric range is on a separate fuse system; it isn't connected to the main entrance panel. Check this possibility if the range doesn't function.
3. Many electric ranges have an in-range fuse system. It usually is located under the range's cooktop or inside the oven. Generally, you can reach the fuse assembly by lifting one of the rear cooktop elements, removing the drip pan, and unscrewing the fuse plug. In some ranges look for the fuses at the top front of the oven. If a fuse is blown, install a new one with the proper rating—usually it's 15 amps. **Note:** Sometimes, just one half of the fuse system fails, and the range's clock, lights, and timer may work, but the elements will fail to heat properly.
4. Some electric ranges have an in-range circuit-breaker system. To reset it, push the circuit breaker or reset button. The reset button is usually found on the control panel.

Cooktop Heating Elements

In most ranges, each cooktop heating element is connected to a terminal block in the side of the element well. If you are sure the range is receiving power, you'll have to test the elements. Follow these steps:

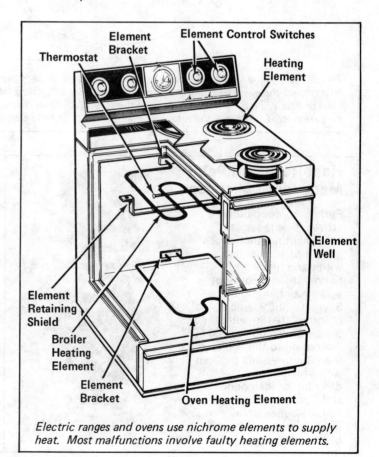

Electric ranges and ovens use nichrome elements to supply heat. Most malfunctions involve faulty heating elements.

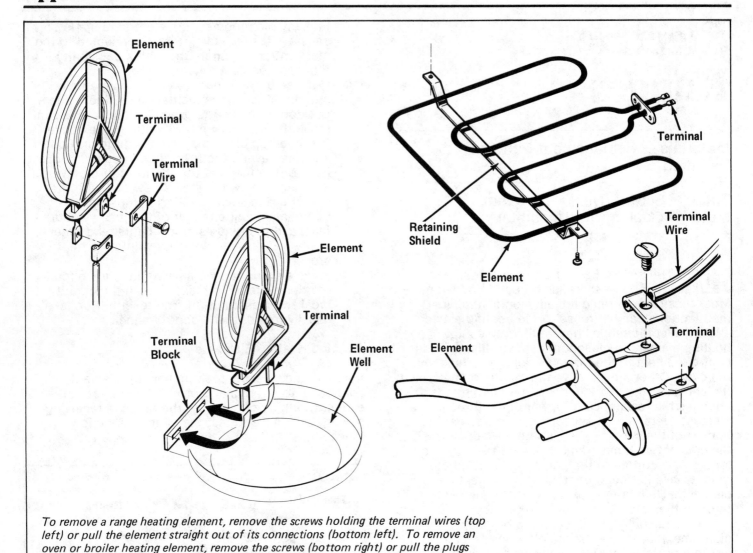

To remove a range heating element, remove the screws holding the terminal wires (top left) or pull the element straight out of its connections (bottom left). To remove an oven or broiler heating element, remove the screws (bottom right) or pull the plugs that connect it. Remove the retaining shield and lift out the element.

Heat-Resistant Paint Made for Appliances

Furnaces, wood-burning stoves, fireplaces, and other heating appliances need a paint that can withstand high temperatures. Hot Spot spray paint, made by Seymour of Sycamore, Inc., is formulated to withstand temperatures up to 1200° F. According to the manufacturer, the product won't blister, peel, discolor, or lose adhesion. Hot Spot paint comes in a 16-fluid-ounce spray can, in aluminum, white, and black colors.

Electrical Work Goes Faster With a Wire Stripper

A wire stripper makes electrical work go faster and look more professional. Eight gauges of wire can be stripped— or cut—accurately with the model No. 69 adjustable wire stripper from General Hardware Manufacturing Co., Inc. The tool handles 12- through 26-gauge wire. It has an adjustable dial that can lock the tool's spring-loaded jaws to protect them from damage when the stripper isn't in use.

1. Unplug the range. *Caution: Before doing any work on an electric range or oven, make sure it's unplugged, or turn off the power to the unit by removing one or more fuses or tripping one or more circuit breakers at the main entrance panel or at a separate panel. If the range is fused at a separate panel, this panel may be located adjacent to the main panel or in a basement, crawl space, or other location. If there is a grounding wire to the range, disconnect it. Make sure the power to the unit is off.*
2. Lift the nonworking heating element and remove the drip pan that's under it.
3. Remove the element. It is either held by two retaining screws, or simply unplugs from the terminal block.
4. Remove a heating element that works from its terminal block.
5. Connect the working element to the malfunctioning element's terminal. The working element doesn't have to fit perfectly; however, it must not touch the edges of the element well.
6. Turn on the power to the range.
7. If the working element heats, the suspected element is malfunctioning and needs to be replaced. If the working element doesn't heat, chances are good that the terminal block wiring or the switch that controls the element is faulty. Call a professional for this repair.
8. Turn off the power to the range, remove the working element, and replace it in its original well.
9. If the nonworking element was defective, install a new element.
10. Restore power to the range.

Oven and Broiler Elements

Oven and broiler elements are easier to test and replace than cooktop elements. Follow these steps:

1. Make sure the oven is receiving power.
2. Turn on the oven.
3. If the element doesn't heat, turn off the power.
4. Remove the element retaining shield, which is held by screws.
5. Disconnect the element from the power wires by unscrewing or unplugging it from its terminals.
6. Remove the element from the brackets that hold it in position in the oven; the brackets are held by screws that turn counterclockwise for removal.
7. If you don't have a volt-ohm meter (VOM), you'll have to take the element to an appliance service center for testing. If it's faulty, buy a new one. If you have a VOM, proceed to the next step.
8. Set the VOM to the R × 1 scale.
9. Connect one probe of the meter to each of the element's terminals. If the meter reads from 15

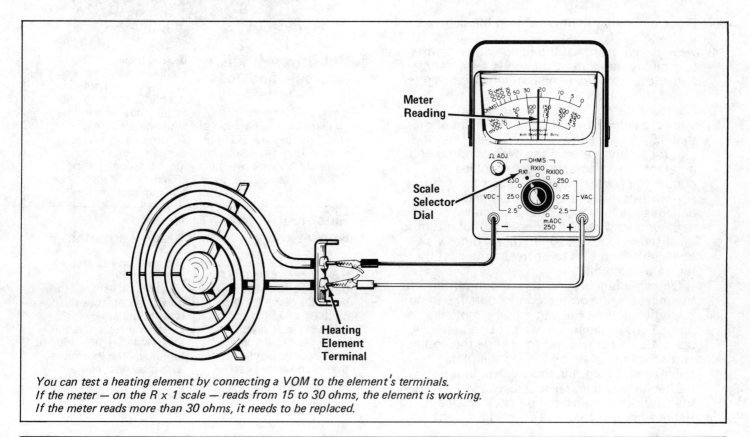

You can test a heating element by connecting a VOM to the element's terminals.
If the meter — on the R x 1 scale — reads from 15 to 30 ohms, the element is working.
If the meter reads more than 30 ohms, it needs to be replaced.

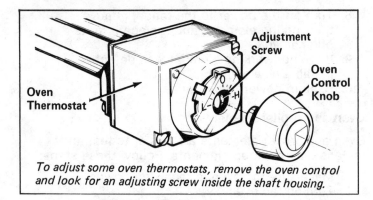

To adjust some oven thermostats, remove the oven control and look for an adjusting screw inside the shaft housing.

to 30 ohms, the element is okay. If the meter reads more than 30 ohms, the element is defective, and needs to be replaced.

10. If the element checks out okay, the problem is in the terminal block or wiring. Call a professional for service.

Oven Thermostats

Many electric ranges have ovens that use a capillary-tube thermostat to detect and maintain the proper temperature level. The thermostat usually is not serviceable; if part of the thermostat fails, the entire control must be replaced—a job for a professional. But, if the thermostat is out of calibration by more than 25° F, you usually can adjust it. Follow these steps:

1. Place a cooking thermometer in the center of the oven.
2. Turn on the oven, set the temperature control to a mid-range setting, close the oven door, and allow the oven temperature to stabilize for about 30 minutes.
3. Compare the thermometer reading with the control setting. If you find a difference of more than 25° F between the thermometer and the control setting, remove the oven control knob and look for an adjusting screw inside the control knob shaft housing. Insert a screwdriver into the shaft so the blade engages a screw slot. Turn the screw counterclockwise about one-eighth of a turn to raise the heat about 25° F; turn it clockwise one-eighth of a turn to decrease the heat by the same amount.

   On some ranges, you simply pull off the thermostat knob on the control panel. Behind it are two screws holding a round, notched plate. Loosen these screws but don't remove them. Use a screwdriver to change the notch setting on the plate by turning the plate counterclockwise; for every one-eighth turn, the temperature increases about 25° F. To turn the heat down, move the plate clockwise.
4. Repeat the test to check your adjustment.

Look for Hidden Fasteners

Sometimes, appliance housings are force-fitted, and may be hard to take apart. Never force parts apart; look for hidden fasteners. If there are no visible fasteners—screws, bolts, or clips—it may appear impossible to disassemble an appliance, but take a second look. Fasteners are often hidden under a nameplate or company logo, behind a scarcely visible plastic plug, under a cork pad on the bottom of the appliance, or under an attachment plate. Carefully pry up the part that is hiding the fastener. When you reassemble the appliance, snap the concealing part back over the fastener, or, if necessary, glue it in place. If you can't find hidden fasteners on force-fitted parts, warm the parts slightly with a heating pad; the heat may make disassembly easier.

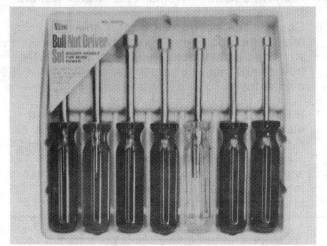

Nut Drivers a Must for Appliance Jobs

If you work around appliances, you can use a set of nut drivers. Bull nut drivers, from the Vaco Products Co., are available in a set of seven hex sizes: ³⁄₁₆ inch, ¼ inch, ⁵⁄₁₆ inch, ¹¹⁄₃₂ inch, ³⁄₈ inch, ⁷⁄₁₆ inch, and ½ inch. The handles, which are larger than standard handles to provide better turning power, are fluted with smooth, chamfered edges; and, they're color-coded for quick identification. The set, No. 89979, comes in a plastic hang-up storage tray.

Electrical Tape Know-How

PVC or plastic electrical tape is considered by the pros to be the best insulating tape for the majority of wiring projects. It is safe at temperatures up to 180° F. If you are working with appliances that produce heat at temperatures higher than this, use fiberglass tape instead of plastic tape.

How to Clean Terminals

The best way to clean power terminals on toasters, skillets, clothes irons, and other appliances is with fine steel wool. Polish the terminals until they shine brightly. Plug-in terminals can be cleaned with electrical contact cleaner, which is available in spray cans at electrical supply outlets.

Water Heater Maintenance

Materials • Newspapers • Rags • String • Thin Wire • Pipe Joint Compound • Replacement Parts as Required

Tools • Screwdriver • Continuity Tester • Adjustable Wrench • Pipe Wrench • Vacuum Cleaner • Wire Brush • Putty Knife

OF ALL THE APPLIANCES in your home, the water heater will probably give you the most trouble-free service. Only a periodic cleaning and draining is necessary to keep a water heater in top working condition. If problems do arise, run through the following checklist before you attempt any repairs or call in a professional service person.

- Is the power on? Check for blown fuses or tripped circuit breakers at the main entrance panel.
- Is the pilot light burning?
- Are the temperature controls set properly?
- Is the exhaust vent open?
- Have you pushed the power reset button?
- Is the drain valve fully closed?

Pilot Light Problems

Gas water heaters have a pilot light that is located next to a burner unit. The pilot light operates much like the one on a gas range. It is controlled by a combination temperature control near the bottom of the heater. Follow the relighting instructions that are usually on a metal plate near the heater control or at the top of the heater. If the instructions are not available, you can follow the procedure in "Pilot Lights" in this chapter.

Temperature Setting Control

All water heaters have a temperature setting control that regulates the temperature of the water in the tank. The control is usually located at the base of the heater. The proper setting for the water heater is between 120° F and 160° F, or "normal" to "hot" if the control doesn't have degree settings. To adjust the control, follow these steps:

1. Turn the control to 140° F, or the "normal" position. Some manufacturers recommend a 160° F, or "hot" setting if you operate a dishwasher.
2. Check the temperature of the hot water. If the manual control doesn't affect its temperature, the problem is probably in the thermostat, not the manual control dial. Call a professional for repairs.

Electric Heating Elements

If your water heater is electric, the tank has an upper and a lower heating element. Each element also has a thermostat, which is directly in back of its control. On some models, the elements are sealed in the tank; any tests or repairs should be left to a professional. If, however, you have access to the elements and you suspect that one is faulty, follow these steps:

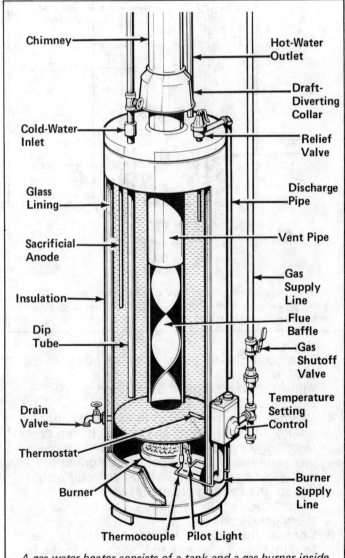

A gas water heater consists of a tank and a gas burner inside an insulated glass-lined cabinet. Clean the chimney at least every other year.

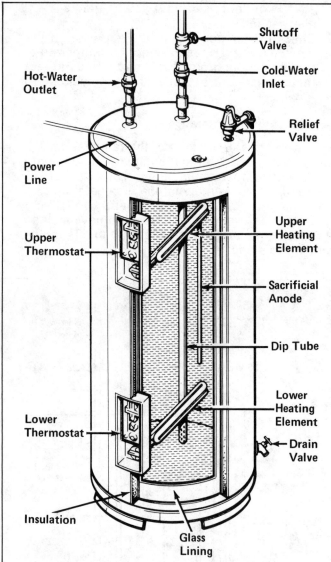

Most electric water heaters have two heating elements — an upper and a lower one — controlled by corresponding upper and lower thermostats.

Labels on figure: Shutoff Valve, Cold-Water Inlet, Hot-Water Outlet, Relief Valve, Power Line, Upper Thermostat, Upper Heating Element, Sacrificial Anode, Dip Tube, Lower Heating Element, Lower Thermostat, Drain Valve, Insulation, Glass Lining

1. Turn off the water supply and the power to the heater.
2. Allow the water in the heater to cool.
3. Drain the water heater.
4. Remove the access panel to the thermostat control housing by prying the panel open or removing several retaining screws. If there is any insulation in the housing, pull or cut it away, but save it to replace when you finish.
5. Locate the heating elements, which are directly behind and slightly below the thermostat controls.
6. Connect the clip of a continuity tester to one terminal of an element and touch the probe to any retaining bolt inside the housing. If the tester lights, the element is faulty. Replace it.
7. Repeat the test on the other element.

8. To replace an element, make sure the water supply and power are turned off.
9. Disconnect the power wires to the element, and remove the retaining screws that hold the element to the housing. Pull the element out of the tank.
10. Install the new element and connect the power wires. Also install a new gasket to seal the element. Then bolt the element into place on the tank flange. Replace the access panel and, if there was any, the insulation.
11. Fill the tank with water, turn on the power, and make any necessary temperature adjustment.

Leaking Heater Drains

All water heaters have a drain valve that looks like an outdoor sillcock. If the heater is new, you should drain the heater about every two months, letting the water run until it is clear. Use a bucket to catch the water, or if you have a basement drain, hook a garden hose to the valve for draining. If the heater has never been drained, don't drain it; opening the valve could cause leaks. To fix a leaking heater drain, follow these steps:

1. Turn off the water supply and power to the heater, and drain the water from the tank.
2. Use a screwdriver to remove the handle from the drain valve.
3. Use an adjustable wrench to remove the packing cap from the drain valve housing.
4. Replace the handle temporarily and turn out the stem of the drain valve; remove the handle.
5. Install a new washer on the end of the stem.
6. Replace the stem, screw on the packing cap, and replace the handle.

Note: The procedure for repairing a drain valve is similar to replacing a washer on a standard compression-type faucet. If the faucet has to be removed, turn off the power and water supply, and drain the tank. Then, with a pipe wrench, remove the faucet. Coat the male threads of the new faucet with pipe joint compound and install the faucet on the heater.

The Relief Valve

Most water heaters have a relief valve that permits water to escape through a discharge pipe when the water pressure in the tank exceeds a predetermined limit—usually 150 pounds per square inch (psi). You should check this valve twice a year to make sure it is working. To test the valve, follow these steps:

1. Squeeze the lever on the valve, which is located near or at the top of the water heater. The squeezing pressure should open a drainpipe, releasing a small amount of water.

2. If the relief valve doesn't work, have it repaired or replaced by a professional.
3. Each time you drain the water heater, open the relief valve; this makes draining the tank easier.

Cleaning the Heater

All water heaters must be kept clean. At least once a year, you should vacuum the outside of the heater to remove dirt and dust.

The chimney of a gas water heater should be cleaned at least once every two years. The chimney of an oil water heater is best left to a professional. Cleaning can result in fuel savings and cut down on any repair and service bills. Electric water heaters don't have chimneys so they don't require the same overall cleaning as gas water heaters. To clean a gas water heater chimney, follow these steps:

1. Turn off the power and gas to the water heater, and let the heater cool.
2. Spread newspapers around the base of the heater to protect the floor.
3. Open the inspection door at the bottom of the heater and spread several layers of newspapers over the burners.
4. Disassemble the chimney. Its sections may be held by self-tapping metal screws at the joints. If so, remove the screws. Start at the top of the chimney and work down. Number the sections as you go so you can reassemble them correctly.
5. Wad up balls of newspaper and push the paper through each section of pipe. This is a very sooty job, so have plenty of newspapers and rags handy. A brush or a putty knife can be used to remove heavy soot buildup.
6. After most of the soot has been removed, vacuum it up, and wipe the chimney sections clean with rags.

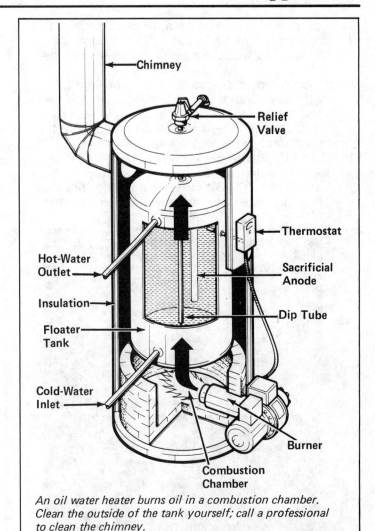

An oil water heater burns oil in a combustion chamber. Clean the outside of the tank yourself; call a professional to clean the chimney.

7. Remove the draft-diverting collar around the top of the chimney and clean it.
8. If there is enough room overhead, remove the flue baffle from the tank and clean it. The

Water Heater Connectors Help Prevent Corrosion

To help prevent corrosion—always a problem around water—flexible copper connectors for water heaters from Chicago Specialty Manufacturing Co. feature threaded steel nuts and dielectric insulators. The connectors are available in 12-inch, 18-inch, and 24-inch lengths, and are designed to fit standard ¾-inch pipe threads. Because the connectors may be bent into a 180-degree curve, they can reduce the number of fittings needed for installation. The connectors can also be used to repair broken sections of pipe or to make connections where piping is roughed in and doesn't quite line up with the existing connections.

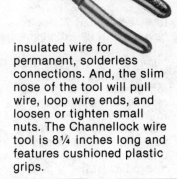

Handy Tool Does the Work of Five

When you wire an appliance, you need a number of tools to do the job right. The No. 908-G wire tool, made by Channellock, Inc., is designed to do the work of five different tools. It can strip wire without damaging the conductor; cut machine bolts without damaging threads; and cut wire with a clean scissors action. The tool also will crimp insulated and non-insulated wire for permanent, solderless connections. And, the slim nose of the tool will pull wire, loop wire ends, and loosen or tighten small nuts. The Channellock wire tool is 8¼ inches long and features cushioned plastic grips.

baffle looks like a piece of twisted metal; its purpose is to slow hot air rising through the chimney so that the heat is transferred to the cold water in the tank.

9. If you removed the baffle, clean the vent pipe in the tank with crumpled newspapers with an attached string. Drop the newspaper wad into the top of the pipe and pull it through with the string until the pipe is clean.

10. Clean up the mess. Then remove any dirt from the burner in the base of the heater by vacuuming it. Make sure the burner orifices are clear; you can open them with a piece of thin

wire. **Note:** Don't use a matchstick or toothpick to clean the gas ports. The wood could break and clog the ports. If the burner is extremely dirty, have a professional service it.

11. Replace the baffle in the tank and reassemble the chimney. If the slip joints in the pipe are loose, you can connect them with self-tapping metal screws—one screw to a joint.

12. After the chimney is assembled, turn on the power and water to the heater.

13. To make sure the pilot light works, turn the temperature dial down until the burner goes out. Then turn it up again to its proper setting.

Water-Heating Heat Pump Can Save Energy

The cost of heating water has risen dramatically and many people are trying to reduce the amount of hot water they use. According to E-Tech, Inc., you don't have to with its Efficiency II water-heating heat pump. The device operates on the same principle as a refrigerator—only in reverse. It removes heat from surrounding air and transfers it to the water in your water heater. Cooling and dehumidification are a by-product of the

Efficiency II, which uses electricity to run its compressor, a more efficient use of energy than is used by an electric—or oil—water heater. E-Tech says that the 100 Series Efficiency II can save 50 percent or more in fuel costs, and can be easily connected to a storage tank or water heater by the homeowner. Instructions are furnished with the installation kit. Model 101 operates on 115 volts/10-14 amps; model 102 operates on 230 volts/5-7 amps. Both come with a five-year limited warranty on parts and labor.

Soldering Gun Is Cordless and Has Automatic Feed

A cordless soldering gun is handy and practical for appliance and other repairs. The Iso-Tip cordless soldering gun, made by Wahl Clipper Corp., not only operates on rechargeable nickel-cadmium batteries, but also features a self-contained automatic solder feed. Solder is fed through a tube at the tip of the gun each time the trigger is fully depressed.

The gun's solder spool is easily refillable. The Iso-Tip No. 7900 kit includes the soldering gun with automatic solder feed, solder spool, plug-in recharger, a high-temperature beveled tip, a chisel tip, and instruction booklet. The recharger, which plugs into any 110-120-volt outlet, can provide a full recharge overnight. There are also 14 other snap-in tips available. The Iso-Tip No. 7920 kit includes the gun without the solder-feed feature. The products carry a one-year warranty.

Long-Reach Pliers Useful for Working on Appliances

Pliers that allow you to reach into difficult places are useful when making appliance repairs. The No.

378 long-reach duck-bill pliers made by Channellock, Inc., are just such a tool. The 8-inch-long pliers have a serrated nose; polished steel finish; and optional, blue plastic grips.

Controller Reduces Appliance Power Load

Dr. Watt is the name of an energy-conserving device— a motor energy loss controller—from EnerCon, Inc., that you can connect to an appliance with a continuously running induction motor, including clothes washers, refrigerators, gas dryers, air conditioners, freezers, and furnaces. It measures the minimum amount of power the motor needs to run efficiently and delivers only that amount. As a result, the manufacturer claims that you save electricity and that the motor runs quieter and cooler. To use, the appliance is plugged into the device which, in turn, is plugged into an electrical outlet. The

National Aeronautics and Space Administration developed the patented device used in Dr. Watt, and EnerCon, under NASA license, modified it for use with home appliances that have induction motors of ½ horsepower or less. Dr. Watt has a built-in safety fuse for line protection and comes with a 30-day money-back guarantee.

When You Need an Extra Hand— Here's Help

Screw-holding attachments for screwdrivers provide a "third hand" when you're driving or removing screws in appliances. The Clip'n Grip attachments for round-shaft screwdrivers set and start screws. Then, by flicking the screwdriver, the clips release the screws. Made by Stanley Tools, the screw-holding attachments are ideal for working in confined areas. The clips come in a set of three to fit any ³⁄₁₆-inch, ¼-inch, and ⁵⁄₁₆-inch diameter screwdrivers.

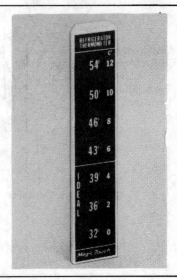

Brush Designed for Cleaning Refrigerator Coils

A refrigerator with dirty coils and fan wastes energy and costs you money. The Energy Saver brush, made by Empire Brushes, Inc., is designed for cleaning refrigerator coils and the fan. Its tapered design allows it to go where most other brushes can't go. According to the manufacturer, the model No. 21-4100 brush can help reduce power consumption by your appliance up to 10 percent.

This Refrigerator Thermometer Has a Digital LCD Readout

A digital thermometer that lights up to show you the exact temperature in your refrigerator is extremely easy to read. The Magic Touch digital refrigerator thermometer, made by Magic Touch Manufacturing Corp., has a liquid-crystal digital readout. It attaches quickly to the refrigeration compartment, and can be mounted flat or at an angle for easy viewing.

Use Your Clothes Dryer for Heating

You can use your clothes dryer to provide extra heat and humidity to the laundry area during the winter. The Extra-Heat EX12, made by Deflect-o Corp., is a clothes dryer heat-saving device and lint trap. It's made of white, high-impact polypropylene. The damper has a handle so that dryer air can be vented indoors or outdoors. The product, which is easy to install with a hanger bracket, is designed to be used with 4-inch vinyl hose or metal duct pipe. There's also a pop-off valve for dryer safety. According to Deflect-o, the Extra-Heat EX12 is made to resist temperatures to 250° F on a continuous basis.

Thermostats

Materials • Cardboard • Tape • Steel Wool • Replacement Thermostat

Tools • Plastic Squeeze Bottle • Thermometer • Artist's Brush • Screwdriver • Carpenter's Level

---

THERMOSTATS ARE electromechanical devices that control the heating and, sometimes, cooling in your home. They seldom need maintenance or replacement. Since the energy crunch, manufacturers have redesigned thermostats to include set-back and timed cycle features so that the heating or cooling unit automatically saves fuel while maintaining various temperature levels.

The most common thermostat problem is dirt on the internal mechanisms, which can affect the thermostat's calibration and interfere with its operation. Other thermostat problems can be traced to loose or corroded electrical connections. All of these problems can be easily corrected.

Checking Calibration

If your thermostat is causing problems, follow these steps to check its calibration:

1. Tape a glass tube thermometer to the wall a few inches from the thermostat; put a small piece of padding, such as cardboard, under the thermometer so it doesn't touch the wall.

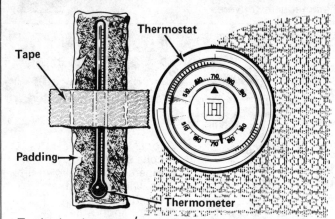

To check a thermostat's accuracy, tape a thermometer a few inches away, and compare the temperature readings.

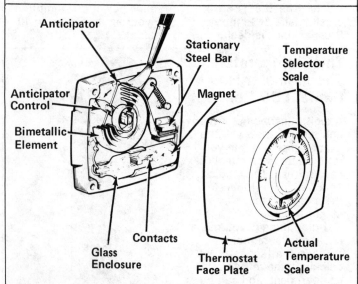

You can clean a thermostat by lightly dusting the inner parts with a small artist's brush.

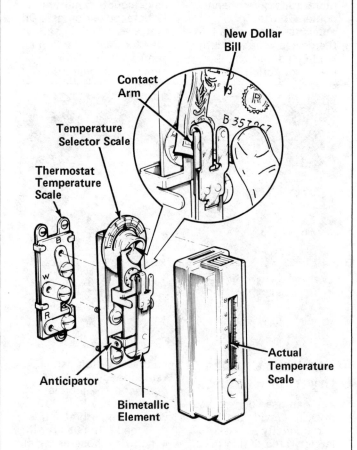

To examine the thermostat, remove the face plate or cover; usually it's held by a snap or friction catch. If it has open contact points — not sealed within a glass enclosure — run a new dollar bill between the points to clean them. Don't use sandpaper or emery cloth!

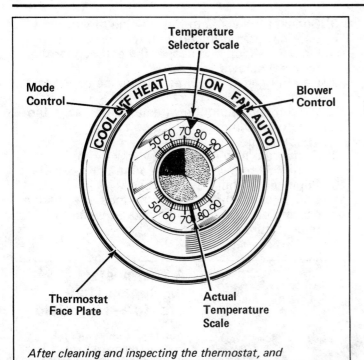

Temperature Selector Scale

Mode Control

Blower Control

Thermostat Face Plate

Actual Temperature Scale

After cleaning and inspecting the thermostat, and comparing its temperature with a thermometer taped to the wall nearby, you can reset the instrument to compensate for any difference of 3° F or more. Or you can replace the thermostat.

2. After waiting about 15 minutes for the thermometer to stabilize, compare the reading on the thermometer with the temperature on the thermostat. If there is a difference of 3° F or more, the thermostat may be dirty or require calibration.

3. Remove the face plate or cover from the front of the thermostat; usually it snaps in place.

4. Lightly dust the inner parts of the thermostat with a small artist's brush, or blow away any dirt by squeezing air from an empty plastic bottle. If the thermostat has open contact points—not sealed within a glass enclosure—rub a new dollar bill between them to clean these spots. Do not use sandpaper or emery cloth. *Caution: Don't use a vacuum cleaner; the suction from the vacuum cleaner is too powerful and may damage the device.*

5. Check the switches and wire connections on the thermostat. If the terminal screws are loose, tighten them; if they are corroded, clean them with steel wool.

6. If the thermostat has a mercury vial inside, make sure the unit is level. If it isn't, loosen the mounting screws and adjust the thermostat until it is level; then retighten the screws.

7. Replace the thermostat cover and repeat Steps 1 and 2. If the calibration is still off, you can reset the thermostat dial to compensate for the difference or replace the device.

Changing a Thermostat

Changing a couple of wire connections is about all that's involved in replacing a thermostat, even if the new one has energy-saving features. Be sure to obtain a thermostat that operates on the same voltage as the old one. This information is marked on the thermostat.

Note: A heating and cooling thermostat should be placed on an interior wall in a central location. If it isn't in such a location, it should be relocated by a professional.

When installing a thermostat it's important to be careful with the device; the parts are delicate and can be damaged easily. Follow these steps:

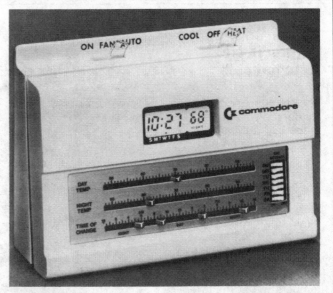

Set-Back Thermostat Can Save You Money

Whether your home heating and cooling system uses gas, oil, electricity, or other fuel source, the Commodore microelectronic thermostat can save you money. According to Commodore Consumer Products Group, only a screwdriver is needed to install the automatic set-back thermostat in place of your old model. The device is 5¼ inches wide, 3½ inches high, and 1½ inches deep. Its controls are sliding levers that handle both temperature and time settings. To operate, you move the levers to the desired temperatures, select the times to fit your household schedule, and leave the thermostat alone. The thermostat automatically selects the proper temperature at the times you have programmed. The thermostat features a continuous LCD digital display of the time in hours and minutes, a continuous display of the actual room temperature, and an electronic arrow indicator that automatically shows the day of the week. Instructions for installing and using the thermostat are provided. The company offers a one-year limited warranty.

Heating and Cooling

1. Turn off the power to the thermostat's circuit by removing the proper fuse or tripping the proper circuit breaker to the "off" position.
2. Remove the cover of the thermostat.
3. The thermostat is held to the wall with screws in a back mounting plate; remove these screws to release the thermostat from the wall.
4. Disconnect the wires to the thermostat by turning the terminal screws on the back of the device. Have someone hold the wires after you disconnect them to prevent them from falling inside the wall. Or secure the wires with a piece of masking tape to prevent this.
5. Buff the ends of the wires with steel wool until the ends are shiny.
6. Connect the wires to the new thermostat terminals; bend the ends of the wires in a clockwise loop and secure the ends under the terminal screws.
7. Carefully push the wires into the holes in the wall.
8. Wrap tape around the wires at the holes in the wall to prevent cold air inside the wall from affecting the thermostat.
9. Fasten the new unit to the wall with the mounting screws; make sure the unit is level.
10. Replace the thermostat's cover.
11. Check to see that the new thermostat turns the heating or cooling unit on and off when the temperature setting is changed.

A Built-In Heater Controls Bathroom Heat Automatically

The Nautilus model N134 fan-forced wall heater, made by Nautilus Industries, is one that you can install in your bathroom using household tools. The model N134 has a decorative chrome grille with a fingertip control panel that allows you to turn on the heater and obtain heat in seconds. An automatic thermostat maintains the bathroom temperature at the level desired. The built-in heater comes with easy-to-follow installation instructions.

A Thermostat for Rooms That Are Hot—Then Cold

Modern furnaces operate from a thermostat that "tells" the furnace when to go on or off. However, rooms located some distance from the thermostat may be colder than other rooms because the heating plant doesn't come on soon enough to get heat to these rooms; the rooms may be hot, then cold, and then hot again. There is no heat balance. You can correct this situation by installing a thermostat that regulates both the temperature and the on/off cycling of the furnace.

Thermostat Switches Automatically From Heating to Cooling

A digital clock thermostat made by Jade Controls, the model H/C-CL, automatically switches from heating to cooling, and back again. Called the Smart thermostat, the instrument can be programmed for eight different temperature settings in four different time periods throughout the day. It features simple operation, a constant LED display of time and temperature, and a recall button that permits you to return to the originally programmed setting. The thermostat is 6⅜ inches high, 5⅝ inches wide, and 1¾ inches deep. Voltage requirements are 18 to 30 volts AC/3 amps maximum; the unit accommodates all 24-volt systems, except heat pumps. Some oil and hydronic furnaces may require an accessory kit (No. OFK-1) for installation. Instructions for mounting are included. The thermostat, which has a 54-degree range, carries a one-year warranty.

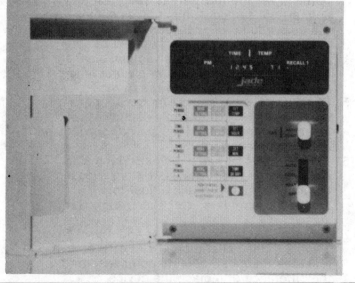

Gas and Electric Furnaces

Materials • Stick Matches • No. 10 Non-Detergent Motor Oil • Belt Dressing • Rags • Bearing Grease • Replacement Parts as Required

Tools • Straight Pin or Wire • Screwdriver • Pump-Type Oil Can • Adjustable Wrench • Toothbrush • Vacuum Cleaner

WITH EITHER A GAS or electric furnace few repairs are possible by the homeowner; most repairs require the attention of a professional. However, a program of regular maintenance can reduce the frequency of repairs, and keep your furnace running more efficiently.

If your gas or electric furnace won't run at all, go through the following checklist before you attempt any repairs or call a professional:

• Is the power to the furnace turned on? Check for blown fuses or tripped circuit breakers at the main entrance panel. **Note:** Many furnaces operate on separate circuits. Don't assume that the furnace is connected to the main entrance panel. Look for another panel, especially in an older home.

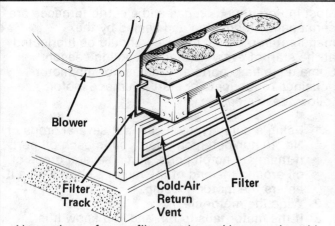

Almost always, furnace filters are located between the cold air return and the blower; most are disposable. Some furnaces have exposed filters that fit into U-shaped tracks (above); these are pulled out for replacement or cleaning.

• If there is a separate power switch on or near the furnace, make sure this switch is turned on.
• Is the thermostat set properly? Try raising it 5° F.
• Did you push the reset button on the furnace motor?
• On a gas furnace check the gas supply line. Is the gas valve to the furnace turned on? Is the pilot light on? *Caution: Gas furnaces and heaters have control shutoffs to prevent gas leaks, but they are not fail-safe. If there is a smell of gas in your house, do not turn any lights on or off, or try to shut off the gas leading to the furnace. Get out of the house, leaving the door open, and go to a telephone; call the gas company or the fire department immediately to report a leak. Don't reenter your home until it's safe to do so.*
• On an electric furnace check the unit's own fuse system for a blown fuse.

Furnace Filters

A dirty air filter on a gas or electric furnace can restrict the amount of heat distributed throughout your home. The filter or filters (some furnaces have two), should be cleaned or changed at the start of every heating season and once a month while the furnace is in continuous use. If the furnace has an air conditioner linked to it, the filters also serve this unit. Therefore, clean or change the filters every month during the cooling season.

Almost always, furnace filters are located between the cold air return and the blower; most are disposable. To gain access to the filter, look for a metal panel on the front of the furnace near the cold air return; usually it is marked "filter." You can remove the panel by unscrewing it from the furnace housing or lifting it off hooks. Some furnaces have exposed filters that fit into U-shaped tracks; these can be pulled out.

When installing a new filter, use one that is the same size as the old one. Also make sure the filter is installed correctly. Directional air flow arrows are shown on the edge of the filter along with the size. Install the filter so that the arrows point in the same direction as the air flow, from the cold air return toward the blower.

Drive Belts

V-belts that drive the blower on gas and electric furnaces can become noisy; they also can become frayed or break. These belts should be checked annually. Follow this procedure:

1. If the belt is noisy and is slipping, apply automotive fan belt dressing to the belt.
2. If the belt is worn or broken, replace it with a new belt that is the same size; the size should be embossed on the belt. If it isn't, take the

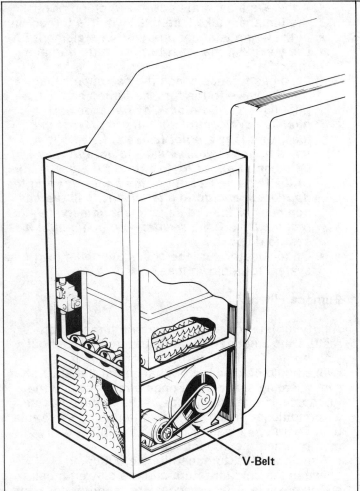

V-belts that drive the blower on gas and electric furnaces can become noisy; they also can become frayed or break. These belts should be checked annually.

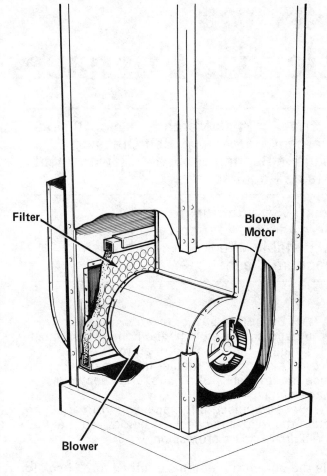

With a little maintenance, the blower on a gas or electric furnace will run trouble-free. At the beginning of every heating and cooling season, lubricate the blower's bearings.

old belt with you when you purchase a replacement. *Caution: Before doing any work on the furnace, make sure the power to the furnace is turned off.*

3. To replace a belt, loosen the bolts that hold the motor to its mounting bracket by turning them counterclockwise with a wrench.
4. Slide the motor toward the blower assembly.
5. Remove the old belt from the pulleys. **Note:** Although you must move the motor to install a new belt, you can also remove the old belt by simply cutting it with a knife.
6. Slip the new belt over the pulleys. Make sure it is seated properly.
7. Push the motor back on its mounting bracket and tighten the bolts.
8. Test the deflection in the belt. It should deflect about ½ inch when you press down on the belt midway between the two pulleys. If the belt is too loose or too tight, move the motor to adjust it properly.

Furnace Motors

Most motors found on gas and electric furnaces are permanently lubricated and sealed by the manufacturer. Some, however, should be lubricated at the start of every heating or cooling season. Some units have ports at each end of the motor housing. To lubricate or start a furnace motor, follow these steps:

1. Using a pump-type oil can, put several drops of No. 10 non-detergent motor oil in each oil port. If there are no oil ports, pump several drops of oil around the end of the motor's shaft where it enters the motor housing.
2. Wipe the motor clean.
3. If the motor fails to run and you know it is receiving power, let the motor cool for 30 minutes. Then push the reset button on the motor.
4. If the motor doesn't start, press the reset

button several more times. If the motor still won't run, call a professional.

Furnace Blower

With just a little maintenance, the blower on a gas or electric furnace will run trouble-free. At the beginning of every heating and cooling season, lubricate the blower's bearings. If the blower shaft has oil ports, lubricate them with No. 10 non-detergent motor oil. If the shaft has grease cups, fill the cups with bearing grease. Clean the blower at the start of the heating season and midway through it, or at any time it appears dirty. Use an old toothbrush to clean each fan blade. Remove any debris with a vacuum cleaner.

The Limit Switch

The limit switch is a safety control switch found on gas furnaces. It is located on the furnace just below the plenum. If the blower on your gas furnace runs continuously, the problem may be caused by the limit switch. To check this, follow these steps:

1. Check the blower control on the thermostat to see if it has been turned to the "on" position; if it has, turn the dial to the "auto" position. If the control is already on "auto," the limit switch needs adjusting.
2. Remove the cover on the limit switch with a screwdriver.
3. One side of the toothed dial under the limit switch cover is marked "limit"; don't touch this side. The other side is marked "fan"; set the upper pointer on the "fan" side to 115° F and the lower pointer to 90° F.
4. Replace the cover and check the blower. If it still runs continuously, call a professional.

Relighting the Pilot

Drafts can cause the pilot light on a gas furnace to go out. Instructions for relighting the pilot light usually are fastened to the furnace. If the instructions aren't available, follow this general procedure:

1. Turn the pilot light's gas valve to the "off" position and wait about five minutes.
2. Turn the gas valve to the "pilot" setting.
3. While you push the reset button on the pilot control panel, hold a lit match to the pilot light orifice; keep the reset button depressed until the flame is burning brightly.
4. Release the button and turn the gas valve to the "on" position.
5. If the pilot light won't stay lit, make sure the orifice isn't blocked; clean it with a piece of wire or a straight pin. If the pilot light won't

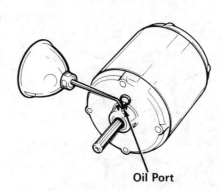

Oil Port

If the furnace motor has oil ports, put several drops of No. 10 non-detergent motor oil in each oil port. If there are no ports, pump several drops of oil around the end of the motor's shaft where it enters the motor housing.

stay lit after several attempts, the thermocouple may be faulty. The procedure for replacing a thermocouple is outlined below. **Note:** Some gas furnaces have electronic devices to ignite the fuel. If your furnace is equipped with this type of system, call a professional for service.

The Thermocouple

Located near the pilot light burner on a gas furnace, the thermocouple is a safety device. If it

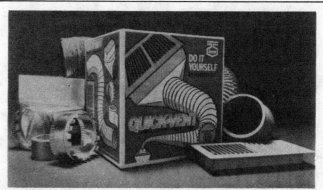

Vent Extension Easy to Install

Quick-Vent is a do-it-yourself kit for extending heating and cooling ductwork into the floor or ceiling of room additions, attics, basements, enclosed porches, and garages. Made by Acme Metal Manufacturing Co., the vent kit includes a 4- by 10-inch damper-controlled register; a 4-inch by 10-inch by 5-inch register boot; 12 feet of 5-inch-diameter flexible duct; a crimped starting collar; duct tape; and an illustrated instruction booklet. Additional 4-foot lengths of flexible duct with a connector collar are also available.

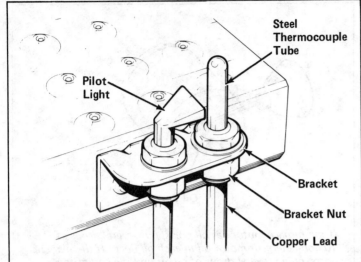

You can adjust the thermocouple by gently tightening the nut that holds the thermocouple in its bracket.

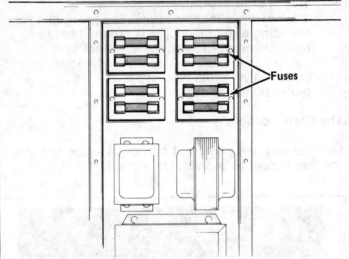

The heating elements on an electric furnace are fused on a separate panel located on or inside the furnace housing.

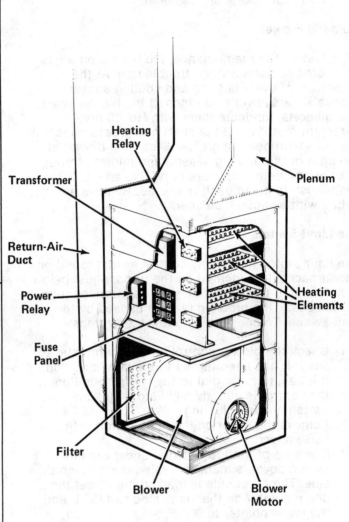

Electric furnaces use heating elements, controlled by relays, to warm the air. For those components that are the same — the motor, blower, filters, and drive belts — maintenance and repair is identical to a gas furnace.

malfunctions, the gas won't come on at the burners or at the pilot light. If this is the case, follow these steps:

1. Try adjusting the thermocouple. Gently tighten the nut that holds the thermocouple in its bracket; don't overtighten it.
2. Try lighting the pilot light. If the pilot stays lit and the burners work, the problem is solved. But if the pilot won't stay lit, you'll have to replace the thermocouple.
3. Unscrew the copper lead and connection nut at the threaded connection to the gas line.
4. Unscrew the bracket nut that holds the tube in place; it is under the mounting bracket at the thermocouple tube.
5. Insert a new thermocouple into the bracket;

the steel side should be up and the copper lead down.
6. Screw the bracket nut over the tube.
7. Push the connection nut to the threaded connection where the copper lead connects to the gas line. Make sure the connection is clean and dry.
8. Screw the nut tightly in place, but don't overtighten it. Both the bracket nut and connection nut should be slightly tighter than finger-tight, and the tip of the pilot light flame should just touch the thermocouple tip.

Electric Furnace Repairs

Electric furnaces operate in much the same way as gas furnaces do except the heating plant is

Cure for Annoying 'Furnace Whistle'

Perhaps your furnace worked fine until the filter was changed. Now, the furnace whistles. If this is your problem, it's easy to solve. The new filter probably isn't seated properly in its track. The noise is caused by air movement whenever the blower goes on and pushes air around the filter instead of through it.

Belt Dressing May Halt Slipping and Squeaking

If a belt is slipping or squeaking on a motor, a belt dressing may stop it. Bondo Belt Grab, made by Dynatron/Bondo Corp., is non-flammable and formulated to halt slipping and squeaking on belt-driven appliances, such as furnaces and central air conditioners. The product also may be used on autos, lawn mowers, power tools, and boats. To use, you squeeze a few drops on the inside of the belt. Belt Grab comes in 1.5-fluid-ounce tubes.

Solution for Steam Pipe Chatter

If the steam pipes in your hot water heating system chatter from time to time, check to make sure that the valves on the radiators are opened fully. Also, check to make sure that the pipes are not sagging along the route from boiler to radiator. If you see a sag, support the pipe at such a point with pipe hangers.

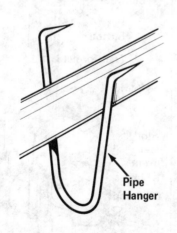

Pipe Hanger

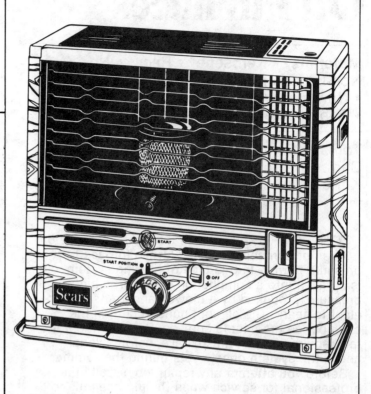

Wick-Type Heater for Spot Heating

Efficient wick-type space heaters are popular in Japan and, recently, their use in the United States is increasing. The No. 32 A 40202L reflection-type, wick heater, which is sold by Sears, Roebuck and Co., may be used near a wall, draperies, or furniture because it radiates heat in only one direction. With your central heating thermostat turned down, the 9300-BTU unit is ideal for heating a family room, workshop, and other areas. It has a safety "tip switch" that extinguishes the system, automatically turning it off should it be accidentally jarred or tipped over. It also has stainless steel burner components and mirror reflector. The removable 1.1-gallon fuel tank allows you to refill the heater with kerosene while it's running, and one tankful provides more than 15 hours of operation. The model 32 A 40202L comes with a woodgrain enamel finish, and is 21½ inches wide, 18½ inches high, and 11 inches deep.

different; the furnace uses electric resistance elements instead of gas to produce heat. For those components that are the same—the motor, blower, filters, and drive belts—maintenance and repair is identical to a gas furnace. If an electric furnace won't heat or the motor won't run, check for a blown fuse or a tripped circuit breaker at the main electrical service panel. Many electric furnaces are on separate circuits, sometimes located in a separate fuse box away from the main panel.

The heating elements on an electric furnace have a separate fuse system located on a panel on or inside the furnace housing. If the furnace won't heat, be sure to check this separate system for a blown fuse. If changing the fuses or resetting the breakers doesn't restore power to the furnace, call a professional. Do not attempt to repair or replace heating elements, the transformer, heating relays, or power relays yourself; repairs to these components should always be done by a professional.

Oil Furnaces

Materials • Kerosene • Rags • No. 10
Non-Detergent Motor Oil • Bearing Grease
• Newspapers • Refractory Cement
• Replacement Parts as Required

Tools • Screwdriver • Pump-Type Oil
Can • Toothbrush • Bottle Brush • Putty
Knife • Adjustable Wrench

THERE ARE FEW repairs that you can make on
an oil furnace, especially if the furnace is a
pressure burner. In this type of heating system, oil
is sprayed into a combustion chamber at high
pressure, propelled by a blower, and ignited by an
electric spark. The oil continues to burn in the
chamber as the mist is sprayed. Because there are
few repairs you can make, have a professional
check the system once a year during the summer.

Before you attempt any repair job or call in a
professional for service when the furnace fails to
function properly, check this list:

• Is the furnace receiving power? Check for blown
  fuses or tripped circuit breakers at the main
  entrance panel or at a separate circuit panel.
• Is the power switch turned on at or near the
  furnace?
• Does the furnace have fuel, and is the fuel
  supply valve open?
• Is the thermostat control set properly?
• Is the blower control set properly?
• Is the limit switch set properly?
• Did you press the reset button on the furnace
  motor or blower motor?
• Is the electric-eye safety clean?

Furnace Filter

A dirty furnace air filter can restrict the amount of
heat distributed throughout your home. The air filter
should be cleaned or changed at the start of every
heating season and once a month while the furnace
is in continuous use.

Almost always, the filter is located between the
cold air return and the blower; most are disposable.
To gain access to the filter, look for a metal panel
on the front of the furnace near the cold air return;
usually it is marked "filter." You can remove the
panel by unscrewing it from the furnace housing or
lifting it off hooks. Some furnaces have exposed
filters that fit into U-shaped tracks; these can be
pulled out.

When installing a new filter, use one that is the
same size as the old one. Also make sure the filter
is installed correctly. Directional air flow arrows are
shown on the edge of the filter along with its size.
Install the filter so that the arrows point in the same
direction as the air flow, from the cold air return
toward the blower.

Drive Belts

V-belts that drive the furnace blower can become
noisy; they also can become frayed or break. These
belts should be checked annually. Follow this
procedure:

1. If the belt is noisy and is slipping, apply
   automotive fan belt dressing to the belt.
2. If the belt is worn or broken, replace it with a
   new belt that is the same size; the size should
   be embossed on the belt. If it isn't, take the

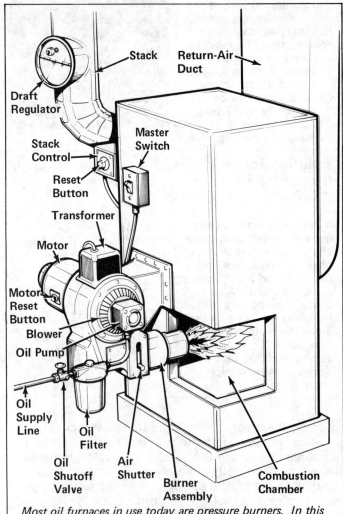

*Most oil furnaces in use today are pressure burners. In this
type of system, oil is sprayed into a combustion chamber at
high pressure. There are few repairs that you can make on
such a furnace.*

old belt with you when you purchase a replacement.

3. To replace a belt, use an adjustable wrench to loosen the bolts that hold the motor to its mounting bracket.
4. Slide the motor toward the blower assembly.
5. Remove the old belt from the pulleys. **Note:** Although you must move the motor to install a new belt, you can also remove the old belt by simply cutting it with a knife.
6. Slip the new belt over the pulleys. Make sure it is seated properly.
7. Push the motor back on its mounting bracket and tighten the bolts.
8. Test the deflection in the belt. It should deflect about ½ inch when you press down on the belt midway between the two pulleys. If the belt is too loose or too tight, move the motor to adjust it properly.

Furnace Motors

Most oil furnace motors are permanently lubricated and sealed by the manufacturer. Some, however, should be lubricated at the start of every heating or cooling season. Some units have ports at each end of the motor housing. To lubricate or start a furnace motor, follow these steps:

1. Using a pump-type oil can, put several drops of No. 10 non-detergent motor oil in each oil port. If there are no oil ports, pump several drops of oil around the end of the motor's shaft where it enters the motor housing.
2. Wipe the motor clean.
3. If the motor fails to run and you know it is receiving power, let the motor cool for 30 minutes. Then push the reset button on the motor.
4. If the reset button doesn't start the motor, press the reset button several more times. If the motor still won't run, call a professional.

Furnace Blower

A furnace's blower usually causes little trouble. At the start of every heating or cooling season, lubricate the bearings on the blower. If the blower shaft has oil ports, lubricate them with No. 10 non-detergent motor oil. If the shaft has grease cups, fill the cups with bearing grease. Clean the blower at the start of the heating season and midway through it, or at anytime it appears dirty. Use an old toothbrush to clean each fan blade. Use a vacuum cleaner to remove the debris.

The Limit Switch

The limit switch is a safety control switch that is located on the furnace just below the plenum. If the

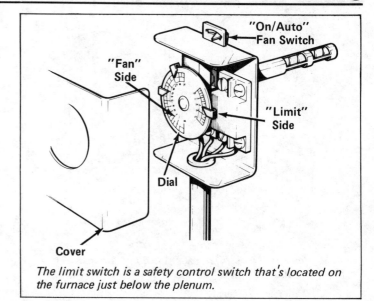

The limit switch is a safety control switch that's located on the furnace just below the plenum.

blower runs continuously, the problem may be caused by the limit switch. To check this, follow these steps:

1. If the blower control on the thermostat has been turned to the "on" position, turn the dial to the "auto" position. If the control is already on "auto," the limit switch needs adjusting.
2. Remove the cover on the limit switch with a screwdriver.
3. One side of the toothed dial under the limit switch cover is marked "limit"; don't touch this. The other side is marked "fan"; set the upper pointer on the "fan" side to 115° F and the lower pointer to 90° F.
4. Replace the cover and check the blower. If it still runs continuously, call a professional.

The Oil Filter

The oil filter should be changed or cleaned at the start of the heating season and about midway through the season. Follow these steps:

1. Close the oil shutoff valve between the fuel tank and filter.
2. Unscrew the bottom or cup of the filter housing. If the filter is disposable, remove it from the cup and insert a new one of the same size and type. If it is a permanent filter, remove the filter and wash it in kerosene. *Caution: Kerosene is flammable; be careful when cleaning a permanent oil filter.* For best service, such a filter should be cleaned every 45 to 60 days during the heating season.
3. Install the new or cleaned filter in the filter housing.
4. After installing a new or cleaned filter, replace the old filter gaskets with new ones.

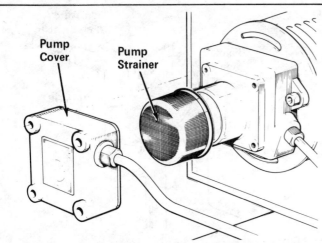

Pump Cover

Pump Strainer

After cleaning the oil filter, clean the pump strainer. To reach the strainer, unbolt the cover of the pump housing, and lift off the cover.

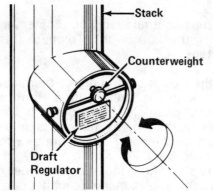

← Stack

Counterweight

Draft Regulator

The draft regulator on the stack opens automatically when the burner is running. To increase the air flow, screw the counterweight inward.

5. Screw in the bottom of the filter housing and open the oil shutoff valve.

The Pump Strainer

Some oil furnaces have a pump strainer, which is located on the pump that is attached to the burner/blower unit. Whenever you change or clean the oil filter, you should clean the strainer. Follow these steps:

1. Unbolt the cover of the pump housing where the oil line enters the burner; lift off the cover.
2. Remove the main gasket around the rim of the housing.
3. Remove the strainer; it is a cylindrical unit that has a wire mesh screen.
4. Soak the strainer in kerosene, and remove any sludge or debris with an old toothbrush. If the screen is ripped or bent, replace it with a new one of the same type.
5. Replace the strainer, install a new gasket, and bolt the cover back on.

The Draft Regulator

The draft regulator, located on the stack, is closed when the burner is off. When the burner is running, it opens automatically to let air into the chimney. Soot and rattling are signs that the regulator needs adjustment. Follow these steps:

1. Open the regulator and wipe it as clean as possible with a rag. This job is very messy, so wear old clothing and cover the floor with newspapers.

Radiant Heater Is Designed for Medium-Size Rooms

With the rising cost of energy, many people are turning to space heaters to help reduce their heating bills. The Aladdin Temp-Rite 9 radiant heater, model S-381, has an output of 9600 BTU's per hour—enough to heat a medium-to-small size room. The unit, marketed by ALH, Inc., has automatic lighting and shut-off features, and a removable fuel tank to ease refueling. The Temp-Rite 9 can operate 17 to 22 hours per 1.2 gallons of kerosene. No outside venting is required.

The unit is 23½ inches wide, 17½ inches high, and 13 inches deep; it weighs 25½ pounds.

Two D batteries supply the ignition source. The Temp-Rite 9 radiant heater is UL Listed.

Keep Steam Heating System Gauge Clean

Most steam heat systems have a water gauge on the front of the boiler assembly. This gauge's glass dial cover usually becomes so dirty that it can't be read. Cleaning, however, is easy. To clean the gauge, turn off the valves at the top and bottom of the gauge. Then, with a wrench, loosen and remove the nuts and washers that hold the gauge to the pipe. Pull the glass up and out of the bottom of its housing and wipe the gauge dial and glass clean.

2. After cleaning, screw the counterweight on the front of the regulator counterclockwise to increase the air flow or clockwise to decrease the air flow. If you have a professional service the furnace before each heating season, a regulator adjustment is part of regular maintenance.

The Stack Control

The stack control, which is located in the stack, is a safety device that monitors the operation of the oil burner. If the burner fails to ignite, the stack control may be the cause. Check it by following these steps:

1. Press the reset button on the stack control just once.
2. If the burner doesn't ignite, turn off the electrical power to the furnace.
3. Remove the bolts that hold the control to the stack.
4. Withdraw the sensor and its housing.
5. With a bottle brush dipped in soapy water, remove all soot from the control. Wipe the control dry.
6. Spread newspapers on the floor and disassemble the stack; it is slipped together in sections.
7. Clean each section of debris by tapping it on the newspaper-covered floor.
8. Carefully reassemble the sections in reverse order.
9. Replace the stack control in the stack.
10. Reseal the connection to the chimney with refractory cement, troweled on with a putty knife.

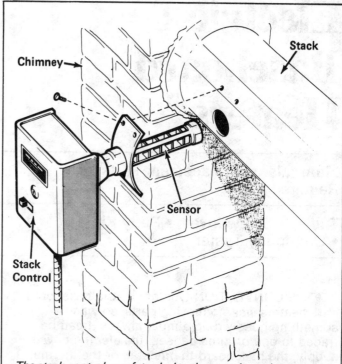

The stack control, a safety device that monitors the operation of the oil burner, should be cleaned monthly. To remove the control, turn off the power to the furnace; then back out the bolts that hold the control in the stack.

Burner Adjustments

Oil furnace burners are not very complicated, but they do require special equipment to service. It is recommended that you call a professional to clean and adjust the burner.

Device Recovers Wasted Flue Heat

It's estimated that from 30 to 50 percent of the heat produced by any central heating plant goes up the chimney. The Spiraflo heat reclaimer, made by Air Control Industries, Inc., delivers much of the heat that normally escapes up the flue by distributing this heat into cool areas. To install the unit, you remove a 24-inch section of flue pipe, replacing it with the heat reclaimer. Then, plug the device into an electrical outlet. When hot gas begins moving up the flue, a thermostatically controlled blower comes on. Cool air from the room is then swirled through heat-gathering fins, absorbing up to 50 percent of the heat going up the flue and delivering it to the area of your choice. The Spiraflo heat reclaimer is designed for 6-inch pipe, although reducers and enlargers are available for smaller and larger pipes. The device will work on central furnaces, wood-burning stoves, and free-standing fireplaces. The UL Listed product, which carries a one-year limited warranty, comes with installation instructions.

Some Oil Furnaces Have Electric-Eye Safety Switch

Instead of a stack control, some oil furnaces have an electric-eye safety switch, which serves the same purpose as a stack control. The electric-eye safety switch also can be cleaned. To clean the switch, turn off the power to the furnace. Remove the access cover over the photocell; it's held by hooks or retaining screws. Wipe the cover and switch clean to remove accumulated soot. Then, reassemble the switch, replace the cover, and turn the power back on.

Electric Baseboard Heaters

Materials • Replacement Parts as Required

Tools • Screwdriver • Putty Knife • Continuity Tester

THE CONVECTION-type of electric baseboard heaters has no moving parts, so when something goes wrong almost always it can be traced to one of three causes: the electric power supply, the baseboard thermostat, or the thermal cutout safety device. Sometimes, the heating element may fail; if it does, call a professional for repairs or replacement.

There is no routine maintenance you can perform on such heaters because nearly all problems are electrical in nature. When an electric baseboard heater fails to heat, follow these steps:

1. Check for a blown fuse or tripped circuit breaker at the main entrance panel. Some electric baseboard installations are on a separate circuit, especially in older homes. Look for a separate power panel if the main entrance panel checks out okay.
2. If you are satisfied that the baseboard is receiving power, turn off the power at the main entrance panel or subpanel.
3. Remove the front or end panels from the unit to gain access to the wiring. These panels usually are held by self-tapping metal screws; remove the screws to release the panels. Or the panels may be held by clips; lift them out, using a putty knife, if necessary, to pry them free.
4. Examine the wiring, making sure that it is connected properly. The wires are usually connected with wire nuts. Remove the wire nut at each connection, and make sure the wires are twisted together properly.
5. Replace the wire nuts, turn on the power, and test the unit. If it works, reassemble the unit.
6. If the unit still won't heat, check to see if it has a reset button near the wiring terminals to reactivate the thermal cutout. If it does, press the button and turn the thermostat up about 10 degrees.
7. If the heater still won't work, turn off the power, and disconnect one of the power leads to the thermal cutout. Then set the thermostat about 5 degrees above room temperature.

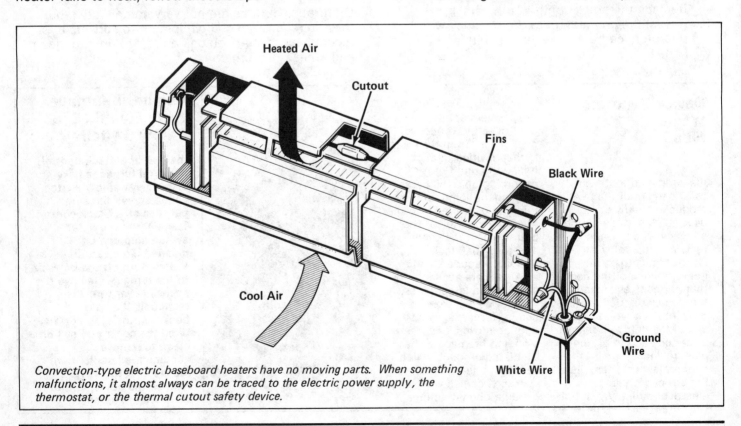

Convection-type electric baseboard heaters have no moving parts. When something malfunctions, it almost always can be traced to the electric power supply, the thermostat, or the thermal cutout safety device.

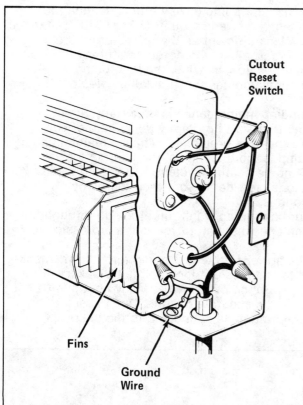

If the heater still won't work after checking the wiring connections, check to see if it has a reset button to reactivate the thermal cutout. If it does, press the button and turn the thermostat up about 10 degrees.

8. Clip the wire of a continuity tester to one terminal on the thermal cutout and touch the probe of the tester to the other terminal. If the tester lights or buzzes, the thermal cutout is okay. If not, install a new cutout device.
9. The cutout device is held to a mounting plate with two screws or bolts. Disconnect the wire from the other terminal and remove the mounting screws.
10. Install a new cutout device and connect the wires.
11. Turn on the power and test the heating unit. If it still won't work, the problem is probably the heating element; have a professional check the voltage rating in the resistance wire. If the element is faulty, have the element replaced. **Note:** If the heat is controlled by a wall thermostat, the thermostat could be faulty or malfunctioning. Refer to the section on "Thermostats" in this chapter.

If low heat—not no heat—is the problem with an electric baseboard heater, make sure that the unit is not being blocked by draperies, furniture, or other obstructions. If this is the problem, move the obstructions, reset the thermostat, push the reset button on the cutout device, and test the unit.

Portable Heater Uses Convection Principle to Heat a Room

The Flo-Aire convection heater made by Patton Electric Co., Inc., is designed for supplemental heat in a room. The portable heater pulls in cool air from the floor area and heats it through a network of heating fins. The warm air then flows out the top of the unit into the room. According to the manufacturer, the appliance never gets red hot, so it's safe around children, pets, and furniture. There are no moving parts, and the heater is quiet when operating. The Flo-Aire convection heater is available in two sizes; model H-12 is a 40-inch-long unit, and model H-15 is a 50-inch-long unit. The product, which has a woodgrain finish, carries a five-year warranty.

Portable Heater for Large Rooms

A portable spot-heater can heat a room inexpensively. The model 217 Watt Wattcher from Hamilton Beach, a division of Scovill, Inc., is designed to spot-heat a 12- by 12-foot room. At the "Hi" setting, the Watt Wattcher 217 uses 1500 watts. When the desired temperature in the room is reached, the heater automatically resets itself to 750 watts to maintain the comfort level. At the "Lo" setting, it maintains heat at 750 watts only. Cool air is drawn into vents at the top of the heater; warm air is discharged by a fan at the bottom. The control panel has a thermostat control, indicator light, and a positive on/off switch. The UL Listed Watt Wattcher 217 has a woodgrain finish, and is 16 inches high, 10 inches wide, and 6 inches deep. There also is a safety "tip switch" and overheat protector.

Heat Pumps

Materials • Rocks or Gravel • Pipe Insulation

Tools • Screwdriver • Vacuum Cleaner • Carpenter's Level • Pry Bar or 2 × 4

A HEAT PUMP functions on the same principle that refrigerators and air conditioners are based on; a liquid absorbs heat as it turns into a gas, and releases heat as it returns to a liquid state.

During the summer, the heat pump operates like a standard central air conditioner. During the winter, the heat pump reverses itself, and extracts heat from the cold air outside and releases it inside the house. The heat pump is very efficient when the outside temperature is around 45° to 50° F, but it becomes less efficient as the temperature drops. Thus, in areas where winter temperatures are consistently below freezing, the heat pump is usually supplemented by an auxiliary electric furnace.

Heat pump maintenance is important. Small problems that aren't promptly taken care of can lead to expensive problems. Because maintaining a heat pump is more technical than caring for the average home heating system, you should call a professional service person when the pump malfunctions.

If your heat pump won't run at all, go through the following checklist before you call a professional:

• Is the power to the heat pump turned on? Check for blown fuses or tripped circuit breakers at the main entrance panel. **Note:** Many heat pumps operate on separate circuits. Don't assume that the heat pump is connected to the main

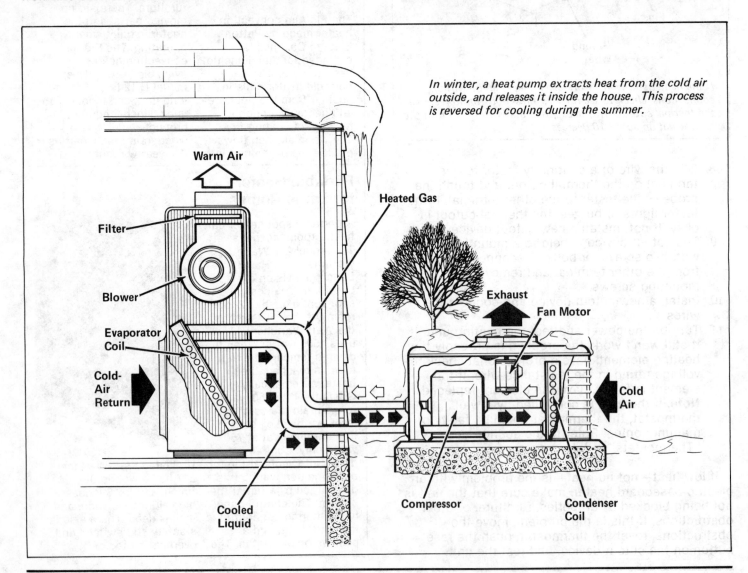

In winter, a heat pump extracts heat from the cold air outside, and releases it inside the house. This process is reversed for cooling during the summer.

entrance panel. Look for another panel, especially in an older home.

- If there is a separate power switch that controls the heat pump, make sure the switch is turned on.
- Is the thermostat set properly? Try raising it 5° F if the heat pump won't work in the heating mode; if it won't work in the cooling mode, try lowering the thermostat 5° F.
- After waiting 30 minutes, try pushing the reset button on the outside cabinet. Repeat if necessary.

Outdoor Maintenance

Like central air conditioners, heat pumps have outdoor units, which should be kept free of dirt and debris. To maintain the outdoor heat pump unit, follow these steps:

1. Turn off the electrical power to the heat pump.
2. Take out the retaining screws that hold the unit's grille in place, and remove the grille.
3. Clean out leaves, grass clippings, or other debris that may be blocking the updraft fans.
4. If you can, insert a vacuum cleaner hose between the fan blades to remove debris from the sides and bottom of the unit.
5. Check the concrete base of the heat pump to make sure it's level. Place a carpenter's level on the top of the unit and check front to back and side to side.
6. If the concrete base isn't level, lift it with a pry bar or length of 2 x 4, and wedge rocks or gravel under the base to level it.
7. Check the insulation on the pipes that run from the heat pump to the house. If the insulation is faulty, install new insulation, available at heating supply stores. Installation instructions are normally provided.

Reversing Problems

A reversing valve on the heat pump automatically switches the pump from the heating mode to the cooling mode and back again, as needed. If there is a heavy buildup of ice on the condenser coil, the heat pump is not defrosting properly; if there is no ice at all, or if the heat pump stays in the defrosting cycle for longer than about 15 minutes, the pump is stuck. Follow these steps:

1. Check the heat pump unit; if leaves, snow, or other debris are blocking the flow of air, clear the obstructions away.
2. If removing any blockage doesn't relieve the problem, wait one hour.
3. If the ice hasn't disappeared after one hour, set the heat pump control to "emergency heat," which turns the pump off and keeps it from running. Call a professional immediately.

Power Interruptions

If a heat pump has been off for more than an hour because of a blown fuse, a tripped circuit breaker, or a utility power failure, the unit should not be put into operation for about six to eight hours. If it is, the valves could be damaged. Follow these steps:

1. Set the heat pump control to "emergency heat." This turns the pump off and keeps it from running.
2. Leave the heat pump in this mode for about six to eight hours.
3. After waiting, switch the pump to its normal heating or cooling setting.
4. If little or no heat is generated at this point, or if the heat pump isn't cooling (if you are using it in the cooling mode), call a professional.

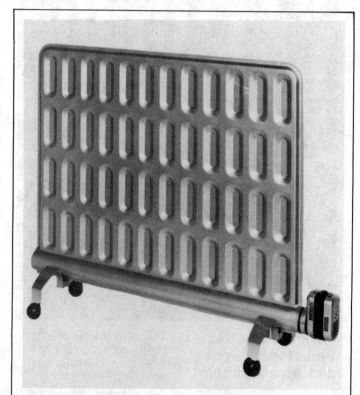

Panel Radiators Feature Slim Design

When people think of radiators, they think of the usual finned column radiator that's common in many older homes. But there's also a slim panel radiator such as the portable models made in England by Dimplex Heating Ltd., and marketed in the United States by Dimplex, Inc. Due to their design, Dimplex panel radiators provide a balance of half radiant heat and half convected heat. The 750-watt model B310 delivers 2559 BTU's; the 1000-watt model C220 provides 3412 BTU's; and the 1250-watt model ER316 yields 4265 BTU's. All three panel radiators may be easily rolled from room to room. They are UL Listed and available in white or gold colors.

Insulate Ducting Through Rooms Not Air Conditioned

Over a period of time, you can save money by insulating the ducts that carry cooled air through non-air-conditioned rooms. Ducts that aren't insulated invite heat gain, which cuts down on the efficiency of the cooling unit. Also, uninsulated ducts can cause condensation troubles.

Portable Electric Radiator for Spot and Area Heating

The DeLonghi electric radiant and convection heater, made in Italy and marketed by DeLonghi-America, is a permanently sealed, oil-filled, portable radiator. The unit features an energy-saving thermostat that responds to room air temperature—not the temperature of the radiator itself—and shuts off the heating element when the selected room temperature is reached.

The oil in the radiator continues to radiate heat after the thermostat has shut down the heating element. The radiator also features a low surface temperature that DeLonghi-America says makes it ideal for children's rooms and nurseries. According to the manufacturer, the radiator emits no fumes, odor, or dust. It's 18 inches long, 25.4 inches high, and 6.3 inches wide. The radiator, which weighs 38 pounds, can be easily rolled from room to room. It operates on regular house current.

Portable Heater Designed for Use in Tight Quarters

A lightweight, portable electric heater that can be put to work most anywhere it's needed, even in tight quarters, is made by Air Care Industries, Inc. The company's model 6200 Big Heat portable heater weighs 3 pounds, 8 ounces, and is 4¾ inches wide, 5 inches high, and 6 inches deep. The heating element has a coil-type design; a squirrel-cage blower circulates heat evenly. An easy-to-operate thermostatically controlled heater, the model 6200 has a four-position switch that includes a 1,200-watt setting and a 1,500-watt setting, which is the maximum allowed under UL regulations. A fan-only setting is designed for summer cooling. The Big Heat heater has a low center of gravity to resist tipping, a safety tip-over switch, and an overheat protector. The steel case has a vinyl woodgrain finish and a chrome front grille. There's a handy retainer strap on the 6-foot-long power cord. The product is UL Listed. There are two other Big Heat models available from Air Care Industries.

Tape Seals Ducts Permanently

Forced-air heating ducts that are leaking at connections can cost you plenty in fuel. With Insta-Seal duct sealer tape, ducts can be made leakproof, moistureproof, and dustproof. The tape, a product of Diversified Specialties, Inc./Durkee-Atwood Co., is available for square or rectangular ducting, No. DS5256, and round or oval ducts, No. DS5261. The duct tape is 100-percent butyl rubber with a pressure-sensitive

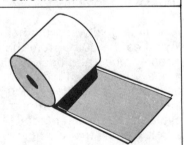

backing. It comes with either an aluminized or Tedlar facing; its surface temperature range is −45° to 280° F. According to the manufacturer, the tape conforms easily to ducting, won't crack, and always stays pliable because it never dries.

Central Air Conditioning

Materials • Household Detergent • Liquid Bleach • Wire Coat Hanger • Duct Tape • Condenser Coil Cleaner • Rags • Pipe Insulation • Gravel or Rocks • Condenser Cover and Cord • Furnace Filter

Tools • Screwdriver • Stiff Brush • Hand Mirror • Soft Brush • Plastic Spray Bottle • Fin Comb • Carpenter's Level • Pry Bar or 2×4

MOST CENTRAL air conditioners are hooked to a home's heating plant so the same motor, blower, and ductwork used for heating are used to distribute cool air.

When the air conditioner is operating, hot air inside the house flows to the furnace through the return-air duct. The hot air is moved by the blower across the cooled evaporator coil in the plenum of the furnace, and is then delivered through the air ducts to cool the house. When the air conditioner is working but the house doesn't cool, the problem is probably in the distribution system.

A central air conditioning system should be professionally inspected and adjusted before the start of every cooling season, but don't limit your maintenance to this annual checkup. While there are not many repairs you can make, there are specific maintenance and troubleshooting procedures you can follow.

Before attempting any diagnosis or repairs, or calling a professional, run down the following checklist when the system develops a problem:

- Is the system receiving power? Check for blown fuses or a tripped circuit breaker at the main entrance panel, or at a separate fuse panel.
- Did you push the reset button on the furnace or air conditioning control panel or the blower motor?
- Lower the thermostat setting 5° F, and try starting the unit.

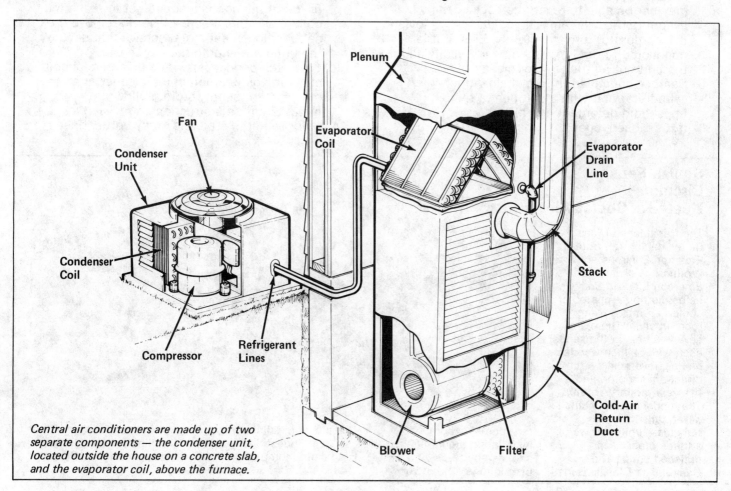

Central air conditioners are made up of two separate components — the condenser unit, located outside the house on a concrete slab, and the evaporator coil, above the furnace.

Heating and Cooling

Caution: Before doing any work on the air conditioning system, make sure the power to the system—both the condenser and evaporator assemblies—is turned off. Shut off the power to the air conditioner at the main entrance panel. Many air conditioners operate on separate circuits; look for another fused circuit, especially if you own an older home.

The Evaporator

The evaporator is located directly above the furnace in the plenum. If the plenum has foil-wrapped insulation at its front, you generally can clean the evaporator. If the plenum is a sealed sheet-metal box, don't attempt to open it. To clean an evaporator, follow these steps:

1. Turn off the electrical power to the system.
2. Remove the foil-wrapped insulation at the front of the plenum; usually, it is taped in place. Save the tape; you can use it later.
3. Use a screwdriver to remove the screws that secure the access plate behind the insulation.
4. Use a stiff brush to clean the entire underside of the evaporator. A hand mirror can be helpful in letting you see what you're doing. **Note:** You may not be able to reach the back of the evaporator for cleaning. If you can't, try moving the evaporator forward slightly. Even if it is connected to rigid pipes, you can usually slide the unit out a little way for cleaning.
5. Remove and clean the tray below the evaporator unit with a solution of mild household detergent and bleach.
6. If it's closed, open the weep hole in the tray with a short length of wire coat hanger. Then, pour a little liquid household bleach into the weep hole to help prevent fungus growth. **Note:** In extremely hot weather, check the drain line and tray every day or two. If there is much moisture in the tray, the weep hole from the tray to the drain line may be clogged. Keep it open with a short length of wire.
7. Replace the tray, move the evaporator unit back into position, attach the access plate, and replace the insulation.

The Condenser

In most central air conditioning systems, the condenser unit is outside the house where accumulated dirt and debris can prevent the unit from operating efficiently. Because the condenser fan moves air across the condenser coil the condenser unit must be cleaned on the intake side. Before you turn off the power to the unit, check to see which direction the air moves across the coil. Then turn off the power and follow these steps:

1. Cut any grass, weeds, or vines that have grown around the condenser unit.
2. Remove the grille or metal panel from the side or top of the condenser cabinet to reach the condenser. Use a screwdriver to remove the self-tapping sheet metal screws that secure the grille or panel to the condenser.
3. Clean the condenser with a commercial coil cleaner; you can obtain the cleaner at a refrigeration supply store. Follow the manufacturer's instructions.
4. Using water in a plastic spray bottle, rinse

Stylish Fans Circulate Heated or Cooled Air

The Casablanca Classic Series ceiling fan from Emerson Environmental Products, a division of Emerson Electric Co., helps distribute heated or cooled air into a living room in style. There are seven models in the series, each with 52-inch wooden blades, reversing switch, direct-drive motor, and a five-year motor warranty. The model choice includes seven fans in four finishes—white, brown, antique brass, and polished brass. The Casablanca Classic Series fans come with an installation mounting kit and step-by-step instructions. And, if you have any installation or servicing questions, you can call Emerson's ceiling fan installation telephone "hot line" for help. Other ceiling fan models are designed for other rooms in your home.

away the cleaner from the condenser coil. Don't use a garden hose; the water pressure will be too great.

5. Clean the condenser fins with a soft brush. If the fins are bent, straighten them with a fin comb, but use the fin comb carefully; the fins are easily damaged. Fin combs are sold at most appliance parts outlets.

6. Check the concrete base of the condenser to make sure it's level. On the top of the unit use a carpenter's level to check front to back and side to side.

7. If the pad isn't level, lift the pad with a pry bar or length of 2 × 4, and wedge gravel or rocks under the concrete to level it.

During the time of year when the condenser unit is not in use, cover it with a commercial air conditioner cover, a tarp, or other weatherproof covering. Secure the cover with a cord. *Caution: Never run the air conditioning system with the cover in place.*

The Filters

A central air conditioning system uses the same filter system as the furnace. For service and maintenance, refer to the procedure outlined in "Gas and Electric Furnaces" in this chapter.

The Refrigerant

Freon refrigerant, made by E. I. duPont de Nemours & Co., is used in air conditioning systems. If the air conditioning system doesn't have the proper amount of refrigerant, little or no cooling takes

You can clean the fins on the condenser with a soft brush to remove accumulated dirt; you may have to remove a protective grille to reach the fins.

place. If you suspect a refrigerant problem, call a professional to recharge the system. *Caution: Don't try to recharge the system yourself; the refrigerant is extremely volatile and can be dangerous.* Done properly, this maintenance procedure requires special equipment.

You can, however, make one repair to the refrigerant system. Examine the refrigerant lines running from the condenser to the evaporator inside the house. If the insulation is damaged or worn, it can reduce the cooling efficiency of the unit. Replace damaged or worn refrigerant-line insulation as soon as possible with new insulation of the same type.

Spray Made to Clean Coils and Fins on Air Conditioners the Easy Way

A clean air conditioner operates more efficiently. Coil & Fin Cleaner, from Con-Serv, Inc., is formulated to dissolve grease and grime on all air conditioners—central and room units—heat pumps, and electronic air cleaners. According to Con-Serv, the product can also reduce air conditioning costs and pitting and oxidation on coils and fins. It is available in a 32-ounce plastic spray bottle.

For use with: **1** window and wall units **2** central air and heat pumps **3** electronic air cleaners

Reduces pitting and oxidation on coils and fins.

Screwdriver Has Ratcheting Action

Searching around for the right screwdriver for an installation or maintenance job can be frustrating. The Pocket Driver, made by Litton Industries, is a self-contained screwdriver set that holds the four most commonly used screwdriver bits inside its handle—two slotted and two Phillips-head bits. The tool features a reversible ratchet head. According to the manufacturer, the Pocket Driver has more than 10 times the turning power of an ordinary screwdriver.

Room Air Conditioners

Materials • Appliance Cord • Household Detergent • Rags • No. 20 Non-Detergent Motor Oil • Wire Coat Hanger

Tools • 20,000-Ohm, 2-Watt, Wire-Wound Resistor • Screwdriver • Continuity Tester • Volt-Ohm Meter • Vacuum Cleaner • Fin Comb • Allen Wrench • Adjustable Wrench

ROOM AIR CONDITIONERS, also called window units, work the same way central air conditioners do. Depending on its size, a room air conditioner may cool only the room it's located in, or it may be able to cool adjoining rooms too.

There are a number of minor repairs that you can make, and regular maintenance will keep your window air conditioner running more efficiently. Before making any diagnosis, repairs, or calling a professional for service, follow this checklist if your room air conditioner develops problems:

- Is the unit plugged into the power outlet?
- Check for blown fuses or a tripped circuit breaker at the main entrance panel.
- Press the reset button—if present—on the control panel or motor housing.
- Lower the thermostat setting 5° F and try starting the unit.
- Reset the control switch.

Caution: Before doing any work on an air conditioner, make sure it's unplugged. Room air conditioners have one or two capacitors, located behind the control panel and near the fan. Capacitors store electricity, even after the power to the appliance is turned off. Before you do any internal work on an air conditioner, you must unplug it and discharge the capacitors, or you could receive a severe electrical shock.

Discharging a Capacitor

To discharge the capacitors on a room air conditioner, follow these steps:

1. Unplug the air conditioner.
2. Locate the capacitor(s); it looks like a large dry-cell battery. It is usually behind the control panel near the fan.
3. Fasten the clips of a 20,000-ohm, 2-watt, wire-wound resistor to the terminals of the capacitor to discharge it. **Note:** If the capacitor has three terminal posts, connect the resistor to one outer terminal and the center terminal;

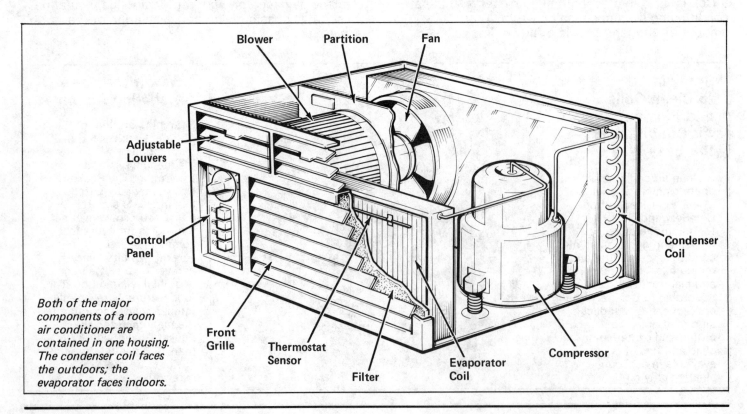

Both of the major components of a room air conditioner are contained in one housing. The condenser coil faces the outdoors; the evaporator faces indoors.

Blower   Partition   Fan

Adjustable Louvers

Control Panel

Front Grille

Thermostat Sensor

Filter

Evaporator Coil

Compressor

Condenser Coil

then to the other outer terminal and the center terminal.

4. Disconnect the resistor.

The Power Cord

The power cord that connects the air conditioner to a wall outlet may become worn, and fail to supply electricity to the appliance. If this is the case, follow these steps:

1. Unplug the air conditioner.
2. Remove the control knobs from the air conditioner's control panel; usually these knobs pull straight off. Or the knobs may have tiny setscrews in their bases; loosen these screws and pull off the knobs.
3. Remove the control panel of the air conditioner. It may be held by self-tapping machine screws, or it fits onto clips or hooks.
4. Disconnect the power cord's wires from their terminal connections, and test the cord with a continuity tester. For details on testing the cord see "Repairing or Replacing Appliance Cords" in the Electrical Work chapter. If the cord is faulty, replace it.

The Filter

The air conditioner's filter should be cleaned—or replaced—at the start of the cooling season. It should then be cleaned once a month during the season. Follow these steps:

1. Unplug the air conditioner.
2. Remove the grille covering the air filter; usually the grille is held in place by clips.
3. Carefully remove the filter from behind the grille to avoid tearing it.
4. Wash the filter with a solution of mild household detergent and water. Rinse it well and dry.
5. Replace the filter and grille.

The Evaporator and Condenser Coils

The air conditioner's evaporator and condenser coils should be cleaned at the start of each cooling season and every month during the season. Dirty coils keep the unit from cooling effectively. If you live in a dusty area, you may have to clean the coils more often. Follow this procedure:

1. Unplug the air conditioner.
2. Remove the grille or front panel or otherwise disassemble the appliance to gain access to the evaporator and the condenser coil.
3. Discharge the capacitor(s), using a 20,000-ohm, 2-watt, wire-wound resistor. Follow the procedure detailed above.

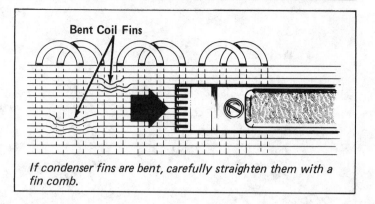

If condenser fins are bent, carefully straighten them with a fin comb.

4. Using a vacuum cleaner and rags, remove dirt and debris from the coil.
5. If any fins on the condenser coil are bent, straighten them with a fin comb. The comb slides into the spaces between the fins. Fin combs are available at most appliance parts outlets. *Caution: The fins are made of thin aluminum; be careful not to damage them.*
6. Reassemble the appliance.

The Selector Switch

The selector switch, which is directly behind the control panel, turns the air conditioner on. Turn the switch on and through its various settings. If the unit will not run at any setting, and it is receiving power, chances are the switch is faulty. Follow these steps:

1. Unplug the air conditioner.
2. Remove the control knobs from the air conditioner's control panel; usually these knobs pull straight off, or they may be held by setscrews.
3. Remove the control panel from the air conditioner.
4. Examine the terminals of the selector switch for signs of burnt insulation or signs of burning on the terminals. If you see any such indications, replace the switch with a new one of the same type.
5. Using a screwdriver, remove the screws that hold the selector switch to the control panel or frame.
6. Disconnect the power wires from the switch terminals.
7. Install the new switch and reassemble the control panel.
8. Test the appliance. If the new switch doesn't solve the problem, call a professional.

The Thermostat

The thermostat for the air conditioner is located directly behind the control panel. It has a special sensing bulb, which extends from the thermostat to

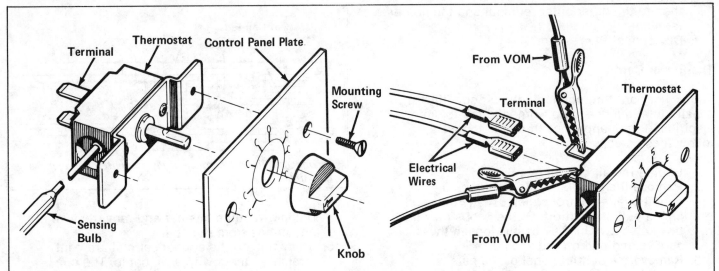

The thermostat, which is located directly behind the control panel (left), has a special sensing bulb that extends from the thermostat to the evaporator coil area. To test the thermostat, disconnect its electrical wires. Then connect one probe of the volt-ohm meter (VOM) to each terminal (right).

the evaporator coil area. If the air conditioner doesn't cool, the thermostat could be faulty. To check and replace a thermostat, follow these steps:

1. Unplug the air conditioner.
2. Remove the control knobs and control panel.
3. Locate the thermostat and remove it by removing its mounting screws. Because the sensing bulb must be returned to its exact position, mark the location of the bulb with a piece of tape before you remove the thermostat.
4. Disconnect the wires to the thermostat.
5. Set a volt-ohm meter (VOM) to the R × 1 scale.
6. Connect one probe of the VOM to each terminal of the thermostat.
7. Turn the thermostat temperature control dial to its coldest setting. If the meter reads zero ohms, the thermostat is operating. If the meter shows a high reading, the thermostat should be replaced.
   Note: If the thermostat has more than two

lead wires connected to it, not counting the sensing bulb, call a professional for service.
8. Install the new thermostat, and replace the control panel and knobs.

The Motor and Compressor

Problems with the air conditioner's motor or compressor can keep the unit from cooling adequately. If your room air conditioner runs but doesn't cool, and cleaning the evaporator and condenser coil and replacing the thermostat doesn't solve the problem, the motor, the compressor, or both could be faulty. Call a professional for service.

The Fan

The air conditioner's fan seldom causes problems, but when a fan does malfunction, the trouble is usually caused by loose or dirty blades. If the fan doesn't work, or if it's noisy, follow these steps:

Air Conditioner Cover Seals Out Dust and Dirt

The air conditioner cover weather seal from Stanley Hardware, a division of The Stanley Works, is designed to seal out dust and draft infiltration through window air conditioners. The cover is made of nylon vinyl material that reportedly resists tearing and remains flexible in cold weather. Covers are sold in three sizes: 16 by 27 by 18 inches, 18 by 27 by 22 inches, and 19 by 28 by 30 inches. The covers, available in white, have a double-strap fastening system to hold them securely in position.

1. Unplug the air conditioner.
2. Disassemble the appliance to gain access to the fan.
3. Discharge the capacitor(s), using a 20,000-ohm, 2-watt, wire-wound resistor. Follow the procedure detailed above.
4. With a vacuum cleaner and a soft rag, clean the fan.
5. The fan is fastened at its hub to a motor shaft by means of a setscrew. Tighten the setscrew with a screwdriver or an Allen wrench, whichever is required. If the unit has a round vent fan, tighten the fan on the motor shaft by inserting a screwdriver with a long shaft through a port to reach the setscrew.
6. If the fan is noisy, check the bolts that attach the fan housing; if they are loose, tighten them with a wrench.
7. Most fans are permanently lubricated and sealed at the factory, but some have oil ports for lubrication. If the fan has oil ports, apply several drops of No. 20 non-detergent motor oil to each port at the beginning of the cooling season.
8. If you suspect that the fan motor is faulty, you can test it with a volt-ohm meter (VOM). Disconnect the wires from the fan motor terminals.
9. Set the VOM to the R × 1 scale.
10. Connect one probe of the VOM to each of the terminals. If the meter reads between about 3 and 30 ohms, the motor is okay. If the meter shows a zero or extremely high reading, replace the motor.
11. To remove the motor, disconnect the power wires and remove the fan and the motor's mounting bolts.
    Note: If the condenser coil must be removed to get the fan out of the housing, don't try to remove the motor. Call a professional.
12. Install a new motor by reversing Step 11.
13. Reassemble the air conditioner.

The Drain Ports

Condensed moisture and water vapor from the evaporator coil are funneled through the drain ports or an opening between the partition barrier between the evaporator coil and the condenser coil. At this point, the fan blows the moisture against the condenser coil, where the water is dissipated.

The air conditioner's drain ports can become clogged with dirt. The result is water leaking from the unit, usually through the bottom of the grille. To prevent clogging, clean the ports twice during the season with a short piece of wire coat hanger.

Also check the condenser side of the air conditioner. Some models have a drain port along the bottom edge of the cabinet frame. If so, clean this port when you clean the other ports.

Weatherstripping Can Seal Window Air Conditioner

Room air conditioners can be difficult to seal, especially where the bottom rail of the window sash meets the top of the air conditioner. An ideal seal can be made with two lengths of self-adhesive foam weatherstripping. Buy the thickest foam that you can. Then, cut a length the width of the bottom rail of the lower window sash and attach it under the sash in two parallel rows—one flush with the outside edge of the window and the other flush with the inside edge. Push the window sash down tight against the air conditioner so the weatherstripping is compressed. Then, with a small finishing nail or wood screw, secure the sash in this position by driving the fastener into the sash channel just above the top rail of the sash. When you want to remove the air conditioner, simply remove the fastener and raise the sash.

Heater-Fan Unit Is Designed to Heat, Cool Entire Room

The Heater Plus Fan, model HF-150, from Patton Electric Co., Inc., uses the convection forced-air principle to provide heating and cooling for an entire room at low cost. According to the manufacturer, the heater never gets red hot. The appliance comes with a 60-minute timer that automatically shuts the unit off as programmed. An adjustable thermostat maintains room temperature at any desired level. The unit has a multi-function control that allows the 6-inch fan to be used independently for cooling in summer. An automatic antifreeze setting can help prevent frozen water pipes, protect porch flowers, and keep other exposed areas from getting too cold. The Heater Plus Fan model HF-150 weighs 4 pounds, and is 16¾ inches high, 11 inches wide, and 7 inches deep.

Humidity Control

Materials • Pipe Insulation • Mildewcide • 6-Mil Polyfilm

Tools • Vacuum Cleaner

DURING WINTER, many homes suffer from a lack of humidity; in summer, many homes have too much humidity. A lack of moisture during the winter can make a house seem cold, even though the heat may be turned up. Low humidity also can cause furniture to dry out, crack, and loosen at the joints, and can cause you discomfort, including cracked lips and dry skin. Static electricity buildup is another problem caused by low humidity.

Too much moisture, or humidity, in the summer makes you feel uncomfortably hot. Cold water pipes drip, air conditioning efficiency is reduced, and your power bills go up.

Adding Humidity

In the winter, there are several things you can do to add humidity to your home. The best way is with a humidifier that attaches to the heating system. Several types are available; most are relatively inexpensive and have been designed for do-it-yourself installation. Complete mounting instructions are furnished with such kits.

Free-standing humidifiers that plug into a wall outlet also are available. These units have a moisture-absorbing belt that turns in a trough of water. A fan blows through the belt to distribute moisture into the air. Some models are connected directly to your home's water supply; others require you to fill them with water every day or two.

Other ways you can add humidity to your home include:

- Place containers of water near the heating plant. The water will evaporate and moisten the dry air that circulates throughout the house.
- Disconnect the duct work on a clothes dryer so that the moisture from the appliance circulates throughout the house.
- Leave a bathroom door open when taking a shower.
- Leave pots and pans uncovered when cooking with water.
- Open the door to the dishwasher and let the dishes air-dry. This also will save money on electric bills.

Dehumidifying

Reducing the moisture in the air during the summer is more difficult than adding it. Mechanical dehumidifiers and air conditioners are helpful, but

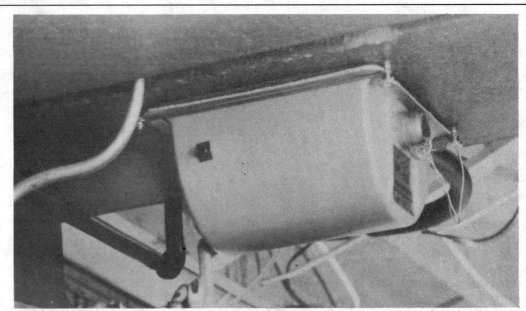

Humidifier Designed for Do-It-Yourselfer

"Good-Bye-Dry" is the name of a whole-house humidifier from Comfort Enterprises Co. It is designed for installation on any forced-air heating system. According to the manufacturer, the humidifer will maintain the comfort level of humidity at 35 to 40 percent. Tools required for installation include a drill and ³⁄₁₆-inch bit, screwdriver, tin snips, and pliers. The humidifier has a 14-gallon-per-day capacity for homes with about 2,000 square feet of living space. The humidifier's design is said to eliminate the need for a humidistat because it only produces moisture when the furnace is operating; an optional humidistat is available for special applications. The unit uses 5 watts of power—about the same as an electric clock. Installation and operating instructions are included.

they aren't the total answer. The best control involves following as many of these steps as you can:

1. Wrap all exposed cold water pipes with pipe insulation.
2. Keep the house well ventilated. A roof vent is helpful; installation instructions are covered elsewhere in this chapter. When taking a bath or shower, open bathroom windows.
3. Keep cooking utensils covered when in use.
4. Vent clothes dryers to the outside and make sure the joints of the ductwork are wrapped tightly with duct tape.
5. Ventilate basement spaces with a window exhaust fan.
6. Use mildewcides to remove any mildew in damp areas.
7. Keep all drains open.
8. Regularly vacuum the coils of the dehumidifier and the evaporator coils on the back panel of the refrigerator.
9. Keep refrigerator drip pans empty and clean.
10. Keep the drain ports of room air conditioners open.
11. Repair house gutters and downspouts so rain water is funneled away from the foundation walls of the house.
12. If insects are not a problem, open the damper to the fireplace.
13. Insulate crawl spaces; lay 6-mil polyfilm over bare earth in crawl spaces. Lap the polyfilm joints 6 inches and weight the material with bricks or stones.

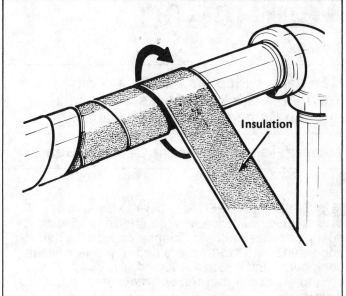

Too much moisture, or humidity, in the summer can make cold water pipes drip. To counter this, you can wrap all the exposed cold water pipes with pipe insulation.

14. Don't leave buckets and other containers filled with water setting anyplace in your home.
15. Keep air conditioning filters clean; change replaceable filters at least twice during the cooling season.
16. Run the range hood vent while cooking.
17. Keep windows slightly open if you don't use mechanical or cooling devices to lower the humidity.

Kit Eliminates Filling Humidifier by Hand

If you own a console humidifier, you know how difficult it is to continually refill the unit with water. You can eliminate this problem with a "Humidify without Buckets" console humidifier automatic water fill kit that may be installed in just minutes with no special tools. Marketed by Comfort Enterprises Co., the product not only eliminates filling by hand, but helps to reduce humidifier mineral scale. The kit includes a self-tapping saddle valve that you connect to a copper or PVC water pipe. Then, you route up to 20 feet of flexible water tubing with the necessary connections to the humidifier. A float valve maintains a constant water level within the humidifier.

Kit Has What You Need to Maintain a Belt-Type Humidifier

If you have a belt-type humidifier, the Vapo-Kit, from Twinoak Products, Inc., has all the chemicals and replacement parts you need for maintenance.

The kit includes a 20- by 63-inch universal belt that can be trimmed to fit if necessary; a 32-ounce bottle of Vapo-Fresh humidifier water treatment; a 32-ounce bottle of Vapo-Eze humidifier cleaner and mineral remover; and an instruction booklet.

Ventilation

Materials • Pipe Insulation • 6-Mil Polyfilm • Bricks or Rocks • Asphalt Roofing Cement or Adhesive Caulking

Tools • Tape Measure • Caulking Gun

HOUSES, LIKE PEOPLE, have to breathe in order to function properly. With efforts to save energy, houses are being blanketed with insulation and sealed with storm doors and windows, caulking compound, and weatherstripping. The result is a structure so tight that trapped moisture vapor can't escape.

Although a house should have all the energy-saving devices possible, it also should have a venting system that works efficiently. The proper use of exhaust fans and vents is, therefore, crucial to keeping a home cool in the summer and dry all year long.

Attics

Because heat rises, attic ventilation is very important. Without proper ventilation an attic can become extremely hot during the summer. The hot air that collects in the attic also carries moisture that should be expelled.

1. If an attic is insulated, a roof ventilator should be installed. The procedure is outlined in "Installing Roof Ventilators" in this chapter.
2. There should be enough soffit vents to ventilate the house adequately. If you don't have enough soffit vents, or if a soffit vent is damaged and must be replaced, you can purchase round and rectangular soffit vents at a home center store.
3. Gable vents are installed in the roof gables at either end of the house. There should be enough vents to ventilate the attic adequately.

Note: Without a vapor barrier on the insulation, figure about 1 square foot of vent for every 300 square feet of ceiling. If there is a vapor barrier you need 1 square foot of vent for every 600 square feet of ceiling. Divide the amount of vent area needed between gable vents and soffit vents.

Moisture-Producing Areas

Any areas of your home where moisture can accumulate needs to be properly ventilated. Excess moisture in bathrooms can loosen wall and ceiling tiles, delaminate wall coverings, pop floor tiles, and rust and corrode fixtures. Other areas where moisture can build up are kitchens, laundry rooms, and basements. To control the humidity in these areas, follow as many of these steps as you can:

1. Open a window slightly when the room is being used. This will expel the moisture.
2. Run the exhaust fan to help reduce the moisture.

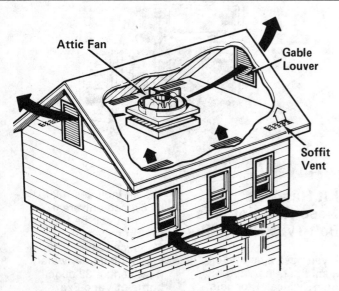

Because heat rises, attic ventilation is very important. Without proper ventilation temperatures in the attic can reach more than 170° F during the summer.

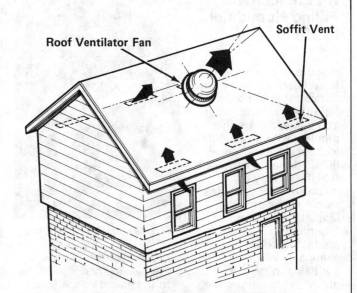

If an attic is insulated, a roof ventilator should be installed. And, there should be enough soffit vents to ventilate the house properly.

3. In an inside bathroom, install a vent fan in the ceiling; vent the air into an attic crawl space, or through ductwork to the outside.
4. When cooking, use the exhaust fan on a range hood to remove moisture.
5. If kitchen moisture is a serious problem, install a vent fan in an exterior wall. Run this exhaust fan when the dishwasher, range, or other heat or moisture-producing appliances are in operation.
6. To control moisture in a basement laundry room, install a basement exhaust fan in a window in or near the laundry area. In an extremely large basement two fans, one at each end, should be used.
7. Wrap all exposed cold water pipes with pipe insulation to prevent condensation.
8. If there is no way to install an exhaust fan, or if opening a window slightly is too troublesome, you can install siding louvers. Siding louvers are vents that are fitted into the siding. Some are round vents that fit into holes drilled in the siding; others are aluminum wedges that are driven under the siding with a hammer. Both types of vents are effective, easy to install, and inexpensive.

   Note: If the paint on the exterior walls covering the kitchen, bathroom, or laundry area bubbles and cracks, siding louvers can prevent this from happening again.

Crawl Spaces

Crawl spaces under a house or enclosed porch need cross-ventilation to prevent moisture buildup. Usually, local building codes specify a certain amount of vent space per square foot of crawl space area. This figure isn't critical; if you have a moisture problem, one or two vents opposite each other should handle the situation. To control moisture in crawl spaces follow these steps:

1. Put down a layer of 6-mil polyfilm in crawl spaces, and under porches and decks to prevent ground moisture from rotting wood supports and siding.
2. Overlap the polyfilm about 6 inches at the seams.
3. At sidewalls, run the polyfilm up the wall about 6 to 8 inches. Hold it in place with a couple of dollops of asphalt roofing cement or adhesive caulking.
4. Weight down the polyfilm with bricks or stones.

Gutters and Downspouts

Don't overlook the moisture from gutters and downspouts that can cause house siding to rot. Gutters and downspouts should be kept in good repair. Use splashblocks under downspouts to carry water away from the house.

Duct Fan Boosts Heating or Cooling Air Flow

If you have a room that's hard to heat or cool, Energaire, a fan device made by Tjernlund Products, Inc., may solve this problem. It fits into an existing round or rectangular duct that is 6 inches or larger, and boosts the air flow into a room that needs it. Only three tools are required to mount the device in the duct—an electric drill, tin snips, and a screwdriver. The Energaire operates on 120-volt AC and uses less than 30 watts. According to the company, its motor never needs re-oiling. The product comes with a one-year limited warranty and installation instructions.

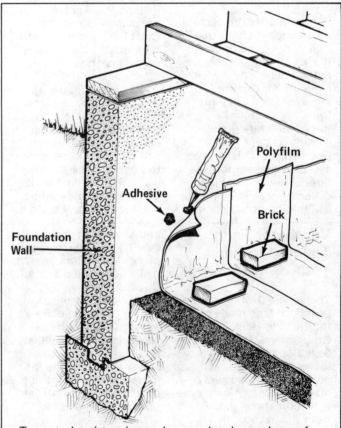

To control moisture in crawl spaces, lay down a layer of polyfilm. You can keep it in place with asphalt roofing cement or adhesive caulking and bricks and stones.

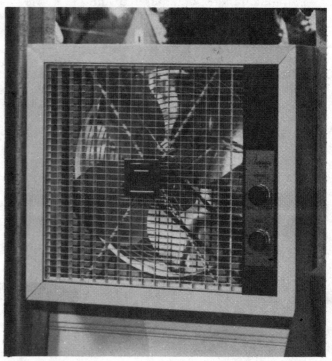

Air Cleaner Designed for Most Forced-Air Systems

"Clear Day" is the name of an electronic air cleaner that is designed to clean the air throughout the entire house. The device, made by Air Control Industries, Inc., fits into the air filter slot of a forced-air heating and cooling system.
Once you've replaced your system's present furnace filter with the Clear Day collector cell, you plug the cell into its power pack.

Then, you plug the power pack into the nearest 110-volt outlet. No tools are necessary for installation. According to the manufacturer, the Clear Day electronic air cleaner attracts up to 99 percent of the pollen and other damaging contaminants in the air, and uses no more power than a 25-watt light bulb. Periodically, you should disconnect the collector cell from the power pack to wash the cell in soapy water. The product is UL Listed and comes with a one-year limited warranty.

Window Fan Can Ventilate the Average Five-Room Home

An easily installed window fan that's designed to perform all the functions of a whole-house attic fan, at less cost, is the Autumaire whole-house window fan made by the Wolverine Fan Co. According to the manufacturer, it moves up to 3,000 cubic feet of air per minute to ventilate the average five-room home.

The model W3000 Autumaire fits into a window opening and is fastened with two screws. You then plug it into the nearest outlet. The fan features a thermostatically controlled, two-speed, $\frac{1}{8}$-horsepower motor that is electrically reversible for air exhaust or intake. Wolverine says the belt-drive and resilient-based permanent-split-capacitor motor provides quiet operation, and operates for about two cents an hour. The model W3000 is UL Listed.

Ventilator Fans Tailored to Fit Your Home's Needs

The series of whole-house ventilator fans made by the NuTone Housing Group offers a wide selection of blade sizes, louver dimensions, and motor and horsepower sizes. NuTone dealers have a specifications guide from which you can choose the model to meet your needs. The NuTone fans feature a belt drive

and sealed fan-drive bearings that never require oiling. The motors are resilient-mounted and offer thermal overload protection. Louvers at the ceiling open and close automatically with the fan's operation, and there is a felt seal on each louver that cushions the louvers for quiet opening and closing. The NuTone fans are tailored to fit standard rafter and truss construction; installation instructions are furnished with each kit.

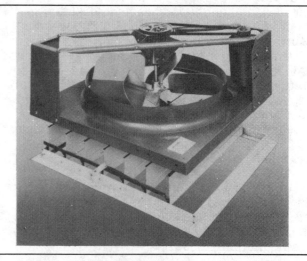

Installing Roof Ventilators

Materials • Turbine Ventilator Kit • 20d Common Nail • String • Chalk • Flashing Sealing Tape • Roofing Nails • Asphalt Roofing Cement • No. 14 Type NM Cable • Wire Nuts • Electrical Tape

Tools • Tape Measure • Ladder • Drill and Bit • Saber Saw • Pry Bar • Wire Stripper • Diagonal Cutters

HEAT BUILDUP in an attic during the summer can exceed 170° F, and if not properly vented, this heat can add a terrific load on cooling equipment for living areas below. The answer is a roof ventilator to remove this excessive heat. If the attic space is insulated, a roof ventilator is almost mandatory.

Roof ventilators are sold in kit form for homeowner installation. There are two choices: wind-driven turbines and power-driven ventilators. The power-type probably is best if you live in an area where there isn't much wind. The difference in price between wind-driven and power ventilators is not prohibitive; installation is almost the same. On an average-size house—about 1,800 square feet—one ventilator is needed. If your home is larger, you may need more than one ventilator. You should be able to calculate this from ventilator capacities printed on the kit. To install a ventilator, follow these steps:

1. Inside the attic space, measure a point down from the peak of the roof between rafters to install the ventilator; the ventilator should be installed near the peak of the roof with just the top of the turbine exposed to wind from all directions.
2. Measure halfway between the rafters—usually 8 inches between parallel rafters—and mark this spot.
3. Drive a 20d common nail on the mark through the roof sheathing, building paper, and shingles. The nail will protrude above the shingles so you can locate the point on the roof from the outside.
4. Measure the diameter of the ventilator.
5. On a day when the surface of the roof is cool, climb onto the roof and locate the nail point.

Caution: Working on a roof can be dangerous, especially on steeply pitched roofs. If the pitch is too great, have a professional install the ventilator.

6. Cut a length of string and tie one end to the nail and the other to a piece of chalk; make sure the length of string between nail and chalk is half the diameter of the ventilator.
7. Using the string and chalk as a compass, mark a cutting circle on the roof.
8. Drill a hole at a point on the marked circle through the roof.
9. Using a saber saw, cut an opening in the roof. Cut completely through the shingles, building paper, and sheathing. Keep the saw blade just inside the scribed circle.
10 After the circle is cut out, save the cutout pieces of roofing shingles; you may be able to use them later for patching.
11. Use a pry bar to lift up the shingles around the circular opening in the roof.
12. Apply a single layer of flashing sealing tape directly onto the roof sheathing around the ventilator opening.
13. Position the roof ventilator over the opening and press the ventilator's flashing into the sealing tape. Then, with roofing nails, nail the ventilator to the roof sheathing. Space the nails about 3 inches apart around the flashing.
   Note: Make sure the opening in the ventilator is aligned exactly over the roof opening before you begin nailing.
14. Coat the joint between the metal flashing and the roof sheathing with asphalt roofing cement; feather the edges of the cement so the surface will be as smooth as possible.
15. Cover the flashing with roofing shingles, using

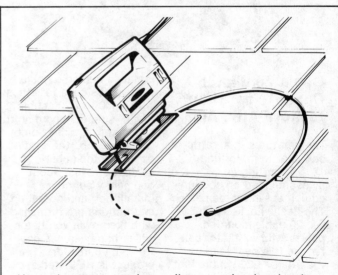

Use a saber saw to cut the ventilator opening, keeping the saw blade just inside the scribed circle. Cut completely through the shingles, building paper, and sheathing.

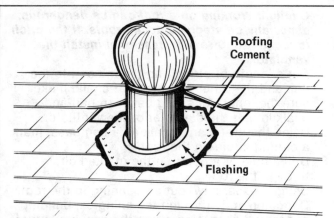

Position the roof ventilator and press the flashing into the sealing tape. Then, nail the ventilator to the roof sheathing. Coat the joint between the metal flashing and roof sheathing with asphalt roofing cement.

the cutout pieces of shingles. Nail down the roofing where possible. Place smaller pieces in position with roofing cement. Then, coat all exposed nailheads and joints in the shingles around the ventilator with roofing cement.

16. Inside the attic, seal the flashing around the opening with roofing cement. If the ventilator is wind-driven, the job is now complete. If the ventilator is power-driven, it must be connected to a house circuit.

17. Run a length of No. 14 Type NM cable from the switch or junction box in the attic to the ventilator.

18. Turn off the power to the circuit you plan to use. Strip about ½ inch of insulation from both ends of both wires in the cable. Connect one end of the cable to the circuit in the switch or junction box; connect black wire to black wire and white wire to white wire. Secure the connections with wire nuts and electrical tape.

19. Connect the other end of the cable to the thermostat/switch wires for the ventilator; secure them with wire nuts and electrical tape. The power ventilator kit will include complete wiring details; follow the manufacturer's instruction.

Note: For a roof ventilator to function efficiently, the house should be equipped with soffit vents. Most homes already have these vents installed. If your home doesn't have soffit vents, see the section on "Ventilation" in this chapter.

Gable Ventilator Costs 1¢ per Hour to Move Attic Air

Temperatures in an attic can soar to more than 170° F, putting an awesome load on cooling equipment in rooms below. The Leslie-Locke model GM-20 gable-mounted, power attic ventilator can reduce this heat load at the rate of 1,200 cubic feet (free air) or 710 cubic feet (installed) per minute. The model GM-20, which is installed behind a gable vent, is designed for attics with 4,800 to 7,200 cubic feet of space. According to Leslie-Locke, a division of Questor Corp., the cost of operating the gable ventilator is just about one penny per hour. Installation and operation instructions are furnished with the power ventilator, which has been designed for do-it-yourselfers. The product is UL Listed and carries a limited lifetime warranty for as long as you own your home.

Wind-Powered Roof Ventilator Keeps Attic Cooler

The temperature in an unventilated attic can reach more than 170° F and force your air conditioning system to work harder to cool living areas. The Whirlybird turbine ventilator, used with intake vents, can help remove such high heat and humidity in attic spaces. The all-aluminum ventilator, manufactured by Lomanco, Inc., has pre-lubricated, sealed ball bearings; rolled vane edges that deflect rain; and a rigid, spider-type construction for strength. The ventilator, according to Lomanco, has been tested in 120-mph winds successfully. The ventilator is available in 8-inch, 10-inch, 12-inch, and 14-inch sizes. Only ordinary hand tools are needed for installation. Lomanco offers a limited warranty for as long as the purchasers own their home.

Cleaning a Chimney

Materials • Chemical Chimney Cleaner • Plastic Sheet or Plywood • Duct Tape • Small Weight • Newspapers • Rags • Bricks • Burlap Bag • Rope • Asbestos Tape

Tools • Chimney Brush • Ladder • Hand Mirror • Flashlight • Vacuum Cleaner • Work Gloves • Screwdriver • Utility Knife

SOOT BUILDUP in a chimney can block it and create a fire hazard. To prevent this, you should clean your chimney every year or two. There are three "tool" choices for cleaning a chimney: a homemade burlap bag swab, chimney brushes, and chemical cleaner. All are efficient, but chemicals and brushes may be less messy.

Chemical Cleaners

There are many chemical chimney cleaners. Some chemicals are specifically designed for soot; others are formulated to rid the chimney of creosote buildup that can become a fire hazard. Check the product's package for the right cleaning formula and follow the use instructions on the package. The general procedures for using chemical cleaners are:

1. Build a fire in the firebox.
2. Sprinkle the chemical on the fire.
3. As the chemical burns, the soot and creosote burns in the chimney and goes up in smoke.

Flue-Lined Chimneys

Although brushes may be used for masonry fireplace chimneys, special chimney brushes work most efficiently in flue-lined chimneys. The brushes fit tightly in the pipes and have a scooping action as well as a brushing one. The brush handles are in sections, and screw or slip together. To use a chimney brush, follow these steps:

1. Make sure there is no fire in the fireplace.
2. Open the fireplace damper.
3. Seal off the fireplace opening from the room with a heavy plastic sheet taped into place, or

a piece of scrap plywood. Make sure there are no cracks or leaks around the edges.
4. Climb onto the roof. *Caution: Working on a roof, especially a steeply pitched one, can be dangerous. If the roof is extremely steep, hire a professional chimneysweep.*
5. Attach a weight below the brush to provide a little added pull.
6. Lower the brush down the chimney until it hits the bottom.
7. Raise and lower the brush several times to dislodge caked soot.
8. If the fireplace has an outside door, open it and remove the soot that's fallen through.
9. Wait an hour or so for the dust to settle; then remove the plastic sheet or plywood from the fireplace opening.
10. Take a large hand mirror and a flashlight and inspect the chimney. Look for any obstructions. If there are any, you will have to go back on the roof and repeat the cleaning procedure.
11. If there are no obstructions, put on gloves and reach over the damper to the smoke shelf.

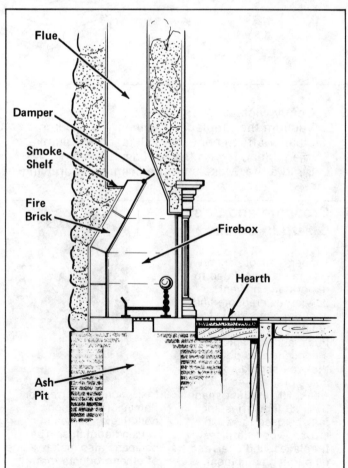

As a fireplace is used, soot builds up in the firebox and on the sides of the flue. To prevent problems, clean the chimney and the ash pit regularly.

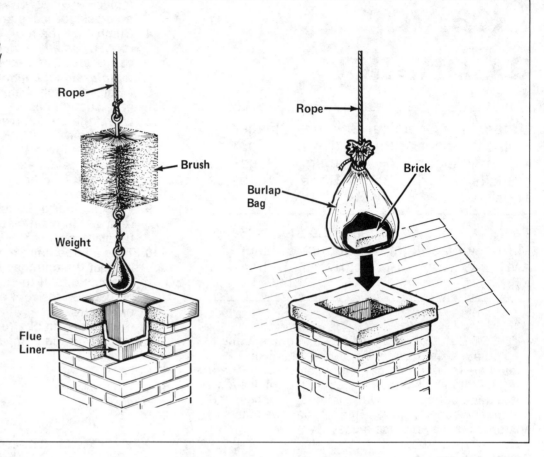

For chimneys with flue liners (right), a chimney brush is the best cleaning tool. Use a brush that is the same shape — round or square — as the flue liner. A burlap bag, filled with crumpled newspaper and weighted with a brick (far right) makes a good cleaning tool for unlined chimneys.

Rope

Brush

Weight

Flue Liner

Rope

Brick

Burlap Bag

Gently wipe away any debris.

12. Vacuum the fireplace. If you have a vacuum cleaner attachment that will reach the smoke shelf, clean it with the vacuum as well.

13. Build a fire. Make sure the chimney is drawing properly. If it isn't, put out the fire and look for obstructions. It's a good idea to use a chemical chimney cleaner at this point. The chemical should burn away any residue you may have missed.

Creosote and Soot Go Up in Smoke

Timber creosote chimney cleaner is formulated to remove and prevent dangerous creosote and soot deposits from building up in chimneys, flues, and stovepipes. It's a concentrated powder that you sprinkle on hot coals or low fires twice a week. The product, made by HMS Industries, Inc., may be used for wood stoves, wood furnaces, fireplaces, and coal- and oil-burning equipment. According to HMS Industries, Timber creosote chimney cleaner is non-

toxic, non-corrosive, non-flammable, and non-polluting. It comes in a 1-pound container. The company also makes a line of other products that include stove paint, stove polish, glass cleaner, and brick and stone cleaner.

Chimney Cleaner Helps Stop Fires

Cleans-Up creosote and soot destroyer, made by Charnas Industries, Inc., can be used for both stoves and fireplaces. According to the manufacturer, the product eliminates the flammability of creosote and soot on contact, and helps eliminate buildup. The liquid cleaner is sprayed on burning wood or coal. It is non-flammable, anti-corrosive, and non-polluting, according to Charnas, and carries a money-back guarantee. It's available in spray bottles.

Masonry Fireplace Chimneys

The soot and creosote buildup in masonry chimney structures can be considerable over a long period of time. Because of the large diameter of the chimney opening, brushes are not practical for cleaning. The best cleaning tool is a burlap bag filled with wadded paper or straw and weighted with a brick or two.

1. Follow Steps 1 through 4 in the previous procedure.
2. Fasten the bag securely to a length of rope long enough to reach to the bottom of the chimney.
3. Lower the bag down one corner of the chimney until it reaches the bottom. Then, raise and lower the bag several times in the chimney opening.
4. Move the bag around the perimeter of the chimney opening, moving it about a foot each time, and repeat this procedure until the entire chimney has been cleaned.
5. Follow Steps 8 through 13 in the previous procedure.

Free-Standing Fireplaces and Wood-Burning Stoves

To clean the round stacks found on wood-burning stoves and free-standing fireplaces a round chimney brush, the same diameter as the flue, is the best cleaning tool. To clean these chimneys, follow these steps:

1. Make sure there is no fire in the heating appliance.
2. The brush will dislodge plenty of greasy soot, so be prepared for a mess. Wear old clothes and gloves, spread plenty of newspapers around the area, and have lots of rags handy.
3. If possible, insert the brush in the chimney pipe or flue at the inside of the firebox. Work the brush up and down in the pipe; try to get about 6 to 8 feet up the pipe before you pull out the brush.
4. Depending on the type of brush—some are very flexible—you may have to disassemble the chimney pipe at the elbows where it comes out of the heating appliance and runs into the main straight pipe section. If the sections are joined by self-tapping sheet metal screws, use a screwdriver to remove them. The sections may be wrapped with asbestos tape. If so, cut the tape with a utility knife.
5. If you can, clean the upper part of the pipe through the firebox or at the elbow fitting. If not, you will have to get on the roof and insert the brush down through the pipe.
   Caution: Working on the roof, especially a steeply pitched one, can be dangerous. If the roof is extremely steep, hire a professional chimneysweep.
6. Attach a weight below the brush to provide a little added pull, and lower the brush down the chimney pipe.
7. Raise and lower the brush several times to dislodge caked soot.
8. When the chimney pipe is reasonably clean, reconnect the sections. If there were screws, replace them. If the pipes were held by asbestos tape, soak new tape in plain water and wrap the tape around the pipe joints. No adhesive is needed; the asbestos tape will shrink and conform to the diameter of the pipe.

Firebrick Yields Eight Hours of Heat

A product that lights easily and produces eight or more hours of heat is the King Koal Solid Fuel firebrick, which is made of coal, cellulose, and other natural ingredients. According to King Koal, a division of Bohanna and Pearce, Inc., the product lights with one match, produces more than 100,000 BTU's of heat, and flames for one to three hours. The company also says that the firebricks are economical to use, are easily stacked and stored, and are clean-burning.

Chimney Cleaning Kit Has What You Need

If you've got a woodburning stove or fireplace, sooner or later it's got to be cleaned. The chimney cleaning kit, made by Schaefer Brush Manufacturing Co., Inc., helps you do a better job on this necessary chore. The kit contains a chimney brush—6-inch, 7-inch, or 8-inch sizes; in both round and square styles to fit your chimney—six 45-inch, flexible fiberglass rods; 25 feet of rope; a curved-handle wire brush; and a pull ring. The flexible rods allow you to clean the chimney from the roof or from the firebox.

Easy-to-Install Fireplace Insert

A fireplace insert designed to provide maximum fuel efficiency and heat exchange for low-cost home heating is available from GlowMaster, a division of T.G. Industries, Inc. The wood-burning unit, which installs in minutes with ordinary household tools, fits most fireplaces. It features twin blowers that pull room air through the airspace created by its firebox and surrounding plenum, both of which are made from heavy-gauge steel. According to the manufacturer, the blowers move up to 16,080 cubic feet of air per hour. The blowers have preset on/off thermostats with a variable speed control. The firebox doors are glazed with tempered glass, and an inner set of steel doors may be closed for additional safety when the fire is left burning unattended. Front draft and damper controls allow you to adjust fuel combustion. The fireplace insert has a black and brass finish.

Device Makes Stoves More Efficient

A device for wood- and coal-burning stoves that is designed to eliminate smoky back-up from the fire and make fire-starting much easier is the Auto Draft made by Tjernlund Products, Inc. According to the manufacturer, the draft-inducing unit also makes stove operation more efficient by controlling the fire. The Auto Draft, which can be easily installed on any wood- or coal-burning stove with a flue pipe from 5 to 8 inches in diameter, doesn't increase the height or diameter of the chimney. A heat-resistant, radial-type blower wheel creates an immediate up-draft from the stove. Then, once the fire is burning, a variable speed control knob on the unit allows you to adjust the device for maximum efficiency and fuel utilization; according to the

manufacturer, only a fine ash residue is left in most cases. The Auto Draft unit features heavy-duty welded construction. A one-year warranty is provided.

Regular Use Reduces Creosote Buildup

A chimney fire is a worry of homeowners who have a fireplace or a wood-burning stove. But Glo-Klén, a powdered combustion catalyst made by Jefco Laboratories, can prevent such fires by reducing creosote or carbon deposits inside the flue, stovepipe, or chimney. According to the manufacturer, Glo-Klén helps wood and coal burn more completely, reducing the creosote or carbon buildup. To use, one scoop of the product is sprinkled on and under the grate before the fire is started. If the fire burns continuously, a second scoop is applied about

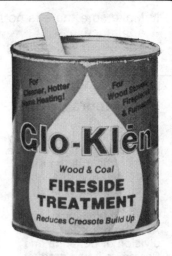

three days later, after the ashes have been removed. During the first month, Glo-Klén is added twice a week. After this, a single scoop weekly is sufficient. Glo-Klén can also be used with oil and other kinds of fuel.

Vertical Heater Offers Wide Coverage

A vertical quartz heater that the manufacturer says will provide wider coverage than any other 1,500-watt quartz heater is available from Boekamp, Inc. The Boekamp quartz heater model 110, which offers you the option of 750 or 1,500 watts with a built-in rocker switch on the front control panel, features a double reflector for a 150-degree angle of coverage. Other features include a guard that virtually eliminates tube breakage, a front safety grille, and a double-slotted heater housing for more ventilation and a cooler surface temperature. The heater is UL Listed.

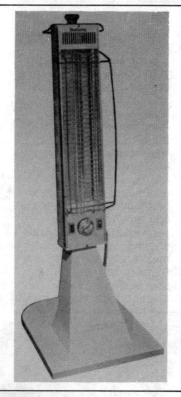

Wall-Mount Heater Offers a Source of Localized Heat

If you need heat in an area of a room, the Dimplex wall-mounted, quartz radiant heater can do the job because it's designed for fast localized heating. The heater is controlled by a fitted, four-position, rotary pullcord switch that's connected to illuminated pilot lights to indicate when the heating element is on. At the control's highest setting, the heater beams heat at an angle of 18 degrees below horizontal; in the lowest setting, it beams heat at an angle 45 degrees below horizontal. There are two models—750 and 1,000 watts. Both are 32½ inches long, 4 inches high, and 4½ inches deep; each weighs 5 pounds. The steel base and frame is gold colored with black-crackle-finish end caps. The UL Listed heater, made by Dimplex Heating Ltd. in England, must be wired through a junction box.

Power Ventilator Moves Attic Air Automatically

Some authorities recommend that a complete change of air in an attic be made every six minutes to remove high heat and humidity in summer. The LomanCool 2000 power roof ventilator automatically can move 1,290 cubic feet of air per minute from attic spaces with air intake vents. A thermostat on the low-profile ventilator, made by Lomanco, Inc., is factory-set to come on when the attic air reaches 100° F; the fan shuts down when the temperature drops to 85° F. The LomanCool 2000 features deep-pitched fan blades balanced for quiet operation; a heavy-duty Westinghouse motor; thermal fusing that automatically shuts off the unit in the event of fire; an automatic, but adjustable, thermostat; and all-aluminum construction. It is available in three colors—white, brown, or black. Or, the unit can be obtained in a mill, or plain, finish. The ventilator is designed to be installed by the homeowner on horizontal, pitched, or vertical roofs. Installation and operation instructions are provided. The UL Listed product carries a two-year limited warranty.

Grate and Basket Works With Wood or Coal

The Champ coal grate and basket, made by the Champ Corp., lets you burn coal or wood in almost any wood-burning stove or fireplace insert in use today. The grate keeps the fire high enough for the bottom drafting needed for coal, yet low enough for the proper top drafting of wood. For example, wood may be burned in the evening for visual effect; coal can be added later for overnight heating without reloading the heating plant. The grate comes in three sizes. The largest model has four movable grates; it is 19½ inches wide, 14½ inches deep, and 6½ inches high. The

medium model, with three moving grates, is 15 by 14½ by 6½ inches. The smallest model, with two moving grates, is 10⅜ by 14½ by 6½ inches. The grates are made from heat-resistant iron alloy.

Heating and Cooling

Attic Fans Install Without Joist Cuts

It would be nice to install a whole-house attic fan without cutting through attic joists or changing trusses. With a new line of attic fans from Emerson Environmental Products, a division of Emerson Electric Co., you don't have to. The shutter mechanism is surface-mounted against the ceiling, and the fan mechanism in the attic is fastened to existing ceiling joists. Rubber isolation mounting throughout the fan offers smooth, quiet operation, according to the manufacturer. A polymeric sleeve liner is used to seal the area between the fan and the shutter. Only five tools are required for installation: a saber or hand saw, utility knife, drill, screwdriver, and tape measure. The Emerson fans are available in 24-inch, 30-inch, and 36-inch sizes; all models are UL Listed and have a five-year motor warranty.

Rack Keeps Towels and Bathroom Warm

A warm towel and a warm bathroom are a luxury everyone can enjoy on a chilly morning. The Dimplex electric towel rack, manufactured in England by Dimplex Heating Ltd., not only keeps towels warm and dry, but also furnishes continuous heat to warm bathrooms. The rack has a special oil that's permanently sealed inside chromium-plated tubular rails. According to Dimplex, the towel rack uses about the same amount of electricity as an electric light bulb to maintain the temperature 24 hours a day. No maintenance is required. The 130-watt towel rack is UL Listed.

Saddle Valve for Fast Water Hookups

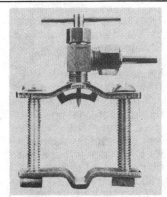

A self-piercing saddle valve, made by Anderson-Barrows Metals Corp., installs in minutes so you can easily hook up a humidifier, evaporative cooler, icemaker, and other appliances. The valve pierces its own hole in ⅜-inch to 1⅜-inch copper or plastic tubing; no drilling or water shutoff is needed for installation, according to the manufacturer. The assembly clamps to a water supply line, and the tubing is secured to the valve assembly. You then turn the valve handle clockwise to pierce the supply line and close the valve. Turn the handle counterclockwise to reopen the valve to the desired water flow. The valve kit comes with installation instructions.

All-Fuel Chimney Comes in a Kit

When you install a freestanding fireplace or heating stove, you need a chimney. A series of Ameri-Vent all-fuel chimney kits are made by American Metal Products Co., for do-it-yourself installation. They feature a reduced outside diameter chimney, a snap-lock coupling system, and triple-wall construction that keeps the chimney's outer pipe cool enough to permit a 2-inch clearance to combustibles. The chimney comes in 6-inch, 7-inch, 8-inch, 10-inch, and 12-inch inside diameters. The model 6FB-RK round kit for example, includes a chimney cap, round flashing, ceiling support, storm collar, and installation instructions. The all-fuel chimney may be used with other low-heat appliances, too, such as cooking ranges, central furnaces, floor furnaces, hot water and steam heating boilers, recessed heaters, unit heaters, and water heaters. There also are kits for flat-ceiling, open-beam, and through-the-wall installations.

Saving Energy

PRODUCTS DESIGNED to save energy in the home have been around for years. But, it took a declared war on energy waste before these products were marketed as energy-savers.

For example, caulking compound has suddenly become an "energy-saver," and it is. But the product has been available for a long, long time to prevent air infiltration. Insulation is another example. Many years ago, people used mud and paper to insulate their homes before fiberglass was developed, and fiberglass has been around for decades. To read many manufacturers' literature, one might think wood- and coal-burning stoves are something new. What *IS* new is the sales emphasis on "new" and "energy-saving."

With these eye-catching energy slogans on thousands of product packages, a homeowner should be cautious when confronted with products that imply fantastic fuel savings. You should—before buying—ask "For what, for how much, and for how long?" Also keep in mind that building codes in your community may prohibit the use of some products and it's up to you to check before buying.

Ten Time-Tested Energy-Savers

The "Big Ten" time-tested home energy-savers are insulation, weatherstripping, caulking materials, storm doors, storm windows, set-back thermostats, fluorescent lighting, window shades and outdoor awnings, furnace and air conditioning filters, and attic ventilating fans.

An investment in these energy-savers will eventually pay off in time—but perhaps not for a number of years. The first significant dividend you get, however, isn't a saving in energy, but comfort. Caulking materials, weatherstripping, and storm windows and doors, for example, stop drafts. The first thing you will notice is comfort. The cost hasn't been realized yet because not much energy has been saved yet.

Many of the "Big Ten" energy-savers qualify for a tax credit on your federal income tax. The deduction may not be much, but it can add up. Be sure to save your receipts and ask the retailer for a leaflet that explains the deducting procedure. Many of them have this information.

Other Energy-Saving Products

Although the "Big Ten" energy-saving products will conserve fuel and save you some money over a period of time, the list doesn't end with ten. The following items—some of them truly new—are recommended products that you should consider:

- Flush tank valves that reduce water consumption.
- Plastic plugs for electrical outlets that stop drafts.
- Reflective film for windows.
- Thermal door thresholds.
- Fireplace heat exchangers.
- Wood- and coal-burning stoves and fireplace inserts.

Insulators Stop Outlet Drafts

Cold air infiltration around electrical outlets is often overlooked by energy-conscious homeowners. Stopdraft electric outlet insulators, made by Pioneer Energy Products, Inc., however, can eliminate most of this problem. Each Stopdraft package contains seven ivory-colored electrical outlet plates and pads, three switch plates, and six plastic plug inserts with gasket insulators to prevent air leaks through outlet holes. The product is UL Listed.

Water-Saving Shower Head

Newer-design shower heads are made to conserve water and energy. The Bubble Stream shower head, model 6002C, made by Wrightway Manufacturing Co., has a push-button feature that turns water on and off without disturbing the temperature setting. According to the manufacturer, it can reduce water flow from 6 gallons per minute to less than 3 gallons per minute, saving both water and energy. The aerating shower head, which has an

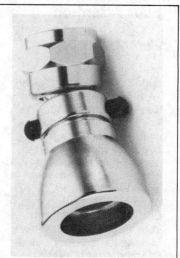

adjustable ball-joint, is chrome-plated solid brass. Only a wrench is needed to install it.

- Plastic sheeting for crawl spaces with earth floors.
- Roof or attic ventilators.
- Clogged-filter indicators.
- Register deflectors for heating and cooling.
- Shade trees and shrubs.
- Reflective roofing materials.
- Reflectant paint.
- Water-saving shower heads.
- Area heating devices.
- Hot water pipe insulation.
- Ducting for clothes dryers.
- Forced-air duct boosters.
- Heat pump replacements for other furnaces.
- Furnace/flue heat-savers.

Maintenance Is an Energy-Saver Too

"New" products can save energy, but don't overlook the maintenance of old products—the ones you already have. For example, furnace filters need to be changed or cleaned four times annually. The filters don't cost much and they're very easy to change. Have you changed yours recently? Chances are your attic is insulated. But is there enough insulation? If not, you can add more at little cost.

These energy-saving products are being pointed out because they often are overlooked in a renewed zeal to save energy. You'll find procedures for using many of these products—and others—in this chapter.

Decorative Ceiling Fan Has Light Fixture

A ceiling fan can not only help cool a house in summer, it also can help save energy costs by redistributing warm air that has risen to the ceiling in winter. The Patton ceiling fan with optional light fixture has hand-rubbed, solid hardwood blades with cane inserts. According to the Patton Electric Co., the manufacturer, the fan consumes as little energy as a light bulb. The fan motor is permanently lubricated and features a variable speed control that ranges from 80 to 240 revolutions per minute. There's also a reverse-rotation switch that permits indirect air circulation. The fan blades are self-leveling for quiet operation and are offered in a choice of two sizes—36 inches or 52 inches. There also is a choice of an optional schoolhouse-style or a five-globe, tulip-design light fixture. The fan is available

in three metal finishes—polished brass, antique brass, or ivory with ivory-finished hardwood blades.

Filter Alarm Whistles to Get Your Attention

Do you know when you should change your heating and air conditioning system filter? With Filter Alert, made by Bede Industries, Inc., you'll know because the device whistles when the filter becomes inefficient—about 60 to 70 percent obstructed. The device sounds softly at first, gradually increasing over a one-week period to gain your attention. Filter Alert is easy to install. It quickly snaps on the filter. When a filter is replaced, you remove the device, rinse it under a faucet, and snap it in the new filter.

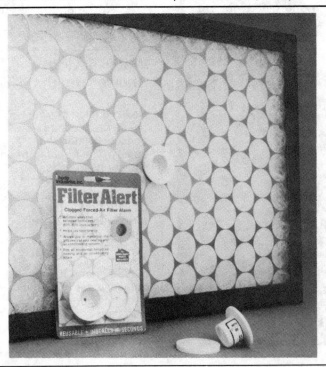

Device Turns Faucet Into a Fountain

A drinking fountain at the kitchen sink would be handy. And, it would save washing glasses. The Bubble Stream fountain, model 806C, made by Wrightway Manufacturing Co., installs quickly on the end of a faucet's spout. Pushing a valve in turns it into a fountain; pushing it out turns it back into a faucet. The fountain is chrome-plated solid brass.

Storm Windows

Materials • Stock Storm Windows or Components as Needed • Caulking Compound • Screws • Adhesive-Backed Foam Weatherstripping • Masking Tape

---

Tools • Tape Measure • Screwdriver • Carpenter's Level • Pencil • Combination Square • Miter Box • Hacksaw • File • Single-Edge Razor Blade • Electric Drill and Bits • Caulking Gun

---

STORM WINDOWS are one of your home's best weapons against heat loss or gain during the heating and cooling seasons. The additional protection they provide can make your home more comfortable and save you plenty in fuel costs. And, storm windows can qualify for a tax credit on your federal income tax. Storm windows are just as important for peak air conditioning efficiency as they are for heating efficiency. If your home has central air conditioning, storm windows should remain in place all year long.

You can buy custom-made storm windows and have them installed. You also can buy stock, pre-hung windows and install them yourself. Or, you can assemble your own storm windows from components available at most home center stores. By comparing the price of custom-made and stock windows, you should be able to determine whether or not making your own windows is worth your time and effort.

Stock Storm Windows

About 20 standard sizes of stock, pre-hung, aluminum storm windows are available. They are the "combination" type of storm window, which includes a sliding screen. You can buy them in a "mill" finish, which is bare aluminum, or in an enameled, or painted, finish; mounting hardware is usually provided. To install a stock exterior storm window, follow these general steps:

1. From the outside, measure the width and height of your window, from just outside the blind stops.

2. Using these measurements, select a pre-hung storm window; you have about ¼-inch margin for error.
3. Remove the glass panes and screen from the storm window frame, and fit the storm window frame against the blind stops of your window frame. If it doesn't fit, return the storm window for an exchange or your money back. If the storm window frame fits, remove it and set it aside.
4. Using a caulking gun, apply a bead of caulking compound suitable for exterior use around the window frame stops.
5. Press the storm window frame into the bed of caulking compound and partially drive a screw at the top of the frame to hold it in place.
6. Use a carpenter's level along the frame's horizontal mullion to level the storm window frame in the window frame.

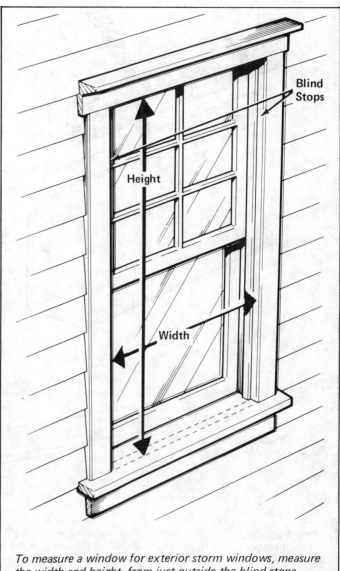

To measure a window for exterior storm windows, measure the width and height, from just outside the blind stops.

7. Once the frame is aligned properly, tighten the top mounting screw and drive in the rest of the mounting screws to secure the frame to the window.

Note: The frame of the storm window has "weep" holes at the bottom. Make sure they are open so that moisture between the window and the storm window can escape.

Assembling Your Own Storm Windows

You can assemble your own aluminum storm windows from components—storm sash sections, corner locks, and window glass—available at home center stores. The important thing is to obtain the correct measurements. Each window should be carefully measured for size. Don't assume that similar windows are the same size. To assemble a storm window from components, follow these steps:

1. Measure the width and height of the window. If the storm window is to be installed on the outside, measure from just outside the blind stops. If it's to be installed on the inside, measure from just outside the inside stops.
2. Use a tape measure and pencil to mark the four sections of aluminum storm sash frame

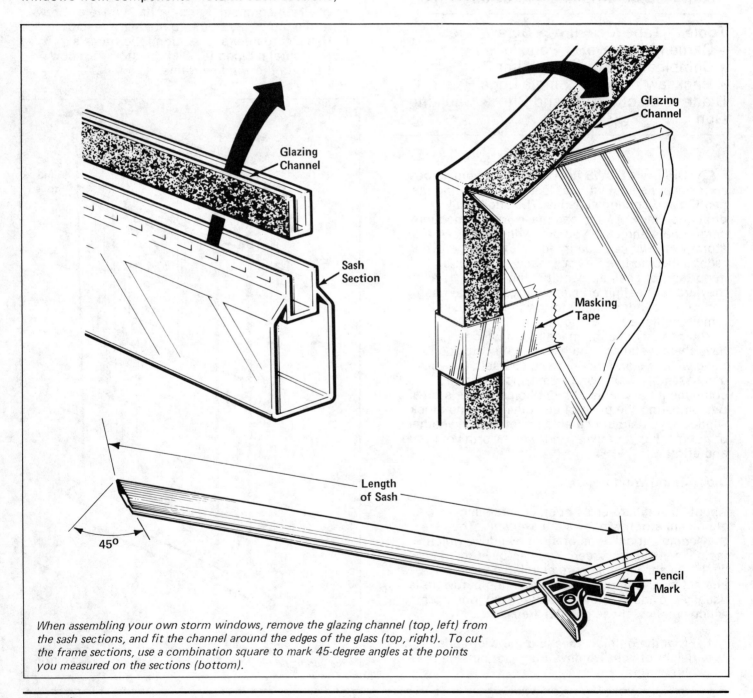

When assembling your own storm windows, remove the glazing channel (top, left) from the sash sections, and fit the channel around the edges of the glass (top, right). To cut the frame sections, use a combination square to mark 45-degree angles at the points you measured on the sections (bottom).

that will fit around the pane of glass. Mark each section of frame—the two side sections and the top and bottom sections—⅛ inch less than your width and height measurements.

3. Remove the glazing channel from the sections of aluminum sash frame.

4. Use a combination square to mark 45-degree angles at the points you measured on the frame sections.

5. Using a miter box and fine-toothed hacksaw, cut the ends of each section at a 45-degree angle. Use a file to smooth each cut end.

6. Have a pane of glass cut—or cut the pane yourself—but take into account the width of the frame sections. Cut the pane ⅟₁₆ inch less than the exact distance between the sash frame channels.

7. Fit the glazing channel around the edges of the glass, mitering or making triangle-shaped cuts with a single-edge razor blade at the corners. Use masking tape to hold the channel in place.

8. Insert corner locks into the side frame sections.

9. Fit the top and bottom frame sections over the edges of the glass and the glazing channel; install the sides of the frame in the same manner.

10. Apply adhesive-backed foam weatherstripping completely around the inside edge of the frame where it butts against the window stops to prevent air infiltration.

11. If you intend to leave the storm window up all

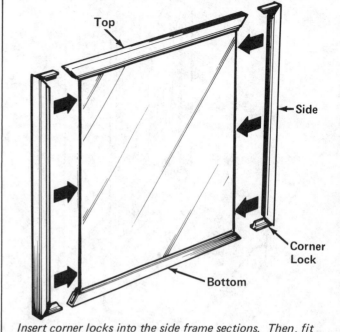

Insert corner locks into the side frame sections. Then, fit the top and bottom sections over the edges of the glass. Finally, install the side sections.

year, apply a bead of caulking compound to the window stops. Then, drill mounting holes through the storm window frame—avoiding the glass and glazing channel—and mount the storm window in place with screws. Or, you can install the storm window with brackets

This Product Pulls the Shade on Heat Loss

A new window insulation system can make saving energy as easy as pulling down a shade. The Minute Man storm window shade kit, from HMS, Inc., provides an airtight seal that blocks out cold, chilling drafts in winter and saves on air conditioning costs in summer. The seal creates an insulating air space between the window and the shade so there's less heat loss through the window. The Minute Man shade installs like an ordinary window shade. It comes as a complete kit that includes all the necessary hardware, including a 25-foot roll of double-faced transparent tape. You apply the resealable tape around the window frame, pull down the clear vinyl shade, and press its edges against the tape. To open, you pull the shade away from the tape and roll it up. The heavy-duty, 6-mil vinyl shade is transparent and, according to the manufacturer, won't discolor or yellow with age. Standard shade sizes available are 37¼ by 68 inches, 43¼ by 68 inches, and 52¼ by 68 inches. The shade also can be cut to smaller sizes with a sharp knife. The shade material can be cleaned with soap and water or any nonabrasive household cleaner.

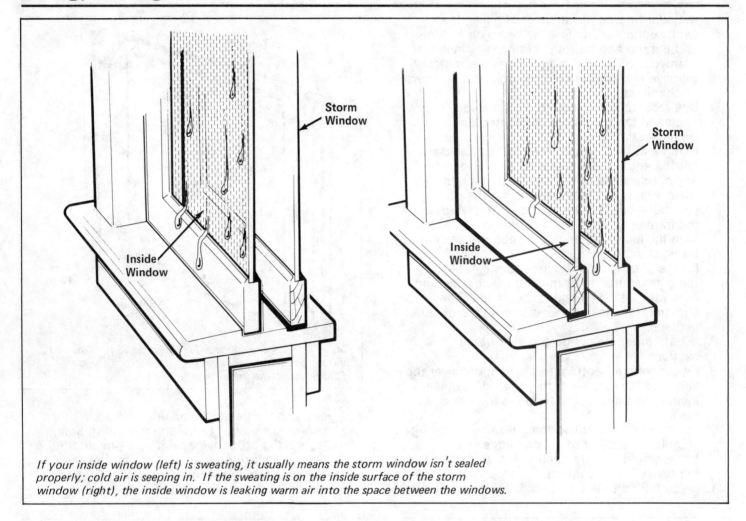

If your inside window (left) is sweating, it usually means the storm window isn't sealed properly; cold air is seeping in. If the sweating is on the inside surface of the storm window (right), the inside window is leaking warm air into the space between the windows.

and hangers made by the storm window manufacturer for this purpose.

12. Drill two small "weep" holes into the bottom of the storm window frame for ventilation.

Sweating and Fogging Problems

One of the benefits of storm windows is that they help prevent window sweating. If you see sweating on the storm windows, however, you should check the seal. If the sweating is on the inside, or prime window, it usually means that your storm window isn't adequately sealed and is allowing cold air to seep in. If the sweating is on the inside surface of the storm window, this indicates that the interior window is leaking warm air into the space between the two windows. Use caulking compound or weatherstripping to solve the problem.

Indoor Storms Snap In and Out

An insulating window that snaps in and out makes it easy to clean your windows. Insul-Pane insulating windows, made by Baxt Industries, snap in and out of self-adhesive molding strips that are installed around the inside of your windows or glass openings in your doors. The product, made of clear styrene, is designed to stop drafts and window fogging in winter, and to reduce heat gain in summer. Standard sheet sizes are 24 by 36 inches, 38 by 56 inches, and 44 by 64 inches; custom sizes can be easily cut on the job. Trim molding is available in lengths of 38, 50, 66, and 80 inches. Installation instructions are included with the product.

Buy the Correct Strength of Glass

When buying window glass for do-it-yourself storm window projects, purchase single-strength glass for small panes that are up to 9 square feet in area. For larger areas, it's best to use double-strength glass. Most stores that sell glass will cut it to your measurements, or you can save money by cutting it yourself.

Vinyl Storm Frames for Acrylic Sheets

Therma Frame is a do-it-yourself storm window frame for acrylic sheet goods. The vinyl frame accommodates 0.080-through 0.100-inch sheets as well as standard glass panels. The window frame, according to Elgar Products, Inc., is easy to cut, assemble, and install. Therma Frame can be cut with a fine-tooth saw, single-edge razor blade, or sharp knife; no special tools are required. And, it can be painted or stained. After assembly and installation, the entire storm window can be removed as a complete unit. Installation instructions are furnished with the materials, which are selected to order. Components include frame sections, sill strips, joiner strips, and clip fasteners.

Window System Comes in Hinged or Sliding Version

If you're looking for an aluminum-frame, do-it-yourself storm window system that is permanently installed, the Aluminum In-Sider storm window system made by Plaskolite, Inc., may be what you're looking for. It is available in a sliding or hinged version; both can be opened for ventilation and cleaning. For glazing, the Aluminum In-Sider system uses either Plaskolite's acrylic safety glazing or window glass. The heavy-duty aluminum frame strips are available in five lengths, fitting windows up to 72 inches square. The strips can be easily cut to size with a hacksaw. The sliding version has aluminum tracks in lengths of 48, 60, 72, and 96 inches.

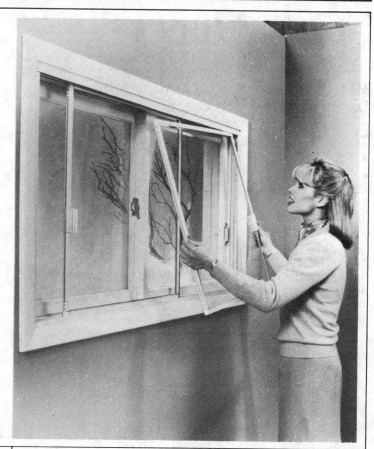

Plastic Sheeting Seals Windows Like Glass Storms

A storm window kit with heavy-gauge vinyl sheeting that can be used around windows, transoms, doors, attic openings, and other areas you want to seal from cold and heat is available from W. J. Dennis & Co. The 4-mil vinyl sheeting in the kit forms a pocket of dead air space similar to insulating glass. The company makes four different size storm window kits to fit the following openings: 24 by 40 inches, 40 by 50 inches, 50 by 80 inches, and 72 by 82 inches. The storm window kit, which is reusable, can be installed in minutes.

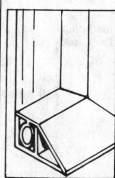

Window Covering Designed for Indoor/Outdoor Use

A storm window covering that you can staple or nail to the inside or outside frame of a window is easy to install. Such a product is the Patrician Energy Saver storm window kit, No. SW36P. If your window has a metal frame, the covering can be stapled to the siding or walls surrounding it. Patrician Products, Inc., also makes a similar kit (No. SW36RS) that contains reflective sheeting, and a kit (No. SW36S) with screening for insect protection. Mounting instructions are furnished.

Storm Doors

Materials • Pre-Hung Aluminum Storm Door Kit • Caulking Compound

Tools • Tape Measure • Pencil • Hacksaw • File • Screwdriver • Carpenter's Level • Caulking Gun

ALTHOUGH WEATHERSTRIPPING can fill the gaps around your home's exterior doors, you can get even more fuel-savings and comfort by installing storm doors. The pre-hung types of storm doors are recommended because they are relatively

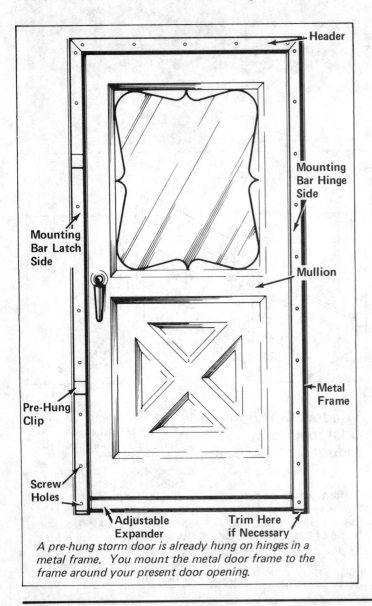

A pre-hung storm door is already hung on hinges in a metal frame. You mount the metal door frame to the frame around your present door opening.

inexpensive, readily available in stock sizes and in several styles and finishes, and easy to hang with ordinary household tools.

A pre-hung door is what the name implies: The door is pre-hung on hinges in a metal frame. The frame is screwed to the casing or wooden frame around your present door opening. The hinges on the pre-hung door should usually be on the same side as the hinges on your present door. To install a pre-hung storm door, follow these steps:

1. Carefully measure the width of the door opening, from one side jamb to the other; take three measurements—at the top, about half way down, and at the bottom. Use the narrowest measurement.
2. Measure the height of the door opening along each side jamb, from the header to the sill. Use the shortest measurement.
3. Buy a pre-hung door that comes closest in size to your measurements. There is approximately a ½-inch margin for error in the width. The length of the door may be shortened or lengthened considerably by means of an adjustable expander section on the door that moves up and down. Most pre-hung doors have this feature.
4. Test the storm door frame in the opening. Usually, you can tell by just setting the door in the opening whether or not it will fit. If it doesn't fit, exchange it.
5. If the storm door has screens and removable glass panels, remove them.
6. Tip the door into position. You may have to trim the bottom of the door frame to fit the opening. If so, make the cuts with a hacksaw and smooth the rough edges with a file.
7. Before repositioning the door frame in the opening, use a caulking gun to apply a bead of caulking compound around the opening.
8. Set the door frame against the bed of caulking compound and drive in—but don't tighten—the screws that fasten the hinge side of the storm door frame to the door opening.
9. Drive in—but don't tighten—the screws that fasten the latch or lock side of the storm door frame to the door opening. **Note:** Some pre-hung storm doors have pre-hung clips along the frame edges. These clips keep the door from "racking" while it's being installed. Usually, the clips are removed after the lock side of the door is fastened.
10. Drive in—but don't tighten—the screws that fasten the header of the storm door frame to the door opening.
11. Test the storm door in the opening to see how it opens and closes.
12. Level the door in the opening by setting a carpenter's level on a door cross member such as the middle mullion or along the latch side,

or both. If necessary, use shims to align the door or have someone help you hold it in position. When the storm door is level, tighten the screws in the frame at the header, along the hinge side, and at the latch side. Although the door opening may not be plumb (vertically level), the storm door must be level in its frame to open and close without binding.

13. Open the storm door and fasten the frame to the side jambs of the door opening.
14. Install the automatic closer. Fasten the jamb bracket first; the closer is attached to it. Then attach the closer to the door bracket. The closer can then be adjusted to "full open" and "full closed" positions. Tension on the closer also can be adjusted at this time. Most manufacturers have instructions for this procedure in the storm door kit.
15. Adjust the expander at the bottom of the storm door up or down so the door sweep just touches the threshold of the door opening. Then, tighten the expander's holding screws.

Door Sweep Has No-Jam Hinge Design

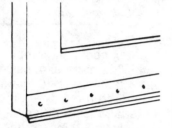

Some door sweeps can jam on carpets or an uneven floor. The Patrician Energy Savers hinged door sweep, however, is designed to prevent this. The door sweep is stapled or nailed to the inside of the door along the bottom. The product, made by Patrician Products, Inc., is available in clear plastic or white or brown colors. One package contains enough material for three doors.

Steel Storm Doors Completely Pre-Hung

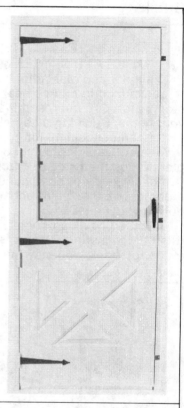

While many storm doors are made of aluminum, there are steel storm doors on the market too. The Lee Haven pre-hung insulated storm door, made by Weather Shield Mfg., Inc., is such a product. There are four styles in white or adobe brown colors. The 1-inch steel door has an interior wood frame and a core filled with polyurethane. There are four steel recessed hinges designed to prevent sagging. The door also features a concealed interior vinyl bottom expander with two flexible vinyl sweeps; the door expands from 79¾ inches to 81¼ to fit most openings.

Patio Door Shade Reduces Heating and Cooling Costs

While sliding glass doors are a definite plus in home design, they can present a problem in trying to heat or cool a room. The patio door shade with cornice, from Sears, Roebuck and Co., is designed to help reduce energy loss in winter by shielding warm room air from the cold glass. In summer, the white back of the shade reflects and deflects some of the sun's rays across the expanse of glass. Available in 12 colors and a choice of open- or closed-weave fabrics, the patio door shade snuggles into the cornice above the door so the door may be easily opened and closed. No. 24 A 68009LH fits a standard 6-foot-wide patio door; No. 24 A 68010LH fits a standard 8-foot-wide door. Only five screws are needed for installation.

Pre-Hung Storm Doors Designed for Do-It-Yourselfers

A storm door helps keep the chill of winter and the heat of summer outside the home. Pre-hung, pre-spaced, and pre-drilled aluminum storm doors are available from Feather-Lite Manufacturing Co. The doors feature distortion-free safety glass, full-pile weatherstripping, fiberglass screening, three bronze-bearing hinges, and U-shaped bottom expander with integral vinyl sweep. Each model includes necessary hardware.

Caulking

Materials • Mineral Spirits • Caulking Compound • Rags or Newspapers • Golf Tee or Large Nail • Stick

Tools • Long Nail or Icepick • Caulking Gun • Putty Knife • Utility Knife • Wire Brush

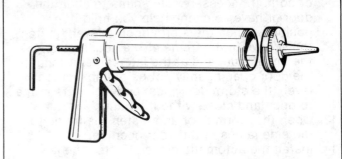

With the barrel-type caulking gun, bulk compound is poured into the barrel. This is, however, messier than using a cartridge-type gun.

CRACKS AND SPACES between and around similar and dissimilar building materials need to be caulked to reduce heat loss and gain, and to stop water, dirt, dust, and insects from entering your home. Caulking also helps to deter wood rot, and it can conceal minor construction irregularities.

Types of caulking compound are almost as plentiful as the types of cracks there are to fill. The five basic kinds of compound include those with an oil or latex base, butyl rubber, silicone, and polyvinyl acetate.

Oil-based caulking compound is inexpensive, but it isn't long-lasting. After a few years, the material tends to shrink, and may fall out of the crack.

Latex caulking compound, often called "painter's caulk," is more expensive than oil-based compound, but it lasts up to 10 years longer. Some manufacturers have combined adhesives with this material, making it serve a dual purpose—an adhesive/caulking compound that sticks to and joins most building materials.

Butyl rubber caulking compound, which is also expensive, is used to fill cracks in masonry, metal, and other similar or dissimilar materials. It requires a solvent for cleanup—as does oil-based caulking compound.

Polyvinyl acetate caulking compound is best used indoors, although it may be used outdoors. It lacks the flexibility of latex, rubber, or silicone caulking compounds. It also dries hard and brittle; this causes separation and caulking compound fall-out.

Silicone caulking compound is long-lasting, but it doesn't adhere too well to painted surfaces—a significant consideration.

Caulking compound is sold in bulk, cartridge, or tube form. In bulk, you fill a caulking gun barrel with the material, which is a messy procedure. Cartridge caulking is what the name implies; the compound is in a cardboard container that fits into a caulking gun. When the cartridge is empty, you discard it. There's no mess. Caulking compound in tubes is usually intended for smaller caulking jobs.

Where to Caulk

Most cracks and splits are obvious; some, however, are not. The following is a checklist of where caulking compound probably should be applied:

- In cracks around window and door casings, moldings, and trim.
- In cracks and splits in wood, metal, and plastic siding.
- In gaps around basement window sash.
- In joints in wood siding, especially where the siding meets vertical and horizontal casing boards.
- At electrical power entrances and exits.

To prevent air infiltration, you should caulk cracks around window and door casings, moldings, and trim.

- Between door thresholds and stoops.
- Around porch steps and railings.
- In cracks between dissimilar materials, such as wood-to-metal, metal-to-masonry, and wood-to-masonry joints.
- At plumbing entrances and exits, especially around outdoor sillcocks.
- Around tubs and showers.
- At gable and roof vents.
- At clothes dryer and exhaust fan outlets.
- Along interior baseboards.

How to Use a Caulking Gun

Loading and using a caulking gun isn't difficult, but there are several procedures you should follow to make the job go easier and to obtain professional results. Follow these steps:

1. Check the caulking gun to make sure it's clean. Remove dried caulking compound with a putty knife and mineral spirits.
2. Cut the plastic nozzle of the caulking compound cartridge at about a 45-degree angle. Some cartridge nozzles are marked to indicate what the inside diameter of the nozzle will be at various cut marks. This is helpful if you will be caulking cracks of a certain width;

for example, ⅛ inch, ³/₁₆ inch, or ¼ inch.
3. Insert the cartridge into the caulking gun.
4. Insert a long nail, icepick, or similar tool in the nozzle to puncture the plastic seal. **Note:** If the plastic seal isn't broken, pressure from the caulking gun plunger can cause the cartridge to break; this will result in a real mess.
5. Activate the caulking gun by turning the plunger rod up or down to engage the ratchet teeth. Squeeze the trigger to force compound out of the cartridge.
6. When caulking, always draw the caulking gun toward you—never move it away from you or "up" the joint or crack. With a little practice, you will learn how fast to move the gun nozzle along the crack or joint while applying pressure to the trigger of the gun.
7. At the end of each caulking run, turn the plunger to disengage it and remove the pressure on the cartridge. Even though the plunger is disengaged, some caulking will always seep out the nozzle; have a rag or newspaper handy to wipe off the nozzle.
8. If you will not continue to use the caulking compound cartridge immediately following a run, plug the nozzle with a golf tee, large nail, or large wood screw to prevent the caulking compound from drying out.

Plumbing entrances and exits, especially around outdoor sillcocks, should be sealed to reduce heat loss and gain, and to stop water, dirt, dust, and insects from entering your home.

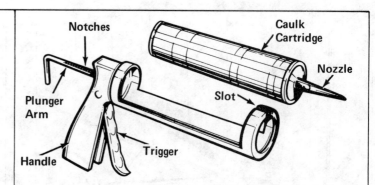

There's little mess with a cartridge caulking gun; when the cartridge is empty, you simply discard it.

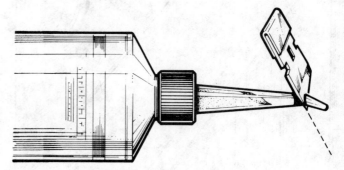

Cut the tip of the caulking compound cartridge at an angle, to the width of the narrowest joint to be filled. Most cartridges are marked with cutting guidelines.

How to Caulk

If a joint or crack has never been caulked, it's easy to spot. If the crack or joint has been caulked, it should be checked to see if the compound in it is still doing a good sealing job. Follow these steps:

1. Use a putty knife to probe the run of caulking compound. If the material feels spongy and resilient, it's still doing its job. If the material is hard and has shrunk in the joint, it should be replaced.
2. To replace caulking compound in a joint or crack, use a putty knife, utility knife, wire brush, or even a large nail to remove the old caulking material. The joint or crack should be as clean as possible and free from any oil, wax, dust, or grit.
3. Select a point along the joint or crack to start caulking. Hold the caulking gun at a 45-degree angle to the work, or at the same angle the nozzle of the cartridge was cut. Draw the caulking gun toward you—never away from you. The caulking compound must fill the crack or joint, slightly overlapping it, for the best seal. **Note:** It's usually best to caulk during warm weather because the caulking compound will flow better.

When caulking, hold the gun at a 45-degree angle to the work, or at the same angle the nozzle of the cartridge was cut.

Aerosol Product Formulated for Frame-to-Foundation Sealing

Air infiltration is the uncontrolled movement of air into and out of a home. One area that usually permits such infiltration in the average home is where the frame and foundation meet on an exterior wall; this area should be sealed. Polycel One foam sealant, made by W. R. Grace & Co., is a product formulated to seal such air infiltration areas. It comes in an aerosol and is dispensed much like shaving cream. Within a few hours, it expands and cures to form a rigid closed-cell urethane foam. According to the manufacturer, Polycel One will never shrink, dry, or harden because it's a non-solvent system. After it has cured, it can be trimmed or sanded and can be painted or stained.

All-Purpose Caulk Bonds and Seals Most Any Material

Caulking is one of the ways that you can protect your home against air infiltration. Polyseamseal all-purpose adhesive caulk, made by Darworth Co., bonds and seals most any material inside or out, including wood, glass, metal, plastic, ceramic, vinyl, porcelain, masonry, and fiberglass. According to the manufacturer, the product resists mildew, won't crack or peel, stays flexible, and cleans up with water. Polyseamseal all-purpose adhesive caulk is available in white, aluminum-gray, black, redwood, and bronze colors.

Weatherstripping Windows

Materials • Weatherstripping Materials as Required

Tools • Tape Measure • Pencil • Tin Snips • Awl • Hammer • Putty Knife

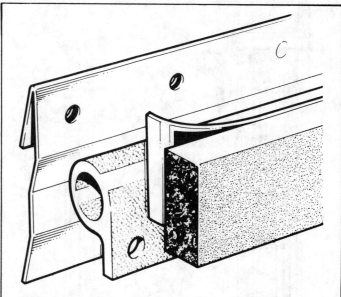

Three of the most popular types of weatherstripping are spring-metal (left), tubular gasket (center), and self-adhesive foam strips (right).

WEATHERSTRIPPING is relatively inexpensive and easy to install on windows. Three of the most popular types are spring-metal, tubular gasket, and self-adhesive strips.

Types of Weatherstripping

Spring-metal weatherstripping is available in V-shaped or flat spring-metal strips that come in bronze, copper, stainless steel, and aluminum finishes. Usually, this long-lasting weatherstripping, which is applied from indoors, is packaged in rolls that include brads for installation. It is an excellent product, but you need some patience to install it. However, once installed, it's impossible to detect when a window is closed. There also are self-adhesive metal strips, which are installed in much the same manner as spring-metal strips that are nailed.

Tubular gasket weatherstripping is a strip of flexible vinyl with a tube running along one edge; the tube compresses and conforms to uneven surfaces. The weatherstripping is nailed to the

outside of a window and, therefore, is visible. The material cannot be painted, but is available in grey or white colors. There also is a foam-filled tubular gasket; foam inside the tube adds strength and holds its shape better than the hollow gasket. Both types, however, are very durable.

Self-adhesive foam strips are probably the easiest type of weatherstripping to install. You simply peel off a protective backing and apply the strips. This type of weatherstripping, however, should only be applied to friction-free parts of a window, such as the bottom rail of the lower sash or the top rail of the upper sash. This inexpensive weatherstripping is available in rubber or plastic in varying lengths and thicknesses. When compressed by a window,

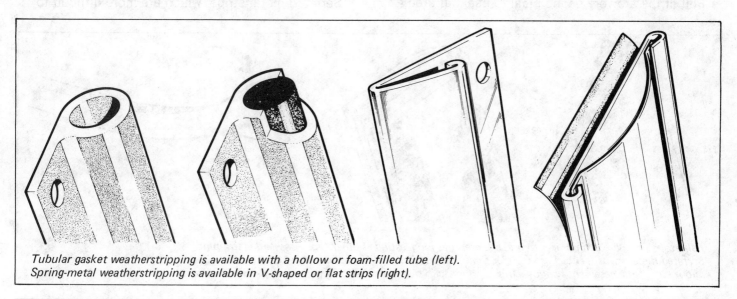

Tubular gasket weatherstripping is available with a hollow or foam-filled tube (left). Spring-metal weatherstripping is available in V-shaped or flat strips (right).

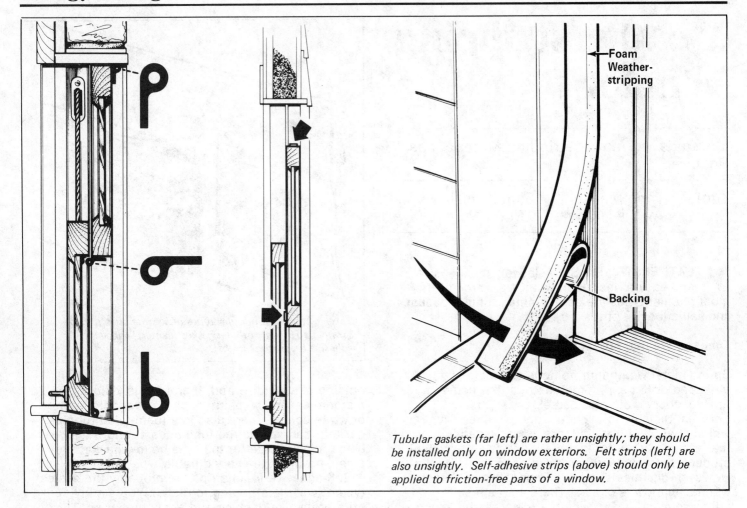

Tubular gaskets (far left) are rather unsightly; they should be installed only on window exteriors. Felt strips (left) are also unsightly. Self-adhesive strips (above) should only be applied to friction-free parts of a window.

the material makes an effective seal. Foam weatherstripping, though, generally doesn't last as long as spring-metal or tubular gasket.

Other types of weatherstripping include felt strips, serrated metal strips, and gaskets designed for jalousie and casement windows.

Felt strips are very economical to use, but aren't as long-lasting as spring-metal or tubular gasket weatherstripping; felt is prone to tear. It comes, however, in a wide range of widths, thicknesses, qualities, and colors. Usually, the strips are stapled or nailed in place but you can buy them with a self-adhesive backing.

Serrated metal strips, which are more difficult to

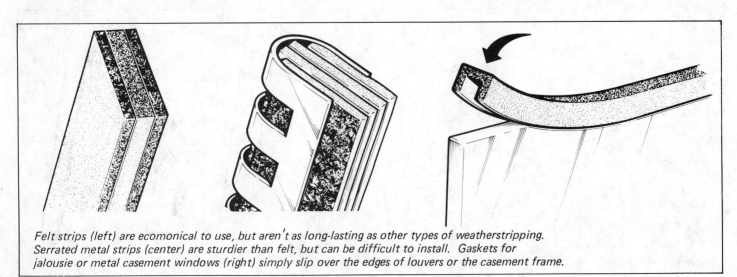

Felt strips (left) are ecomonical to use, but aren't as long-lasting as other types of weatherstripping. Serrated metal strips (center) are sturdier than felt, but can be difficult to install. Gaskets for jalousie or metal casement windows (right) simply slip over the edges of louvers or the casement frame.

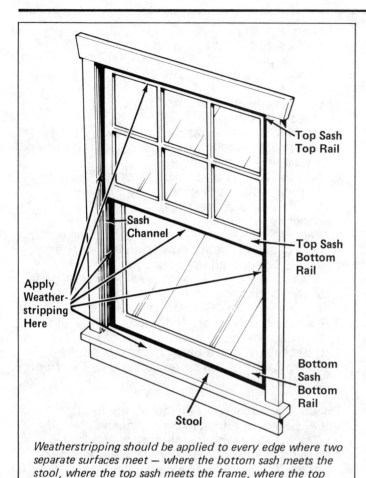

Weatherstripping should be applied to every edge where two separate surfaces meet — where the bottom sash meets the stool, where the top sash meets the frame, where the top and bottom sashes meet, and along every side joint.

install than most other types of weatherstripping, have a felt or vinyl insert running the length of the metal reinforcement.

Gaskets for jalousie or metal casement windows are made of vinyl. They simply slip over the edges of jalousie louvers or the metal casement frame; no tools or fasteners are needed for installation, but adhesive is sometimes used to secure the gaskets.

Installing Spring-Metal Strips

Spring-metal strips are very commonly used on double-hung wood windows. Unlike other types of weatherstripping, they can be installed between moving parts of the window. Usually, they are applied to the sash channels and on the sash rails. They also can be installed to the frame of wood casement windows that don't have built-in weatherstripping. To install spring-metal strips on a double-hung wood window, follow these steps:

1. Measure the length of the upper and lower sash channels.
2. Using tin snips, cut four lengths of strip for the sash channels that are 2 inches longer than your measurements.

Weatherstripping Has Many Uses

Self-adhesive weatherstripping has many uses. Permatite sponge-rubber weatherstripping, from Diversified Specialties, Inc./Durkee-Atwood Co., may be used for cushioning, insulating, and dustproofing. The weatherstripping features an air-tight plastic cover, pressure-sensitive adhesive surface, a nonstretch fabric back, and a sponge-rubber liner. The weatherstripping is available in several sizes, from 3/16 by 3/8 inch to 9/16 by 1 inch. To use, peel off the protective plastic backing and stick it in place.

The Right Size Air Conditioner

Air conditioners are rated by BTU's—British Thermal Units—a heating-cooling technical term. It takes approximately 18 BTU's per hour to cool 1 square foot of space in your home. Therefore, if you have 1,000 square feet of space to cool, you would require an air conditioner with an output of 18,000 BTU's. Other points to remember when you buy an air conditioner are: Buy the right size unit. An oversized unit will not control the humidity in your home; it actually wastes electricity. An underpowered or undersized unit will not work efficiently, and it will wear out quickly. A central air conditioning unit—one that is connected to your heating plant—costs about 20 percent less to operate than a window unit. Although the initial price of the central unit will be more, you can recover the cost over a period of time. And, you will have the advantage of cooling your entire house—not just a room or two.

Weatherstripping Resists Moisture

A product that can be cleaned with soap and water is something to consider. Vinyl-Clad Window & Door Weather Seal, from Stanley Hardware, a division of The Stanley Works, is a general-purpose weatherstripping that has a moisture-proof covering to prevent water absorption. Under the vinyl is a compressible inner foam that can seal large and small gaps in doors, windows, around air conditioning units, and at hatchways. It's available in two sizes: No. V1344-3, which is 1/4 inch by 1/4 inch by 10 feet; and No. V1344-4, which is 1/4 inch by 3/8 inch by 10 feet. To install it, you peel off the protective backing and press the self-sticking strip in position.

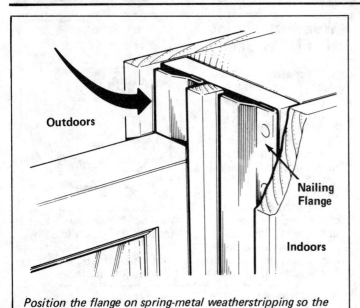

Position the flange on spring-metal weatherstripping so the flared edge faces outdoors and the nailing flange faces indoors.

3. Position one of the strips in a lower sash channel so the flared flange of the strip faces outdoors and its nailing flange faces indoors.
4. Fasten the strip in the channel. First drive a brad at the top of the strip and then at the bottom. Check to see that the strip is straight and in proper position. If it is, drive a brad in the center. Finally, drive the rest of the brads into the strip. **Note:** Some strips may need pilot holes for the brads; if so, use an awl to make them.
5. Repeat the preceeding procedure for the other lower sash channel and the two upper sash channels. **Note:** Use tin snips to make any necessary cuts in a strip to accommodate pulleys or other window hardware.
6. Measure the length of the bottom rail of the lower sash.
7. Cut three lengths of strip to your measurement.
8. Position a strip under the bottom rail of the lower sash; face the flared flange outdoors and the nailing flange indoors.
9. Nail the strip in place with brads as you did with the strips for the sash channels.
10. Mount a strip on the top of the top rail of the upper sash.
11. Raise the lower sash completely and lower the upper sash of the window so that the upper sash's bottom rail is accessible.
12. Position a strip against the inside of the upper sash's bottom rail with the flared flange facing down and the nailing flange facing up.
13. Nail the strip in place with brads as you did the other strips.
14. If necessary, use a putty knife to bend the flared flange of the strips outward so they form a better seal.

On wood windows, weatherstripping that is stapled, nailed, or attached with adhesive can be used. On windows with metal frames, only self-adhesive types of weatherstripping, as a rule, can be applied. You apply the self-adhesive weatherstripping to the top rail of the upper sash—if it moves—and to the bottom rail of the lower sash. If you spot any other gaps on a metal window, you can try attaching a vinyl tubular gasket to the gap with construction adhesive.

Weatherstripping for Doors, Windows Keeps Its Shape

Scandy Super Weatherstrip, which is made of 100-percent, closed-cell EPDM (ethylene propylene diene monomer) rubber, bounces back to its original extruded shape after being compressed. According to the Scandy Rubber Corp., the weatherstripping, which doesn't absorb moisture, is unaffected by ozone, radon, sunlight, or acidic rain. Scandy Rubber offers six different types of weatherstripping to fill different-size window and door cracks from ⅛ to 9⁄32

inch. To install most types, you cut the weatherstrip to length, peel off a protective backing, and apply the adhesive-backed material in position. You then tack or staple each end for added security. Two types are tacked or stapled in place. There also is a weatherstrip designed for garage doors.

Weatherstripping Can Help Stop Air Infiltration

Plenty of cold or hot air can penetrate around unprotected doors and windows. According to the 3M Company, 3M V-Seal weather strip can reduce such air infiltration up to 70 percent on windows and up to 90 percent on doors. To use, unroll the weatherstripping to the length needed. Cut it with scissors, and fold it along a pre-scored line to form a "V" shape. Peel the protective paper backing from the adhesive side of the product and press the strip into place on a

window or door frame with the "V" facing the outside to provide a continuous barrier to infiltration.

Weatherstripping Doors

Materials • Weatherstripping Materials as Required • Soap and Water • Rags • Staples

Tools • Tape Measure • Pencil • Tin Snips • Hammer • Awl • Putty Knife • Scissors • Screwdriver • Hacksaw • Utility Knife • Stapler

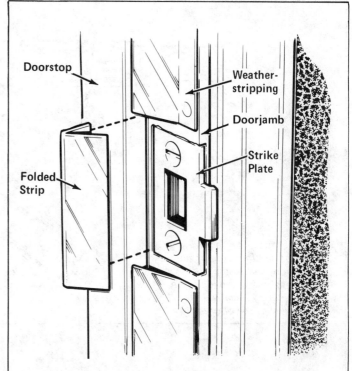

On the latch side, attach the folded strip of spring-metal provided to the edge next to the strike plate; fasten lengths of spring-metal strips above and below the strike plate.

DOORS ARE as easy to weatherstrip as windows—usually easier. In fact, many of the same products used for windows can be used to prevent air infiltration around the top and sides of doors. The most popular types of weatherstripping for doors include spring-metal strips; self-adhesive foam strips; and wood, plastic, or metal strips with plastic tubing, foam, or felt. There also are rubber or vinyl gaskets designed for metal sliding doors.

For the bottom of a doorway, there are door sweeps, which are attached to the bottoms of doors, and thermal thresholds, which are wide strips of aluminum with a "bubble" gasket of vinyl that runs as an insert down the center of the threshold.

Finally, there is weatherstripping for overhead garage doors. This is usually a flexible strip of heavy felt, vinyl, or rubber that comes in rolls to fit standard-size garage doors.

As with windows, weatherstripping that is stapled, nailed, or attached with adhesive can be used on wood doors and door frames. On metal doors or metal frames, only self-adhesive types of weatherstripping, as a rule, can be applied.

Before you apply weatherstripping to a door, make sure the door fits in its frame. If it doesn't fit properly, you may have to plane the edges, install new hinges, reset the doorstop, or replace the door entirely.

Installing Spring-Metal Strips

Spring-metal strip is a long-lasting weatherstripping product. It is packaged in rolls that include brads for installation. To install such strips along the sides and the top of a wood doorway, follow these steps:

1. Measure the top and side doorstop moldings.
2. Using tin snips, cut strips for the top and sides to your measurements.
3. Position a side strip so that the flared flange is facing the doorstop and the nailing flange is against the doorjamb.
4. Mark and trim or cut the strip to go around hinges or other door hardware.
5. Drive in a brad at the top and at the bottom of the strip. Check the strip to see that it's aligned and straight. Then, drive in a brad in the center of the strip. Finally, drive in the rest of the brads. **Note:** Some strips may need pilot holes for the brads; if so, use an awl to make them.
6. Install the strip for the other side of the doorway, and the strip for the top.
7. If necessary, use a putty knife to bend the flared flange of the strips outward so they form a better seal.

Installing Self-Adhesive Foam Strips

Self-adhesive foam strips can be installed on the edge of the doorstop and to the jamb along the top and sides to form a tight seal when the door is closed. This weatherstripping can be used for both wood and metal doorways. Follow this procedure:

1. Clean the mounting surfaces—the doorjamb on the hinge side of the door and the doorstop at the top and lock side of the doorway—

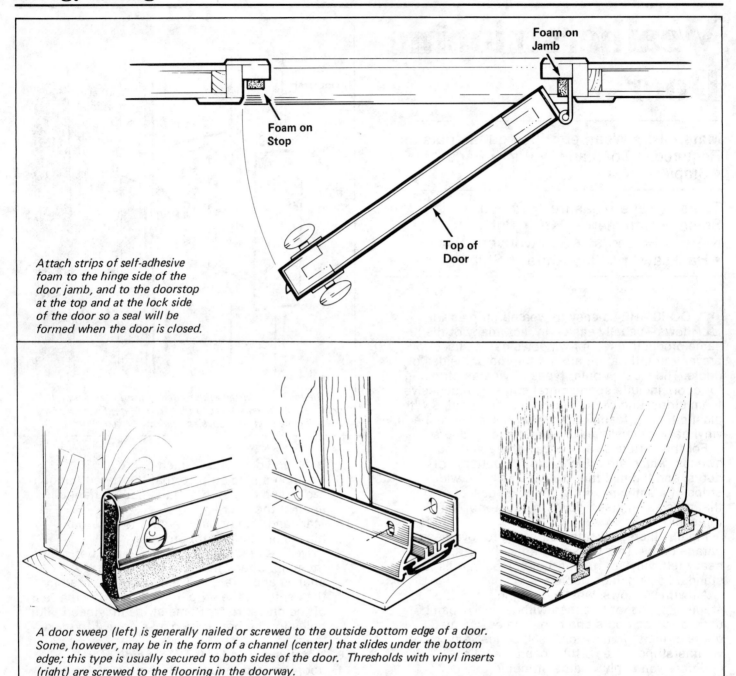

Attach strips of self-adhesive foam to the hinge side of the door jamb, and to the doorstop at the top and at the lock side of the door so a seal will be formed when the door is closed.

Foam on Jamb

Foam on Stop

Top of Door

A door sweep (left) is generally nailed or screwed to the outside bottom edge of a door. Some, however, may be in the form of a channel (center) that slides under the bottom edge; this type is usually secured to both sides of the door. Thresholds with vinyl inserts (right) are screwed to the flooring in the doorway.

where the strips are to be applied; make sure the surfaces are dry.

2. Measure the top and side doorstop moldings.
3. Using scissors, cut strips for the top and sides to your measurements.
4. Begin at one end of the jamb at the hinge side of the door and peel off the protective backing as you press the strip in place on the jamb next to the stop.
5. Mount another length of strip to the doorstop—not the jamb—at the top and at the lock side of the door so a seal will be formed when the door is closed.

Door Sweeps and Thresholds

Door sweeps are generally nailed or screwed to the outside bottom edge of a door. Some, however, may be in the form of a channel that slides under the bottom edge; this type is usually secured to both sides of the door. The flexible part of a sweep should just touch or "sweep" the threshold.

Thresholds with vinyl inserts are screwed to the flooring in the doorway. Before installing it, you will have to remove the old threshold. Then, measure and cut the metal part of the threshold with a hacksaw and the vinyl part with a sharp utility knife.

Brush Strip Seals Gaps in Garage Doors

A special weatherstripping seal for garage doors is made by Sealeze Corp. It is a tough, flexible nylon brush sealed in a bed of durable PVC plastic.

Therm-L-Brush may be attached to one- or two-car garages; kits contain nails and installation instructions. The product, which is available in brown or white colors, may be used with automatic garage door openers. The one-car garage kit covers a door 7 feet high and 9 feet wide; the two-car garage kit covers a door 7 feet high and 16 feet wide. Material for the bottom of the door is not included. Therm-L-Brush installs with ordinary household hand tools. Sealeze also makes kits for sealing gaps around and at the bottom of other doors in your home.

Weatherstripping for Garage Doors

Closed, but loose-fitting garage doors, are a major source of energy loss. Cold air gusting through the bottom can be shut out with 3M garage door bottom weather strip, made by the 3M Company.

This synthetic rubber material, which is nailed in place with galvanized nails, remains flexible at temperatures below −20° F, and it conforms to an uneven cement floor for an efficient seal. This type of weatherstripping is essential if your garage is attached to the house.

Dual-Edge Weather Seal for Door Bottoms

Doors are notorious for allowing air infiltration. The Double Seal Door Bottom Weather Seal, No. V1306, from Stanley Hardware, a division of The Stanley Works, offers protection against draft, cold, heat, and dust infiltration from underneath doors. Made to fit 1¾-inch-thick doors, it has patented dual sealing edges that combine water-repellant polypropylene pile and inner fins to provide extra protection. The 36-inch mounting channel covers existing nicks and scratches near the bottom of the door and protects against further damage. The seal's slip-on design makes it easy to install. Slotted screw holes allow you to adjust it, and minimum pile drag allows the door to open and close easily. The door seal comes in white or brown to match or contrast with light or dark finishes.

Screw or nail the threshold to the floor so that the vinyl insert is compressed by the bottom edge of the door when it is closed.

Garage Door Strip

If your garage is attached to the house, a lot of energy can escape through the crack between the floor and the bottom of the garage door unless flexible weatherstripping is installed. Strips to seal this gap can be made of heavy felt, vinyl, or rubber that comes in rolls. All are installed in a similar way. Follow these steps:

1. Measure the bottom of the garage door.
2. Using a utility knife, cut the length of strip to your measurement.
3. Clean the bottom of the door.
4. Staple or nail the strip to the bottom edge of the door. If you use nails, roofing nails work well. Drive a nail at one end of the strip. Then, just tack the other end to hold it in place. Return to the first nail and begin spacing nails about 2 or 3 inches apart. When you reach the tacked end, remove the partially driven nail and secure the end of the strip. You may have to trim the end of the strip.

Sun Control Film for Windows

Materials • Sun Control Film • Glass Cleaner • Paper Towels • Liquid Dishwashing Detergent • Masking Tape • Clear Fingernail Polish

Tools • Utility Knife • Plastic Squeeze Bottle • Rubber Squeegee • Spray Bottle • Straightedge

When the inside of the window and the sticky side of the film are completely wet, place the sticky side of the film against the glass. Then, slide the film around until it's positioned properly.

SUN CONTROL, or reflective, film for windows not only reflects the sun's heat away from your home in summer, but it also keeps heat in your home in winter. Besides providing all-year energy savings, sun control film filters out glare and reduces the fading effects caused by sunlight on draperies, carpeting, and furniture.

Sun control film is available in silver or bronze tints, and in a number of densities ranging from about 50 percent to 85 percent. A 50-percent film doesn't produce the mirrored effect of the higher-density film, making it more desirable to some people. However, as a rule of thumb, the higher the density, the more energy-saving benefit there is.

Note: Different brands of sun control film may have slightly different application techniques. If in doubt, always follow the manufacturer's installation instructions.

To install sun control film, follow these steps:

1. Clean the windows. Remove all dirt, grease, wax, and paint, and dry the glass thoroughly.
2. Mix 1 teaspoon of liquid dishwashing detergent and 1 pint of water into a plastic squeeze bottle.
3. Spray the window with the solution and wipe it dry with paper towels.
4. Cut the film so that it is about ¼ inch larger on all sides than the window glass.
5. At one corner of the film, attach a short length of masking tape to each side of the film, but don't let the adhesive sides of the two pieces of tape touch each other.
6. Spray the glass with plain water until it is covered.
7. Pull the tabs of masking tape to separate the film from its protective backing.
8. Spray the sticky side of the film with water as you peel the backing off; the entire surface of the film must be wet.
9. Place the sticky side of the film against the glass, and slide the film around until it's

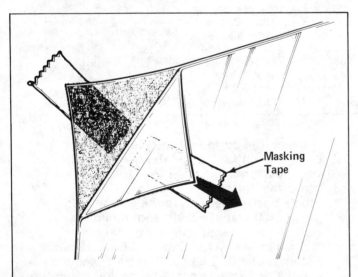

At a corner of the film, attach a short length of masking tape to each side of the film. Then, you can pull the tabs of tape to separate the film from its protective backing.

Masking Tape

Film Reflects Summer Heat

Solar film takes about two hours to install; once it's on, it should last for years. Van Leer Plastics manufactures Valvac Solar Control window film, which can be left on the windows year-round, and can be cleaned with cool water. The film is composed of a thin layer of aluminum, which is covered on both sides with tinted plastic film. Not only does it reflect heat during the summer, but it helps contain heat inside during the winter. Available colors are silver, silver/smoke, and silver/bronze.

Sun Control Film Stops Fabric Fade

Solar film not only reflects the sun's heat, but can help slow the process of furniture, drapery, and carpet fading. Gila Mirror Film, made by Gila River Products, reflects up to 77 percent of the sun's heat, according to the manufacturer. The manufacturer also reports that the film blocks up to 95 percent of the sun's ultraviolet rays—the major cause of fabric fading.

Window kits come in five standard window sizes, in silver, smoke, or bronze colors. The Mirror Film can also be purchased in bulk.

Reusable Solar Film Comes in Three Tints

Summer sunlight pouring through windows can fade your household furnishings. Scotchtint reusable sun control film, made by the 3M Company, rejects from 65 to 70 percent of the sun's heat and 85 to 90 percent of the sun's glare, the company reports. It also cuts ultraviolet rays that cause fading of interior furnishings, such as carpeting, wallpaper, paint, chair and sofa coverings, and paneling. The film can be removed easily for reapplication or left in place over large, glassed areas. Scotchtint sun control film is available in silver, bronze, or smoke tints.

positioned properly. The wet film should slide easily on the wet glass.

10. When the film is in position, spray the back side of the film with plain water to provide lubrication for a rubber squeegee.

11. Using a rubber squeegee, work the water from the center of the film by stroking vertically and horizontally. Small bubbles or haze should disappear in a few days. Don't press the squeegee down along the film's edges until the film is trimmed.

12. With a sharp utility knife and straightedge, trim the film to within about 1/16 inch from the edge of the glass.

13. Squeegee the edges of the trimmed film. **Note:** If the edges of the film ever start to peel, apply a thin line of clear fingernail polish to the problem area and press the film back down again.

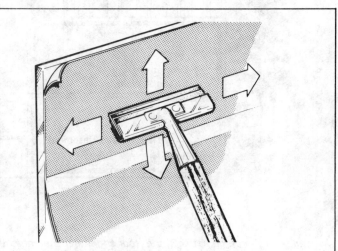

Use a rubber squeegee to work the water from the center of the film. Stroke vertically and horizontally.

Insulation

Materials • Insulation as Required • Plastic Sheeting as Required • Staples • Duct Tape

Tools • Tape Measure • Pencil • Utility Knife • Rake • Hammer or Broom • Stapler • Breathing Mask • Safety Goggles

NEXT TO storm windows and storm doors, weatherstripping, and caulking, insulation is your best buy for saving energy and making your home more comfortable. Like other energy-saving home building products, insulation can qualify for a tax credit on your federal income tax.

Insulation not only saves energy, it also serves as a fire-retardant and offers some sound-deadening qualities. There are nine different types of insulation. You can install all of them yourself, but some are easier to install than others. For example, to install blanket insulation behind a gypsum board wall, the wallcovering has to be removed—a job most homeowners wouldn't want to tackle. The same wall, however, can be filled with a loose-fill insulation, such as vermiculite, which you can do with a rented machine that blows the insulation between the wall studs.

Insulation works by increasing the resistance to the flow of heat through your home's attic, walls, or floor. The measure of how much resistance a material has is called its R-value. The "R" stands for resistance to winter heat loss or summer heat gain. These numbers, which are insulation efficiency ratings, are more accurate than inches as a means of designating performance. For example, one brand of insulation may be slightly thicker or thinner than another, but if they're marked with the same R-value, they'll resist heat flow equally well. The higher the R-value, the more resistant—and effective—a material's insulating capability is.

Nearly all insulation dealers have a chart that gives R-values recommended for use in your geographical area.

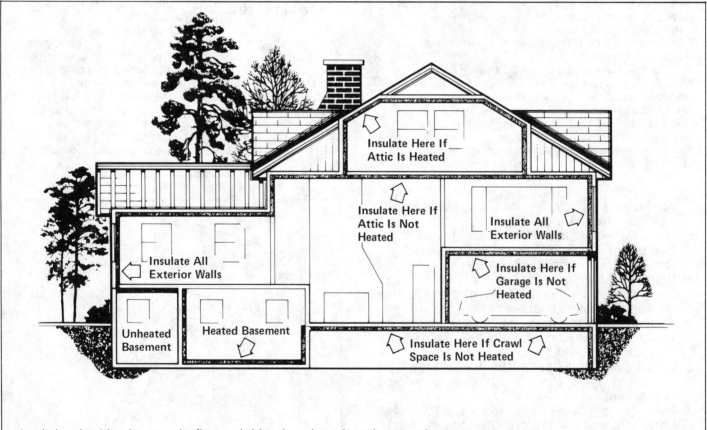

Insulation should go between the floor and either the unheated crawl space or basement, between the ceiling and unheated attic (between the attic and the roof if the attic is heated), and inside all exterior walls, including those adjacent to an unheated garage.

Types of Insulation

The easiest types of insulation for a homeowner to put in are blanket, batt, and loose-fill mineral wool or vermiculite insulation.

To prevent condensation, insulation must always have some type of vapor barrier. Some insulation has this vapor barrier attached to it: the barrier will be either aluminum foil or kraft paper. There is no difference in the quality of the barrier; paper, however, is generally used where there is no risk from fire.

For loose-fill insulation—and batt and blanket insulation without a vapor barrier attached—polyethylene, or plastic, sheeting is used as a vapor barrier.

Regardless of type, the vapor barrier must always face the warm side of the room. If the material is being installed in an unheated attic, the barrier should face the heated rooms below. Between rafters, the barrier faces the room, not the roof. If the attic floor will be covered, use insulation without a barrier between the floors and insulation with a barrier between the rafters. In crawl spaces, the vapor barrier usually goes against the subfloor—toward the warm room above.

The following are popular types of insulation and their R-values:

FIBERGLASS. This material comes in blankets, batts, and loose fill. It is easy to use. The blankets with the vapor barrier attached are stapled to framing members. Batts usually are laid in place, while loose-fill fiberglass is placed between joists and raked level. Fiberglass insulation has a 3.3 R-value per inch of material.

Note: The per-inch figure, when multiplied by the thickness of the material, is not a certain guide to the material's R-value. Therefore, insulation manufacturers indicate the exact R-value on the product or on its package. Loose-fill insulation has the R-value yield inch by inch.

VERMICULITE. This is a loose-fill material that can be poured between framing members and raked level. Or, it can be blown into place with special equipment. Vermiculite is not well-suited for insulating walls because it tends to "pack down" after insulation, reducing the R-value, which is 2.1 per inch.

POLYSTYRENE. This is a rigid-board insulation, and is best used in new construction. Its main use in older homes is behind wall paneling. The insulation may be glued or nailed in place.

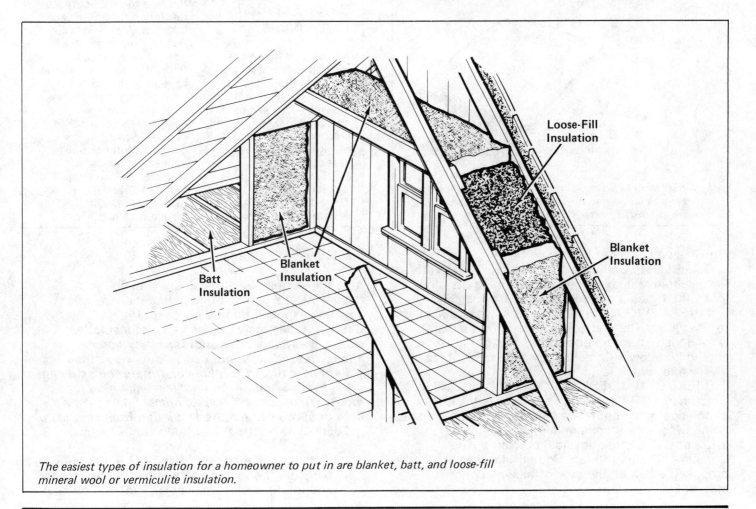

The easiest types of insulation for a homeowner to put in are blanket, batt, and loose-fill mineral wool or vermiculite insulation.

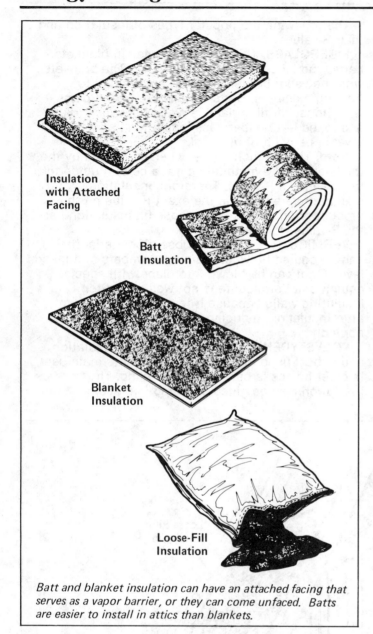

Insulation with Attached Facing

Batt Insulation

Blanket Insulation

Loose-Fill Insulation

Batt and blanket insulation can have an attached facing that serves as a vapor barrier, or they can come unfaced. Batts are easier to install in attics than blankets.

Variety of Blanket, Batt Insulation Is Available

A variety of fiberglass insulation products are available from Johns-Manville Corp. In batts and blankets, for example, the company makes foil- and kraft-faced batts and blankets, as well as unfaced batts and blankets, with R-values ranging from R-11 to R-38. There also are a flame-resistant FSK-25 batt insulation with a fastening flange and an all-purpose insulation for utility use. In addition, Johns-Manville makes a sill sealer for use between masonry foundations and sill plates to reduce air and dirt infiltration, and masonry wall batts that are designed to be installed between furring strips before an interior finish is applied. Johns-Manville also makes acoustical batts and blankets, loose-fill insulation, and insulating sheathing.

The R-value is 3.5 per inch.

CELLULOSE. Cellulose that has been treated for fire resistance is available in blankets, batts, and loose fill. It has a good R-value—3.7 per inch.

MINERAL WOOL. Mineral, or rock, wool is similar to fiberglass. The main difference is that mineral wool doesn't have an odor when wet, but it never should be allowed to become wet because it loses its R-value, which is 3.3 per inch.

UREA FORMALDEHYDE FOAM. This insulation, which has an R-value of 4.5 per inch, is the subject of considerable controversy. After installation, some homeowners have complained about odors, skin irritations, and other physical problems. The Consumer Product Safety Commission has proposed a ban on the sale of this insulation material.

Insulating Attic Floors

Attics are often easy to insulate because you usually have a choice of installing the insulation between exposed floor joists or roof rafters. *Caution: When installing any type of insulation, wear a breathing mask, gloves, safety goggles, and a long-sleeved shirt that can be buttoned at the collar and cuffs. Insulation can irritate the skin and eyes. Every 30 minutes or so, leave the area for a break. When you're finished, immediately take a bath or shower to remove insulation from your skin.*

To insulate an attic floor, follow these steps:

1. Determine the square footage of the attic. Measure the length and width of the attic floor and multiply the dimensions. Batt and blanket

Indoor Cover for Air Conditioner

An outdoor cover on an air conditioner can be stolen or blown away by strong winter winds. An indoor cover cannot, and it's easier to install; you don't need a ladder. The No.

CAC 300 indoor insulated air conditioner cover, made by Con-Serv, Inc., fits all residential window and wall air conditioners. It has a foam lining that blocks out cold air; an "aluminized" layer reflects heat inside. The cover installs in minutes.

Insulated Blanket for Water Heaters

You can help reduce heat loss around an uninsulated water heater and minimize sweating around a water tank with insulation. With Water Heater Insulation Weather Seal from Stanley Hardware, a division of The Stanley Works, only scissors are needed for installation. You wrap the weather seal around the heater or tank, and hold it in place with pre-cut vinyl tape provided with the insulation kit. The seal side wrapper is 1⅝ inches thick with an insulating value of R-6.3; the top plate is 2½ inches thick with an insulating value of R-8.7.

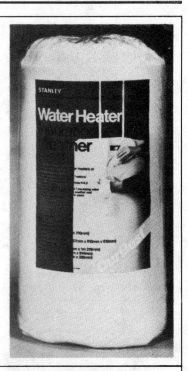

Foil-and-Film Wrap Insulates Ducts

Insulating your ducts is one way to reduce heat or cold air loss. Ductwrap, made by Pioneer Energy Products, Inc., combines closed-cell polyethylene foam and reinforced aluminum foil in a self-adhesive wrap. Ductwrap is available in 6-inch or 12-inch widths, in 15-foot rolls. It can be applied to round or rectangular ducts. The wrap also is effective in helping to reduce noise.

Energy-Saving on the House

If you're planning to reshingle your home's roof sometime soon, take advantage of color. For example, if you live in a cold climate, use darker shingle colors; they absorb more sunlight and heat. If you live in a moderate or warm climate, use lighter shingle colors that reflect sunlight. This can add considerable savings to heating and cooling costs over a period of time.

insulation are sold by the square foot—usually 40 square feet to a package. For example, if the attic area you're insulating is 800 square feet, you will require 20 rolls with a vapor barrier.

Note: If you are installing loose-fill insulation, you also will have to determine how much plastic sheeting you'll need for a vapor barrier. This is sold in large rolls, and will have to be cut into strips with a utility knife to fit between the joists.

2. Measure the distance between the framing members—rafters or joists. Usually, they are 16 inches on center, but some could be 24 inches on center. You can buy insulation to fit these widths.

3. If your attic floor already has some insulation, and you want to increase the R-value, the new insulation may be placed directly over the old material. Batts or blankets can be placed over loose-fill insulation or batts or blankets. If the old insulation is covered by a vapor barrier, slash the barrier with a utility knife and lay the new insulation—vapor barrier up—over the existing insulation.

Note: If you are placing loose-fill insulation over loose-fill insulation, rake the present insulation level and pour in the new material *if* there is an existing vapor barrier under the old loose-fill material. If there isn't, you will have to remove the old insulation, install a vapor barrier, and pour and level the insulation over it.

4. Install the batt or blanket insulation at the eaves and work toward the center of the attic.

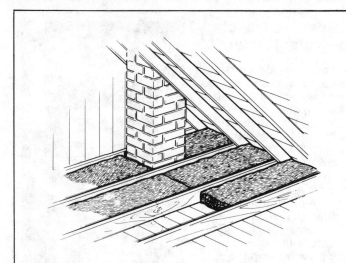

When installing batt insulation, start at the eaves and work toward the center of the attic.

When installing loose-fill insulation, lap edges of plastic sheeting up the face of the joists and staple it in place.

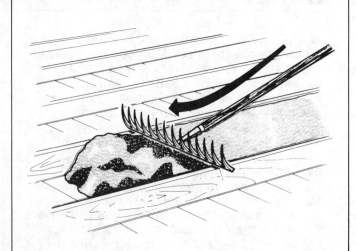

You can level loose-fill insulation between joists with a rake.

When you reach the center, work from the opposite side toward the center. Use a hammer handle or broom stick to push the insulation in position in areas you can't reach. Press the insulation into place between the framing members without compacting it or the material will lose insulation value.

Note: If you're installing loose-fill insulation, install the vapor barrier first. Lap the edges of the plastic sheeting up the face of the joists about 2 or 3 inches and staple it in place. Don't cover vents and heat-producing devices. These items, which can be surrounded by batts, need 3 inches of clearance. Finally, pour the insulation and level it with a rake.

5. If you have to cut a batt or a blanket, use a utility knife. Compress the insulation with a length of board, and use the edge of the board as a straightedge to guide the knife.
6. Trim batts or blankets to fit around vents, recessed lighting fixtures, and exhaust fan motors. Allow 3 inches of clearance between such heat-producing devices and the insulation. *Caution: Don't pull on electrical wiring to move it out of the way.*
7. If the vapor barrier on the insulation should be accidentally ripped, patch the tear with duct tape.

Insulating Walls or Rafters

Insulating exposed wall studs or roof rafters isn't difficult. The procedure, however, is slightly different than insulating an attic floor. Follow these steps:

1. Follow Steps 1 and 2 in the previous procedure to determine how much foil- or kraft-faced insulating batts or blankets you will need for the job.
2. If you are adding insulation to existing insulation with a vapor barrier, slash the barrier with a utility knife and push it down between the rafters or studs if the studs are wide enough to accept it.
3. Hang the insulation from the top down, precutting the material to fit the length of the rafter run or the height of the wall.
4. Staple the insulation to the faces—not edges—of the framing members. Space staples at about 3-inch intervals. The insulation vapor barrier has a tab for staples along each edge. This tab, which is about ¾ inch from the surface of the barrier covering the insulation material, provides an air space between the vapor barrier and the back of a wallcovering. This small air space provides an additional R-value of about 0.94 to the insulation.
5. Trim the insulation to fit around vents,

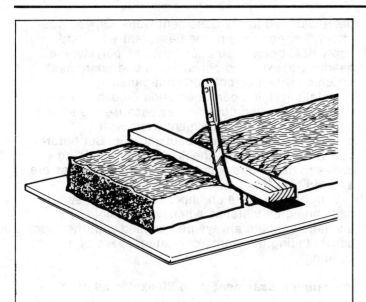

If you have to cut a batt or blanket, compress the insulation with a board, and use it as a straightedge to guide your knife.

recessed lighting fixtures, and exhaust fan motors. Allow 3 inches of clearance between such heat-producing devices and the insulation.

Caution: Don't pull on electrical wiring to move it out of the way.

6. If the vapor barrier on the insulation should be accidentally ripped, patch the tear with duct tape.

Insulation in Covered Walls

Putting insulation between stud walls that are covered on one side with sheathing and siding and on the other side with plaster on gypsum wallboard is a job best left to a professional. Loose-fill material can be blown between the studs, but it's better to have a professional do this. You can, however, rent the necessary equipment in some areas and do the job yourself. It involves drilling holes at the top of each stud spacing and forcing in the loose-fill insulation through a hose.

Install Attic Batts Toward the Center

When insulating an attic with batt insulation, work from the outer edge of the space toward the center. You'll be able to do whatever cutting and fitting is necessary more easily at the center of the attic rather than near the eaves, where there's little headroom. Batt insulation in rolls or rigid-fit batts are made by CertainTeed. The company's products have installation instructions printed on the package, and the batts are striped to indicate R-values. Insulation in the form of rolls is ideal for larger jobs. CertainTeed rolls are 39 feet, 2 inches long, and have an R-value of 19.

Indoor/Outdoor Building Veneer Is Insulated

When you need to insulate and cover a wall, a product that does both can save you time and money. CrystalBrick insulated building veneer, made by Thermo Energy Amalgamated Manufacturing Corp., has an insulating factor of R-13. It is lightweight and suitable for indoor or outdoor application. Easily applied with industrial mastic, the product is made from fiberglass-reinforced cement backed with 1 ¾ inches of polyurethane foam. Each CrystalBrick panel is 24 inches wide, 12 inches high, and 2 inches thick; five panels (10 square feet) are packed to a carton. According to the manufacturer, the product is fire-retardant and termite-proof. It is available in several finishes—Mexican brick, slumpbrick, wirebrick, mountain rock, and antique brick.

Insulating Basements and Crawl Spaces

Materials • Insulation as Required • Staples • Wire Hangers, 1 × 2 Furring Strips, or Chicken Wire • Nails and Wire • Duct Tape • Construction Adhesive • 1 × 3 Furring Strips • Plastic Sheeting • Roofing Cement or Short-Shank Roofing Nails • Bricks

Tools • Stapler • Tape Measure • Utility Knife • Breathing Mask • Safety Goggles • Hammer • Caulking Gun

IF YOUR BASEMENT is unfinished, you can insulate it in one of two practical ways. You can build stud walls to which you staple or friction-fit insulating blankets after the stud walls have been fastened to the basement walls. Or, you could attach furring strips to the basement walls and apply rigid-board insulation, such as polystyrene beadboard, extruded polystyrene, and fiberglass, which can then be covered with paneling.

Installing rigid-board insulation probably is the easiest of the two possibilities because the sheets can be glued to the basement walls with construction cement in a caulking gun. But before you start this project, check your local building codes to determine what types of wallcoverings are allowed over this type of insulating material.

Vapor barriers are an important part of insulation and should be installed whenever possible. Insulation should always be installed with the vapor barrier facing the warm, or heated, space of a building.

Insulating a Basement With Blanket Insulation

To insulate a basement with vapor barrier-backed blanket insulation, follow these steps:

1. Cover the subfloor's header and end joists with insulation blankets; staple the insulation from the subfloor above to the framing below.
2. Measure and cut insulation to fit the length of the ceiling joists. To cut the insulation, sandwich it between two boards to compress it, and using the top board as a straightedge, cut the insulation with a utility knife.
3. If the insulation vapor barrier will face the

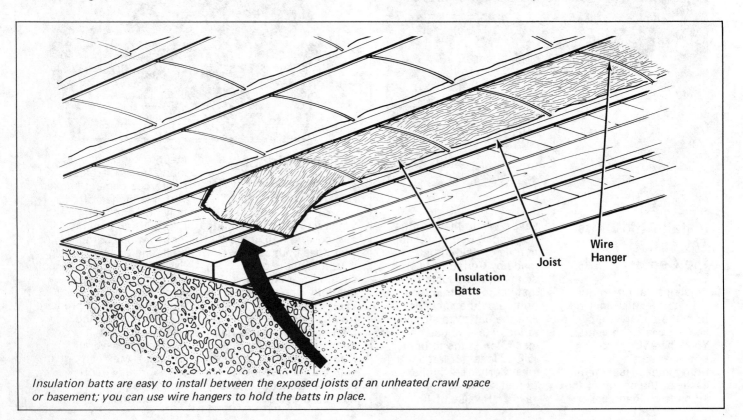

Insulation batts are easy to install between the exposed joists of an unheated crawl space or basement; you can use wire hangers to hold the batts in place.

basement, staple the insulation to the faces—not edges—of the ceiling joists; the insulation has tabs along each side for this purpose.

If the vapor barrier will be facing away from the basement, "hang" the insulation between the joists using wire hangers, which are designed to hold insulation. Space the hangers at about 28-inch intervals. Wire hangers have sharpened ends to pierce the wood; bend them slightly and snap them into place.

Note: If the ceiling will be left unfinished, you can use 1 × 2 furring strips or chicken wire fastened to the joist edges to keep the insulation in place. Or, you can zig-zag wire around nail supports driven into the joists.

4. After insulating the ceiling, measure and cut insulation to fit between the top plate, or header, of the wall studs and the bottom plate, or sill.
5. Staple the insulation to the faces—not edges—of the wall studs with the vapor barrier facing the basement. You can fill space around electrical outlets and other odd openings with wadded-up pieces of insulation. If the vapor barrier should be accidentally ripped, patch the tear with duct tape.

Insulating a Basement With Rigid-Board Insulation

If your basement will not be finished, rigid-board insulation may be installed directly to the basement walls; it isn't suitable for ceilings. If the basement will eventually be finished, the walls will have to be furred so that the wallcovering materials may be attached. For this procedure, follow these steps:

1. Glue and/or nail 1 × 3 furring strips to the basement walls on 16-inch centers; the center of one strip should be 16 inches from the center of the next one.
2. Using a caulking gun, apply a few daubs of construction adhesive on each insulation panel and place it between the furring strips.
3. If necessary, tack sheets of plastic sheeting to the furring strips, completely covering the walls. The plastic, which will serve as a vapor barrier, can hang loosely because the wallcovering fasteners will hold it in place.
   Note: If the rigid-board insulation used is polystyrene beadboard or fiberglass, you'll have to install a vapor barrier. This isn't necessary with other types of rigid-board insulation because they form their own vapor barrier.

If the basement isn't to be finished, the rigid-board insulation can be applied directly to the basement walls with construction cement. Make sure, however, that all joints are flush and tight. The insulation is best installed horizontally; and work from the ceiling downward. After the insulation has been installed, cover the floor with plastic sheeting, lapping it about 2 inches up the insulation and tacking it in place with roofing cement or short-

Don't Forget to Insulate Band Joist

When insulating a basement, you shouldn't forget to protect the band joist—the space between the top of the basement wall and the ceiling above—from winter heat loss and summer heat gain. An uninsulated band joist can mean uncomfortable winter drafts and higher fuel bills for heating and cooling. This area of the basement can be insulated with long strips of unfaced fiberglass insulation, such as that manufactured by Owens Corning Fiberglas Corp. The company makes a wide variety of insulation products, including unfaced and kraft-faced batts and blankets, loose-fill wools, masonry and perimeter insulation, sill sealer, and fiberglass insulating sheathing.

Save Heat and Energy at Your Clothes Dryer

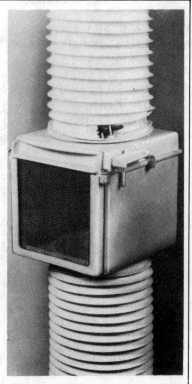

During cold weather, you can save clothes dryer heat and energy. The Clothes Dryer Heat Energy Saver, made by Melard Manufacturing Corp., connects directly into a dryer's vent duct in minutes. All dryer heat can then be transferred to the room of your choice. A self-locking operating lever on the device closes or opens the vent for summer or winter operation. The Clothes Dryer Heat Energy Saver, model No. 2575B, is made of molded, high-heat polypropylene in an off-white color. It features an automatic safety overload valve and a lint screen that can be cleaned easily.

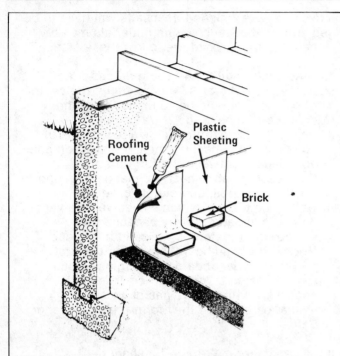

Cover the ground under the porch with plastic sheeting. Where there's a foundation wall, lap the sheeting up the wall about 6 inches and "tack" it in place with daubs of asphalt roofing cement.

1. Measure the area under the porch and cut enough plastic sheeting to fit.
2. Cover the ground with the plastic sheeting. Where there's a foundation wall, lap the sheeting up the wall about 6 inches and "tack" it in place with daubs of asphalt roofing cement.
3. At joints on the ground, lap the sheeting about 6 inches and weight it down with bricks.
   Note: You don't have to insulate between porch floor joists. The purpose of the sheeting is to prevent moisture from the ground from penetrating into the wood above and encouraging rot.

Crawl Spaces

Like attached porches, crawl spaces with earth floors should also be protected. Follow this procedure:

1. Measure the length of the joists over the crawl space and cut lengths of blanket insulation to fit between them.
2. Place the insulation between the joists with the vapor barrier facing the subfloor or heated area above.
3. Secure the insulation with wire hangers at about 28-inch intervals. Or, you can use 1 × 2 furring strips or chicken wire fastened to the joist edges to secure the insulation. Another alternative is to zig-zag wire around nail supports driven into the joists.
4. Finally, cover the earth floor in the crawl space with plastic sheeting, following the procedure in Steps 1 through 3 in "Earth Floors Under Porches."

shank roofing nails. On the floor, sheets should overlap about 6 inches. They also should be weighted down.

Earth Floors Under Porches

Homes with attached porches that have earth floors should have insulation protection. Follow these steps:

This Heavy-Duty Utility Knife Guards Your Knuckles

Skinned knuckles are commonplace whenever you have to cut materials. The heavy-duty utility knife, made by the American Safety Razor Co., features a guard that protects your hand when cutting all sorts of materials. The knife also has three blade positions with a firm lock to prevent wobbling. The utility knife, which is easy to load without tools, stores extra blades in its plastic handle.

Polystyrene Foam Insulation for Foundation Walls

Exposed foundation walls can account for about 10 percent of a typical home's heat loss. Applying Styrofoam TG insulation, made by Dow Chemical USA, on the exposed outside wall allows the foundation to store heat produced inside the house rather than collect and retain cold from the outside. Dow's Stryofoam TG insulation is a rigid, extruded polystyrene foam, manufactured in board form. The boards are

strong, lightweight, and virtually impervious to water. The boards feature tongue-and-groove edges that fit snugly together to insure a tight barrier of protection and to help reduce air infiltration.

Wood- and Coal-Burning Stoves

Materials • Masking Tape • Newspapers or Dropcloths • Plastic Trash Bags • Stove Replacement Parts as Required • Stove Cement • Waxed Paper • Stove Blacking • Newspapers and Kindling • Fuel • Creosote and Soot Cleaner • Salt or Baking Soda

Tools • Pencil • Screwdriver • Flue-Cleaning Brush • Wire Brush • Shovel • Putty Knife • Vacuum Cleaner • Metal Bucket

WOOD- AND COAL-BURNING stoves have been gaining in popularity as alternate sources of energy. But, if you're planning to purchase one to heat part or all of your home, there are a number of safety and installation considerations you should be aware of before you buy. Or, you may already have a stove, but have problems in getting the appliance to burn better and more efficiently. Smouldering fires, fuel that won't ignite, smoke-filled rooms, and most importantly, safety hazards are just some of the daily problems you may be facing.

Safety Considerations

Most stove manufacturers supply instructions for installation with their products. In fact, you should be wary of buying a stove that doesn't have complete instructions. It's also recommended that the product be certified by a recognized testing organization, such as Underwriters' Laboratories. And, before installing a stove, obtain a building permit—if one is required in your area—before putting in the chimney; after it's installed, have building code officials inspect it.

If you are shopping for a new stove, there are some basic requirements for installation that you should check with the retailer before you buy:

1. The top of the chimney should be at least 3 feet above the point where it goes through the roof. It also should be 2 feet higher than

the house at any point within 10 feet; for example, the top of the chimney should be 2 feet higher than the roof ridge if the roof ridge is within 10 feet of the top of the chimney.
2. The chimney should not extend more than 90 feet for 6-inch, 7-inch, or 8-inch pipe sizes, and it should not go beyond 50 feet for 10-inch and 12-inch pipe sizes. If the chimney goes through a wall, it should not extend more than 30 feet beyond the tee section that goes through the wall.
3. The chimney, which can act like a lightning rod, should be grounded; ground the stove as you would any electrical appliance.
4. If the chimney pipe goes through a closet or built-in storage area, such as kitchen cabinets, it must be in an enclosed space. Enclosures for chimney pipes are available from a number of manufacturers.
5. If more than one stove will be connected to a pipe-type chimney, the chimney should be

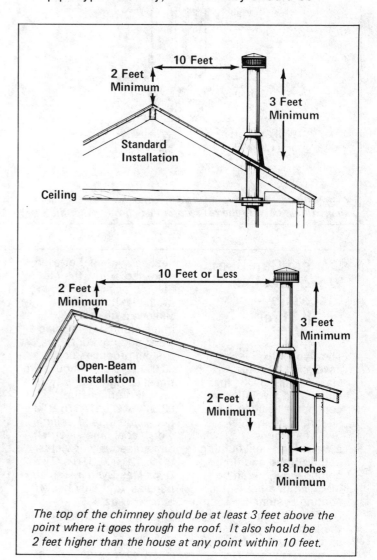

The top of the chimney should be at least 3 feet above the point where it goes through the roof. It also should be 2 feet higher than the house at any point within 10 feet.

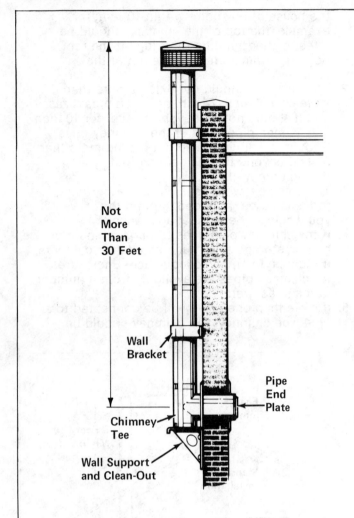

Not More Than 30 Feet

Wall Bracket

Pipe End Plate

Chimney Tee

Wall Support and Clean-Out

If the chimney goes through a wall, it shouldn't extend more than 30 feet beyond the tee section that goes through the wall.

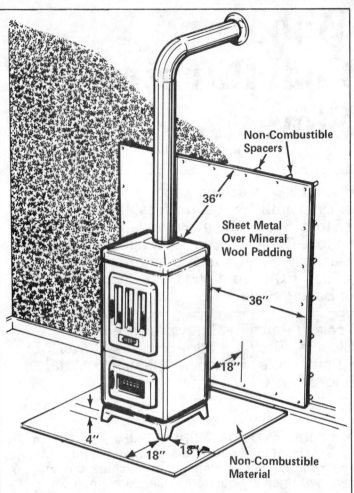

Non-Combustible Spacers

Sheet Metal Over Mineral Wool Padding

36"

36"

18"

4"

18" 18"

Non-Combustible Material

There are minimum clearances for stove installations. For example, floor protection should include a stove mat with at least 4 inches of clearance from stove to floor. The protection should extend at least 18 inches around the stove.

System Can Use Wood, Coal, or Electricity— or All Three!

The Dyna-Max System, developed by Riteway Manufacturing Co., Inc., is billed as a revolutionary concept in residential heating. The system revolves around the Dyna I, a wood- and coal-burning unit. With no additional components, it can be installed in a hot water heating system. By adding the Max-Changer package, the Dyna I can be installed in almost any hot air heating system. For even more versatility, the Max Electric package is available; it includes a 5-kilowatt electric immersion heater. Using wood and coal only, the system produces up to 50,000 BTU's (six-hour burn time); using electricity only, it produces up to 68,300 BTU's (17,075 BTU's per element); and using wood, coal, and electricity simultaneously, it yields up to 120,000 BTU's. The Dyna-Max System can be used as your only heat source or as a supplemental one. It also can be used to supplement a heat pump.

Little Drops Add Up to a Lot

One drop of hot water every second from just one leaky faucet can waste 700 gallons of hot water per year. Not only does the water go down the drain, but so does the heat used to make the water hot. This is about 5½ gallons of oil, 175 kilowatt-hours of electricity, or 700 cubic feet of natural gas. A new washer to stop the leak costs less than five cents, and it should take you less than 30 minutes to install it.

equal in size to the combined area of the connector pipes. Never connect additional wood- and coal-burning appliances, or a fireplace, to a fireplace chimney.

6. Floor protection should consist of an approved stove mat, such as fiberglass batts covered with sheet metal, mortared bricks, stone, or concrete with at least 4 inches of clearance from the stove to the floor. The protection should extend at least 18 inches around the stove so that embers don't fall on an unprotected floor.

7. Minimum wall clearance—where combustible materials such as paneling, gypsum wallboard, and wood studs are involved—is 3 feet. If the walls are protected with mineral wool paddings and have a 28-gauge sheet metal covering with a 1-inch air space between the back of the shield and the wall, the stove may be moved to 18 inches of the wall.

8. Exposed stovepipe must be three times its diameter away from anything that will burn; for example, an 8-inch pipe would have to be at least 24 inches away from a combustible material. If a heatshield is used, this distance may be reduced to a minimum of 9 inches, but check your local codes first.

9. A spark screen should be installed over the outside opening of the chimney to prevent sparks from escaping and causing roof or exterior building fires.

Cleaning a Stove

Both wood- and coal-burning stoves must be cleaned regularly. Creosote and soot buildup can reduce the draft of a stove and cause a serious fire hazard. If the build-up is ¼ inch or more thick, the stovepipe should be cleaned. As a rule of thumb, the stove and stovepipe should be cleaned at the start of each heating season. Follow these steps:

1. If there are many sections to the stovepipe, number them with labels made from masking tape so that you can reassemble them in the correct order.

2. Cover the area around the stove and stovepipe with newspapers or dropcloths.

3. Disassemble the stovepipe. Use a screwdriver to remove the self-tapping screws that hold the sections together; the screws turn counterclockwise for removal.

4. Put the stovepipe sections in a large, plastic trash bag so you can transport them outdoors without dropping creosote or soot on floors and carpeting.

5. Using a flue-cleaning brush, clean the inside of the stovepipe sections. You also may need a wire brush to scrub off stubborn creosote.

6. If a damper in the stovepipe must be removed,

Firescreen and Heat Exchanger Can Conserve Energy

If you have a fireplace, you can conserve energy by installing a glass door firescreen and a heat exchanger. According to Sears, Roebuck and Co., its Heat Screen glass door firescreen reduces air flow through the fireplace opening by 70 to 90 percent. The screen doors may be opened or closed. Interlocking closures and overlapping seals restrict air movement and heat loss. The Heat Screen firescreen used with Sears' heat exchanger can change a fireplace into a more efficient heating system. A two-speed blower next to the fireplace draws cool air into the heat exchanger. The air is then heated by flames and embers. Warm air is forced directly out of the exchanger into the room through vents at the base of the fireplace. Installation instructions are provided with both products.

For a Satin Finish on Black Stoves

A new coat of paint can freshen up an old stove. Stove Black paint from Illinois Bronze Paint Co., resists temperatures up to 1200° F. The company also says that the paint provides a satin finish on the metal that resists peeling and blistering. Stove Black paint is rust- and waterproof, and is available in cans for brushing or spraying. The paint may be used for other items such as barbeque grills, range hoods, fireplace equipment, furnaces, and steam pipes.

Heat Reflector Should Be Clean

Some water heaters have a heat reflector below the heating element. If your heater has this feature, turn off the water heater and clean the heat reflector. A steel-wool soap pad and water works well. Rinse and dry the reflector, and then turn on the heater. A clean reflector will help increase the appliance efficiency.

push the damper handle toward the pipe. Give the handle a quarter turn counterclockwise and pull the handle out of the opening. Remove the damper plate. You reverse the procedure for reassembly. **Note:** If the damper or damper shaft has become rusted or corroded, replace the parts. Also replace any damaged, corroded, or rusted sections of stovepipe.

7. If possible, clean the chimney from the stovepipe opening; refer to the section on "Cleaning a Chimney" in the chapter on Heating and Cooling.
8. After the chimney and stovepipe have been cleaned, remove the grates—if any—from the stove. Clean out all the ashes. And, if the stove has no grates, be careful not to shovel out sand on the firebox floor. **Note:** Cleaning a stove is messy work, so wear gloves and old clothing.
9. Using a wire brush and putty knife, clean all metal surfaces inside the stove that you can reach.
10. If the stove has a baffle system, clean it with a wire brush and putty knife, and vacuum out the debris. Some baffles can be easily removed. If your stove has this feature, remove them to clean them; if not, clean them in place.
11. As you clean, check the metal for any cracks. Apply stove cement to any cracks you find, using your fingers as a "trowel." The cement should dry for at least 24 hours before the stove is fired. Follow the stove cement manufacturer's instructions.
12. Check the seal around the door of the stove. If it's cracked or broken, replace it before firing the stove.
13. Reassemble and install the stovepipe.
14. Replace the firebox grates or sand floor.
15. If the exterior of the stove looks worn, it can be polished by rubbing waxed paper over the metal surfaces. Also, give the stove a coat of stove blacking at least once a year.

Fire-Building Tips

Many people have trouble building a proper fire in a stove. And, if they have a new stove, they may not be aware that it should be broken-in. For the first few weeks, they should only build small fires. If the stove doesn't have an ash pit at the bottom, the bottom should be covered with 2 inches of sand to provide insulation. To build a fire, follow these steps:

1. Open the drafts.
2. Place wadded newspaper at the bottom of the stove; don't use magazines.
3. Place small kindling over the newspaper; then place the fuel over the kindling. Never burn trash in the stove.
4. Light the newspaper and close the stove door.
5. If the fuel doesn't ignite, shovel or otherwise move it to one side of the firebox and repeat Steps 2 and 3. *Caution: Under no circumstances should you pour gasoline, charcoal lighter fluid, or other petroleum products over the fuel to ignite it. An explosion can occur.*
6. After the fire is burning satisfactorily, turn down the damper slightly; the fuel will burn better and more completely with less air.
7. If you plan to leave the house with the stove still burning, open the stovepipe damper and close the air inlet damper.
8. To get the fire going again, open the inlet damper and add fuel to the fire. Allow the fire to burn high for about 20 minutes or so; this helps reduce creosote and soot buildup.
9. When the ash box is full or the bottom of the firebox becomes thickly covered with ashes, remove the ashes. Use a metal bucket because there may be glowing embers and coal in the deposits even though the fire may be out.
10. You can use a commercial creosote and soot cleaner, but your stovepipe and chimney must be clean at the beginning. The cleaner really doesn't "clean" the pipes; it prevents a buildup of creosote and soot in a *clean* chimney.

Coping With a Chimney Fire

Regularly cleaning the creosote and soot from your chimney reduces the chance of a fire. Should you have a chimney fire, follow these steps:

1. Call the fire department immediately.
2. Close the dampers to cut off the supply of air to the stove.
3. Have everyone leave the building. One adult may stay to check for sparks and signs of fire indoors; those outside should watch the roof for signs of fire.
4. You can use a fire extinguisher designed for chimney fires. Never pour or spray water in the stove or chimney.
5. Even if you believe the fire is out, examine the outer surfaces of the chimney and inner walls near the chimney for excessive heat.
6. When the fire is completely out, sweep the chimney and carefully examine the chimney and stove for damage.

Ducts for Use With Evaporative Coolers

If your home is cooled by evaporative air, you can increase the effectiveness of your insulation and keep your attic and ceiling temperatures lower. The Up-dux vent, made by Gila River Products, is installed in the ceilings of rooms to permit up to 900 cubic feet of cooled air per minute to flow from downstairs rooms to upstairs rooms or the attic. And, there's no need to keep doors or windows open. The deluxe model DL101 Up-dux has a molded polystyrene grille with a slide-in styrene thermal panel for winter closure. An emergency system closes automatically in the event of fire. Installation instructions and all hardware are furnished. According to the manufacturer, the device can lower attic temperatures as much as 40° F.

Permanent Covers for Exhaust Fans

When a ceiling or wall exhaust fan isn't operating, heated or cooled air can escape. Drafts can enter. Exhaust fan covers to prevent this are made by The Crest Co. The transparent covers fit over the exhaust fan so that when the fan isn't running the area is blocked. The covers are permanently installed so you don't have to keep putting them on and taking them off during changes of season. Model No. EFC-8-VT is 10¼ inches in diameter; model No. EFC-11-VT is 11⅞ inches square.

FAN ON   FAN OFF

FAN ON   FAN OFF

Solve Heating or Cooling Problems With Duct Kit

When remodeling or adding a room to your home, you often have to find some way to heat or cool the area. The X-Tra Duct kit, manufactured by Tjernlund Products, Inc., is an easily installed duct system that can eliminate the need for supplementary heating or air conditioning units. The kit includes 12 feet of 5-inch-diameter, heavy-duty, flexible ducting that's reinforced and foil-faced. Other components are a 4- by 10-inch, baked-enamel register with adjustable damper; a register boot with

mounting wings; mounting screws; and a 5-inch flanged collar; and a 2-inch-wide roll of duct tape. There is a one-year limited warranty. For longer runs, additional 4-foot-long extension sections of flexible ducting are available separately.

Appliances Are Energy-Rated

Most appliances today are energy-rated; they have an EER number somewhere on them. If the EER rating for an appliance is 10, it's an excellent rating. EER ratings of 8 or 9 are good. Below 8, an appliance begins to become an energy hog.

Acrylic Latex Caulk Is Formulated for Exterior, Interior

If you have gaps in your home's siding and around interior window frames, you need a caulking compound that's suitable for indoor and outdoor use. DAP acrylic latex caulk is a flexible caulking compound for exterior and interior applications. It adheres to most construction materials, including wood, metal, glass, plaster, masonry, drywall, ceramics, and plastics. It is available in an 11-fluid-ounce cartridge for use with a caulking gun or in a 6-fluid-ounce squeeze tube. Cartridge-packaged DAP acrylic latex caulk comes in white and six chalk- and fade-resistant colors—brown, tan, red, gray, olive, and

black. DAP caulk in squeeze tubes is available in white only.

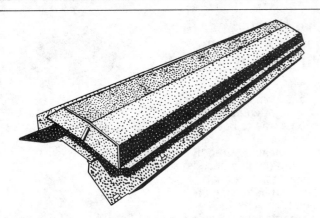

New Concept in Ridge Vents

The Ridge Runner continuous-ridge attic ventilation system, made by Leslie-Locke, a division of Questor Corp., is the most effective approach to static ventilation, according to the manufacturer. It provides top attic ventilation efficiency that is continuous by offering positive air circulation at all roof pitches. The system works on the principle of natural air flow. As the wind blows over the ridge of your home, it creates a low-pressure area that draws warm air out of the attic while allowing replacement air to enter at the eaves. Although a professional should install it, the system consists of 4-foot modular sections made from embossed aluminum, and can be installed with common tools. The Ridge Runner system is guaranteed for the life of the roof shingles upon which the system was originally installed under normal weather and sound roof conditions. The vent system is available in an aluminum finish, or in brown or black colors.

Low-Pressure Sodium Light Saves Power

The Norelco Light is a low-pressure sodium outdoor security light that provides the most light for the least money, according to North American Philips Lighting Corp. It uses 60 watts (lamp and ballast), and one unit can light up to a quarter of an acre. The light produced is the result of the glow of the sodium vapor filling the entire volume of the bulb, as compared to the small glowing filament area in a conventional incandescent bulb. Thus more light is provided and less energy is consumed, says the manufacturer. A sodium-vapor light produces a yellow light that reduces glare, improves visibility, remains cool during operation, and doesn't attract insects. Complete installation instructions are furnished.

Hand-Held Shower/Massager Offers Water Savings

A massage and shower handset that features a water-flow control, which automatically restricts water consumption to 2.75 gallons per minute, is made by Interbath, Inc. The Great Vibrations personal care appliance, called "The Original," always maintains the selected spray setting with no sudden bursts of hot or cold water, according to the manufacturer. Its pulsating massage spray is adjustable from "light" to "forceful." The Original massage handset connects to any bathtub spout quickly and easily. Accessories and

installation instructions are included with the product.

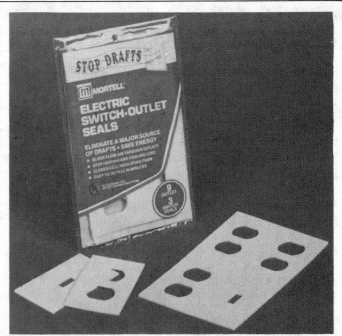

Seals for Electric Outlets and Switches

More cold air than you might think enters your home through the electrical switches and outlets on exterior walls. Electric switch/outlet seals from the Mortell Co. can block this flow of cold air. The seals, made of closed-cell insulating foam, also cut down on heat gain during summer months. Only a screwdriver is needed to install the seals, which fit behind your outlet cover plates. After installation, the seals cannot be seen. One package contains seals for nine outlets and three switches—enough for three average-size rooms. The product is UL Listed.

Squeaking Floors

Materials • Powdered Graphite • Chalk
• Cedar Shingle Wedge • Wood Screws
• 1 × 4's • 8d Common Nails • 8d
Finishing Nails • Wood Filler • Cloth
• Tile Adhesive • Hardwood Block

Tools • Hammer • Drill and Bit
• Screwdriver • Nail Set • Clothes Iron
• Putty Knife

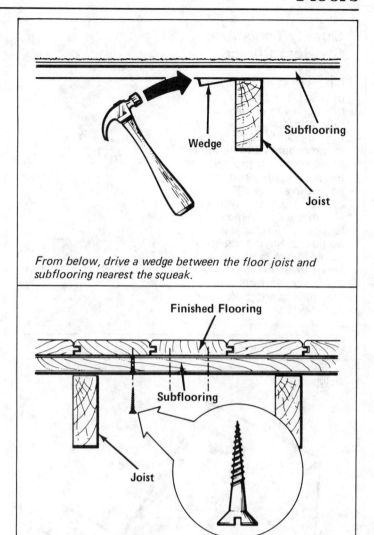

From below, drive a wedge between the floor joist and subflooring nearest the squeak.

If a wedge doesn't solve the problem, drive screws through the subflooring and just into the finish flooring above.

NORMAL SETTLING of your house on its foundation can make floors squeak; most probably the squeak is caused by two pieces of wood rubbing against each other. There are several remedies available to you; if one doesn't work, try another.

The first thing to try—if the squeak isn't too loud—is powdered graphite. Apply this lubricant between the cracks in the finish flooring at the squeaking point. Then hop up and down on the surface to work the powder in. If the squeak is more serious, however, you'll have to take other measures.

Working From Below

If you have access to the subflooring from below, follow these steps:

1. Have someone step on the squeaky spot while you are in the basement. If you can see any movement in the subfloor, mark the spot with chalk.
2. Drive a wedge made from a cedar shingle between the floor joist and subflooring nearest the squeak. Just drive the wedge in about ½ inch or so; you don't want to separate the subflooring from the edge of the joist.
3. If the wedge doesn't solve the problem, drill a pilot hole in the subflooring at the squeaking spot. The pilot hole should go through the subflooring, which is usually ¾ inch thick, and into the finish flooring above, which is usually ⅜ to ¾ inch thick. **Caution: Stop drilling before you reach the surface of the finish flooring.**
4. Drive a screw that's about 1 inch long into the pilot hole, and test the floor. If the squeak hasn't stopped, drill several more pilot holes

around the squeaking spot and drive in screws.
5. If driving screws into the flooring is only partially successful, add joist bridging at the squeaking spot and between other joists around this area. Between parallel joists, toenail a pair of 1 × 4's to the tops and bottoms of the joists with 8d common nails, criss-crossing the bridging. Space pairs of 1 × 4's about 30 inches apart.

Working From Above

If you can't reach the squeaking spot from underneath the floor, you have no choice but to work from above. Follow these steps:

1. Drive 8d finishing nails through the flooring in the subflooring at points around the squeaking boards. Drill pilot holes for the nails into the

Floors

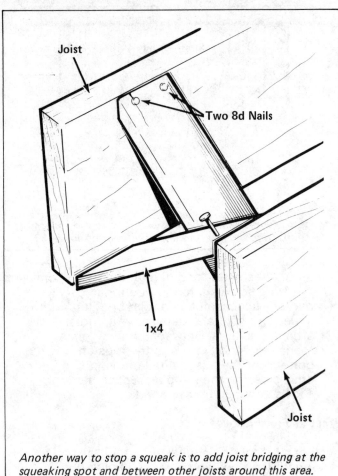

Another way to stop a squeak is to add joist bridging at the squeaking spot and between other joists around this area.

Joist

Two 8d Nails

1x4

Joist

hardwood floor. After the nails are in, countersink them—drive the heads slightly below the surface of the floor—with a nail set.

Then fill the holes with wood filler to match the floor.

2. If the floor is covered with carpet and you can't get at the squeak under the subflooring, you can drive 8d finishing nails down through the pile of the carpeting into the finish flooring and subflooring. After the nails are started, use a nail set to drive the nails. The pile will hide the nail heads so they won't show.

3. If the floor is covered with resilient tile, remove a tile at the squeaking spot. Cover the tile to be removed with a piece of cloth. Press a clothes iron at its medium heat setting over the cloth and tile; the heat will loosen the tile adhesive. Once the tile is loosened, pry up the tile carefully with a putty knife.

4. With the tile removed, drive 8d finishing nails through the floor and into the subflooring at the squeaking spot; countersink the nail heads with a nail set. If there is a joint in the underlayment at this point, put some powdered graphite into the joint.

5. Apply new tile adhesive, replace the tile you removed, and weight the tile with a heavy object for 24 hours.

6. If you can't go through the finish flooring with nails or graphite powder, place a hardwood block, such as a piece of oak, over the squeaking spot. Then, pound on the block with a hammer to try reseating loose nails below. Move the block, spot by spot, in an area of about 3 feet around the squeak, striking the block sharply.

7. If none of the procedures solve your squeaking floor problems, the only solution left is to wait until it's time to refinish the floor. Then, you can re-nail the subflooring.

Squeaking Stairs

Materials • Cedar Shingle Wedges
• Wood Glue • Common Nails • 2 × 2
• Metal Corner Braces With Wood Screws
• Thin Cardboard • Powdered Graphite
• Finishing Nails • Wood Filler

Tools • Handsaw • Hammer • Drill and
Bit • Pencil • Screwdriver • Nail Set

A SQUEAKING STAIRWAY may be just the thing for a mystery story, but the plot changes to irritation when it's your stairs that are involved. Squeaky stairsteps are caused by the same thing that causes floors to squeak—two pieces of wood rubbing together.

Chances are the trouble is a tread rubbing against either the riser or the stringer, because these boards are not fastened securely. By stopping the movement, the squeak usually disappears.

Working From Below

If you can gain access under the stairs, follow these steps:

1. Have someone walk on the stairs, going back and forth on the step that squeaks while you try to spot the movement from beneath the stairway. Look especially for loose nails, split boards, or anything else that could cause movement.
2. Once you locate the squeaking spot, cut wedges from cedar shingles; the wedges should be about 3 or 4 inches long.
3. With a quality wood glue, coat the side of the wedges that will press against a flat surface.
4. Drive the cedar shingle wedges between the rubbing stair members. Lightly tap the wedges into the joint, making them go in as tightly as possible. Don't, however, drive them in so far that they separate the joined wood members.
5. After the wedges are in position, secure them in place with nails, but first blunt the points of the nails with a hammer, or drill pilot holes for the nails, to help prevent the wood from splitting.
6. If any joints are too tight for wedges, cut triangular blocks from 2 × 2 lumber. Cut the blocks diagonally. **Note:** If you prefer to use metal corner braces instead of wood blocks, proceed to Step 10.
7. Drill pilot holes in the blocks for nails.
8. Coat the two faces of the blocks that will go against the joint on the stairs with wood glue.
9. Hold the blocks in position and then nail them; the nails will help hold the blocks until the glue dries. **Note:** Be sure to check the length of the nails; they should not go through the stairs.
10. If you prefer to use metal corner braces, place a brace as a guide to mark the locations of screw holes.
11. Drill pilot holes for screws at the points you marked, but be careful not to penetrate the stairs with the drill bit.
12. Insert a thin piece of cardboard between the metal brace and the mounting surface on one leg of the brace. Then drive the screws into the other leg. The cardboard separates the brace and wood just enough to put tension on the

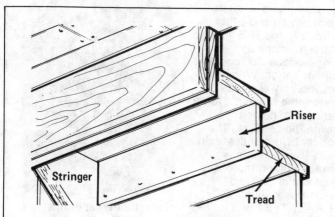

Chances are a squeaking stairstep is caused by a tread rubbing against the riser or the stringer.

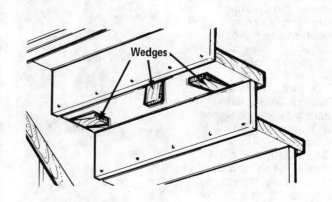

Drive and glue wedges between the rubbing stair members; however, don't drive them in so far they separate the members.

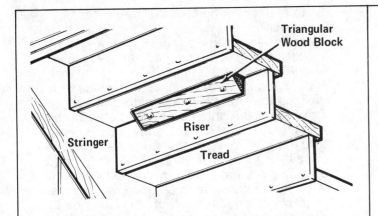

If stair joints are too tight for wedges, glue and nail a triangular wood block made from 2x2 lumber.

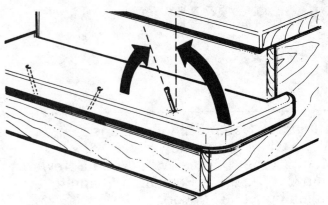

If you can't get under a stairway, you can drive finishing nails into the tread at an angle; countersink the nail heads.

brace when it is completely fastened. This tension draws the open wood joint together.

13. Remove the cardboard and drive in the screws into the other leg.

Working From Above

If you can't get under the stairway, you'll have to try to spot movement in the stairs from above. And, this can take quite awhile because you'll have to work by trial-and-error. Follow these steps:

1. Apply powdered graphite into the joints all around the area that squeaks. Then jump up and down on the area to work in the powder.
2. If the powder doesn't solve the problem, drive finishing nails into the stair tread at an angle so that the nail goes into the riser or the stringer where you think the movement is. Countersink the nails with a nail set. Cover the nail holes with wood filler.
3. If the steps are carpeted, you can drive finishing nails down through the pile of the carpet so the nails won't show. Start the nails into the wood and drive them the rest of the way with a nail set.
4. If the steps are covered with rubber or vinyl tread protectors, you can usually remove the protectors by removing the nails or screws that hold them in place. Be careful that you don't damage the tread protectors during removal. If the protectors are torn or ripped, replace them.

Tool Eases Installation of Stair Carpeting

Getting a professional-looking job on stair carpeting is easier with a tool that can drive the carpeting into a stair crotch—the joint between the tread and the riser. Stair tools, made by Roberts Consolidated Industries, are designed for stair carpeting installations. The No. 10-520 stair tool is 2¾ inches; the extra-wide No. 10-521 is 3½ inches. Both are forged chrome-steel; they also may be used for other home maintenance and improvement projects.

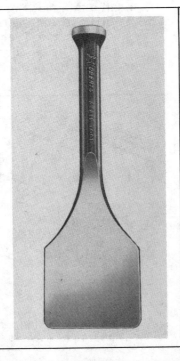

Dry Film Lubricant Stops Wood Squeaks

Squeaky floors or stairs are annoying and often difficult to fix. TFE dry film lubricant, made by the Cling-Surface Co., contains DuPont Teflon. When sprayed between rubbing boards, the product's long-lasting film helps to prevent noise. Spray the lubricant from underneath stairs if possible; any surface film on top of the steps could create a dangerously slippery situation. TFE dry film lubricant has many other uses. It bonds to and lubricates metal, plastic, glass, rubber, and other clean substances. It is available in 6- and 16-ounce aerosol cans.

Fixing a Loose Tile

Materials • Cloth • Container of Water • Floor Tile Adhesive • Rags • Mineral Spirits or Turpentine • Replacement Tile • Sandpaper • Newspapers • Clear Plastic Cement

Tools • Clothes Iron • Propane Torch With Flame-Spreader Nozzle • Putty Knife • Combination Rasp • Notched Adhesive Spreader

NORMAL WEAR and tear on any type of resilient tile floor can cause a tile to loosen at the edges or even pop up completely. It's best to repair such a tile as soon as it's noticed; postponing repairs usually results in having to redo sections of the flooring, or even the entire floor.

Fixing a Loose Tile

To fix a loose floor tile, follow these steps:

1. If the tile is merely loose around the edges, cover the tile with a piece of cloth. Set a clothes iron at a medium-heat position, and press down on the cloth and tile. The heat should soften the tile adhesive so that the tile can be pressed back into place.

   Note: If a clothes iron won't soften the adhesive, you can use a propane torch with a flame-spreader nozzle. Carefully apply the torch flame directly to the tile—there's no need for the cloth. ***Caution: Be extremely careful with the propane torch; you don't want to scorch or otherwise damage the tile.*** Hold the flame at least 4 inches away from the surface of the tile. Have a container of water handy in case the tile, adhesive, or flooring begins to burn.

2. If this doesn't solve the problem, repeat the heating procedure, and when the adhesive is warm, carefully pry up the edges of the tile with a putty knife.

3. Clean out the old adhesive under the edges of the tile as best as you can. Apply new tile adhesive under the edges with a putty knife. Then press down on the tile and weight it with heavy objects.

4. As weight is applied to the tile, adhesive will probably ooze from the edges. Clean the adhesive up immediately. If the adhesive is water-based, the excess may be removed with water; if mineral-based, use mineral spirits or turpentine to remove the excess adhesive.

5. Before you remove the weight, let the adhesive dry. Follow the manufacturer's directions for drying time.

To remove a damaged tile, soften it with a propane torch and a flame-spreader nozzle; be careful not to damage surrounding tiles.

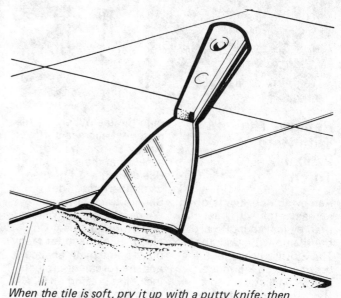

When the tile is soft, pry it up with a putty knife; then scrape the old adhesive off the floor so new adhesive will bond properly.

Replacing a Tile

If a loose tile is damaged, it often is easier to replace the tile with a new one than attempt to stick down pieces of the damaged one. Follow this procedure:

1. Cover the tile with a piece of cloth. Set a clothes iron at a medium-heat position and press down on the cloth and tile. The heat should soften the adhesive so that the tile can be removed carefully with a putty knife.

   Note: If a clothes iron won't soften the adhesive, you can use a propane torch with a flame-spreader nozzle. Carefully apply the torch flame directly to the tile—there's no need for the cloth. *Caution: Be extremely careful with the propane torch; you don't want to scorch or otherwise damage the surrounding tiles.* Hold the flame at least 4 inches away from the surface of the tile. Have a container of water handy in case the tile, adhesive, or flooring begins to burn.
2. After the tile has been removed, clean the floor of all excess adhesive. Use a putty knife for this and, if necessary, sandpaper. Sweep away the debris.
3. Check the replacement tile on the floor. If the tile is slightly larger than the opening, you can trim it with a combination rasp run lengthwise along the edge of the tile. Also check the replacement tile to make sure the pattern matches the surrounding tiles.
4. If the replacement tile is slightly smaller than the tile you removed, take pieces of the old tile and rasp the edges over some newspaper until you get a small pile of tile particles. Set it aside.
5. Apply tile adhesive to the floor using a notched adhesive spreader.
6. Position the new tile, removing any excess adhesive at the joints.
7. After the replacement tile is in position, mix a paste from the particles of old tile and clear plastic cement. Fill any small gaps in the joints around the tile with the mixture. It won't be a perfect match, but it will be better than having gaps in the joints.
8. Weight the tile with a heavy object until the adhesive dries.

Remove Tile With Help of Propane Torch

Removing floor tile is often an easier job with heat than by just trying to pry the tile up with a scraper. The Spitfire propane brazing torch kit, model 307, is packaged with a flame-spreader attachment that is ideal for spreading the flame from the torch onto the tile. When the tile material becomes soft, you simply scrape the tile away from the subflooring. Use care, however, when using the torch. The Spitfire torch kit, made by Wingaersheek, a division of Victor Equipment Co., also may be used for many other home maintenance and improvement projects, including brazing and sweating copper tubing. An instruction manual is included in the kit.

Cure for Curled Tile

Sometimes, floor tile will curl at the edges. This is an adhesive problem that often can be corrected with a little heat from a clothes iron. If just a fraction of the tile has popped loose from the floor—about 1 inch or less—cover the tile with a clean heavy rag. Set the clothes iron in the medium range and press the curled edge of the tile back into position with the iron. The heat from the iron softens the tile adhesive, and the pressing from the iron seats the tile in place. Don't give up too quickly if the tile won't stick immediately; you may have to work with the iron for several minutes until the adhesive is tacky enough to stick. If the iron technique won't work, the tile should be removed from the floor and the tile and the floor cleaned of all adhesive and dirt. Spread new tile adhesive on the floor and reset the tile, weighting it until the adhesive dries—about one day.

Notched Trowel Puts Down Floor Adhesive

When applying floor-covering adhesive, you need a trowel with the proper notch pattern. Because different patterns are designed to serve different purposes, be sure to check the can of adhesive to find out which pattern best suits your needs. Harrington Tools makes the Throw Away adhesive spreader, which is ideal for the one-time floor project, in several patterns. Featuring a 6⅜-inch-wide toothed area, the spreader is made of heavy-gauge steel.

Installing an Underlayment

Materials • Water Putty • Sandpaper • Tempered Hardboard or Particle Board as Required • Matchbook or Thin Cardboard • Wood Strips or Cedar Shingle Shims • Subfloor Adhesive • Threaded or Ringed Underlayment Nails

Tools • Pry Bar • Screwdriver • Hammer • Nail Set • Wood Chisel • Broom • Vacuum Cleaner • Tape Measure • Pencil • Chalk Line • Block Plane • Carpenter's Level • Carpenter's Square • Crosscut Saw • Coping Saw • Caulking Gun

ALMOST WITHOUT exception, floor coverings such as resilient tile, resilient sheet flooring, parquet blocks, and carpeting need a smooth and solid underlayment. If you are planning to cover your floors, make sure the present flooring, underlayment, or subflooring is smooth and solid. If it isn't, follow these steps:

1. Move all furniture out of the room.
2. Remove the doors to the room and store them.
3. Remove all moldings and trim at the base of the walls. See "Replacing Molding" in the Walls chapter. Also remove any registers, electrical outlet covers, pipe escutcheons, and so on.
4. Remove any carpeting. Inspect other types of flooring material—tile, blocks, hardwood—to make sure it's solidly in place. If not, the covering should be removed or at least fastened down with adhesive, nails, or other permanent fasteners.
5. Drive in protruding nail heads with a nail set and flatten all bumps and ridges you find; you may have to use a chisel for this. All large holes and cracks must be filled with water putty and sanded smooth.
6. After making repairs, inspect the floor. It should be just as smooth as you can make it. Then, sweep the floor and vacuum it.
7. Stack the underlayment around the room in which it will be installed for about 36 hours before installation; this allows the material to adjust to the room temperature and humidity. **Note:** When you buy underlayment, it's better to get 4- by 4-foot panels rather than 4- by 8-foot ones if possible. The smaller panels are easier to handle and fit.
8. With a tape measure, find and mark the exact center of each wall. Stretch a chalk line across the floor between opposite center points. Snap the chalk line. Where the lines intersect is the room's center.
9. Position the first underlayment panel at the center point on the floor using the chalk lines as a guide for the edges of the panel.
   Note: If the underlayment is tempered hardboard (don't use standard or perforated hardboard), the slick side should be facing down. If the underlayment is particle board, either side of the panel may be used. However, be extremely careful when handling particle board because the edges chip very easily.
   Also, before laying each hardboard panel, you'll have to chamfer, or bevel, the top edges with a block plane. One swipe with the plane should be sufficient.
10. Nail the underlayment panel every 6 inches around its perimeter. In hardboard, the nails should be about ½ inch from the edge. In particle board, the nails should be about 1 inch from the edge to prevent chipping.
11. Place the next panels against those laid and nailed. If possible, the panels should not have common joints on all four sides; stagger the joints as much as you can. Four corners should never meet. Also, space the panels about 1/32 to 1/16 inch between joints to allow for

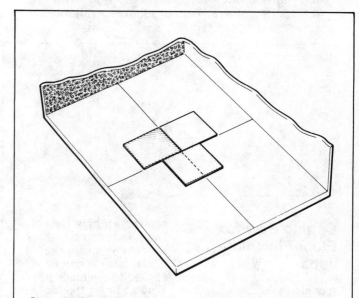

Place the first underlayment panel at the centerpoint on the floor using the chalk lines as a guide for the edges of the panel. Place the next two panels against the first so there are no common joints.

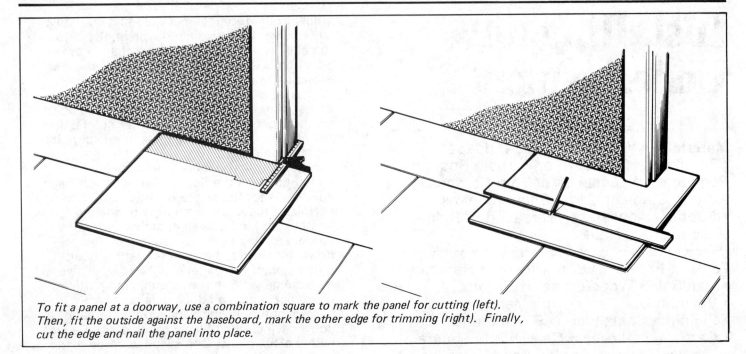

To fit a panel at a doorway, use a combination square to mark the panel for cutting (left).
Then, fit the outside against the baseboard, mark the other edge for trimming (right). Finally,
cut the edge and nail the panel into place.

expansion and contraction from humidity. This is about the thickness of a matchbook cover. Or, you can use a thin piece of cardboard.

12. As you set each panel, check to see they are level. If they are not, you can raise them slightly with thin wooden strips or shims made from cedar shingles; however, make sure that the underlayment over these strips is solid.

13. Set trimmed panels against the walls, next to doorways, and other places to complete the job. For smaller pieces, you should both glue and nail the underlayment to the floor with subfloor adhesive. This product is available for use in a caulking gun. Apply the adhesive to the floor. Then, press the underlayment down and pick it up again. Then reset it and nail it. Pressing the panel down and picking it up before resetting it helps spread the adhesive over the surface for a better bond.

14. After all underlayment panels have been fastened down, carefully walk over the floor. If you find any loose or spongy spots, nail the panels in such places with underlayment nails; the floor should be as solid as possible before the finish flooring is installed. Complete the job by vacuuming the floor.

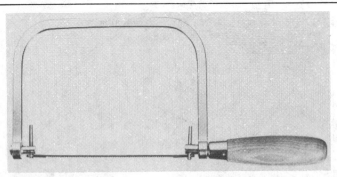

Coping Saw for Floor-Finishing Jobs

A coping saw can make most any flooring project easier, especially when you have to install trim. The model 7CP Eclipse coping saw from Neill Tools, Inc., can cut at almost any angle. The proper tension can be applied to the blade by simply turning the tool's handle. The depth of bow is 4¾ inches so that the saw can handle most any thickness of flooring.

Screw Nails Can Help Eliminate Floor Pops

Subfloors are nailed to framing members. The movement of the framing members can loosen nails, causing them to pop and the subflooring to loosen. You can help reduce this problem with flooring screw nails that hold better than ordinary box, common, or finishing nails. Hillwood Manufacturing Co. makes several types of flooring nails: Nos. 400 and 500 underlayment nails with a ring-barb and Nos. 800 and 900 flooring screw nails. Each package contains 20 to 40 nails, depending on nail size.

Laying a Resilient Tile Floor

Materials • Mineral Spirits • Rags • Sandpaper • Floor Tiles • Floor Tile Adhesive • Thin Cardboard • Paper • Caulking Compound

Tools • Hammer • Screwdriver • Putty Knife • Tape Measure • Pencil • Chalk Line • Vacuum Cleaner • Notched Adhesive Spreader or Brush • Rolling Pin or Tile Roller • Scissors • Carpenter's Square • Compass • Caulking Gun

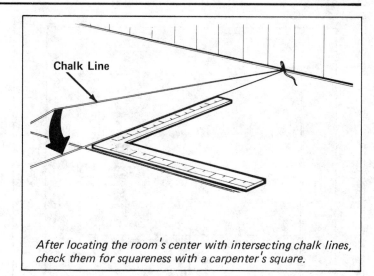

After locating the room's center with intersecting chalk lines, check them for squareness with a carpenter's square.

THE BEAUTY of a resilient tile floor is its finished appearance plus the relative ease of installation. In fact, most do-it-yourselfers should be able to tile an average-size 12- by 15-foot room in less than four hours. Follow these steps:

1. Remove the moldings and trim from the bases of the walls. See "Replacing Molding" in the Walls chapter. Also remove any metal thresholds in doorways, heating and cooling register covers, and other items that might interfere with the job. You'll need a hammer, screwdriver, and a stiff-bladed putty knife, which makes an excellent tool for prying up moldings. Its wide surface helps prevent splitting and breakage.

2. Clean the floor, removing all wax, dirt, grease, and any other debris from the surface. Sand down any high spots, and make sure there are no nails sticking up. **Note:** Because resilient tiles are flexible and tend to conform to whatever is under them, any irregularities in the floor will eventually show through. Make sure the floor is clean and solid or tiles may become loose in time.

   If there is an old floor covering that is tightly bonded to the subflooring, you may not have to remove it. If, however, the old floor covering is in poor condition, remove it. If old tile has to be removed, the best way is with a flat tiling spade or long-handled ice scraper; remove one tile and wedge the spade or scraper under the adjoining tiles and pry up.

3. With a tape measure, find and mark the exact center of each wall. Stretch a chalk line across the floor between opposite center points. Where the lines intersect is the center of the room. Lay a carpenter's square along each line to check for squareness. Do this at the center point in the middle of the floor. If the lines aren't square, correct them.

4. With uncemented or unpeeled self-adhesive tiles, check the measurements in the room by laying a full row of tiles along one wall; begin at the wall's centerline, aligning the edge of the first tile with the line. If the last tile in either direction is less than half the width of a full tile, snap a new chalk line mark beside the original center line, moving the center line half a tile in either direction. This trick will give you even-sized end tiles at both ends of a room and save cutting and fitting time. Repeat the procedure for the other centerline.

5. Pick up the tiles and thoroughly clean the floor. Vacuum all dust and dirt particles.

6. Before you lay any tiles, store the tile in the room to be tiled for about 24 hours; this lets the material adjust to the temperature and humidity within the room. **Note:** Tiles should be laid when the room temperature is 70° F or more. This temperature level also should be maintained for about 10 days after the job has been completed.

7. Start working at the center of the room—in one quarter—where the chalk lines cross. The first tile is extremely critical because it is the keystone for all other tiles to be laid, so make sure it is aligned perfectly along the centerline marks.

8. If you are using tile adhesive, spread enough adhesive for about six to eight tiles at a time. This number may vary, depending on your arm reach. Just set as many tiles as you can

Floors

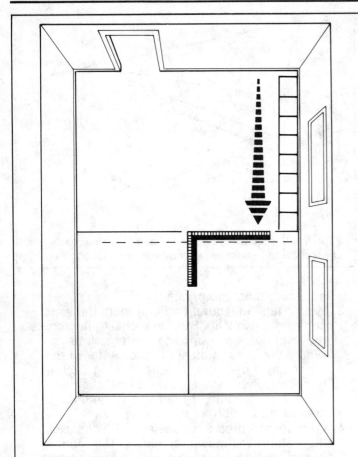

With uncemented tiles, lay a row of tiles from the centerline. If the last tile is less than half the width of a full tile, snap a new chalk line, moving the center line half a tile.

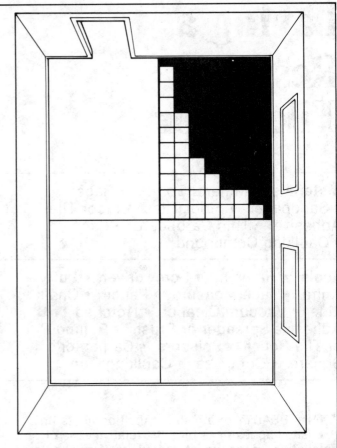

Start laying tile at the center of the room — in one quarter — where the chalk lines cross. Set tiles alternately toward each wall, building a sort of pyramid.

comfortably reach without sticking your hand in the adhesive for support.

If you are using self-adhesive tiles, peel the backing off on each tile as you go. Don't peel a number of tiles and set them aside. *Caution: The adhesive on peel-and-stick tiles is extremely sticky and bonds tightly. Once the tile is in place, you may not be able to remove the tile for refitting without damaging it.* After the backing has been removed, bend the tile slightly and butt just the edges of the tile against the adjoining tiles on two sides. Then "drop" it in position, using the straight edges on the adjoining tiles as guidelines.

If you are setting the tiles with floor adhesive, tiles should be set in place the same way as self-adhesive tiles, using adjoining tiles as guidelines. With floor adhesive, however, the tiles may be slid slightly into alignment. **Note:** Make sure the floor adhesive that you are using is made for the type of tile being laid—vinyl adhesive for vinyl tile; asphalt adhesive for asphalt tile, and so on. Most floor adhesives are applied with a notched spreader, although some may be brushed on. Either

way, follow the adhesive manufacturer's recommendations. Also be sure to note adhesive setting times. Some adhesives must be allowed to cure for 20 minutes or so before the tiles are applied.

9. After the first, or key, tile is set, lay tiles alternately toward each wall, building a sort of pyramid. Do just one quarter of the room at a time, except for the row of tiles along the walls.

   Note: Some tile products—especially those with patterns—have directional arrows printed on the back of each tile. If the product you're using has these arrows, make sure that the tile is laid so the arrows point in the same direction.

10. Clean up any adhesive that oozes from the tile joints as you work; it's easier to do this now before the adhesive dries.

11. When you finish laying tiles in one quarter of the room, go over the tiles with a rolling pin to compress the tiles evenly into the adhesive. You may want to rent a tile roller—by the day—for this job.

12. Once you've laid the tiles in one quarter of the

Mending a Dent in Floor Tile

What do you do when a floor tile is dented by a dropped skillet or a heavy chair or table leg? Often, it isn't necessary to replace the tile. Try shaving very small pieces from the edge of a spare matching tile with a sharp utility knife. Make the shavings as small as you can. Then, clean the dent in the tile; the area should be free from dirt, wax, and grease. Mix the shavings with a small amount of clear varnish to form a thick paste about the color of the floor tile. Use a putty knife to trowel the paste, leveling it in the dent. Allow the mixture to dry. Then, very lightly buff the patched surface with extra-fine steel wool; you just want to smooth it. If it's already smooth to your satisfaction, don't use the steel wool. Finally, hard wax the patched area and then wax the entire floor.

Resilient Flooring Has Foam Backing

New flooring materials are a far cry from the days of linoleum. For example, the foam backing on GAF's GAFSTAR flooring provides a very comfortable feel as you walk on it. Much thicker than old-fashioned flooring, GAFSTAR is so resilient that you can actually drop dishes on it without breaking any, the manufacturer says. GAFSTAR, made by GAF Corp., never needs waxing, but you may find that you have to restore the gloss in high-traffic areas. GAF's Brite-Bond floor finish is formulated to do that.

room, set tiles in another quarter of the room until you're finished, following the procedure in Steps 8 through 11.

13. Cut and fit the border tiles along the walls. To fit a border tile, place a tile precisely on top of a tile in the row adjoining the border row to be laid. Then, butt a second tile against the wall, with its sides aligned with the first tile. Mark the first tile where the first and second tiles overlap, using the second one's edge as a guide. Cut the first tile along your mark; it should fit exactly.

    Note: Some types of tile products, especially asphalt tile, can be cut easier if they are heated until they are pliable. This is especially helpful when you must cut small pieces and irregular shapes.

14. To fit tiles around objects such as a pipe, heat register opening, toilet, or bathtub, you have a choice of two methods. One way is to use a compass with a point on one leg and a pencil on the other leg. Guide the pointed leg along the irregular surface of the object while the pencil draws this shape on a tile that is positioned exactly on top of the tile in the adjoining row, as explained in the previous step.

    Another way is to use thin cardboard that is the exact size of the tile, and cut a template to fit around the irregularity. Make a pattern of the obstacle from the cardboard on paper, trace it onto the tile, and then cut the tile along your marks.

15. With lots of effort, you can make each tile fit perfectly against the wall surfaces. However, the easiest way to cover any imperfections along the walls is with the molding or trim that you removed before the job started, or with new molding or trim that you plan to buy. When the entire floor has been laid, add the molding along the walls and across the thresholds of doorways. Also, reinstall heat register covers and anything else you removed. Caulk any joints that butt against bathtubs or pipes.

16. Don't scrub the new tile floor for about 10 days. You should, however, clean up any excess adhesive as soon as the floor is down.

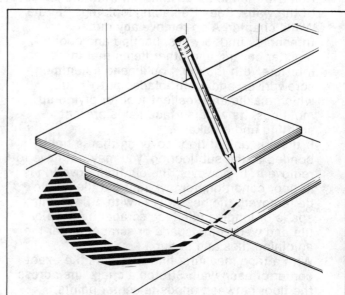

To fit a border tile, place a tile precisely on top of the tile in the row adjoining the border row. Then, butt a second tile against the wall with its sides aligned with the first tile. Mark the first tile where the first and second ones overlap. Cut the first tile; it should fit exactly.

Laying Parquet Flooring

Materials • Finishing Nails • Mineral Spirits • Rags • Sandpaper • Concrete Patch • Parquet Tiles • Parquet Adhesive • Caulking Compound

Tools • Hammer • Nail Set • Screwdriver • Putty Knife • Flat Tiling Spade or Ice Scraper • Tape Measure • Pencil • Chalk Line • Carpenter's Square • Vacuum Cleaner • Notched Adhesive Spreader • Buffer Block • Rolling Pin or Tile Roller • Wire Cutters • Utility Knife • Coping Saw • Scribing Compass • Caulking Gun

TODAY, PARQUET hardwood flooring is almost as easy to lay as resilient flooring. The parquet—some of it with a self-adhesive backing—is in the form of tile blocks. There is a variety of wood tones and colors from which to choose. To lay a parquet floor, follow these steps:

1. Remove the moldings and trim from the bases of the walls. See "Replacing Moldings" in the Walls chapter. Also remove any metal thresholds in doorways, heating and cooling register covers, and other items that might interfere with the job. You'll need a hammer, screwdriver, and a stiff-bladed putty knife, which makes an excellent tool for prying up moldings. Its wide surface helps prevent splitting and breakage.
2. If there is an old floor covering that is tightly bonded to the subflooring, you may not have to remove it. If, however, the old floor covering is in poor condition, remove it. If old tile has to be removed, the best way is with a flat tiling spade or long-handled ice scraper; remove one tile and wedge the spade or scraper under the adjoining tiles and pry up.
3. With a tape measure, find and mark the exact center of each wall. Stretch a chalk line across the floor between opposite center points. Where the lines intersect is the center of the room. Lay a carpenter's square along each line to check for squareness. Do this at the center point in the middle of the floor. If the lines aren't square, correct them.

4. Using uncemented or unpeeled self-adhesive tiles, check the measurements in the room by laying a full row of tiles along one wall; begin at the wall's centerline, aligning the edge of the first tile with the lines. If the last tile in either direction is less than half the width of a full tile, snap a new chalk line mark beside the original center line, moving the center line half a tile in either direction. This trick will give you even-sized end tiles at both ends of a room and ease cutting and fitting later. Repeat the procedure for the other centerline.
5. Pick up the tiles and thoroughly clean the floor. Vacuum all dust and dirt particles.
6. Before you lay any parquet, store the tile in the room to be tiled for about 24 hours; this lets the material adjust to the temperature and humidity within the room. **Note:** Tiles should be laid when the room temperature is 70° F or more. This temperature level also should be maintained for about 10 days after the job has been completed.
7. Start working at the center of the room—in one quarter—where the chalk lines cross. The first tile is extremely critical because it is the keystone for all other tiles to be laid, so make sure it is aligned perfectly along the centerline marks.
8. If you are using tile adhesive, spread enough adhesive for about six to eight tiles at a time. This number may vary, depending on your arm reach. Just set as many tiles as you can comfortably reach without sticking your hand in the adhesive for support. If you are using self-adhesive parquet blocks, peel the backing off on each tile as you go. Don't peel a number of tiles and set them aside. *Caution: The adhesive on peel-and-stick parquet blocks or*

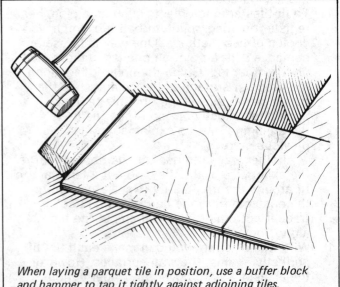

When laying a parquet tile in position, use a buffer block and hammer to tap it tightly against adjoining tiles.

tiles is extremely sticky and bonds tightly. Once the tile is in place, you may not be able to remove the tile for refitting without damaging it. After the backing has been removed, butt the edges of the tile against the adjoining tiles on two sides. Then "drop" it in position, using the straight edges on the adjoining tiles as guidelines. Use a buffer block to tap each tile tightly against the adjoining tiles.

If you are setting the tiles with floor adhesive, tiles should be set in place the same way as self-adhesive tiles, using adjoining tiles as guidelines. With floor adhesive, however, the tiles may be slid slightly into alignment. **Note:** Make sure the floor adhesive that you are using is made for hardwood parquet tile. Most floor adhesives are applied with a notched spreader. Follow the adhesive manufacturer's recommendations. Also be sure to note adhesive setting times. Some adhesives must be allowed to cure for 20 minutes or so before the tiles are applied.

9. After the first, or key, tile is set, lay tiles alternately toward each wall in the quarter of the room, building a sort of pyramid. Do just one quarter of the room at a time, except for the row of tiles along the walls.
10. Clean up any adhesive that oozes from the tile joints as you work; it's easier to do this now before the adhesive dries.
11. When you finish laying tiles in one quarter of the room, go over the tiles with a rolling pin to compress the tiles evenly into the adhesive. You may want to rent a tile roller—by the day—for this job.
12. Once you've laid the tiles in one quarter of the room; set the tiles in another quarter of the room until you're finished, following the procedure in Steps 8 through 11.
13. Cut and fit the border tiles along the walls. Parquet tiles are laminated strips of hardwood; each strip may be held to another with a wire spline in the edge of the wood. Each of

Sanding Discs Reach Floor's Edges

A disc sander is the tool to use to get into the edges and corners that a big sander cannot reach. The 3M Co. makes coated abrasives for every type of sander and for every sanding function, and its 3M Resinite sanding discs come in all the popular grits in discs that are made to fit all makes and sizes of machines from 5 to 16 inches in diameter. Be sure to buy enough sanding discs so that you can replace spent ones readily. Trying to stretch the life of a worn-out disc results in a poor sanding

job, and it produces an unattractive floor finish.

Retractable Rule Is a Handy Tool

Many do-it-yourself projects demand measurements, and a retractable steel rule is a good measuring tool. The 20-foot, retractable steel rule from Disston, Inc., is a quality measuring device. It offers a positive locking system that engages with just a push of your thumb,

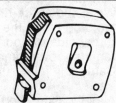

and its smooth power return automatically retracts just as easily. The Mylar-coated blade has red and black markings on white or yellow. It also features a belt clip.

Repairing a Minor Scratch in a Wood Floor

If a scratch in a hardwood strip or parquet floor isn't too deep, you often can repair the damage by lightly buffing the scratch with fine steel wool and a liquid solvent cleaner, such as mineral spirits. The trick is to use a buffing motion with the steel wool, going in the direction of the wood grain. When the scratch disappears, clean the area with a wood cleaner—not soap and water—and wax the wood.

Self-Sticking Parquet Flooring in Solid Oak

The look of solid oak on a floor gives a room a warm, substantial look. Hartco prefinished, solid oak parquet tile has a foam backing with 144 adhesive dots covered by a peel-off paper backing. After measurements have been made and the subfloor has been properly prepared, you simply peel off the backing and stick the parquet flooring tile in position. Three different types of oak block tiles are available—Windsor oak finish, standard oak finish, and old brown oak finish. The manufacturer also makes matching baseboard, quarter-round, and shoe moldings. And,

once the floor is down, you can maintain it with a series of Hartco floor care products.

Parquet, Plank Flooring for Most Any Decor

Hardwood floors that are properly finished are among the easiest of all floor surfaces to keep clean and new looking. A variety of wood parquet and plank flooring materials is available from Bruce Hardwood Floors, a division of Triangle Pacific Corp. The selection includes ¾-inch solid oak parquets, ⁵⁄₁₆-inch solid oak and teak parquets, and ⅜-inch laminated oak parquets. Also available are ¾-inch solid oak planks and ⅜-inch laminated oak planks, both of which have factory-installed pegs.

Accurate Rule for Flooring Measurements

Some tape measures are difficult to read. The Powerlock rule, made by Stanley Tools, a division of The Stanley Works, has a window on the top of the case to show you the exact measurements at a glance. The rule is ideal for inside measurements, something you often encounter when you lay any type of flooring. The Powerlock rule features a Mylar-protected blade, black-and-red graduations on a yellow background, a true-zero hook that slides automatically to allow for its own thickness for inside or outside

measurements, and a belt clip. Two models are available: No. 33-910 is a 10-foot rule; No. 33-912 is a 12-foot rule.

these strips can be "folded" and broken apart so that the pieces can be fit along the walls. Bend the individual strips back and forth until they break free. You may have to cut the spline with wire cutters.

If you are using self-adhesive parquet blocks, score the protective backing between the strips with a utility knife. Then bend the strips back and forth until they break free.

If an individual strip is too wide to fill an opening, you can cut the strip to size with a coping saw. Go completely through the wood strip, adhesive, and protective backing. If the saw becomes clogged with adhesive and sawdust, clean the residue with a wiping cloth moistened with mineral spirits.

If the blocks are not laminated strips, but rather pieces of wood scored to resemble parquet blocks, the tiles may be cut to fit this way:

Place a tile precisely on top of a tile in the row adjoining the border row to be laid. Then, butt a second tile against the wall, with its sides aligned with the first tile. Mark the first tile where the first and second tiles overlap, using the second one's edge as a guide. Cut the first tile along your mark; it should fit exactly.

Note: Border tiles should be about ¼ to ½ inch from a wall or any vertical obstruction. This allows for expansion and contraction of the parquet blocks as humidity in the room changes.

14. To fit tiles around objects such as a pipe, heat register opening, toilet, or bathtub, use a compass with a point on one leg and a pencil on the other leg. Guide the pointed leg along the irregular surface of the object while the pencil draws this shape on a tile that is positioned exactly on top of the tile in the adjoining row, as explained in the previous step.

    Note: Because some parquet tiles may be separated into individual strips, you may want to cut several tiles this way and fit the pieces around irregularities as you match them. If so, you can use adhesive to stick the small pieces into place.

15. With lots of effort, you can make each tile fit perfectly against the wall surfaces. However, the easiest way to cover any imperfections along the walls is with the molding or trim that you removed before the job started, or with new molding or trim that you plan to buy. When the entire floor has been laid, install the molding along the walls and across the thresholds of doorways. Also, reinstall heat register covers and anything else you removed. Caulk any joints that butt against bathtubs or pipes.

16. Avoid walking on the floor as much as possible for about 24 hours to allow the adhesive to set properly. Because most parquet flooring is pre-finished, don't clean the floor with water or a water-based product. Use special cleaners and top waxes recommended for wood flooring or follow the recommendations of the manufacturer.

Installing Wall-to-Wall Carpet

Materials • Wood Putty • Carpet Tack Strips • Carpet Padding • Staples • Carpet Tape • Carpet • Doorway Strips • Common Nails

---

Tools • Tape Measure • Pencil • Screwdriver • Hammer • Nail Set • Vacuum Cleaner • Staples • Utility Knife • Carpet Stretcher • Scissors • Carpet Tape Heater • Putty Knife

---

WALL-TO-WALL carpeting, also called "tacked-down" carpet, must be stretched so that it's under tension. If it isn't, the carpeting is likely to ripple and wad, causing cleaning and appearance problems. Installation isn't too difficult, but there are some tricks to doing the job correctly. Follow these steps:

1. Measure the room to be carpeted to determine how much carpet you will require.
2. Move all furniture out of the room to be carpeted.
3. Remove the doors to the room and any metal thresholds.
4. Remove all tacks—if any—remaining from previous carpet installation. Also eliminate any squeaks in the floor, and drive in any protruding nails with a nail set and hammer. If there are large cracks in the floor, fill them with wood putty.
5. Scrub and vacuum the floor.
6. Nail carpet tack strips to the floor all around the perimeter of the room, leaving a ¼-inch space between the strips and the walls. The teeth of the strips must face the walls.
7. Install the carpet padding by stapling it to the floor. Space staples at about 12-inch intervals just so the padding won't slide. The padding, which should go right to the edge of the tack strips, can be trimmed if necessary with a utility knife after it is in place.
8. If necessary, seam the carpet. **Note:** Many carpet retailers will cut and seam the carpet you buy before delivery. There is, however, a charge for this. If you want to do your own seaming, use standard, double-faced carpet tape or the kind that is activated by a special heat device available from some carpet retailers and tool rental firms. The heat-activated tape usually works better for seaming than the standard tape. Be sure to match the carpet pattern pile direction carefully to obtain invisible seams.
9. Move the carpeting into the room and unroll it.
10. Center the carpet in the room. Use a carpet stretcher, or knee-kicker, to stretch the carpet.
11. After the carpet has been stretched, hook the edges over the tack strips around the perimeter of the room. **Note:** As you stretch the carpeting, have someone stand directly in back of you to weight the material so you can hook

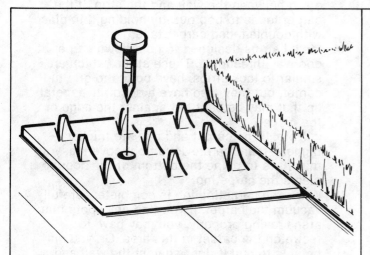

Carpet tack strips are nailed all around a room's perimeter, leaving a 1/4-inch space between the strips and the wall.

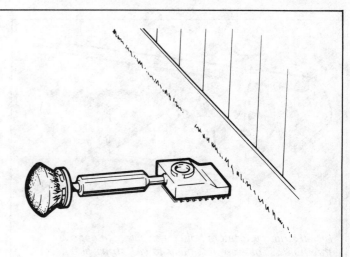

Use a carpet stretcher, or knee kicker, to stretch the carpet. Then, hook the edges over the tack strips.

Carpet Casters Designed for Heavy Furniture

Heavy furniture can be difficult to move on carpeting. The Coronet decorative metal ball caster is especially designed for heavy furniture on carpeting. The caster has a plate so it can be screwed directly to the furniture's frame. There is a choice of two finishes: antique or bright brass. There are also two sizes: a 2- and a 2½-inch ball/plate. Load capacity for the 2-inch model is 320 pounds; it's 400 pounds for the 2½-inch model. The casters, manufactured by the Faultless Division of Bliss & Laughlin Industries, are packaged two or four to a card.

Knee Kicker for Carpeting

A carpet stretcher is a handy tool for wall-to-wall carpet installation. The Roberts Golden Touch knee kicker from Roberts Consolidated Industries is a stationary length kicker with a wide head. Guaranteed for three years by the manufacturer, the tool features a pin adjustment dial with a visual indicator that shows the exact depth of penetration. The tool, however, doesn't include a bumper and nap-grips, which are available separately.

Wooden Tack Strips Cover Perimeter

For tacked-down carpet installations, you must cover the perimeter of the room with tack strips. Sears, Roebuck and Co. offers wooden tack strips in 4-foot lengths, packaging 25 strips to a box. You merely tack the strips to the floor; the strips grab and hold the carpet taut around the edges of the room.

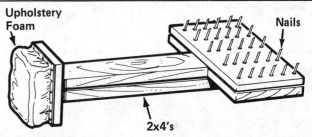

Upholstery Foam

Nails

2x4's

You Can Make a Homemade Knee Kicker

A homemade knee kicker to help you install wall-to-wall carpeting is simple to make. Because the padded part of the tool must be thick enough for comfort when you hit it with your knee, glue a thick scrap of upholstery foam to one side of an 8-inch square of scrap wood. Make the body of the kicker out of two 12-inch 2 × 4's assembled in a T-shape, and use nails driven at an angle through another 8-inch square of wood as the stretcher pins. Be sure to angle the nails—hardened steel nails work best—so they'll grip the carpet when pushed down. Assemble the other wooden pieces to the kicker body with wood screws, and your carpeting tool is finished. Swift knee movement against the foam pad stretches the carpet. Then, when the forward push stops, the carpet hooks over the angled spikes in the tack strip.

the edges without having the carpet slip backward.

12. Trim the edges of the carpet with heavy-duty scissors and utility knife, leaving about ⅜ inch of carpet beyond the tack strips.

13. Use a wide putty knife to poke excess carpet down between the wall and the strip. If the carpet tends to pop out, try holding it in place with double-faced carpet tape.

14. Install strips designed to hold down carpet at doorway thresholds. These strips, which are similar to tack strips, have points to grip the carpet, but they also have a decorative metal lip that may be bent flat against the edge of the carpet.

    Note: If the carpet and pad are thicker—higher—than the previous floor covering, you may have to plane the bottom of the door so it clears the carpeting.

15. When the carpeting job is complete, carefully vacuum the carpet. If you find any spots that aren't laying properly, you may have to restretch the carpet in this area. Or, you may be able to pull it tight against the wall and tack it with nails; the carpet pile should conceal any nail heads.

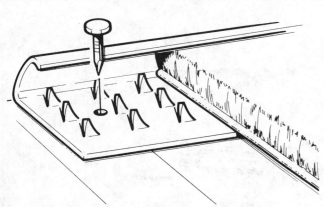

Install strips designed to hold down carpet at doorway thresholds. These strips, similar to tack strips, also have a decorative metal lip that can be bent flat against the edge of the carpet.

Installing Bathroom Carpet

Materials • Bathroom Carpeting • Brown Wrapping Paper or Newspapers • Cellophane Tape • Carpet Tape • Piece of Plywood

Tools • Tape Measure • Pencil • Heavy-Duty Scissors • Felt-Tip or Ballpoint Pen • Utility Knife

WALL-TO-WALL bathroom carpeting is easy to install. The key to the installation is making accurate measurements and transferring them to a paper pattern. To install bathroom carpeting, follow these steps:

1. Measure the bathroom. Multiply the length by the width to obtain the square footage.
2. Take the figures to a carpet retailer so the retailer can determine how much carpeting you'll need.
3. Make a paper pattern of the bathroom. You can buy rolls of brown wrapping paper for this purpose, or you can tape sheets of newspaper together. The pattern will be easier to handle if you make the pattern in several sections, and then tape them together.

   For example, to make the pattern for around the toilet, fold the paper in half and place it along one side of the toilet. Press the paper against the bottom edge of the toilet so you can get an outline of the base. Pencil this shape onto the paper and then cut out the shape with scissors. Check the fit as you mark and cut. Once the folded paper section fits half of the toilet shape, unfold it and cut a straight line in the paper from back of the toilet opening in the pattern to the wall behind the toilet. Fit the pattern around the toilet and refine the pattern so it fits exactly. You can use this technique for any other fixtures that can't be easily removed.
4. When all sections are cut out, piece them together on the bathroom floor to make sure they fit the room precisely. Then tape the

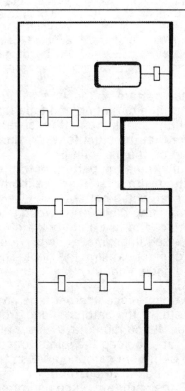

Make a paper pattern of the bathroom. You can buy a roll of brown wrapping paper for this or you can tape sheets of newspaper together.

To cut the pattern for a toilet, fold a sheet of paper in half and place it against the fixture (top). Pencil the outline on the paper and cut it out. Once the folded paper fits half of the toilet shape, unfold it and cut a straight line (bottom) from the back of the toilet opening to the wall behind it.

Floors

Tape a Patch or Whole Carpet

Never lay a carpet without securing its edges; it can be dangerous. MYRO, Inc. markets CarpeTape, a double-faced tape that does all the things carpet tape should do and does them well. In addition, you will probably discover a multitude of other uses for MYRO CarpeTape around the house. For example, it does a good job of holding posters to a teenager's wall, leaving no ugly holes or unsightly residue. MYRO also makes bathtub seam-sealing tapes, bathtub safety treads, and other adhesive products.

Sweep Up the Daily Dirt

A carpet sweeper can be handier to use for small cleaning chores than a vacuum cleaner. The Century II carpet sweeper, made by Bissell, Inc., features two small brushes at the front corners of the unit to get dirt that is right against the wall—dirt that other sweepers might miss. The unit adjusts in height to be effective on any floor surface from bare floors to shag carpets. Bissell also markets

several carpet cleaning compounds, including a dry carpet cleaner that the

company says eliminates all possibility of staining or fading.

Rug Shears Cut Carpets Cleanly

While you can cut most carpeting with nearly any good pair of heavy-duty scissors, Clauss rug shears offer one big advantage—shape. The

offset handles make carpet-cutting much easier. Made of hammer-forged molybdenum steel with double-plated chrome over nickel, the Clauss rug shears, from Clauss Cutlery Co., have exceptionally sharp 8-inch knife blade edges.

Padding Can Make a Big Difference

You can make inexpensive carpet feel several times thicker and plushier by placing a good padding material beneath it. For padding under a bathroom carpet, try one of the rubberized types because fiber padding is too susceptible to moisture. If you plan to carpet over resilient flooring, use double-faced tape to hold the padding down.

sections together. Mark the word "TOP" on the pattern.

5. In another room with plenty of working space, lay the carpeting face down on the floor.

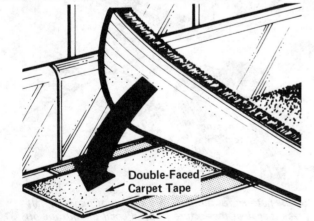

Place double-faced carpet tape around the perimeter of the bathroom, install the carpet, and press the edges against the carpet tape.

6. Turn the pattern so the word "TOP" is facing down on the carpeting and tape it to the carpeting. Check the pattern several times to be sure that the cutouts will accurately be located on the carpeting.
7. Carefully trace the pattern onto the back of the carpeting with a felt-tip or ballpoint pen, whichever works better.
8. Place a scrap piece of plywood under the carpeting, and use a utility knife to cut along the marked lines; move the plywood so the knife doesn't damage the floor. The carpeting should slice smoothly. Make any trim cuts with scissors.
9. Place double-faced carpet tape around the perimeter of the bathroom and around the fixtures. If you must have a seam in the carpet, apply tape to keep the joints together. **Note:** Some bathroom carpeting doesn't have to be taped to hold it in position.
10. Install the carpet in place and press the edges against the carpet tape. If you need to move the carpet, you can quickly peel it up from the tape and then stick it back down again.

Repairing Burns in Carpeting

Materials • Latex Adhesive • Scrap of Matching Carpet • Carpet Tape

Tools • Fingernail Scissors • Tuft Setter

AFTER A PARTY, you may find some evidence of an accident: a cigarette burn in your carpet. Although you can't repair the damage completely unless you have the carpet rewoven, there are several ways to hide the burned spot very effectively. Follow these steps:

1. Using fingernail scissors, clip away all blackened carpet fibers. If the burn didn't go all the way down to the carpet backing, you may not have to do anything else but trim the burned fibers; the low spot may not be noticeable. If the burn did reach the backing, scrape the charred matter away.
2. If the backing shows, clip new fibers from a carpet scrap so you can glue them in the hole. If you don't have a piece of matching scrap carpet, you may be able to obtain enough fibers to clip at the edge of the carpet next to the baseboard molding.
3. Apply latex adhesive in the hole. When the adhesive gets tacky enough to support the

Stick Carpet Edges Together With Binding Adhesive

Instead of trying to bind the edges of a carpet patch with needle and thread to prevent raveling, you can try Mister Quick, a specially prepared binding adhesive. Made by the Carpet Products Co., it comes in a plastic squeeze bottle with a spout that lets you apply it along the carpet edge quickly. Because it dries clear, Mister Quick is ideal for carpet burn repairs.

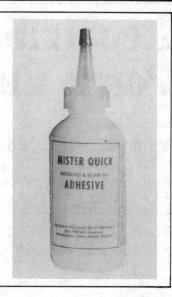

fibers, carefully place a few fibers at a time upright in the adhesive.

Note: For deep burns, you can also retuft the carpet, using a tuft-setting tool to insert carpet fibers one by one. Ravel the edge of a piece of scrap carpet, pulling out individual tufts; each piece should be twice the depth of the carpet pile. Fold a fiber in half, making a V-shaped tuft. Place it in the fork of the tuft-setter and drive it into the backing of the glued area, striking the tool lightly with a hammer.

4. If the damage is severe, cut a square out of the carpet and replace it with a matching scrap piece cut to the exact size of the cutout. Use double-faced carpet tape to hold the patch in place. Make sure that the nap of the carpet patch lays in the same direction as the nap of the carpet.

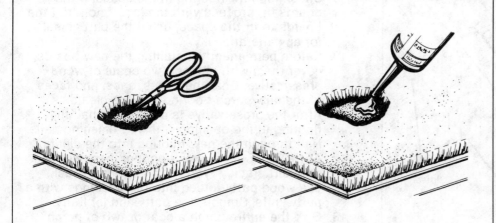

To repair a burn that isn't extensive, clip away blackened fibers (left), apply latex adhesive in the hole (right), and when the adhesive gets tacky enough to support the fibers, carefully place a few fibers at a time upright in the adhesive.

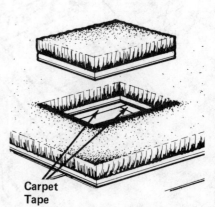

Carpet Tape

If the burn damage is severe, cut a square out of the carpet and replace it with a matching piece; use double-faced tape to hold the patch.

Repairing a Porch Floor

Materials • Porch Boards as Required
• 2 × 4 Lumber • 10d Common Nails • 10d Finishing Nails • Wood Preservative
• Wood Putty • Porch and Deck Enamel

Tools • Carpenter's Square • Pencil
• Brace and ¾-Inch Wood-Boring Bit
• Keyhole or Saber Saw • Pry Bar • Butt Chisel • Hammer • Paintbrushes • Putty Knife

MOISTURE FROM a crawl space below porch flooring usually is the cause of rotting porch floor boards and supporting framing members. The best way to deter this is to cover the earth with plastic sheeting. See "Insulating Basements and Crawl Spaces" in the chapter on Energy-Saving.

If the framing members are beyond support—or repair—they must be replaced. This is a job for a professional, especially if the porch has a roof. If just the boards are rotted, you can make repairs. Follow this procedure:

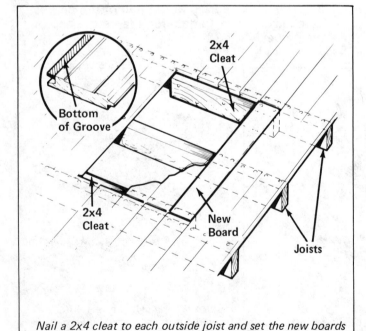

Nail a 2x4 cleat to each outside joist and set the new boards into the opening; cut off the bottom of the groove on the last board.

1. With a carpenter's square, outline the damaged porch floor area with a pencil, confining the outlined area between joints of the boards.
2. Use a brace and wood-boring bit to drill ¾-inch holes at the four corners of the penciled outline, in boards that are not rotted; the holes should be inside the lines. **Note:** The holes should be bored just through the layer of porch flooring; don't bore into the framing members.
3. Using a keyhole or a saber saw, cut along the marked lines to connect the four holes.
4. Pry out the damaged boards.
5. Measure and cut new boards to fit the space.
6. Porch flooring usually is made of tongue-and-groove boards. To slip the patch into adjoining boards, you will have to square the bottom of the groove of one board so the board may be inserted. Do this with a butt chisel.
7. If necessary, add wooden cleats to the sides of joists to support the boards. You can use scrap porch flooring for the cleats, or you can use scrap lengths of 2 × 4 lumber.
8. Nail the cleat supports to the joists with 10d common nails. The tops of the cleats must be flush with the top of the joists.
9. Check the new flooring in the space. If the boards fit, proceed with the job. If not, trim the boards to fit the space, using the butt chisel for any alterations.
10. Before permanently installing the new boards, cover them with at least two coats of wood preservative. Coat the edges, ends, and faces of the new porch flooring and the cleats.
11. After the preservative is dry, fit and nail the flooring in the opening with 10d finishing nails. Nail through the new flooring into the cleats.
12. At the ends of the new flooring, there will be a saw kerf crack. If you want to fill this crack, use wood putty forced into the openings with a putty knife. Smooth the putty and let it dry.
13. Give the entire porch a coat or two of porch and deck enamel. This will conceal the patch.
14. Although it isn't an easy job, you should paint the underside of the porch flooring and support members with a couple of coats of wood preservative to prevent future rot.

Stain Preservative for Wood Flooring

Mister Thinzit clear stain penta wood preservative has a 5-percent penta formula that makes it ideal for exterior use on flooring and other wood products. The product, made by Michlin Chemical Corp., is water repellent, and can be painted. According to the company, it reduces wood shrinkage, warping, swelling, checking, and other dimensional changes caused by moisture; it also

protects against wood insects such as termites and carpenter ants.

Chisel Designed for Cutting Tongues

When you replace floor boards that have a tongue and groove, often the tongue must be removed so you can slip the board patch in position. To help you do this, Neill Tools, Inc., designed a floorboard

chisel for cutting the tongue from the board without too much danger of splitting the board. The floorboard chisel, No. CB776A, has a 2½-inch blade and is 9 inches long. You should always wear safety goggles and gloves when working with this type of tool.

Modular Flooring and Matting for Home Use

If you are troubled by an area that's often wet and damp, there's a flexible floor covering that provides excellent drainage. Matéflex home flooring and matting is a modular, polyethylene material designed in a flow-through honeycomb pattern. It comes in 13-inch interlocking squares. According to Matéflex/Mele

Manufacturing Co., the product is ideal for indoor or outdoor flooring, matting, and runners in game rooms, basements, laundry rooms, porches, decks, walkways, and mud rooms. Rain, cold, snow, and dirt have no effect on the material, the company says. The flooring comes in orange, white, brown, light blue, dark blue, yellow, red, sand, and green colors. The tiles may be assembled in solid colors or mixed to form patterns.

Carpet Tape for All Floors

Carpet tape is great for holding down all kinds of carpeting. Mystik's carpet tape is double-faced and helps hold carpeting to wood, tile, and linoleum floors. According to the company, Mystik Corp., the carpet tape can reduce sliding, slipping, and other potential accidents. The tape, which has a peel-off liner, eliminates tacking and stapling. Each roll of No. M-959 tape is 1½ inches wide by 14 yards long.

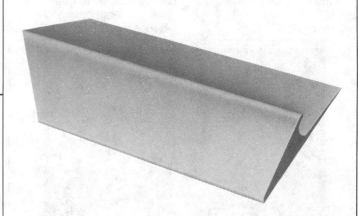

Entry Edging Is Finishing Touch

Even with carpeting that is taped in place, there's always the possibility that someone will catch a heel on the edge when entering the room. You can prevent such accidents by installing one of the many different types of edging strips made of metal or plastic to accommodate both the carpeting and the flooring in the adjoining room or hall. Mercer Plastics Co., Inc., offers a wide variety of vinyl edgings for resilient floors and carpets, including its Imperial carpet reducer, which is made of vinyl. The edge molding is available in black, brown, avocado, gold, red, or blue colors.

Latex-Based Adhesive for Vinyl-Asbestos or Asphalt Tile

For vinyl-asbestos or asphalt tile, you can use a latex-based vinyl tile adhesive. Gulf reinforced vinyl tile adhesive, from Gulf Adhesives and Resins, Gulf Oil Chemicals Co., is such a product. It can be rolled or brushed on the tile or floor. It is formulated for the installation of vinyl-asbestos and asphalt tile on wood or concrete floors, where moisture is not a factor. The Gulf

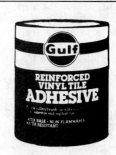

adhesive features good spreadability, a strong tack, and freeze/thaw stability. According to the manufacturer, it is also non-flammable and alkali- and moisture-resistant. The adhesive is available in quart, gallon, 3½-gallon, and 5-gallon containers.

Adhesive for Vinyl Flooring

For installing felt-back and vinyl sheet goods, vinyl tile, or indoor/outdoor needle-punch carpeting, you can use a good multi-purpose carpet/flooring adhesive. Such a product is made by Gulf Adhesives and Resins, Gulf Oil Chemicals Co. Gulf multipurpose carpet/flooring adhesive, however, is not to be used for vinyl-backed carpet. The material spreads easily and has excellent tack and re-bond qualities. It also is alkali and water-resistant, non-flammable, and freeze/thaw stable, according to Gulf. The product comes in quart, gallon, 3½-gallon, and 5-gallon containers.

Spray Cleaner Can Handle Spot-Cleaning

Most spots on resilient flooring can be removed with one of many spray cleaners available at grocery and hardware stores. For example, Formula 409, made by the Clorox Co., is an all-purpose cleaner that can quickly rid floors of food and grease stains, heel marks, and other spots and substances that can attack your floors. It works on linoleum as well as vinyl flooring, but like most spray cleaners, Formula 409 will remove wax if left on for a long period of time. Thus, the key to spot removal is to spray it on and wipe it off immediately.

Flooring and Construction Adhesive

If you're joining plywood or particleboard subflooring to joists, you can use a construction adhesive such as Gulf flooring and general construction adhesive (FGC). It also is made for flooring installations. The product is a quality, light-color mastic formulated for joining plywood and particle-board subflooring to joists. The use of this FGC adhesive, from Gulf Adhesives and Resins, Gulf Oil Chemicals Co., can help eliminate floor squeaks, increase floor stiffness, and reduce nail-popping, according to the manufacturer. It is available in a 30-ounce cartridge that fits standard caulking guns.

Metal Trim for Almost Any Floor

A variety of aluminum trim in a bright finish, hammered aluminum finish, or hammered gold finish for almost any floor covering is made by Reynolds Metal Co. The strips, which can be used with carpeting, tile, linoleum, and wood block, include edging, seam and edge binder bars, saddle thresholds, carpet bars, and stair nosing. The strips come in 3- and 6-foot lengths.

Dirty Grout in Ceramic Tile Floors

The grout between ceramic tiles in floors usually becomes dirty through use; the white grout lines become black, especially in high traffic areas. This is a normal condition. Even tile sealer doesn't satisfactorily solve the problem. The best way to restore the grout lines is to clean them out with a 10d nail driven through the end of a short piece of 1 × 2 or 1 × 3. Just remove the top layer of grout with the point of the nail—perhaps a ⅛ inch or so. Vacuum the residue. Regrout the tile joints with a fairly thick mixture of grout that is about the consistency of thick whipped cream. Let the grout dry, and then clean the haze from the top of the tiles. Complete the project by sealing the floor with a quality tile sealer.

Casters for Hard Surfaces

For hard surfaces such as tile, terrazzo, linoleum, wood, concrete, and so on, rubber-tread casters on furniture pieces are best. Shepherd rubber tread casters have the rubber permanently bonded to the wheels. The rubber is oil-resistant—an important feature. The Shepherd casters are available in several models.
They also feature an enclosed design that eliminates caster flutter and keeps out foreign matter. Models with conductive treads are available where static electricity may be a problem. The products are manufactured from die-

cast metal alloy with self-lubricating acetal resin bearings. Sizes range from 2¼- to 5-inch wheel diameters. Treads are black or gray; the black treads are conductive. Finishes include antique copper, bright brass, bright chrome, and satin chrome. They are also available unfinished.

Floor Adhesive for Most Coverings

A multi-purpose adhesive can do the job of a lot of other adhesives. Weldwood multi-purpose floor adhesive, made by Roberts Consolidated Industries, is a non-flammable, latex-based adhesive that may be used on almost any carpeting material—indoors or outdoors. The product is easy to apply and cleans up with water. The adhesive is available in

quarts, gallons, and 3½- and 5-gallon pails.

When Floors Sag

An adjustable jack post is the answer to sagging floors, provided the sag isn't too great. Jack posts are inexpensive and extremely simple to use. Set the jack post under the sag on a short length of 2 × 10. Bridge the joists with a length of 2 × 10 sandwiched between the jack post and the edges of the joists. Every two days, give the jack post one quarter turn—no more or no less. Do this every two days until the floor is level. At this time, you can either leave the jack post in position for support or remove the jack post and replace it with an inexpensive Lally column. This steel column is designed for sagging floor problems. Use the Lally with 2 × 10's—as with a jack post—or as building codes in your area specify.

Brush-On Adhesive for Vinyl-Asbestos Tile

For bonding vinyl-asbestos tile to concrete or plywood subfloors and to lining felt on double-strip wood floors, you should use an adhesive formulated for this type of job. United States Gypsum Co. makes Durabond brush-on vinyl tile adhesive that is designed for rapid application of vinyl-asbestos tile to subfloors. When dry, it's water-resistant. According to the manufacturer, the product also is freeze/thaw stable. The adhesive's paint-like consistency makes it easy to apply with brush, roller, or notched trowel. Coverage is about 250 to 300 square feet per gallon.

Slate Laymanship

Slate floors, which are used mostly in foyers where water from the outdoors is a problem, are not especially difficult to install with adhesive and a cement-type grout. Slate, however, is heavy, so you must be sure that the floor framing is adequate to handle the weight. In an average-size foyer—for example, one that is 5 by 7 feet—the structure probably is more than adequate to support the weight. If you are going to lay a lot of slate, however, it's recommended that you consult a construction professional about the support framing. Slate may be laid over wood, concrete, or composition floors. The only requirements are that the floor should be tight, fairly smooth, and reasonably level.

Pour a Floor

Once used only for industrial purposes, pouring an epoxy onto the floor and then adding chips of color for depth and beauty can now be done in the home. For a tough seamless floor covering, check out a Dur-A-Flex installation. The density and color of the chips allow you to vary the effect to suit your surroundings. Dur-A-Flex, Inc., also markets the epoxy in a number of solid colors.

Try Adhesive for Flooring, Underlayment

Nails and staples are great mechanical fasteners for installing subfloors, underlayment, and some finished flooring materials. These fasteners, teamed with subfloor adhesive, do even a better holding job. Franklin Sub-Floor & Plywood Adhesive is available in 29-fluid-ounce cartridges for caulking guns. The adhesive may be used for glued floor systems, wood parquet, and vinyl floors as well as for wall paneling, ceilings, countertops, and other applications.

Replacing a Ceramic Tile

Materials • Ceramic Tile as Required • Ceramic Tile Adhesive • Masking Tape or Toothpicks • Tile Grout • Towel • 1 × 2 Scrap • 8d Finishing Nail

Tools • Electric Drill With Carbide Bit or Straightedge and Glass Cutter • Cold Chisel • Hammer • Safety Goggles • Putty Knife • Utility Knife • Sponge

REMOVING AND replacing just one broken ceramic tile can be very difficult. And, finding a new tile that matches the old can be time-consuming, too. But once you have the right tile, follow this procedure for removing a broken tile and putting in a replacement—or a series of replacements:

1. Drill a hole in the center of the damaged ceramic tile with a carbide bit locked in the chuck of a portable electric drill. If you don't have an electric drill, you can use a straightedge to scribe an "X" on the surface of the tile with a glass cutter.
2. Use a cold chisel and hammer to break away the tile. Take care not to damage any surrounding tiles. *Caution: Wear safety goggles when using the hammer and chisel.*
3. Clean the bed on which the old tile rested, making the surface as smooth as possible. Then, remove any loose grout around the opening with a putty or utility knife.
4. Spread ceramic tile adhesive over the back of the replacement tile. Keep the adhesive about ½ inch away from all four edges.
5. Hold the tile by its edges and put it in place. Press until the new tile is flush with the surrounding tiles.
6. Position the tile so there's an even space all around it, and then tape it in place or insert broken toothpicks to keep gravity from pulling the tile down before the adhesive sets up.
7. Allow 24 hours for the adhesive to cure, and then mix tile grout according to the manufacturer's directions. Be sure to mix the grout until it is completely smooth, and only mix what you can use in about 15 minutes.

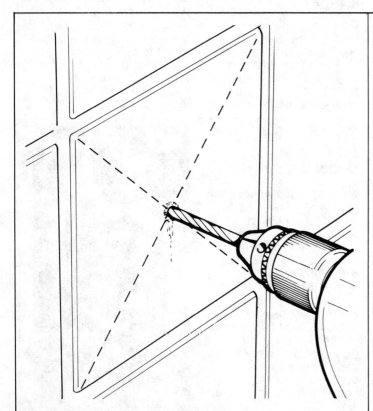

To remove a tile, drill a hole in the center with a carbide bit locked in the chuck of an electric drill.

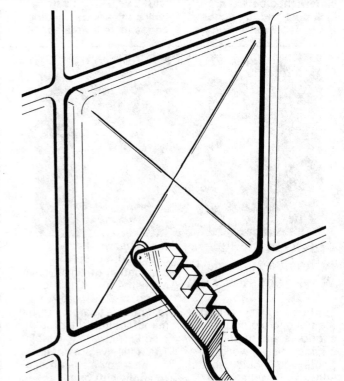

If you don't have an electric drill, scribe an "X" on the tile with a glass cutter, and use a cold chisel and hammer to break away the tile.

Carbide-Tipped Masonry Bit Goes Through Ceramic

A drill bit set from General Hardware Mfg. Co., Inc., contains five tungsten-carbide-tipped bits for use with a ¼-inch drill. In addition to drilling ceramic tiles, these bits can cut through concrete, brick, and stone, and they are spiral-fluted to assure fast dust removal without clogging. Because you only need one of the smaller bits in the set for drilling out a ceramic tile, you may wish to buy these General Hardware drill bits individually; on the other hand, once you own the set you will probably find plenty of uses for the other sizes.

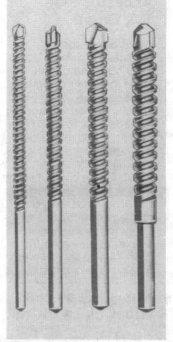

Cutting Mirror Tile Isn't Hard

The best tool for cutting mirror tile is a glass cutter. Use a carpenter's or combination square as a straightedge to run the glass cutter against. Just make one cut along the intended line; don't go back and forth over the line with the cutter. Then snap the tile at the scored line. If you have lots of tile to cut, have several glass cutters handy because cutting wheels dull quickly.

Disaster Follows Inaccurate Measuring

Many projects, both professional and amateur, have gone astray due to inaccurate measurement. The Exact aluminum rule, from the Exact Level & Tool Mfg. Co., is truly parallel and accurate. The edges are smooth, square, and straight, and the tool's numbers are large and easy to read. One edge has calibrations in eighths and the other in sixteenths. Exact aluminum rules range in length from 24 to 120 inches.

8. Fill in the space all around the tile with the grout mix. Dip a sponge or your finger into the mix, and apply it until you fill the space entirely. You will do no harm if you get the grout on surrounding tiles. Use a moistened index finger to smooth the grout lines so they are slightly concave.
9. After the grout has set for about 30 minutes, take a damp towel and gently remove any excess on surrounding tiles. Just be careful not to dig out any of the grout from between the tiles.
10. Wait about 24 hours, and then rub a damp towel vigorously to remove all traces of grout, and to polish the tile. If the tile you replaced is in a shower, make sure that you avoid getting any water on it until the grout has set up completely; a three-day period is recommended.

Note: You can fix loose tiles using the procedure above, except that you can skip Steps 1 and 2. Use a utility knife or a short length of 1 × 2 with an 8d finishing nail sticking through it to scrape out all the grout around the loose tile. Then, gently pry out the tile with a putty knife.

If you will be working on one tile, you should check all the others to see if they are loose. Loosened tiles usually are caused by shifting in the foundation of the house—a normal condition. Therefore, several tiles often come loose at the same time. Light tapping on the tiles with a putty knife handle will show you where any loose ones are.

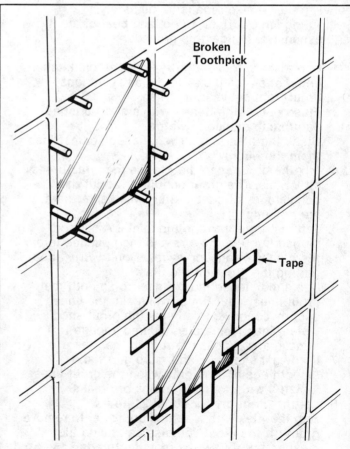

Until the adhesive sets up, tape the ceramic tile in place or insert broken toothpicks to keep gravity from pulling the tile down.

Regrouting Tile

Materials • Tile Grout • Coarse Towel or Tile Cleaner • Silicone Tile Grout Spray

Tools • Mixing Container • Putty Knife, Kitchen Knife, or Ice Pick • Paintbrush • Sponges

THE ABSENCE of grout between ceramic tiles looks unattractive. It also invites mildew. And in time, water will seep behind the tiles, loosen them, and decay the drywall or plaster to which the tiles are mounted. The result is a major remodeling job. You may even have to replace the framing members, because the water will soon rot them.

Whenever you spot loose or crumbling grout between tiles, make repairs immediately. Regrouting isn't difficult to do, and best of all, it isn't expensive. Follow this procedure:

1. Use a sharp tool—a putty knife, an old kitchen knife, or an ice pick—to dig away all loose grout from between the tiles.
2. Flush out all the debris with a short-bristled paintbrush dipped in water.
3. Clean the tiles to remove all soap scum. Rinse them thoroughly.
4. Mix the grout according to the manufacturer's directions. The grout should be about the consistency of cake batter. Make sure there are no lumps.
5. Jab the grout into the tile joints. A sponge dipped into the mixture and then pushed into the cracks often works well. Don't worry about getting the grout on the tiles.
6. Use a moistened index finger to smooth the grout lines. Your finger will make the lines slightly concave; this helps the grout shed water. Then, use a clean, damp sponge to remove any excess grout from the tiles.
7. If any gaps remain, add more grout and smooth again. Stop only when the grout lines look full with no indentations or breaks.
8. Let the grout dry for about 24 hours.
9. Rub the tiles with a coarse dry towel to remove grout off the tiles. You also can buy a tile cleaner, but follow the manufacturer's directions for its use.
10. When the grout has cured thoroughly, seal the grout lines with a silicone tile grout spray.

Asbestos-Free Tile Grout

Tile grout, made by the Synkoloid Co., may be used for grouting the joints between ceramic, plastic, and mosaic tile. The asbestos-free product is white in color and available in two sizes—2½- and 6½-pound packages. To use the grout, let the tile adhesive set for 24 hours. Then, mix the grout according to package directions and apply to the tile surface with a rubber-faced trowel. Work the trowel in an arc, holding it at a slight angle to force grout between the tiles. When the grout starts drying, wipe the excess from the tiles with a damp cloth. After the grout is completely dry, rinse the wall with water and wipe it with a clean trowel.

Spray Keeps Tile Grout Lines Clean

One of the biggest problems with tile is keeping the grout lines clean. The lines start off gleaming white, but they fade and yellow as time goes by. Magic American Chemical Corp. markets a special Tile 'N Grout Spray—the cap is a handy brush/sponge combination—that not only cleans and whitens the grout but also polishes the tiles.

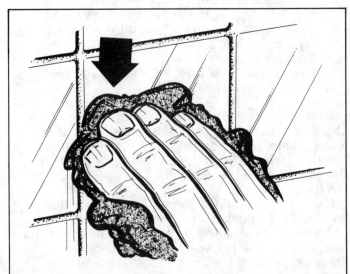

After the grout has dried for about 24 hours, rub the tiles with a coarse dry towel to remove grout from the tiles.

Recaulking Fixtures

Materials • Caulking Compound
• Cleaning Solvent • Rags

Tools • Putty Knife • Utility Knife or
Single-Edge Razor Blade • Caulking Gun

Chemical Kills Mildew on Contact

Mildew can often be a problem on walls in damp areas. But if you squirt some of the mildew remover, No. 0288, made by Red Devil, Inc., on the mildew in your kitchen, laundry, or bathroom, the chemical kills the mildew on contact, according to the manufacturer. Red Devil says the mildew remover requires no scrubbing or scouring; you simply spray it on and rinse it off with clean water. The product comes in a 16-ounce bottle with a spray applicator.

W HEN CAULKING compound breaks loose around a bathtub or sink, the crack may not look too bad, but it should be refilled with caulking compound immediately. As long as there is a gap between the fixture and the wall or floor, water is seeping into the opening. In a very short time, the seepage will rot the wallcovering, cause mildew, and damage the framing.

The caulking compound that you use should be made especially for cracks around bathtubs, showers, sinks, lavatories, toilets, and so forth. This information will be on the product. An adhesive caulk is recommended, although it is a bit more expensive than standard compounds. Some caulking compound manufacturers also offer compound in colors so you can match the color of your fixtures. If you can't find a matching color, however, white compound will look fine no matter what color your fixtures are. To caulk around your fixtures, follow these steps:

1. Remove all of the old caulking material. Use a putty knife or utility knife, but be careful not to chip the surface of the fixture or the edges of the bottom or adjoining row of wall tiles.
2. Use a cleaning solvent to clean away any soap residue in the crack.
3. Rinse away the solvent with water.
4. Make sure that the crack and surrounding area is completely dry by wrapping a dry rag around a putty knife blade and running it through the crack.
5. Cut the nozzle of the tube of caulking compound at an angle and at a point where the size bead that comes out will be slightly wider than the gap around the fixture. Use a utility knife or single-edge razor blade to cut the nozzle.
6. Squeeze the tube of compound to form a continuous bead all around the fixture. **Note:** If the compound is in a hand-squeezed tube, apply it by moving the tube away from you. If the compound is in a caulking gun, draw the

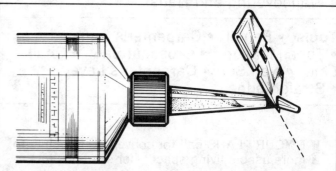

Cut the nozzle of the caulking compound tube at an angle so that the size bead that comes out will be slightly wider than the gap around the fixture.

Apply compound from a hand-squeezed tube by moving the tube away from you; squeeze the tube of compound to form a continuous bead all around the fixture.

gun toward you. This will result in a smoother and fuller joint.
7. Dip your index finger in water, and then press the compound into the gap. Keep your finger moist and smooth the compound as you push it in.

Framing a Partition Wall

Materials • 2 × 4 or 2 × 3 Lumber as Required • 10d Common Nails • 16d Common Nails • Cedar Shingle Shims • Wallcovering and Nails

Tools • Pencil • Carpenter's Square • Tape Measure • Crosscut Saw • Chalk Line • Nail Set • Carpenter's Level • Straightedge

IF YOUR PLANS call for converting a room into more usable living space—for example, in a basement or attached garage—you will probably have to build a partition wall. Even if you have never done many carpentry projects, you will find that framing a wall isn't difficult at all.

The basic components of a partition wall include the top plate; the sole, or floor, plate; and the wall studs. The studs are usually on 16-inch centers, which means that the distance from the center of one stud to the center of the next measures 16 inches. All framing lumber for a project is of the same size, usually 2 × 4's or 2 × 3's.

Note: The framing described here is for a non-load-bearing partition wall. Because it isn't designed to support the ceiling or the floor above, you need not worry about the roof caving in. All you have to strive for is making the finished wall look as attractive as possible. Remember that minor cosmetic faults in the framing will be covered over by the wallboard or paneling.

To build a partition wall, follow these steps:

1. Plan the wall, making sure that you consider all the uses the room will be put to and what furniture or equipment will go in it. Think about the best place for a door.
2. When the planning is completed, cut the top plate and sole plate for the wall. Use long lengths of lumber (10-foot, 12-foot, or 16-foot lengths) to make the plates all one piece, if possible. Remember that the sole plate doesn't run through a doorway.
3. After these plates have been cut, lay them side by side and mark them for stud locations. The studs may be 16 or 24 inches on center; however, the 16-inch measurement is recommended.

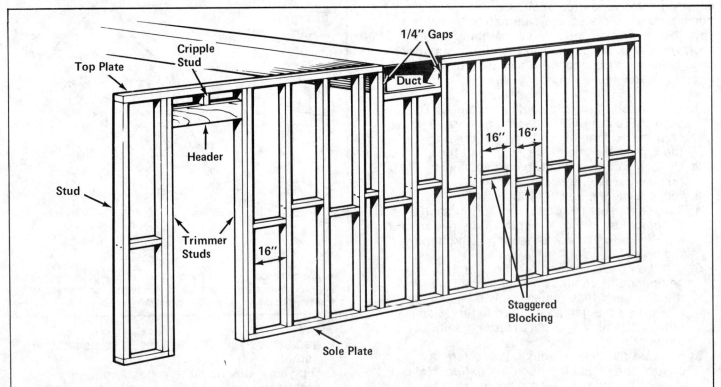

The basic components of a partition wall include the top plate; the sole, or floor, plate; and the wall studs. All framing lumber for a project is of the same size, usually 2x4s or 2x3s.

4. If the wall runs across the joists in the ceiling above, you can nail the top plate to each joist. If the wall runs parallel to the joists and cannot be positioned so that the top plate can be nailed to a joist, then you must install bridging of 2 × 4's to provide solid nailing for the top plate. Space the bridging pieces on 16-inch centers, and nail them to the joists with two nails through each end of each bridging piece.
5. Snap a chalk line on the floor where the sole plate is to go to guide you as you install it.
6. Install the sole plate by nailing it; make sure it's aligned with your chalk line. If necessary, shim under the plate with cedar shingles to compensate for any unlevel sections of flooring.
7. With the plate in place, use a long, straight 2 × 4 to determine where the top plate should go so that it will be directly above the sole plate. Place the straightedge against the 2 × 4, and use a level to make it vertically level, or plumb.

     Note: If a heating and cooling duct is in the way of the top plate, you will have to cut the top plate at the duct and continue it on the other side. Butt the top plate against the duct, leaving about ¼-inch gap on each side for expansion of the wood. Then, install a stud against one side of the duct and nail it to the top plate and to the sole plate. Do the same on the other side of the duct. Run a length of 2 × 4 across the bottom of the duct and nail it to the studs on both sides. Finally, under the midpoint of this horizontal 2 × 4, install another stud for support, nailing it to the 2 × 4 under the duct and to the sole plate.
8. If the floor and ceiling are even, assemble the studs and top plate on the floor as a unit, which will be raised as an assembly. This allows you to nail through the top plate and straight into the top of each stud. If the studs must vary in length, however, install the top plate, cut each stud to fit, and then toenail each stud in place. **Note:** Toenailing consists of driving 16d nails into the side of the stud at about a 45-degree angle so that the nails penetrate the top plate. Drive two nails into each side of the stud, plus one nail into the edge.
9. Toenail the studs in place to the sole plate.
10. Openings for doors in the framing must be about 3 inches wider and about 1½ inches higher than the actual size of the door. Nail extra 2 × 4's—called "cripples" or "jack studs"—on both sides of the door opening; and a header at the top. Then, place shorter cripples between the header and the top plate, and nail them in place.
11. Nail 2 × 4's between studs at the midpoint of

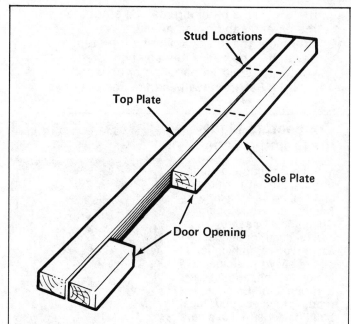

After cutting the top and sole plates, lay them side by side and mark them for stud locations.

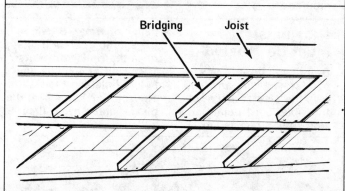

If the wall runs parallel to the joists, you can install bridging made of 2x4's to provide solid nailing for the top plate.

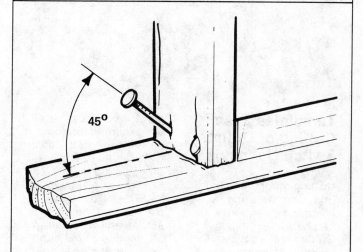

Toenailing consists of driving a nail into the side of a stud at about a 45-degree angle.

the wall. This blocking may be staggered so the pieces can be end-nailed.

12. Complete the job by covering the stud partition. You can apply any type of surface you want, such as paneling or drywall.

   Note: Partition walls can be insulated to lower sound transmission between the two "new" rooms. Insulation, however, doesn't reduce noise to a great degree. A better sound-absorbing product would be acoustical ceiling tile, which can absorb about 66 percent of the airborne sound striking it.

Connectors Made for Framing Jobs

Metal clips that join studs to the plates at the floor and ceiling can make framing a snap. Carpentry Connectors, made by Teco, can be used for almost every type of framing joint; all are easy to use, quick in application, and render a strong joint. Be sure, though, to check your local building code to make sure that this sort of installation conforms with regulations.

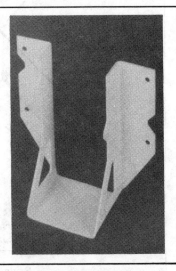

New Plaster Must Be Treated

Before you cover a new plaster wall with anything, give the plaster a coat of this solution: 1 pound of zinc sulphate mixed in 1 gallon of water. Brush on the solution. When it dries, rinse the walls with water. Then wait at least 12 days before finishing the wall. The solution helps seal the plaster and prevent lime salts.

Crumbling Cork Can Be Cured

Cork tiles, especially thick ones, have a tendency to crumble at the corners as they are being installed. When this happens, fill the damaged corners with a little daub of cork tile adhesive and simply press in pieces of cork that have crumbled off. You can level the cork patch with your fingers.

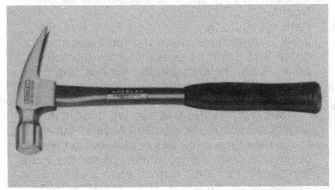

Framing Hammer Has Extra Heft

When you frame a wall, you need a heavy hammer. The Stanley framing hammer, made by the Stanley Tools Division of The Stanley Works, is a little heavier than an all-purpose hammer. It has a 22-ounce mill-checkered face. All Stanley hammers with fiberglass handles feature a tapered assembly design to eliminate the possibility of the head flying off. The head, forged of high carbon steel, is secured with epoxy resin adhesive. The comfortable grip is made of vinyl.

Templates Ease Cutting of Outlet, Switch Openings

Cutting an opening in drywall or paneling for an electrical outlet or switch can be tricky. Cutout Guides are templates for marking accurate cutout lines for electrical outlets and switches, telephone jacks, vents, ducts, wall fans, thermostats on paneling, drywall, and other wallcoverings. The products are made by Construction Templates, Inc. The patterns are marked for mounting screws and wire pathways so junction boxes can slip right into the opening without damaging the wallcovering.

Combination Plumb Bob and Chalk Line

Anytime you want something straight up and down, you should use a plumb bob. Some plumb bobs are no more than a weight on a string, while others are almost precision instruments. One handy version is the combination plumb bob and chalk line called the Strait-Line Chalk Line Reel, made by the Irwin Auger Bit Company. The unit consists of the line, a container from which the line unreels, a handle to

reel it back in, and the chalk dust. The container, which is pointed at the bottom, acts as the weight for the plumb bob. There is a small trap door in the container through which the chalk dust is poured. Blue chalk dust refills are available at hardware and paint stores.

Installing Drywall

Materials • Drywall as Required • 2 × 4 Lumber • Common Nails • Coated Drywall Nails • Coarse, Medium, and Fine Sandpaper • Cornerbeads • Drywall Joint Compound • Drywall Joint Tape • Primer, Sealer, Paint • Wallcovering

Tools • Pencil • Tape Measure • Hammer, 13- and 16-Ounce Claw • Saw • Utility Knife • Straightedge • Carpenter's Square • Sawhorse • Sanding Block • Drill and Bit • Keyhole Saw • Drywall Taping Knife • Paintbrush

SHEETS OF 4- by 8-foot drywall, or gypsum wallboard, go up fast to finish off framed walls. Once up, drywall can be paneled, wallpapered, or painted. In fact, almost any type of finish wallcovering may be applied to this material.

Although it's easy to figure how much drywall to buy (just compute the square footage of the walls and ceiling), it takes some planning to end up with as few joints as possible. The standard-size sheets for walls are 4 by 8 feet. You usually install them with the long side running from floor to ceiling, but you can place them horizontally if by doing so you eliminate a joint. You can buy larger-size sheets for the ceiling. All drywall sheets are 4 feet wide, but many building material outlets offer 10-foot lengths. Other sizes may be specially ordered through a distributor, but not a retailer.

As to the number of nails, rolls of tape, and the amount of joint compound you will need, consult a dealer to learn how much of each is required for the square footage involved. For example, 1,000 square feet of ⅜-inch-thick wallboard—the best home thickness—requires about 7 pounds of coated drywall nails, a 5-gallon pail of joint compound in mixed form, and a 500-foot roll of tape. Each outside corner requires one metal cornerbead; drywall tape is used for inside corners.

Installing Drywall

To install drywall, or gypsum wallboard, on the ceiling and walls of a framed room, follow these steps:

1. Cover the ceilings first. If possible, try to span the entire width with a single sheet of gypsum wallboard to reduce the number of joints. Before you can work on the ceilings, though, you need to construct a pair of T-braces from 2 × 4's that are about 1 inch longer than the distance from floor to ceiling. Nail 2 × 4's about 3 feet long to one end of each longer 2 × 4 to form the T's, and then position and wedge the braces against the drywall sheet to hold it in place until you finish nailing it.
2. Drive nails at 4-inch intervals into all the joists covered by the sheet. Start in the center of the drywall panel and work out.
3. After you drive each nail in, give it an extra hammer blow to dimple the surface slightly. Take care, though, not to break the face paper.
4. When you need to cut panels to complete the coverage, use a sharp utility knife along a straightedge. All you want to do with the knife is cut the face paper. After you make the cut, place the board over the edge of a sawhorse, a 6-foot length of 2 × 4 laid flat on the floor, or some other type of support, and snap the scored section down. The gypsum core will break along the line you cut. Then turn the panel over, cut the paper on the other side, and smooth the rough edges with very coarse sandpaper on a sanding block.
5. When the ceiling is finished, put up the walls. Again space the nails 4 inches apart, but start nailing 4 inches from the ceiling. Butt the wall

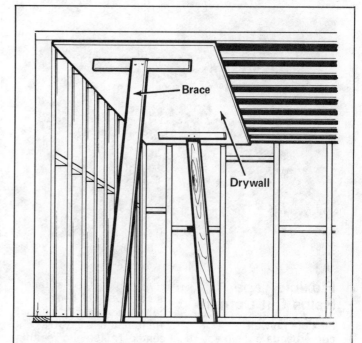

When installing drywall on a ceiling, use T-braces made from a pair of 2x4s to hold the drywall in place until you can nail it in place.

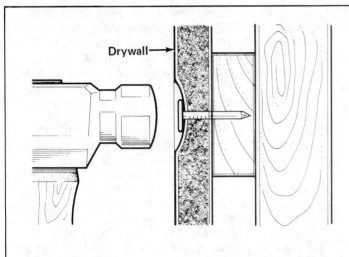

After you drive each nail in, give it an extra blow to dimple the surface slightly; don't break the face paper, however.

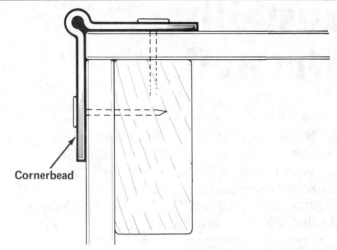

If outside corners are involved, nail the metal outside cornerbeads in place; there's no need to dimple these nails.

panels against the ceiling sheets.
6. Dimple all nails.
7. If outside corners are involved, nail the metal outside cornerbeads in place.
8. Be sure to measure carefully for any cutouts in the drywall wallboard including electrical outlets, switches, or light fixtures. To make cutouts in the drywall, draw a pattern of the cutout on the wallboard, drill a hole, and then use a keyhole saw to follow the pattern.

Taping Procedure

Once you are through applying the board to the walls, you face the problem of covering up all the nails and joints. This is where you use joint

Flexible Tape Helps Cut Corners

Flexible drywall cornerbeads enable you to fit the cornerbead to any angle. Goldblatt Tool Company's Flex Corner drywall metal corner tape is composed of two galvanized steel strips that are joined to a flexible center. The steel gives this cornerbead tape durability, while the flexible center allows it to fit any angle.

Self-Tapping Screws Drive in Easily, Quickly

Hanging drywall walls is easier with self-tapping and self-countersinking drywall screws that can be installed with a punch and portable electric drill equipped with a Phillips-head drill bit. Screws To Go screws are designed for installation in drywall, wood, and sheet metal (up to 20 gauge) in less time than conventional fasteners. The secret, according to Screws To Go, the manufacturer, is the very sharp point. The screws also feature a self-countersinking bugle-style head or round washer head. A No. 2 Phillips head bit tip is used with the fasteners. Once driven in, the screws will not pop out; they must be unscrewed. Sizes include 1-inch through 3-inch lengths in ¼-inch increments for the bugle-style screws, and ½- and 1¼-inch lengths for screws with the round washer head.

compound and joint tape in a technique called taping and bedding. Follow this procedure:

1. Use a drywall taping knife to spread joint compound into the slight recess created by the tapered edges of the drywall sheets. Smooth the compound until it is even with the rest of the board surface.
2. Center the drywall tape over the joint and press it firmly into the compound. Because some compound will squeeze out, you should make sure that there is still a good bed underneath.
3. When you get the tape imbedded into the compound all along the joint, smooth it with the taping knife.
4. When the compound is completely dry—usually 24 hours later—apply a second very thin coat of compound that extends out a few inches to either side of the first coat.
5. After the second coat dries completely, apply a third coat, extending it out to about 6 inches to either side.
6. When the third coat is dry, feather all the edges with a sanding block covered with medium-grit sandpaper.
7. Fill all the dimples with compound. They also require three coats as well as drying time between coats. After the final coat, sand to

feather and smooth the dimpled spots.
8. Inside corners, including spots where the walls and ceiling meet, must also be taped and bedded. Cut the tape to length and then fold it in half. After laying the bed of compound, press the folded tape into the compound and then feather the compound out at least 1½ inches to each side. The corners also require three coats, and the last coat should extend out about 8 inches to each side. Sanding is required here, too.
9. If you have any outside corners, apply three coats that taper up to the bead. The last coat should extend the compound on each wall to about 8 inches wide. Sand here too.
10. If there are cracks at the floor and ceiling, install molding to hide them. Always attach baseboards at the floor.
11. Let the walls dry for five days.
12. If you are installing paneling, you can apply it directly over the gypsum wallboard. If you are going to paint or wallpaper, give the surface of the drywall a coat of primer made for paint or wallpaper. When the primer is dry, sand the drywall surface lightly with fine-grit sandpaper on a sanding block. Be sure to sand between each additional coat of paint with fine-grit sandpaper. New drywall should receive at least three coats—a sealer, primer, and finish coat.

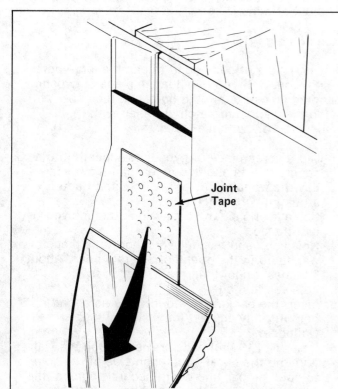

Spread joint compound into the slight recess of butting edges, center the tape over the joint, and press it firmly into the compound.

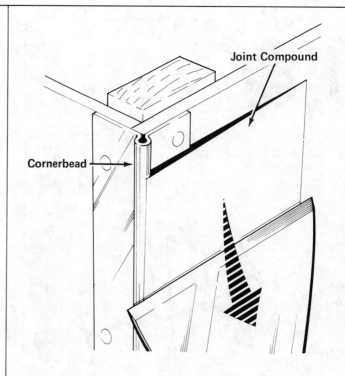

On outside corners, apply three coats of compound that taper up to the cornerbead. The last coat should extend about 8 inches on each side of the bead.

Patching Holes in Drywall

Materials • Tin Can Lid • Wire • Stick • Spackling Compound • Board • No. 10 Flathead Screws • Drywall Scrap • Fine Sandpaper • Primer • Paint

Tools • Tape Measure • Pencil • Keyhole Saw • Awl • Utility Knife • Carpenter's Square • Drywall Taping Knife • Diagonal Cutters • Brush or Trowel • Screwdriver

THE EASE and economy of drywall construction sometimes is marred by the fact that drywall, or gypsum wallboard, can develop a hole the first time someone slams a door knob against it or rams a metal toy through it. At first, the hole looks like complete disaster, but you will be amazed at how easily you can patch it. Small holes require one type of backing; larger holes need another technique.

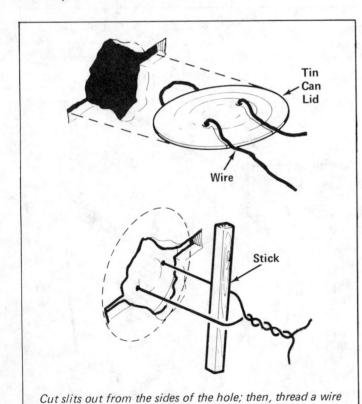

Cut slits out from the sides of the hole; then, thread a wire through a tin can lid, and slide it in. Pull the lid flat on the inside of the wall, and hold it in place with a stick.

Patching Small Holes

To patch a small hole, follow these steps:

1. Remove any loose material around the hole.
2. Select a tin can lid that is bigger than the hole and measure across the lid. Then, use a keyhole saw to cut a slit extending out from both sides of the hole so that you will be able to slip the lid into the hole sideways.
3. With an awl, punch two holes in the center of the lid and run a length of wire through them.
4. Slip the lid through the slit, holding onto the wire. With the lid inside, pull the wire until the lid is flat against the inside of the wallboard.
5. Twist the wire around a pencil or a stick that is long enough to span the hole; this will hold the lid in place to serve as a backing plate.
6. Plaster the hole with spackling compound. Cover all of the backing plate, the slit, and the edges, but avoid trying to make the main body of the patch level with the rest of the wall.
7. When the patch dries, remove the stick and snip the wire off flush with the patch.
8. Apply a second coat of spackling compound, bringing the surface up level with the rest of the wall.
9. Use a brush or trowel to texture the patch so that it matches the rest of the wall.
10. Let the patch dry overnight before applying a coat of primer.

Patching Large Holes

Applying layers of compound to patch a large hole doesn't work well at all. Instead, a piece of gypsum wallboard is inserted in the hole, and the gaps around the wallboard patch are filled with compound. Follow these steps:

1. Cut a scrap piece of gypsum wallboard into a square that is slightly larger than the hole.
2. Lay the wallboard over the hole and trace around it with a pencil.
3. Use a keyhole saw to cut along the line you just traced.
4. Now you need backing to support the piece of wallboard in the opening. Select a board about 6 inches longer than the widest span of the hole you just cut.
5. Insert the backing board into the hole, and hold it firmly against the inside of the wallboard.
6. Insert No. 10 flathead screws through the wall and into the backing on each side of the hole to hold the backing board securely against the inside of the wall. Keep turning the screws until the flat heads dig down below the surface of the wallboard.
7. Coat all four edges of the wallboard patch with

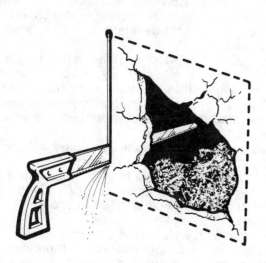

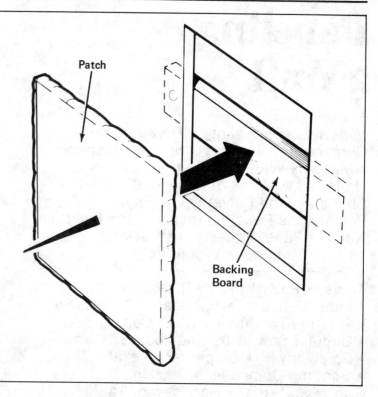

Cut a patch piece of drywall larger than the hole; then cut out the damaged area to exactly the same size and shape as the patch (left). Secure a backing board on the inside of the wall to brace the patch; then coat the edges of the patch with compound and set it into place in the hole (right).

spackling compound and spread compound over the back of the patch where it will rest against the backing board.

8. Carefully put the patch into place, and hold it there until the compound starts to set up.

9. When the compound is dry, fill up the slits around the patch with compound. Then cover the entire patch—plus the screw heads—with

compound, using a brush or trowel to make the compound match the texture of the rest of the wall. Leave the compound slightly higher than the surrounding wall surface because it tends to shrink as it dries.

10. After the entire area is dry, sand the repair with fine sandpaper. Then prime and repaint the wall.

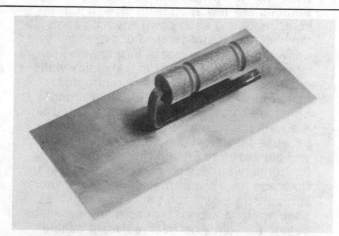

Smoothing Trowel for Wall Patches

Large patches in wall materials, such as spackling compound in drywall, require a long straight tool for smoothing. The model No. 440 finishing trowel from Warner Manufacturing Co. provides this feature; it has a 4½- by 10-inch steel surface. The trowel has a triple-riveted blade and a painted hardwood handle.

Crack Cleaner and Undercutter

When you patch cracks in plaster and drywall walls, the cracks generally have to be cleaned and undercut for the patching compound. An excellent tool for cleaning and undercutting is an old beer can opener—the kind with a pointed end. The point of the opener is ideal for this purpose.

Cover Small Cracks With a Stick

There are sticks for filling hairline cracks in plaster or drywall that do the job quickly and easily. Plaster-Stik, from Embee Corp., is one such stick that can also fill cracks in wood, stone, or any hard surface that will be painted over. All you do is work the stick back and forth over the crack in a circular motion. Usually, there is no need for sanding because any excess can be removed with a putty knife or even with your finger. After 24 hours, you can paint over the patched crack with any kind of paint.

Paneling a Wall

Materials • Paneling • Drywall Joint Compound • Furring Strips • Sandpaper • Masonry Waterproofing • Masonry Nails • Two Sawhorses • Cedar Shingle Shims • 4-mil Polyethylene Sheeting or Polystyrene Paneling Insulation • Panel Nails • Panel Adhesive • Masking Tape • Molding • Wood Putty

Tools • Putty Knife • Pry Bar • Pencil • Tape Measure • Hammer • Saber Saw With Fine-Toothed Blade or Coping Saw • Circular Saw With Fine-Toothed Blade • Screwdriver • Carpenter's Level • Scribing Compass • Caulking Gun • Scissors • Handsaw or Table Saw • Electric Drill and Bits • Keyhole Saw • Miter Box and Backsaw • Nail Set

On uneven or cracked walls, nail a grid of furring strips to the studs. Shim low spots solidly by wedging shingles under the strips.

THERE IS A TREMENDOUS selection of wall paneling available. Your biggest problem may be choosing the right paneling for the room you want to redo.

You can buy plywood paneling that is finished or ready-to-finish. Or, you can buy hardboard panels in finishes ranging from barn siding to marble. Some paneling has a composition-type core. This material, however, breaks easily and should always be used over drywall or plaster walls.

The plastic-coated finishes on both hardboard and plywood panels are almost impervious to scratches and stains, and they are washable so long as you don't soak them; to clean, just go over the finish lightly with a damp cloth and mild detergent.

The ease with which panels go up makes paneling a wall a simple do-it-yourself project. Modern adhesives virtually eliminate nailing, and the preparation and basic installation steps are the same for both plywood panels and hardboard.

Note: You can apply panels directly to the wall studs where you have new construction, but because the panels tend to give a little and are far from soundproof, it is best to provide a drywall backing. Nevertheless, if you decide to apply paneling directly to the studs, make sure that the studs are free of high or low spots. Plane away high spots and attach cedar shingle shims to compensate for any low spots.

Follow this procedure:

1. Remove the molding and trim from the walls and check for high or low spots by moving a long straight board against the wall and watching for any gaps as you draw it along. Build up any low spots with drywall joint compound, and sand down any high spots. If the walls are badly cracked or extremely uneven, you should install furring strips on which to attach the paneling. Masonry walls must always be furred and waterproofed.

2. Install furring strips, if necessary. Furring strips are 1 x 2's or 1 x 3's that are nailed to the wall. It's recommended that you use 1 x 3's because they provide a better bearing surface and are easier to install. Nail the furring horizontally on 16-inch centers, starting at the floor and finishing at the ceiling. Place short vertical strips between the horizontal strips, spacing them every 4 feet so that they will be behind the joints between adjacent panels. Nail furring strips to the wall with masonry nails, compensating for low spots by wedging shingles under the strips. A 4-mil polyethylene vapor barrier should be placed over the furring of masonry walls and on any other type of walls where moisture might be a problem. Or, you can cement 2- by 4-foot polystyrene paneling insulation between the furring strips.

3. At electrical wall switches and outlets, compensate for the increased thickness of the wall. Remove the cover plates and reset the electrical boxes out the necessary distance. ***Caution: Turn off the electrical power to the circuits you are working on before removing the cover plates.***

4. Stack the panels in the room to be paneled with strips of boards between each one. Leave them there for at least 48 hours before installing them. This step is very important for a successful paneling job because it allows the panels to adjust to the moisture content of the room.

5. After the panels have stabilized to the humidity and temperature in the room, lean them against the walls as you think they should be installed. This gives you a chance to match the wood graining in the most pleasing manner. When you have the panels arranged the way you want them, number the panels.

6. Measure the distance from floor to ceiling at several different points. If the panels have to be cut for height, you can cut all of them the same, provided that there is no more than a ¼-inch variance. If there is more variance than ¼ inch, you should measure the height for each panel and cut it to fit. If you are not going to use a ceiling molding, each panel must be cut to conform to the ceiling line, but if you do use ceiling moldings—and you should—leave a ¼-inch gap at the top. There also should be a ¼-inch gap at the floor, which will be concealed by floor molding.

7. Because very few corners are plumb (vertically level), place the first panel that is to go in a corner next to the wall and check the plumb with a level. Get the panel plumb and close enough to the corner so that you can span the space with a scribing compass. Then run the compass down the corner, with the point in the corner and the pencil marking a line on the panel. Cut the panel along the marked line with a saber saw equipped with a fine-toothed blade or with a coping saw. **Note:** Install this first "key" panel so it's perfectly plumb. If it isn't, the error will compound itself on other panels.

8. If you plan to nail the panels, use matching nails. You can use 3d finishing nails to attach the panels to furring strips, but if you must go through wall material to reach the studs, be sure to use nails long enough to penetrate about 1 inch into the studs. Drive nails about every 6 inches along the edges of the panel and about every 12 inches through the center; check frequently to make sure you are nailing into the furring strips.

If you are using panel adhesive, get it in cartridges so it can be applied with a caulking

Match Your Nails to the Paneling

Rather than countersinking and then applying wood putty over the nails that hold your paneling to the wall, you can save yourself some work by using nails that match the panel color. Most paneling manufacturers market such nails, and many fastener makers specialize in colored nails. Philstone Nail Corp. markets a line of nails for just about every paneling color available.

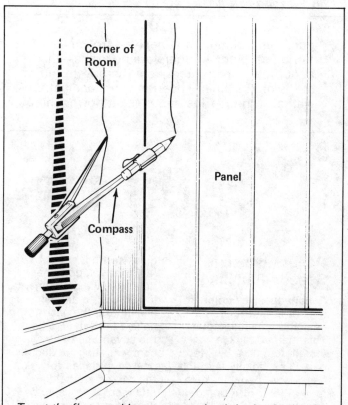

To set the first panel in a corner so that it is plumb, align it using a level. Then, run a compass down the corner, with the compass point in the corner and the pencil marking a line on the panel. Trim the marked edge of the panel carefully.

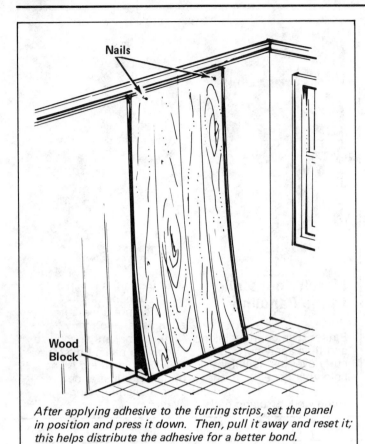

After applying adhesive to the furring strips, set the panel in position and press it down. Then, pull it away and reset it; this helps distribute the adhesive for a better bond.

gun. Run a ribbon of adhesive across all furring strips or—if there are no strips—in about the same pattern as if there were furring strips on the wall. Place the panel against the wall or furring strips and press it down. Then,

pull it away from the wall and reset it; this helps distribute the adhesive for a better bond. Nail the panel in place at the top with a pair of nails. Then, pull the bottom of the panel out from the wall and prop it with a scrap block of wood until the adhesive gets tacky. When this happens, remove the block and press the panel against the wall. Then, secure the panel by pounding it with a padded block and hammer.

9. When you come to a door or window, use one of the large sheets of paper that came between the sheets of paneling and make a pattern. Tape the paper in place, press it against the door or window frame, mark it with a pencil, and cut it to fit with scissors. Use this pattern to transfer the marks to the panel, which you can then cut with a fine-toothed crosscut hand saw or with a power saw equipped with a fine-toothed blade. **Note:** If you use a handsaw or a table saw, cut the panel with the face side up. If you use a hand power saw, cut with the face side down.

10. To make cutouts for electrical outlets or switches, trace the outline of the switch or outlet box on the panel, and drill pilot holes at opposite corners. Then use a keyhole saw to connect the corners with a saw kerf.

11. Next comes the finishing touch—the application of molding. Most panel manufacturers offer prefinished moldings to match. You can get floor moldings, ceiling moldings, inside or outside corner moldings, and just about anything else you need. Use a miter box and a fine-toothed backsaw to cut the moldings. Be sure to countersink the nails and fill the holes with matching wood putty.

Panel Adhesive Speeds Paneling

Panel adhesives come in bulk or in cartridges for use with a caulking gun. This method makes installation of 4- by 8-foot panels especially fast and easy. Most panel makers market their own brand of panel adhesive, but there are many other good ones. Goodyear Plio-Nail panel adhesive, for example, is quick-setting, but not so fast that you don't have time to make adjustments. In addition to almost eliminating the need for nails, Plio-Nail also has the advantage of compensating for slightly uneven surfaces to which the panels are being attached. It can also be used to attach drywall, hardboard, or rigid-foam insulation to most wall surfaces.

Touch-Up Pen Covers Scratches

Woodwork that is marred by scratches or nicks is annoying, but it can be repaired quickly. Scratch Fix, made by the K. J. Miller Corp., is an easy-to-use, felt-tip, touch-up pen that can cover scratches and nicks in wood finishes. The manufacturer says that Scratch Fix produces a durable, waterproof finish. It can be used on paneling, doors, moldings, wood furniture, kitchen cabinets, and picture frames. The product is available in four hues—black-brown, dark brown, light brown, and red-brown.

Stud Finder Can End Your Frustration

Ever try to find a stud in the wall when you need strong support for a heavy object? Most people find it a frustrating task and wind up hammering a nail or driving a screw into every place but the stud. Fortunately, Stanley Tools Division of The Stanley Works has come to the rescue with a special tool for locating wall studs easily. The tool, Stanley's Magnetic Stud Finder, consists of a strong cylindrical magnet in a red

sleeve that is housed in clear plastic. The blue base of the stud finder is grooved so that you can mark the stud location precisely with a pencil. This can be one of the handiest tools in your toolbox.

Wall Paneling Covers Decorating Spectrum

No matter what your decorating motif, there is an appropriate wall paneling pattern available. And, Masonite Corp. probably makes it. Finishes closely resemble woods of all kinds, as well as other materials, such as marble. Masonite also has a line of companion products, including color-matching nails, panel adhesives, moldings and trims, and putty sticks that cover up nail holes and scratches.

Estimating 4 × 8 Wall Paneling

If you know the dimensions of the room you plan to panel, it's easy to estimate how many 4- by 8-foot panels you need. Use this table:

Perimeter of Room	Panels Needed
20 Feet	5
24 Feet	6
28 Feet	7
32 Feet	8
60 Feet	15
64 Feet	16
68 Feet	17
72 Feet	18
92 Feet	23

Install Paneling With Adhesive

You can use color-matched paneling nails to install paneling but panel adhesive is a good alternative. Gulf Panel and General Construction Adhesive is formulated for bonding gypsum, hardwood plywood, and hardboard wall panels to wood stud framing.

According to Gulf Adhesives and Resins, Gulf Chemicals Corp., the adhesive helps reduce nailing requirements and produces a high racking strength. The manufacturer also says the product is light in color, is resistant to water and oxidation, and has gap-filling properties. It comes in 11- and 30-ounce cartridges.

Wood Veneer Panels Are Attractive

Paneling with a veneer of real wood is hard to beat for warmth and beauty. The variety of real wood paneling from Georgia-Pacific Corp. is so great that you should go to a paneling outlet and compare the different styles before you decide on your project. The manufacturer offers face veneers in birch, oak, pecan, cedar, pine, fir, and other woods. There also is a selection of paper overlaid and printed panels. And, there is paneling with V-grooving or channel grooving.

'Shingles' for Interior Use

Have you ever considered using shingles inside your home? Sugarhouse Slats are thin strips of prestained wood that create the effect of rustic shingles on your walls. The product, designed for interior application, can be used to accent walls in kitchens, family rooms, studies, home offices, and other rooms. Made by Vermont Weatherboard, Inc., Sugarhouse Slats are easy to apply to almost any interior wall. The only tools needed are a hammer, paneling nails, and a fine-tooth saw.

Line and Chalk for a Plumb Bob

Absolute plumb is necessary to frame a wall and to hang most wallcoverings, including wallpaper and paneling. Establishing this vertical line can be difficult unless you use a steel or metal plumb bob for the job. Besides the plumb bob, you need chalk and a chalk line. You apply the chalk to the line, find vertical level, and snap the line on the framing or wall surface to guide you. The model No. 134 lump chalk, line, and plumb bob kit, made by Warner

Manufacturing Co., has a piece of lump chalk, an 8½-foot length of line, and a metal plumb bob. Replacement lump chalk also is available from Warner.

Papering a Room

Materials • Wallpaper as Required
• Wallpaper Paste or Vinyl-to-Vinyl Paste
• Medium Sandpaper • Fine Sandpaper
• Spackling Compound • Wall Sizing
• Tack • Dropcloth

Tools • Wallpaper Steamer • Putty Knife
• Vacuum Cleaner • Wall-Cleaning Sponge
• Tape Measure • Chalk Line • Plumb
Bob • Carpenter's Level • Scissors
• Water Tray • Paste Brush • Stepladder
• Smoothing Brush • Utility Knife • Seam
Roller • Straightedge

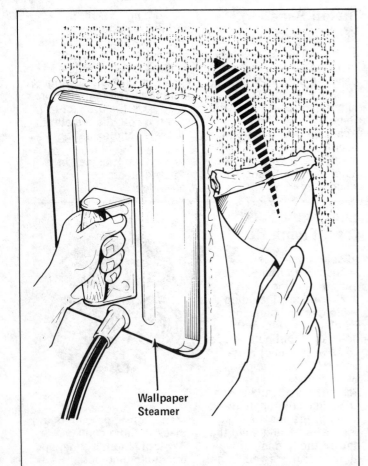

Wallpaper Steamer

Removing old wallpaper is no easy job. You can rent a steamer but you still have to scrape off most of the covering with a wide-blade putty knife.

ADHESIVES AND special papers and fabrics manufactured today have made the once dreaded job of wallpapering almost pleasant to do.

Vinyl wallcoverings are extremely popular because they are washable, fade-resistant, and most are strippable. That last advantage is especially important when you have to recover the walls later. Strippable coverings can be peeled off the wall in one piece, eliminating messy steaming, soaking, and scraping.

Prepasted coverings are also popular because they are easy to use and less messy than unpasted coverings. Prepaste coverings, however, require the use of a water tray. You must put the strip in the water tray to activate the paste.

If you select a covering that is not prepasted, you must be sure to use the prescribed type of paste. For example, if you are applying a vinyl covering, use one of the special vinyl adhesives that are much stronger and more mildew-resistant than wheat paste.

Figuring how many rolls of wallcovering to buy is strictly a mathematical exercise, but you have to know the rules. No matter how wide the roll is, any wallcovering roll contains approximately 36 square feet. A roll 24 inches wide is 18 feet long, while a roll that is 27 inches wide is only 16 feet long.

Because of trim and waste, you can never use all 36 square feet on a roll. The actual yield is usually only about 30 square feet. To figure how many rolls you will need, measure the perimeter of the room and multiply that figure by the room's height. That gives you the square footage. Deduct one roll for every two openings—such as doors and windows—and then divide the total by 30 square feet. The final figure is the number of rolls to purchase.

Wall Preparation

Before covering a wall, you must prepare the wall surface. Follow these steps:

1. A paper wallcovering can be applied over old paper, provided that the old wallpaper is sound. If it isn't, remove any loose paper and feather the edges with medium-grit sandpaper. If there are more than two layers of old paper, or if you are applying a vinyl wallcovering, you should remove all of the old covering. Removing old paper, however, is no easy job. You can rent a steamer but you still have to scrape off most of the covering with a wide putty knife.
2. An unpapered wall that is textured should be sanded to remove all the bumps. You need to sand it very smooth with fine-grit sandpaper. If you don't, the bumps will show through the new wallcovering unless it is a burlap or grass-cloth covering. Remove the gloss from any enameled surfaces.

3. Fill all cracks and holes with spackling compound.

4. Vacuum the room thoroughly and go over the walls with a wall-cleaning sponge.

5. Apply sizing (a sort of glue) over the wall. Absolutely necessary on new dry wall, unpainted plaster, and other such surfaces that would absorb paste, sizing also works well on most other surfaces. Talk to your wallpaper dealer; he can tell you which sizing is compatible with the adhesive you are using.

6. Remove cover plates from electrical outlets and switches in the room.

Applying the Paper

After preparing the wall, you are ready to hang the wallpaper. Follow this procedure:

1. Select the most inconspicuous corner of the room, and measure out along the wall, adjacent to that corner, a distance that is 1 inch less than the width of the wallpaper roll.

2. Drop a chalked plumb line from that point, and snap it to show the true vertical. A plumb line is nothing more than a string with a weight on one end. Tack the chalk-coated string at the ceiling so that the weight almost touches the floor. When the weight stops moving, the string is vertical. Hold the bottom end tight against the wall and snap the string to place a vertical chalk line on the wall surface to guide you. Check the line with a level to make sure it's accurate.

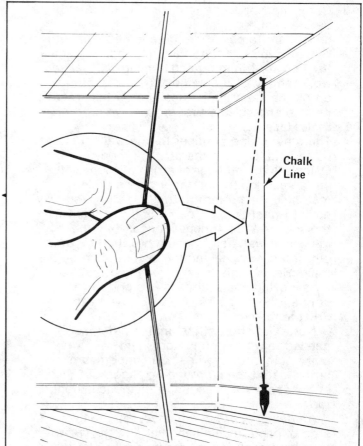

Chalk Line

To place the first strip of wallpaper, measure the paper's width from a corner, less 1 inch. Then, snap a chalk line. Check the chalk line with a level to make sure it's accurate.

Make Regular Wallpaper Strippable

Apply this undercoater to the walls you plan to cover with regular wallpaper and you will be able to strip the wallpaper later without damage to the under surface—including new drywall. Peelz Wallpaper Release Coating, from Wm. Zinsser & Co., Inc., is a fast-drying latex coating that primes, sizes, and seals wall surfaces before wallpaper or any other wallcoverings are applied. According to the manufacturer, it will adhere to most porous surfaces including plaster, painted surfaces, old wallcoverings, and wood. When the wallcovering is to be removed, no steamers, chemicals, or heavy scraping are necessary, the company says. The undercoating cleans up with soap and water. One gallon covers up to 800 square feet— enough for 24 to 28 rolls of paper.

Chemical Eases Removal of Wallpaper

Removing old wallpaper can be a problem. Chemical removers, however, can speed up the job. DIF wallpaper stripper is a two-part formula that combines enzymes with a blend of wetting agents. This combination re-wets more thoroughly and breaks down the molecular structure of the paste more completely than many other wallpaper strippers, according to the manufacturer. That means less hacking and scraping to remove the paper. DIF may be sprayed or sponged on, after which it should be allowed at least 15 minutes to work. With waterproof coverings, you must first score the surface so the mixture can penetrate and reach the adhesive. DIF, made by William Zinsser & Company, Inc., is available at many stores selling wallpapering materials and tools.

3. Cut wallpaper strips to cover an entire wall before pasting them up. Measure the wall, baseboard to ceiling, to determine the length of paper you need. Add about 4 inches to this to allow for trimming and slippage. Cover your work table with a clean plastic dropcloth and unroll the paper on it. Measure off the length needed and cut the first strip; leave it on the table, face up.

4. The other strips of paper for the wall must be pattern-matched to the preceding ones. Calculate the number of strips needed. Roll out a second strip of paper on the table, matching the pattern to the first strip; you may have to waste paper to match the strips. Cut the second strip 4 inches longer than the measured wall height and move the first strip out of the way, leaving the second strip on the table. Repeat this matching and cutting, each time moving one strip farther along the wall, until all the strips for one wall have been cut. Be sure to keep them in order.

   Note: Cut short strips, still in order, as needed to work around doors and windows; make sure both overhead and underneath strips match the surrounding paper. Cut these strips about 4 inches longer than measured, too.

5. If your wallpaper is prepasted, roll the first strip of paper loosely and set it in the water tray; let it soak for the recommended time.

   For unpasted papers, mix the paste, following the manufacturer's instructions. Lay the strip face down on the work table, with one end hanging over the table end. Spread paste on the table end of the strip, smoothing it on with the paste brush, to cover about half the strip. Fold this pasted end over on itself—paste to paste—and slide the folded strip down the table so that the other end of the strip can be pasted. Spread paste on the other end of the strip and fold this end too back on itself—paste to paste—forming a folded-in "U" of paper. Keep the edges even, and don't crease the folds or the finished wall will also have creases in it.

6. Move the stepladder into the marked corner. To pick up the strip of pasted paper or moistened prepasted paper, slide your fingers under the edges of the folded-in strip, at the center of the "U." Lift the paper carefully, holding the top edge with your thumbs and forefingers.

7. Unfold the top half of the paper strip and start applying the paper at the ceiling. The long edge of the paper strip must line up *exactly* with the snapped chalk line on the wall. Leaving about 2 inches extra above the ceiling line, unfold the top half of the paper strip, lining up the right edge on the chalk line. Smooth the paper with your hand, working back from this edge toward the corner of the room. Fold the extra inch of paper at the far side of the strip around the corner and onto the other wall.

8. When the top part of the wallpaper strip is securely in place, carefully unfold the rest of the strip and smooth it onto the wall, making sure it lines up exactly with the snapped chalk line. Smooth the paper firmly with the smoothing brush to remove air bubbles and excess paste, working toward the edges.

9. To secure the wallpaper around the corner and along the ceiling and the baseboard, use the

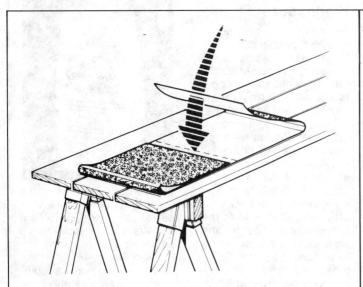

Spread paste on half the strip at a time; fold the ends over paste side in, all edges even.

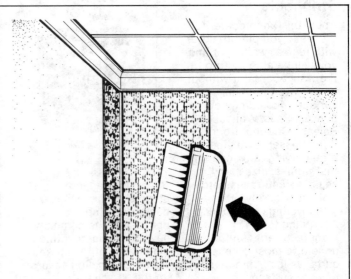

To secure the wallpaper around a corner and along the ceiling and baseboard, use the edge of the smoothing brush.

edge of the smoothing brush head-on, as a pounding tool. Strike the bristles against the edges and into the corner of the wall to push the paper firmly into place. Leave the edges untrimmed until the next strip of paper is hung.

10. Repeat the previous procedure all across the wall, making sure each new strip of paper is matched to the one before it. To place each strip correctly, match the pattern near the top edge, set the paper against the wall next to the previous strip, and slide it to butt exactly against the already pasted paper.

11. As each new strip is set into place and smoothed, pound its top and bottom edges into place. Then trim the excess from the top and bottom of the preceding strip, using a sharp utility knife and following the wall-ceiling joint carefully. Press each new seam carefully with a seam roller.

12. To work around a door, a window, or a similar interruption, set the precut short strip into place above the opening, handling it exactly like a full-length strip. Repeat, being careful to match the pattern, with strips under windows. Trim the edges and roll the seams as before.

13. Use the same papering technique to hang paper all around the room, matching and trimming as you go. Paper right over outlets and switches, then go back and cut out the opening.

Note: If a strip of paper ends exactly in a corner, fold the next strip around to overlap it slightly. Cut closely along the overlapping edge with a sharp utility knife and a straightedge; fold back the top layer of paper, peel off the trimmed-off strip beneath it, and restick the new edge.

Save some scraps of wallpaper in case the wallcovering becomes damaged or later develops a blister or other problem.

Choosing Adhesives for Wallcoverings

Different types of wallcoverings require different adhesives. Here are some types of flexible wallcoverings and the appropriate adhesive to use:

Wallcovering	Adhesive
Regular wallpaper	**Wheat or stainless paste**
Backed burlap/Foils	**Vinyl adhesive**
Strippable	**Wheat paste**
Unbacked burlap	**Wheat or stainless paste**
Backed cork/Vinyl	**Vinyl adhesive**
Fabrics	**Stainless paste**
Prints/Flocks/Murals	**Vinyl adhesive**

Paperhanging Knife for Paper Trimming

Most wallcoverings are ready to hang because they are pre-trimmed. Some papers, especially foils, have selvage for matching purposes and must be trimmed to match patterns. The No. 72 paperhanger knife, from Warner Manufacturing Co., is designed for this kind of trimming. It has a tempered ground blade of cutlery steel and a stained wooden handle. The blade is 3 inches long and 1⅛ inches wide. The tool should be used with a straightedge guide for best results.

Textured Paper Camouflages Wall Bumps and Cracks

What do-it-yourselfer hasn't wished for a wallpaper that can hide bumps and cracks on a wall? Wall Sculpture, a textured paper that has an embossed layer laminated to a backing, can cover many problem wall surfaces. The paper, which is imported from England by Decor International Wallcoverings, Inc., is available in 26 designs including basketweaves, straw looks, pebble textures, stucco, and a design inspired by an old-fashioned tin ceiling. A double roll covers 57.5

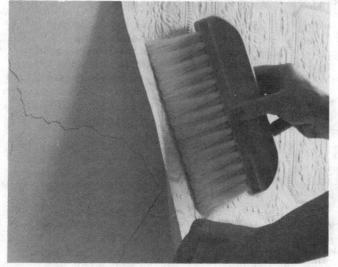

square feet. All designs come in white; 22 are also available in color combinations. Wall Sculpture paper can be painted with a good-quality latex paint, and once painted, it's washable.

Tips for Removing Wallpaper

If old wallpaper must be removed before a new wallcovering is installed, the best way to remove the old paper is with a wallpaper steamer. This tool can be rented. The secret to using a steamer is letting the tool do the job. The more the paper is steamed, the easier it comes off. In fact, if you let the steamer do the job, the wall scraper will hardly have to be used; the paper will actually fall off the ceiling or wall. If you can't rent a steamer, use chemical wallpaper remover. Give the chemical plenty of time to work.

Imported Vinyl Wall System Covers It All

Problem areas like basement cinder block, old ceramic tile, paneling, and even cracked and uneven walls are hard to cover. Paris Wall, a cushioned vinyl wall covering made in France and marketed by Forbo North America, Inc., however, can cover them all. The heavy-duty wall covering comes in pre-cut 9½-inch by 31½-inch rolls.

Its durable surface is a clear, nonporous vinyl that seals in the design and keeps spots and spills out. Three-level embossing on a dense, vinyl, foam-cushion core helps mask wall imperfections. Paris Wall's Pariglas back is non-woven, glass fiber-backing that bridges minor surface gaps and ridges because it retains its shape. The product can be used in bath areas because it's waterproof and moisture-resistant.

Rollers to Flatten Wallpaper Seams

With the exception of flocked and some foil wallpaper, all wallpaper seams, especially those that are lapped, should be rolled, or pressed firmly against the wall surface. To do this, you need a seam roller. Warner Manufacturing Co. makes three models of hardwood seam rollers. All are double-bracketed, have heavy brass bearings, and mahogany-stained wooden handles. The model No. 30 is 1 inch wide with a flat surface; No. 31 is 1 inch wide with an oval surface; No. 32 is 2 inches wide with a flat surface.

Special Shears for Paperhangers

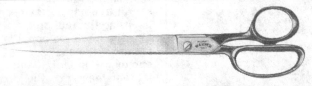

The scissors used by professional paperhangers are longer and skinnier than standard household shears. Warner Mfg. Co., a firm that makes just about every paperhanging tool, markets lightweight, imported paperhanging shears that are made of forged steel. The shears are 12 inches long.

Not Much to Do About Nail Pops

Nails popping from drywall walls and ceilings are common because the framing shrinks and loosens the nails. To fix popped nails, hit the pop with a hammer so the wallboard is slightly dented. Just above or below the pop area, drive a threaded gypsum wallboard nail (drywall screw) into the framing member. Hit the nail so it is set below the wall surface. This usually eliminates the pop problem in this area forever. You can hide the dimples with spacking compound pressed with a putty knife. Leave the compound slightly high; it will shrink a bit when it dries. Then, lightly sand the patches and paint, wallpaper, or apply whatever covering you desire.

Brushes Designed to Smooth Wallpaper

A paperhanging brush is essential to smooth wallpaper as you apply it. Paperhanging brushes from Warner Manufacturing Co. have two rows of bristles that help get the wallcovering smooth fast. The model No. 451 brush is 12 inches long—plenty of length for smoothing jobs on standard, flocked, and foil papers as well as grass and burlap mats. Vinyl wallcovering brushes, model Nos. 453 and 454 also are available from the company.

Match Adhesive to the Covering

Using the wrong kind of adhesive for the wallcovering can result in disaster; strips can fall off or curl up at the seams, while the paste can mildew underneath and smell up the entire house. Be sure to use the adhesive made for your type of covering. If you aren't certain, ask the dealer when you buy your wallcovering.

First-Rate Trimmer Cuts Accurately

Considered by many to be one of the best tools of its type, the Hyde Century trimmer, made by Hyde Mfg. Co., can be positioned instantly alongside a straightedge. Its sharp blade—individually hardened, tempered, and honed—runs true for an accurate cut with no wobble or sway. When the long-lasting blade does wear out, you can replace it quickly and without difficulty. Although the Hyde Century trimmer is an excellent tool, it may be too expensive to buy for just a one-room paper-hanging assignment. For considerable paperhanging, it can be a good tool investment.

Wallpaper Repairs

Materials • Wallpaper Paste or Vinyl-to-Vinyl Paste • Straight Pins • Wallpaper Scraps as Required • Kneaded Eraser • Mild Detergent • Colored Ink Pens

Tools • Small Artist's Brush • Seam Roller • Single-Edge Razor Blade • Sponge

IF YOUR WALLS are covered with wallpaper, sooner or later you're bound to have some problems with the wallcovering. But keeping wallpaper in shape isn't as difficult as it may sound. It's best to fix a loose seam, a slight tear, or a puffy bubble as soon as possible or it is sure to become a larger and more unsightly problem later. Follow this procedure for various problems:

1. Seams that come unstuck can be simply repasted. Save a small container of paste for that purpose, and squirt a bit under the loose flaps or spread it on with a small artist's brush. Then use a seam roller to press the paper back down. It's also a good idea to "clamp" the seam until the paste dries by using straight pins stuck through the paper into the wall. If the paper is patterned or textured, the tiny holes won't show. **Note:** If you have overlaps in a vinyl covering that refuse to stay down, use special paste made for vinyl-to-vinyl adhesion. An application of this special paste will do the job.

2. If your newly applied wallpaper has bubbles, slit them twice to form an "X" across the center of the blister. Then peel back the tips of the slit and squirt paste into the blister. The tips of paper may overlap a little, but such overlapping is seldom noticeable. If you notice the blister shortly after you finish papering—but after the paste has dried—the thick blob under the blister may still be wet paste. Try sticking a pin in the blister and then forcing the paste out. If that trick doesn't do the job, slit and repaste.

3. Patching a torn section of wallpaper is easy to do—provided you saved some scraps from the original papering job. Select a scrap section that matches the pattern, and tear the patch in

Wallpapering Over Paneling

If you are planning to cover grooved paneling with wallpaper, cover the grooves with fiberglass tape. Also fill all nicks, dents, nail heads, and other imperfections with spacking compound; you may have to enlarge the holes slightly so that the spackling compound will hold. Then, give the surface a light sanding and coat the paneling with one coat of penetrating sealer. Sand the surface lightly and apply the wallpaper.

an irregular shape so that the edge can be feathered back under the patch. Such a patch blends in much better than if it were cut evenly.

4. When nonwashable paper gets dirty, use a kneaded eraser—available at an art store—to rub away the dirt.

   Note: Nonwashable wallpaper can be made washable with an application of a transparent coating that is available. Be sure to test the coating on a scrap, however, before covering the entire wall with it. You can sponge washable wallcoverings with a mild detergent and even scrub some vinyls, but to find out just how much rubbing your paper can take, work on a scrap first.

5. If some of the wallpaper's design has rubbed off and you don't have the scraps to patch over it, you might consider using colored inks to redraw the design.

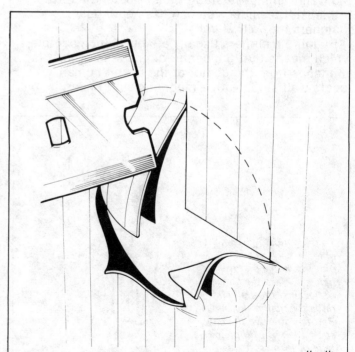

To repair a blister in the paper, slit it twice to form an "X." Then, peel back the tips of the slit, squirt paste into the blister, and smooth the paper down.

Wall Fasteners

Materials • Nails • Swag Hooks, Screw Hooks, or Screw Eyes • Spackling Compound • Picture Hangers • Cellophane Tape • Plastic or Nylon Wall Anchors

Tools • Stud Locator • Tape Measure • Hammer • Putty Knife • Screwdriver • Drill and Bits

THERE IS A wide variety of hardware designed to hang almost any object you would want to hang on a wall. The selection ranges from lightweight picture hooks to heavy screw hooks and screw eyes that will support items weighing hundreds of pounds.

Because most wall framing is covered with drywall about ⅜ inch thick, most hanger hardware is designed to hug the surface of this material for support. Any heavy object, such as a large mirror, should be supported by hardware that is attached to the wall framing—a stud or joist—behind the wall. If this isn't feasible, you can use heavy-duty fasteners for hollow walls.

Framing members usually are on 16-inch centers, which means that the center of one stud or joist is 16 inches from the center of the next. You can locate wall studs with a magnetic stud finder. If you

To hang most lightweight objects, such as small pictures, use a picture hanger. Place the hanger flat against the wall and drive the nail in the hanger. Before you drive the nail, stick a tab of cellophane tape over the spot to prevent the drywall from crumbling when the nail is driven in.

don't have this handy device, measure 16 inches from a corner of the room (there is always a stud in a corner). Then, drive a small nail through the wall. If the nail hits a stud, use this point as reference for other other stud locations farther along the wall. You can remove your "locater" nail later and patch the tiny hole with spackling compound.

Hanging Light Objects

To hang most lightweight objects, such as small pictures, use a picture hanger. Place the hanger flat against the wall and drive the nail in the hanger. Before you drive the nail, stick a tab of cellophane tape over the spot to prevent the drywall from crumbling when the nail is driven in and later removed.

Hanging Medium-Weight Objects

To hang medium-weight objects, such as drapery rods, use plastic or nylon wall anchors. Buy the anchors made for the size screws you have, and examine the package to find out what size drill bit to use for the holes. Then, to install these anchors, follow these simple steps:

1. Drill a hole in the wall to accommodate the plastic anchor.
2. Tap the anchor in all the way in the wall with a hammer.
3. Insert the screw through the item it is to hold, and then turn it into the anchor; the screw expands the anchor to make it grip the sides of the hole.

Hanging Medium-Weight and Heavy Objects

When hanging heavier objects, such as shelves and mirrors, the best device is the expansion anchor, or bolt. This type of fastener comes in different sizes to accommodate differences in wall thickness and in the weight of the things they are to hold. Once you get the right fastener, here is how to install it:

1. Check the package to see what size drill bit you must use, and then drill a hole in the wall.
2. Lightly tap the fastener in place with a hammer.
3. Turn the slotted bolt clockwise. When you can't turn it any more, back it out. The fastener is then secure against the inside of the wall, and you are ready to hang the object.
4. Put the bolt through the object or its hanger, and reinsert the bolt in the expansion anchor.

Hanging Very Heavy Objects

For really heavy objects, such as cabinets or a bookshelf unit, use toggle bolts. Available in several

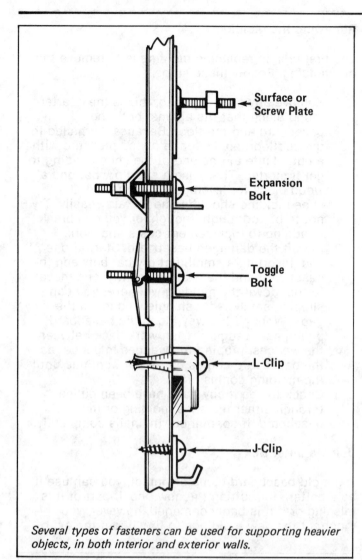

- **Surface or Screw Plate**
- **Expansion Bolt**
- **Toggle Bolt**
- **L-Clip**
- **J-Clip**

Several types of fasteners can be used for supporting heavier objects, in both interior and exterior walls.

sizes, toggle bolts also require you to drill holes in the wall. If you buy the packaged kind, you will find the size of the hole specified on the package. Here is how to install them:

1. Drill the proper-size hole.
2. Remove the bolt from the flange.
3. Put the bolt through the object to be hung or through its hanger before you insert it into the wall; you can't remove the bolt after the toggle bolt device is in the wall without the flange falling down between the wall. Reinsert the bolt in the flange.
4. Squeeze the flange with your thumb and forefinger and push it into the hole. Of course, you must hold the object you are hanging right next to the wall as you insert the toggle bolt. When the flange goes through, pull the bolt back toward you until you feel the flange open and hit the back of the wall.
5. Turn the bolt clockwise until the hanger or the item itself is flat and secure against the wall.

Covers to Conceal Different Fasteners

If you could hide screw, nail, or rivet heads, a job can look more professional. Now you can with Snap Caps fastener covers from Bostik Consumer division of Emhart Corp. The system uses a special washer and cap. The washer goes under the fastener head; the cap snaps onto the washer, concealing the fastener head. Snap Caps fastener covers are available in a wide range of sizes in white, black, or brown colors.

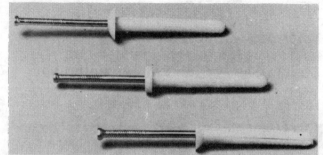

Nylon Fastener Anchors Nearly Anything Anywhere

It can be difficult to mount objects to hard surfaces like concrete block and then remove the object later. The Pro-Set Tap-It nylon fastener, made by U.S.E. Diamond, Inc., functions as an anchor, a toggle, a blind fastener, or a rivet. The fastener works in solid or hollow construction, and in all types of materials including concrete, plaster, glass, metal, wood, stone, and plastic. According to the manufacturer, it can anchor virtually any object to any material with an exceptional grip. Installation requires only a drill and a hammer. Screw threads and slot permit easy removal so the fastener may be used again. Tap-It is available in flush-head, flat-head, round-head, round-(recessed) head, and mushroom-head styles.

Permanent Fastener for Hollow Walls

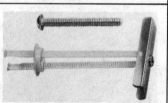

For permanent installation of shelving, mirrors, cabinets, and other heavy items on a hollow wall, you need a strong fastener. KapToggle, made by Universal Fastenings Corp., is three times stronger than any other hollow-wall fastener, according to the manufacturer. To install, the KapToggle fastener is inserted into a hole drilled in the wall. A steel toggle is pulled against the back of the wall by means of two plastic strips attached to it. A washer on the strips is pushed forward until it is seated inside the hole. The mounting screw can then be driven into the fastener. A 2-inch screw or less is all that's needed. KapToggles are available in ⅛-inch, ³⁄₁₆-inch, and ¼-inch sizes. Each carded package contains four fasteners.

Replacing Molding

Materials • Molding as Required • Cedar Shingle Wedges • Wood Block • 4d and 6d Finishing Nails • Paint or Stain • Wood Putty • Medium-Grit Sandpaper

Tools • Putty Knife • Pry Bar • Hammer • Miter Box • Backsaw or Fine-Toothed Hacksaw • Pencil • Tape Measure • Coping Saw • Nail Set • Paintbrush

FOR WIDE SEAMS, joints, and gaps between materials, molding—along with wood putty, caulking compound, and other "fillers"—is the solution for a neat-looking job. When the molding itself gets damaged, however, you can't hide the problem. You must replace at least the section of molding that is damaged.

Because baseboards are down at floor level where they can be struck by all sorts of objects, they are the most easily damaged moldings. The following procedures guide you on how to replace baseboard molding, but you can also apply the same techniques to other types of moldings.

Removing the Molding

The first task in replacing molding is to remove the old molding. Follow these steps:

1. Remove any shoe molding; this is the quarter-round piece that fits against both the baseboard and the floor. Because it's nailed to the subfloor, apply gentle prying pressure with a putty knife at one end of the shoe molding to get it started. Then, use a short pry bar and a wood block for leverage. Once started, the shoe molding should come up fairly easily. Try not to be too rough, though, or you can break it, adding to replacement costs and work.
2. Pry off the damaged baseboard. Start at one end, inserting a small, flat pry bar between the baseboard and the wall. Pry gently, and move further down the molding whenever you can, slipping small cedar shingle wedges in the gaps. Work all the way along the baseboard prying and wedging. Then work back between the wedges, tapping the wedges in deeper as the baseboard comes out more. Continue until the molding comes off.
3. Check to see if any nails have been pulled through either the shoe molding or the baseboard. If so, pull out the nails completely.

Using a Miter Box

If the old baseboard came off intact, you can use it as a pattern for cutting the new one. If part of it is missing or if it is badly damaged, however, you must cut the new moldings to fit without the aid of

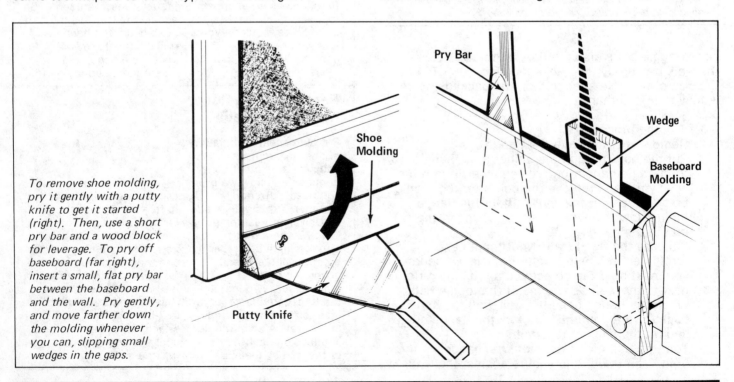

To remove shoe molding, pry it gently with a putty knife to get it started (right). Then, use a short pry bar and a wood block for leverage. To pry off baseboard (far right), insert a small, flat pry bar between the baseboard and the wall. Pry gently, and move farther down the molding whenever you can, slipping small wedges in the gaps.

Shoe Molding

Putty Knife

Pry Bar

Wedge

Baseboard Molding

a pattern. You will need a miter box to cut the moldings; an inexpensive wooden miter box will be adequate for this work. Slots in the box will allow you to cut molding at 45-degree angles, and you should use either a backsaw or a fine-toothed blade in a hacksaw to do the sawing. **Note:** Be sure to place the molding you are about to cut next to the molding against which it will rest to make certain that the cut you plan to make is the correct one. To make two 45-degree cuts to join molding so it forms a right angle, follow this procedure:

1. Place a length of molding in the miter box.
2. Make sure that the lip of the miter box presses against the edge of a table or bench so that you can hold it steady.
3. Hold the molding tightly against the side of the miter box to prevent it from slipping as you saw a 45-degree cut at one end.
4. Repeat the procedure for the other length of molding; the two lengths should form a perfect right angle.

How to Cope Molding

If you must cut an inside right angle, you'll have to cope the joint, using a coping saw. The blade of the saw is mounted so it may be turned to match the cutting angle, if necessary. Follow these steps:

1. Blunt-cut a piece of molding to fit tightly into the corner along one wall. Hold the molding in place or fasten it lightly with a 2d finishing nail driven partway in.
2. Hold a second blunt-cut piece of molding—a scrap will do—along the other wall, butted against the corner-fitted piece.
3. With a pencil, trace the outline of the second piece of molding carefully onto the side of the fastened piece, keeping the pencil at a constant angle so the traced outline will be exact.
4. Unfasten the corner-fitted molding and cut it slowly and carefully along the traced line with a coping saw, following the pencil mark exactly.
5. Complete the coped joint by installing a blunt-cut piece of molding along the wall you traced from; then install the traced and trimmed piece of molding in place against it.

Installing the Molding

When you finish all the mitered and coped joints, you are ready to install the new baseboard molding and to reinstall the shoe molding. Follow this procedure:

1. Fit all the pieces together before nailing to make sure that you cut them correctly.
2. Nail the baseboard in place with finishing nails. Then use a nail set to drive the nail heads below the surface of the molding.
3. Install the shoe molding with finishing nails as well. Shoe molding, however, must be nailed to the floor and not to the baseboard. Drive the nail heads below the surface of the shoe molding with a nail set.
4. Paint or stain the moldings to match your walls.

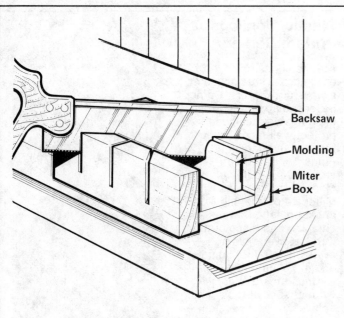

You can make 45-degree miter cuts easily using a miter box and a backsaw.

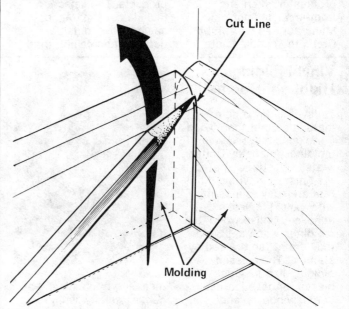

To cope molding, outline the cut area by butting the two molding pieces together and marking it with a pencil.

Walls

Pre-Finished and Unfinished Trim Is Available

Moldings are an important part of an interior finishing job; they hide many seams, joints, and gaps from view. A complete line of moldings is made by the Colombia Moulding Co., including pre-finished and unfinished trim, jambs, and moldings in wood, cellular, and rigid PVC. Standard sizes in lengths and widths are available, too. Shapes include window and door casings, outside corners, stops, baseboards, shoes, caps,

and inside corners. Moldings are available in ranch and colonial patterns.

Wide-Blade Knife Helps You to Tape Wallboard

Whenever you do drywall work, you need a good taping knife. The Iowa Broad Knife is the Marshalltown Trowel Company's medium-priced taping knife. Ideal for the home handyman, the stiff 10-inch blade and handle are fuse-welded into a one-piece tool that gets drywall jobs finished quickly. A better quality model comes in 8-inch, 10-inch, and 12-inch widths. The tempered blade is

fashioned from the highest grade blue clock steel, and it has no exposed rivets or ridges. If you do a great deal of drywall work, you should consider buying this more expensive model.

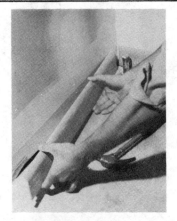

Pre-Finished Moldings Can Save Time

Pre-finished moldings can save you plenty of installation time. The Aztra line of pre-finished moldings has 18 different profiles in ranch and traditional styling. Manufactured by Abitibi Corp., the moldings are

available in standard lengths for floors, walls, and ceilings. The company's products are approved by all major building codes. The moldings are not only for paneling installations, but may be used for decorative trim on other building products. The selection includes crown, ranch casing, cove, outside corners, and ceiling trim.

Estimating the Amount of Ceramic Tile You Need

Most ceramic tile is 4¼ inches square. You can use the table below to estimate how many of these tiles you need per linear foot:

Length of Row	Tiles Required
5 feet	15
6 feet	17
7 feet	20
8 feet	23
9 feet	26
10 feet	29
11 feet	32
12 feet	34

Vinyl Moldings Highlight Rooms

Today, moldings come in materials other than wood. For example, Gossen moldings, made by United States Gypsum Co., are pre-finished vinyl moldings that are easy to install with nails, staples, or adhesive. Unlike wood, the moldings won't split and the "grain" isn't raised by staining. The Gossen molding line includes pieces for baseboards, doors, windows, and ceiling trim. There are many colors and patterns,

including birch, pine, teak, pecan, hickory, walnut, oak, gray, black, charcoal, white, and sienna.

Plastic Moldings Protect Corners

Are the edges of entranceways damaged or always dirty? Miller Corner Saver transparent corner moldings are designed to protect wallpaper, paint, plaster, and paneling. Fingerprints wipe off easily with a damp cloth. Manufactured by the K. J. Miller Corp. from high-impact plastic that resists chipping and discoloration, Corner Saver molding is available in 4-foot lengths and in ⅜-inch and ¾-inch widths. It installs quickly without special tools, and comes in two versions—with self-adhesive or screw mountings.

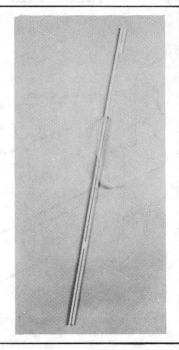

Drywall Glue Sticks Tight

If you are applying drywall to wood or metal studs, or laminating studs with conventional foil-back drywall, you should use the proper adhesive. Gulf Drywall Adhesive, from Gulf Adhesives and Resins, Gulf Chemicals Corp., is designed to bond drywall to such framing. It

also may be used for installing insulating sound-deadening board, cork, and most other insulation material except for foam. The adhesive, which is light in color, has a high resistance to oxidation, according to the manufacturer. It should, however, be used when temperatures are at 75° F or higher. Gulf Drywall Adhesive comes in a 30-ounce cartridge.

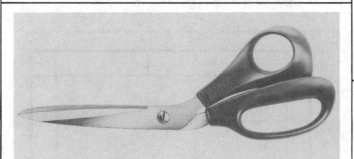

Heavy Wall Fabric Requires Heavy-Duty Scissors

The household scissors you now have may not do the job on some fabrics used for wallcoverings. If they don't quite "cut it," so to speak, you'll end up not only with sore and aching hands but probably with a sloppy job as well. The precision-made Wiss

Contura-lite shears from The Cooper Group are what you need. Though extremely lightweight, they can make a sharp clean cut in all types of fabrics. Made in 8- and 9-inch versions, the Wiss Contura-lite shears are the only featherweight scissors in which the steel blades extend fully into the cushioned, contoured handles, providing strength and comfort.

Fastener for Solid or Hollow Walls

Especially designed to support mirrors, pictures, cabinets, bathroom and electrical fixtures, and other light-to-medium-heavy objects, Molly well nuts can be used for both hollow- and solid-wall construction. To use the fastener, you drill a hole in the wall material the size of the nut base. Then, remove the screw from the

fastener and stick it through the object to be mounted. Finally, drive the screw into the base of the fastener. The all-purpose fastener is ⅜ by ⁹⁄₁₆ inch; it requires a ¼-inch hole in gypsum wallboard, plaster, tile, and plywood. The Molly well nut is made by Bostik Consumer division of Emhart Corp.

Fasteners for Hollow Walls

A fastener, which is designed for any hollow wall, floor, or ceiling covered with gypsum wallboard, plywood, paneling, or other material that leaves space between the framing members, is the original Molly drive fastener, made by Bostik Consumer division of Emhart Corp. You punch a hole in the wall for the base of the fastener. Then, insert the fastener. Remove the screw in the fastener and thread it through the object to be mounted. Then, turn the screw into the base. The base "fans" out behind the wall and grips the wall to

hold the object securely. Molly drive fasteners are available in a wide variety of sizes.

Wall Fastener for Any Wall

A wall fastener that will work in any wall—gypsum or plaster wallboard—is very useful. You drill a hole, push in the Toggler screw anchor, run a screw through the item to be mounted or hung, and twist the screw into the fastener. The Toggler screw anchor, made by Mechanical Plastics Corp., is plastic. On solid plaster, the shank of the fastener grips the sides of the hole for staying power. On hollow walls, the Toggler "fans" out to hug the back

of the wall like a toggle bolt. The system works on any wall thickness from ⅛ inch. Any size screw from Nos. 6 through 14 may be used with the versatile fastener.

Toggle Bolt Springs Into Action

For hanging or mounting items on hollow walls, you need a special fastener. The Star Snapin toggle bolt has a spring within the winged head that causes it to open automatically once the head gets through the hole in the wall. Made in a wide range of sizes, toggle bolts made by Star Expansion Co. come carded with two

bolts to the pack. They also come in three head styles: round, flat, and mushroom. Instructions on the package tell you what size drill bit you need to make the proper-size hole.

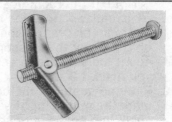

Tiling a Ceiling

Materials • Ceiling Tile • Tile Adhesive • 1 × 2 or 1 × 3 Furring as Required • 6d Common Nails • Staples • 4d Common Nails • Cove Molding

Tools • Stepladder • Tape Measure • Chalk Line • Carpenter's Square • Pencil • Utility Knife • Putty Knife • Crosscut Saw • Hammer • Staple Gun

THE FAST WAY to have a new ceiling is to install ceiling tiles directly to the plaster or drywall ceiling. If the ceiling surface isn't suitable, the tiles can be stapled to furring strips. And, if the ceiling is in really poor condition, you can lower the ceiling with a suspended ceiling system—provided the ceiling is high enough. The procedure for installing a suspended ceiling is covered elsewhere in this chapter.

Installing Tile With Adhesive

If you plan to apply tile directly to the existing ceiling surface with adhesive, follow this procedure:

1. Determine how much tile you need; multiply the room's length by the width to obtain the square footage. Most tile is sold in boxes containing 64 square feet, although smaller quantities are available. To find how much tile you need, divide 64 into the square footage; allow for some extra tiles in case of mistakes.
   Note: If the room doesn't have a square or rectangular shape, you can draw a sketch of the room on graph paper, using each square on the paper to represent 1 square foot. Then, count the squares to determine how many tiles you need.
2. Find the center of the ceiling. Measure and mark the mid-point of each wall. Stretch a chalk line between opposite mid-points and snap the chalk line; where the lines cross is the center. Check it with a carpenter's square to make sure the lines form 90-degree angles.
3. Measure the ceiling to determine the width of the tiles that will go around the edges of the room; measure in feet and inches, across both chalked center lines.

Note: To calculate the width of border tiles, consider only the inches measured past the last full foot in each direction—5 inches, for example, from 17 feet 5 inches. Add 12 inches—the width of one full tile—and divide by 2. The result is the width of the border tiles at each end of each row of tile laid in that direction. If the inch measurement is 5, for example, border tiles in rows across the direction measured will be 8½ inches wide.

4. Calculate the width of border tiles along both directions. Start in one corner of the room; from this corner, measure out the width of the border tiles in each direction. Mark these points on the ceiling. Snap a chalk line on the ceiling at a right angle through each of these points, making sure each of the two new lines is parallel to one of the chalk lines across the center of the ceiling.

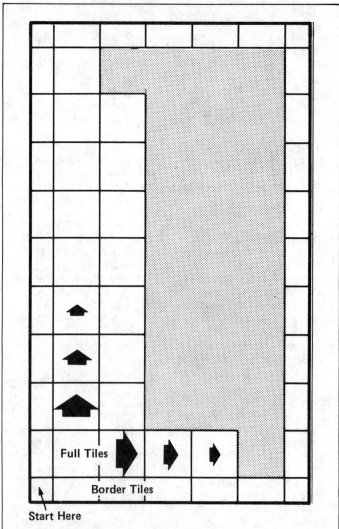

Start by setting the corner tiles first. Then, cut border tiles to work out along the corner walls. Fill in between the border tiles with full tiles.

5. Set the corner tile first. Mark it to the measured size with a pencil; cut it, face up, with a sharp utility knife and a steel straightedge.

   Note: Ceiling tiles are made to lock together, with two grooved edges and two tongued edges. The tongued edges of the starter tile must face toward the center of the room, so cut the grooved edges to trim the corner tile to size. The border tiles along the two starter walls will also be trimmed along a grooved edge; the tiles bordering the two far walls will be cut along the tongued edges.

6. Apply adhesive to the back of the trimmed corner tile with a putty knife, putting daubs of adhesive in the center of the tile and about 1½ inches in front of each corner. Place the tile into the corner, tongued edges out, and slide it into position exactly within the two chalked

lines. Press it firmly into place.

7. Cut border tiles to work out from the corner tile along the two corner walls. As you work, slide the grooved edges of each tile over the exposed tongues of the last tiles to lock the tiles firmly together.

8. Fill in between the border tiles with full-size tiles in an expanding wedge pattern, gradua extending the rows of border tiles and fanr tiles out to cover the entire ceiling.

   Note: To work around light fixtures, hold tile up to the ceiling before applying adhesi carefully mark and cut off the portion to be removed, then apply adhesive and slide the tile into place.

9. Continue setting tiles until you reach the far corner of the room. Before cutting border tiles for the two far walls, measure the gap left beyond the last full tile. Mark and cut border

Forget About Furring

To eliminate wooden furring strips, Armstrong World Industries, Inc., developed a system of lightweight steel channels that were designed for attaching the company's ceiling tiles to plaster, drywall, or exposed joists. The Easy Up channels are manufactured in 12-foot lengths. The channels are sold in kits, which contain enough tracks, clips, and nails to install 20 to 24 square feet of ceiling tile.

Sound-Condition a Noisy Room

Ceiling tile can add extra dimension and sound-conditioning to any room of your home. Gold Bond Decorator ceiling tile, made by Gold Bond Building Products, a division of National Gypsum, is available in a number of patterns. Most ceiling tiles are a standard 12 by 12 inches in size. But there are Gold Bond "Just Ceilings" tiles in a 12- by 24-inch size.

Hand Stapler Can Use Five Sizes of Staples

If you plan to install ceiling tiles by stapling them to furring strips, you need a quality stapler. The model CT-859A Duo-Fast stapling gun from the Duo-Fast Corp. can handle five sizes of staples: ¼-inch, ⁵⁄₁₆-inch, ³⁄₈-inch, ½-inch, and ⁹⁄₁₆-inch staples. Other features include a variable power control adjustment; reversible screen/fabric and wire attachment; fast-release front assembly for cleaning and jam-clearing;

contoured handle with a hand stop; and a handle hold-down clip. The chrome-plate steel tool operates smoothly, with about medium-grip pressure to fire the staples.

Wear Gloves When Putting Up Ceiling Tile

The pros do it, and you should do it, too: Wear gloves when installing ceiling tile. Clean gloves help protect tile surfaces from finger smudges. Boss No. 641 Hevy gloves, from Boss Manufacturing Co., are made of 8-ounce canvas fabric. They feature a clute cut and a knit wrist. When the ceiling tile project is completed, you can use the gloves for other home maintenance and improvement jobs.

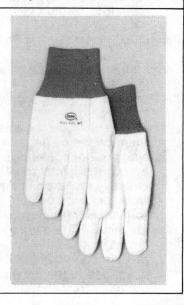

Ceilings

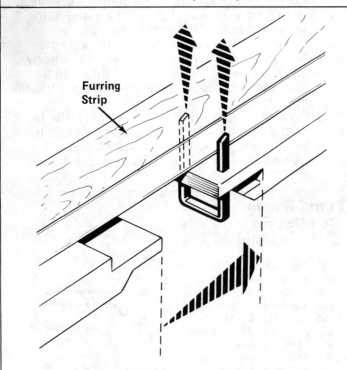

Staple the tile to furring strips along grooved edges. Slide in tongued edges to lock the tile firmly.

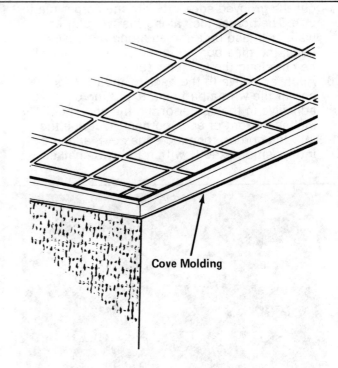

Finish the tiling job by installing cove molding along the edges of the ceiling.

tiles along these walls one by one to make sure they fit the gap.

10. Finish the job by installing cove molding along the edges of the ceiling.

Installing Tile on Furring Strips

To install tile over an uneven or badly damaged ceiling, nail furring strips across the ceiling. Follow these steps:

1. Locate each ceiling joist in the room, and mark them on the ceiling.
2. Nail 1 x 2 or 1 x 3 furring strips at right angles across the joists and along the edges of the ceiling with 6d common nails, 12 inches apart from center to center; use a carpenter's square to make sure the strips are even and properly angled. Cut the strips to fit, if necessary, with a crosscut saw.
3. Measure and calculate border tile width as described in the previous procedure. To mark the lines from the starting corner for the corner tile and the first two border rows, carefully snap a chalk line each way on the furring strips.
4. Cut the corner tile and set it into place, grooved side toward the center of the room and centered on the furring strips. Staple it to the furring strips, setting three staples along each exposed grooved edge. Nail the other two sides firmly into place with 4d common nails, as close to the walls as possible.
5. Continue across the room, setting border tiles and then filling in with full tiles, sliding new tiles in to lock over old ones as you go. Staple each new tile with three staples along each grooved edge.

   Note: To fasten border tiles into place at the wall, drive three nails along each trimmed tongued edge, as close to the wall as possible. These nails will be covered by molding. Trim and set border tiles for the far walls one by one as you work.
6. Finish the job by installing cove molding along the edges of the ceiling.

Tiling Around Beams and Ductwork

Materials • Ceiling Tile • Tile Adhesive • Prefinished Metal Wall Angle for Suspended Ceilings • Panel Adhesive • Cove Molding • Two 1 × 3's • ½-Inch Plywood (CDX) • 10d Threaded Nails

Tools • Pencil • Tape Measure • Stepladder • Crosscut Saw • Utility Knife • Hammer • Hacksaw

THERE ARE TWO methods of installing ceiling tile around ductwork and metal support beams. Which one you use depends on how far down from the ceiling the obstruction is and its shape. If it is just a matter of a few inches, you can build a plywood "box" around the duct. If the distance is a foot or more, the tile may be applied directly to rectangular ductwork. The plywood box method is best for metal support beams and other irregularly shaped obstructions.

Covering Rectangular Ductwork

Tiles may be installed directly on rectangular ducts. Follow these steps:

1. Install ceiling tile to the edge of the metal duct. The fit doesn't have to be perfectly accurate because cove molding will be used to hide the joints.
2. Use tile adhesive to stick the tiles to the sides and bottom of the duct. If strap duct hangers won't let the tile lay flat, mortise the back of the tile slightly with a series of saw kerfs made with a crosscut saw.
3. After the tile has been installed over the duct, measure, cut, and install a strip of prefinished metal wall angle made for suspended ceilings on the bottom edges of the duct over the tiles. Because the wall angle is very light in weight, you can affix it over the tile with tile adhesive or panel adhesive.
4. At the top of the duct—where the ceiling tile meets the tile covering the sides of the duct—install prefinished cove molding with panel

Stay Clean Along With the Tile

Installing ceiling tile with adhesive can turn into a messy job. Your hands will become covered with adhesive, which picks up dirt. The dirt is then smudged onto the tile. These smudges can be very difficult to remove because they are adhesive-based. When working with ceiling tile, wear clean, inexpensive cotton gloves. You should buy three pairs. This way, you can put on a clean pair while the dirty ones are being laundered.

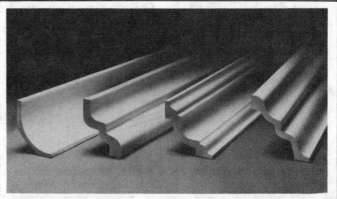

Ceiling Borders Hide Defects Between Materials

Ceiling borders can add a nice finishing touch to a room. Designer's Touch decorative ceiling borders are available in scallop, cove, and crown styles. Made by the Decoration Division of Nomaco, Inc., the borders are packaged in 6½-foot lengths. According to the manufacturer, the borders may be painted, stained, or finished with any latex-based product. The borders, which are made of an extruded polymer, are attached with an adhesive and all joints are filled with a filler made for the borders. Installation instructions are provided with the borders.

Non-Sagging Adhesive for Ceiling Tile

You should use a quality adhesive when installing ceiling tile. According to Gulf Adhesives and Resins, a division of Gulf Chemicals Corp., Gulf ceiling tile adhesive (CTA-43) retains its plasticity and won't sag. The product, which has a buttery consistency for fast tile application, is also non-freezing and easy to apply from 40° to 100° F. The adhesive is formulated for mounting wood fiber wallboard and other semi-rigid materials such as insulation board,

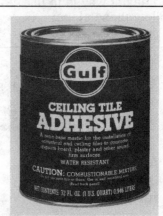

hardboard, gypsum wallboard, masonry, white plaster, or concrete. The product, however, isn't recommended for use on wood, galvanized steel, or uninsulated concrete roof decks.

Ceilings

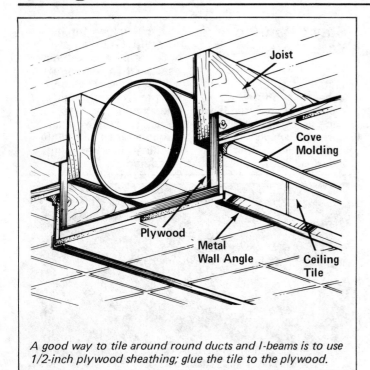

A good way to tile around round ducts and I-beams is to use 1/2-inch plywood sheathing; glue the tile to the plywood.

adhesive. You will probably have to hold the molding for several minutes until the adhesive has time to set enough to adhere to the tiles.

Note: You can use a pair of 1 × 3's wedged between the floor and the molding to hold the molding until the adhesive sets.

Round Ducts and I-Beams

You can use 1 × 3 furring strips to go around round ducts and I-beams, but it's a lot of work. A faster and easier way is to use ½-inch plywood sheathing. Follow these steps:

1. Cut the plywood sheathing into strips for the sides of the obstruction; they should match the width and the height (distance from ceiling to bottom of duct or beam) of the obstruction.
2. Using 10d threaded nails, nail one strip of plywood to the side of the joist nearest the duct or beam. Then nail the other strip of plywood on the other side to the nearest parallel joist.
3. Bridge the two plywood strips with a strip of plywood for the bottom of the obstruction. Nail through the face of the bottom strip into the edges of the vertical strips. Use threaded nails and panel adhesive on the edges for strength. When you are finished, you have a boxed enclosure onto which you can glue or staple the ceiling tile.

   Note: If the obstruction is below the ceiling joists and makes 45- or 90-degree turns within the room, you may not be able to use this technique. A suspended ceiling may be the answer.
4. Tile the ceiling up to the plywood-sheathed obstruction. Then, cover the plywood enclosure with ceiling tile.
5. Measure, cut, and install a strip of prefinished metal wall angle made for suspended ceilings on the bottom edges of the enclosure over the tiles. Because the wall angle is very light in weight, you can affix it over the tile with tile adhesive or panel adhesive.
6. At the ceiling joists along the enclosure, install cove molding with panel adhesive. You will probably have to hold the molding for several minutes until the adhesive has time to set enough to adhere to the tiles.

   Note: You can use a pair of 1 × 3's wedged between the floor and the molding to hold the molding until the adhesive sets.

A Good Handsaw Is Fine for Framing

A good crosscut handsaw works fine for mortising ceiling tile, and for cutting studs, plates, cripples, headers, and so on. Moreover, a well-made saw will last for many years. The Nicholson Professional Silver Steel crosscut saw, made by The Cooper Group, is just what you need for ceiling tasks, but it can also handle many other cutting chores around the house. A crosscut saw is made to cut across the grain of the wood. A good crosscut saw should be 26 inches long and have 10 teeth per inch.

Staples Make Tiling a Ceiling Easy

One squeeze of Arrow's T-50 heavy-duty, all-purpose staple gun drives a staple wherever a nail can be driven—into the hardest of woods and even into light metals. When equipped with the Ceiltile wire staple, the gun is ideal for fastening ceiling tiles. Made by the Arrow Fastener Company, the T-50 staple gun can also be used for hundreds of do-it-yourself chores with the five other staple sizes it is designed to use. It

even comes in a T-50 MP kit with attachments for screens, wiring, and shades; three boxes of staples, including Ceiltile; and a staple lifter.

Ceilings

Replacing Damaged Tiles

Materials • 4-Pound Cut White Shellac
• Ceiling Tile as Required • Paint • Rags
• Tile Adhesive

Tools • Stepladder • Paintbrush
• Keyhole Saw • Carpenter's Square
• Utility Knife • Pliers • Putty Knife

WHEN YOU LOOK at a ceiling covered with tile—all neatly and tightly butted together—the idea of replacing a damaged tile somewhere in the middle of the ceiling may seem impossible. Actually, it probably will be easier to replace the damaged tile than to find and buy a matching tile for the project.

If a tile or a series of tiles have been damaged by water and have become stained, you may not have to replace the tiles. Instead, brush a coat of 4-pound cut white shellac over the tiles, and allow the shellac to dry for one hour. Then, paint the tiles with a color to match the undamaged tiles. The shellac seals the tile surface so the stain won't "bleed" through the paint.

To remove and replace one or more damaged tiles, however, follow this procedure:

1. If the tile is applied to furring, cut a hole in the center of the damaged tile large enough to stick your hand through. Use a keyhole saw for cutting the hole, but be careful you don't damage adjoining tiles or anything behind the tile. Carefully remove the damaged tile with your fingers. If it's glued directly to a plaster or drywall ceiling, you'll have to make a hole with some sharp tool and carefully pry the pieces off.
2. Using a carpenter's square or a straightedge, cut the tongue or grooved edges from the replacement tile with a utility knife. The edges you should remove can be determined by holding the tile in position over the opening in the ceiling.
3. Match the cut tile to the opening. It may need special trimming to fit. Use the utility knife for sharp, clean-cut edges.
4. Remove any old staples or adhesive from the furring strips or ceiling. Be careful not to damage the edges of adjoining tiles.
5. Place a walnut-sized daub of ceiling tile adhesive at each corner of the new tile and press the new tile into the opening. Hold the tile in position for several minutes until the adhesive sets enough to support the tile.
6. Before the adhesive dries, examine the tile. If it is not aligned with surrounding tiles, you can slip the tile into the proper position before the adhesive dries.

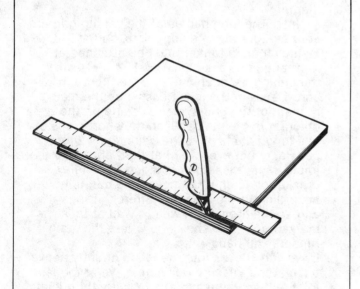

Before installing a replacement tile, cut the tongue or grooved edge with a utility knife; you can determine which by holding the tile in position over the opening.

Adhesive for Ceiling Tile and Wallboard

Especially formulated for installation of acoustical ceiling tile, pre-finished hardboard, and tile board, Franklin Ceiling Tile Installation Adhesive has a quick initial grab and high cohesive strength, according to Franklin Chemical Industries, the manufacturer. The adhesive also allows long open or working time for adjustment and positioning of materials without having them pull away from the base or framing members. Two sizes are available: quarts and gallons.

Suspended Ceilings

Materials • Graph Paper • Suspended Ceiling Panels • Metal Wall Angles • Main Runners • Cross Tees • 12-Gauge Hanger Wire • 6d Common Nails • String • Screw Eyes

---

Tools • Stepladder • Tape Measure • Pencil • Chalk Line • Carpenter's Level • Tin Snips or Hacksaw • Diagonal Cutters • Pliers • Straightedge

---

A SUSPENDED ceiling can cover a lot of flaws and obstructions, including pipes, wiring, and ductwork. It works best where you can afford to lose some ceiling height.

Suspended ceiling panels are sold in 2- by 2-foot and 2- by 4-foot sizes; use the smaller size for smaller rooms.

To install a suspended ceiling, follow this procedure:

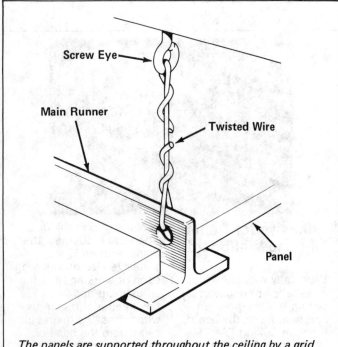

The panels are supported throughout the ceiling by a grid of main runners and cross tees. These are attached to the ceiling with wire and screw eyes.

1. Measure the ceiling and plot it on graph paper, marking the exact locations of windows and doors. Mark the direction of ceiling joists. Mark the joists on the ceiling itself, using a pencil or chalk to draw the joist lines across the ceiling.
2. Take the diagram with you when you buy the ceiling materials. With the dealer, plan the layout for the ceiling, figuring full panels across the main ceiling and evenly trimmed partial panels at the edges. To calculate the width of the border panels in each direction, determine the width of the gap left after full panels are placed all across the dimension; divide by 2. The dealer should help you calculate how many panels you'll need, and should also tell you how many wall angle (in 10-foot lengths), main runner (in 12-foot lengths), and cross tee (in 4-foot or 2-foot lengths) grid sections, and how much 12-gauge hanger wire to buy.
3. Begin by marking the level the new ceiling will hang at; allow at least 4 inches clearance between the panels and the old ceiling. Snap a chalk line at this height across each wall, using a level to keep it straight. Make sure the lines meet exactly at the corners of the room.
4. Nail wall angle brackets along the chalk line all around the room, with the bottom leg of the L-angle facing into the room and flush along the chalk line. Use 6d common nails to fasten the brackets, setting them every 1½ to 2 feet. Cut the bracket to the required lengths with tin snips or a hacksaw.
5. Locate the points where screw eyes should be driven in by consulting your final ceiling layout diagram.

   Note: The long panels of the ceiling grid are set parallel to the ceiling joists, so the T-shaped main runner must be attached at right angles to the joists, every 4 feet across the ceiling. Hanger wire threaded through screw eyes in the joists suspends the main runners of the grid system. Locate on the diagram the joints between the short sides of two long panels; if you're using 2- by 2-foot panels, count every joint at right angles to the joists. Mark these points along the angle bracket on each wall, measuring carefully according to the diagram. Stretch strings across the room from wall to wall at these marked points to show you where the main runners will hang.
6. Drive screw eyes into the joists directly above each string, placing one screw eye at the last joist on each side and one in every third joist across the ceiling. If you're covering a finished ceiling, drive the screw eyes at the marked joist lines; use long screw eyes to hold through the thickness of the ceiling.

Suspension System Installs Easily

Suspended ceilings are popular. The suspension systems from Chicago Metallic Corp. feature grids with non-directional main runners and cross tees that can be connected at either end. This eliminates lots of mistakes and lets you suspend a ceiling easier. The CMC system is available in walnut grain, black, bronze, or baked white enamel. According to the manufacturer, the grid systems require no special fasteners or accessories. They can be installed with regular workshop tools.

Panels for Ceiling Are 2 by 2 Feet for Different Look

Most ceilings are covered by 12-inch-square tiles or 2- by 4-foot panels. But, 2- by 2-foot panels are available to give ceilings a different look. The Waverly II No. RE 192 pattern, from The Celotex Corp., is such a panel. It features a "reveal edge," a specially indented edge that drops below the suspended grid for a three-dimensional look. The acoustical panel contains non-directional fissures, and a black grid contrasting against white Waverly II panels can set them off beautifully.

Ceiling Panels Are Flexible and Add Insulation to Rooms

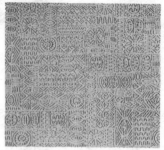

If you're installing a suspended ceiling, you can now obtain ceiling panels that are flexible so they can bend and yet spring back and stay flat without damage. The panels also add insulation to your home. The ceiling panels, which are made by Owens-Corning Fiberglas Corp., are backed with Fiberglas acoustical insulation, and they carry a 10-year limited warranty against warping. According to the manufacturer, they're lightweight and easy to cut with a knife. There are four series of panels available in a number of patterns. Three of the series have 2- by 4-foot panels. One series—the Thermal Series—has panels in 2- by 4-foot sizes as well as 4- by 4-foot; 4- by 8-foot; 4- by 12-foot, 6 inch; and 4- by 16-foot sizes. The two largest sizes, however, must be special-ordered from an Owens-Corning dealer.

Keep That Ceiling Level

Ceiling tile must be level on the ceiling whether the tile is fastened to furring strips, placed in a suspended ceiling grid system, or glued directly to the ceiling. The Mark III Uni-Vial level, from Mayes Brothers Tool Manufacturing Co., has vials that are larger than most for better visibility; they also are adjustable for plumb or horizontal level. The Mark III level, which is 28 inches long, has an extruded aluminum frame with a baked-enamel finish that the company says won't peel or chip. And, the level's end caps are swedged on so they won't work loose.

7. Cut a length of hanger wire for each screw eye—long enough to fasten securely through the screw eye, extend down to the stretched runner string and fasten the runner. Thread a wire through each screw eye and twist the end firmly around the dangling wire. Exactly at the point where the wire crosses the string beneath it, bend the wire sharply with pliers to a 90-degree angle.
8. Set the main runners into place. Cut T-shaped main runner sections to required lengths with tin snips or a hacksaw; if you must put two sections together to cover a long span, snap the pieces together with the preformed tabs.
9. Lift each long main runner and set one end into place on the wall angle bracket at one side of the ceiling, with the single leg of the "T" up; swing the other end up and position the runner exactly along the marker string and under the screw eyes in the joists. Thread the bent end of each hanging wire through a hole in the runner leg; bend the end of the wire up and secure it. Check each runner with a level and adjust the length of the hangers if necessary. Repeat until all main runners have been installed.
10. Working from your ceiling diagram, install the cross tee sections of the ceiling grid. These sections snap into place in slots in the main runner sections; because they're sold in 4-foot lengths, no cutting is necessary. Snap the sections into place every 2 feet along the main

Ceilings

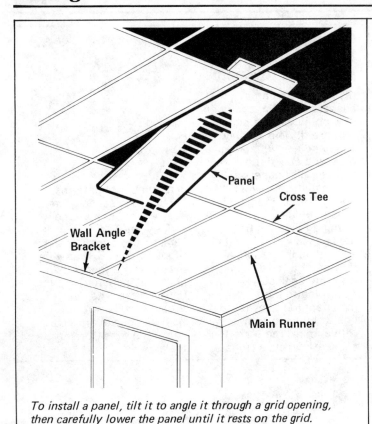

To install a panel, tilt it to angle it through a grid opening, then carefully lower the panel until it rests on the grid.

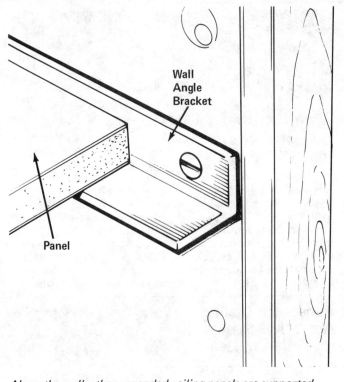

Along the walls, the suspended ceiling panels are supported by wall angle brackets fastened to the wall.

runners. If you're using 2- by 2-foot ceiling panels, use 2-foot cross tees to divide each 2- by 4-foot panel in half; snap the sections together firmly.

11. After all main runners and cross tees are in place, install the panels. Tilt each panel to angle it through a grid opening, then carefully lower it until it rests on the bracket edges of the grid sections. Measure border panels carefully; cut them to size with a utility knife.

12. If you have to fit a panel around a post, carefully measure across the opening to the

post in both directions; sketch the opening and mark the post. Measure the diameter of the post. Mark the panel lightly where the post will go through it; cut the panel in two exactly through the center of the post, across the shorter dimension. Carve an opening for the post on the inside cut edge of each panel, forming two semicircular or rectangular cutouts. Cut only a little at a time; hold the cut sections up to the post frequently to fit them exactly. Set the two sections into place in the suspension grid; the cut will show hardly at all.

Ceiling Fan Is Decorative Yet Practical Too

A ceiling fan is a decorative touch that's also practical. The model No. JU-01 ceiling fan from JAB Industries, Inc., is designed to save energy by circulating cool or heated air throughout rooms. According to the manufacturer, the fan can spread the breeze evenly over a large area quietly. The fan has an optional lighting attachment and reverse switch. The motor is a capacitor type with ball bearings top and bottom. A solid-state, variable-speed control regulator is hooked to the motor by a pull chain and provides a speed range from 45 to 275 rpm. The fan blades are balanced to provide maximum air displacement. The UL Listed product comes with a five-year guarantee.

Installing Recessed Lighting

Materials • Lighting Fixture With Mounting Hardware • Light Diffusion Panel • Nails • Wire Nuts • Expansion Fasteners, Toggle Bolts, or Masonry Anchors

Tools • Stepladder • Screwdriver • Hammer • Wire Stripper • Drill and Bit

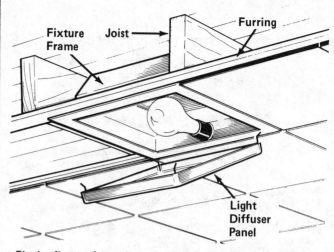

Fit the fixture frame into the opening and mount it with the hardware supplied by the manufacturer. After connecting the wiring, install the reflector, the light bulb, and the light diffuser panel.

RECESSED LIGHTING fixtures are readily available for a variety of ceilings. For ceilings with 12-inch square tiles on furring strips over joists, the fixtures are the size of a single tile. For suspended ceilings with 2- by 4-foot panels, you can buy fixtures that fit above a single panel and attach to the joists, subflooring, or to the main tees of the suspended system. A special light panel replaces the ceiling panel below the light fixture.

To power a lighting fixture, you may be able to use an existing ceiling fixture junction box and wall switch or route wiring from an existing circuit into a ceiling junction box for the new fixture. If a new circuit is required, call a professional. In any case, the wall switch and wiring for the fixture should be routed to the site of the ceiling fixture before the ceiling tile or panels are installed.

At the fixture site, fasten a junction box to the joists, using hangers for the box that span the joists. **Note:** Some fixtures are "prewired" with their own junction boxes. With this type of fixture, the circuit wires can be connected directly to the fixture's junction box with wire nuts.

After the wiring has been routed to the site of the fixture, you can proceed to install the ceiling tile or suspended ceiling system.

Lighting in a Tiled Ceiling

Lighting fixtures for a ceiling with 12-inch square tiles are usually incandescent lighting fixtures that fit between joists above furring strips; the light fixtures mount to the furring strips and/or joists. Follow this procedure:

1. Tile the ceiling to the location of the fixture.
2. Fit the fixture frame in the opening and mount

it in place with the hardware provided by the manufacturer.
3. Turn off the power to the fixture circuit by removing the proper fuses or tripping the proper circuit breaker to the "off" position.
4. Connect the circuit wiring to the fixture, using wire nuts to join white wire to white wire, black wire to black wire, and bare or green wire to the fixture's green wire or grounding clip.
5. Install the reflector in the fixture according to the manufacturer's instructions; it usually snaps into position around the light socket and the fixture frame.
6. Screw in the light bulb and install the light diffuser panel over the frame of the fixture and reflector, according to the manufacturer's instructions. On some fixtures, the diffuser is hinged to the fixture frame and is snapped into place.
7. Restore the power to the fixture's circuit.

Lighting in a Suspended Ceiling

Lighting fixtures for suspended ceilings are almost always fluorescent fixtures. To install such a fixture in a suspended ceiling, follow these steps:

1. Install the suspended ceiling.
2. Turn off the power to the fixture circuit by removing the proper fuse or tripping the proper circuit breaker to the "off" position.
3. Disassemble the new fluorescent fixture, if necessary, to expose its wires. Have someone hold the fixture while you connect the circuit wiring to the fixture; attach black wire to black wire, white wire to white wire, and bare or green wire to the fixture's green wire or

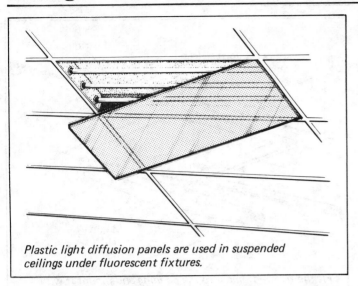

Plastic light diffusion panels are used in suspended ceilings under fluorescent fixtures.

grounding clip. Then, reassemble the fixture, if necessary, and position it against the ceiling.

4. Mount the fixture with the hardware provided. Most fluorescent fixtures come with installation screws. Use these screws if you can drive them into ceiling joists or some other solid wood; otherwise, use expansion fasteners or toggle bolts for drywall or plaster ceilings, or masonry anchors and screws for concrete ceilings. Drill pilot holes to size for bolts and anchors; drill pilot holes of slightly smaller diameter for wood screws. Then firmly screw or anchor the fixture to the ceiling.
5. Place the fluorescent tubes into the fixture's contact slots, and restore the power to the circuit.
6. Install the plastic light diffusion panel into place in the ceiling.

Ceiling Panels Fit Standard Grids

Recessed ceiling lights, installed in a standard grid system ceiling, offer an easy way to provide lighting that reduces glares and shadows. Baxt Luminous Ceiling Panels are available in standard 2-by 4-foot sizes to fit most ceiling systems. They are lightweight, and are reported to be easy to cut and install. For the most effective lighting, use the panels with 40-watt, 4-foot fluorescent tubes. The space above the light fixture should be painted white, and the tubes should be spaced 4 inches from the panel. The Luminous Ceiling Panels, from Baxt Industries, Inc., are available in four basic styles. The Cracked Ice panels have an overall pattern of highlights, and are available in white or clear polystyrene. Prismatic panels have a prism pattern for glare-free light; they are available in clear or white, made from either polystyrene or acrylic. Acry-Lene panels are smooth, white, and translucent; they are available in polystyrene. Louvered panels—both Econo-Louver and Difus-a-

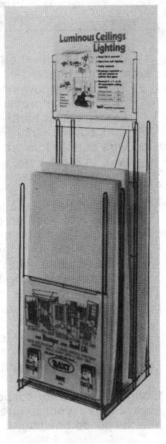

Louver—provide free air circulation through open cubes. The diffusing panels are available in white acrylic, or aluminum in black, gold, mill-finished aluminum, or baked-on white enamel. Panels in 2- by 2-foot sizes are available by special order.

Fluorescent Fixtures for Suspended Ceilings

Two popular types of fluorescent fixtures for suspended ceilings are the kind that attaches to the grid by means of mounting brackets or rests directly on the grid. Armstrong World Industries, Inc., makes both types of fixtures. Gridmate fixtures attach to the grid by brackets using only a screwdriver; Troffermate fixtures, which are completely preassembled, rest directly on the grid. Troffermate fixtures have four lamps and come with a clear prismatic lens panel. With Gridmate there's a choice of either two or four lamps, and of several embossed panels that coordinate with various ceiling designs. All fixtures have rapid-start 40-watt lamps (20-watt lamps are also available with Gridmate) and ballasts guaranteed for two years. All are wired for 120 volts and are UL Listed.

Fluorescent Lighting for Ceilings

The Grid Master fluorescent lighting fixture, made by Liteway Corp., is designed for T-bar suspended tile ceilings. The fixture is mounted directly to the T-bars and becomes a part of the ceiling system. Wide, white reflectors and wide lamp spacing provide glare-free fluorescent light spread throughout the room below, according to the manufacturer. The fixture is made for standard 2- by 2-foot and 2- by 4-foot grids. The fixture is 4¾ inches deep. There are models with two or four 20- or 40-watt tubes. Fluorescent tubes, however, are not included with the fixtures.

Rosettes Add Detail to Ceilings

Rosettes once were designed from plaster by craftsmen. This is virtually a lost art today. But simulated rosettes are available and they are difficult to tell from the real thing. You can use them to surround ceiling or wall-mounted lighting fixtures, or simply as decorations. Designer's Touch rosettes, from the Decoration Division of Nomaco, Inc., are available in many sizes, ranging from 2½-inch-diameter round-button to a 26¾-inch-diameter round rosette. There also is a 24¼- by 17¼-inch oval rosette. According to the manufacturer, the closed-cell structure of the rosettes resists all changes in moisture and temperature; they won't peel or crack, and they need no touch-up once installed with adhesive and filled.

Plaster Patch for Ceilings

For patching ceilings and walls, a quick-setting plaster of paris is desirable. Synko plaster of paris, from the Synkoloid Co., a division of Dutch Boy, Inc., sets hard in about 10 to 15 minutes. It can be used for sculpting, casting, modeling, and mounting, as well as patching. After it hardens, the product may be drilled, sanded, filed, carved, or painted. You mix two parts of the plaster of paris with one part water. Three sizes are available: 2½-pound, 5-pound, and 25-pound packages.

Who Hid the Grid?

Grids for suspended ceilings don't have to be obvious. Armstrong's Headliner suspended ceiling system goes up fast, but the best part is that the Headliner panels and grids blend harmoniously. The ceiling appears to be a continuous unbroken surface. The Headliner system made by Armstrong World Industries, Inc., can be used in full suspension, attached directly to exposed wood joists. Armstrong Headliner panels are 2 by 2 or 2 by 4 feet and come in several designs; recessed fluorescent fixtures are also available for the Headliner system.

Acrylic Formulation Adds Texture to Walls and Ceilings

Drab-looking walls can be enlivened by giving them texture. RUFF-IT acrylic sculpture coat, made by the Z-Brick Co., is a formulation that adds texture to wall and ceiling surfaces. After it's applied, you can use anything that will make an impression in the wet product—trowel, whisk broom, taping knife, roller, and so on. The product can be applied to almost any clean, dry, non-oily, stable surface such as plaster, drywall, plywood, concrete block, cement, or metal. A 2-gallon container will

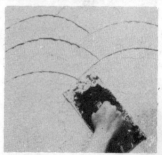

cover about 80 square feet, depending on the thickness of the application. RUFF-IT acrylic sculpture coat is pre-mixed and pre-colored in Oxford brown, Dover white, Tudor red, Putney tan, Windsor gold, and Hampton green. The product isn't recommended for bathrooms or other areas with high humidity.

Unsticking Windows

Materials • Candle, Bar Soap, or Silicone Spray • Wood Block • Piece of 2 × 4 • Replacement Window Channels • Stop Molding as Required • 6d Finishing Nails • Sealer • Paint or Stain • Plastic Sheeting • Tape

Tools • Putty Knife • Hammer • Sanding Stick, Rasp, Butt Chisel, or Hobby-Size Power Tool • Pry Bar • Jack or Jointer Plane • Tape Measure • Nail Set • Paintbrush

WINDOWS STICK for a number of reasons: humidity, unsquare frames, damage. One of the main reasons is failure to unlock the window. Another is a thin paint film along the window joint where the sash meets the window stops.

If you are confronted by a sticking window, follow these steps:

1. Examine all around the frame to see if paint has sealed the sash to the stops. Usually, the seal is complete all the way around.
2. Insert a putty knife—a medium-wide putty knife is ideal—where the crack should be between the sash and the stops. If you cannot get the knife in the crack, tap the knife's handle lightly with a hammer. If the window was painted both inside and out, cut the seals on both sides.
3. With the seal broken all around and the window still not moving, check the channels above. If the paint is too thick in the channels—preventing the window from sliding—remove the excess with a sanding stick, rasp, butt chisel, or a hobby-size power tool. Once the window is open, lubricate the sash's channels. Rub a candle or a bar of soap along the channel, or apply some silicone spray.
4. If the window still refuses to budge, use a small flat pry bar on it. Pry carefully from the outside if possible, and place a scrap block of wood under the bar.
5. If it still won't move or moves only slightly, tap the frame away from the window with a hammer and a piece of 2 × 4; even the slightest movement may be enough to free the sash.
6. If the preceding treatment fails to open the window, remove the inside stop molding with a putty knife, pry bar, or chisel. You'll probably break the molding and it will have to be replaced.

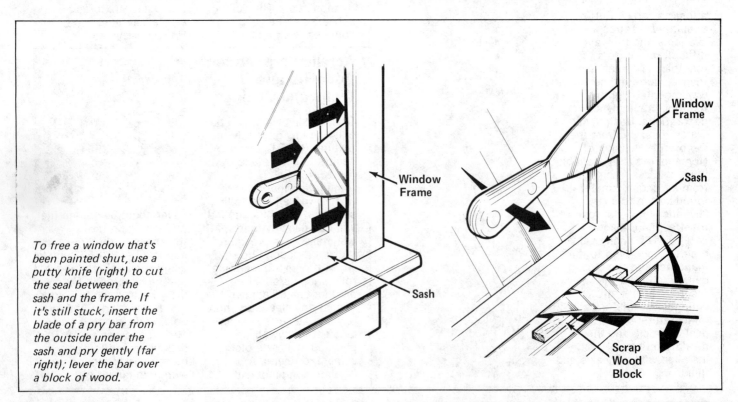

To free a window that's been painted shut, use a putty knife (right) to cut the seal between the sash and the frame. If it's still stuck, insert the blade of a pry bar from the outside under the sash and pry gently (far right); lever the bar over a block of wood.

Window Frame

Sash

Window Frame

Sash

Scrap Wood Block

7. Remove the window sash from the channels.
8. Use a jack plane or jointer plane to remove excess wood from the sides of the wooden sash. Apply sealer to the bare wood.

   Note: You may be able to purchase replacement "channels" for the windows. These are installed after top and bottom window sashes have been removed. The channels are U-shaped tracks in which the sash rides; they are fastened to the side jambs. Installation instructions are furnished with the replacement channel kits.
9. Replace the window sash in its channels, and temporarily install the stop molding.

10. Test the window. If it slides to your satisfaction, remove the molding and the window sash again.
11. Paint the stop molding, giving it two coats. Lightly sand the surface between coats. If the molding is stained, give it two coats of stain, sanding lightly between coats.

    Note: Because the sash is out of the window while the painted or stained molding is drying, cover the open window with plastic sheeting and tape to keep out insects and the weather.
12. After the paint or stain is completely dry, set the window sash back in place and install the molding, using 6d finishing nails.

Product Cleans and Lubricates Windows

A cleaner and lubricant in one package is a handy idea. Window Fixer spray, from Quaker City Manufacturing Co., cleans and lubricates sash channels so that windows won't stick. To use, you wet the sash channel with Window Fixer, which comes in an aerosol can, and wipe away the residue with a soft cloth. Then, you apply a second coat of the product. In a few minutes, it cures to a lubricating film that makes windows easier to open or close.

Lubricate Sash Once a Year

Once every year you should lubricate a window sash along the edges of the stop moldings. One of the best lubricants is a block of paraffin because it doesn't collect dirt and grit, and paraffin is inexpensive. Sash lubrication keeps the window parts moving. Left unlubricated, a window can become stuck so tightly that you may have to pry off the stop to free it.

Heavy-Duty Pry Bar for Stubborn Windows

Some stuck windows require a heavy-duty tool. The Enderes pry bar from Enderes Tool Co., Inc., is just such a tool. Just be sure not to damage wood on or around the window any more than is absolutely necessary when using a pry bar. The tool is made of drop-forged high-carbon tool steel that is heat-treated.

Condensation on Windows

If the window glass inside the house has condensation or "sweat" on it, the problem is cold air entering in or around a storm sash or piece of molding or weatherstripping that doesn't fit properly. If the window glass in a storm window has condensation on it, the problem is a leaky interior window. Check the trim and molding and any weatherstripping that may be causing the air leak.

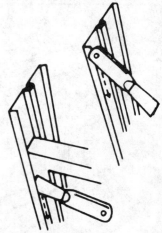

Replacement Sash Channels Can Cure Drafts

If the windows in your home stick shut—or open—or produce lots of drafts, the sash channels may be at fault. The permanent solution to such problems may be Window Fixer replacement channels, made by Quaker City Mfg. Co. The replacement channels, made of aluminum and stainless steel, have a spring-powered center bead that seals out drafts better than ordinary weatherstripping, according to the manufacturer. Also, the channels hold the sash securely in any position, while letting the sash slide smoothly when lifted or closed. The channels fit all double-hung windows with standard 1⅜-inch wood sash with ½-inch parting bead. The channels come in a baked-white enamel finish. Installation instructions are furnished.

Replacing Sash Cords

Materials • Sash Cords or Chain • Small Weights

Tools • Single-Edge Razor Blade • Wide Putty Knife • Pry Bar • Hammer • Utility Knife • Screwdriver

M ANY DOUBLE-HUNG wood windows are operated by a system of cords, pulleys, and weights hidden behind the side jambs of the window. The cords are attached to the top and bottom window sashes, pass over pulleys, and are tied to weights that serve as counterbalances to

Many double-hung windows are operated by a system of cords, pulleys, and weights hidden behind the side jambs of the window.

keep a sash at the level to which it has been raised.

When a sash cord breaks, the weight falls to the bottom of the jamb casing and the window won't stay in a raised position. If the cord is badly frayed, the window can become extremely difficult to open or close.

When a cord on a double-hung window frays or breaks, you can easily replace it with a new cord or, even better, sash chain. Follow these steps:

1. Remove the stop molding from the side of the window where the broken or damaged cord is, but do it carefully or the molding may break. If there's a paint seal along the molding strip, cut it with a single-edge razor blade. Then, use a wide putty knife or a flat pry bar to pry the stop molding off.
2. With the stop strip removed, angle the window sash out of the window frame to expose the sash pocket in which the sash cord is knotted.
   Note: If the broken or damaged cord is in the upper sash of a double-hung window, follow this same procedure, except that you will have to remove the channel parting strip after removing the lower sash, so you can gain access to the upper sash.
3. Untie the knot in the sash cord and remove it from the pocket in the side of the sash frame.
4. Ease the sash out of the channel on the other side of the window, and untie the cord there too. Set the window sash out of the way.
5. Look for the access plates. You should be able to locate them in the lower parts of the channel on both sides of the window. If they're hidden by paint, tap each channel with a hammer until the plates' outlines are revealed. Then, cut along the outlines with a utility knife. Also locate the screws holding the plates in place, and remove them. **Note:** Some windows don't have access plates; if this is the case, you'll have to remove the side jambs and casings to reach the weights inside.
6. With the access plates removed, lift each weight out.
7. Untie the old sash cords and use one to determine the approximate length needed for new sash cords or sash chain.
8. Weight one end of each new cord or chain with something small enough to pass over a pulley, and feed the cords or chain in over the pulleys.
9. When each cord or chain reaches its access plate opening, pull it through the opening.
10. Knot the other end of each cord or chain to prevent it from slipping over its pulley; also remove the small weights on the ends of the cord or chain.
11. Tie one end of each cord or chain to a window sash weight, and put the weights back through the access holes.
12. If you're using sash cord, tie a knot in the

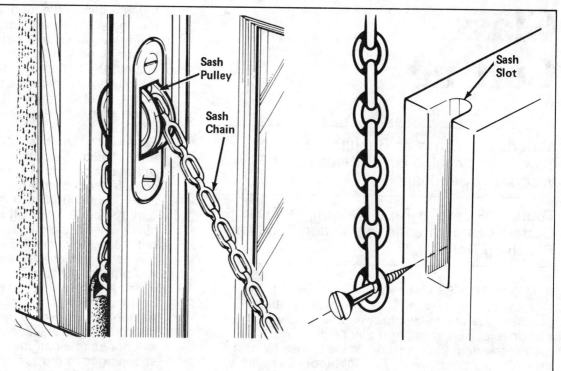

Sash Pulley

Sash Chain

Sash Slot

Before attaching a new sash chain, weight one end and feed it in over the pulley (right). After the chain is attached to the weight, attach the other end to the slot in the side of the sash with a wood screw (far right).

other end of each cord and insert it into the pocket on the sash frame. If you're using sash chain, fasten the end of each chain to the sash frame pockets with screws.

13. Replace the window sash in its channels and hold it against the parting strips as you raise the sash to the top of the window.

14. With the sash raised, check the weights of the access openings; they should be about 3 inches above the window stool; if not, adjust the cords or chain at the sash.

15. After the sash cords or chain have been properly adjusted, replace the access plates and the stop strip.

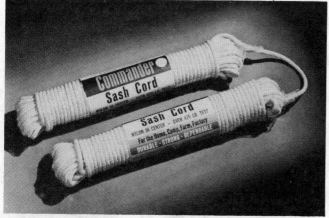

Sash Cord Must Be Strong

After all the trouble you go through to replace a sash cord, it would be a shame were the cord to break in a year or two. Prevent such

disasters by using a strong cord. King Cotton nylon center sash cord, made by the King Cotton Cordage Co., is made to resist extra wear and abrasion. It comes in several thicknesses and in hanks of 50 or 100 feet.

Sash Chain Is a Long-Lasting Alternative

A metal chain is a long-lasting sash cord replacement. The sash chain from Campbell Chain comes in packages

and in rolls. In replacing sash cord with a chain, you use the same weights and the same pulleys. The main installation difference is that you attach the end of the chain to the sash with a wood screw instead of knotting the cord end to hold it in place.

Glass Cutting

Materials • Glass as Required • Paper Towels • Machine Oil or Kerosene • Fine Wet or Dry Sandpaper

Tools • Gloves • Tape Measure • Glass Cutter • Straightedge • Wooden Pencil or Finishing Nails

MOST STORES that sell glass will cut it to your exact specifications. Or, you may be able to purchase standard-size glass panes. If, however, you do a lot of glazing, or if you do your own picture-framing, you can save some money by doing the cutting yourself. With the right tools and a little practice, you should be able to cut glass to size every time—just like a professional.

Follow this procedure:

1. Select a flat surface on which to work, and place the piece of glass on it.

   Caution: Glass edges are very sharp and can cut you quickly. Until you become expert at cutting glass, you should wear tight-fitting gloves that allow you to "feel" the cutter at work, yet protect your fingers.

2. Clean the surface of the glass.
3. Lubricate the tiny wheel on the glass cutter with machine oil or kerosene. You should also brush a film of the lubricant on the glass along the line you intend to cut.
4. Hold the glass cutter between your index and middle fingers, with your index finger resting against the flat area on the handle. Your thumb should be on the handle's bottom side. Grip the cutter firmly but not too tightly.
5. Place a straightedge along the line to be cut, and hold it firmly in place.
6. Position the cutter so that it is almost at a right angle to the glass.
7. Start your cut about ⅛ inch or less from the edge farthest from you. The stroke must be an even flowing motion toward you that continues until the cutter goes off the near edge of the glass. The idea isn't to cut *through* the glass, but merely to *score* it. Experiment with scrap pieces of glass to discover how much pressure you must apply to attain an even scoring. Never let up on the cutter and never go back over the line you score.
8. As soon as you score the glass, make the break. Glass heals, and if you wait too long it will not snap along the line. The idea in snapping is to provide a raised area under the scored line. Some people position the glass so that the cut is along the edge of a table, and then they snap the glass along the table edge. Others place a wooden pencil under the glass and center it on the line, while still others place finishing nails at each end of the scored line. To make the snap, press down on the glass firmly on both sides of the line.
9. Smooth the newly cut edge with fine wet-dry sandpaper.
10. Lubricate the glass cutter before storing it. Keep the wheel of the glass cutter well lubricated between uses, and protect the wheel from anything that might nick or dull it.

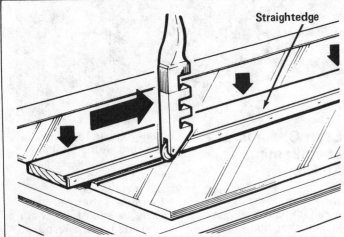

When cutting a piece of glass, apply even pressure, never let up on the cutter, and never go back over the line you score.

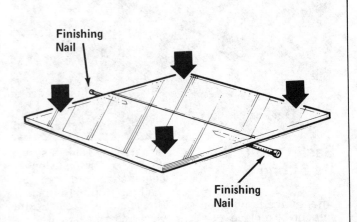

After scoring the glass, you can place a finishing nail at each end. Then, press down on the glass firmly on both sides of the scored line.

Replacing a Broken Pane

Materials • Linseed Oil • Glass Pane • Glazier's Compound or Putty • Glazier's Points or Spring Clips • Paint • Rags

Tools • Stepladder • Hammer • Putty Knife • Propane Torch • Paintbrush • Wire Brush • Tape Measure

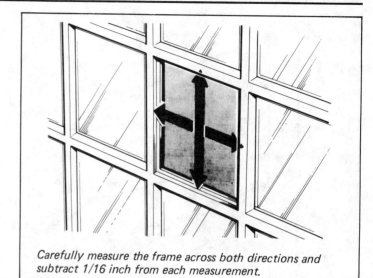

Carefully measure the frame across both directions and subtract 1/16 inch from each measurement.

THE NEXT TIME a window pane is broken, you can easily do the repair job yourself. In fact, window pane replacement is one of the easiest home repair jobs; it requires only a few tools.

Most stores that sell replacement glass will cut the glass to size for you. Or, you can cut the glass yourself. To replace a glass pane, follow this procedure:

1. Remove all the old glass. *Caution: Glass edges are very sharp and can cut you quickly. You should wear gloves to protect your hands.* Be careful as you wiggle the pieces back and forth until you free them. If there are pieces that are too firmly imbedded in the putty to come loose with wiggling, take a hammer and knock them out from inside the room.
2. When the glass has been removed, scrape away all the old putty from the frame. You can soften dried putty by carefully applying heat from a propane torch, or—if you don't have a torch—you can brush the puttied areas with linseed oil and let it soak in. The linseed oil should soften the putty sufficiently to allow you to scrape it away. As you remove the old putty, look for little metal tabs—in a wooden frame—or spring clips—in a metal frame. The tabs, called glazier's points, and clips are important when you install the new pane.
3. Use a wire brush to remove the last traces of putty, and use a paintbrush to coat the wooden area where the putty was with linseed oil.
4. Carefully measure the frame across both directions, and subtract $\frac{1}{16}$ inch from each measurement to compensate for the fact that most frames are not perfect rectangles and for the expansion and contraction of the frame. In

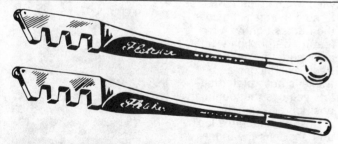

General-Purpose Glass Cutter

Every homeowner should have a glass cutter. The model 01-DC Gold-Tip general-purpose glass cutter, made by the Fletcher-Terry Co., has a cutting wheel made from special steel that the manufacturer says will last longer, and cut easier and smoother; it also offers clean break-outs of glass. For hard glass, such as Cathedral and foreign glass, a hard glass cutter, model 06-DC, is available.

Picking Up Pane Can Be a Pain

After you cut a pane of glass and it's lying flat on the table, how do you pick it up? The easy answer is with a vacuum cup made for this purpose. Red Devil, Inc., makes a single-cup version consisting of a thick rubber disc and channel-type vacuum levers. The base is made of cast aluminum. When properly seated, the cup will hold the glass until the vacuum is broken with the vacuum lever. Red Devil also makes double- and 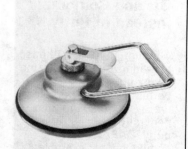 triple-cup models with 4-inch, 5-inch, and 6-inch cups. A vacuum cup helps eliminate the danger of cutting your hand on sharp edges.

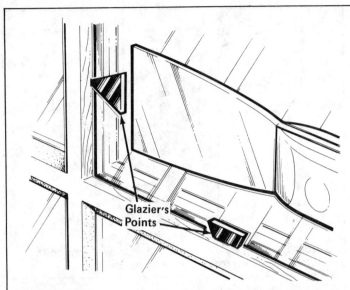

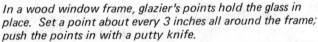

In a wood window frame, glazier's points hold the glass in place. Set a point about every 3 inches all around the frame; push the points in with a putty knife.

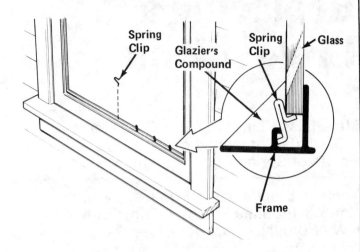

In a metal window frame, the glass is held by spring clips instead of glazier's points. Install the clips by snapping them into the holes in the frame.

fact, if there is a wide lip on the frame, subtract as much as ⅛ inch from the vertical and horizontal measurements.

5. Roll glazier's compound or glazing putty—compound is preferable—between your hands

to form a "string" about the same diameter as a pencil. Press this string of the compound against the outside of the frame where the glass is to fit.

6. When the compound completely covers the lip

Glass Replacement in Window Units

The glass in windows—and doors too—that is prone to breakage should be replaced with tempered glass whenever possible.

Tempered glass is a type of safety glass that breaks into tiny pieces like automobile glass. Danger from severe cuts is lessened considerably. Tempered glass also is stronger than standard single-strength glass.

You Should Use Glazing Compound Instead of Putty

Although putty is still used for window repairs, glazing compound usually works better. It is easier and less messy to work with, and generally outlasts regular putty. DAP '33' glazing compound, for example, works equally well on wood and metal window frames and can even be used on unprimed wood, although a coating of linseed oil over bare wood is recommended. Most importantly, DAP '33,'

made by DAP, Inc., doesn't dry out and harden as putty does, and it takes paint with good results.

Point Driver Speeds Glazing, Picture Framing

The Red Devil model 1602 automatic point driver operates much like a staple gun, except that it drives zinc-coated, diamond metal points into window and picture frames to hold the glass against the frames tightly. A big feature of this lightweight, aluminum tool, made by Red Devil, Inc., is a framer's nose plate that lets you use the tool in any position or at a sharp angle. An adjustable lock unit shortens the trigger stroke for less power. To use the point driver, position the tool flat against the glass or frame backing and squeeze the trigger; a spring drives a point into the wood. It comes with a starter package of ½-inch zinc-coated points.

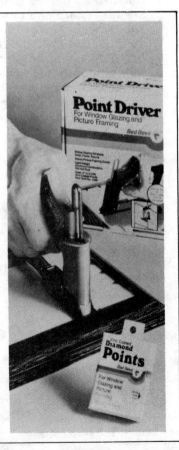

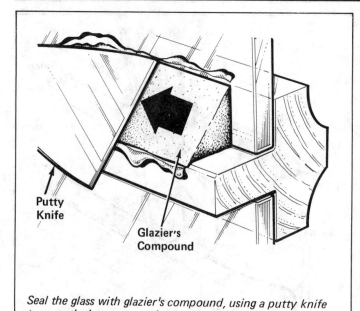

Seal the glass with glazier's compound, using a putty knife to smooth the compound at an angle; match it to the bed of compound on adjacent windows.

of the frame, press the glass in place against the compound. Press firmly, and pay no attention to the fact that some of the compound is pushed out around the frame.

7. With the pane pressed firmly in position, insert glazier's points or spring clips to hold the glass in place. The clips snap in holes, while the points must be pushed into the wood. Use your putty knife to push them in; they need not be pushed in very far. The points should go in about every 3 inches all around the frame.

8. Apply compound around the outside edge of the glass. The object is to make this bed of compound match the others on adjacent windows. The best way is to place blobs of compound all around the glass against the frame, and then use your putty knife to smooth them out at the same bevel or angle. If the putty knife seems to stick to the compound, pulling it away from the glass and frame, dip the knife in linseed oil or even water to stop it from doing so. Or, you can "scour" it by plunging the blade several times in the ground; this will clean the blade. Wipe the blade with a rag.

9. Remove the excess compound from both inside and outside the frame, and put the compound back in the can.

10. Allow the compound to cure for at least three days, and then paint it. Paint all the way from the frame up to the glass, letting a little paint get over on the glass to seal the compound completely between the glass, compound, and frame.

Glass Cutter Has an Iron Handle

Every homeowner should have a glass-cutting tool. The GC glass cutter from Allway Tools has a cast-iron handle with an alloy steel glass-cutting wheel. According to the manufacturer, the durable glass cutter provides easy cutting for almost any type of glass.

Push Points Mean Fewer Broken Windows

Those little triangles called glazier's points have accounted for more than a few broken windows. Many people try to install the points with a few taps of a hammer, but one misplaced tap can break the new pane. Push points from Warner Manufacturing Co. are different because they have a projection that lets you push them into place with the end of your putty knife; no hammer blows are needed and no glass breakage is likely to occur.

Tool for Smooth Glazing Lines

Removing and replacing glazing compound or putty around window sash is easy, but the Window Tool, No. 4044, from Red Devil, Inc., makes the project even easier. It has a V-shaped end that packs, shapes, and trims new glazing, and a flat end that removes the old glazing. The blades of the tool are stainless steel; the handle is made of tough plastic.

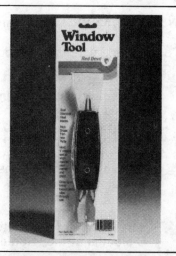

Linseed Oil Makes Glazing Easier

By brushing the frames of windows where the bed of putty or compound will lie with boiled linseed oil, you can prevent the wood from drinking oils from the material. Raw linseed oil, moreover, is great for making old and dry putty workable again. Just add a few drops of raw linseed oil to the unused putty, and then knead it until it is again soft and pliable. Raw linseed oil can even help in the removal of dried and hardened putty on the frame; brush the raw linseed oil over the surface and let it soak in before attempting to chop it out with your chisel.

Screen Replacment

Materials • Short Lengths of 2 × 4's
• Replacement Screen • Staples
• Splining Material

Tools • Putty Knife • Pliers • C-Clamps
• Tape Measure • Staple Gun • Scissors
or Tin Snips • Hammer • Splining Tool

WHEN YOU NOTICE a hole in a screen door or window screen that is too large to patch, the screening should be replaced. Also, if the screen has rusted, it should be replaced.

Many stores sell replacement screening materials in standard sizes for doors and windows. Installation of the new screen isn't difficult, providing the screen frame is still in good condition. The secret to any good rescreening project is getting the screen wire taut.

Working With Wooden Frames

To replace a screen in a wooden frame, follow this procedure:

1. Use a putty knife to remove the molding from around the edges of the damaged screen, but be sure to pry carefully so you don't damage the molding. Leave the brads in the molding.
2. Remove the old screen. Be sure to remove all the old tacks or staples that secured it with pliers.
3. Bow or arch the frame. You can do this by placing a length of 2 × 4 under the top of the screen, one at the bottom, and by using C-clamps at the middle of each side.

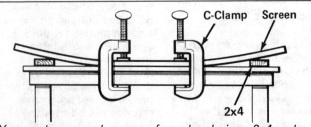

You can bow or arch a screen frame by placing a 2x4 under the top and bottom of the screen, and by using C-clamps at the middle of each side.

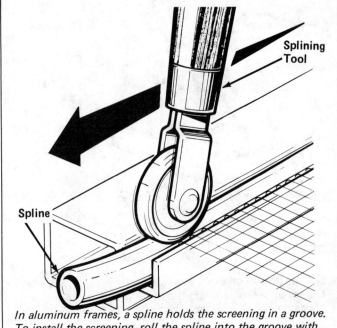

In aluminum frames, a spline holds the screening in a groove. To install the screening, roll the spline into the groove with a splining tool.

4. With the frame arched, use a staple gun to fasten the screen at the top and bottom; stapling is much quicker than tacking. Staple every 2 or 3 inches all along the top and bottom of the frame. Then, staple the sides.
5. When the screen is fastened securely to the frame, remove the clamps. The screen should be very taut as the frame straightens out.
6. Trim off any excess screening or molding.

Working With Aluminum Frames

If the screen frame is aluminum, examine the spline that holds the screening in the frame. If it isn't in good condition, replace it too. Spline is available in many sizes and thicknesses.

To replace a screen in an aluminum frame, follow these steps:

1. Remove the old screen and spline from the frame.
2. Position the new screen over the frame, aligning one end and one side of the screen with the corresponding edges of the frame.
3. Use the end of a splining tool with the convex roller to push the screening down into the groove in the frame, working on the end and side you just aligned. Then do the remaining two sides. The screen should be taut.
4. Use the other end of the splining tool—the concave wheel—to work the spline into the groove all the way around the frame.
5. Trim off any excess screening as close to the spline as possible.

Screen Repairs

Materials • Clear Fingernail Polish or
Shellac • Thin Wire or Nylon Thread
• Screening Material as Required
• Aluminum Foil

Tools • Ice Pick • Small Artist's Brush
• Needle • Clothes Iron

To mend a tiny hole in a metal screen, separate the strands of wire and push them back into place with an ice pick or some other pointed tool or object to close the hole.

NO MATTER WHAT type of screening—metal or fiberglass—you have, it alway seems to develop holes somehow. Patching is the easy solution to the problem. However, this depends on the size of the hole. If the hole is large, the screening should be replaced, not patched. But if the hole is small, a patch will do. Follow this procedure:

1. For a tiny hole, use an ice pick or some other pointed tool or object to move as many wire strands as possible back toward the hole. If

none of the wire strands are torn, you can close the hole back up and make the screen as good as new.
2. If there are torn wire strands, close up the hole by painting over it with clear nail polish or shellac. Brush on a coat and let it dry; then keep applying more coats until the hole has been sealed.
3. If the damage is a long rip, you may need to stitch it back together. Once again, close the gap with a sharp-pointed tool, and then use a strand of wire or a strong nylon thread to bind

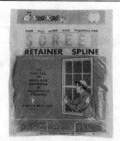

Spline for Aluminum Screen May Need Replacing

When replacing wire or fiberglass screening in screens with aluminum frames, check the spline, which holds the screen to the frame. It may be time to replace the spline too. Frost-King screen retainer spline is made by Thermwell Products Co., Inc. The 5/32-inch spline is packaged in a 25-foot-long roll.

Dowel Can Secure Screen Frames at the Joints

Wooden screen frames often break at the frame joints where the sides meet the top and bottom members. You can use a metal mending plate to secure the joint, but a better way is with dowels. Clamp the loose joint tightly. With a brace and bit or a bit locked in the chuck of a portable electric drill, bore a hole through the side member into the top or bottom member. Cut a dowel that is the length of the hole. Then insert the dowel with glue and trim off any protruding part. The dowel will hold the joint tight and won't be visible.

Fix Up Screens With Splining Tool

You could use a screwdriver to push the spline into an aluminum screen's frame, but a splining tool does the job better. An inexpensive device, the splining tool consists of two rollers with a handle in between. One roller is used to push the screen down into the track of the frame, while the other inserts the spline that holds the screen in the groove. If the spline in your aluminum screen frames is worn or damaged, replace it with spline of the correct diameter. Frost-King's spline and splining tool, products of Thermwell, Inc., can take care of most aluminum screen problems.

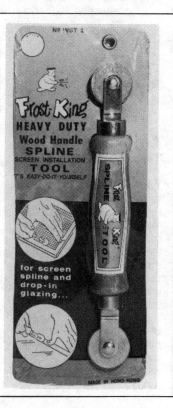

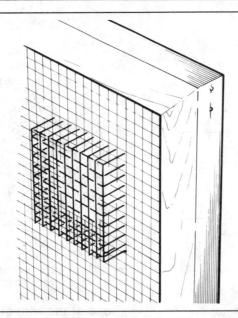
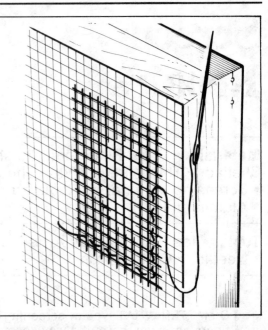

To patch metal screening, remove the edge wires of a patch to make a fringe. Bend the fringe wires at a right angle and press the patch over the hole (right). Fold the fringe toward the center of the patch on the other side, and stitch around the patch with nylon thread.

up the gap. A needle will make the sewing go quicker, and a few coats of clear nail polish or shellac will prevent unraveling.

4. For a bigger hole, cut a square—at least 2 inches bigger than the hole all the way around—from a scrap piece of screening.

5. Pick away at the strands of wire on all four sides to leave about ½ inch of unwoven strands sticking out.

6. Fold the unwoven edges forward—at a 90-degree angle—and insert these wires into the screen over the hole.

7. Fold the unwoven strands toward the center of the patch on the other side, and stitch around the patch with a needle and nylon thread. Once again, apply a few coats of clear nail polish or shellac to seal the patch and stitching in place.

8. Repair fiberglass screening by laying a patch of the material over the hole and running a hot clothes iron around the edges. The heat melts and fuses the patch in place. Be sure to place a scrap of foil over the screen itself to prevent the iron from touching it.

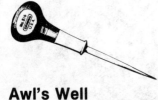

Awl's Well That Ends Well

You need a sharp pointed tool for many screen repairs. General Hardware Manufacturing Company offers a trio of scratch awls, all with blades of hardened and ground tool steel. Awls of this quality, of course, can serve many more purposes than just repairs. They can be used to create starter holes for screws in soft wood and for lining up and marking screw and bolt holes.

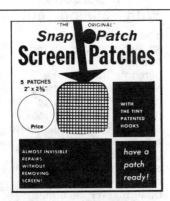

Screen Patches Snap in Place

If you don't have scraps of screening on hand for patching material, you can buy a kit. The Screen Patch Company markets Snap-Patch, small patches that are ready for installation. They consist

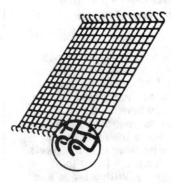

of regular screening in 2- by 2⅜-inch segments, but the ends of the patch wires have tiny hooks that snap into place over the hole in the existing screen. Once the Snap-Patch is in place, it is virtually invisible. Sold in packages of five, Snap-Patch come in either aluminum or galvanized screening.

Flat Screening Reduces Sun's Heat

Most metal and fiberglass screening is ribbed, but Phiferglass SunScreen, which is woven from a vinyl-coated yarn, is flat. This, according to the manufacturer, Phifer Wire Products, Inc., makes for a stable screening that reduces the possibility of damage. The company also says that SunScreen can reduce the amount of solar heat gain by up to 70 percent. The product is easily adapted to most standard window and framing systems. SunScreen is available in charcoal, silver-gray, bronze, chaqua, gold, and white colors.

Window Shades

Materials • Rag • Cardboard Shims • Medium Sandpaper • Graphite Powder or Dry Lubricant

Tools • Stepladder • Pliers • Screwdriver • Hammer

A NY SHADE that refuses to go up or down and stay up, down, or in any position you put it, is a problem. Some shades are so wound up that they could almost lift you off the ground, while others are so slack they fail to go up at all. In most cases, the remedy is just a matter of adjustment; but to know how to adjust a shade properly, you should understand how one works.

Look at the wooden roller. One end is hollow with a concealed coil spring in it. There is a pin at each end of the roller; the one at the spring end is flat and rotates, winding or unwinding the spring. When you pull the shade down, the spring winds tight. When you stop pulling, a little lever—the pawl—falls in place against a ratchet at the spring end of the roller. The pawl prevents the spring from winding the shade back up. When you want to raise the shade, you tug down slightly on the shade, moving the pawl away from the ratchet and allowing the spring to carry the shade back up. Now that you know how a shade works, you should have no problem in figuring out what you have to do to adjust it.

Follow this procedure:

1. The shade that refuses to go back up as far as you would like usually lacks sufficient spring tension. To increase the tension, pull the shade down about two revolutions of the roller, and then remove the flat pin from its bracket. Now roll the shade up by hand. When you get it all the way up, put the flat pin back in its bracket and test the tension. If the shade still won't go up far enough, repeat this procedure until the spring tension is just right.
2. If the shade has too much tension, take the flat pin out of its bracket while the shade is up, and unroll it by hand about two revolutions; then return the pin to its bracket and test the shade. Repeat if necessary until the tension is just right.

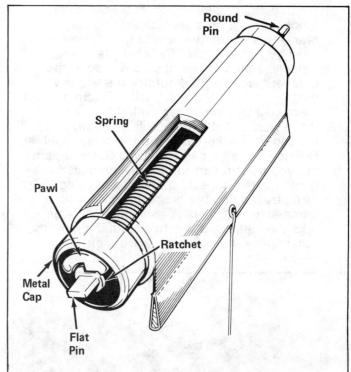

The shade is operated by a spring inside the roller. At the roller's flat-pin end, a pawl-and-ratchet mechanism stops the movement of the spring when the shade is released.

3. If the shade fails to stay down, the pawl is not catching for some reason. Remove the metal cap from the flat-pin end of the roller; then clean the pawl-and-ratchet mechanism.
4. A shade that wobbles when it goes up or down usually has a bent pin. Apply gentle pressure with pliers to straighten a bent pin.

Window Shades Can Save Energy

There are window shades that can reduce heat gain in summer and heat loss in winter. Properly installed Energy Guard shades from the Clopay Corp. can reduce heat gain by as much as 66 percent and heat loss up to 24 percent, the company says. Energy Guard shades are available in four widths: 37¼, 46¼, 55¼, and 73¼ inches. All shades are 6 feet long. The shades are made from white, light-blocking and linen-embossed vinyl, and they are mounted on an adjustable steel roller.

5. When a shade falls out of its brackets, the brackets must be moved closer together. If the brackets are mounted inside the window casing, glue a shim to the brackets. Usually, a piece of cardboard will do. If the brackets are mounted outside the window casing, you can either reposition them or bend them slightly toward each other.

6. If the shade binds, the problem usually is caused by brackets that are too close together. Outside brackets can be moved farther apart, but you must resort to other techniques for those mounted inside the window casing. First, try tapping the brackets lightly with a hammer. If that doesn't move them enough, take the metal cap and fixed round pin off the roller, and sand down the wood a bit.

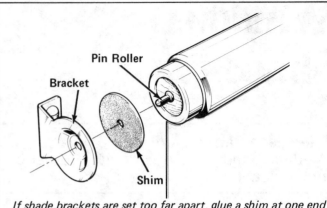

If shade brackets are set too far apart, glue a shim at one end between the bracket and the roller; add more shims as needed at both brackets.

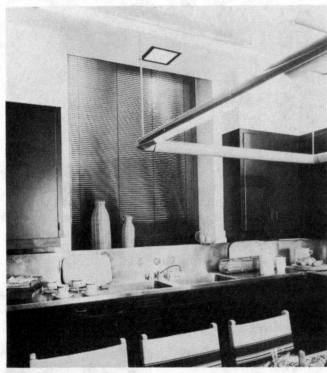

Window Blinds Made to Absorb or Reflect Sun's Heat and Light

Window blinds can contribute to conserving energy in the home. The Cryotherm blind, a new mini-slat blind made by Levolor Lorentzen, Inc., is designed to absorb or reflect its sun's rays or reflect its heat. The blinds are normally finished with a light-absorbing black color on one side, and a light-reflecting bright finish on the other. There are, however, seven options—a bright metallic finish on both sides through convex/concave, concave/convex combinations of a bright finish with brushed aluminum, low-gloss black, or alabaster. The blinds can be made for installation inside or outside the window frame, and can be perforated or striped.

Screening Can Block Glare From the Sun

Screening can be used to block glare from the sun. Hanover's Imperial alodized aluminum screening is almost invisible from the inside, yet reduces the sun's glare by as much as 30 percent, according to Hanover Wire Cloth, the manufacturer. The screening also is highly resistant to mortar stains, if you have a brick or block home. The company's Alodine treatment reduces oxidation of the aluminum screening strands, which helps increase the life of the product. The screening is installed the same way as any window screening. Other Hanover screening available includes Staralum Alclad aluminum, Starlife electro-galvanized steel, Starbrite commercial bronze, Starglas fiberglass, and stainless steel.

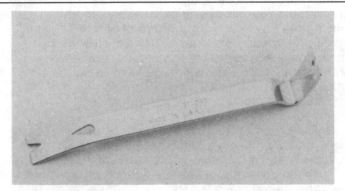

Every Toolbox Should Include Pry Bar

There should be a pry bar in every toolbox. The Easco Dyna-Mo pry bar is a heavy-duty model, and yet it is only 14½ inches long. Made of spring-tempered forged steel, it has an ideal shape for prying away window sash but can also be used for other lifting and prying chores. The tool, made by Easco Tools, Inc., features a tiny notch for pulling hard-to-reach nail heads. It is covered by a warranty against defects in workmanship and materials.

Drapery Hardware

Materials • Drapery or Curtain Rods and Hardware • Cardboard • Plastic Wall Anchors or Expansion Bolts • Screws

Tools • Stepladder • Tape Measure • Carpenter's Level • Pencil • Scissors • Scratch Awl • Drill and Bit

SOMETIMES, WHEN you try to hang curtain or drapery rods, they wind up sagging at one end. If you fail to solve this problem, the whole unit may fall off its brackets when you open or close the drapes. There are ways to hang standard and traverse rods faster, easier, and better.

Hanging Curtain and Drapery Rods

To hang curtain or drapery rods so that they stay in place and operate as they should, follow these steps:

1. If the rod will be attached to a wooden window frame, use the frame as a guide for getting the rod up straight. You can position the end brackets at the outside corners of the frame and install a center brace—if required—at the frame's center. Make sure that the screws you use to hang drapery or curtain rods are at least ¾ inch long.
2. If there is no window frame to use as a guide, or if you want the draperies out away from the actual opening, measure out laterally from the top of the opening and make a mark. Then measure from the mark to the ceiling. Repeat the procedure for the other side to determine the bracket locations. Place each bracket in position, and mark where the screws will go. Check the position of the brackets with a level.
3. Drill pilot holes for the screws at the spots you marked on the wall. If the wall is hollow, use plastic wall anchors or expansion bolts. If there are wall studs where you want to hang the brackets, use screws that are long enough to go through the wallcovering and into the studs.
4. Attach as many center support brackets as are needed to prevent the rod from sagging.
5. Adjust the end brackets and center supports

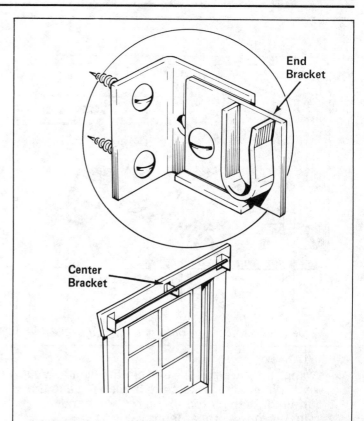

Mount drapery rods on brackets at the top of the frame. Use center brackets for rods that are more than 48 inches long.

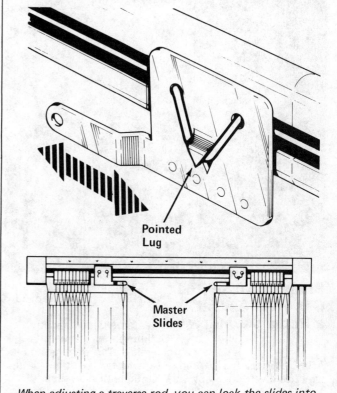

When adjusting a traverse rod, you can lock the slides into operation by hooking the loop on the second master slide over the pointed lug.

Windows

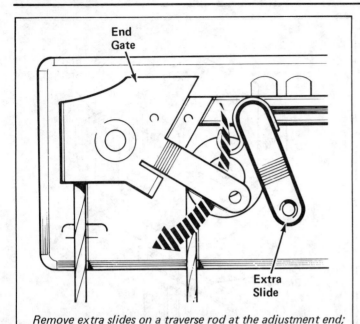

Remove extra slides on a traverse rod at the adjustment end; push the gate down, pull the slides out, and replace the gate.

so that they are as far out from the wall as you want. When all brackets are in place, place the curtain or drapery rod in the brackets and adjust it to the proper length.

Adjusting Traverse Rods

Traverse rods should be installed so that when you hang the draperies and pull them, panels on both sides will open at the same time and go all the way to the ends. Similarly, when you close them, you want the rod to carry the drapery panels back to the center and not leave a gap in the middle. Here is how to adjust a traverse rod to draw the drapes properly:

1. Lift the rod out of the brackets and lay it on the floor face down.
2. Pull the outer cord at the side to bring the master slide on that side all the way over as far as it will go toward the cord.
3. While holding the cord tight, manually slide the other master slide over as far as it will go.
4. On this second slide there is a loop of cord running through two holes. Lift the loop and hook it over the lug just below it.
5. Now replace the rod back in the brackets and lock it in place. Insert drapery hooks through the plastic slides, and remove any extra slides at the end gate.
6. Test the draperies to see if you have made the adjustments properly. If necessary, repeat the procedure.

Brass Traverse Rod Can Help Accent a Room's Window

After redecorating a room, why not give its windows a new look? The Summit traverse rod, made by the Kirsch Co., will accent draw draperies on windows ranging from 30 to 170 inches wide. It features wide-spaced fluting and sceptered finials. The traverse rod is available in a bright or an antique brass finish, at curtain and drapery shops, department stores, and other outlets.

Use Screws to End Wobbly Brackets

Curtain rod brackets fastened to window casings with small nails get loose and pull out over a period of time. Instead of constantly re-driving the nails, which can be quite a job because you can't get a full swing with a tack hammer, use small screws. The screws not only hold better longer, they're easier to drive especially if the screwdriver has a screw-starter attachment.

Push-Pin Hangers Are Decorative

A rose, an eagle, a fleur-de-lis, and other traditional designs have been incorporated into push-pin hangers that will secure almost any lightweight object. You simply push the Homecraft decorative pins into the wall and hang the object on the hook that is a part of the design. The tempered-steel pin is strong enough to be hammered into hard plaster walls if your fingers are not powerful enough. Each package has three hangers in a gilt or antique brass finish. Each hanger is about 1⅜ inches. The product is made by Gries Dynacast, a division of Coats & Clark, Inc.

Venetian Blinds

Materials • Venetian Blind Cord • Ladder Tape • Staples

Tools • Pencil and Paper • Pliers • Scissors • Stepladder • Staple Gun

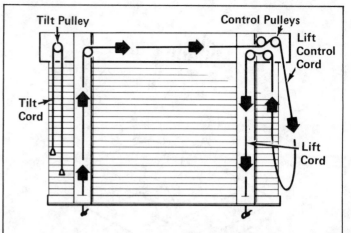

The lift cord is threaded up one side of the blind, over a pulley, across the top and through the control pulleys, and then down the other side. A loop of cord from the control pulleys forms the lift control. The tilt cord is separate.

ALTHOUGH YOU may have trouble adjusting venetian blinds, you'll find the job of repairing them is a relatively simple task.

The two major venetian blind problems involve the ladder tape, or webbing, and cords. These components are prone to becoming broken or frayed. Because replacements are readily available and easy to install, most venetian blind problems are really not major ones at all.

There are two sets of cords. One set, called the "lift cord system," raises and lowers the blinds. The other, called the "tilt cord system," changes the amount of light coming in by altering the angle at which the blinds tilt. Most replacement kits come with both sets of cords, and it is a good idea to change both cord sets at the same time.

Replacing the Cords

To replace venetian blind cords, follow this procedure:

1. Make a sketch of the venetian blinds to help you get the cords back in their proper places.
2. Open the blinds so the slats are horizontal.
3. Start with the lift cord by examining the knots under the tape at the bottom of the bottom rail. The tape may be stapled on, or—if the rail is metal—it may be held in place by a clamp. Untie the knots and remove the cord by pulling on the loop as if you were going to raise the blinds.
4. Starting at the side next to the tilt cord, feed the new cord through from the bottom up through the openings in the slats. Be sure that the cord goes on alternate sides of the ladder tape, or webbing, as you feed it in.
5. Go up to and over the pulley at the top of the blinds.
6. Run the cord along the top until you reach the mechanism at the other side. Thread the cord *under* the first and *over* the second pulley.

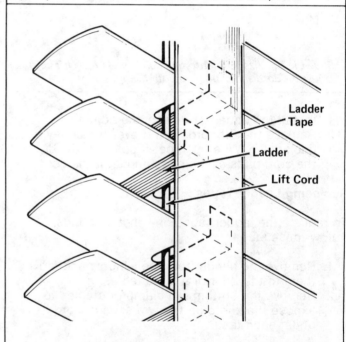

Thread the lift cord between the front and back ladder tapes, on alternating slides of the connecting strips.

7. Bring the cord down through the lift cord locking device.
8. Go back and knot the other end of the cord, and then pull the cord until the knot is nearly against the bottom rail.
9. Feed the unknotted end of the cord back into the top rail, over the other pulley or pulleys, and down through the slats in the same manner as you did on the other side.
10. When you get the cord all the way through, adjust it to set the size of the loop. Then snip off the excess cord from the unknotted end before tying the knot.

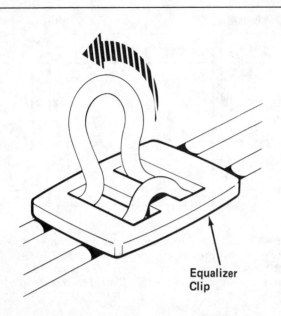

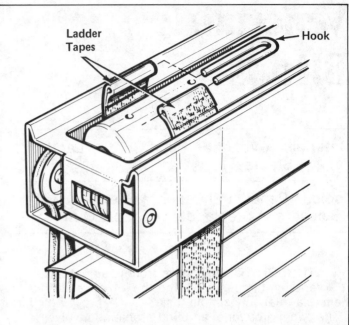

Ladder Tapes

Hook

Slide the equalizer clip onto the looped end of the lift cord; adjust the cord and clip for smooth lifting.

At the top of the blind, slide the hooks into the sleeves in the front and back ladder tapes at the tilt tube.

11. Install the equalizer device and adjust it.
12. Replace the tilt cord. Run it over the pulley and back down. When you get it positioned, add the cord pulls at the ends and knot the cord.

Replacing Ladder Tapes

To replace the ladder tapes on venetian blinds, follow these steps:

1. Remove the blinds from the window and move them to the floor or a large table.
2. Remove the bottom rail clamp or staples to expose the knots on the two ends of cord under each tape.

3. Untie the knots and pull the cords up through the slots all the way up to the top of the blinds.
4. The slats will now come out of the tapes; remove them.
5. Unhook the top of the tape from the tilt tube by removing the hook.
6. Hook in the new tape at the tilt tube.
7. Insert the slats in the new tapes.
8. Weave the cord back through the slots, making sure that the cord goes on alternate sides of the ladder tapes.
9. Knot the cord under the bottom rail.
10. Replace the clamp or staple the ends of the tapes.

If Blind Repairs Leave You in Dark, Get a Kit

There are kits designed to tackle venetian blind problems. The Venetian Blind Renew Kit from Globe Products Corp. will handle just about any problem that can afflict your blinds. Consisting of 11 feet of plastic tape with cross-slat holders, 27 feet of cord, a pair of plastic pulls, and a metal equalizer, the kit allows you to renew anything on blinds up to 64 inches long. Another kit is made for blinds up to 72 inches long. On the back of the kit are instructions covering disassembly of the blinds, removal of the old tape and cord, and the subsequent reassembly. No special tools are required. A pair of scissors can take care of everything, unless the new tape must be stapled to the bottom rail.

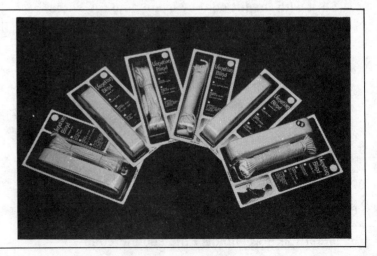

Window Blinds With a New Slant

Window blinds help you conserve energy and they provide privacy and light control. Levolor Lorentzen, Inc., offers vertical aluminum blinds in 115 colors and in 35 fabric coverings. The blinds may be ordered so vanes stack to the left or right, or to both left and right. The blinds have cord controls for both traversing and tilting, or a cord for the traverse and a clear plastic wand for the tilt. According to Levolor Lorentzen, the blinds may be mounted inside or outside a window's frame. If a vane becomes misaligned, simply closing and reopening the blind will correct it.

Stained Glass Cutter Has Replaceable Wheels

Stained glass is extremely hard so it's difficult to cut. With the heavy-duty Gold-Tip stained glass cutter, made by the Fletcher-Terry Co., the job is easier because you have full-wheel visibility and a handle that has been designed for heavy-duty cutting. The wheel unit of the tool is offset at the end of the cutter head; you can see the cut whether it is straight or curved. The cutter's tapered wheel unit also can be replaced when it becomes worn. Two wheel units are available—carbide-tapered or steel-tapered. Both models have a wheel unit with a 134-degree hone angle.

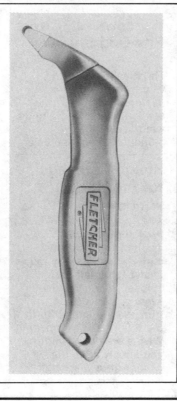

Nail Set Sinks Nail Heads

Nails should be hidden. The tool for driving the nail heads below the surface of wood is called a nail set. Nail sets come in various sizes, and it is important to match the point of the nail set to the head of the nail; otherwise, you can damage the wood while trying to hide the nail. The Mayhew nail set, made by Mayhew Steel Products, Inc., is made of high-grade tempered steel. It has a knurled body with a polished point and a square head.

Covers to Fit Most Window Wells

Window well covers keep snow, rain, and debris out of the wells and help prevent window well accidents to children and pets. Wind-O-Cove window well covers, from BQP Industries, Inc., range in size from 40 inches long by 15 inches wide to 60 inches long by 22 inches wide to fit most window wells. The covers, which are made of heavy-duty butyrate plastic, are mounted to the rim of the metal well insert.

Device Makes Even Large Windows Easier to Open

Do you have to wrestle with your windows to open them? Quaker Power Lifters are designed to provide added lift so window sashes—even large windows—can be opened or closed more easily. The product, made by Quaker City Mfg. Co., features glass-filled nylon pulley assemblies to give a friction-free, noise-free operation. According to the manufacturer, an integral cord guide eliminates tangles; the cord used is 180-pound-

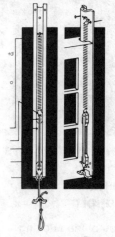

test pre-stretched Dacron. Power Lifters, however, can only be installed on windows with plowed sashes.

Frame Your Blinds?

Have you thought about framing window blinds? The "Definition" frame by Levolor Lorentzen, Inc., consists of 1-inch-wide aluminum strips that may be joined to a window blind's top brackets to match or contrast with its slats. When matched by a valance and bottom rail, the slats form a complete frame around the blinds. The frame can be installed on new or already installed blinds. The "Definition" frame, according to the

manufacturer, helps to reduce drafts.

Repairs for Leaded Glass

Leaded glass windows require little maintenance, but in time the leading "stretches," causing the glass to pull away from the metal. To make repairs, you can apply a neutral-colored glazing compound in the tiny crack between the lead and the glass. This joint, however, should be cleaned thoroughly with a toothbrush before the glazing goes into the joint. The lead channels also can be soldered, but this is an exacting and time-consuming job. You can use 60/40 solid-core solder with oleic acid flux. You can also use a universal flux for all metals.

Planing Windows Is a Job That Needs Support

If you plane sticking window sashes, or cut doors to size, you need support. For this kind of job, McCoy Industries, Inc., has sawhorses that are solidly built of western wood. The sawhorses are packaged ready to assemble. The wood is smoothly finished with pre-drilled, countersunk holes; all screws are included. You only need a Phillips-head screwdriver to assemble the sawhorses, which come in three sizes.

Devices Can Replace Sash Cords

When a sash cord breaks, you can replace it with new cord, sash chain, or with one of several window remodeling kits on the market. These kits replace the cord-pulley-weight arrangement. One is a tubular spring device. Another is a tape-and-roller assembly; the tape is fastened to the window sash and is wound up in a roller in the side jamb of the window channel. Still another alternative is a window channel kit. With this kit, you replace the sash stops with a channel unit in which the window sash moves; the channel unit puts tension on the sash so it may be raised and stopped wherever you wish. The above products are usually sold as "sash balances," "spring lifts" or "spring tapes." All three products come with installation instructions.

Window Well Cover Fits Odd Shapes

The Plaskolite, Inc., window well cover is designed to fit semicircular or rectangular window wells as well as standard types. The clear-plastic cover is ribbed for extra strength and rigidity. The product can be mounted to brick, wood, or masonry with small brackets. It may be left over the window well in the summer to prevent heat gain and save on air conditioning bills.

Rough Openings for Pre-Hung Windows

Pre-hung windows, available at most building material outlets, are much easier to install than "piece" windows where every part has to be trimmed and nailed to fit the rough window opening. With a pre-hung window, you simply slide the window into the rough opening, shim the header, sill, and jambs, and nail the window into position. Rough opening margins for pre-hung windows are from about 1 to 1½ inches from the jambs and header. For example, if you were installing a 3-foot-wide window, the rough opening would have to be about 39 inches wide—1½ inches per side. This extra space gives plenty of room for shimming and leveling the window.

Hanging an Interior Door

Materials • Door and Door Hardware • Fine Sandpaper • Wooden Wedges • Finishing Nails • Cardboard • Stop Molding • Wood Putty • Wood Sealer or Other Finish • Cedar Shingle Shims

Tools • Stepladder • Tape Measure • Pencil • Sawhorses • Crosscut Saw • Straightedge • C-Clamps or Hand Screws • Jack or Jointer Plane • Sanding Block • Butt Marker • Hammer • Wide Butt Chisel or Utility Knife • Screwdriver • Miter Box and Backsaw • Nail Set • Carpenter's Level • Paintbrush

HANGING A DOOR is an exacting job that must be done correctly for the door to open and close properly. If you are replacing a door and take your time, the job isn't very difficult. If you are installing a new door, for example in a new partition wall, you might consider a pre-hung door so you don't have to build the door frame yourself; a pre-hung door comes with a frame.

Replacing a Door

Before buying a door, measure the inside of the door opening exactly, top to bottom and jamb to jamb. Be sure to measure between the side jambs of the frame—not between the stops. Allow ⅛-inch clearance at the top of the door and ¼-inch clearance at the bottom. If the door will open or close over carpeting, allow ⅞-inch clearance at the bottom. Subtract this clearance from the measured top-to-bottom height of the opening. Allow ⅛-inch clearance at each side; subtract ¼ inch from the measured side-to-side width of the opening.

To install the door, follow these steps:

1. Place the door across sawhorses and cut off the stile extensions, if any, at the top.
2. Cut off enough at the bottom of the door to provide the necessary clearance in the door opening.
3. With a pencil, draw a line parallel to the latch edge of the door to indicate how much must

be trimmed off so the width of the door is exact.

4. Place the door on the floor—hinge-edge down—and clamp the door to a workbench solidly; it must be perfectly vertical.
5. With a jack or jointer plane, plane the latch edge of the door down almost to the pencil line. Before you plane down to the line, however, set the door in the opening to make sure the planed edge is parallel to the jamb; the jamb, of course, should be properly set. If the edge of door isn't parallel to the jamb, mark the edge of the door accordingly, and finish planing.
6. After you have planed the door to the correct size, bevel, or chamfer, the latch edge of the door backward very slightly to allow it to clear the jamb as the door swings open and shut.
7. Round off all of the door's corner edges slightly to prevent them from splintering, and sand all surfaces smooth; use fine-grit sandpaper on a sanding block.
8. Set the door in the opening and force it tight against the hinge jamb by driving a wooden wedge into the gap on the latch side.

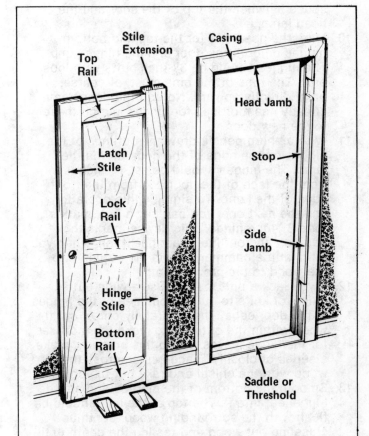

Before buying a door, measure the inside of the door opening exactly, top to bottom and jamb to jamb. Be sure to measure between the side jambs — not between the stops.

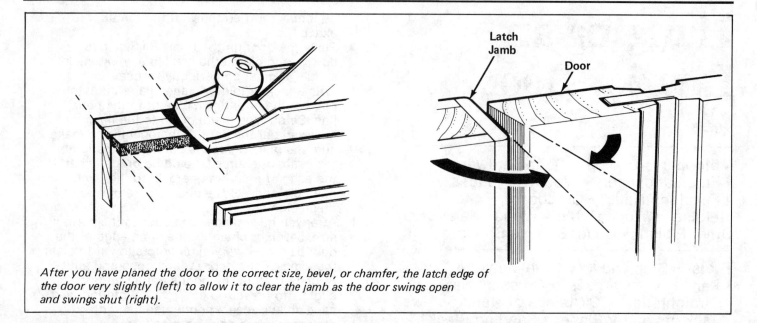

After you have planed the door to the correct size, bevel, or chamfer, the latch edge of the door very slightly (left) to allow it to clear the jamb as the door swings open and swings shut (right).

9. Lay a 6d nail across the top of the door and drive a wooden wedge under the door until the nail is snug against the head jamb; this procedure provides the proper amount of space between the top of the door and the head jamb.

10. Mark the positions for the top and bottom hinges on both the door and the hinge jamb. The hinges should be 3½-inch butts with loose pins. The tops of the pins must, of course, point directly upward. **Note:** If the door frame already has mortises for hinges, match these to the new door.

11. With a sharp pencil, draw the outlines of the hinges on the edge of the door and on the jamb. The hinges should be set 1⅛ inches in from the face of the door and from the front edge of the jamb. To simplify this operation and the next one, you can buy a butt marker for a 3½-inch hinge. This device marks the position and outline of a hinge; then, when you hit it with a hammer, it cuts the outline into the wood to the proper depth.

12. If you lack a butt marker, use a wide butt chisel or knife to cut the outlines of the hinges in the door edge. Then, carefully chisel out the wood within the outlines to make the mortises for the hinge leaves. To do this properly, make a series of closely spaced cuts across the wood with the chisel and rake out the chips.

13. Smooth the bottom of the mortise and set the hinge leaf into it. The top of the leaf should be flush with the surrounding wood; continue chiseling out wood and testing the depth until the leaf is flush with the surface.

14. After you complete the mortises in the jamb and in the edge of the door, take the hinges apart and screw the leaves firmly into the door edge. Screw the other leaves into the jamb, but drive in only one screw per leaf; don't make the holes for the other screws yet.

15. Set the door into the opening and fit the hinge leaves together. If they fail to fit, loosen the jamb leaves slightly and try again. If you still cannot make them fit, adjust the jamb leaves up or down in the jamb as necessary.

16. When you get the right fit, slip the hinge pins into the hinges. Then, finish driving the remaining screws into the jamb.

17. If the door strikes the latch jamb when you push it closed or if there is too much of a gap between the door and the latch jamb, loosen the screws in the jamb and insert narrow cardboard shims under the leaves. A shim placed under the inner edge of a hinge forces the door away from the latch jamb; placed under the outer edge (pin edge), the shim forces the door toward the latch jamb. The thicker the shims, of course, the greater the movement of the door.

18. Step into the room and pull the door shut. Draw pencil lines on the jambs around the sides and top of the door.

19. Cut stops to fit around the door, position them along the pencil lines, and tack them to the jambs temporarily.

20. Close the door against the stop moldings. If the door fits snugly against them, nail the stops, and countersink the nail heads with a nail set. If the stops don't fit snugly against the door, remove the tack nails and reposition the moldings. The door must be plumb—vertically level—in the opening to swing properly; make sure it's plumb before you nail the stops.

21. Fill any nail holes with wood putty and finish

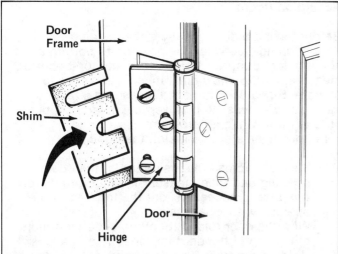

To shim a hinge, loosen the screws on the door frame side. Cut a shim from thin cardboard, with slots to fit around the screws, and slide it behind the hinge.

the moldings and door—including the edges—with sealer, stain, paint, varnish, shellac, or whatever finish you wish. The entire door must be sealed or the door will warp.

Pre-Hung Doors

Pre-hung doors are the easiest to install. These doors come already set in a frame, and one side of the frame has been trimmed with molding. Usually, the hardware has been installed, too, making installation even easier. To buy a pre-hung door, you need to know the size of the rough door opening. There are approximately 3 inches at the side jambs and 1½ inches at the head jamb for fitting purposes. To install a pre-hung door, follow this procedure.

1. Set the pre-hung door into the rough opening, and plumb—make vertically level—the jamb sides, filling any gaps at the top and sides with cedar shingle shims.
2. Nail the head and side jambs to the rough framing, using 16d finishing nails. Countersink the nail heads into the face of the jambs. Fill the holes with wood putty.
3. Nail the furnished casing or molding to the doorway with 10d finishing nails; countersink the nail heads. Fill the heads with wood putty.
4. Apply wood sealer to both sides of the door and the top, bottom, and side edges. Seal the casing and door moldings, too.

Seal the Entire Door to Stop Warp

Doors can warp very badly unless the entire door is sealed with paint, stain, varnish, shellac, or other finish. Don't seal just one side of the door; the back and front, and all edges must be coated with a sealer to prevent warping. The type of sealer really doesn't matter. Its purpose is to stop moisture from penetrating the wood.

Unfinished Interior Doors Made of Pine

Interior doors in your home need not be plain-looking. There's a style of door available that can add much to a room's decor. Wing Industries, Inc., has a series of Early American or Colonial design interior doors that are doweled and glued with top cross, lock, and bottom rails and stiles. The model 4030 Colonial-style doors have a height of 80 inches and a thickness of 1⅜ inches. The model 4040 Early American door is 1⅜-inch thick and 80 inches high. On all model doors, the height to the center of the lock rail from the bottom of the door is 36 inches.

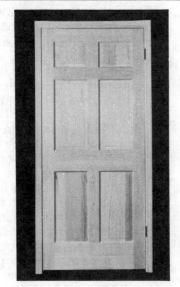

Lock rail dowels are on 3-inch centers. The doors are made from unfinished pine.

Professional-Type Miter Box for Home Craftsman

The home craftsman, who enjoys construction projects as well as repair tasks, should own a quality miter box; an inexpensive plastic or wooden miter box is only suitable for the occasional job. Hempe Manufacturing Co., Inc., makes a series of miter boxes ranging from economy to professional models. Hempe's model 36241 professional miter box is precision-machined for accurate work. It features a roller guide system for precise mitering. The miter box has saw hangers that can hold a backsaw in the "up" position, a bracket that can be used on either end of the box for clamping and cut-offs, and a lever that locks the pivoting arm at any angle from 45 degrees right to 45 degrees left. The miter box measures 18 inches long, 13 inches wide, and 14 inches high. The box comes with a 4- by 24-inch, 11-point backsaw.

Hanging a Folding Door

Materials • Folding Door and Mounting Hardware • Scrap Wood

Tools • Tape Measure • Pencil • Hacksaw • Drill and Bits • Screwdriver • Hammer • Chisel • Rubber Mallet • Plumb Bob • Handsaw

IF YOU NEED a door where there just isn't room for it to open, you might install a folding door. It can be an accordion door, which takes no more space than the depth of the door frame, or a bi-fold door, which uses only half the space of a regular door.

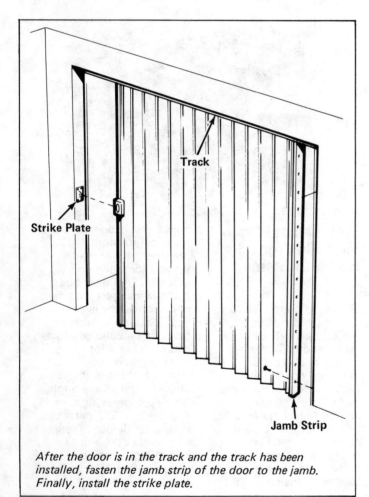

After the door is in the track and the track has been installed, fasten the jamb strip of the door to the jamb. Finally, install the strike plate.

Accordion Doors

Before buying a door, measure the inside of the door opening—between jambs—top to bottom and side to side. Subtract ½ inch from the top-to-bottom measurement to allow clearance for the door to operate. Buy a door to fit the measured size; you must allow at least ½-inch vertical clearance, but a little extra width is no problem.

Follow these steps to install the door:

1. Measure across the inside top of the door opening and then measure the metal track for the door. If necessary, cut the track to fit the opening with a hacksaw.
2. With the door folded together, slide the rollers at the top of the door into the metal track.
3. Holding the track with one hand, set the door in the opening so that its front folds align with the front edges of the jambs; if there is an old strike plate in the door frame, make sure the latch of the new door is on the same side. Mark the position of the track on the top of the door frame.
4. Remove the door from the track, and set the track into position across the top of the door opening, as marked. Mark the locations for screw holes at the top of the doorway along the track and set it aside.
5. Drill pilot holes for the screws across the top of the door opening.
6. With the door still folded together, slide the rollers into the metal track. Set the track in position in the door opening, aligned over the screw holes. Slide the door to one end of the track and attach the other end with the screws provided; then slide the door to the secured end and fasten the rest of the track.
7. On the hinge side, the accordion door will have a long wood or metal strip; this strip must be fastened to the jamb on that side. If nails are provided for installation, nail the strip firmly into place along the jamb, using the nail holes punched in the strip; be sure the edge of the door hangs straight in the door opening. If screws are provided, mark the screw holes, drill pilot holes, and screw the strip into place.
8. Install the strike plate for the door. If there is an old strike plate in the door frame, remove it. Extend the accordion door so that its latch touches the jamb; mark the exact position of the latch on the jamb. Open the door. Set the new strike plate in position; if it replaces an old strike plate, mark the screw holes, drill pilot holes, and screw the plate into place.

   If there wasn't an old strike plate, set the plate in position and outline it on the door jamb. Use a hammer and a sharp chisel to cut out the outlined area so that the plate is set flush with the jamb. With the chisel held parallel to the jamb, make a series of small, closely spaced cuts down the length of the outlined area, to the depth of the strike plate's thickness. Cut out the scored wood. At the point where the latch of the door will enter the strike plate, drill a hole as large and as deep as necessary to accommodate the latch. Then, mark and drill the screw holes and screw the strike plate into place.

9. Test the door for proper operation. If it binds or doesn't hang evenly, adjust it according to the manufacturer's instructions.

Bi-Fold Doors

Bi-fold doors are available with as few as two panels or as many as eight; two panels fit a standard door opening. Before buying a bi-fold door, measure the inside of the door opening. Subtract 1¼ inches for vertical clearance and ½ inch (or, for a four-panel door, ¾ inch) for horizontal clearance. Buy a door cut to fit this size opening; make sure the panels are already hinged together and the

necessary pivots are included. Install the door so that the face of the door aligns with the front edges of the jambs.

To install the bi-fold door, follow this procedure:

1. Insert the top pivot bracket into the metal track that guides the door, as directed by the manufacturer. If you're installing a four-panel door, insert the second top pivot bracket into the other end of the track as directed.
2. Set the track in position across the inside top of the door opening, with the edge of the track flush with the edges of the jambs. Mark the location for screw holes along the track and set it aside.
3. Drill pilot holes for screws as directed by the manufacturer and fasten the track into place.
4. With the top pivot bracket at the corner of the opening where the door will fold together, drop a plumb bob from the center of the pivot bracket to the floor. Set the bottom pivot bracket on the floor at this point, so that the holes in the two brackets line up exactly. Mark

Folding Doors in Wood, Vinyl

Accordian-type folding doors can be used for many interior applications, including closets, passthroughs, laundry areas, and as room dividers. Pella folding doors, which are made of real wood veneers or vinyl, are manufactured by the Rolscreen Co. The company's Designer Series features folding doors with raised wood panels and real wood veneers. The Classic Series of doors have smooth panels of wood veneers. The Vinylwood Series of doors are ideal for areas where high humidity or frequent cleaning might take its toll on other doors. Vinylwood doors are vinyl over a stabilized wood core, in pecan, dark oak, or walnut wood-grain finishes, or in a textured white finish.

Bifold Doors Offer Advantages

Bi-fold doors can offer privacy, sound control, and more free floor and wall area. Four bi-fold styles are available from Wing Industries, Inc.—full louver, louver and panel, Colonial with raised panels, and flush bi-fold. The doors are available in unfinished or finished pine, and come with Acme steel hardware and hanging instructions. The panel thickness is 1⅛ inches, and panel height varies from 78¾ to 79 inches. The all-flush bi-fold door model has a 7-ply hollow core; the other models are doweled and glued. The bottom pivots are all fingertip adjustable. A heavy-duty jamb bracket prevents sagging without under-blocking when the doors are mounted above floor height.

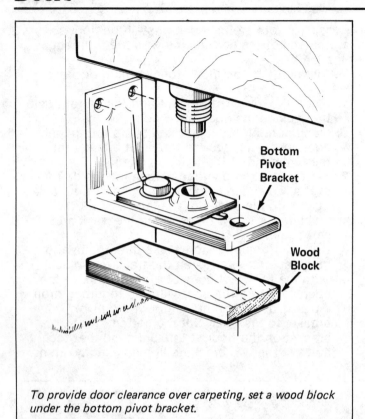

Bottom
Pivot
Bracket

Wood
Block

To provide door clearance over carpeting, set a wood block under the bottom pivot bracket.

carpeted area, allow adequate clearance over the carpeting. Determine the position of the bottom pivot bracket or brackets as before, but don't attach them. Trace the outline of each bracket exactly on a block of scrap wood that is the same thickness as the carpeting. With a handsaw, cut the block of wood to the same size as the bracket. Set the block in place and screw the bottom pivot bracket into the block and the door frame.

6. Fold the door panels together. The pivot panel has pivot pins at top and bottom to fit into the pivot brackets; the guide panel has a wheel that moves along the track. Set the bottom pivot pin into place in the bottom pivot bracket and tilt the folded-together door into the door frame. Slide the top pivot bracket over to the top of the tilted door and insert the top pivot pin into the bracket. Tilt the door slowly into position, sliding the top bracket back toward the pivot corner; insert the guide wheel in the track as soon as the angle of the door allows. Open the door to bring it firmly upright.

   Note: If you're installing a four-panel door, repeat this procedure to install the second pair of panels on the other side of the door frame.

7. Test the door for proper operation. If it sticks or doesn't hang evenly, adjust it according to the manufacturer's instructions.

8. Complete the installation by attaching the doorknobs provided on both sides of the hinge joint. Mark and drill pilot screw holes, if necessary; then, screw in the knobs with the screws provided.

   Note: If you're installing a four-panel door, attach doorknobs to each set of panels; close the door and attach the aligner plates provided to hold the panels firmly together.

the screw holes for the bottom pivot bracket.

5. Drill pilot holes for the screws and screw the bracket into position on both the floor and door frame.

   Note: If you're installing a four-panel door, install the second bottom pivot bracket in the same way, aligning it exactly under the top pivot bracket at the other side of the door frame. If you're installing the door in a

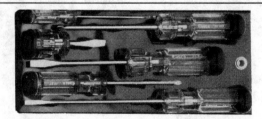

Quality Tool Is a Good Investment

Screwdrivers are among the tools most commonly picked up at the bargain bin, but in most cases the bargain screwdriver should be left in its bin. Buy good screwdrivers and take care of them; they'll provide a lifetime of good service.

Easco Tools, Inc., makes a quality screwdriver. The cross-ground chrome-vanadium blade is strong and durable due to the high-strength steel alloy used. It is machine-ground and rustproofed, the tip is ground accurately, and the plastic handle is big enough and shaped properly for good gripping.

Replacement Hardware for Doors, Windows

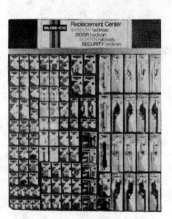

Broken door, window, screen, and security hardware can be tough to replace because brand-name manufacturers don't always have parts readily available. Slide-Co, however, makes such hardware as tension spring rollers, locking handles, screen clips, tub enclosure rollers, shower door latches, shower door splines, top-hung rollers, and bottom adjustable rollers. The parts will fit

most original products. Installation instructions are printed on each package.

Installing a Lockset

Materials • Lockset • Medium Sandpaper

Tools • Tape Measure • Pencil • Brace and Bits or Electric Drill With Hole Saw Attachment • Combination Square • Butt Chisel • Rubber Mallet • Screwdriver

YOU CAN OFTEN upgrade the locks on the doors in your home by just removing the old lockset and installing a new one. The new locksets are not limited to exterior doors. You can buy handsome sets for interior doors, bathroom doors, closets, cabinets, and any other type of door.

If you just want to replace an existing lock with a better one, look for a new lock that will fit in the existing holes. Sometimes, however, you won't be able to cover the old holes with the new lock, but you can generally cover large openings with a large decorative escutcheon plate. If need be, you can usually enlarge mortises and holes to accommodate the new lockset.

Also, when you buy a replacement lock, the most important measurement to take is the thickness of the door.

To install a lockset in a new door, follow this procedure:

1. Wrap the paper or cardboard template that comes with the new lockset around the edge of the door, according to the manufacturer's directions; it is used to locate two holes. One hole is for the lock cylinder; the other hole goes into the edge of the door for the bolt. Mark the centers for these two holes on the door.
2. Use a brace and an expansion bit or a power drill with a hole saw attachment to drill a hole of the size specified for the lock cylinder. Be careful not to damage the veneer on the opposite side of the door. When you see the point of the drill coming through, stop and go around to the other side to finish boring the hole.
3. Drill a hole of the appropriate size for the bolt into the edge of the door. Be sure to drill at a perfect right angle to the door, and keep drilling until you reach the cylinder hole. Use a combination square against the edge of the door and the drill bit to keep the bit at a right angle to the door.
4. Smooth the edges of the holes with sandpaper.
5. Insert the bolt into its hole, and place the bolt plate in position over it. Then, trace the bolt plate's outline on the edge of the door.
6. Remove the bolt, and mortise the edge for the bolt plate so it will be flush with the surface. Use a butt chisel to cut the mortise and a rubber mallet to drive the chisel.
7. Insert the bolt and plate in the mortise, and drill pilot holes for the mounting screws.
8. Install the screws to secure the bolt in place.
9. Insert the outside lock cylinder so that the stems or the connecting bar fits into the bolt assembly.

Wrap the paper or cardboard template that comes with the new lockset around the edge of the door, according to the manufacturer's instructions.

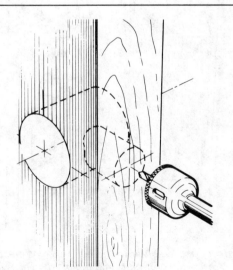

After drilling the hole for the lock cylinder, drill a hole for the bolt into the edge of the door. Be sure to drill at a perfect right angle to the door.

Deadbolt Locks Offer More Security

A deadbolt lock is probably the best security lock you can install on a door. The low-profile, 1-inch Yale security deadbolt, made by the Scovill Security Products Division, has a tapered wrench ring and pin-tumbler cylinder that project from the door only ¹⁵⁄₁₆ inch. A 2⅜-inch backset is included. The deadbolt may be installed on doors from 1⅜ to 1¾ inches thick. The lock is available in bright or antique brass.

Adhesive Can Replace Nails on Many Projects

Door and window trim don't necessarily have to be installed with nails; you can use construction adhesive. Macco Liquid Nails construction adhesive can be used for this purpose as well as for installing paneling, parquet tile, veneer brick, and foamboard insulation. According to Macco Adhesives, Glidden Coatings & Resins, a division of SCM Corp., Liquid Nails is a waterproof general-purpose construction adhesive formulated for bonding pre-finished panels of all types.

Replacing Casing Board Not Difficult

Casing is a trim board that goes around doors and windows. Unfortunately, casing often rots where the boards touch dissimilar materials such as a concrete porch or patio. At first sight, the replacement looks difficult but it isn't. Simply pry off the old casing board and replace it with a new one that is the same width and length. Seal all surfaces of the new casing board with paint, stain, or wood perservative. Then nail the board in position with 10d finishing nails. Countersink the nail heads with a nail set, fill the holes with caulking compound or wood putty.

10. Attach the interior lock cylinder and secure it with screws.
11. Locate the proper spot for the strike plate on the jamb.
12. Drill a proper-size hole in the jamb.
13. Using the strike plate as a pattern, mark the jamb for mortising, and cut the mortise.
14. Install the strike plate with screws so that it fits flush with the jamb.
15. Test the operation of the lock.

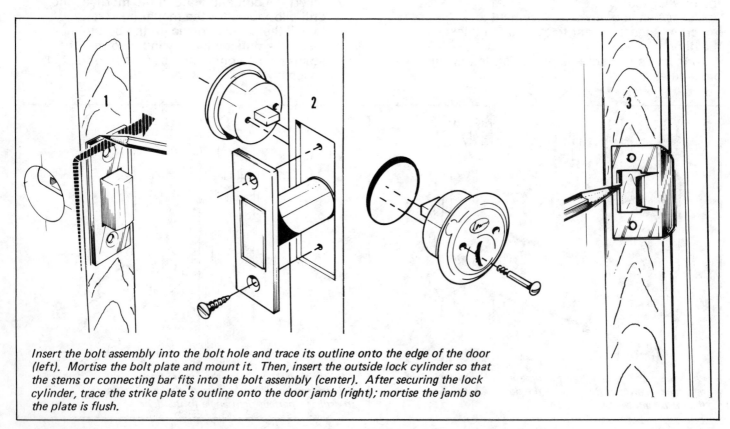

Insert the bolt assembly into the bolt hole and trace its outline onto the edge of the door (left). Mortise the bolt plate and mount it. Then, insert the outside lock cylinder so that the stems or connecting bar fits into the bolt assembly (center). After securing the lock cylinder, trace the strike plate's outline onto the door jamb (right); mortise the jamb so the plate is flush.

Replacing Door Sills and Jambs

Materials • Doorjamb Board • Wood Sealer or Other Finish • 10d Finishing Nails • 16d Finishing Nails • 4d Finishing Nails • Wood Putty • Door Sill • Caulking Compound • Porch and Deck Enamel

Tools • Tape Measure • Pencil • Screwdriver • Pry Bar • Hammer • Crosscut Saw • Carpenter's Level • Paintbrush • Nail Set • Butt Chisel • Rubber Mallet • Broom • Wood Rasp • Caulking Gun

A DOOR SILL, or saddle, is that part of the exterior door framing that the threshold is fastened to. A doorjamb is the framing member on each side of the door frame. Both have something in common: rot.

The decay problem is commonly found at the bottom ends of the jambs and at the corners of the sill where the sill tucks under the jambs and door casing. To spot the rot, you may have to stick a jackknife into the wood. If the knife penetrates the wood easily, the sill or jamb should be replaced.

Replacing Jambs

There's not much work to replacing a doorjamb. To do so, follow this procedure:

1. Measure the width of the jamb boards and determine the length; buy replacement boards.
2. Remove the door and the door hinges.
3. Remove the stop moldings on the jambs at the top and sides of the doorway.
4. Remove the threshold at the bottom of the doorway.
5. Using a short pry bar or ripping hammer, remove the side jambs. You don't have to be careful about splitting the wood because the jambs will be replaced. **Note:** You may have to remove the head jamb to remove the side jambs. If so, be careful not to damage it.
6. Measure and cut the new jambs to fit.
7. Apply a coat of quality penetrating sealer,

wood preservative, or paint to the jambs. Allow the finish to dry.
8. Face nail the jambs to the framing members with 10d finishing nails. Countersink the nail heads with a nail set.
9. Hang the door. You may have to cut new mortises for the hinges. If so, use a butt chisel for this and follow the procedure for "Hanging a Door" elsewhere in this chapter.
10. Nail the stop molding with 4d finishing nails. Countersink the nail heads with a nail set.
11. Fill any nail holes with wood putty.
12. Paint the jambs and molding.

Replacing a Sill

Replacing a door sill, or saddle, looks difficult, but it isn't. You must have patience, however, because you have to fit the new sill underneath the jambs. Don't force the sill into position; just tap it into place under the jambs and nail it. To replace a sill, follow this procedure:

1. Remove the door.
2. Using a butt chisel and rubber mallet, split out the old sill, being careful not to damage the casing or the jambs. **Note:** If you think these

Replacing a door sill, or saddle, looks difficult, but it isn't. You must have patience, however, because you have to fit the new sill underneath the door jambs.

components will be damaged, carefully pry them off so they may be renailed after the new sill has been installed.

3. Clean out the wood debris under the side jambs, and sweep the area with a broom.

4. Measure, cut, and fit the new sill under each side jamb and seat it properly against the rough framing. The sill must fit as tightly as possible. If trimming is necessary, use a butt chisel and wood rasp, and take off small amounts of wood at a time, cutting and fitting as you go.

5. When the new sill fits, seal all sill surfaces with a quality penetrating sealer, wood preservative, or paint.

6. Install the new sill, nailing it to the framing at the sill plate and side jambs with 16d finishing nails. Countersink the nail heads with a nail set.

7. Caulk the joints at the side jambs and wherever you see a crack with exterior caulking compound.

8. Fill any nail holes with wood putty and paint the sill with at least two coats of porch and deck enamel.

9. Replace the threshold and the door.

Curing Veneer Pops on Flush Doors

Many flush panel doors—both interior and exterior—are skinned with veneers just like plywood. Sometimes, these veneers separate due to dampness and humidity. You'll probably first notice the problem at the edges of the door along the top and bottom. When this happens, coat the back of the veneer and the front of the veneer core—the backing—with a quality water-resistant adhesive.

Use a small artist's brush to distribute the adhesive. Then press the two surfaces together and clamp them until the adhesive dries—at least 24 hours. If possible, sandwich a wide glue block between each jaw of each clamp and the door to help distribute the pressure evenly. When the adhesive has set, remove the clamps and the blocks, and refinish the face panels and edges of the door with varnish, paint, stain, or other sealing material.

'Invisible' Hinges for All Types of Doors

Hinges on doors don't have to be visible. Michigan Products Grinding Co., Inc., a division of Core Industries, Inc., makes Soss invisible hinges for all types of doors. No portion of the hinge is visible when the door is closed. The Soss hinges also are tamper-proof; create a flush, smooth closed surface with a close fit; and are reversible, except for one hinge model. The hinges, in four finishes—brass,

bronze, dull chrome, and cadmium—open to 180 degrees. The hinges come with a full-size installation template and instructions.

Tape Measure Is an Important Tool

Measuring carefully before cutting framing members will help you end up with a better wall. Generally, a zigzag or folding rule is ideal for a framing project, but if you plan to invest in just one measuring device, a retractable steel tape unit would be best. Lufkin—the Cooper Group—makes a variety of tape measures. The Lufkin 25-foot Ultralok power tape with automatic return can be locked in any extended

position. The 50- and 100-foot Lufkin Speedwinder models feature a pointed end-hook so you won't need someone to hold the tape as you unroll it.

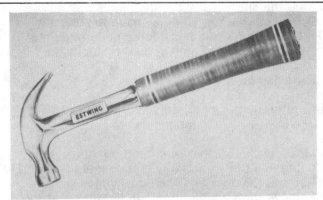

Claw Hammer Is All-Round Performer

The all-purpose 16-ounce claw hammer—16 ounces refers to the weight of the head—is available in versions with wooden handles, fiberglass handles, or with steel handles. Like many of the hammers and hand axes from Estwing Manufacturing Company, the firm's 16-ounce claw model features a steel handle and a leather grip. Because it's a quality hammer, this Estwing hammer should last a lifetime. It also has excellent balance.

Hinge Pins May Not Be Standard

Removable hinge pins on both interior and exterior doors are usually standard in size, but there can be a difference. If you are replacing a hinge pin, it's a good idea to take the pin that you will replace to the store for matching purposes. Don't rely on "standardization."

Garage Door Maintenance

Materials • Rags • Petroleum-Based Solvent • Machine Oil or Silicone Lubricant • Paint • Garage Door Weatherstripping

Tools • Stepladder • Carpenter's Level • Adjustable Wrench • Hammer • Screwdriver • Paintbrush

MOST GARAGES constructed over the past 30 years have overhead doors. There are two types: the roll-up door and the swing-up door. Both rely on a heavy tensioned spring for ease of operation.

When a garage door becomes difficult to open or close, many homeowners try to remedy the problem by adjusting the spring. Usually, the spring isn't the problem. If, however, you determine that the spring is the problem, be extremely careful. The spring is under tension and releasing it can be dangerous. It is recommended that you have a professional handle this kind of repair.

To troubleshoot and maintain your garage door, follow this procedure:

1. Check the vertical tracks with a level to be sure they are plumb (vertically level). If they are not, adjust the tracks by loosening the brackets that hold the tracks to the wall, and then tap them back in alignment.
2. Check all tracks for any crimps. If you find any, straighten them out or replace the track.
3. Be sure that the tracks are positioned so that the rollers don't bind in the track.
4. Inspect the tracks for dirt. Old grease can collect dust and dirt, and you might need to swab out the track with a petroleum-based solvent to dissolve old grease and remove the dirt.
5. Lubricate the track, the rollers, and the pulleys, if any. Use machine oil or silicone lubricant on the rollers and pulleys; use a multi-purpose grease in the tracks.
6. Look for any loose hardware such as hinges, tracks, or brackets. Any of these can cause balky operation when they loosen. Tighten any loose fittings.
7. After you have checked everything else, you can go to work on the spring. If you have the type of roll-up door with a spring on either side, try shortening the spring cable while the

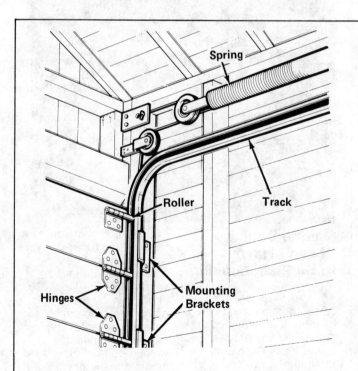

On a roll-up door, check the vertical tracks with a level to be sure they are plumb vertically.

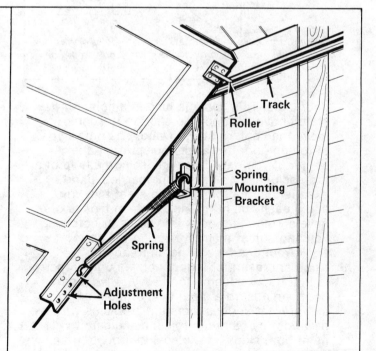

On swing-up doors, check the horizontal tracks for crimps. If you find any, straighten them or replace the track.

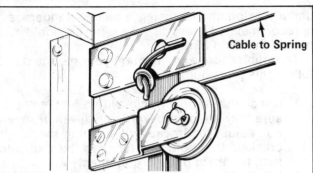

If your roll-up door has a spring on either side, you can shorten the cable when the door is up by moving the knot in the plate above the door.

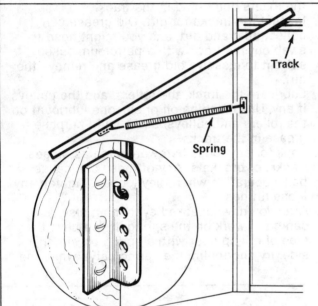

Swing-up doors have springs that hook into holes or notches. You can adjust them by moving the spring hook from one hole or notch to another.

Transmitter for Garage Openers

A digital hand transmitter for a garage door opener is extremely convenient. The Stanley digital garage door opener hand transmitter is designed for Stanley U-Install model openers—models 1100, 2100, 3100, and 4000. It allows you to set your own code for added security; there are 1,024 possible combinations so you can change the setting as often as you wish. The unit comes with an LED indicator light to show battery strength and signal transmission. A car visor clip and battery are included. The product is made by Stanley Hardware, a division of The Stanley Works.

Spring Adjustment for Garage Doors

Some garage doors are counterbalanced with a coil-type spring that runs along the door tracks and connects to a header arrangement at the ceiling or joist level. These springs are under high tension, and when the door won't open or close properly, the problem usually is lack of spring tension. Some springs have an adjusting nut on the spring at the header connection. You may be able to use an adjustable wrench to increase or decrease this tension by turning the adjusting nut. It will be a trial-and-error project so don't give up too quickly. If you don't seem to correct the tension problem, call a professional. Special tensioning equipment is sometimes needed. Also, highly-tensioned springs can be dangerous, so any disassembly should be left to a pro.

Garage Door Doesn't Have to Be Plain-Looking

Today, garage doors can be more than plain-looking. The model 38 garage doors from Clopay Corp. include three distinctive series of patterns including Monterrey, Belmonte, and Arlington. The choice, says the manufacturer, lets you buy a door that best conforms to the design of your home. The Model 38 doors may be fitted with optional glazed panels for different accents. The panels are made of vacuum-formed plastic set in kiln-dried lumber. A wide range of sizes also is available.

door is up. This cable is held in a hole in a plate above the door. To shorten the cable, move the knot, or stay, inward. The other type of roll-up door has a torsion spring in the center. If you have this type, seek the help of a professional who has the proper tools and experience; the torsion is so great that you could easily be hurt. The swing-up type doors have springs that hook into holes or notches; you can adjust them by moving the spring hook from one hole or notch to another.

8. Another reason for a door not working properly is that it has become too heavy. A wooden door can absorb a great deal of moisture. You can prevent serious moisture problems with a new door by painting it; just make sure to paint both sides and to seal the top, bottom, and sides. Also, apply garage door weatherstripping to the bottom of the door; this can help deter moisture.

Installing an Automatic Garage Door Opener

Materials • Automatic Garage Door Opener Kit • Rags • No. 10 Non-Detergent Motor Oil or Silicone Lubricant • Multi-Purpose Grease • 2 × 4 Lumber • 16d or 20d Common Nails • Lag Screws

Tools • Screwdriver • Hacksaw • Stepladder • Tape Measure • Pencil • Drill and Bits • Carpenter's Level • Adjustable Wrench • Hammer

CONVENIENCE AND safety are two major reasons for installing an automatic garage door opener. Many of today's models are designed for do-it-yourself installation and come with complete instructions.

The key to buying an opener is the amount of space between the top of your garage door and the ceiling level of the garage. Measure this distance before you go shopping. If the headroom is especially narrow you can buy adaptor kits.

Buy an opener made specifically for the size and type—swing-up or roll-up—of garage door you have. Choose a preassembled opener that can be plugged in at an existing outlet, and make sure it has an automatic reverse switch.

Once you select an opener, here is a general procedure for installing it properly:

1. Before installing the opener, make sure the garage door operates correctly. Clean the tracks to remove grease and dirt; lubricate the rollers with oil or silicone lubricant, and the tracks with garage door lubricant or powdered graphite. If the door binds, repair it as necessary. Finally, remove the lock on the garage door or saw off the locking bar with a hacksaw.
2. Measure across the top of the inside garage door frame and mark the center point.
3. Attach the header bracket—including the automatic reverse switch—to the beam over the door, centered exactly on the marked point and at least 2 inches down from the ceiling. Mark the screw holes for the bracket, drill pilot holes for them, set the bracket into place, and fasten it with the screws provided.
4. Attach the hanger straps—the door opener you're installing may have one set or more. If the ceiling has exposed beams, mount the straps directly to the side of a beam about three-quarters of the length of the opener track back from the door. Measure across the beam to position the straps exactly centered on the beam, directly aligned with the header bracket; attach the straps with 1½-inch lag screws and an adjustable wrench.

   Note: If the ceiling is finished, nail a 3-foot 2 × 4 to the appropriate beam above the ceiling with 16d or 20d common nails; center the 2 × 4 on the beam. Attach the hanger straps for the door opener to the 2 × 4 with 1½-inch lag screws; position the straps exactly centered on the beam to align with the header bracket.
5. With preassembled openers, no further preparation is necessary. If your unit isn't preassembled, attach the power unit firmly to the track, following the manufacturer's instructions exactly; attach the carrier and the hanger clamp to the track as directed.
6. Set the door end of the track into place in the header bracket over the garage door; bolt it into place, but don't tighten the bolt.
7. Have someone help you lift the power unit end of the track and slide the hanger clamp into position over the hanger straps. Bolt the clamp and the straps firmly together with the hardware provided; then tighten the bolt that holds the track in place in the header bracket.

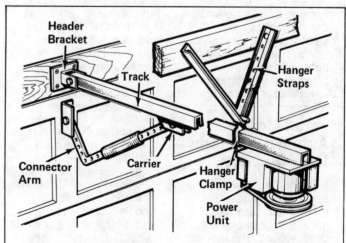

Mount the header bracket to the beam over the door; mount the hanger straps directly back from it. Attach the power unit to the track, bolt the track to the hanger straps, and attach the connector arm to the carrier.

8. Attach the connector arm that moves the door. Center the bracket plate at the top of the garage door, directly below the header bracket; mark locations for screw holes, drill pilot holes, and attach the plate with the hardware provided.

9. Set the end of the connector arm into place against the bracket, as directed by the manufacturer, and screw or bolt it into place.

10. Attach the track end of the connector arm to the carrier in the track with the hardware provided; turn the unit by hand to slide the carrier out to the free end of the arm.

11. Remove the power unit cover and connect the control wires to the terminals in the power unit; follow the manufacturer's instructions exactly to connect the wires.

12. Install batteries in the hand transmitters; if the opener includes a garage light, screw in a light bulb. Replace the cover on the power unit and plug the opener in.

13. Check the installation by opening and closing the door several times; adjust it, as necessary, according to the manufacturer's instructions. Adjustments for proper fit in the door opening are made at the power unit; adjustments to the automatic reverse are made at the header bracket. Following the manufacturer's instructions, make sure the door closes and the automatic reverse functions properly.

Garage Door Opener With Electric Eye System

There are many garage door openers, but Chamberlain Manufacturing Corp., has developed one with an electric eye system that retracts a descending door when the door is confronted by a person or obstacle— without touching the person or obstacle. The Chamberlain device is called "The Protector," which is part of its model 444 H.D. Plus automatic garage door opener system. The garage door also retracts if the electric eye system is knocked off-kilter, if a short-circuit occurs in the electrical system, or if dirt obscures the contact between the electric eye and receiver. The system, activated by a light sensor, is not affected by changes in natural or manufactured lighting. The garage door opener's other safety back-up systems include a weight/pressure release device that retracts the door on contact; a 30-second timer that automatically retracts the decending door if it does not close and lock within that time period; and an emergency hand-pull device that lets the homeowner retract the door manually when all other systems fail.

Combination Lock for Garage Door With Opener

How to get into a garage with its door controlled by an automatic opener can be a problem for family members when the opener is in the car and they are not. The Domino electronic combination lock, which mounts outside the garage door, may be the answer.

When a garage key or transmitter isn't available, the Domino lock can be used. It has a 3-digit combination with a 30-second delay if the wrong number is pressed. The device's wiring is protected and secured. The Domino electronic combination lock, made by Domino Engineering Corp., measures 5 inches high, 1¾ inches wide, and ¾ inch deep.

Three Models of Automatic Garage Door Openers

Designed for homeowner installation is a line of three basic automatic garage door openers from Clopay Corp. The models have three different type drives at three different prices. The lowest-priced Clopay Duralift opener operates on a chain-and-cable drive, but there is a mid-priced model with continuous chain drive; the highest-priced model has machined screw-drive. The mid- and high-priced models have transmitters with digital coding, and up to 1,000 different codes are possible, the company says. All models are backed by a one-year warranty against defects.

Deadbolt Lock for Storm Doors

You may be able to discourage a burglar if you install a deadbolt lock on your storm door. The Wartian model DB-800 deadbolt key lock for storm doors, made by Wartian Lock Co., is surface-mounted and may be attached high on the door stile so it's out of the reach of children. The positive lock requires a ¾-inch hole through the

storm door, and it will fit wood or aluminum doors up to 1¾ inches thick.

Removing Broken Keys in Locks

A key broken off in a cylinder lock can be difficult to remove, especially if the key has twisted inside the cylinder. If this happens, don't try to fish the key out. Instead, remove the setscrew from the lock and unscrew the cylinder. Hold the cylinder face down and tap the back of it with a hammer. This often loosens the key so you can flip it out with a straightened paperclip. Work the paperclip along the top of the keyway; this helps "push" down the tumblers in the lock and free the stub of the broken key.

Pick a Padlock

For extra security on many doors around the home, a padlock may be the answer. The American Lock Company has three series of padlocks, which are rated "Best Security," "Better Security," and "Good Security." The "Best Security" locks have 15-year warranties; the "Better Security" locks have 10-year warranties; and the "Good Security" locks come with 5-year warranties. According to the manufacturer, the padlocks are so secure that American Lock will refund your money if any American Lock fails to perform for any reason including damage, tampering, or misuse. There is a wide variety of lock sizes, cylinders, shackles, and case materials from which to choose. All locks are made from solid brass or

hardened steel. The locks are key- or combination-operated. The key-operated locks have the double-locking heel-and-toe shackle system, which has been recommended by the National Crime Prevention Institute. American Lock also makes hasps to match the padlocks.

Sliding Mirror Door Framed in Solid Oak

A wardrobe door with a full-length mirror is a convenience in any bedroom. The Oak Fantasy model sliding mirror door from Contractors Wardrobe, Inc., features 2⅛-inch-wide bands of solid oak to frame the quality plate mirror. The door has bottom rollers with 1½-inch-diameter wheels. The corners of the oak frame are mitered, stapled, and glued. An oak fascia is finished to match the frame. The door is available in standard widths: 48, 60, 72, 84, 96, 108, 120, and 144 inches. All Contractor's Wardrobe doors meet all federal impact tests including Category II, the company says.

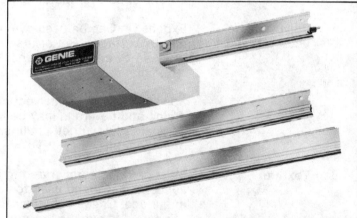

Garage Door Opener Is Partially Assembled

A garage door opener that is partially assembled makes it easier for the do-it-yourselfer to install. The Genie garage door opener, made by Alliance Manufacturing Co., Inc., takes lots of work out of assembly. According to the manufacturer, you can install the model GS-850 Deluxe Screw Drive System, in less than three hours by following five basic steps. Features include direct screw drive, ⅓-horsepower motor, automatic light delay, emergency release, safety reverse, and security-coded Cryptar II digital radio controls. The opener also has an extra touch of safety: You push once to open it, twice to close.

Guide to Paint Selection

THERE ARE so many different types and colors of paints available for so many different types of surfaces and materials that it can boggle the mind. For the novice painter, the best thing to do is to visit a paint store with the measurements of what you want to paint and let a knowledgeable dealer show you his wares. Consider the alternatives, the choice is yours.

The accompanying tables show basic types of interior and exterior coatings to help you narrow down the type of paint you need. They also show recommended methods of application.

Interior Paint

Type	Characteristics, Use	Recommended Application
Acoustic	For ceiling tile. Water-thinned and water cleanup.	Spray (preferable) or roller.
Alkyd	Same as exterior alkyd. Solvent-thinned and solvent cleanup. Don't apply over unprimed drywall.	Brush or roller.
Epoxy	Expensive. Solvent-thinned and solvent cleanup. May require special mixing; check container. Can be used over metal and glass.	Brush.
Polyurethane and Urethane	Expensive. Can be used over most finishes and porous surfaces. Better than most varnishes. Primer may be required; check manufacturer's recommendations for primer and type of solvent.	Brush.
Oil	Solvent-thinned and solvent cleanup. Slow-drying and coverage may be limited as compared to synthetic paints. Odor may be objectionable.	Brush, roller, or spray.
Texture	Must be constantly stirred to keep aggregate suspended. Can be used to cover minor defects in surface. Check container for recommended thinners and cleanup information.	Brush, roller, pad, trowel, broom, sponge, and many others.
Metal	Excellent primer; any paint may be applied over it. Some paints are water-based; check container label.	Spray or brush.
Latex	May be used over almost all surfaces. Water-thinned and water cleanup. Available in gloss, semi-gloss, and flat finishes. Usually requires two coats.	Brush, roller, or pad.
One-Coat	*Caution: Use one-coat only if surface has been sealed.* Water-thinned or solvent-thinned; check container label for recommendations for thinners and cleanup information.	Brush, roller, or pad.

Natural Bristle Brush for Oil-Based Paints

Natural bristle brushes are recommended for applying oil-based paints, varnishes, lacquers, and other finishes because natural fibers resist most strong solvents. The Rubberset Company makes a variety of natural bristle paintbrushes, including the Rubberset No. 1060 wall brush. Intended for professional and industrial use, this model has long black bristles, precision ferrules, and natural-color

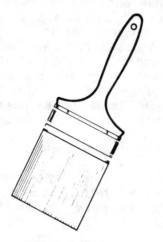

beavertail handles. The brush is available in 3-inch and 4-inch sizes.

Quality Paint Will Last Longer

No one wants to paint his home every year or even every two or three years. To keep such big projects as infrequent as possible, you should use a top-quality exterior paint. Sears, Roebuck and Co., has premium-quality Survivor exterior acrylic latex house paint, which is available in 50 colors, in flat or satin finish. According to Sears, the paint is a one-coat product that is non-yellowing and has no chalk washdown.

Exterior Paint

Type	Characteristics, Use	Recommended Application
Acrylic	Type of latex. Water-thinned and water cleanup. Use on any building material and over primed metal.	Brush, roller, or pad.
Alkyd	Qualities similar to oil-based paint. Solvent-thinned and solvent cleanup. Use over oil or alkyd paint, or according to manufacturer's recommendations. Good covering quality.	Brush, roller, pad, or spray.
Latex	Same qualities as acrylic with easy water cleanup. Mildew-proof and may be applied over damp surfaces. Don't apply over oil-based paint unless specified by manufacturer.	Brush, roller, pad; apply thickly with little spreadout.
Oil	Very durable, but slower drying than acrylic, alkyd, and latex paints. Odor may be objectionable.	Brush, roller, pad, or spray to very dry surface.
Masonry	Can be latex, epoxy, Portland cement, rubber, alkyd, or special mixtures with bonding cement. Check container labels.	Brush or roller.
Primer	For new wood or any new building material, or old materials that are badly worn. Provides good surface for top coat paint. Use primer formulated for top coat paint.	Brush, roller, or pad.
Porch/Deck	Alkyd, latex, epoxy, rubber, oil, or polyurethane. All synthetics dry quickly; oil-based paint slow-drying but durable. Limited color choice.	Brush, roller, or mop.
Stain	Water- or solvent-thinned; both types durable. Also choice of transparent, semi-transparent, or solid-stain pigmentation.	Brush, roller, or spray.

Interior Painting

Materials • Spackling Compound • Rags • Mild Detergent • Sponges • Fine Steel Wool or Liquid Deglosser • Tack Cloth • Dropcloths • Newspapers • Masking Tape • Plastic Bags • Interior Paint • Cardboard • Fine Sandpaper

Tools • Hammer • Putty Knife • Scraper • Stepladder • Screwdriver • Pliers • Paintbrushes • Roller With Extension Handle • Mixing Sticks • Roller Tray • Sanding Block

OF ALL HOME improvements, interior painting probably produces the most dramatic change in a short period of time. Any paint job takes more patience than skill, and the key to professional-looking results is preparation, which, of course, is the most difficult procedure and the one that takes the patience. However, even if you have never painted before, you can become a professional fast by following these suggestions.

It will pay you to buy a high-quality interior paint, because such a paint lasts longer, saving you the work of recoating the surfaces too frequently. Also, high-quality paint is easier to apply, cleans up quickly, and you can wash the painted surfaces after the paint dries fully without damaging the appearance of the surfaces.

Preparing the Surface

Although you may be tempted to begin painting quickly, restrain yourself. Preparation of the surface to be covered is extremely important. Follow these steps:

1. Inspect walls and ceilings for any popped nails. If you find any, drive them back in and cover them with spackling compound.
2. Patch any cracks or holes.
3. Scrape away any loose or flaking paint.
4. Clean the wall and ceiling surfaces. If they are merely dusty, brushing or wiping may be all that you need to do. If there are grease spots or other dirt, however, wash the walls and ceilings with water and a mild detergent. Then, rinse them and allow them to dry.
5. Degloss any shiny surface. You can buy liquid deglossing preparations at a paint store or use fine steel wool.
6. Move all furniture, pictures, draperies, and carpet out of the room if possible. Protect

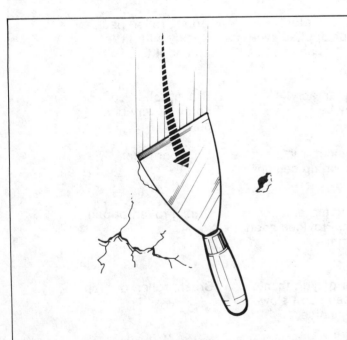

When preparing a surface for painting, patch small flaws with spackling compound; smooth it firmly to keep the patched surface even.

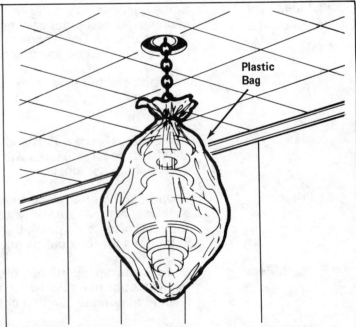

To keep paint off light fixtures, loosen the fixtures and let them hang down. Wrap them in plastic bags to protect them.

everything that must stay in the room with dropcloths or newspapers.

7. Mask all trim that is adjacent to wall areas that will be painted.
8. Remove electrical outlet and switch plates.
9. Loosen light fixtures and let them hang down. Wrap the fixtures in plastic bags to protect them from paint splatters.

Painting the Ceiling

After you have prepared the surface, you can start painting. Do the ceilings first, walls next, and all woodwork including doors, windows, and trim last. For ceilings, you can use a roller with an extension handle, but you'll have to trim at the ceiling line—where the walls meet the ceiling—with a brush or corner paint pad. Follow this procedure:

1. Mix the paint thoroughly.
2. Use a brush to paint a border along the edge of the ceiling and next to moldings. Avoid getting paint on the molding. This technique is called "cutting in."
3. Fill the roller tray with paint, load the roller, and roll it across the tray grid to remove excess paint.
4. Start painting with the roller next to the painted cut-in strip. Use slow steady strokes, working back and forth over the width of the ceiling. Fast strokes spin the roller and can sling paint. Use cross strokes to smooth the paint on the ceiling.
5. Keep working in strips across, always working over the wet edge of previously painted strips. If you allow a strip of paint to dry, you may leave streaks when you paint over it. Therefore, be sure to paint the entire ceiling without letting wet paint edges dry.

Painting Walls

Walls are painted in much the same manner as ceilings, but they are easier to paint. Follow these steps:

1. Paint the walls following the basic procedure used for ceilings. Begin by cutting in at corners and around doors and windows.
2. Start in the left-hand corner if you are right-handed, or right-hand corner if left-handed. Begin at the top and work up and down all the way, moving across as you finish each strip. Again, use cross strokes to smooth; always work against the wet edge; and avoid stopping in the middle of a wall.
3. Apply the roller horizontally to paint the narrow strips over doors and windows.
4. If you didn't mask the woodwork with tape, hold a strip of cardboard in one hand as a

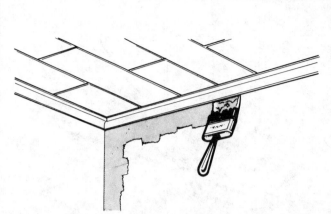

Use a brush to paint a border along the edge of the ceiling next to moldings; also paint next to corners. This technique is called "cutting in."

When using a roller, work in strips across, always working over the wet edge of previously painted strips. Paint the entire ceiling without letting wet paint edges dry.

moving masker. Should you happen to get some wall paint on the trim, use a rag moistened with solvent to wipe it off as you go.

Painting Woodwork

Molding, trim, doors, windows, and other woodwork should be painted with a semi-gloss enamel in a color to match the wall or ceiling color. You may, however, use the same wall or ceiling paint on the wood, but the wood will look better if enamel is used. Because an enamel has some gloss, it is easier to clean than flat wall or ceiling paint with just an occasional wiping.

To paint woodwork, follow this procedure:

Cardboard
Masker

When painting trim like baseboard, use a piece of cardboard as a moving masker to avoid getting paint on adjacent surfaces.

1. Clean all trim surfaces and remove the gloss with sandpaper, steel wool, or by applying a chemical deglosser available at paint stores. These chemicals degloss and also leave a tacky surface that makes the new paint adhere better; be sure to follow the directions on the label.

2. Mix the enamel paint thoroughly.

3. Although you can use rollers or foam pads to paint large flat areas, appropriately sized brushes are better for painting most woodwork. An exception would be flush-panel doors.

4. Start by painting the ceiling moldings, then the baseboards; use a moving cardboard masker as you paint.

5. Paint the windows next, but be sure to mask the panes of glass and to open the sash about 3 or 4 inches before you start painting. Then, after you paint but before the paint starts to set, move the sash up or down to prevent it from sticking.

6. Paint the doors and door frames last. Remove all hardware before painting the doors, and make sure that the enamel is dry before reinstalling the hardware.

   Note: Door surfaces usually require two coats of paint. For a good-looking finish, sand the door lightly with fine-grit sandpaper on a sanding block. Then, paint the door. When the paint dries, sand the surface again lightly, and remove any sanding residue with a soft rag. Then, apply a final coat of paint.

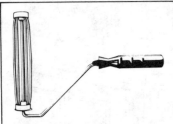

Paint Rollers Come in Different Sizes

Paint rollers can cover flat areas much more quickly than a brush. But there are differences among paint rollers. For one thing they are available in different sizes. The model 7422 paint roller frame from the Rubberset Company is a 9-inch roller with a three-wire cage frame and polypropylene end caps. It has a ¼-inch steel shank and a threaded plastic handle. You can do a job faster with such a large roller, but keep in mind that it will be heavier to use.

Texture Paint for Ceilings

If your ceilings have minor blemishes, you can probably cover them with a textured paint. Textone Ready-Mixed texture paints, from United States Gypsum Co., are designed to give a three-dimensional effect to flat and slightly damaged ceilings. The paint may be applied with a paintbrush or roller. Once on, Textone paint has the look of a professionally applied spray paint job, according to the manufacturer. Four types of paint are available: light sand texture, smooth design texture, interior/exterior stucco texture, and coarse ceiling texture. The paints clean up easily; if you splatter, globules may be removed with a joint knife.

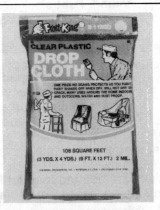

Protect Furniture Before Painting

Whether you use a brush or a roller on your painting project, it's a good idea to cover the room's furniture with dropcloths. Frost-King polyethylene dropcloths, made by Thermwell Products Co., Inc., can save furniture from paint splatters. There are 10 different sizes, ranging from 9 by 12 feet to 12 by 25 feet.

Exterior Painting

Materials • Caulking Compound • Medium Sandpaper • Rags • Primer • Fabric Dropcloths • Plastic Bags or Sheeting • Large Containers • Exterior Paint • Screening or Coarse-Mesh Material

Tools • Stepladders and Scaffolding • Caulking Gun • Scraper • Wire Brush • Nail Set • Hammer • Mixing Sticks • Paintbrushes • Rollers • Roller Tray • Garden Hose • Bucket Hooks

AS IN INTERIOR painting, preparation is the key to a successful exterior paint job. In many cases, preparing the exterior surface of a house will take much more time than the actual painting. You'll obtain the best results when the temperature is mild, the humidity is low to moderate, and there is no rain forecast.

Preparing the Surface

Before you begin painting, you'll have to prepare the surface properly. Follow this procedure:

1. Caulk around all doors and windows and any other joints that might let in moisture or air.
2. Repair or replace any damaged wood or other exterior siding material.
3. Remove all loose paint with a scraper and a wire brush. Feather any chipped edges by sanding away the sharp edges of the remaining paint.
4. Reset any loose nails with a nail set and hammer.
5. Prime all bare spots with a primer recommended for use with the paint you have selected. Latex exterior paint offers the same ease of application and cleaning as latex interior paint, and—when used properly—it provides long-lasting coverage. Nevertheless, oil-based paint is a dependable, quality product for exterior use.
6. Be sure to remove any mildew on exterior surfaces. Add a mildewcide to the paint if mildew is a problem or buy a paint with a mildewcide, but don't expect the mildewcide to kill the existing fungus. You must do that with

Cleaner, Coating for Aluminum Siding

In time, pre-finished permanent siding can stain, mildew, chalk, and soil. Aminco Tackle and Aminco Guard are two aluminum care products, from Aminco Industries, Inc., that can be used on aluminum siding, gutters and downspouts, shutters, trailers, mobile homes, doors, lamp posts, and other items. Aminco Tackle is a water-based, phosphate-free, nonflammable cleaner. According to the manufacturer, it's also biodegradable and won't harm most plants or shrubs. One gallon of the cleaner covers about 1,600 square feet of siding—depending on its condition. Aminco Guard is a protective finish applied with a paint pad; it minimizes chalking, restores the appearance of siding, and acts as a barrier to dirt. Aminco also says that it has the same biodegradable qualities and coverage as Tackle cleaner. Directions for use are on each product.

Synthetic Bristles Absorb Less Water Than Natural Bristles

Synthetic bristle brushes are made from nylon or polyester. Nylon brushes are recommended for both latex and oil-based paints because the fiber absorbs less water than natural bristle brushes do, while resisting most strong paint and lacquer solvents.

Polyester brushes are recommended for use with latex and oil-based paint, shellac, and varnish. Both types are easy to clean. The Rubberset Company makes a full line of polyester and nylon paintbrushes. For example, there is the No. 3110 angular sash brush with polyester bristles for painting sash and trim. It has a long handle and angle cut for easy access to corners. It is available in 1½- and 2-inch sizes.

How to Estimate Paint for Home's Exterior

You can estimate the amount of paint that you need to paint the exterior of your home by counting the number of rooms in the house. For example, if the house has seven rooms, you will need seven gallons of paint. For every gable area, add one gallon of paint to the total. And, if the exterior surface is extra dry, add two more gallons.

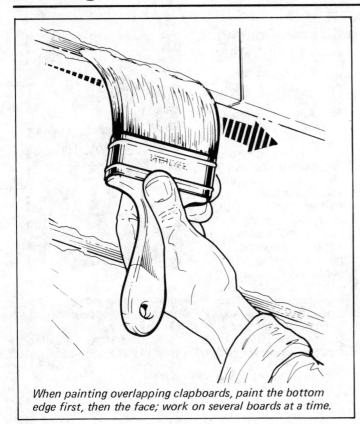

When painting overlapping clapboards, paint the bottom edge first, then the face; work on several boards at a time.

a mildewcide solution before you paint.

7. Make sure that all surfaces you intend to paint are clean. Hose off any loose dirt, working from the bottom of the siding to the top, to prevent streaking.

8. Wait until the surfaces are dry before starting to paint.

Pad-Type Tool Replaces Wire Brush

Preparing a surface for painting is often tougher than painting. Stroke of Genius Clean Stroke is a pad-type scraper that the manufacturer says is faster than a wire brush in removing loose and flaky paint, preparing glossy and chalky surfaces, and removing surface rust, corrosion, and mildew. Made by EZ Paintr Corporation, the pad is on a base with a handle that also fits any threaded extension pole. Replacement pads for the Clean Stroke scraping tool are also available.

9. Cover walks, drives, patios, and shrubs with tarps or fabric dropcloths. Plastic suit bags from the dry cleaners are handy for covering shrubbery.

Painting Procedures

After preparing the surface, you are ready to begin painting. If you will be working on a ladder, always make sure that the ladder is on firm footing, positioned about one-fourth its length from the foundation of the house to its feet, and lapped at least three rungs, if the ladder is an extension type.

Always climb a ladder just one rung at a time. Also work "within" the ladder, keeping both hips inside the rails of the ladder. Don't overreach. Instead, move the ladder to the work. When changing lengths of an extension ladder, always make sure the extension hooks are firmly locked on the supporting rungs. And, watch out for electric power lines when carrying or setting an extension ladder.

If you use a stepladder, always try to lean the ladder against the work instead of opening the ladder. If the ladder is open, the scissors braces must be locked and any paint tray placed in a down position. Never stand on the upper three steps of a stepladder.

Caution: Scaffolding can be very dangerous. However, if you must use scaffolding, be sure to have the proper scaffolding and the ladder jacks that support it. Don't jerry-rig scaffolding from 2 x 10 planks; rent the proper scaffolding and equipment. The cost isn't prohibitive.

To paint an exterior surface, follow these steps:

1. Mix the paint thoroughly. If you are using several gallons of paint, mix all of the paint together in one or two large containers. Then "box" the paint by pouring the paint from one container to another. This is especially important if color paint—not white paint—is being used. Paint colors tend to vary slightly even though they have been mixed by the manufacturer. If the large containers cannot be sealed, you should pour the paint back into the smaller buckets after boxing and seal the buckets.

2. If there are lumps and "skin" in the paint, strain the paint through a wire screen or coarse-mesh material.

3. Start painting at the top, completing all broad main areas first. Work in a band across the width, painting a swath of about 3 to 4 feet wide, and continue painting such bands all the way down. Avoid painting in the hot sun.

4. When you finish the main part of the house, go back and paint the trim.

5. After the first coat is completely dry, apply a second coat.

Painting Doors, Windows, and Shutters

Materials • Paint • Rags • Medium and Fine Sandpaper • Scrap Wood • Nail

Tools • Mixing Stick • Paintbrushes • Pry Bar, Screwdriver, or Wide Butt Chisel • Hammer

PAINTING DOORS, windows, and shutters isn't difficult, but you will obtain better results if you follow the procedures used by professionals.

Painting Doors

Plain doors are easy to paint, but doors with inset panels can be tricky. No matter what type of door you're painting, paint the entire door without stopping. Follow this procedure:

1. Start painting the inset panels at the top of the door. Paint all the panels and the molding around them. **Note:** You may want to mask door hardware before painting.
2. Paint across the top rail of the door.
3. Paint down to cover the other horizontal rails.
4. Finish the door by painting the stiles.
5. If both sides of the door need painting, follow Steps 1 through 4 on the other side of the door before painting the edges of the door.
6. Paint the top edge of the door, followed by the hinge and latch edges.

Painting Windows

The job of painting windows will go faster if you purchase a "sash tool" brush. This type of brush is angled slightly across the bottom of the bristles so that you can push the brush into 90-degree corners. A 2- to 2½-inch-wide brush is recommended. If you're using oil-based paint, use a natural bristle brush. Never use such a brush with a water-based paint.

Follow these steps for painting windows:

1. Raise the bottom sash more than half way up, and then lower the top sash until its bottom

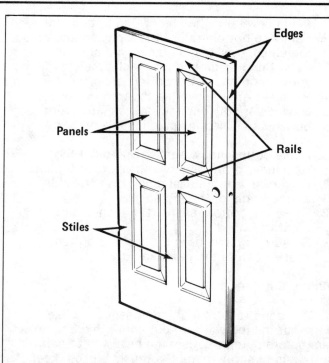

When painting a door, paint the panels first. Then paint the rails, the stiles, and finally the edges, working from the top to the bottom of the door.

Paint double-hung windows in the sequence shown, moving the top and bottom sashes for access to all surfaces. Paint horizontal surfaces first, then verticals; sash channels first, then frames.

rail is several inches below the bottom sash.
2. Paint the bottom rail of the top sash and on up the stiles, or sides, as far as you can go.
3. Paint the outside and inside channels as far as you can go above the bottom sash.
4. Paint the area above the top window sash.
5. Now lower both window sashes, and paint the outside and then inside channels on both sides.
6. Raise both window sashes and paint the remainder of the two channels on both sides.
7. Lower the bottom sash and finish the stiles and top rails of the top sash.
8. Raise the bottom sash a few inches and paint it.
9. Be sure to move both the top and bottom sashes before the paint can dry.

Painting Shutters

Shutters don't require a painting sequence like doors, but the job will turn out better if you remove them before painting. Also, the best way to paint shutters is to spray them. If a brush is used, keep it fairly "dry" with paint to prevent runs and sags.
To paint shutters, follow this procedure:

1. Examine the shutters to see how they are fastened. Decorative shutters often are nailed or screwed in place, even to masonry walls.
2. Remove the shutters, if possible, using a short pry bar, hammer, screwdriver, or wide butt chisel. Be careful to avoid damaging the shutter material.
3. Stand the shutters upright, if possible, to paint them. A good way is to hang them from a ceiling joist with a short length of scrap wood nailed to the shutter and the ceiling joist. If you can't do this, lay the shutters flat and finish an entire shutter unit at one time. This lets you catch paint runs and sags while the paint is fresh.
4. If you drip paint on unpainted shutter surfaces—especially new shutters that haven't been finished—remove this paint immediately. If you don't, the paint will form a "ridge" under a coat of paint that will be visible. If the paint drip has dried before you can brush it out, remove the paint with fine-grit sandpaper. Don't paint over the dried drip or run.
5. Use a narrow brush—a 2-inch-wide brush is recommended—and paint the louvers first, the frame second, and the edges last.

Have the Dealer Shake Your Paint

Even if you aren't going to use a new gallon of paint for several weeks, always have the dealer where you purchase the paint shake the can for you. This takes a couple of minutes, but it can save you plenty of mixing later. Paint pigments settle in the bottom of a container but this process usually takes considerable time. The only exception is pigmented stains, which should be constantly stirred as you use them.

Variety of Spray Paint Colors Offered

For many indoor or outdoor painting projects, an aerosol spray enamel paint is ideal. Krylon spray paints, made by Borden Chemical, a division of Borden, Inc., are available in 58 different colors.

There also are primer, clear, fluorescent, metal flake, high-heat, and engine color paints, as well as a line of touch-up car, van, and truck colors. According to the manufacturer, Krylon spray paints are formulated to resist runs and drips; they also have a fast-drying formula.

Sash Painter Reduces Mess

When painting windows, do you get paint on the glass? The Sashline Wand from EZ Paintr Corp. takes the mess and aggravation out of sash painting, trimming, and touch-ups, according to the manufacturer. The tool comes with three individual paint pads so you can change them quickly for different colors. You simply dip the pad in any type of paint and brush it on the surface to be painted.

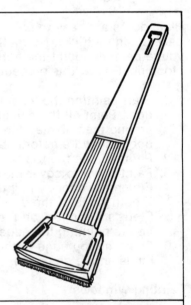

Quality Paint Doesn't Cost As Much As You Think

The cost of paint may frighten you, especially the cost of high-quality paint. Look at it this way, however. A good-quality paint job will last from 8 to 10 years. An inexpensive paint may last 5 years— probably less. Divide the cost of the quality paint by 10; the answer is your cost per year. Do the same for the inexpensive paint, but multiply by 20. You'll find that the difference isn't that much when you figure the expense on a yearly basis, especially if you consider your labor and how much the painting accessories cost.

Paint Problems

Materials • Wedge-Type Siding Vents • Sandpaper • Primer • Paint • Rags • Household Bleach • Household Detergent • Mildewcide

Tools • Extension Ladder • Stepladder • Hammer • Screwdriver • Nail Set • Wire Brush • Sanding Block • Paintbrushes • Garden Hose • Broom

VERY SELDOM are paint problems due to the paint. Most often, paint failures are caused by the painter. And most failures stem from the lack of proper preparation of the surfaces to be painted.

If you have properly prepared the surface to be painted and the paint still fails, many manufacturers will refund the cost of the paint. But you will have to reasonably prove that proper preparation was done. The following are some common paint failures and their causes:

PEELING. When paint curls away from the surface, it is usually because of moisture in the wood. You have to find out where the moisture is coming from and stop it before you can expect a good paint job. You may be able to use wedge-type siding vents to help dispel moisture vapor in problem areas. Often, peeling is the result of painting over wet wood. It can also be from moisture within the house pushing its way out. If you cannot control the moisture, try latex primer coat and latex paint. Latex will allow some moisture to pass right through the paint. Another cause of peeling is that the paint was applied over a dirty or a glossy surface. To undo the damage, all loose paint flakes must be scraped off with a wire brush and the surface sanded to feather any sharp edges. Bare spots must be primed.

ALLIGATORING. This problem looks just like its name implies—paint crawls into islands. It results from the top coat not adhering to the paint below. It can be caused when a paint not compatible with the paint below is used, or it can be caused when the second coat is applied before the first is completely dry.

BLISTERING. This is paint that rises from the surface and forms hollow blisters. It has the same cause as peeling—moisture in the wood.

WRINKLING. The paint forms an uneven surface.

Mildewcide Can Be Added to Any Paint

If mildew is a problem, you can use paint that contains a mildewcide. This is a chemical that helps deter the spread of mildew. If the paint you want doesn't come with a mildew inhibitor, you can buy a mildewcide additive that can be mixed with the paint.

This can occur when the paint you are using is too thick and the surface starts to dry before the bottom layer does. It can also happen if you paint in cold weather; the cold surface slows drying underneath. To recoat, make sure the new paint is the proper consistency and be sure to brush it out as you apply. Before doing this, you will have to sand the wrinkled area smooth, and in some cases, remove the paint altogether.

CHALKING. This is paint that has a dusty surface. Oil-based exterior paint is generally made to chalk. When it rains, a very fine powdery layer is removed, cleaning the painted surface. In most cases, this is desirable; however, it isn't desirable if the chalking runs down over the brick below. In that situation, you will need a non-chalking exterior paint. Excessive chalking is not desirable and indicates that you will be repainting much sooner than you should. Too much chalking is caused by a chemical imbalance. This can be due to an inferior paint that never had a proper chemical balance. It can also be caused by a previous coat of paint that was too thin or was placed over a porous surface that absorbed too much of the paint's binders. To repaint over a chalking surface, you should hose down the surface with a strong spray, then use a stiff broom to remove the powder. If this doesn't remove all the chalking, after it dries try this solution: mix a quart of household bleach, a tablespoon of household detergent, and enough warm water to make a 2-gallon mixture. Scrub with this solution and then hose it off.

MILDEW. This is a painted surface that has a moldy growth on it. This is not a paint failure. However, if you paint over a mildewed surface, the mildew will come through the new coat of paint. The mildew problem will have to be solved before you can repaint. Use a commercial mildew preparation according to manufacturer's directions

RUNNING SAGS. This is paint with a wavy, irregular surface. The probable cause is poor brushing technique in which you failed to brush out the paint to a consistent thickness. To correct it after it is dry, you will have to sand and repaint.

PAINT WON'T DRY. When a painted surface remains tacky it's a sign of inferior, low-quality paint. If you apply the paint too thickly or during too humid a period, an inferior paint will be slow to dry. A good paint, however, will dry. If you have applied poor-quality paint, removing it and repainting is the only answer.

Paintbrush and Roller Care

Materials • Aluminum Foil or Plastic Bags • Household Detergent • Rags • Paint Thinner or Turpentine • Wood Alcohol • Lacquer Thinner • Containers • Scrap Wood or Newspapers • Linseed Oil • Brush Cleaner

Tools • Paintbrush Comb • Wire Brush or Putty Knife

ALWAYS BUY quality paintbrushes. And, always give them the care that they deserve and they will properly spread paint for many years. There is, however, one exception. If the paint job isn't too critical or the job is very small, you can buy disposable brushes. It is usually cheaper to junk them than to buy cleaner to rinse them out for re-use.

How to Use a Paintbrush

Care of a paintbrush begins with its use. Follow these steps with your paintbrushes:

1. Never use a brush to stir paint. To do so could cause it to become floppy. Instead, use a wooden mixing stick, often given away free at a paint store when you buy paint.
2. Never dip a brush into the paint bucket more than half way up the bristles. You should try to prevent paint from getting into the heel of the brush.
3. Never paint with the side of a brush; it causes curling.
4. To remove excess paint, tap the brush against the inside of the can instead of drawing the brush across the lip of the can. The latter method can cause the bristles to "finger," which means that they separate into clumps.
5. Never leave the brush in the bucket. Its own weight will bend the bristles against the bottom of the can and cause them to curl.
6. If you stop painting for a short period of time while applying any paint, wrap the brush in aluminum foil or insert it in a plastic sandwich bag. Latex paint dries quickly, and partially dried paint in a brush can stiffen the bristles. Oil-based paint dries somewhat slower.

7. Pick the right brush for the job. For example, use only nylon brushes for latex paint. No brush is capable of doing all painting, and forcing a brush to do things it is not shaped or sized to do can damage the brush.

Brush Maintenance

You will get the most mileage out of a paintbrush when the brush is cleaned immediately after each use. To maintain a paintbrush properly, follow these steps:

1. Use the correct solution to clean a brush. For latex paints, use soap or detergent and warm water; avoid putting nylon brushes in solvents. For oil-based paints, use paint thinner or turpentine. For shellac, use wood alcohol. For lacquer, use lacquer thinner. For varnish, use paint thinner or turpentine.
2. Let the brush soak for a few minutes to saturate the bristles completely. Make sure to use enough cleaner to cover all of the bristles. Suspend the brush in such a way that the bristles don't rest on the bottom of the container.
3. Work the brush against the side of the container or on a scrap wood surface or on newspaper for several minutes to get the paint out.
4. Squeeze the bristles with your hands. Start at the heel of the brush against a section of newspaper to remove excess solvent and to check whether all the paint is gone. If there is still some paint present, repeat the cleaning process.

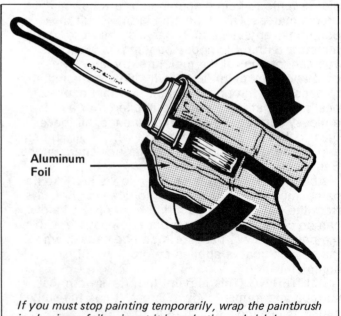

Aluminum Foil

If you must stop painting temporarily, wrap the paintbrush in aluminum foil or insert it in a plastic sandwich bag.

Brush, Roller Cleaner for All Types of Paint

A product that can clean natural or synthetic bristle brushes used with oil- or water-thinned paints is very useful. Klean-Strip Brush & Roller Cleaner, made by Klean-Strip division of W. M. Barr, is formulated to do just that with hard or soft brushes. It also cleans rollers. After soaking, old paint, varnish, or lacquer can be washed away with water, the

manufacturer says. The product is available in pint, quart, and gallon cans.

Pad Applicator Designed for Rough Surfaces

If you need to paint rough surfaces such as brick, stucco, concrete, or rough-hewn wood, an ordinary roller probably won't cover the surface well. The Padco Ruff Painter pad applicator is designed for rough surfaces. Made by Padco, Inc., the applicator is used with a light scrubbing motion. It measures 8 inches by 3½ inches.

Save a Brush by Soaking It

An empty 2-pound coffee can with a plastic lid makes an ideal paintbrush soaker because most brushes can be suspended in solvent without the bristles touching the bottom of the container. The lid with a hole cut in it for the brush handle seals the container so the solvent doesn't evaporate. To make the brush soaker, cut an X-shaped slit in the plastic lid for the brush handle. Then, drill a small hole in the ferrule of the brush and insert a length of wire coat hanger through the hole; this suspends the brush in the container.

Salvage Paint-Hardened Brushes With This Powder

Every do-it-yourselfer probably has a few paint-hardened brushes that were ignored until it was too late to clean them easily. Before you discard expensive paintbrushes, you should try to salvage them. Red Devil, Inc., makes Sav-a-Brush paint brush cleaner and restorer, which is part of the company's D-I-Y product line. It's a concentrated powder that can remove hardened paint from brushes, overalls, and dropcloths. Three ounces

of the powder makes a quart. It comes in 3-ounce and 9-ounce packages.

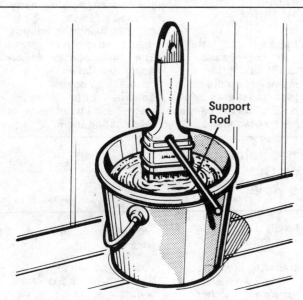

When cleaning a brush, suspend the brush in such a way that the bristles don't rest on the bottom of the container.

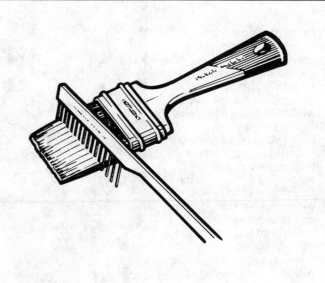

When the brush is clean, shake out the excess solvent or water, and comb out the bristles.

5. With latex paint, rinse the brush out by holding it under a running faucet.
6. When the brush is clean, shake out the excess solvent or water and comb out the bristles.
7. Wash solvent-cleaned brushes in warm, soapy water, and comb them again to separate the inner bristles and to allow the brushes to dry straight.

Brush Storage

Even a clean brush must be stored correctly or it will go bad before you need to use it again. Follow this procedure:

1. Always let brushes dry by suspending them with the bristles down.
2. Wrap natural-bristle brushes in aluminum foil after they have dried. Wrap carefully to hold the brush in its proper shape during storage, and pour in a little linseed oil before crimping the foil around the handle.

Renewing Bristles

You won't be able to reclaim all old brushes that are caked with paint, but it is worth trying to restore them because brush cleaner costs much less than a good brush.

If you neglected your brushes and now they are hard with caked paint, follow these steps to restore them:

1. Use a commercial brush cleaner on the paintbrush. Some are liquid, while others are dry and must be mixed with water.
2. Let the brush soak in the cleaner. If there is dried paint up under the metal ferrule, make sure that the brush is dipped in the cleaner as far as the ferrule.
3. When the cleaner has softened the paint sufficiently, use a wire brush or putty knife to scrape the residue away; work from the ferrule downward.
4. Rinse the brush in the cleaner. If you still can see caked paint, soak the brush some more and repeat the cleaning process.
5. Follow the procedure for cleaning a brush after using it in "Brush Maintenance" in this section.

Roller Cleaning

Roller covers are cleaned almost the same way as brushes: under a faucet with detergent if you are using a water-based paint or with paint thinner if you are using an oil-based paint. After they have been cleaned, store roller covers in aluminum foil.

Unfortunately, roller covers don't respond to cleaning like paintbrushes. Some paint residue usually remains in the nap of the roller, and this dried paint causes marks on a newly painted surface when the roller is used again.

Roller covers, however, are fairly inexpensive, and it is suggested that you purchase a new cover for every paint job to obtain the best results.

Hand Cleaner Does the Job Without Water

No matter how hard you may try, working around your house can get your hands, wrists, and forearms dirty. One good way to remove the dirt is with SupraSoap. Made by Sparkle Plenty, Inc., SupraSoap is a foaming, waterless hand cleaner that comes in a 9-ounce aerosol can. You simply foam it on your hands, wipe your hands together and over other soiled skin areas, and wipe SupraSoap off. According to the manufacturer, the product will also remove lipstick and gasoline odors from your skin. It has a pleasant lemon fragrance.

Use the Right Brush for Water or Oil Paints

Don't use a pure bristle brush for water-based paints. If you do, the bristles will soon clump together. Use a pure bristle brush for oil-based paints only. For water-based paints, use a brush with synthetic bristles, such as nylon. Most brushes or their packages are clearly marked as to the type of paint or finish the bristles have been made to spread. The same recommendations apply to paint roller covers. Use covers specified for oil-based or water-based paints—never interchange them.

Corner Paint Pad Trims Out for a Roller

Painting a 90-degree angle is difficult. The problem is solved with the corner paint pad from Padco, Inc., which fits the 90-degree inside angle wherever one surface meets another. You can use it to paint both surfaces, or just one  surface, at one time. The pad is made of cushioned Nylfoam, a foam plastic that conforms to uneven surfaces.

Painting Masonry

Materials • Masonry Joint Patching Compound • Muriatic Acid • Concrete Degreaser • Block Filler • Masonry Primer • Masonry Paint

---

Tools • Stepladder • Extension Ladder • Putty Knife • Tuckpointing Trowel • Joint Strike • Hoe • Wire Brush • Safety Goggles • Gloves • Scrub Brush • Vacuum Cleaner • Paint Roller • Paintbrushes

---

PAINTING MASONRY—brick, blocks, stone, concrete—is generally more difficult than painting other types of surfaces. However, a masonry paint job doesn't have to be a problem, if you follow several rules before, during, and after the paint is applied.

Moisture is a major cause of masonry painting problems. Most masonry is porous, and water that comes through it pushes at the paint, causing small particles to come off. In addition, the alkalinity in most masonry affects the adhesiveness of some paints and attacks the pigments in others. Of course, paint that goes on masonry surfaces designed for rough treatment—floors, patios, walks, drives, and so on—must be tough to withstand the punishment. Paint selection, therefore, is of crucial importance, and preparation must be thorough.

There are a number of latex-based masonry paints, all of which offer the advantages of easy cleaning and easy application; in addition, they can be used in damp conditions without adhesion problems. Cement-based paints, those with actual Portland cement in them, are frequently used on previously unpainted concrete where very low pressure moisture is a problem.

Epoxy paints are often applied where a hard finish that resists moisture and chemicals is needed. Just make sure that the paint you use is compatible with the existing paint—if any—and with the type of masonry you are covering. If you tell the paint retailer your painting plans, you stand a better chance of leaving the store with the best paint for your purposes.

The first phase of any masonry painting task is preparation. To do the job right, follow these steps carefully:

Interior and Exterior Waterproofing Paint

Formulated for use on both interior and exterior masonry surfaces such as bare block, stucco, brick, and vertical placed concrete, Enterprise latex waterproofing basement paint contains Syncon 1206, a water-repellent shield. According to the Enterprise Companies, the non-flammable paint keeps moisture and dampness from penetrating walls, and resists mildew. The paint is said to apply easily and smoothly with a roller; there is no mixing and troweling. The paint cleans up with soap and water.

Concrete Paint for High-Traffic Areas

A coat of paint can spruce up high-traffic areas on concrete. Drylok latex concrete floor paint is formulated for masonry surfaces such as basement and garage floors, patios, and stairs that are subjected to foot or auto traffic. According to the manufacturer, United Gilsonite Laboratories, the product endures scuffing, moisture, weather, and repeated washing. It is a latex-type paint so no thinners are required during application; tools clean up with soap and water. It is available in quart and gallon sizes.

Special Tools for Texture Paint

If cracked and broken plaster or drywall is a problem in your home, texture paint may be able to hide the imperfections. You can apply the texture paint with any one or all of the special products from the EZ Paintr Corporation: deep texture roller covers, a texture roller for corners, and texturing and stipple brushes. The roller covers, Nos. 409-DTR-90 and 407-DTR-90, fit standard roller cages. The texture brush, No. TEXT-40-73, has fairly short bristles needed for rough work. There also is a choice of a deep texture brush, No. TEXT-20-73, and a complete kit of texture painting tools in two sizes, Nos. 930-DTR-90 and 730-DTR-90.

Painting

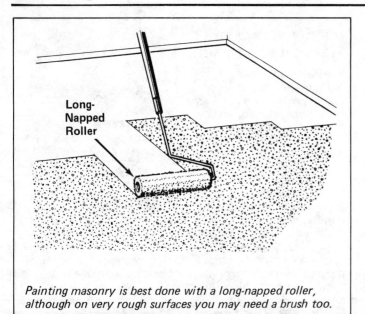

Painting masonry is best done with a long-napped roller, although on very rough surfaces you may need a brush too.

1. Repair and patch all cracks and holes. Allow the patching compounds to cure fully.
2. Remove efflorescence, the whitish bloom that appears in spots on brick and concrete, with a mixture of four parts water to one part muriatic acid. Scrub the surface with the mixture, let it stay for four hours, and then flush it away. *Caution: Wear gloves and safety goggles when working with muriatic acid.*
3. Clean the surface, removing any loose or chalking paint. Driveways and garage floors must be free of grease and oil. To clean such surfaces, you can use a prepared concrete degreaser.
4. Vacuum the surface just before painting.
5. Very rough and porous masonry surfaces should be coated with a block filler, a fairly thick mixture available at a paint store. Be sure the type you get is compatible with the paint you are planning to apply. You can try applying the block filler with a roller, but if the roller fails to get into the pores of the masonry surface, use a brush.
6. Be sure to read all the directions on the paint can label. Various paints require special preparation procedures.
7. Painting masonry is usually best done with a long-napped roller, although on very rough surfaces you may need a brush too.
8. Allow the paint to dry thoroughly before walking on the surface. When painting a swimming pool, be sure to wait the full time specified on the paint before you fill the pool.

Note: Some homeowners decide on the spur of the moment to paint the exterior brick of their homes. If you are considering this, remember that while painted brick can be attractive, in many instances, once painted, brick cannot easily be restored to its original appearance without sandblasting. Moreover, unpainted brick requires no periodic touching up as does painted brick.

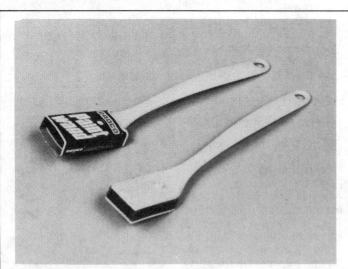

Pad Applicator for Small Areas

Specially designed paint pad applicators can speed painting of window sash, trim, shutters, and other things around the home. The Paint Wand, made by Padco, Inc., is designed for painting smaller areas such as window sash. The pads pop off the wand with the push of a button for cleaning or replacement. The pad size of the Paint Wand is 1⅛ by 1¾ inches.

Lightweight Aluminum Ladder Works Well for Painting Tasks

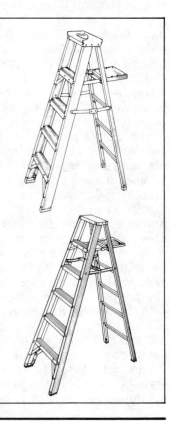

An aluminum stepladder is ideal when working on many household projects, the only exception being work involving electrical wiring. Lightweight yet sturdy, the Bauer aluminum ladder, made by the Bauer Corp., has a foldout shell plus tool-holder holes in the top step. Available in several sizes (4- and 5-foot sizes are the most popular for general household purposes), the Bauer aluminum ladder is braced for extra stability and strength and features Shur-grip safety shoes.

For Large Jobs Mix All Paint at the Same Time

If you are starting a project that requires several gallons of paint, it's a good idea to mix all of the paint together at one time so the color is sure to be the same. You can buy a clean, empty 5-gallon container for this job. Pour all the paint from the gallon cans into the large one. Then, thoroughly mix it. If you have to use two large containers, pour the paint back-and-forth between them. Although this mixing procedure takes a little more time, it's important for color-blending, especially if the color is a shade of green, red, blue, or yellow.

Spray Spackling for Plaster, Drywall

Spackling compound is available in an aerosol can. Kracks Away spackling compound, from the Homagic Division of Midco Products Co., Inc., is sprayed into cracks and nail holes in drywall and plaster walls. The formulation sets up quickly, dries hard, and doesn't dry out in the can, according to the manufacturer. Kracks Away spackling compound can be painted and sanded. The spray application forces the spackling compound deep into crevices. A smoothing applicator, enclosed under the cap of the container, means you don't need any other tools for the repair.

Paint Remover Sprays On, Peels Off

Stripping paint can be a time-consuming, messy job. Strip-O-Magic paint remover, made for Design & Funding, Inc., can remove almost every type of paint from almost any surface. According to the manufacturer, the product removes paint, ink, tar, asphalt, grease, wax, glue, varnish, shellac, decals, and labels in short order, and it can be rinsed off with water or wiped off with a rag. However, the product isn't recommended for terrazzo, vinyl tile, plastic laminates, styrene, and other types of plastics. Before using, carefully read the product cautions; it contains methanol, which cannot be made non-poisonous.

Tack Cloth for Painting Jobs

Before you paint anything, the surface must be free of all debris. The best way to remove this debris is with a tack cloth. The No. 0570 super activated tack cloth from Red Devil, Inc., has treated cotton fiber that helps eliminate dust, lint, and sanding particles on all surfaces. The cloth measures 18 by 36 inches.

Sanding Blocks Have Two Sanding Grades

Preparing the surface can be the most difficult job in painting. Red Devil, Inc., a manufacturer of painters' hand tools and do-it-yourself sealant products, has four flexible sanding blocks that offer more sanding area than many other abrasive blocks, the company says. Ideal for both wet and dry sanding on both contoured and flat surfaces, the aluminum oxide abrasive blocks each have two sanding grades—coarse and medium or fine and medium. Both are available in two sizes—5 by 3 by 1 inch and 4½ by 2¾ by 1 inch.

Paint Tray Made for Pads

If you're using a pad applicator, you should have a paint tray made for pads—not a roller tray. Padco, Inc., makes a tray designed for paint pads. According to the manufacturer, the tray's Dispensa-Wheel offers uniform, no-drip paint-loading without dipping. As the pad is drawn over the wheel, it turns to bring paint up to the pad surface. The tray will rest on any flat surface or it can be hung from a ladder rung or step.

Painting

Texture Paints Can Provide Several Effects

If you're tired of the same old painted walls, why not add a texture to them? Artisan paints, from the Evans Product Co., patch, paint, and pattern in one step, the manufacturer says. There are three latex-based paints—Smooth Texture, Sand Texture, and Stucco Texture. The Sand Texture paint produces a rough sandy effect and covers minor cracks and irregularities. The Smooth Texture coating can hide defects and uneven places in walls or ceilings, while the Stucco Texture paint hides defects and provides the appearance of Mediterranean or Old World styling; the stucco also provides the heaviest textured appearance of the three paints. The products can be applied with a brush or roller; a notched trowel, crumpled plastic or cellophane, putty knife and other items can be used to achieve different effects.

Spackling Paste for Use on Wood, Plaster, Drywall

Ready-to-use spackling paste from the Synkoloid Co. may be applied to cracks and gouges in wood, plaster, or drywall. It also can be used to smooth and resurface plywood. According to the manufacturer, the asbestos-free spackling paste requires no mixing. It can be painted immediately after application with a minimum of shrinkage.

Paint, Varnish Remover for All Finishes

People are often confused about what to use to remove a finish. Sunnyside Premium Remover, however, will work on any paint or varnish finish, according to the manufacturer. The Sunnyside Corp. says its product will work on latex, oil, lacquer, vinyl, epoxy, polyurethane, and marine paint and varnish on wood, metal, or plaster. The remover has a non-flammable gel that is formulated to stick to vertical surfaces. It is water rinsable for both antique and modern finishes. If fine woods are involved, the remover can be rinsed with mineral spirits or paint thinner instead of water. It comes in pint, quart, and gallon containers.

 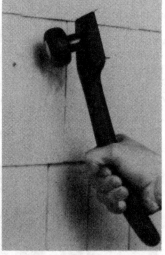

Scraper and Hammer in One Tool

When scraping old paint, you often run across a popped nail. There's a tool that can handle both jobs. The Stanley "Best" model scraper has a curved handle for better leverage and a design to prevent scraped knuckles. It also will drive popped nails with its steel-core hammer-head knob. The "Best" model comes in three sizes: 6, 7, and 8 inches with 1-inch, 1½-inch, and 2-inch-wide blades. Blades are changed by turning a screw. The scraper is made by Stanley Tools, a division of The Stanley Works.

Aggregate Adds Texture to Paint

If you want to add texture to painted walls, you can buy an aggregate and mix it with your interior paint. D.I.Y. aggregate, made by Schalk Chemical for Red Devil, Inc., is formulated to be added to paint for textured or sand finishes. According to the manufacturer, the material may be mixed with any type or color of interior paint. Complete mixing instructions are on the package. The product comes in a 6-ounce bag.

Spray Paint May Be the Nearest Thing to Chrome

Appliances, household and outdoor furniture, picture frames, and many other objects in and around your home have chrome trim. New York Bronze Powder Co., Inc., manufactures Nybco "The Nearest Thing to Chrome," a chrome aluminum spray enamel that can be used to touch-up or refinish chrome items. The spray enamel, which comes in an aerosol can, can also be used to apply a chrome look on almost any non-porous surface, including wood, metal, and hard plastic. According to the manufacturer, the product produces a shiny and

bright finish, but the company doesn't claim the paint has the durability or toughness of real chrome; occasional respraying may be necessary depending on use.

Primer/Sealer for Most Surfaces

When applying a top coat finish, you need a good surface to cover. Zinsser Wonder Base latex sealer, made by William Zinsser & Co., Inc., was primarily developed for use under wallcoverings, but it's also recommended as a primer and sealer for most surfaces under any type of paint, except for high gloss or gloss latex paints where it has been applied over gloss enamel. Wonder Base latex sealer is a fast-drying, semi-transparent

acrylic latex coating that cleans up with soap and water. A gallon covers about 800 square feet.

Paint Mixer for Electric Drill

You can homogenize paints fast with an electric paint mixer. A two-bladed paint mixer that locks into the chuck of a portable electric drill is distributed by Symonds & Co. The mixer has an upper blade that pulls paint down to the center, while a lower blade pulls paint from the bottom of the container. The blades also are set at

a special angle so there is no splattering while mixing.

Snap-on Device Helps Eliminate Much Paint Mess

When you paint from a 1-gallon can, paint usually fills the lid's grooves quickly. And, when you pour from the can, paint is likely to run down the outside of the can. The Mess Less paint pour cap is a simple device that is designed to prevent such problems. The plastic cap snaps into the grooves of any 1-gallon paint can to prevent paint from getting in those grooves or on the side of the can. It also features a spout that avoids any mess while

pouring paint from the can. There's a "balance ledge" for resting the paintbrush temporarily. The Mess Less paint pour cap, from Vic Heath Enterprises, has an opening that is large enough to stir the paint and work with a 4-inch-wide paintbrush.

Undercoat Is Key to Quality Paint Job

Before you paint, you have to prepare the surface well for good results. The undercoat is the key to a quality job. According to William Zinsser & Co., Inc., Zinsser 3-Purpose B-I-N primer-sealer can save you time, trouble, and extra coats of paint. The product, the manufacturer says, dries to the touch in about 15 minutes and is ready for the finish coat of paint in 45 minutes; it also

adheres well to porous and nonporous surfaces.

Texturizer for Interior Surfaces

If you're trying to achieve the look of stucco or other textured finishes on your interior walls, Tex-Appeal interior latex texturizer, made by Sandstrom Products Co., can do the trick. It is a polyvinyl chloride terpolymer-based coating that may be applied to drywall, wallboard, plaster, concrete, cement block, or wood. According to the manufacturer, there's no mixing; you just pour it into a roller tray and apply it. The product, which is

not washable, is tack-free in about two hours and dries to a hard cure in 24 hours.

Sagging Support Beams

Materials • 4 × 4 Lumber • 2 × 10 Lumber • Nails • Adjustable Jack Posts

Tools • Screw-Type House Jack • Tape Measure • Pencil • Crosscut Saw • Hammer • Sledgehammer • Carpenter's Level • Stepladder

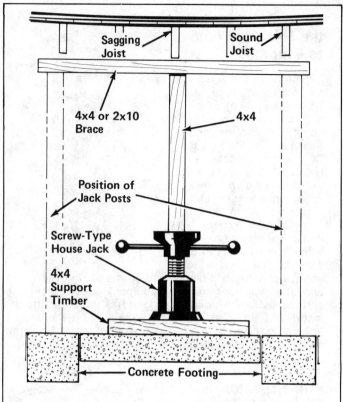

Set the jack on a 4x4 timber base. Then, nail a 4x4 or 2x10 brace across the sagging joists. Use a 4x4 between the jack and the brace.

SOMETIMES A cracked wall, sticking upstairs door, or even a roof leak is caused by a basement problem—the joists under the floor are sagging. Once the joists give a little, the sag continues. Before you start trying to remedy the results upstairs, therefore, you need to take care of the cause in the basement.

Although the cure is simple, you first must check local building codes to see that what you plan to do conforms to the regulations. Once you know, you can follow these steps to remedy sagging supports:

1. Buy or rent a screw-type house jack. They are commonly called screw jacks.
2. Place a 4 × 4 timber directly under the center of the sag to serve as a support.
3. Cut another 4 × 4 or 2 × 10 to run across the sagging joists and beyond to several non-sagging joists on each side. Nail this beam in place across the joists.
4. Place the screw jack on the support base.
5. Measure from the top of the lowered screw jack to the bottom of the beam you nailed up and cut a third 4 × 4 to this length.
6. Install this third piece as a vertical member between the jack and the beam. Because it must be plumb, use a level to set it.

7. Turn the handle of the screw jack until you feel resistance, and **STOP**. *Caution: The leveling process must be very gradual; otherwise, you can crack your walls and do considerable damage to the house.*
8. Wait 24 hours, and then turn the screw jack handle only one quarter turn. The handle will probably be very easy to turn, and you will be tempted to turn more, but be patient. Continue to make no more than a quarter turn every 24 hours. If you miss a day, don't compensate for it with additional turning.
9. When the sagging beams begin to straighten out, start checking them with a level every day.
10. When the beams are all level, install support columns at each end of each beam to secure them. There are adjustable jack posts that work like the screw jack; these are the easiest supports to set.
    Note: No matter what type of supports you install, make sure that the footing below them is sound. The common concrete basement floor is not reliable enough. You should remove a 2-foot section of the old floor where each support post will go. Place a concrete footing that is at least 1 foot thick, and make it level with the rest of the floor. When it has cured, you can put the support posts on the footing.

Telescoping Post Takes Sag Out of Supports

By installing a telescopic Adjusta-Post, you can cure sagging support beams and have a permanent post to prevent future problems. The Sturdy "R" series of posts, made by Adjusta-Post Mfg. Co., offers a 15,000-pound capacity and a safe load of 10,000 pounds. The posts are ball-and-socket jointed and have a ½-inch turning bar. They use a 1-inch screw with 6 inches of threads, and feature two pins in the adjustment holes for greater strength.

Foundation Maintenance

MOST TROUBLE in foundation walls can be blamed on the house structure settling. This is a normal condition; all houses settle because they are extremely heavy.

Settling is caused by movement of the soil on which the foundation is constructed. And moisture is generally the cause of the shifting soil. Too much or too little moisture causes enough expansion or contraction of the soil to move the entire house. If the movement is uniform throughout the structure, the foundation may not suffer. It is unequal movement that causes twisting, bending, and other problems in your home's foundation.

Because unequal movement usually is the product of changes in the moisture content of the soil, be aware of the possible harmful effects on your foundation of plumbing leaks, excessive watering of flower beds adjacent to the house, poor drainage away from the house, or an obstruction that allows water to collect in one spot. The following are some preventive maintenance procedures to follow to minimize the risk of foundation woes:

1. Check the grade around the house to be sure it slopes away from the foundation.
2. Make sure that the natural channels for drainage haven't been dammed or filled. These low places—they shouldn't be ditches—were either created when the property was originally graded or they formed naturally, but uninformed homeowners often fill in such required low areas to make lawns level.
3. Inspect gutters and downspouts to be certain that they are effective and that rainwater is being deposited far enough away from the foundation so as not to cause a problem.
4. Check flower beds next to the house to be sure they are sloped and that the curb or edging doesn't act as a trap for water.
5. Avoid planting shrubs and trees right next to the house. They absorb moisture from the soil, and too little moisture can lead to foundation problems as well.
6. Be sure to water lawns and, particularly, flower beds uniformly—even to the extent of watering where there may be no plants—so that the moisture content will be as equal as possible.
7. Never allow a plumbing problem to go unrepaired any longer than absolutely necessary.

Evidence of unequal settling or upheaval shows itself in spaces developing between the walls and the doors and the windows, cracks in the inside walls, doors that suddenly fail to fit their frames properly, and, of course, cracks in the foundation itself. You can let problems inside the house slide for a while, but take care of exterior cracks and spaces at once. Fill in foundation cracks and caulk spaces around doors and windows before additional moisture can get in and cause more damage.

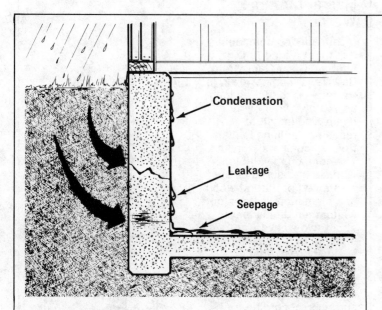

Water in a basement may be due to condensation, leakage, or seepage. If seepage is the problem, inspect the ground around the house to be sure it slopes away from the foundation.

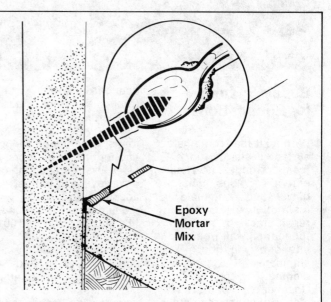

Evidence of unequal settling can show itself in cracks or in spaces between joints. You can fill floor-wall joints with an epoxy mortar mix to prevent seepage. Smooth the joints with the back of a spoon.

If your foundation problems continue to worsen after you correct the moisture imbalance, call a professional. Slab foundations may have to be raised and shored with a process called "mud-jacking," which involves pumping soil cement grout under pressure to lift the slab and chemically stabilize the soil. Doing a foundation leveling and repair job correctly requires engineering skill, experience, and equipment. Done properly, this kind of foundation repair should not have to be repeated.

Masonry Work Requires a Line Level for Accuracy

If you are building a retaining or foundation wall from any masonry material, the job almost always requires a line level and chalk line for accuracy. The No. 75-L3 True Temper line level is lightweight and has single-vial construction. It is 3 inches long and grooved for use on pipes. It features a no-sag string hook design and a handy pocket clip.

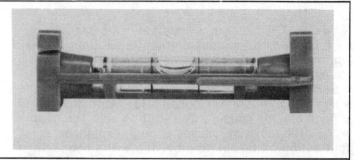

Repair System for Foundations

With a kit that contains a surface sealer cartridge, resin cartridges, nozzles, entry tees, plugs, nails, gloves, and a complete instruction sheet, you can repair cracks in a foundation wall from the interior of your house. This eliminates all exterior digging. The Thermal-Chem crack repair system also is workable on cold and wet surfaces, and will weld the concrete together, preventing water, dust, insects, and other debris from entering through the crack. Made by Thermal-Chem, Inc., the system works on cold joints, base plate sealing, and for cracks in floors, sidewalks, garage slabs, driveways, and patios, according to the manufacturer. The product fills cracks down to 0.002 inch, chemically and mechanically welding the concrete together and restoring the structural properties such as compressive, tensile, and flexural strengths. The kit has enough material to weld one 8-foot-long crack together.

Preventing Structural Wood Rot

You can help prevent wood rot in house structural members that are exposed to high levels of moisture and humidity by coating the wood with a quality preservative. There are three excellent preservatives available: pentachlorophenol, copper naphthenate, and creosote. All three may be applied with a brush or by dipping the wood into a bucket filled with the preservative. Several coats are recommended. If you use copper naphthenate, which leaves a green cast to the wood, let the wood weather for six to eight months before you paint it. The other two products should be dry before you finish them, and the finish used over creosote should have an asphalt base.

Caulking Compound Has a 'Lifetime' Warranty

Most caulking compounds don't last a long time. Lifetime Clear Caulk from Red Devil, Inc., however, is warranteed to last as long as you own your own home. The moisture-repelling caulking is made from silicone and acrylic. The compound will blend with colored surfaces such as stained or natural wood and aluminum. It flows out white, then dries clear in about two weeks. The material can be used to seal windows, door frames, and outdoor fixtures without having to repair the original surfaces, according to the manufacturer. It adheres to plaster, wood, masonry, or tile. The caulking comes in an 11-ounce cartridge.

Damp Basements

Materials • Tape • Hydraulic Cement • Splash Blocks • Mortar Mix or Oakum Caulking • Waterproofing Compound • Pipe Insulation

Tools • Safety Goggles • Gloves • Hand Mirror • Hammer • Baby Sledgehammer • Cold Chisel • Brick Chisel • Stiff Brush • Garden Hose • Trowel • Stepladder • Extension Ladder • Tiling Spade • Flat Spade • Dehumidifier • Exhaust Fan

UNLESS YOUR home is constructed over an underground spring or river or next to a natural watershed, there's no reason why you can't convert a damp basement into usable living and storage space.

The first step toward solving a dampness problem is to determine where the moisture is coming from. Usually, you'll find that a leaking or badly sagging gutter is to blame. Or, a downspout is not positioned so rainwater can flow away from the foundation wall.

Assuming that there is no plumbing problem, the dampness must result from leakage, seepage, or condensation. Leakage is outside water that comes in through cracks. Seepage is also outside water, but it is in such abundance that it makes its way through pores in the concrete. Condensation is inside water that exists as humidity in the air until it condenses on the cool masonry walls or cold water pipes.

You can tell when the problem is leakage because the moisture will only be around cracks. Seepage and condensation may appear much alike, however. To find out which one it is, tape a hand mirror against the wall in the middle of a damp spot, and leave it there overnight. If the mirror is fogged over the next day, you have condensation; if not, you have seepage.

Curing Leakage

If your problem is caused by leakage through a crack, follow these steps:

1. Patch the crack with hydraulic cement, the kind that is quick-setting and can actually set up with water coming in through the crack.
2. If the crack is larger than a hairline, undercut it using a hammer and chisel to make the crack wider beneath than it is on the surface; undercutting lets the cement lock itself in place.
3. Clean away all loose debris, and hose out the cavity with water.
4. Mix the hydraulic cement according to directions.
5. Push the mixture into the crack with a trowel, making sure to fill the entire cavity.
6. Smooth the surface and let the patch cure according to directions.

Steps for Seepage

If seepage is the problem, you should try to divert the outside water that has been penetrating the foundation of the house. Follow this procedure:

1. Check gutters and downspouts. They must be free of debris, pitched properly to carry rainwater off, and the ground on which the downspouts spill should be sloped to carry the water away from the house. The gutter pitch should be $\frac{1}{16}$ inch per foot. Also install concrete or plastic splash blocks.
2. Inspect the ground around the house to be sure it slopes away all around. If not, fill it in until there is good run off, and then roll and

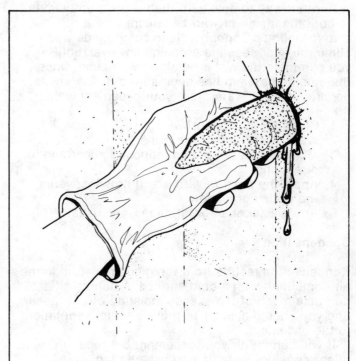

You can plug an open leak with hydraulic cement. Force a long plug of cement into the hole and then trowel the patch smooth.

seed—or sod—to prevent the soil from washing away.

3. Examine flower beds to be sure they are not trapping water that should be running off.
4. Be sure patios and walks next to the house are sloped away, and check the joints to see that they are sealed and curved properly. If they aren't, use a chisel and hammer to undercut the joints, and then fill them with a mortar mix or oakum-type caulking material.

Tiling and Waterproofing

Some outside conditions can be cured only by digging down around the foundation and laying drains. You should have experience in such work.

If you want to tackle it, though, you must dig down to a level below the basement floor—but not below the footing—set drain tile alongside each wall, and extend the drain out into the yard and a dry well to carry the water away. The drain is made of sections of clay tile pipe covered with about 2 feet of gravel. While you have the outside wall exposed, coat it with a waterproofing compound.

There are companies that have a process for pumping a special sealing compound into the ground under pressure. The compound flows along the same paths that the water takes and then seals the wall. Be sure to check with your local Better Business Bureau, however, before contracting for such a treatment because there are some dishonest companies in the field.

Another way to deal with the seepage problem is to coat the inside of your basement with a waterproofing compound. Such compounds won't eliminate your seepage problem, however, unless you eliminate the water outside your house. Once the outside problem has been solved, follow these general steps to waterproof your basement walls:

1. Clean the basement walls.
2. Wet the surface of the walls.
3. Mix the waterproofing compound according to directions.
4. Apply the mixture with a stiff brush, covering the walls completely.
5. Apply a second coat if necessary; usually it is.

Condensation

Condensation results from too much moisture in the air combining with a cold surface. A dehumidifier can take much of the excess moisture out of the air, and you should also try to provide better ventilation in the basement.

If you cannot air your basement out regularly, you might consider installing an exhaust fan. In addition, be sure to wrap exposed cold water pipes with the type of insulation designed to stop pipes from sweating.

Waterproofer for Most Porous Materials

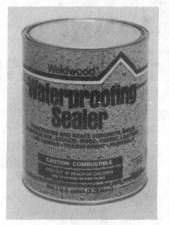

A product that can be used to waterproof a variety of porous materials is extremely useful. Weldwood waterproofing sealer can be used on virtually all porous surfaces including masonry, fabric, drywall, leather, and canvas. According to the manufacturer, Roberts Consolidated Industries, the waterproofing sealer, which contains no silicones, produces a moisture-repellent surface. It can be applied with a brush or roller, by dipping, or by a flooding spray. Coverage is about 150 square feet per gallon. Odorless when dry, the waterproofing sealer also is colorless when dry and can be painted. It is available in 12-ounce spray cans, 32-ounce containers, and 1-gallon, 5-gallon, and 55-gallon sizes.

System Waterproofs Inside and Out

Thoro System Products offers two waterproofings in powder form: Waterplug and Thoroseal. Waterplug, applied to all cracks and joints, is quick-setting and effective even against running water. In fact, Waterplug becomes harder when exposed to water, the manufacturer says. Thoroseal, a heavy cement-base waterproof coating, seals pores. Painted on, Thoroseal comes in white, gray, and other colors to decorate as it seals your basement walls. The products can be used in combination, or separately.

Combatting Mildew

Getting Rid of Mildew

Because mildew is always around, you must continually combat it, which you can do easily with modern chemicals that can even be added to paint. Here are several steps you can take to get rid of mildew easily:

1. Cover all the mildew spots you can see with household bleach. Because most of the fungus will be along the grout lines between tiles or in corners, a good way to apply the bleach is with a plastic squeeze bottle, such as a shampoo or dish detergent bottle. Be sure to observe all of the caution notices on the bleach bottle regarding dangers to your skin and respiratory system.
2. Most of the mildew spots will disappear in a few minutes, but stubborn spots may need additional bleach and perhaps a light scrubbing. An old toothbrush is ideal for scrubbing between tiles and in the corners.
3. When all the mildew is gone, thoroughly rinse the bleach away with water.
4. When you are absolutely sure that none of the bleach remains on the walls, wash the walls with household ammonia. *Caution: Never mix bleach and ammonia. The combination releases potentially fatal chlorine gas.*

Materials • Household Bleach • Plastic Squeeze Bottle • Household Ammonia • Dehumidifier or Exhaust Fan • Mildew Eradicator • Household Detergent

Tools • Stepladder • Toothbrush • Stiff Brush or Broom • Garden Hose • Rubber Gloves

MILDEW IS an airborne fungus. Mildew spores must have moisture and dirt to feed on, and can settle on a wall, ceiling, siding, foundation—wherever conditions are favorable. For example, soap scum is mildew's favorite food, and bathroom walls are among the most common places for the fungus to grow.

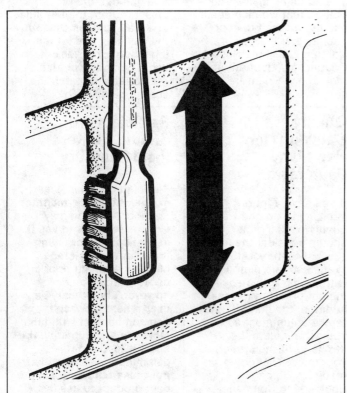

Stubborn mildew spots often need additional work to remove them. An old toothbrush is ideal for scrubbing between tiles and in corners.

Mildew Stains Can Be Removed on Contact

Removing mildew stains from laundry, bathroom, and kitchen areas can be a tough chore. Magic Mildew Stain Remover, from the Magic American Chemical Corp., however, removes such stains on contact without scrubbing, according to the company. The product, which is sprayed on and rinsed off, comes in a 1-pint plastic bottle with sprayer. Magic American Chemical also markets other household aids including Tile 'n Grout Magic that removes stains from ceramic tile and grout lines; Fiberglass Tub & Shower Magic that cleans surfaces such as plastic tub enclosures; and Stainless Steel Magic that removes grease and stains from ovens, range hoods, and other appliances.

Find the Source

New mildew can't get started when you eliminate the conditions that allow it to thrive. Find out what is causing the excess moisture in areas where you have experienced mildew problems. If the mildew occurs in a bath, kitchen, or laundry room, you know where the moisture comes from, and your problem is to discover a way to exhaust the excess moisture. A dehumidifier or an exhaust fan may be the answer, or regular airing of the room may do the job.

If the moisture comes from a leak under the house or bad drainage, you must correct the problem to eliminate your mildew problem for good.

Naturally, it is always a good idea to keep walls free of dirt, grease, and soap scum.

Mildew also forms outside. Many people think that they can kill the fungus when they paint their homes with a mildew-retardant paint. Usually, however, the mildew grows back in weeks.

No paint can kill mildew; you must kill mildew before painting. To get rid of mildew from exterior walls, mix a solution of 1 quart chlorine bleach, ⅔ cup mildew eradicator, ⅓ cup household detergent, and 3 quarts warm water. Scrub the affected areas with a stiff brush or broom, then hose them off thoroughly. Be sure to trim back trees and bushes that prevent air and sunlight from reaching mildew-prone areas.

Grout Cleaner for Floor or Wall Tile

Grout lines between tiles get dirty as time goes by. Tile and grout cleaner, No. 0336, from Red Devil, Inc., is formulated to clean dirt, grit, and stain from grout lines between floor and wall tiles. The product removes and cleans soap film and contains no abrasives, according to the company. A 6-ounce package makes 3 pints of solution.

You Need a Ladder for Ceiling Work

Unless you're very tall, you need a ladder for most ceiling work. The Job-Master Type I stepladder is ideal for ceiling jobs because it has a tool tray that can hold paint, tools, nails, and other materials. The ladder, which is made by R. D. Werner Co., Inc., has double-riveted construction, 3-inch side rails, and 1¼-inch rear rails.

Silicone Rubber Patches Basement Wall Leaks

There is a brush-on/roll-on silicone rubber coating that you can use to patch hairline cracks in masonry and concrete as well as handle many other sealing jobs around the house. You can use it to seal around joints inside and out, protect wooden posts against rot, and to coat flashings. It is Dow Corning's Silicone Rubber Coating. You just stir and then apply it right from the can.

Patching Splits in Plywood

Plywood siding sometimes splits at grooved joints, or the top veneer breaks loose from its core. To patch this material, drive threaded or ringed nails around the split. Use plenty of nails. Then, force a quality caulking compound into the break. You can get lots of pressure from the flat side of a wall scraper. Smooth the caulking and let the job alone for a week or two. Then paint or stain the surface to match the surrounding siding.

Acrylic Latex Caulk Is Formulated for Indoor or Outdoor Use

Some caulking compounds can be used to fill seams around doors and windows, cracks between the foundation and siding, joints in gutters, and seams between flashing and roof shingles. Macco Super Caulk LC-130 is such a product. According to Macco Adhesives, Glidden Coatings and Resins, a division of SCM Corp., Super Caulk is a flexible acrylic latex caulking compound that is durable and fast-drying. It's recommended for use in residential construction for sealing cracks and exposed joints between similar or dissimilar

materials, such as wood, metal, brick, stone, and masonry.

Quality Caulking Gun Has Many Features

If you have a lot of caulking to do and want a quality caulking gun, you should consider the Albion 139-3. It features Albion's ¼-inch square piston rod with thumb-activated instant pressure release. In addition, the gun offers a stroke adjustment so that you can regulate the stroke to fit the size of your hand. The tool is made by Albion Engineering Company, which makes other caulking tools and accessories.

Particleboard Should Be Kept Inside and Dry

Particleboard makes an excellent underlayment for flooring. And, you may even be tempted to use it as a sheathing or siding for an outdoor storage building or porch floor or deck. Particleboard, however, should only be used where it doesn't come in contact with high moisture and humidity. If it does, it tends to delaminate and crumble. For these outdoor jobs, the best product to use is plywood with an exterior glue bond or tempered hardboard.

Replacing Damaged Siding

Materials • Aluminum Nails • Acrylic Latex Caulk • Paint • 16d Common Nails • Scrap Wood or Cedar Shingle Wedges • Electrical Tape

Tools • Hammer • Caulking Gun • Paintbrush • Butt Chisel • Hacksaw or Backsaw • Tape Measure • Pencil • Carpenter's Square • Block Plane • Putty Knife • Electric Drill and Bit

Y OU DON'T HAVE to rip off the whole side of your house to replace a damaged or rotted length of clapboard or shingle siding. If the damage isn't extensive, it can be accomplished in a morning or an afternoon.

If the clapboards or shingles are only cracked or split, you may be able to repair them instead of replacing them. Tap the break together with a hammer and drive in aluminum nails 1 inch apart through each side of the split. Then, caulk the crack and paint the caulk to match the siding.

If rot is a problem on the siding, you'll have to stop the source of the rot—probably gutters or downspouts in poor condition. Moisture penetrating the siding from inside the house can also cause siding rot. Vent inside moisture with a fan or aluminum siding vents, or by installing insulation with a moisture vapor barrier facing *inside* the house.

Clapboard Siding

Follow this procedure for replacing a length of damaged clapboard siding:

1. Make wedges from scrap wood or use cedar shingles as wedges.
2. Drive the wedges up under the damaged siding to pull the siding away from the underlapped siding and the sheathing. Locate and remove all nails; if you can't remove them with a hammer, cut the nails with a hacksaw. Then drive wedges under the course of siding that overlaps the damaged siding, and remove all nails.
3. Use a backsaw or a hacksaw—or the blade removed from a hacksaw and wrapped at one end with electrical tape for a handle—to make two cuts through the siding, one on each side of the damaged area. Make a complete cut through the siding on each side. You may have to move the wedges around while cutting.
4. Slide the length of damaged siding down and out. If it is difficult to remove, use a butt chisel to complete the bracket cuts. If the siding still won't pull out, hack at the damaged siding with the chisel, removing it in pieces. Don't hack at the siding until the bracket cuts have been made.
5. Measure, mark, and cut a new length of siding to fit, and test-fit the new piece. The clapboard should underlap the top piece slightly and overlap the bottom piece. Plane the edges for a tight fit after you've made the initial cuts.
6. Prime the new piece of siding with a coat of paint—both sides and the edges—and prime the cut edges of the old siding. Let the paint dry completely.
7. When the paint is completely dry, insert the primed siding into the gap and nail it with 16d nails to the siding above and below it.
8. Caulk the cracks with acrylic latex caulk; smooth the caulk with a putty knife or your finger. Let the caulk dry; then paint the new siding.

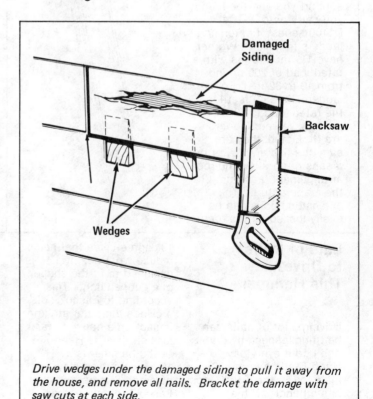

Drive wedges under the damaged siding to pull it away from the house, and remove all nails. Bracket the damage with saw cuts at each side.

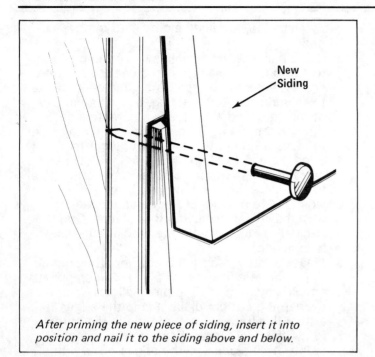

After priming the new piece of siding, insert it into position and nail it to the siding above and below.

New Siding

Shingle Siding

To replace damaged shingle siding, use this procedure:

1. Drive wood or cedar shingle wedges under the course of shingles above the damaged area.
2. Use a hacksaw blade to cut the siding nails if the nails can't be removed with a hammer. Wedge out and cut the nails on the shingles below the damaged shingles, if necessary.
3. Remove the damaged shingles.
4. Insert new shingles and nail them into position; use aluminum nails for this job. If the nail holes are not predrilled in the shingles, drill pilot holes with a small bit to prevent splitting and to make nailing easier.

   Note: Instead of using new shingles, it's a good idea to replace damaged shingles with shingles from an inconspicuous part of the house. This way, the shingles for the patch will be weathered properly to match the shingles surrounding the patch.

Climb Onto Structures With Safety

If the job requires a ladder, be safe with a ladder that is strong enough to support you and the loads you carry onto it. The D1100 series of extension ladders from R. D. Werner have 1½-inch rungs with a rated load of 200 pounds from 16 to 32 feet. For ladders 36 to 40 feet long, the rated load is 225 pounds. Werner ladders are UL Listed; they are easy to raise and lower by means of a pulley-and-rope arrangement, according to the manufacturer. The extension hooks can be easily locked on the rungs.

Cure for Curled Lap Siding

Lapped siding sometimes warps and curls. And it is almost impossible to renail the siding because the pressure from the warped wood pops the nails. Instead of nails, use a couple of wood screws to solve this problem. Drill pilot holes for the screws and countersink them. Then, drive in the screws, and paint or stain the heads so they blend in with the siding's finish.

Nail Holder Saves Your Thumb

The next time you drive nails don't take a chance of smashing your thumb. Use the Molly Thumb-Saver nail holder from Bostik Corp. The tool is designed to hold tacks, brads, or nails safely and securely. It works on fasteners from a ½-inch brad to a 10d nail.

Lots of Nails to Drive? Try This Hammer

Driving a lot of nails can be tiring, especially if you don't do it every day. The Hand-Tastic hammer, made by Easco Tools, Inc., has a handle with a 19-degree curve that helps reduce wrist flex. It also is designed to fit the shape of a cupped hand. This, according to Easco Tools, provides a greater striking impact on a nail with far less strain. The Hand-Tastic hammer is a 16-ounce curved claw hammer. It is backed by an Easco Tool guarantee.

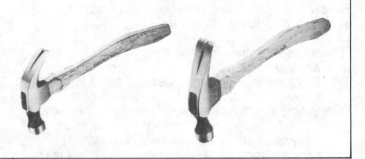

How to Replace Damaged Siding Shingles

Split and damaged siding shingles are common, and they usually can be replaced very quickly. Use a hammer and short pry bar to remove the nails that hold the shingle to the sheathing. These nails are under or on the shingle directly above the damaged one. The damaged shingle also is nailed through its face to the shingle directly below it. When the nails are out, pull the damaged shingle down and out. If the replacement shingle will show, you may want to remove a good shingle from another part of the house where a replacement won't show. This way, the replacement shingle will be weathered the same as the surrounding shingles. The new shingle can go into the void left by the replacement.

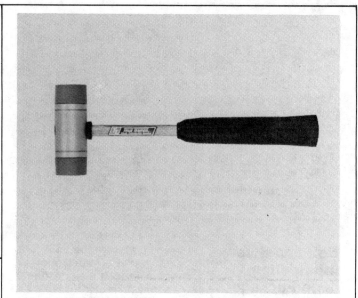

Wood Chisel Set Can Handle a Variety of Projects

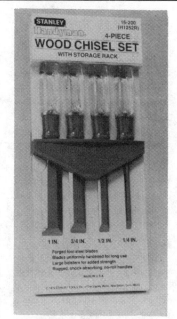

Every homeowner should have a set of wood chisels. They can be used for a variety of projects ranging from mortising a door hinge to removing damaged siding. A four-piece set of wood chisels is available from Stanley Tools, a division of The Stanley Works. The Handyman No. 16-200A chisel set includes 1-inch, ¾-inch, ½-inch, and ¼-inch chisels and a storage rack. The tools have impact-resistant clear handles and a blade and bolster that is forged in one piece from high-grade tool steel, heat-treated and beveled. The blades have a polished finish.

Power Saw Can Cut Studs Quickly

A power saw makes any construction job easier. A circular saw, like Black & Decker's 7¼-inch model, can cut all the studs for your framing job in a matter of minutes. The combination blade does both cross-cutting and ripping. Though not an expensive saw, this unit, made by Black & Decker (U.S.), Inc., with its 1½-horsepower motor will do nicely for the average home handyman.

Soft-Tip Hammers for Assembly Jobs

Soft-head hammers should be used so you don't damage the object or surface you're striking. True Temper Soft-Tip hammers have aluminum or shot-loaded heads, fiberglass handles, and non-slip molded cushion grips. A special compound used for the tips is formulated to outlast any other soft-faced tip material, according to True Temper Corp. Alternate tips are available; they range from medium-hard to tough, and can be interchanged on the hammers, which True Temper says aren't affected by dampness, dryness, heat, cold, or common chemicals.

Jack Screws Fight the Sags

You can combat structural sags with jack screws. A heavy-duty jack screw is available from Montgomery Ward in four sizes to handle weights from 5 to 18 tons. Short and stubby, the heavy-duty jack screw is best used in a crawl space where a standard jack post could not be. It is made of a high-tensile iron for strength and painted to resist rust. The wide bell bottom gives the jack screw a firm footing, and the hot-forged one-piece steel turn screw (you'll need a wrecking bar to turn it) has precision-cut threads. The product is available through Montgomery Ward's catalog—not in retail stores.

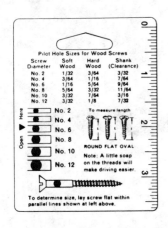

Bolt and Screw Information Is on Package

Bolts and screws are easy to use. The problem is knowing where and how to use the fasteners. Rockford Products Corp. has solved this problem on its packages of screws and bolts. On the back is a table that provides pilot hole sizes. It includes the screw diameter for Nos. 2 through 12; the hole sizes for each in soft and hard wood; shank clearance; how-to-measure information; head types; and a 3-inch ruler. A wide range of screw and bolt sizes and types are available.

Bridging Expands as Lumber Shrinks, Stopping Squeaks

Bridging can prevent or cure squeaky floors. Kant-Sag Speed Bridging, No. O-16, is inserted between floor joists and positioned. The lower prongs of the bridging are hammered into the joist at the bridging points. As the joists shrink from drying out, the bridging automatically expands to take up the slack. This, says the manufacturer, United Steel Products Co., prevents or cures squeaky floors. The bridging may be installed any time. It fits 2 × 6 to 2 × 12 joists set 16 inches on center. No nailing is necessary, although you can use one nail at the bottom prong point if you wish.

Framing Ties for Strength in Structures

Framing ties add strength to construction. One standard and two extended-style Kant-Sag rafter ties are available from United Steel Products Co., for fabricating decks, porches, and even room additions. The standard style, Nos. RT-1 through RT-4, ties the top plate to a rafter. It has a grip-tooth design that helps you hold the framing member while you nail it. Nos. RT-5 through RT-8 are extended-style ties for nailing top plates to rafters. This style, however, doesn't have grip teeth. The nails go through predrilled holes in the ties. Nos. RT-9 and RT-10 are extension-style ties to support studs to two top plates and a rafter; both are reversible. The ties are made of 18-gauge galvanized steel.

Tool Detects Hidden Studs

Finding studs in back of walls so paneling, pictures, and other materials and objects may be hung sometimes can be a hard job. With the No. 2805 Stud Finder from Red Devil, Inc., the hunt is easier. The stud finder tool has a magnetic needle that indicates where studs are as you move the tool over the wall and it passes over a nail in the stud or any other framing. The best place to use the tool is along the wall at the baseboard where the baseboard has been nailed to the studs.

Removing Dents in Aluminum Siding

The best way to repair those long and shallow dips in aluminum siding is with the suction cup of a plumber's plunger. Push the suction cup down on the flat surface of the siding so there is a good vacuum between the cup and the siding. Then, pull on the handle. You may have to repeat this process several times before the metal pops back.

Repairing Leaks

Materials • Aluminum or Copper Flashing • Asphalt Roofing Paper • Asphalt Roofing Cement • Shingles as Required • Roofing Nails

---

Tools • Stepladder • Extension Ladder • Flat Spade • Hacksaw Blade • Hammer • Pliers • Short-Bristled Paintbrush

---

L EAKS IN ROOFS can do all sorts of damage to the structure of your home. Repairing the leak is often an easy task, but because leaks are very elusive, locating the leak can take much longer than fixing it.

For example, water can enter at one point in your roof and follow a rafter for many feet before it drips down onto the ceiling. Sometimes, a leak occurs only when the wind is blowing from a certain direction and with enough force to blow rain in under a broken shingle or through some crack. You frequently have to be in the attic when it is raining to track down the spot, but the leak may even be in a place where you cannot spot it from inside the attic; then you have to look outside—but not while the roof is wet. Look for such things as missing shingles, split shingles, loose nails, or bad flashing. Once you find the leak, mark it well so that you know where to go to work when the roof is dry.

Assuming that you have located the leak, you are ready to make repairs.

Caution: Roof repairs often involve climbing a ladder. Make sure the ladder is extended three rungs above the eaves of the house and that it is pulled back one-fourth of its length from the foundation at the ladder's base. It also is important that the ladder extension hooks are securely in place on the support rung, and that the ladder extension laps at least three rungs. As you raise the ladder, be careful not to contact any electrical power wires. And, make sure the ladder is on a firm footing and someone is holding the base of the ladder while you climb from the ladder to the roof and from the roof to the ladder.

Wood Shingle Roof

For fixing a leak in a wood shingle roof, follow this procedure:

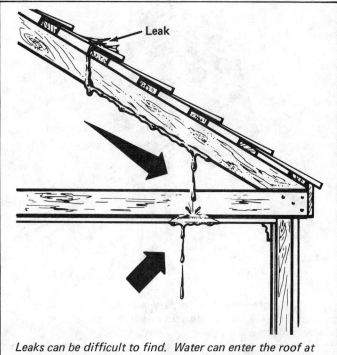

Leaks can be difficult to find. Water can enter the roof at one point and follow a rafter for many feet before it drips down onto the ceiling.

1. Replace a split shingle or stop the leak in the old one. If you decide not to replace the shingle, try slipping a piece of aluminum or copper flashing under the split or inserting some asphalt roofing paper under it. First, pry up the overlapping shingle with a flat garden spade, using your foot on the handle to apply pressure. If you cannot get the patch as far back under the shingle as you think it should go, use a hacksaw blade to cut any nails that are in the way. Then, apply asphalt roofing cement to anchor the patch. If you need to drive new nails that leave exposed heads, put a dab of cement over each head.
2. Replace any missing shingles as soon as you notice their absence. Pry up the overlapping shingles, cut any nails that prevent your getting the new shingle in far enough, and use a combination of asphalt roofing cement and nails to anchor the new shingle.
3. If the problem involves the ridge shingles, buy a bundle of ridges and install them with roofing nails rather than try to piece them together.

Composition Shingle Roof

For repairs on a roof with composition, or asphalt, shingles, follow these steps:

1. If asphalt shingles have curled corners, put a dab of asphalt roofing cement about the size

Roof Work

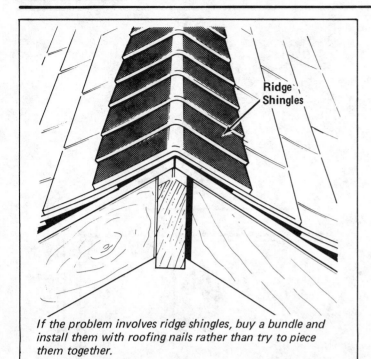

If the problem involves ridge shingles, buy a bundle and install them with roofing nails rather than try to piece them together.

of a quarter under each and press the corners down.
2. Patch holes or rips with roofing cement. Lift up the shingle, dab the cement under the hole, and press the shingle back down.

3. If you must replace a shingle, you can usually get to the nails holding the faulty shingle by raising the overlapping shingle with a flat tiling spade. Raise it gently so as not to crack the shingle. Then, loosen and remove the nails, and slip the bad section out. Put the new one in its place and renail using only two nails. Dab cement on the nail heads and on the overlapping shingle to anchor it down. You will find that warm composition shingles are much more pliable and, therefore, easier to work with.

Damaged Flashing

You can patch most damaged flashing with asphalt roofing cement. The problem is locating the trouble. A gap in a flashing joint is easy to locate and easy to patch, but detecting a nearly invisible pinhole is something else again. When you see any spots that might possibly be pinholes, cover them with cement. In addition, dab some cement on any exposed nail heads in the flashing.

Flashing should be "painted" once every two years with asphalt roofing cement that is made for this purpose. Include chimney, roof vent, and valley flashing on your maintenance list. See the section on "Valleys and Flashing" in this chapter.

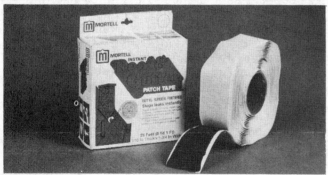

Roof and Gutter Patch Tape

If a gutter or downspout is leaking, the problem may be repaired with tape. Mortell instant roof and gutter patch tape is cut to size and pressed firmly over the leak in a gutter, downspout, vent and chimney flashing, or shingles. Then, you remove the paper backing. The tape is made of elastic butyl rubber that won't dry out, crack, or shrink, and it will conform to irregular surfaces, according to the manufacturer. The patching tape is also an ideal product to seal roof ventilators between the bottom of the ventilator flashing and the roof sheathing. The tape, made by the Mortell Co., comes in 25-foot rolls that are 1¾ inches wide and ¹⁄₁₆ inch thick. The tape sticks to damp surfaces for emergency patches, but it does best when the surfaces are clean and dry.

Wood Ladders With No-Sway Extensions

Wood ladders can carry a load and be just as safe as metal ladders. The Type I, Series No. 20 wood extension ladder, made by Rich Ladder Co., has no-sway extensions and a 250-pound duty rating that meets OSHA requirements, according to the manufacturer. The rungs of the ladder are made from Appalachian hardwood with fully rodded construction. Ladder sizes are 16, 20, 24, 28, 32, 36, and 40 feet, with 13- to 35-foot maximum extended lengths. A professional tip: Never paint a wooden ladder; the paint can hide any damage. Instead, coat the wood with linseed oil mixed with a small amount of turpentine. Wipe it dry.

This affords plenty of wood protection.

Valleys and Flashing

Materials • Flashing • Asphalt Roofing Cement • Shingles as Required • Roofing Nails • Mortar

Tools • Stepladder • Extension Ladder • Hammer • Tape Measure • Pencil • Putty Knife • Brick Chisel • Caulking Gun • Paintbrush • Trowel • Wire Brush

MOST ROOFS are constructed with roof sheathing, a layer of asphalt building paper, and the shingles. In roof valleys—where two sections of roof meet—and around chimneys, vents, and stacks, metal flashing is used under the shingles to prevent leaks. The flashing usually is made of aluminum or copper, although galvanized steel sometimes is used.

Most flashing is simply nailed to the roof sheathing with roofing nails. The flashing is then coated with asphalt roofing cement; the shingles overlap this ribbon of metal.

All flashing should be checked periodically and repaired anytime you spot a leak in the metal. All flashing should be coated with asphalt roofing cement at least every other year to prevent leaks. Asphalt roofing cement, used for both asphalt and wooden shingles, is available in quart, gallon, and 5-gallon containers. You also can buy it in cartridges for use in a caulking gun.

Chimney Flashing

To replace flashing around a chimney, follow these steps:

1. Remove the old cap flashing—the outer or covering layer—that has come loose. However, some installations may not have any.
2. If necessary, remove the shingles around the flashing. Take care particularly with composition shingles because replacements may not be easy to find. Cautious prying can usually save shingles.
3. Remove the flashing and save it for use as a pattern to cut a replacement.
4. Examine the base flashing to see if it needs to be replaced. If there is any doubt, replace it too, but be careful so you don't damage the

roofing paper beneath it.
5. Chisel away all the old cement that held the flashing in place between the bricks.
6. Apply the front base flashing first, using liberal amounts of asphalt roofing cement to hold it in place. When nails must be used, be sure to cover nail heads with the cement. Roofing cement, applied with a putty knife, is usually best for covering nails.
7. When all the base flashing is in place, replace the cap flashing, using as much of a lip going into the mortar joints as possible. This lip should be at least 1½ inches wide.
8. Set the cap flashing in place with either roofing cement or mortar, both of which are available in cartridges for use with a caulking gun.
9. Replace the shingles and cover all exposed nail heads and all edges with roofing cement.

Flashing on Vertical Surfaces

Vertical surfaces can be treated in much the same way as described in the procedure for "Chimney Flashing," unless there is siding on the vertical

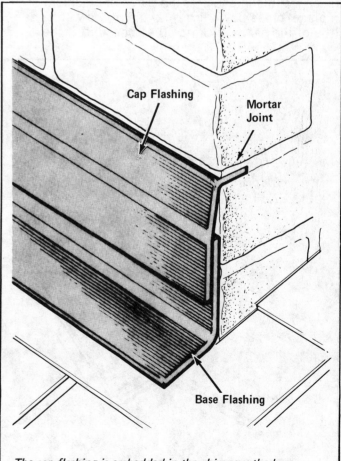

The cap flashing is embedded in the chimney; the base flashing is sealed to the roof. Both must be firmly anchored.

surface. In such a case, bring the flashing up under the siding.

Pipes that stick out through the roof—such as vent pipes—must also be flashed. If the flashing around the pipes is in poor condition, you can generally buy a complete flashing unit that slips over the pipe.

Remove enough shingles above the vent to expose all of the old flashing, and then remove the old flashing. Slip the new unit in place and nail it down, covering all the edges and nail heads with cement. Then, replace the shingles. Avoid exposed nail heads, but if lots of nails are necessary, cover their heads with roofing cement.

Valley Flashing

Valley flashing is treated differently. Fortunately, most roof valley problems result from holes, and every effort should be made to patch rather than replace sections of roofing.

When you locate a hole, cut an aluminum or copper patch to fit over it and use asphalt roofing cement to hold it in place. Always apply aluminum to aluminum, copper to copper, and steel to steel. Mixing metals sets up a corrosive action, which can cause trouble later. After the patch and cement are in place, press down firmly so that there will be as little of the patch sticking up as possible. If the

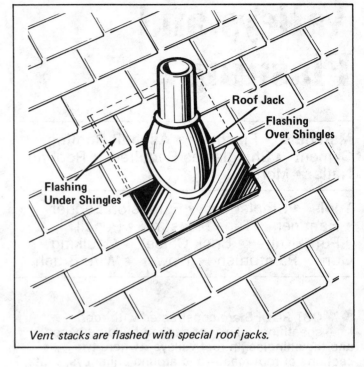

Vent stacks are flashed with special roof jacks.

hole is under the shingles, pry up the shingles carefully and patch. Apply a dab of cement over any exposed nails that you must drive into the shingles. Avoid exposed nail heads whenever possible.

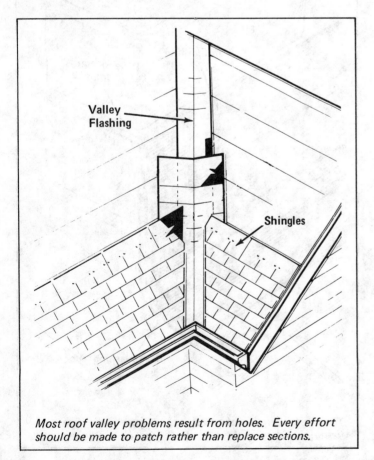

Most roof valley problems result from holes. Every effort should be made to patch rather than replace sections.

You Can Buy Aluminum Valleys in Rolls

Howmet Aluminum Corporation markets valley material in 10-foot-long rolls. The material is 0.016 inch thick and comes in 14- and 20-inch widths. Because they don't rust or discolor, aluminum valleys can be left unpainted to weather to a soft gray color. If your aluminum valleys come in contact with masonry or with a dissimilar metal, however, you should coat them with a bituminous paint to avoid electrolytic action between the surfaces. Moreover, you should only use aluminum nails.

Estimating Shingles

Shingles are sold by the "square." A square is 100 square feet, or enough shingles to cover this amount of area. Three "bundles" of shingles comprise one square. A bundle is 33 square feet.

You will need 1½ pounds of roofing nails to install one square of shingles. You'll also need one quart of roofing cement or two tubes of roofing cement in caulking cartridges to install one square. The cement is used to seal nail heads and stick down curled shingles.

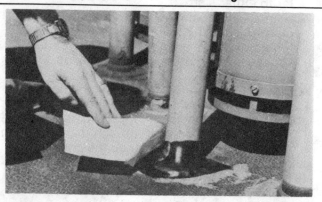

Resilient Tape Seals Concrete, Other Materials

Miracle Seal tape, which comes in a roll, is very pliable so you can press the material into place. According to the manufacturer, Revere Chemical Corp., it will stick to almost any surface. Then, you peel off a protective covering to complete the job. Miracle Seal will repair flashing, copings, cracks, seams, gutters, downspouts, and almost any other building product on the market, the company claims. The product is resistant to all weather conditions, won't oxidize, and molds readily to irregular surfaces. You can paint it immediately after application with an asphalt, tin, or aluminum coating. The product is available in 2½- and 8-inch-wide rolls.

Seal Flashing With Aluminum Tape

Flashband, a peel-and-stick self-adhesive aluminum flashing that comes in rolls, has a strong asphalt adhesive that will stick to almost any clean, dry surface of virtually all conventional building materials, the manufacturer says. Developed for professional roofers, Flashband is available to the homeowner in rolls of 2, 3, 6, or 9 inches wide by 20 feet long. Water and air tight, it can be used to create a permanent seal

around flues, chimneys, and skylights, but it also comes in a Patch Pak for smaller spot jobs. Flashband is made in England, but it is distributed in the United States by the 3E Corp.

Elastomeric Roof Coating for Sealing Flashing

If your roof flashing needs some sealing, you'd better do it soon before the damage gets worse. Parr, Inc., makes Storm King Polar White roof coating that protects against corrosion, prevents moisture penetration, resists sunlight deterioration, reflects heat, and deadens sound, the company says. The elastomeric coating is easily applied and can be thinned with solvent.

Universal Adhesive for Almost Any Kind of Material

A glue, sealer, hardener, weatherproofer, dustproofer, and bonding agent in one product is extremely useful. Weldbond can bond and seal asbestos, bricks, carpets, cement, ceramics, cord, cardboard, fabrics, glass, gypsum, hardboard, metal, paper, plywood, roofing, slate, stone, foam plastic, veneers, and dozens and dozens of other materials. You mix Weldbond with water and apply it with a brush to the surface of the material you want sealed. The mixture dries clear, and according to Frank T. Ross & Sons, Inc., it is impervious to gas, oil, grease, salt, molds and fungi, and weak alkilis and acids. After setting, Weldbond withstands all climatic conditions. Undiluted, Weldbond can cover about 400 to 550 square feet per gallon. Diluted with three parts water, the coverage is 1,800 square feet per gallon.

Lighten Snow Loads on Roof

Snow is heavier than you might think and it can cause roofs to weaken and sometimes collapse if it isn't removed. Garelick Manufacturing Co. makes a roof snow rake that is aluminum with an angled blade for easier snow removal. The model 89421 rake is 21 feet long, which is enough length for most single-story homes. Extensions are available for higher structures.

Gutter and Downspout Care

Materials • Asphalt Roofing Cement • Wire Screening • Gutter Hangers • Roofing Nails • Rivets • Self-Tapping Screws

Tools • Stepladder • Extension Ladder • Whisk Broom or Plastic Scraper • Gloves • Garden Hose • Drain-and-Trap Auger • Wire Brush • Tin Snips • Paintbrush • Carpenter's Level • Hammer • Rivet Tool • Drill and Bit, Nail, or Icepick

GUTTERS AND downspouts require lots of attention. They must be kept clean, and any damaged section must be repaired or replaced as soon as you notice it. If you don't, water from gutters and downspouts can spill over onto and into the structural and finishing materials of your home.

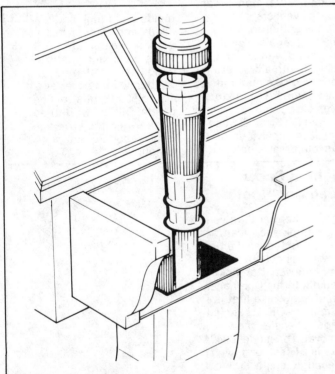

Flush out the gutters and downspouts with a hose. If downspout is clogged, use a drain-and-trap auger to break through the clog.

The result can cost you thousands of dollars in repairs.

Cleaning Gutters

To clean your gutters, follow this procedure:

1. Use a ladder that is long enough to reach the gutters, and be sure to play it safe; move the ladder often so that you never have to reach far to either side.
2. Remove all the debris from the gutter. Use a discarded plastic plate scraper or a whisk broom to rake the leaves out of the gutter. If you clean the gutters with your hands, wear gloves.
3. Flush out the gutters with a garden hose.
4. Flush out the downspouts with the hose. If you discover that they are stopped up, use a drain-and-trap auger to break through the clog. Then flush with the hose. Or, stick the hose down the downspout and turn on the water full to flush it.
5. While cleaning, look for rust spots, holes, loose supports, and sags in the gutters and downspouts. Check the runoff to be sure the gutters are still pitched properly, and be sure the strainers are in place and unclogged. The gutters should be pitched $\frac{1}{16}$ inch per foot, and hangers should be spaced every 3 feet.

Patching Gutters

Gutters may be patched, but consider the patch as a temporary measure to stop a drip or leak. The gutter should be replaced as soon as possible. Follow this procedure to patch a gutter:

1. Remove all rust and any other loose metal by cleaning the area with a wire brush. Cover the bad spot with asphalt roofing cement.
2. Cut a patch from wire window screen material. The patch must cover the hole and extend about ½ inch beyond it. Or, cut the patch from an asphalt shingle or scrap of roll roofing material.
3. Coat the area around the hole with asphalt roofing cement.
4. Put the patch down over the cement and press it in place.
5. Brush the cement over the patch.
6. When the first coat sets up, cover it again with cement. You can patch tiny holes without using the patching material; the cement will fill in by itself. You may have to apply several coats.

Sagging Gutters

A gutter that sags usually has a loose hanger. There are three types of gutter hangers in use today. One

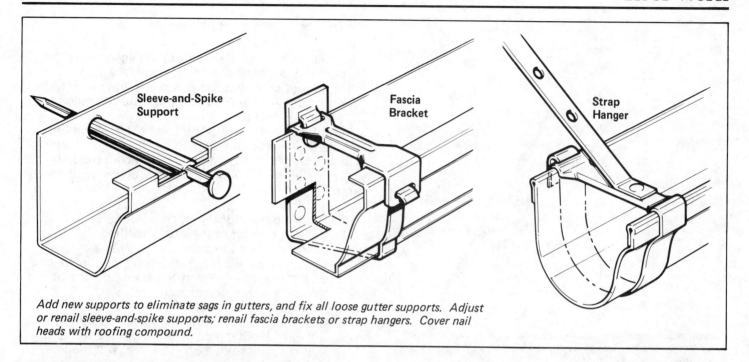

Add new supports to eliminate sags in gutters, and fix all loose gutter supports. Adjust or renail sleeve-and-spike supports; renail fascia brackets or strap hangers. Cover nail heads with roofing compound.

employs a gutter spike driven through a sleeve and into the roof board. If the spike comes loose, you can drive it back in with a hammer. Another type of hanger features a strap that is nailed to the roof under a shingle. Be sure to use galvanized roofing nails to resecure a loose strap, then put a dab of asphalt roofing cement over the heads and old nail holes. A third type of gutter hanger is a bracket nailed to the fascia under the gutter. Because you may not be able to get to the loose nails with this type of gutter hanger, add an auxiliary support of another type to eliminate the sag. Sometimes a gutter sags because it lacks sufficient support points. There should be support about every 3 feet.

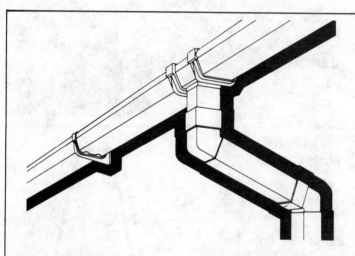

Vinyl Gutters Snap Together Fast

Designed for do-it-yourself installation, GSW snap seal vinyl rain goods—gutters and downspouts—are easy to install on your home. Made by Jackes-Evans Mfg. Co., a division of GSW, Inc., the products include end caps, elbows, downspout clips and connectors, shoes, roof rafter brackets, drip edge, gutters, downspouts, ends, joiners, and hooks. Complete assembly instructions and all hardware are furnished with the products.

When It Rains, This One Rolls

Hook the Benson Down Spout-O-Matic to the opening of a downspout. Normally, it is rolled into a tight cylinder to stay out of the way. When it rains, however, the device automatically rolls out over the lawn. When it stops raining, the product rolls up automatically. The product, made by Benson Mfg. Corp., has holes throughout its roll-out section. The rain squirts out of these holes to spread evenly on the lawn. The Benson Down Spout-O-Matic comes in 4-foot, 8-foot, and 12-foot lengths. The device, made of polyethylene, slips over the downspout and buckles in place with a strap.

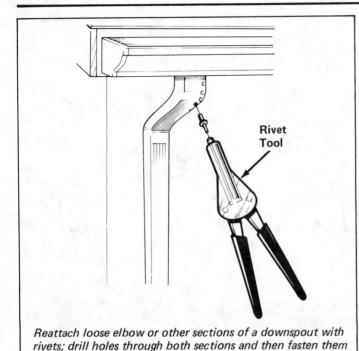

Reattach loose elbow or other sections of a downspout with rivets; drill holes through both sections and then fasten them together with a rivet tool.

Rivet Tool

Repairing a Downspout

If an elbow or other section of a downspout keeps separating, an easy way to fasten it is with a riveting tool that punches rivets into the metal from the outside surface. You don't have to reach inside to secure the rivet.

Another way is to join the two sections and bore a hole through the metal with a drill, nail, or icepick. Then, drive a self-tapping metal screw in the hole.

To install rivets with a riveting tool, follow these steps:

1. Place the two loose sections together.
2. Using a drill bit of the size specified to accommodate the size rivet you have, drill through both pieces. Make two such holes, one on either side or one at the front and one at the back of the downspout.
3. Insert the rivet into the hole in the tool, and then place the tip into the holes you drilled.
4. Squeeze the handles of the tool together until the rivet shaft pops off. The rivet will then be permanently in place.

Stop Ice Dams With Heat Cable

Ice and snow won't form on gutters and roof overhangs if you use heating cable that melts the ice and snow as it forms. The add-on roof and gutter de-icing system from Easy Heat/Wirekraft comes in sections as you buy and use only the footage that you need.

During a mild winter, for example, you may not need much cable. In a severe winter, you may need more cable, which you can add-on quickly. Components are sold in two basic packages. One contains one 25-foot section of heating cable, mounting hardware, and installation instructions. The other has the base unit, which is the power cord.

Hacksaw Cuts Guttering to Size

Although you shouldn't have to do much cutting when installing gutters and downspouts, be sure to use a good hacksaw equipped with a fine-toothed blade for whatever cutting must be done. The

Millers Falls hacksaw frame, No. 300-01, made by the Millers Falls Co., does a good job. Able to handle both 10- and 12-inch blades, it has a lever tensioning device that makes blade changing quick and easy. The unbreakable Tenite handle is comfortable, a feature that is especially welcome.

Splashblock With Cleats

House foundations and lawns or gardens should be protected from downspout flows. The Rain-Away downspout water deflector, made by Vydel Corporation of America, is a one-piece plastic splashblock that is cleated in back so that you can anchor it in the ground. Besides protecting house foundations from water seepage, it also helps to eliminate standing and stagnant water.

Patch Tape for Fixing Roof, Gutters

If your roof or gutters need patching, you can use Frost-King Roof & Gutter Patch Tape. According to Thermwell Products Co., Inc., it's an economically fast way to seal any dry building material. The tape is self-adhesive and usable in a temperature range from 65° F to 180° F. The product, the company says, expands and contracts with heat. The

patch tape comes in a roll that is 2½ inches wide, ⅛ inch thick, and 30 inches long.

Aluminum Under-Eave Louvers

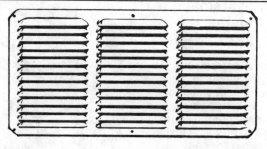

When you insulate your attic space, the space should be ventilated at the gable ends, or through a roof ventilator, and along the soffits. You can install under-eave louvers, manufactured by Anderson Metal Products Corp. (AMCOR), with little more than a drill, keyhole saw, tape measure, and screwdriver. The louvers are screened aluminum that come with a mill (plain) or white-painted surface. The UA-series is available in two sizes: 16 by 8 inches and 16 by 4 inches.

Roof Leak Plugger Works in the Rain

Fixing roof leaks is a job that has to be done quickly to prevent extensive damage. Leak Plugger plastic roof cement, made by Parr, Inc., will plug roof leaks even when the roof is wet. The all-purpose, all-weather cement provides either a temporary or permanent water-stopping repair, according to the manufacturer. The material, which is troweled onto the wet or dry roof surface, is black in color with inert fibered reinforcing fillers in a blended asphalt base. The cement sets in 24 to 72 hours for a flexible, lasting repair. The product comes in a 1-gallon can.

What to Do When Skylights Leak

Skylights can leak. So, your skylights should be inspected yearly for damaged flashing, broken or hardened skylight seals and glazing, and broken glass or plastic dome covering. The flashing can be sealed with regular asphalt roofing cement. If the dome is glazed, remove the old glazing and fill it with new. Regular glazing compound can be used. Damaged seals often can be replaced by loosening several screws or clips that hold the seals in place. The seals are available at outlets that sell skylights. If the dome is plastic and it is cracked, try sealing the crack with butyl caulking compound. This material will stick to the slick plastic better than most similar products. If the dome is glass and the glass is cracked or broken, replace the glass with tempered safety glass.

Skylights Have Double-Dome Design

A skylight can shed natural light on dark areas in your home. Baxt Solar Vu skylights, made by Baxt Industries, Inc., are available in flush-mounted or curb-mounted styles. Both feature an insulating airspace between an inner dome and an outer dome. The curb-mounted model has a condensate gutter and weep hole at the mounting flange. According to Baxt, once a Solar Vu skylight is installed, it should require no maintenance. Normal rainfall keeps the skylight clear, although washing with soap and water will not damage the unit. No petroleum-based cleaners should be used. The skylights come in clear/clear, clear/white, and bronze/clear. The opening sizes are 22¼ by 22¼ inches, 30¼ by 30¼ inches, 22¼ by 46¼ inches, 30¼ by 46¼ inches, and 46¼ by 46¼ inches. Installation instructions come with each skylight. Installation is not guaranteed, but the products are.

The Search for Roof Leaks

Finding a leak in a roof can be difficult. The next time you are faced with the problem, go into the attic or attic crawl space on a sunny day. Look for sunlight coming through the sheathing. At these points, stick a length of thin wire up through the holes. When you go onto the roof, you can see the wire protruding from the shingles. This is where to seal the shingles. If you can't get into the attic, the next best way is to climb onto the roof and carefully look for damaged shingles and flashing. Remember, leaks often are "below" the damaged area on the roof. For example, a water leak near the eaves could start at the ridge of the roof.

Aluminum Soffits Require Little Maintenance

Aluminum components require little maintenance. The aluminum soffit system, from Sell-Even, Inc., is fast and simple to install for new construction and remodeling, according to the manufacturer. The soffits are 12-inch wide panels with deep V-grooves for strength. Sell-Even claims that the soffit will never rust, rot, or split. The adjoining fascia is made from heavy gauge 0.024 aluminum. Parts you can buy include frieze runners, soffit panels, vented soffit panels, double channel, cove molding, and aluminum nails. The only tools needed for installation are a hammer, tape measure, level, and tin snips. Instructions for installing the system are provided.

All-Purpose Sealant for Flashing

Leaks in roof flashing, gutters, and downspouts should be repaired as soon as they're noticed. Ruscoe Permanent-Sealer, from W. J. Ruscoe Co., is an all-purpose nitrile rubber-based sealant that can be used as a flashing seal, gutter seal, weather seal, concrete seal, and bathroom caulk. According to the manufacturer, it rainproofs flashing on wood, metal, and any type shingles, and remains permanently flexible in all weather conditions. The product, which is available in clear, white, and aluminum colors, comes in 10½-fluid-ounce cartridges and 4-ounce squeeze tubes.

Glass Fabric Reinforcement for Roof Repairs

When you need to reinforce a roof repair, you might try Storm King glass fabric reinforcing material, made by Parr, Inc. The product is designed for use with Storm King Plus heavy-duty roof coating. The material is strong, rotproof, fireproof, light in weight, and easily handled and applied, according to Parr. The reinforcement is used by pressing it into the layer of roof coating.

Patching Strip for Roof Repairs

If your roof has a crack or blister, you can use Storm King Flash-Patch, a press-on elastomeric black roof patch. According to Parr, Inc., the manufacturer, Flash-Patch has good quick-seal ability and tenacious adhesion to clean surfaces. You also can use it to form a vapor barrier seal on air ducts, ventilators, and conduit and pipe entrances. To use, you press the patch in place and pull off its specially treated paper.

Rain Systems Are Plastic; Won't Rot or Rust

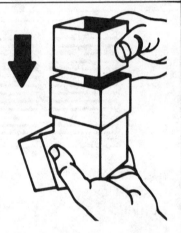

Rust and corrosion is always a threat to metal gutters and downspouts. Genova Raingo vinyl gutter and downspout systems are made of solid vinyl and engineered for do-it-yourself installation. The system simply snaps together; there is no solvent welding or cuts to make. The company guarantees the system forever against rust, rot, or corrosion. The color goes completely through the product, so the system never needs painting. The insides of the gutters have ridges designed to prevent debris from resting directly on the bottom of the gutter. If ice builds up in the gutter, the ridges help lift the ice away from the gutter base. Component parts include end caps, gutter strap hangers, gutter brackets, slip joints, corners, drop outlets, elbows, and the lengths of gutter and downspout. Assembly and installation instructions are provided with the product.

Repairs for Built-Up Roofs

"Built-up" roofs, or tar-and-gravel roofs, consist of sheathing and roofing paper over which tar and gravel has been spread and sprinkled. Repairs or maintenance on this type of roof is easy. You simply add more tar and gravel over the leaking spots or worn areas. The best "tar" product to use is plastic asphalt roofing cement that is "fibered"; the word "fibered" will appear on the label of the product. The gravel can be rip-rap or plain washed gravel you can buy in 80-pound bags. Spread the cement over the area to be patched. Use plenty; you want a fairly thick layer. Then sprinkle the gravel over the cement and imbed it with the flat side of a garden spade. If just gravel is missing, you can lightly coat the base roof with roofing cement and sprinkle new gravel into the cement.

Patching Holes and Cracks in Concrete

Materials • Ready-To-Mix Concrete Sand Mix • Portland Cement or Concrete Bonding Agent • 2 × 4 Lumber • Tarp or Plastic Sheeting • Plastic Lid • Sand

---

Tools • Safety Goggles • Gloves • Hammer or Baby Sledgehammer • Cold Chisel • Garden Hose • Paintbrush • Wheelbarrow • Hoe • Small Trowel or Putty Knife • Steel Finishing Trowel • Wood Float • Fiber Push Broom

---

I T'S NORMAL for a concrete drive, walk, patio, or other surface to develop cracks and holes, especially if the concrete has been in service for a number of years. The trick is to fill such cracks and holes as soon as you notice them. This preventive maintenance can save you plenty of work.

Patching Holes

Holes in concrete usually are caused by the ground underneath the concrete sinking slightly. Or, the concrete in the hole area was not properly troweled at the time it was finished. To patch a hole, follow this procedure:

1. Remove every last bit of the loose concrete with a hammer or a baby sledgehammer and a cold chisel. Hose out the cavity with water until it is perfectly clean. *Caution: Wear safety goggles to protect your eyes and gloves to protect your hands.*
2. Get a sack of ready-to-mix concrete—called a sand mix—and a small can of bonding agent. The bonding agent is the key to creating a patch that is bonded permanently to the old concrete. **Note:** You can buy patching mix that includes a bonding agent, but if you are patching many holes, the cost of the mix might be prohibitive.
3. Remove any standing water from the hole to be patched.
4. Brush on the bonding agent, following the manufacturer's directions.
5. Prepare the sand mix according to directions.

Make sure that all of the sand is coated with the mix, and make sure to use only the prescribed amount of water. A watery mix may be easier to work with, but it can lose much of its strength. A metal wheelbarrow makes an ideal container for mixing.

6. Pour the mix into the hole, and then use a trowel to pack it in place completely.
7. Seesaw a 2 × 4 across the top of the patch to level it.
8. When the water sheen disappears from the top of the patch, start to smooth the patch with a wooden float. You will soon see some water back on the surface, and when you do notice a sheen again, stop the smoothing process.

A metal wheelbarrow makes an excellent container for mixing concrete sand mix.

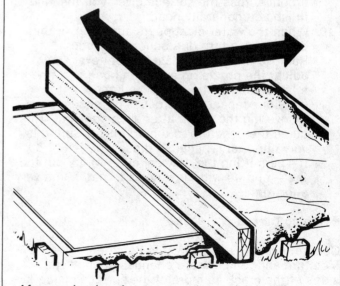

After pouring the mix, use a trowel to pack it in. Then, seesaw a 2x4 across the top of the concrete to level it.

Brick and Masonry

Tamp Down Earth and Sand to Improve Concrete Work

An inexpensive tamper like the one from Marion Tool Corporation can be a great help in establishing a solid base for your concrete work. It measures 8 by 10 inches, a good size for a hand tamper. Wooden-handled tampers like this one should occasionally be treated with a coat of boiled linseed oil. The linseed oil preserves both the handle and your hands.

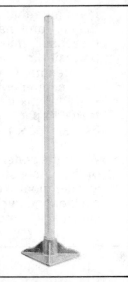

'Veneering' Concrete

Adding a thin layer of new concrete over a layer of old, broken concrete seldom is satisfactory because the new concrete won't bond properly to the old. In a short time, the "veneer" concrete will pop away from the old. This problem can be solved with a bonding cement that can be "feathered" to a 1/16-inch edge. Bonding cement has a special binder mixed with the cement. You simply add water and stir it to the consistency of whipped cream. Bonding cement is expensive, but the result can be worth it.

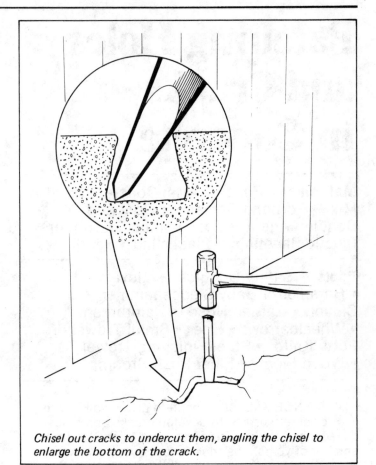

Chisel out cracks to undercut them, angling the chisel to enlarge the bottom of the crack.

9. If additional smoothing is necessary, wait until the surface sheen goes away again, and then smooth with a steel finishing trowel. Remember, though, that most outdoor concrete projects should have a fairly rough finish for better traction. Pulling a fiber push broom across the surface gives you the kind of finish you generally need.
10. When the water disappears again, cover the patch with a tarp or a sheet of plastic.
11. Remove the tarp or plastic sheet every day, adjust the nozzle on a garden hose to a fine mist, and spray the concrete lightly. If possible, repeat this process for six days, recovering the patch after each spraying. This cures the concrete to a hard finish. Curing is very important, because those who fail to do it—permitting the new concrete to dry out too fast—end up with new holes to patch in a very short time.

Patching Cracks

Concrete cracks can grow into concrete holes. Moisture and temperature changes push at the sides of the crack as more of the surface inside the crack becomes loose. To fix a crack, follow these steps:

1. Use a cold chisel to convert the crack to a groove that is at least 1 inch deep and ½ inch wide. *Caution: Wear safety goggles to protect your eyes and gloves to protect your hands.* For additional safety you can cut X-shaped slits in a plastic coffee can lid and slip it over the chisel to shield you from flying fragments.
2. Undercut the groove to make it wider at the bottom; undercutting helps lock in the patch. When finished, the crack should have an inverted V-shaped configuration.
3. Brush and wash out all the loose concrete with a stiff broom and strong spray from a garden hose. If the crack goes all the way through the slab, tamp in a sand base.
4. Leave all surfaces wet, but get rid of any standing water.
5. Coat all surfaces with a creamy mix of Portland cement and water, or use a bonding agent.
6. Prepare either a stiff sand mix or one with small gravel.
7. Tamp the mix into the crack.
8. When the new concrete begins to stiffen—usually about 45 minutes later—smooth it with a trowel or a 2 × 4.
9. Let the patch cure six days. Refer to Step 11 in the previous procedure.

Patching Concrete Steps

Materials • Boards or Plywood • 2 × 4 Lumber • Nails • Concrete Bonding Agent • Ready-to-Mix Concrete Sand Mix • Concrete Bonding Cement • Tarp or Plastic Sheeting

Tools • Safety Goggles • Hammer • Baby Sledgehammer • Cold Chisel • Garden Hose • Mixing Container • Shovel • Hoe • Steel Finishing Trowel • Wooden Float

NO MATTER how well they're built, the edges of concrete steps are the weakest point of the construction. Once edges start to break and crumble, the concrete will keep eroding until the steps pose a safety hazard.

To fix crumbling concrete steps, follow this procedure:

1. Undercut the crumbling edge of the steps with a hammer or baby sledgehammer and a cold chisel. The cut should be an inverted V-shape configuration into solid concrete to help hold the patch in position. *Caution: Wear safety goggles to protect your eyes.*
2. Remove all loose concrete, and clean the area thoroughly with the strong spray from a garden hose.
3. Build a form by placing a board against the riser of the step and securing it with several bricks; that should hold the board firmly in place. Select two planks or pieces of plywood that are wide enough and place them against the sides. Then angle a 2 × 4 as a brace, and nail it in place. Make sure that the top of the form is level with the step.
4. Paint the area of the step to be covered with a concrete bonding agent, following the directions on the can. If the patch will be thin, use a concrete bonding cement; it can be leveled to $\frac{1}{16}$ inch thick.
5. Use ready-to-mix concrete with sand mix formula. Add no more water than the directions specify, and mix completely until all the sand is coated with the cement.

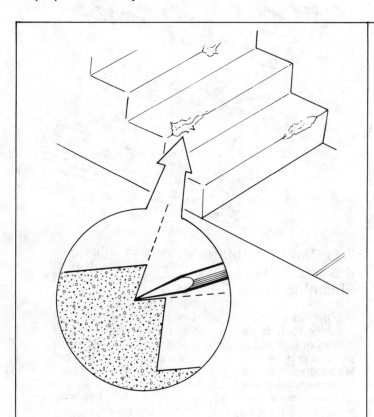

Chisel out each worn edge to remove crumbling concrete and form a clean open angle along the top of the step.

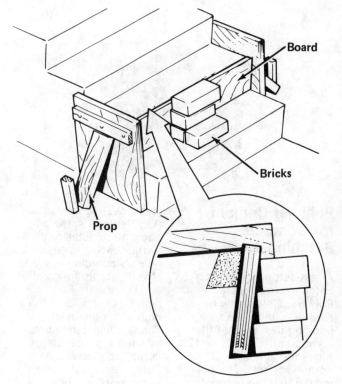

Build a form for each step; wedge boards upright at the sides and prop a board flat against the riser.

6. Use a trowel to pack the concrete mix in place, and check to be sure that you leave no air spaces back in the V-shaped groove.

7. Finish off the concrete patch so that it is level with the rest of the step. You can use a trowel or a wooden float to level the patch.

8. Make the patch match the texture of the rest of the step, and then cover it with a tarp or a sheet of plastic.

9. For 6 days, lift the cover and spray the new concrete with water. Adjust the hose nozzle to its fine mist setting.

10. Leave the forms in place during the curing process to reduce the likelihood of someone accidentally stepping on the patch before it is fully cured.

Anchoring and Patching Cement

An anchoring and patching cement that can be used outside and inside the home is Rockite, which anchors bolts, posts, hand rails, awnings, shelving, motors, seats, columns, and almost any other building component. It also patches floors, walls, stairs, ceilings, and so on. Rockite anchoring and patching cement comes in a bag and is mixed with water. On floor jobs, you can pour it in place. For vertical surfaces, you make a thick mixture and apply it with a trowel.

According to Hartline Products Co., Inc., the manufacturer, Rockite is fast-setting, strong, permanent, and safe to use.

Watch Concrete Set-Up Times

Fresh concrete may be worked about 45 to 60 minutes after it has been placed and screeded, depending on the temperature and humidity. If the final job calls for a steel-trowel finish, the surface must be struck with a wooden float and then steel-troweled. You must work very fast to do this in the time span. If, however, the set time gets away from you, immediately sprinkle the entire surface very lightly with water from a garden hose. Don't use too much water; you just want to dampen the concrete surface. Then, with a wooden float, go back over the surface and leave it alone. You won't have a slick finish, but you won't have a half-finished, wavy, and pockmarked surface either.

Polymer Cement for Concrete Patching Jobs

A fast-setting concrete patch makes a job go fast. Poly Repair-It, made by Kwik Mix, Inc., is a self-bonding cement that the manufacturer says has 12 times the adhesion of normal concrete. This means that the product can be feathered to a very thin section for patching and veneering concrete. Poly Repair-It sets up in about 10 minutes and is traffic-bearing in eight hours. According to Kwik Mix, it sets to the color of aged concrete, won't shrink or crack, and has a high abrasion resistance. The bonding cement may be used to repair steps, curbs, walkways, patios, floors, ramps, sills, holes, joints, pots, moldings, and so on. It comes in 5- and 50-pound plastic pails.

You Can't Complete the Job Without Finishing Tools

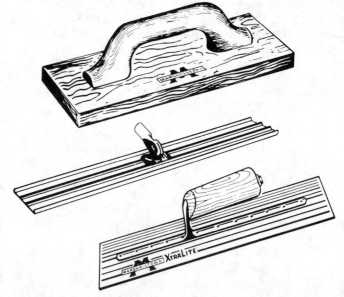

You'll need several finishing tools in the course of completing an average concrete job. The Marshalltown Trowel Company makes every concrete tool you might require. The company's magnesium bull float can be fitted with either a magnesium or fiberglass handle. Marshalltown also makes a wooden float. The Marshalltown metal finishing trowel, in the company's Xtralite line, has a spring-steel blade and aluminum mounting. Marshalltown also makes a long-handled metal trowel, a groover for creating joints between slab, and an edger for rounding off the edges of a slab.

Repairing Blacktop Surfaces

Materials • Blacktop Patch • Plywood • Blacktop Caulking • Rags • Mineral Spirits • Blacktop Sealer

Tools • Safety Goggles • Hammer or Baby Sledgehammer • Cold Chisel • Broom • Shovel • Caulking Gun • Putty Knife • Sealer Applicator

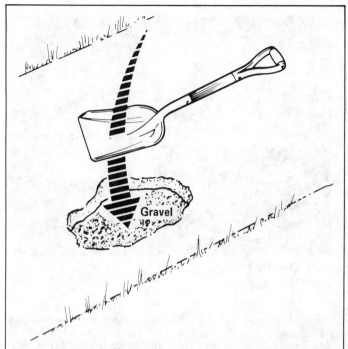

After removing loose blacktop, fill deep holes partially with gravel, and pound the gravel down firmly before adding the blacktop patch.

BLACKTOP DRIVEWAYS need attention almost every spring. The asphalt material is prone to cracking and drying out. When either occurs, large and costly maintenance repairs usually follow.

Holes and Large Cracks

Blacktop patching material comes in 40- and 80-pound bags. It is ready to place directly into holes in asphalt. Follow this procedure:

1. Chip away at the loose asphalt material until you reach a solid surface. Use a hammer or baby sledgehammer and a cold chisel. **Caution: Wear safety goggles to protect your eyes and gloves to protect your hands.**
2. Brush out all of the loose material.
3. Pour in the blacktop patch from the sack, adding enough to make a patch about ½ inch higher than the surrounding area.
4. Use the back of your shovel to pack the patch down thoroughly. If you can pack the patch material below the surrounding surface, pour in more and tamp it down. Just make sure that the patched area is slightly higher than the surrounding asphalt surface.
5. Place a piece of plywood over the patch.
6. Drive the wheels of your automobile over the plywood; the weight of the car will compact the patching material firmly into the hole.
7. Remove the plywood.

Small Cracks

If the crack in the blacktop isn't large enough for a blacktop patch or not small enough for driveway

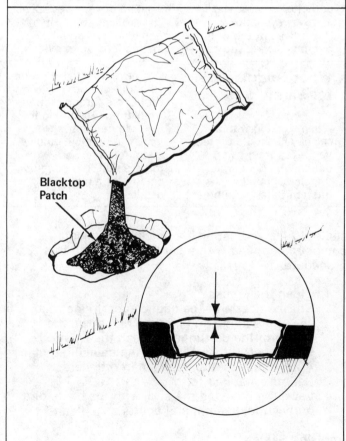

Fill the hole with the blacktop patch; tamp it firmly, add more, and tamp again to make a solid patch.

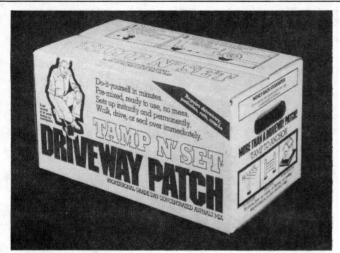

Pre-Mixed Patch for Driveways

If your driveway has developed potholes and cracks, it's time to repair it. Tamp 'N Set driveway patch is a pre-mixed material that can patch potholes, cracks, and ruts in driveways quickly. Regardless of the weather or temperature, you can scoop the product directly out of its package and into the hole. Then, tamp it firmly. The result is a permanent surface that can be walked and driven on, or sealed immediately. The finished patch, according to HMS Industries, Inc., is similar in appearance to existing driveway surfaces. The product comes in a 20-pound package. Instructions are provided.

Cleaner for Oil, Grease on Driveways, Patios, or Garage Floors

A dirty, oil- and grease-stained driveway, patio, or garage floor can mar an otherwise attractive home. And, often the grime is tracked into the house. Garage Magic, a cleaner from the Magic American Chemical Corp., is formulated to deal with grease and oil spots. After allowing it to work for a few minutes, the cleaner can be flushed easily with a garden hose, according to the manufacturer. Garage Magic comes in a 1-pint aerosol spray can.

Nails for Fastening Lumber, Sheet Metal to Concrete

When you must attach lumber or sheet metal to concrete, you can often do so without drilling. Helyx tempered concrete screws are driven with a hammer. Made by Hillwood Manufacturing Co., the concrete screws are available in lengths from ¾ inch to 3 inches.

Wear Goggles for Safety

When working with a chisel you should protect your eyes from flying debris. The E-5 series goggles, made by Eastern Safety Equipment Co., have a soft vinyl frame with four plastic ventilators for indirect ventilation. According to the manufacturer, the lenses are optical quality, distortion-free, and replaceable. The goggles come with a rubber headband.

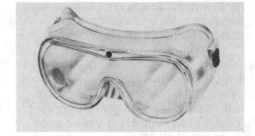

---

sealer to fill, you can use a blacktop caulking compound applied with a caulking gun. Use this procedure:

1. Clean the crack.
2. Cut the nozzle of the caulking cartridge at a 45-degree angle and insert a nail down the nozzle of the cartridge to break the plastic seal. Insert the cartridge in the caulking gun.
3. Apply the blacktop caulking into the crack until the crack is full.
4. Level the caulking material with the blade of a putty knife; use mineral spirits as a cleaner.

Applying Sealer

About every two or three years, depending on the climate, an asphalt driveway should be resealed. Blacktop sealer, which comes in a 5-gallon bucket, is thick like paint. You also can buy an application tool that has a brush on one side and a squeegee on the other side of a wooden block. To apply sealer to your blacktop drive, follow these steps:

1. Clean the asphalt surface of all mud, grease, and other debris.
2. Patch and fill any holes or cracks with blacktop patch or caulking, as described in the previous procedures.
3. Dump and spread the asphalt sealer at the top of the driveway and distribute the liquid downward with the applicator's squeegee. Then, smooth the liquid with the brush.
4. Wait about one week for the sealer to dry. Drying time will be noted on the sealer container.

Tuckpointing Mortar Joints

Materials • Mortar Mix Cement • Mortar Coloring • Corrugated Cardboard

Tools • Safety Goggles • Gloves • Hammer or Baby Sledgehammer • Cold Chisel • Concrete Mixing Container • Water Bucket • Tuckpointing Trowel • Joint Strike • Steel Finishing Trowel • Stiff Fiber Brush • Garden Hose

"TUCKPOINTING" is the professional term for removing old mortar between bricks, block, and stone and replacing it with new mortar. Loose or crumbling mortar should be replaced as soon as you discover it, or it will allow moisture to penetrate. Moisture can damage walls to such an extent that they must be replaced. You can tuckpoint mortar joints by following this procedure:

1. Clean out the loose or crumbling joints with a hammer or baby sledgehammer and a cold chisel. *Caution: Wear safety goggles to protect your eyes and gloves to protect your hands.* Cut down to a depth of at least ½ inch, attacking the vertical joints first and then the horizontal ones.
2. Flush away all loose mortar and dust from the joints with a garden hose.
3. Mix the new mortar. The mix may be an entirely different shade when it dries than when you first mix it, so mix a trial batch and apply it to a piece of corrugated cardboard. The porous cardboard will suck out most of the water, and the mortar that is left will be about the same shade it will be when dry. The next step is to add some color—available at hardware stores—to the mortar so that it will match the rest of the walls. When you arrive at a match on the cardboard, you will have a good idea of what the wet mix should look like to achieve the desired results.
4. Dampen the joints to be tuckpointed.
5. Force mortar into the joints with a tuckpointing trowel, filling the vertical joints first and then the horizontals. Press the mortar into the new joints firmly to make certain that you leave no cavities.
6. Strike the joints with a joint strike before the mortar sets up. Strike the vertical joints first, then strike the horizontal joints.
7. Remove any excess mortar from the face of the bricks by giving them a swipe with the edge of a steel trowel.
8. When the mortar is dry—wait one week—use a stiff fiber brush to clean the face of the bricks. Water from a garden hose usually will dislodge any mortar stains and debris.

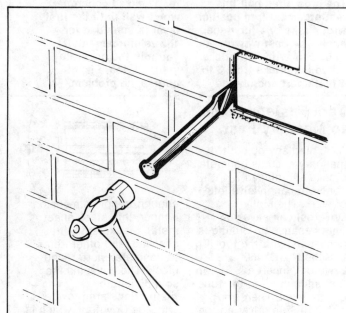

Cut out the crumbling mortar, at least 1/2 inch deep, to provide a sound base for the new mortar joints.

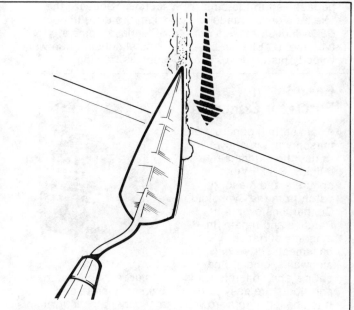

Fill the cleaned joints with mortar, packing it in tightly; first fill vertical joints, then horizontal joints.

Wear Gloves to Protect Your Hands

When working with a hammer and a cold chisel, you should wear gloves to protect your hands. The model 5501 "The Original Plastic Dot" cotton work gloves, made by Boss Manufacturing Co., are made of 10-ounce canvas fabric. They feature tiny plastic dots on the palm, thumb, and index finger to provide better gripping power on tools and other objects, an important consideration when using a chisel. The gloves have a

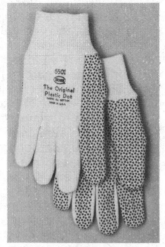

clute cut and a natural knit wrist.

Silicone Sealant for Masonry

Cracks in cellar walls and foundations can be sources of heat loss due to cracks. GE silicone masonry seal, made by General Electric Co., can be used for cracks in foundations as well as around pipe and vent entrances, outdoor sillcocks, doors, windows, walls, stairs, porches, and electrical outlets. The 8.5-ounce caulking cartridges dispense about 42 linear feet of the material using a ³⁄₁₆-inch diameter cut on the end of the plastic nozzle. The seal may be used at temperatures as low as −35° F, but the surface must be frost-free.

Bang! Bang! and Your Project Is Framed

If you've got a lot of studs to fasten to masonry, a stud driver can do it fast. The Remington 473 stud driver drives a series of fastener pins into masonry so framing members can be fastened to the pins. The stud driver, made by DESA Industries, is a gun-type tool that has a low-velocity piston drive. The piston is activated with .22 caliber standard crimp-cartridges—without the bullet, just the primer, casing, and powder. You load the fastener into the gun. Then, position the muzzle of the tool over the spot you want the fastener. Squeeze the trigger to drive the pin. The SP series of pins are for general construction work such as framing.

Supporting Reinforcing in Concrete

If the walk, driveway, or patio you will place will have steel rod or mesh reinforcement, the steel must be positioned at about half the width of the total thickness of the slab. The pros often pull this reinforcement into position with a rake or a juryrigged hook. The best way for you to do it is with half bricks. Place the bricks from 3 to 4 feet apart and lay the rods or mesh on top of the bricks. The reinforcement should be tied lightly with wire where it overlaps or crosses. Another method is to place about half the thickness of the concrete and lay the reinforcement on top of it. Then place the rest of the job. The trouble here, however, is that most truck drivers who deliver ready-mixed concrete won't wait until the first layer is screeded for the reinforcement. If you mix the concrete yourself, there is, of course, no problem.

Fast-Setting Patch for Concrete

A fast-setting concrete and masonry patch allows you to use the patched area quickly. Synko Vinyl concrete and masonry patch from the Synkoloid Co. hardens overnight. Patches and repairs in masonry surfaces, basements, driveways, sidewalks, cinder block, patios, and concrete walls and floors are easy to fix. It is applied with a trowel or putty knife after the surfaces are cleaned and

dampened with water. Synko concrete and masonry patch is available in 4- and 25-pound packages.

Tool Fastens Items to Masonry Fast

Attaching any object to masonry such as concrete blocks and placed concrete can involve lots of work. The Molly Drivetool can save you time because no drilling is necessary with the tool. To use the No. DT460 Drivetool, insert a fastening pin into the tube of the driver. Then, you strike the pin driver on top of the tool with a baby sledge. The pins are strong

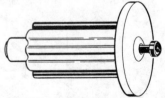

enough to hold dimension lumber, thin steel, sheet metal, brackets, fixtures, shelving, and other items to concrete, mortar, and block. The drivepins are sold by length. Instructions are provided with the Drivetool, which is made by Bostik Consumer division of Emhart Corp.

Replacing a Brick

Materials • Mortar Mix Cement • Mortar Coloring • Replacement Brick • Concrete Patching Cement

Tools • Safety Goggles • Gloves • Hammer or Baby Sledgehammer • Cold Chisel • Bucket • Wire Brush • Garden Hose • Steel Trowel • Tuckpointing Trowel • Joint Strike • Stiff Fiber Brush

LOOSE BRICK must be reset and a damaged or broken brick should be replaced just as soon as you notice the problem. If left unattended, moisture will get behind the brick and crumble mortar joints, In time, the entire wall may have to be replaced. Follow this procedure:

1. With a hammer or baby sledgehammer and a cold or brick chisel, remove the mortar from around the loose or damaged brick. If the brick must be replaced, use the chisel to break it out of the opening. If the brick is just loose, be careful not to break it. ***Caution: Wear safety goggles to protect your eyes and gloves to protect your hands.***
2. After the brick comes out, chip away all the mortar that is still clinging to it.
3. Place the brick in a bucket of water.
4. Go back to the hole and chip away all remaining mortar. You may have to use a wire brush to get the hole really clean. When you get all the mortar out, hose down the cavity with water.
5. Mix the mortar, adding mortar coloring to shade the mixture so that it matches the rest of the wall, if necessary.
6. With a steel trowel, lay a bed of mortar down on the damp bottom of the hole where the brick will go.
7. Take the brick out of the bucket of water, but don't dry it; just shake off any surface water. Apply mortar to the two ends and the top of the brick.
8. Insert the brick in the hole and press it in place, lining it up with the other bricks.
9. Use the trowel to force back into the cavity all the mortar that was pushed out when you inserted the brick.

How to Break a Brick Neatly

The pros can hit a brick with the edge of a trowel and break it cleanly in half. But unless you're an expert, don't try this. Instead, lightly score the surface of the brick with a brick chisel tapped with a baby sledgehammer. Wear safety goggles and gloves for protection. The scored line should be about 1/16 inch deep. When the brick has been scored, lay the scored line over the edge of a short length of 2 x 4. Then lightly tap the protruding part of the brick with the sledge to fracture the brick. You may have to practice scoring and fracturing until you get the hang of it. But when you do, the brick will break very cleanly.

---

10. With the edge of a tuckpointing trowel, "slice" away the excess mortar hanging over the face of the surrounding bricks.
11. Strike the mortar joints with a joint strike. Do the vertical joints first and then the horizontal joints; the strike makes the new mortar slightly concave in configuration so water drains from the joints. Also, the joint strike helps pack the new mortar into the joint.
12. Let the job set for one week. Then with a stiff fiber brush and water, clean the mortar stains from the brick.

Note: Small hairline cracks in mortar joints, can be repaired with a special concrete patch contained in a caulking-type cartridge. Instructions for use are on the product.

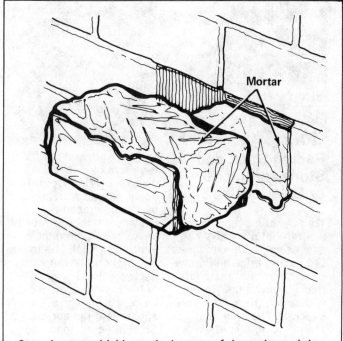

Spread mortar thickly on the bottom of the cavity and the brick's top and sides, and press the brick firmly in.

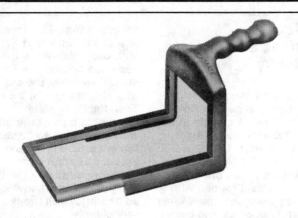

Brick Tool Meters Out Mortar Mix

Applying the correct amount of mortar between courses of bricks can be tough to do consistently if you're not a professional bricklayer. The Brickmate tool helps you maintain the correct amount of mortar consistantly between each brick and between courses of bricks. It also provides proper alignment at the same time. Manufactured of cast aluminum by Brickmate Industries, Inc., the tool is rustproof and easily cleaned with just water. The tool fits all standard and modular-size bricks, and besides turning you into a professional-type bricklayer, it can save plenty of mortar.

You'll Need a Hoe for Hand Mixing

Many people use a mortar mixer hoe for mixing concrete. The Atlas hoe, made by the Union Fork & Hoe Co., is a heavy-duty tool, featuring a 10- by 6-inch blade that helps the mixing go faster. The 66-inch handle fits into an 8-inch Tapertite ferrule. Atlas makes a full line of industrial-quality shovels, scoops, wheelbarrows, and rakes, all designed for rugged use.

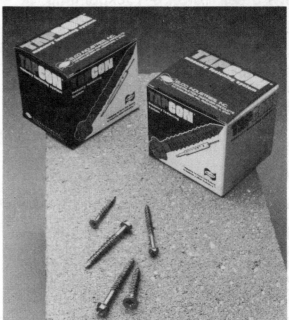

Facing Brick and Stone for Interior or Exterior Use

Traditional masonry has warmth but it's heavy and expensive. Design Images Ltd. facing brick and stone is an all-mineral material that gives you the warmth without all the weight and expense. The brick and stone facing materials, which can be used indoors or outdoors, are firesafe and fully guaranteed for ten years by Z-Brick, a division of VMC Corp. To apply, spread adhesive, press and embed the individual bricks or stones, strike or smooth mortar joints, and seal. The facing material can be cut with a hacksaw. Brick, available in burnt sienna and mesa beige, covers up to 4 square feet per carton. Stone, in graystone and sandstone, covers up to 3 square feet per carton.

Masonry Screws Without Plugs

A masonry fastening system that eliminates the need for fiber or lead plugs in the masonry to hold screws tightly is the patented Tapcon masonry fastening system. The threads of a Tapcon fastener cut threads into masonry materials when driven. There are two sets of threads: one is "high" and the other "low." The high thread cuts the thread in the masonry; the low thread provides stability. The fastener shank is tapered so it creates a progressive tapping action to improve holding power. The result is a kind of self-tapping screw for masonry. Made by Elco Industries, Inc., Tapcon fasteners come with a carbide-tipped drill bit, and the correct depth for the fasteners is reached by drilling the full length of the bit. In all cases, the hole must be at least 1/4-inch deeper than the fastener embedment. The company also recommends that a hammer-drill be used for drilling into masonry materials—especially placed concrete.

Minimum-Maintenance Landscaping

REGARDLESS OF what you do, if you have a yard it will take some maintenance to keep it presentable. Even if you surface the ground with concrete and paint it green, you would still have to paint it every year or two and patch the cracks. By planning ahead, you can keep your yardwork to a minimum and still have a good-looking lawn.

Here are some suggestions to make caring for your yard easier:

MOWING AND EDGING. Mowing in itself is not a problem unless there are slopes or other tough-to-mow areas. If there are steep slopes, you could plant a ground cover, terracing with rocks or stones or changing the slope. There are no easy solutions, but after they are done, the mowing problem is licked. Depending on the size of your lawn, you may be able to eliminate all mowing by using a ground cover instead of grass. There are growing ground covers such as ivy, ajuga, sedum, and other such plants and inert ground covers such as pebbles, bark, or gravel. The next mowing-edging problem is with the places where the grass ends. You can install mowing strips where the lawn meets a flower bed, or where the lawn runs to a wall. Mowing strips are strips that are flush with the lawn and wide enough for the mower wheels to ride on. You can make these from bricks, concrete blocks, railroad ties, or landscaping ties. Be sure to put a good bed of sand or gravel under the mowing strip so it doesn't sink. If flower beds are not a big part of the yard, corrugated edging strips help prevent grass from getting into the beds.

WATERING. The best answer to watering problems is to install an underground sprinkler system and automate it. Short of that, be selective in the sprinkler you get. Moving sprinklers are better than a steady spray. Let the shape and size of your yard guide you in selecting a sprinkler. Buy one that will adjust to odd shapes without too much waste, but also get one that will cover as much territory as possible without your having to move it. To accomplish this, you may need to have more than one sprinkler. Water only when there is a need. Overwatering or everyday shallow watering isn't as good as deep-watering when needed.

WEEDS. Some homeowners fight weeds and never win. In flower beds, cover empty spaces with mulch or inert ground cover. Mulch does other good things for the beds like retain moisture. For the lawn, there are herbicides that will kill weeds. They will also kill other plants including the grass unless you are careful and use the right type for your lawn. One of the most effective ways to control weeds is to feed your lawn with a quality fertilizer distributed with a spreader, give it plenty of water, and mow regularly. A healthy lawn will kill weeds, and keeping them cut down won't allow them to seed. Add some hand-pulling to that, and you should get rid of them altogether.

INSECTS. The biggest problem is identifying the insect, choosing the proper insecticide, and using it at the time that will be the most effective. The use of combination fertilizer-insecticides will usually do a good preventive job, although you will need specific formulations for some bugs. Picture charts of insects for identification purposes with matching insecticides to kill them are available at stores that sell garden and lawn supplies.

LEAVES. There isn't much you can do about leaves if you have trees that shed their leaves each fall. If you are going to plant new trees, find out what trees are native to the area that will serve your purpose, but with less of a leaf problem. Some trees, such as mimosas, not only drop leaves, but shed beans, flowers, and sap at different times of the year. If you have a big leaf problem, get a power lawn vacuum or a leaf blower.

One of the most effective ways to control weeds is to feed your lawn with a quality fertilizer distributed with a spreader.

Other Ways to Reduce Maintenance Time

In addition to the five biggest problems already discussed, there are some more things to consider so you might further reduce maintenance time:

- Don't cut the lawn area into separate sections.
- Don't try to grow grass where it won't grow, as in areas that receive little sunlight.
- Determine what type of grass grows best in your area.
- Plant trees native to the area. You can get other species to grow, but they might require more time and effort.
- Plant for the future. Remember that trees will spread. Don't plant them too close.

Trim Grass, Weeds the Electric Way

For general purpose use, the Utility model 8201 grass and weed trimmer from Black & Decker (U.S.), Inc., has a 7-inch cutting swath with nylon line. There is an automatic line cut-off, and the tool is double insulated so it needs no grounding. Other features include a wishbone cord connection for quick attachment and easy release of the extension cord, an instant release switch with a trigger; it weighs 2½ pounds. The motor, which runs at 12,000 rpm, uses 1.1 amps of 120-volt AC current.

Building Masonry Retaining Walls

If you plan to build a garden retaining wall with any masonry unit, such as brick, block, or stone, the wall should have a footing for support. The footing doesn't have to be fancy. Just lay out the job, dig a trench, and fill the trench with concrete. Smooth the top of the concrete level. The trench doesn't have to be formed for the concrete, although several reinforcing rods driven vertically along its length will provide stability. Make sure the rods are below the ground surface, and space them about 3 feet apart.

Get a Good Rake

If you're just starting your lawn, you may not see much need for buying a garden rake, but you'll need one before long. When you do buy a rake, get a good one. True Temper Corp. makes a quality rake called the T-14 Level Head garden rake. It is 14¾ inches wide and has 5½-foot handle. Each of its 14 slim tapered teeth is 2¾ inches long.

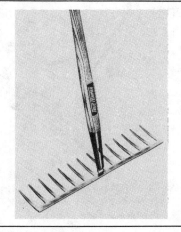

Lawn Edging Comes in Many Sizes and Colors

A variety of lawn edging is available from Patrician Products, Inc. It comes in the following sizes: 3¾ by 40 inches; 4 by 20 inches; 4 by 25 inches; 4 by 40 inches; 6 by 20 inches; 6 by 40 inches; 8 by 20 inches; and 10 by 25 inches. The edging can be purchased in green, white, brown, tan, or black—either in solid colors or with a top white edge. The edging is made of plastic so it can't rust or corrode; there are no sharp edges. According to Patrician, the edging is easy to handle, shape, and install.

Trimmer for Yards With Big Growth

If you have a lot of grass and weeds to trim weekly, it may pay you to have a heavy-duty trimmer. The model B280 Ryan trimmer has a rear-mounted 31cc two-cycle engine. Made by the Ryan Lawn-Care System of Outboard Marine Corp., the trimmer has solid-state ignition, an on/off switch, bump head line release, head-mounted clutch drive, and complete handlebar operation. The trigger throttle control is bar-mounted on the Ryan, which uses 0.105-diameter line. An adjustable shoulder strap is included.

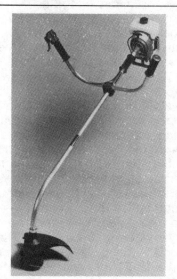

Planting a Lawn

Materials • Lime or Gypsum • Peat Moss • Grass Seed • Fertilizer • Chemical Weed Killer

Tools • Hose and Sprinkler • Tiller • Tine Rake • Spreader • Shovel • Roller • Lawn Mower

O WNING A HEALTHY, green lawn not only makes your home look attractive but the grass helps fight air pollution, provides some oxygen, prevents soil erosion, and reduces noise pollution. A super lawn takes super care; an occasional mowing doesn't provide that well-manicured look.

The type of grass that grows best in your area varies with the climate, moisture, and soil. You can and should talk with experts, but one of the best ways is to pick out several healthy-looking lawns in the neighborhood and ask the owners what they did to achieve such results. Find out which species of grass is most successful and how much trouble it is to maintain. The owners will be flattered, and you should learn a great deal.

Planting a New Lawn

After you select which type of grass you want, learn which time of year is the best for planting. Here are some general steps to follow when putting in a new lawn:

1. If the grading hasn't been done yet, you should have it done or do it yourself. The ground should slope gradually away from the house in all directions.
2. After grading, check for low places by turning on a sprinkler and looking for spots where water collects.
3. Check the soil; it should have the proper pH. The only way to find out about the soil's pH is to test it. Most county agents and many seed stores will test your soil at no or little cost to you. Lime is added to soil that is too acid, and gypsum is added to soil that is too alkaline. The soil should also be crumbly. Squeeze a handful tightly in your fist and release it. If the blob fails apart, the soil is too sandy. If it looks like a mud ball, it contains too much clay.

4. Make whatever soil additions are indicated by the tests, and then till the soil. You can rent a tiller if you don't want to buy one. When tilling, avoid making the soil too fine. Marble-sized lumps are better than fine dirt.
5. Wet the soil to pack it down and then wait 24 hours.
6. Spread the grass seed at the rate recommended for the specific variety of seed you are planting. Don't spread the seed too thickly; if you do, the young seedlings will compete for nutrients and most will die.
7. Rake the ground lightly to cover the seeds partially with soil.
8. Go over the ground once with a roller to press the seeds into the soil. Don't try to bury them.
9. Feed the lawn as soon as you finish the seeding if this is recommended by the company that packaged the seed. Use the fertilizer recommended for your variety of grass and follow the directions on the bag.
10. Water as soon as you finish fertilizing. During the next two weeks, water two or three times a day, keeping the top layer of soil damp at all times. When the seedlings are up, revert to regular morning waterings.
11. Wait until the sprigs are 2 inches tall before mowing. Mowing will help to spread the root system and make the lawn thicker.
12. Mow weekly until you note the proper thickness; then mow as needed.

When tilling the soil, avoid making the soil too fine. Marble-sized lumps are better than fine dirt.

Note: Never use a weed killer on a new lawn. Pull the bigger weeds and mow the rest. As your lawn thickens, many of the weeds will be choked out. You can use a weed killer the second year your lawn is in.

Re-Doing an Established Lawn

The maintenance of a lawn depends on the species of grass planted, the soil condition, and the climate. A lawn specialist or county agent can tell you what type of fertilizer you should have and how often you should apply it, as well as how much water you should be using.

If your existing lawn is in poor condition, try to renovate it. If there is at least 50 percent of the area still covered with grass, plant new grass in the bad spots. Here are the steps to follow:

1. Get rid of all weeds. Apply a chemical weed killer according to the manufacturer's directions.
2. Mow the existing grass very close.
3. Rake the yard to remove all grass clippings and leaves and, also, to loosen the surface of the soil. Test the soil as described in the procedure for "Planting a New Lawn."
4. Follow Steps 6 through 12 in the previous procedure for planting a new lawn to seed the bare spots.

Good Spreader Helps Grow a Healthy Lawn

Despite its utilitarian appearance, the model BSS Cyclone broadcast spreader is well designed. It has a stainless steel hopper as well as other stainless parts, and it holds up to 40 pounds of fertilizer, seed, granular pesticides, or other dry ingredients. The micro dial insures good coverage, and the tapered feathered edge spread prevents stripes and streaks. A comprehensive spreading chart is included with

every Cyclone spreader made by Cyclone Seeder Co., Inc., a division of Jackson Mfg. Co.

The Numbers on Fertilizers

All fertilizer is numbered; for example, 5-10-5, 24-3-3, 10-10-10, 1-1-1. The numbers stand for chemical contents of the products. The first number is for the amount of nitrogen. The second number is for the amount of phosphoric acid. And the third is for the amount of potash. Because the numbers and names are difficult to remember, try this system: "Up." "Down." "All Around." The first number makes the grass grow *up* and green. The second number makes the roots grow *down* and healthy. The third number increases the root growth *all around*. So, if you want your grass to be extremely green, choose a fertilizer with a high first number. If you are just starting a new lawn or reshuffling the old one, you want a high second number to encourage root growth. If you want a root growth that is healthy and even across the lawn, you want a fertilizer with a high third number.

Pads Take Misery Out of Lawn Work

No matter how you plan it, there are going to be times when you must crawl around in the yard to pull up crabgrass or other weeds. Crawling can be a little rough on the knees, but if you wear a pair of Judsen knee pads, you can save yourself a great deal of misery. Judsen lightweight knee pads are made of rubber and give the soft pillow treatment to your knees. Made by the Judsen Rubber Works, Inc., the knee pads come in handy for plenty of other household chores.

Lawn Edger Keeps Yards Looking Neat

An easy way to keep a lawn from spreading into a flower bed and to curb erosion is to install edging. Patrician Landscape Lawn Border is decorative and easy to install. It comes in a 20-foot roll, in black, white, green, brown, or redwood colors. Extender connectors are included so that additional lengths can be attached. According to the manufacturer, the product will not lose its shape, and remains flexible in all kinds of weather.

Planting a Shrub

Materials • Shrub or Bush • Top Soil

Tools • Gloves • Shovel • Wheelbarrow • Utility Knife • Pruning Shears • Garden Hose • Tape Measure

WHAT DO YOU want a shrub to do? Screen a bad view? Help stop erosion? Accent the design of your home—or hide it? Buy the type of shrub that will do the job best. A nursery will help you make this decision; there are hundreds of shrub and bush varieties from which to choose.

Most nurseries and garden centers certify that their shrubs and bushes are free from insects, disease, and other growth problems. Get this in writing so the plant will be replaced if it dies through no fault of yours. If you spot cankers, leaf rot, spots, insects, or other problems, don't buy the shrub. Follow these basic steps:

1. Dig a hole about 8 inches wider and 6 inches deeper than the balled roots of the plant.
2. Carefully place the root ball into the hole. If the ball is wrapped with burlap, cut the string that holds the burlap to the plant. If the ball is in a plastic or metal container, remove it by lightly tapping down on the container while you hold onto the base of the plant; it should drop right out.
3. Spread out the plant's root system in the hole, and cover the roots with top soil—or a good rich soil mixture.
4. Cover the roots with soil and lightly pack it down and against the base of the plant.
5. Prune any stalks that are broken or dead. **Note:** In fall, when the plant is dormant, prune the stalks back about a third of their length; it will promote better growth.
6. Deep-water the roots. The soil must be kept damp until you see growth on the plant. The dealer where you purchased the plant should be able to tell you the best watering schedule; follow it.
7. If you are planting a hedge, you can plant it in a trench instead of individual holes. The trench should be deep and wide enough to accept the root system without crowding it. If you want the hedge to grow about 6 feet high, the hedge plants should be spaced about 20 inches apart. If you want the hedge to grow higher, space the plants about 3 feet apart.

Plant the shrub in a hole about 8 inches wider and 6 inches deeper than the balled roots of the plant.

Lawn and Garden Materials Mover

For work in the yard, you should have a wheelbarrow. The Big 4 model KB-4 wheelbarrow, made by Kelley Manufacturing Co., is the best size for homeowners with an average to large-size lot. The tray, which has a rounded front for easy dumping, is finished with baked-on yellow enamel. The wheelbarrow comes with long hardwood handles for leverage and a 16-inch pneumatic tire on a stamped wheel. The length is 59 inches; width is 27 inches. It has a 4-cubic-foot capacity.

Pruning Trees

Materials • Wound Compound

Tools • Stepladder • Gloves • Pruning Tools • Paintbrush

ALTHOUGH IT IS sometimes difficult for people to trim away perfectly healthy foliage, trees should be pruned for several good reasons. Pruning gives trees a more desirable shape, strengthens them by improving their structure, removes dead limbs and diseased portions, and increases the production of foliage, flowers, and fruit. Follow this basic procedure for pruning trees:

1. Sharpen all pruning tools; dull tools lead to ragged cuts, and ragged cuts can lead to problems.
2. Select the right size and type of tool for trees. Too large or too small a tool can make ragged cuts.
3. Make all cuts as close as possible to the base of the piece being removed without damaging the larger limb to which it is attached.
4. Try to do as much of the pruning work as possible while standing on the ground. When you must work from a ladder, never try to reach very far; move the ladder frequently and make certain that it is always on solid ground. Position yourself and your ladder so that the limbs you prune fall free and nowhere near you. If you are cutting away large limbs, make certain that there is no chance of them falling against electric power lines.
5. Seal all cuts with wound compound.
6. Winter is the best time for pruning trees because that is when most trees are dormant. Naturally, trees that exude sap during the winter should not be pruned until the following spring. **Note:** Because their root systems have usually been greatly reduced, newly transplanted trees should be pruned no matter what the season of the year.
7. In spring, prune most trees lightly for shaping purposes.
8. Remove broken limbs anytime of the year, but prune dead limbs in the fall.
9. When heavy pruning—the removal of as much as a third of the tree—is needed, don't perform all of the pruning during a single season. Do it, instead, in stages over a two- or three-year period.

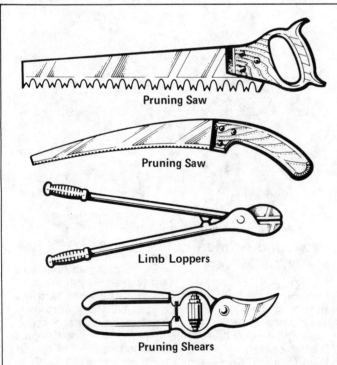

Before pruning a tree, sharpen all pruning tools. Dull tools lead to ragged cuts, which can lead to problems.

Pruning Saw

Pruning Saw

Limb Loppers

Pruning Shears

The root systems of newly transplanted trees have usually been greatly reduced, so prune the branches back too.

Moss Removal

Moss, that green plant that is supposed to grow only on the north side of trees but grows almost anywhere it wants, can be removed from a surface with hydrated lime. Dip a moistened scrub brush in the lime and scrub away the moss. Wear rubber or heavy gloves to protect your hands from the lime.

Versatile Hose Reel for Large Lawns

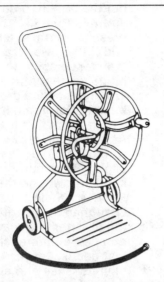

If you've got a large lawn, watering it can be difficult and so can hose storage. The No. 23-805 Ames Deluxe-Truk hose reel may be the thing. It holds 150 feet of ⅝-inch plastic garden hose. It features a zinc-coated handle and wheel guards, a base pan for hauling when the hose reel is detached, 1¼-inch wide-track wheels, and a 4½-foot leader hose. The hose reel is finished in an avocado color.

Types of Landscaping Stone

Stones that are used for landscaping are generally sold in three classifications: "Rubble" is stone that hasn't been cut to a specific shape. "Trimmings" is stone that was specially cut to form a building component such as a sill or molding. "Ashlar" is stone that has been cut to resemble brick.

Two-Hand Lopping Pruner Handles Heavy Pruning

The Bartlett two-hand pruner is typical of the heavy-duty limb loppers that every tree pruner needs. Rugged and made for heavy pruning, it features drop-forged tool steel blades and white ash handles. For easier cutting, place the blade next to the main limb or the trunk of the tree with the hook handles in your left hand. This locks the tool in place so that all the power of the right hand can be devoted to cutting instead of steadying. The Bartlett Manufacturing Company markets other tree pruning equipment as well as garden shears.

Pruning Saws Are Different for Different Purposes

Pruning saws come in several different types. Disston makes several pruning saws. The model No. 32 Deluxe full-length pruning saw has a 24-inch blade and is made for cutting big limbs and tough branches. The model No. K-40 Standard double-edge pruning saw does double duty for the homeowner. The coarse side is for big limbs, while the other side has an eight-pointed edge for cutting smaller branches. The Disston model No. 38 folding pruning saw has a curved blade that permits accurate reach-in cuts on green wood.

No Need to Climb to Trim Trees

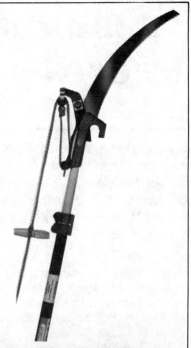

A pruning tool that has a long handle to give you maximum leverage makes it possible for you to prune your trees without risking your own limbs. The Snap-Cut tree pruner and saw features a "Multi-Power" cutting action to increase your leverage. The saw is a 16-inch blade with needle-point teeth to cut through green wood and large limbs; it can prune limbs up to 1⅛ inch in diameter. The lightweight aluminum alloy poles telescope from 6 to 12 feet with a simple twist. The Snap-Cut line of garden equipment is made by Seymour Smith & Son, Inc.

Storage Structure Keeps Gear Together

If you've got the space, a storage building keeps all your yard equipment and materials handy and safe. The Neverust Division of Nichols-Homeshield, Inc., offers more than a dozen different storage buildings made of aluminum so rust-out won't be a problem. The structures range in size from 10 by 11 feet to 24 by 47 inches. The buildings are easy to assemble. With reasonable care, says the manufacturer, the structures will retain their polyester finish for more than 15 years. All that the building should need is a hosing or washing down once a year; painting and patching isn't necessary. The roof and wall panels are ribbed and embossed for rigidity. The structural members are one-piece extruded channels and frames. The doors also are framed for strength and to prevent racking. Several colors are available, including green, white, red, and brown.

Trimming Hedges

Materials • Wound Compound

Tools • Gloves • Tape Measure • Hedge Clippers • Pruning Shears • Tree Saw • Paintbrush • Rake or Lawn Broom

I T TAKES A steady hand, plenty of patience, and practice to trim a hedge. The technique can vary, however, depending on how you want the hedge cut. Follow these steps to trim a hedge:

1. If the hedge is new, cut it so it has a good leaf growth from top to base. If the bottom of the hedge doesn't have many leaves, it probably was pruned incorrectly when it was planted. Just after the plant is in the ground, you should cut back the foliage at least one-third to as much as one-half; this will induce bushy growth, especially next to the ground.
2. If the plant has a fairly good upper and lower growth, trim about half the growth. If the hedge has just a few low branches, trim them to about 8 to 10 inches from the ground.
3. If the plant is established—several years old—but the bottom branches are sparse, cut several of the lowest branches to half their present length. After two seasons have passed and if the lower branches are still thin, trim them once again to half their length at the branches that formed on the old stems.
4. When the hedge grows back to its original height after trimming, cut it once again to within about 4 inches of the last cut.
5. As the hedge grows, prune it to the height you want it to be, but you should vary the cuts slightly from cutting to cutting to eliminate knotty growth on the plant stems. **Note:** Hedges should always be cut wider at the base than at the top.
6. In fall, after tree leaves have turned and dropped from branches, clean the hedge of leaf debris. Leaves left in the hedge can cause plant disease and encourage insect breeding.
7. If you cut especially large stems—those ½-inch in diameter or larger—the cut ends should be covered with wound compound.

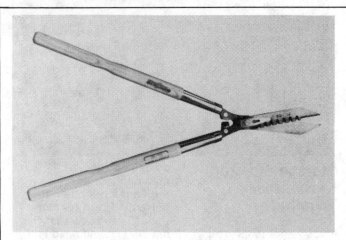

Long-Reach Shears for Wide Hedges

If you have hedges that are wide, standard hedge clippers won't let you do the cutting job very easily. Ames extra-long-reach Miracle Hedge Shears, No. 23-088, feature 22½-inch-long handles to make such chores easier. The tool can also tackle many hard-to-reach cutting situations with less effort. The blades are made of tempered, hollow-ground steel with precision-honed cutting edges. Notches and serrations in the blade prevent branches from slipping out during cuts. The handles are made of smooth northern ash finished with a sealer. Ames is a McDonough Company.

Log Lifter for Chain Saw Cutting

You should lift the log off the ground to cut it with a chain saw. If you don't lift the log, dirt and debris can clog the chain of the saw and cause all sorts of problems. The Oregon Lift 'n Cut log lifter made by Omark Industries, Inc., is designed to hook around the log and raise it off the ground for cutting in just one operation. The heavy steel claws and base pod of the tool are fitted with a rugged 32-inch maple handle for plenty of leverage. The lifter is 42 inches long and raises the log 12 inches off the ground.

Pruning Shears for Yard Work

For keeping hedges, shrubs, and other yard plants in shape, you need pruning shears. Ames No. 23-800 "Our Best" Professional by-pass pruning shears have precision cutting blades, a heavy-duty spring, and easy tension adjustment. The blades are replaceable. The tool is 7¾ inches long. Ames is a McDonough Co.

Mower Maintenance

Materials • Rags • Penetrating Oil
• Replacement Blade • No. 20 Non-Detergent Motor Oil • Household Detergent
• Kerosene • Spray Lubricant • Spark Plug • Replacement Spark Plug Cable
• Points and Condenser

Tools • Block of Wood or C-Clamp
• Adjustable Wrench • Metal File • Pencil
• Screwdriver • Stiff Brush • Vacuum Cleaner • Spark Plug Wrench • Wire Gapping Gauge or Book of Matches
• Flywheel Puller • Pliers

G ASOLINE-POWERED lawn mowers and electric mowers, too, are simple, hard-working machines that will last for years if they are properly maintained and you clean away lawn debris, such as fertilizer and chemicals after each mowing session. If you do nothing more than annually change the spark plug, clean the air filter, change the oil, and hose chemicals off the metal housing, the lawn mower should run trouble-free.

The following procedures are for maintaining a gasoline-powered lawn mower. Electric lawn mowers have a motor that is best serviced by a professional if problems arise. However, the housing of the electric unit is maintained in much the same way as a gas-powered engine. Follow these steps:

1. Disconnect the spark plug cable before inspecting or servicing the mower. *Caution: Disconnect the spark plug wire to prevent accidental starting of the engine.*
2. Tilt the mower over so that you can inspect the blade. If it is not sharp, remove the blade and sharpen it, or replace the blade. To remove the blade, block the blade so it will not turn with wrench pressure. A block of wood and a C-clamp should work. Usually, you will have to apply some penetrating oil on the nut to loosen it. Follow the manufacturer's directions in the mower's instruction manual, if available.
3. Dress the cutting edges of the blade with a file, giving each cutting edge the same number of strokes with the same amount of pressure on the file. Don't worry about nicks in the blade. Before the blade is replaced, it must be balanced. This can be done by filing a notch along the blade on the heavy side. However, don't notch the cutting edge. Rest the blade on a pencil to check its balance.
4. Clean the housing underneath. Clippings that are caked on can be scraped away.
5. Clean the fins that are sticking out on the engine. If these are not clean, the mower can run hot. A stiff brush will usually do the job.
6. Clean the air filter. Most filters are foam sponge. They can usually be cleaned with warm water and detergent. After the filter is clean, squeeze it out and coat it with lightweight oil. Squeeze out excess oil. Be sure the filter is secure in its housing. The dry-type filters can be cleaned with a vacuum cleaner and by brushing. However, when they refuse to come clean, replace them. **Note:** Some mowers have an oil-bath-type filter. They are cleaned with a solvent. Be sure it is a safe solvent such as kerosene. *Caution: Never use gasoline as a solvent; it is too dangerous.* Air dry the parts of the filter and the filter assembly, and put in new oil.
7. Check the spark plug. To remove it, you need a spark plug wrench. If you have a socket set, you can buy a special socket for spark plugs. If not, you can get an inexpensive wrench made just for spark plugs. **Note:** Because lawn mower spark plugs are not expensive, it is best to replace it annually or even twice a year if

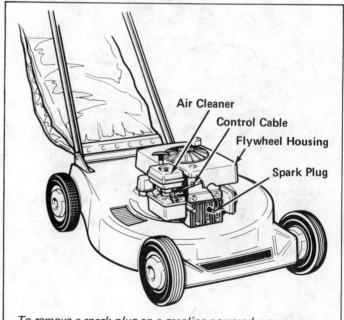

To remove a spark plug on a gasoline-powered mower, you need a spark plug wrench. If you have a socket set, you can buy a special socket for spark plugs.

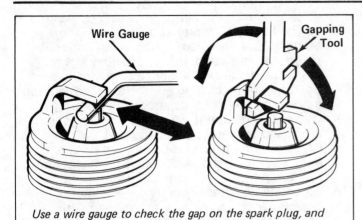

Use a wire gauge to check the gap on the spark plug, and use a gapping tool to set the correct gap according to your owner's manual.

the mower is used to cut a large lawn—about 3 acres or so.

8. Set the gap on the plug. Use a wire gapping gauge made for this purpose. Or, if a gauge isn't available, try using a match book cover. Your owner's manual is the best guide. If you don't know the correct gap, 0.025 inch should work. The exact gap will do better, however. When putting the plug back in, be sure its threads are clean. Oil them. Hand-tighten the plug and then give it about a third of a turn with the wrench. Don't over-tighten.

9. Inspect the spark plug cable. If it is frayed,

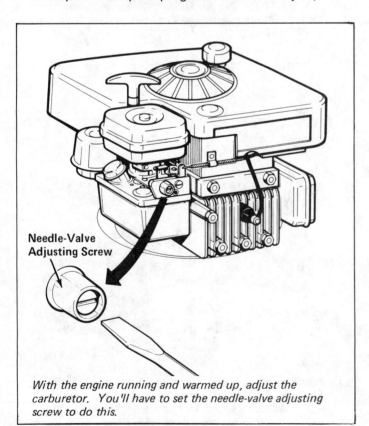

Needle-Valve Adjusting Screw

With the engine running and warmed up, adjust the carburetor. You'll have to set the needle-valve adjusting screw to do this.

replace it. Some are not easily replaced because doing so requires the removal of the flywheel, and to do this, you will need a special puller made for your mower's engine and engine size. These tools, however, are available at lawn mower repair centers. Be sure that cable connection is tight. If the cable terminal fits loosely on the plug, squeeze it gently with pliers.

10. Check the oil level. If the oil is dirty, change it. It will drain more completely when hot. **Note:** Oil should be changed at the end of each mowing season, no matter how dirty or clean it may appear.

11. Lubricate all moving parts on top of the mower. Also use a spray lubricant on the throttle and cable.

12. Check to see if the choke is properly adjusted. To do this, remove the air filter unit, and look into the carburetor. There will be a round plate. With the control set to "choke," this plate should move down to close the opening. If not, loosen the screw and clamp that hold the choke cable in place. Move the cable forward until the plate closes. Tighten the cable and check again. Replace the air filter.

13. Reconnect the spark plug cable and start the mower.

14. With the engine running and warmed up, adjust the carburetor. Turn the needle-valve adjusting screw clockwise one-eighth turn. Wait a few seconds, then make another one-eighth turn. Do this until the engine slows. Now turn counterclockwise in one-eighth turns counting the eighths. When the engine falters, stop. Divide the number of one-eighth turns by two and turn back—clockwise—that number of eighths. That sets the needle-valve to its best setting. To set proper idle, turn the throttle to its top speed and then back to its slowest speed. Turn the idle speed adjustment screw until the engine sounds as if it is running at about half the maximum speed.

15. If the lawn mower won't start, and you know that the spark plug is okay, chances are that the mower needs new points and a condenser. A clue to this is how the mower stopped running—quit suddenly without sputtering—or how it won't start—absolutely no kick-over at all. The condenser and points are located directly under the flywheel. You will need a flywheel puller to get at these parts for replacement. *Caution: Don't try to pry up the flywheel with a wrench handle or screwdriver; the force will break the flywheel.* Once the flywheel is off, a round metal container should be visible. Remove the lid and the points and condenser will be exposed. You can buy points and condenser kits for mower tune-ups at most outlets selling lawn and garden supplies.

'Upside Down' Mower Blades

Replacement blades for lawnmowers often are packaged "upside down." The surface you see faces the lawnmower, not the grass. Some manufacturers stamp the metal "grass side." However, you must look very closely to see this imprint, which is on the opposite side of the label stickers on the blade.

Tune-Up Kit Gets Mower Purring Again

If your mower isn't giving you the power and performance you expect from it, it probably needs a tune-up. Look for a Prestolite Tune-Up Kit for your mower model. The kit features the company's mini-plug, designed for your mower. There are different kits to take care of just about every mower, snowmobile, garden tractor, and chain saw; individual components within the kit are available separately. You can find Prestolite Tune-Up Kits, made by the Prestolite Electrical Division of Eltra Corp., wherever mower parts are sold.

Metal-Handled Hedge Shears

Seymour Smith and Son, Inc., makes a line of quality garden tools. An example is the Snap-Cut No. 354-9T hedge shears. The tool features 9-inch hardened and serrated blades, and spring-steel blade tensioner and shock absorber. The handles are top-quality metal, strong yet light.

A Paint for Grills

Barbecue grills last for years, but they can become rusty and grimy. The solution is Plasti-kote Bar-B-Q Paint from the Plasti-kote Co., Inc. According to the manufacturer, the paint is heat-resistant and can be applied with little or no preparation. You just push a button and spray on the paint. Plasti-kote says it dries quickly and won't rub off, crack, or peel. The paint, No. 150, is black in color and comes in a 16-ounce aerosol container.

Make Use of Grass Clippings

The best thing you can do with grass clippings is to spread them out evenly on a garden bed. A thin layer of clippings makes an excellent mulch. The worst thing you can do with grass clippings is to pile them in a corner like a haystack. The stack not only will smell bad in a short period of time but it will serve as an excellent breeding spot for flies.

Automatic Bug Killers Have Optional Photo Eye

Electric insect killers can do a good job of removing flying pests from your yard. Three sizes of electronic bug killers are offered by the Emerson Environment Products Division of Emerson Electric Co. All feature an optional photo cell that turns on the device at dusk and turns it off at sunrise. The bug killer's ultraviolet light also permits the unit to double as a security light. The electronic bug killers are available in 15-, 25-, and 50-watt sizes; all are UL Listed. Other features include a GE Lexan housing and easy lamp changings. The devices can be plugged into any UL Listed, grounded outdoor extension cord or grounded 120-volt outlet. An outer grid prevents fingers from coming into contact with the charged inner grids. Mounting accessories are sold separately.

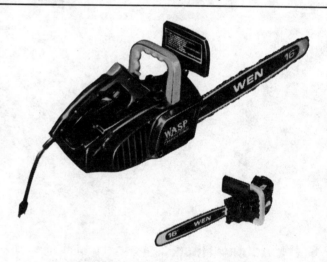

Electric Chain Saw Cuts Wood Fast

If you cut your own fireplace logs, a chain saw speeds the job. The model 2600 Wasp 16-inch electric chain saw has a 16-inch capacity that will handle most log-cutting for average fireplaces. The tool also may be used for tree-trimming and other chores. The Wasp chain saw features an automatic oiler with manual override, non-slip handles, and a 16-inch reversible bar with a low-profile chain to minimize kick-back. The saw, manufactured by Wen Products, Inc., also has a bar-tensioning mechanism, chain catch, and bucking spike. It operates off 120-volt AC and is double insulated with a 12-amp, 5200-rpm motor.

Gas-Powered Chain Saw for Big Jobs

If you have lots of wood to cut for your fireplace or wood stove, you may be happier with the Homelite 330 gas-powered chain saw. The Homelite chain saw, made by the Homelite Division of Textron, Inc., features a 3.3-cubic-inch engine displacement, automatic oiling, a capacitor-discharge ignition, low-operating sound levels, and an anti-kickback chain device. The chain saw also has excellent balance and a new vibration isolation system. You also get a chain catcher, cushioned rubber-coated handlebar, and a throttle interlock.

Powerful Hand Sprayer Has Many Uses

An essential garden tool—indoors or outdoors—is a hand sprayer. The Spray Pal, made by Thiokol, the AFA Corp., is a 32-ounce, all-purpose plant and garden sprayer that you operate by hand. The nozzle of the model S-69 is adjustable and the refillable bottle is unbreakable, according to the manufacturer. You can adjust the spray from a fine mist to a full stream, which makes the sprayer an ideal tool for insecticides, plant foods, water, or any low-viscosity liquid.

Setting Posts in Concrete the Easy Way

You don't have to mix and dump concrete into a post hole to set the post. First, dig the hole to the depth you want. Throw in a couple of handfuls of gravel for drainage. Set the post in the hole. Then, pour ready-to-mix concrete mix into the hole, filling the hole about one-third full. Pour a half bucket of water on top of the mix and puddle it with a short length of 1 × 3. When the mixture is packed tight and the water disappears, fill the hole two-thirds full. Add water and puddle it again. Finally, fill the hole full and add water and puddle. When you are finished, trowel the top of the concrete so it slopes away from the post; this is for water drainage.

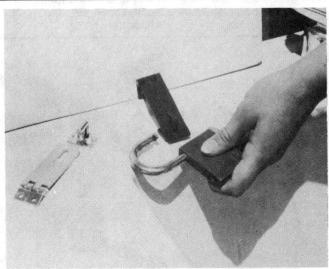

Self-Latching Hasp Provides Security

An outdoor storeroom door should have a lock. The Snap-Tite hasp, when it is closed, has a stainless steel retaining clip on a locking-T padeye that automatically retains the hinged latch securely. You don't have to fumble with an awkward swivel eye, pin, or padlock. The padeye and latch may be installed the usual way where the door and casing are on the same level. Or, either part may be mounted on a surface higher or lower than the other. The hasp, made from aluminum alloy, has a tensile strength of about 36,000 psi; the strength is 80,000 psi for the stainless steel clip and hinge pin. The hasps and hinges are available with a polished or anodized satin black finish. The latch is 3 inches long (closed) and 1⅛₆ inches wide. The product is made by Moeller Manufacturing Co., Inc.

Hose Storage Reel Keeps Hose Safe and Handy

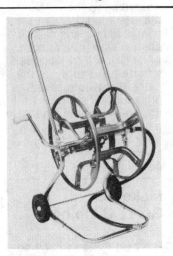

By keeping a garden hose properly stored—instead of lying out in the yard where mowers, bikes, cars, and people can crush it—a hose should provide years of trouble-free service. The No. 23-868 Douglas portable hose reel keeps a hose safe. The front-loading reel has two bearing points and a low center of gravity for easier operation and storage. It has a 150-foot hose capacity with a 54-inch connector hose. The wheels are molded; the reel is 17 inches in diameter. It has a chrome-plated frame.

Hose-End Sprayers for Bugs, Weeds

A sprayer that attaches to the end of a garden hose can be economical to use. There are three Acme Burgess hose-end sprayers with top-mounted controls. The nozzle adjusts the spray upward, downward, or in a jet stream. Model 427, a 2-gallon sprayer, is ideal for flowers, vegetables, and for spraying wettable powders, insecticides, and fungicides. Model 428, with a 6-gallon capacity, is

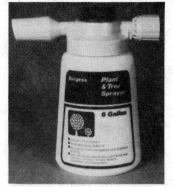

ideal for plant, shrub, and tree spraying. Model 429, a 15-gallon sprayer, is designed for spraying lawns and soil.

Bug Zapper Replaces Bug Sprays Outdoors

If you have a small yard or spend a lot of time on your patio or balcony, you could use an electronic bug killer to make evenings more enjoyable. The Patio Web is an electric bug killer that can eliminate backyard pests without aerosol chemical pesticides, according to the manufacturer. It can be used for backyards up to one-half acre as well as for patios and balconies. The Patio Web, manufactured by Weber-Stephen Products Co., uses less than 30 watts. The manufacturer says this is cheaper than the cost of one aerosol can of pesticide. The device is made of porcelain-sealed, heavy-gauge steel. It comes ready to hang in position and use.

Net Provides Protection for Your Garden

If birds and small animals cause damage in your garden, a net may be the answer. The Ross garden net is designed to protect shrubs, trees, gardens, and other plant life. It also may be used as a winter wrap for plantings and for erosion control and temporary fencing. The netting comes in several sizes: 6½ by 21 feet, 13 by 13 feet, 13 by 45 feet, 13 by 75 feet, and 26 by 26 feet. According to Ross Daniels, Inc., the net won't interfere with normal growth. Also, it isn't affected by crop sprays and it won't rot. To use, drape the net over the planting or stake it out.

Lattice Growing in Popularity

Lattice can screen bad views, add architectural interest to poor construction, block the wind, and add privacy. Prefabricated lattice panels from Wing Industries, Inc., are available in 2- by 4-foot, 2- by 8-foot, and 4- by 8-foot panels. The lattice strips are ⅛ inch thick and 1⅛ inches wide. Spacing of the lattice strips is 1¾ inches. The panels are made from pine and are fabricated to withstand years of weathering and hard knocks. The lattice is ready to stain or paint.

Pest Protection That You Paint on

An insecticide that you apply with a regular paintbrush to stop and control ants, crickets, firebrats, spiders, silverfish, and roaches is Pest-Aid 180. The product, according to the manufacturer, Velsicol Chemical Corp., keeps these insects under control for up to six months. Velsicol says that the material is transparent, odor-free, and durable after it dries. Then, the application may be cleaned, washed, and exposed to foot traffic and weather without destroying its effectiveness. Pest-Aid 180 is available in quart and gallon containers. Application instructions come with the product.

Drill Grinding Kit Can Sharpen Many Home and Garden Tools

Home and garden tools get dull quickly. The General drill grinding kit consists of a drill grinding attachment and grinding wheel that is able to accurately sharpen twist drills. The attachment can be used for fractional drills ⅛ to ¾ inch; for number size drills 30 to 1; for letter size drills A to Z; and for millimeter size drills 3.0 to 19.0mm. Although designed for use with the No. 825 drill grinding attachment, the 6- by

1-inch No. 826 grinding wheel in the kit is also suitable for reshaping and resharpening most home and garden tools.

Basic Tools

AFTER YOU'VE acquired the most basic tools—hammer, pliers, screwdrivers, and wrenches—what are the essentials? For most jobs, you'll need measuring and marking tools, saws, and a drill; planes, files, and clamps are next in line. Add tools and accessories as your budget permits. Power tools do what hand tools do—faster and, usually, easier.

There is only one cast-in-concrete rule about tools: Buy good ones. Quality tools are safer and easier to use, and most will last a lifetime if you take care of them. You can spot a quality tool by its machining: The metal parts are smooth and shiny and the tool is well balanced. Inexpensive tools are often painted to hide the defects or roughness of the metal parts, and the machining is crude. You can also tell quality by the price tag—you'll pay an average of 25 percent more for quality equipment. But cheap tools are no economy—you get what you pay for.

Measuring and Marking Tools

Measuring Rule or Tape Measure: Flexible tape measures are available in lengths of up to 50 feet; a tape that is 16 to 24 feet is usually adequate. Buy a tape at least ⅝ inch wide, so it will stay rigid when extended. Many rules have an automatic power return.

Folding Rule. Folding rules are available in 4-foot, 6-foot, and 8-foot lengths; they're used for laying out projects where absolute accuracy is necessary. The rules fold down to 6 inches; care must be taken not to strain the metal joints at the folding points. Some rules have a metal insert in the first 6 inches. This insert is pulled out of the rule for use as a depth or marking gauge, or for extremely critical measurements. It can also be used for measurements inside door or window frames or between parallel surfaces.

Carpenter's Square. The standard sizes for carpenter's squares are 18 or 24 inches (body) by 12 or 18 inches (tongue); the size is important for laying out projects on plywood and hardboard. Carpenter's squares are steel or aluminum; they have multiple scales for figuring board-foot requirements, brace (rafter) height, stairstep stringer angles, and rafter cuts.

Combination Square. For small jobs, a combination square is easier to use than a carpenter's square because the combination square is smaller. The body of the square slides along a

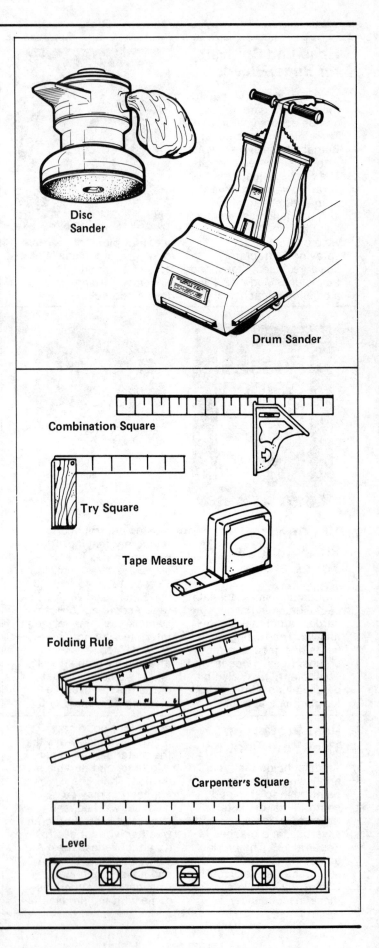

Disc Sander

Drum Sander

Combination Square

Try Square

Tape Measure

Folding Rule

Carpenter's Square

Level

handle, and the blade can be fixed at any point with a thumbscrew. The handle of the square may incorporate a small bubble level or a scratch awl, which can be used for leveling and marking. This square can also be used as a depth gauge, a miter square, and, with the blade removed, as a straightedge and ruler.

Try Square. This tool looks like a small carpenter's square with a wood handle. The measurements go across the metal blade only (not the handle). The square is generally used to test the squareness of edges in planing and sawing work. It can also be used to check right-angle layouts. The tongue has a maximum length of 12 inches; it is fairly wide, but it can be used as a straightedge, ruler, and depth gauge.

Level. Two- and three-bubble levels are standard for most leveling and plumbing (vertical level) projects. Some of the bubbles are in vials that can be moved for angle "leveling"; these vials can sometimes be replaced if they are damaged or broken. The edges of a level can be used as a straightedge. Laid flat against a vertical surface, the level can determine both horizontal and vertical levels—often needed when installing cabinets, hanging wallpaper, or hanging pictures. Level frames are either wood or lightweight metal such as aluminum; lengths range to 6 feet.

Chalk Line. Chalk lines are available in a metal canister or case, or in a ball like heavy twine. In the canister type, the line is chalked with powdered chalk poured into the canister. In the ball type, the chalk is hard chalk similar to that used for blackboards. To use a chalk line, stretch it taut along a surface and snap the line; the chalk leaves a blue line along the work for measuring and cutting. A chalk line is also used to suspend plumb bobs, for vertical lines, and to lay out walks, driveways, and foundations.

Handsaws

Crosscut Saw. The crosscut saw, as its name implies, cuts across the grain of the wood. Crosscut saws have from 5 to 10 or more teeth per inch to produce a smooth cut in the wood. They are used for cutting plywood and hardboard panels, and sometimes to cut miters. They can be used for ripping but aren't as fast as the ripsaw.

Ripsaw. The ripsaw cuts along the grain of the wood, called "ripping." Its teeth are spaced from 3 to 5 teeth per inch. The ripsaw's teeth are wider-set than those of the crosscut saw, so they slice through the wood like a chisel. The final cut of a ripsaw is fairly rough, and the wood usually has to be planed or sanded to its final measurement.

Backsaw. A backsaw has a reinforced back to stiffen the blade; its teeth are closely spaced—like those of a crosscut saw—so the cut is smooth. A backsaw is generally used for making miter cuts

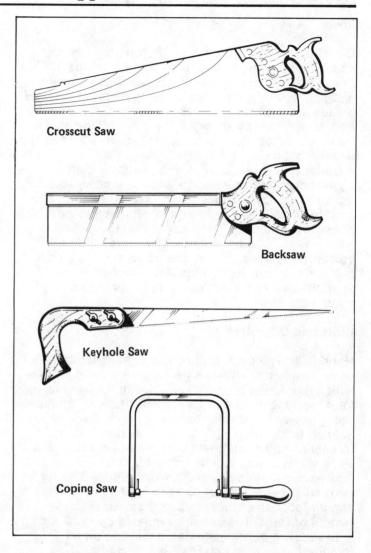

Crosscut Saw

Backsaw

Keyhole Saw

Coping Saw

and for trimming molding. It's designed for use in a miter box; the reinforced back serves as a guide.

Keyhole Saw. This saw has a 10- to 12-inch tapered blade; it's used to cut openings for pipes, electrical boxes, and almost any straight or curved internal cuts that are too large for an auger bit, drill, or hole saw. Quality keyhole saws have removable blades with a variety of tooth spacings, for various materials such as wood, plastic, metal, and hardboard. Similar to the keyhole saw is the compass saw, which has a blade 12 to 14 inches long. A compass saw is used like a keyhole saw, but the keyhole saw can make a tighter turn.

Coping Saw. This saw looks like a C-clamp with a handle. The blades are thin, and replaceable; the blade is secured with two pins at the ends of the saw, and the handle turns to put the proper tension on the blade. A variety of blades is available, with both ripsaw and crosscut tooth spacing. Blades can be inserted into the frame to cut on the forward or backward stroke, depending on the sawing project; the pins can also be turned to set the blade at an angle for special cuts.

Appendix: Useful Information

Power Saws

Circular Saw. A portable electric tool, the circular saw is the power version of a crosscut or ripsaw. The guide on the saw can be adjusted to cut miters and pockets in almost any building material. Several blades are available: crosscut, rip, masonry, metal, and plastic. Accessories for the saw include a table, so the saw can be mounted to work as a small table saw.

Saber Saw. The saber saw, sometimes called a jigsaw, consists of a short—about 4 inches—blade, driven in an up-and-down reciprocating motion. This portable power tool is designed with a wide variety of blades for a wide variety of materials, including wood, metal, plastic, masonry, ceramic, and high-pressure laminate. This is the power counterpart to the keyhole and the coping saw; it will make smooth fine-line or contour cuts either with or across the grain.

Drills and Drill Bits

Hand Drill. The hand drill is like an eggbeater; a drive handle moves bevel gears to turn a chuck in which a drill has been locked. This drill can't make large holes, but it can make small-diameter, shallow holes in wood and soft metals.

Push Drill. The push drill requires only one hand to use; as you push down on the handle, the shank turns a chuck into which a small bit fits. This is a limited-capacity tool, but it's excellent for making pilot holes, and is handy for setting hinges and similar jobs. The bits are usually stored in the handle of the drill; sizes are available up to ¼ inch.

Brace. The hand brace has a rotating offset handle that turns a chuck with a ratcheting mechanism; auger bits, countersinks, and screwdriver attachments are available, and the ratchet also lets you work in restricted areas. The large-capacity chuck accommodates bits that will cut holes up to 1½ inches in diameter. The brace is the counterpart of the electric drill, but a hand brace chuck isn't designed for twist drills, unless the drills have a special shank for hand use.

Electric Drill. Three sizes of chucks are available for power drills: ¼-, ⅜-, and ½-inch capacity. The two popular sizes are ¼ and ⅜ inch. The ¼-inch chuck has a capacity of ¼-inch drills in metal and ½-inch in wood; it can handle only a limited range of drilling

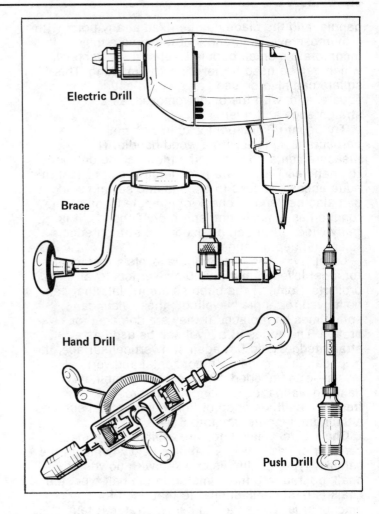

Electric Drill

Brace

Hand Drill

Push Drill

operations, but it's the least expensive type of electric drill. It should not be used for prolonged hard jobs. Accessories are available.

The ⅜-inch drill can make ⅜-inch holes in metal and ¾-inch holes in wood; a hole saw can also be used with this tool, to cut holes up to 3 inches in diameter. Many ⅜-inch drills have a hammer mode that permits drilling in concrete, along with a reversing feature handy for removing screws. A variable-speed drill is recommended; this type can be started slowly and then speeded up. A variety of attachments and accessories is available, including wire brushes, paint mixers, and even a circular saw attachment.

Drill Bits. The most common drill bits include those shown in the accompanying table:

Bit	Drill Type	Use
Twist Drill	Hand, power, or drill press	Small-diameter holes in wood and metal.
Spade Bit	Power or drill press	Holes up to 1½ inches in wood.
Auger Bit	Hand	Holes up to 1½ inches in wood.
Expansion Bit	Hand	Holes up to 3 inches in wood.
Fly Cutter	Drill press	Holes up to 6 inches in wood; smaller holes in other materials.
Hole Saw	Power or drill press	Holes up to 3 inches.

Planes

Jack Plane. The jack plane removes excess wood and brings the surface of the wood to trueness and smoothness. The plane is 12 to 14 inches long. Depending on the job, it can also be used to true long edges for gluing.

Smoothing Plane. This plane, slightly smaller than the jack plane, is used to bring wood to a final finish. The plane measures from 6 to 9 inches long.

Block Plane. The block plane is small, and is designed to smooth and cut the end grain of wood. The plane has a low blade angle that permits smooth cutting, and only one hand is needed to use it. Although the block plane is a cabinetmaker's tool, it can be used to smooth almost any soft material, even aluminum. For large jobs, a smoothing or jack plane should be used, because both are longer and wider.

Wood Files

A wood rasp, with a rasp and/or curved-tooth cut, is used to remove excess wood; the piece of wood is final-smoothed with a single- or double-cut file. As a starter set, buy an assortment of flat files—wood rasp, bastard, second-cut, and smooth files.

Clamps

Clamps are very inexpensive, and they're essential for many jobs. Start with several C-clamps and a set of bar clamps; if you plan to work on furniture, get strap clamps too.

C-Clamps. These clamps are made from cast iron or aluminum, and have a C-shaped body; a screw with a metal pad applies the tension on the material being clamped. Because C-clamps can exert lots of pressure, buffer blocks of scrap wood or other materials should be inserted between the jaws of the clamps and the material being clamped. A wide range of sizes is available.

Screw Clamps. These clamps have parallel wood jaws; they are the basic woodworking clamps. Tension is applied by hand with two threaded wood spindles; the clamps can be adjusted to angles by moving the spindles. Screw clamps are expensive.

Bar Clamps. These clamps are made to fit on long metal rods or pieces of pipe, tension is applied by tightening a screw. Bar clamps are used for gluing boards together and on wide surfaces where the throats of C-clamps are too shallow to accept the work. Bar clamp fixtures and bars or pipe can be purchased separately.

Strap or Web Clamps. These clamps are simply webbing straps, usually nylon, with a sliding tension clamp. The clamp is used for four-way tensioning on odd-shaped or four-cornered pieces. Because the clamps are fabric, the pressure won't damage the material being clamped.

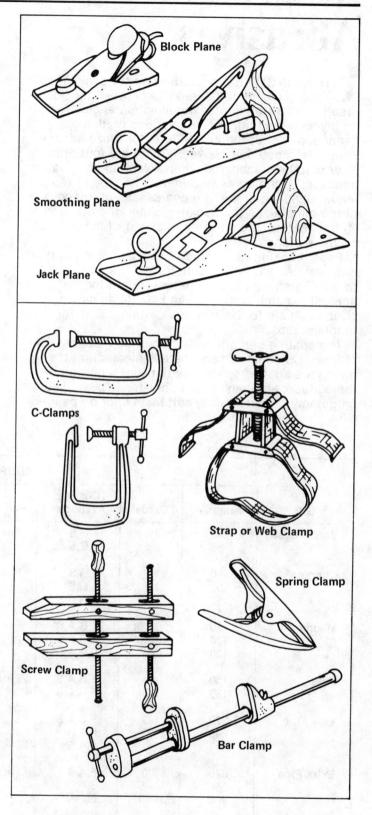

Block Plane

Smoothing Plane

Jack Plane

C-Clamps

Strap or Web Clamp

Spring Clamp

Screw Clamp

Bar Clamp

Spring Clamps. These clamps look like large metal clothespins; they're used for clamping light jobs, such as veneers glued to core material. Spring clamps also come in handy as holding devices. They are very inexpensive.

Abrasives

CHOOSING THE proper abrasive for a given job usually means the difference between mediocre results and a truly professional appearance. Most do-it-yourselfers still refer to various grades of "sandpaper," but the proper term for these sanding sheets is "coated abrasives." There are four primary factors to be considered when selecting any coated abrasive: (1) the abrasive mineral, the type of rough material; (2) the grade, the coarseness or fineness of the mineral; (3) the backing, paper or cloth; and (4) the coating, the nature and extent of the mineral on the surface.

Paper backing for coated abrasives comes in four weights: "A," "C," "D," and "E." "A" (also referred to as "Finishing") is the lightest weight for the lightest sanding work. "C" and "D" (also called "Cabinet") are for heavier work, while "E" is for the toughest jobs.

The coating can either be "Open-Coated" or "Closed-Coated." "Open-Coated" means that the grains are spaced so as only to cover a portion of the surface; an open-coated abrasive is best used on gummy or soft woods, soft metals, or on painted surfaces. "Closed-Coated" means that the abrasive covers the entire area. Naturally, closed-coated abrasives provide maximum cutting, but they also clog faster; a closed-coated abrasive is best used on hard woods and on hard metals.

There are three popular ways to grade coated abrasives. Simplified markings (fine, very fine, etc.) provide a general description of the grade. "Grit" actually refers to the number of mineral grains that, when set end to end, equal 1 inch. The commonly used "O" symbols are more or less arbitrary. The coarsest grading under this system is 4½, and the finest is 10/0, or 0000000000.

Although the coated varieties definitely include the most popular forms of abrasives, there are other types of finishing abrasives that you should know about. The best known of these other types are pumice, rottenstone, rouge, and steel wool. Pumice is a volcanic abrasive powder used for fine finishing; it is generally lubricated with water or oil and comes in several grades. Rottenstone is a fine powder, finer even than pumice, that is used to render a high sheen. Rouge is an abrasive powder used primarily in the polishing of metal. Steel wool comes in many grades of coarseness, and you should be careful to apply the correct grade of steel wool to the work you have at hand.

Grit	Number	Grade	Coating Available[1]	Common Uses
Very Coarse	30	2½	F,G,S	Rust removal on rough finished metal.
	36	2	F,G,S	
Coarse	40	1½	F,G,S	Rough sanding of wood; paint removal.
	50	1	F,G,S	
	60	½	F,G,A,S	
Medium	80	0(1/0)	F,G,A,S	General wood sanding; plaster smoothing; preliminary smoothing of previously painted surfaces.
	100	00(2/0)	F,G,A,S	
	120	3/0	F,G,A,S	
Fine	150	4/0	F,G,A,S	Final sanding of bare wood or previously painted surfaces.
	180	5/0	F,G,A,S	
Very Fine	220	6/0	F,G,A,S	Light sanding between finish coats; dry sanding.
	240	7/0	F,A,S	
	280	8/0	F,A,S	
Extra Fine	320	9/0	F,A,S	High finish on lacquer, varnish, or shellac; wet sanding.
	360	—[2]	S	
	400	10/0	S	
Superfine	500	—[2]	S	High-satinized finishes; wet sanding.
	600	—[2]	S	

SANDPAPER

[1] F = flint; G = garnet; A = aluminum oxide; S = silicon carbide. Silicon carbide is used dry or wet, with water or oil.
[2] No grade designation.

STEEL WOOL

Grade	Number	Common Uses
Coarse	3	Paint and varnish removal; removing paint spots from resilient floors.
Medium Coarse	2	Removing scratches from brass; removing paint spots from ceramic tile; rubbing floors between finish coats.
Medium	1	Rust removal; cleaning glazed tiles; removing marks from wood floors; with paint and varnish remover, removing finishes.
Medium Fine	0	Brass finishing; cleaning tile; with paint and varnish remover, removing stubborn finishes.
Fine	00	With linseed oil, satinizing high-gloss finishes.
Extra Fine	000	Removing paint spots or stains from wood; cleaning polished metals; rubbing between finish coats.
Superfine	0000	Final rubbing of finish; stain removal.

ABRASIVE CLOTHS

Type	Grades	Common Uses
Emery	Very coarse through fine	General light metal polishing; removing rust and corrosion from metal; wet or dry sanding.
Crocus	Very fine	High-gloss finishing for metals.
Aluminum Oxide	Very coarse through fine	Power sanding belts.

ABRASIVE POWDERS

Type	Grades	Common Uses
Pumice	F through FFF	Rubbing between finish coats; final buffing; stain removal.
Rottenstone	None	Buffing between finish coats; final buffing; stain removal.
Rouge	None	Metal polishing.

Plywood Grading

KNOWING EVERYTHING you can about plywood can save you money as well as mean the difference between a successful project and one that fails. For example, there's no reason for you to buy an expensive piece of plywood that's perfect on both sides if only one side will ever be seen. Similarly, there's no sense in paying for ⅝-inch thickness when ¼-inch plywood is really all you need. Plywood also comes with different glues, different veneers, and different degrees of finish. By knowing these characteristics you may be able to save quite a bit of money, and you certainly will improve your chances of getting the right material for the work you have in mind.

Plywood is, in several respects, better than lumber for some jobs. It's strong, lightweight, and rigid. Its high impact resistance means that plywood doesn't split, chip, crack all the way through, or crumble; the cross-laminated construction restricts expansion and contraction within the individual plies. Moreover, you never get "green" wood with plywood. Easy to work from cutting to fastening to finishing, plywood is available at home centers, hardware stores, and lumberyards.

When you buy a sheet of plywood, you know exactly what size you're getting. A 4- by 8-foot sheet of ¾-inch plywood measures exactly 4 by 8 feet and is ¾ inch thick. This contrasts with the distinction between nominal and actual measurements that affects other types of lumber.

When you buy plywood, look for a back-stamp or edge-marking bearing the initials APA or DFPA. APA stands for American Plywood Association, while DFPA is the Douglas Fir Plywood Association. These two organizations represent most of the plywood manufacturers and they inspect and test to insure that plywood quality is high and that grading is accurate. Their stamp is your assurance that what you see is what you get.

Plywood is broadly categorized into two types: exterior and interior. Exterior plywood is made with nothing but waterproof glue, and you should always select exterior plywood for any exposed application. Interior plywood, made with highly resistant glues, can actually withstand quite a bit of moisture. There is interior plywood made with IMG (intermediate glue), which is resistant to bacteria, mold, and moisture, but no interior plywood is made for use outdoors. The reason is that in most cases the inner plies of interior plywood are made of lower grade woods.

The most critical plywood grading category for most home projects is the appearance grade of the panel faces. Check the accompanying table before you buy any plywood.

The "Plywood Grades" tables indicate the various uses for each grade. The first letter indicates the face grade, while the second indicates the back grade.

PLYWOOD GRADES

Interior Grade	Face	Back	Inner Plies	Common Uses
A-A	A	A	D	Cabinet doors, built-ins, and furniture where both sides show.
A-B	A	B	D	Alternate for A-A. Face is finish grade; back is solid and smooth.
A-D	A	D	D	Finish grade face for paneling, built-ins, and backing.
B-D	B	D	D	Utility grade. One paintable side. For backing, cabinet sides, etc.
C-D	C	D	D	Sheathing and structural uses such as temporary enclosures, subfloor. Unsanded.
Underlayment	C-Plugged	D	C,D	For underlayment or combination subfloor-underlayment under tile and carpeting.
Exterior Grade	Face	Back	Inner Plies	Common Uses
A-A	A	A	C	Outdoors, where appearance of both sides is important.
A-B	A	B	C	Alternate for A-A, where appearance of one side is less important. Face is finish grade.
A-C	A	C	C	Soffits, fences, base for coatings.
B-C	B	C	C	For utility uses such as farm buildings, some kinds of fences, base for coatings.
C-C (Plugged)	C-Plugged	C	C	Excellent base for tile and linoleum, backing for wallcoverings, high-performance coatings.
C-C	C	C	C	Unsanded, for backing and rough construction exposed to weather.

Fasteners

NAILS, SCREWS, and bolts are fasteners that every do-it-yourselfer uses. But very few know all the different types and their specific uses. The following are many of the most common types of fasteners.

Nails

The easiest way to fasten two pieces of wood together is with nails, and nails are manufactured in a variety of shapes, sizes, and metals, to do almost any fastening job. Most commonly, nails are made of steel, but other types—aluminum, brass, nickel, bronze, copper, and stainless steel—are available for use where corrosion could occur. Nails are also manufactured with coatings—galvanized, blued, or cemented—to prevent rusting and add holding power.

Nail size is designated by penny size, originally the price per hundred nails. Penny size, almost always referred to as "d," ranges from 2 penny, or 2d—1 inch long—to 60 penny, or 60d—6 inches long. Nails shorter than 1 inch are called "brads"; nails longer than 6 inches are called "spikes."

The length of the nails is important: At least two-thirds of the nail should be driven into the base, or thicker, material. For example, a 1 × 3 nailed to a 4 × 4 beam should be fastened with an 8-penny, or 8d, nail. An 8d nail is 2½ inches long; ¾ inch of its length will go through the 1 × 3, and the remaining 1¾ inches will go into the beam.

Bulk nails are usually sold by the pound; the smaller the nail, the more nails to the pound. You can buy bulk nails out of a nail keg; the nails are weighed and then priced by the retailer. Or, you can buy packaged nails, sold in boxes ranging from 1 pound to 50 pounds.

There are several different types of nails: common, box, casing, and finishing nails; brads, spikes, and nails for special applications.

Common Nails. Common nails are made from wire, cut to the proper length; they have thick heads, and can be driven into tough materials. They're used for most medium-to-heavy construction work. Common nails are available in sizes from 2d to 60d.

Box Nails. Box nails are similar to common nails, but they are both lighter and smaller in diameter. Box nails are designed for light construction and household use.

Finishing Nails and Casing Nails. Finishing nails are lighter than common nails, and have a small head. They're used primarily in building furniture. Casing nails are similar, but are heavier; they're used mostly for woodwork.

Brads. Nails less than 1 inch long are called

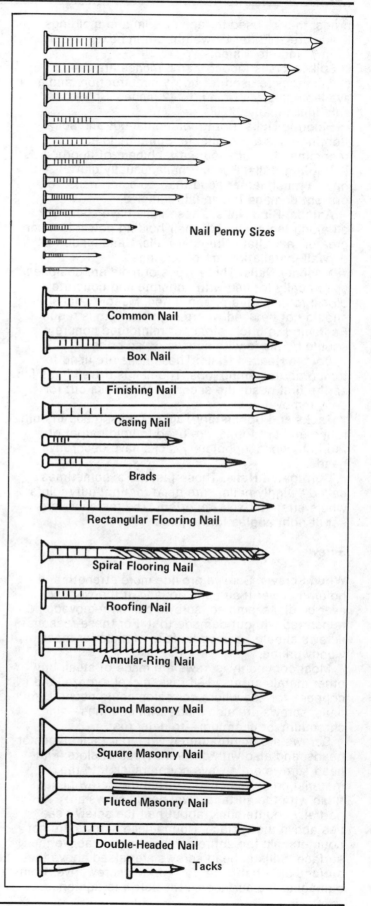

Nail Penny Sizes

Common Nail

Box Nail

Finishing Nail

Casing Nail

Brads

Rectangular Flooring Nail

Spiral Flooring Nail

Roofing Nail

Annular-Ring Nail

Round Masonry Nail

Square Masonry Nail

Fluted Masonry Nail

Double-Headed Nail

Tacks

brads; they're used to tack on trim and moldings. Brads are sold not by weight but in boxes, by size, from ³⁄₁₆ inch to 1 inch.

Spikes. Nails longer than 6 inches are called spikes; they're used for heavy construction, and are available in sizes from 6 to 12 inches. Spikes are sold individually.

Flooring Nails. Both rectangular-cut and spiral flooring nails are available. Spiral nails are recommended for secure attachment of floorboards.

Roofing Nails. Roofing nails, usually galvanized, have a much larger head than common nails, to prevent damage to asphalt shingles.

Annular-Ring Nails. These nails have sharp ridges all along the nail shaft; their holding power is much greater than that of regular nails. Nails made for drywall installation are often ringed.

Masonry Nails. Three types of nails are designed specifically for use with concrete and concrete block: round, square, and fluted. Masonry nails should not be used where high strength is required. Fastening to brick, stone, or reinforced concrete should be made with screws or lag bolts.

Double-Headed Nails. These nails are used for temporary fastening jobs. The nail is driven in as far as the first head; the second head sticks out for easy removal.

Tacks and Upholstery Tacks. Tacks, made in both round and cut forms, are used to hold carpet or fabric to wood; upholstery tacks have decorative heads.

Corrugated Nails. These fasteners, sometimes called "wiggly nails," are used for light-duty joints where strength isn't important. The fasteners are set at right angles to the joint.

Screws

Wood Screws. Screws provide more strength and holding power than nails do; and, if the work will ever be disassembled, screws can be removed and reinserted without damage to it. For these reasons, screws should be used instead of nails for most woodworking.

Most commonly, screws are made of steel, but other metals are used—brass, nickel, bronze, and copper—for use where corrosion could occur. Like nails, screws are also made with coatings—zinc, chromium, or cadmium—to deter rust.

Screws are manufactured with four basic types of heads, and also with different types of slots. Flat-head screws are always countersunk into the material being fastened, so that the screw head is flush with the surface. Oval-head screws are partially countersunk; about half the screw head lies above the surface. Round-head screws are not countersunk; the entire screw head lies above the surface. Fillister-head screws are raised above the surface on a flat base, to keep the screwdriver from damaging the surface as the screw is tightened.

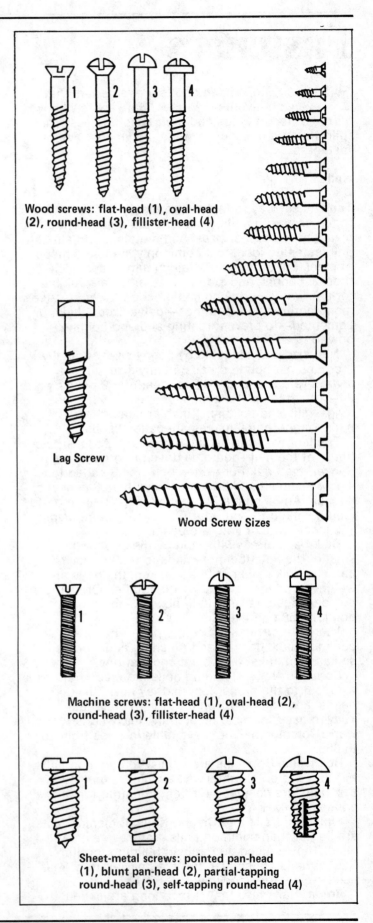

Wood screws: flat-head (1), oval-head (2), round-head (3), fillister-head (4)

Lag Screw

Wood Screw Sizes

Machine screws: flat-head (1), oval-head (2), round-head (3), fillister-head (4)

Sheet-metal screws: pointed pan-head (1), blunt pan-head (2), partial-tapping round-head (3), self-tapping round-head (4)

Most commonly, screws have plain slots, and are driven with regular blade screwdrivers. Phillips-head screws have crossed slots, and are driven with Phillips-head screwdrivers. Stopped-slot screws are less common; they're driven with a special screwdriver.

Screw size is measured in two dimensions: length, and diameter at the shank. Shank diameter is stated by gauge number, from 0 to 24. Length is measured in inches: in ⅛-inch increments from ¼ to 1 inch, in ¼-inch increments from 1 to 3 inches, and in ½-inch increments from 3 to 5 inches. All lengths are not available for all gauges, but special sizes can sometimes be ordered.

The length of screws is important: In most cases, at least half the length of the screw should extend into the base material. For example, if a piece of ¾-inch plywood is being fastened, the screws that hold it should be 1½ inches long.

To prevent the screws from splitting the materials being fastened, pilot holes must be made before the screws are driven. For small screws, pilot holes can be punched with an awl or ice pick, or even with a nail. For larger screws, drill pilot holes with a small drill or a combination drill/countersink.

Sheet-Metal Screws. Sheet-metal screws, used to fasten pieces of metal together, form threads in the metal as they are installed. There are several different types of machine screws. *Pointed pan-head screws* are coarse-threaded; they are available in gauges from 4 to 14 and lengths from ¼ inch to 2 inches. Pointed pan-heads are used in light sheet

DRILLING FOR WOOD SCREWS

Gauge Number	Decimal Diameter	Fractional Diameter	Shank Hole Twist Bit	Shank Hole Drill Gauge	PILOT HOLE HARDWOOD Twist Bit s	HARDWOOD Twist Bit p	HARDWOOD Drill Gauge s	HARDWOOD Drill Gauge p	SOFTWOOD Twist Bit s	SOFTWOOD Twist Bit p	SOFTWOOD Drill Gauge s	SOFTWOOD Drill Gauge p	Auger Bit Number	Threads Per Inch
0	.060	1/16 −	1/16	52	1/32	—	70	—	1/64	—	75	—	—	32
1	.073	5/64	5/64	47	1/32	—	66	—	1/32	—	71	—	—	28
2	.086	5/64 +	3/32	42	3/64	1/32	56	70	1/32	1/64	65	75	3	26
3	.099	3/32 +	7/64	37	1/16	1/32	54	66	3/64	1/32	58	71	4	24
4	.112	7/64 +	7/64	32	1/16	3/64	52	56	3/64	1/32	55	65	4	22
5	.125	1/8 −	1/8	30	5/64	1/16	49	54	1/16	3/64	53	58	4	20
6	.138	9/64 −	9/64	27	5/64	1/16	47	52	1/16	3/64	52	55	5	18
7	.151	5/32 −	5/32	22	3/32	5/64	44	49	1/16	3/64	51	53	5	16
8	.164	5/32 +	11/64	18	3/32	5/64	40	47	5/64	1/16	48	52	6	15
9	.177	11/64 +	3/16	14	7/64	3/32	37	44	5/64	1/16	45	51	6	14
10	.190	3/16 +	3/16	10	7/64	3/32	33	40	3/32	5/64	43	48	6	13
11	.203	13/64 −	13/64	4	1/8	7/64	31	37	3/32	5/64	40	45	7	12
12	.216	7/32 −	7/32	2	1/8	7/64	30	33	7/64	3/32	38	43	7	11
14	.242	15/64 +	1/4	D	9/64	1/8	25	31	7/64	3/32	32	40	8	10
16	.268	17/64 +	17/64	I	5/32	1/8	18	30	9/64	7/64	29	38	9	9
18	.294	19/64 −	19/64	N	3/16	9/64	13	25	9/64	7/64	26	32	10	8
20	.320	21/64 −	21/64	P	13/64	5/32	4	18	11/64	9/64	19	29	11	8
24	.372	3/8	3/8	V	7/32	3/16	1	13	3/16	9/64	15	26	12	7

s = Slotted head   p = Phillips-head

metal. *Blunt pan-head screws* are used for heavier sheet metal; they are available in gauges from 4 to 14 and lengths from ¼ inch to 2 inches. Both types of pan-head screws are available with either plain or Phillips-head slots.

Partial-tapping round-head screws have finer threads; they can be used in soft or hard metals. They are available in diameters from ³⁄₁₆ inch to 1¼ inches. *Self-tapping round-head screws* are used for heavy-duty work with thick sheet metal; they are available in diameters from gauge 2 to ¼ inch and in lengths from ⅛ inch to ¾ inch. Both types of round-head screws are available with either plain or Phillips-head slots.

Nail-type sheet-metal screws are pounded in, not screwed in; they have spiral thread-cutting shafts with pointed ends. The heads of these screws are not slotted. They are used for heavy-gauge sheet metal and for fastening other materials to metal.

Machine Screws. Machine screws are blunt-ended screws used to fasten metal parts together; they are commonly made of steel or brass. Like other fasteners, they are also made with coatings—brass, copper, nickel, zinc, cadmium, and galvanized—to deter rust. Machine screws are manufactured with the four basic types of heads—flat-head, oval-head, round-head, and fillister-head—and with both plain and Phillips-head slots. They are available in gauges 2 to 12 and diameters from ¼ inch to ½ inch, and in lengths from ¼ inch to 3 inches.

Lag Bolts. Lag bolts, while known as bolts, are actually heavy-duty screws. They are driven with a wrench, and used primarily for fastening to masonry. For light work, lead, plastic, or fiber plugs can be used to hold large screws. For larger jobs and more holding power, lead expansion anchors and lag bolts are used. The anchors are inserted into holes drilled in the masonry, and the lag bolts driven firmly into the anchors.

Bolts

Bolts are used with nuts or locknuts, and sometimes with washers. The three basic types are carriage bolts, stove bolts, and machine bolts. Other types include the masonry bolt and anchor and the toggle and expansion bolts, used to distribute weight when fastening to hollow walls.

Machine bolts are manufactured in two gauges, fine-threaded and coarse; carriage and stove bolts are coarse-threaded. Bolt size is measured by shank diameter and by threads per inch, expressed as diameter × threads—for example, as ¼ × 20. Carriage bolts are available up to 10 inches long, stove bolts up to 6 inches, and machine bolts up to 30 inches; larger sizes must usually be special-ordered.

Carriage Bolts. Carriage bolts have a round head with a square collar; they are driven with a wrench. When the bolt is tightened, the collar fits into a prebored hole or twists into the wood, preventing the bolt from turning. Carriage bolts are used in making furniture; they are coarse-threaded, and are available in diameters from ³⁄₁₆ to ¾ inch and lengths from ½ inch to 10 inches.

Stove Bolts. Stove bolts are available in a wide range of sizes. They have a slotted head—flat, oval, or round, like screws—and are driven with a screwdriver or a wrench. Most stove bolts are completely threaded, but the larger ones may have a smooth shank near the bolt head. Stove bolts can be used for almost any fastening job; they are coarse-threaded, and are available in diameters from ⁵⁄₃₂ to ½ inch and lengths from ⅜ inch to 6 inches.

Machine Bolts. Machine bolts have either a square head or a hexagonal head, and are fastened with square nuts or hex nuts; they are wrench-driven. Machine bolts are manufactured in very large sizes; the bolt diameter increases with length. They are either coarse- or fine-threaded, and are available in diameters from ¼ inch to 2 inches and lengths from ½ inch to 30 inches.

Masonry Bolts and Anchors. These bolts work on the same principle as the lag bolt or screw; a plastic sleeve expands inside a predrilled hole as the bolt is tightened. Various types and sizes are available.

Hollow-Wall Bolts. Toggle bolts and expansion bolts are used for light-duty fastening to hollow walls. Toggle bolt wings are opened by a spring inside the wall; the bolts are available in diameters from ⅛ to ½ inch and lengths up to 8 inches. Expansion bolts are inserted into an expansion jacket, which expands as the bolt is tightened; they are available for walls as thick as 1¾ inches.

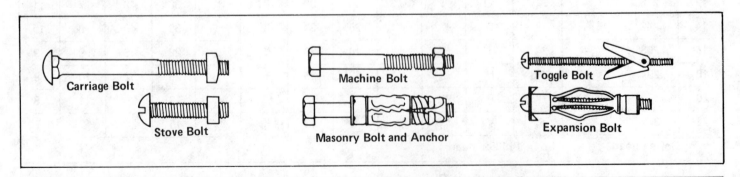

Carriage Bolt

Stove Bolt

Machine Bolt

Masonry Bolt and Anchor

Toggle Bolt

Expansion Bolt

Adhesives

IF YOU FAIL to use the right adhesive in the proper manner, you'll end up with a poor joining job every time. Here's some information on adhesives do-it-yourselfers use most frequently:

Multipurpose Adhesives

White Glue (Polyvinyl Acetate). PVA glue is a white liquid, usually sold in plastic squeeze bottles; it's recommended for use on porous materials—wood, paper, cloth, porous pottery, and nonstructural wood-to-wood bonds. It isn't water-resistant. Clamping is required for 30 minutes to one hour, until the glue sets; curing time is 18 to 24 hours. School glue, a type of white glue, dries more slowly. PVA glue dries clear. It is inexpensive and nonflammable.

Epoxy. Epoxies are sold in tubes or in cans. They consist of two parts—resin and hardener—which must be thoroughly mixed just before use. They are very strong, very durable, and very water-resistant, and are recommended for use on metal, ceramics, some plastics, and rubber; they aren't recommended for flexible surfaces. Clamping is required for about two hours for most epoxies. Drying time is about 12 hours; curing time is one to two days. Epoxy dries clear or amber. It is expensive.

Cyanoacrylate (Instant Glue). Cyanoacrylates are similar to epoxy, but are one-part glues; they form a very strong bond. They are recommended for use on metal, ceramics, glass, some plastics, and rubber; they aren't recommended for flexible surfaces. Apply very sparingly. Clamping is not required; curing time is one to two days. Cyanoacrylates dry clear. They deteriorate gradually when exposed to weather, and weaken in temperatures above 150°F. They are expensive.

Contact Cement. A rubber-based liquid sold in bottles and cans, contact cement is recommended for bonding laminates, veneers, and other large areas, and for repairs. It can also be used on paper, leather, cloth, rubber, metal, glass, and some plastics; it dries flexible. It isn't recommended for repairs where strength is necessary. Contact cement is applied to both surfaces and allowed to set; the surfaces are pressed together for an instant bond. No repositioning is possible once contact has been made; a sheet of paper can be used to prevent contact until positioning is correct. Clamping isn't required; curing is complete on drying. Contact cement is usually very flammable; it is also fairly expensive.

Polyurethane Glue. This high-strength glue is an amber paste, sold in tubes; it forms a very strong bond, similar to epoxy. Polyurethane glue is recommended for use on wood, metal, ceramics, glass, most plastics, and fiberglass; it dries flexible, and can also be used on leather, cloth, rubber, and vinyl. Clamping is required for about two hours; curing time is about 24 hours. Polyurethane glue dries translucent, and can be painted or stained; its shelf life is short, and it is expensive.

Silicone Rubber Adhesive or Sealant. The silicone rubber glues and sealants are sold in tubes; they're similar to silicone rubber caulk. They form very strong, very durable, waterproof bonds, with excellent resistance to high and low temperatures. They're recommended for use on gutters and on building materials, including metal, glass, fiberglass, rubber, and wood; they can also be used on fabrics, some plastics, and ceramics. Clamping is usually not required; curing time is about 24 hours, but the adhesive skins over in less than one hour. They dry flexible, and are available in clear, black, and metal-colored forms. They are expensive.

Household Cement. The various adhesives sold in tubes as household cement are fast-setting, low-strength glues. They are recommended for use on wood, ceramics, glass, paper, and some plastics; some dry flexible, and can be used on fabric, leather, and vinyl. Clamping is usually not required; setting time is 10 to 20 minutes, curing time up to 24 hours. Household cements are inexpensive.

Hot-Melt Adhesive. Hot-melt glues are sold in stick form and used with glue guns. A glue gun heats the adhesive above 200° F; for the best bond, the surfaces to be joined should also be preheated. Hot-melt adhesives are only moderately strong, and bonds will come apart if exposed to high temperatures; this type of glue is recommended for temporary bonds of wood, metal, paper, and some plastics and composition materials. Clamping isn't required; setting time is 10 to 45 seconds, and curing time 24 hours. Hot-melt adhesives are medium-priced; a glue gun is necessary, but the gun can be reused.

Wood Glues

Yellow Glue (Aliphatic Resin, Carpenter's Glue). Aliphatic resin glue is a yellow liquid, usually sold in plastic squeeze bottles, and often labeled as carpenter's glue. Bulk quantities are also available. Yellow glue is very similar to white glue, but is recommended specifically for general woodworking, and forms a slightly stronger bond. It is only slightly more water-resistant than white glue. Clamping is required for about 30 minutes until the glue sets; curing time is 12 to 18 hours. Yellow glue dries clear; it doesn't accept wood stains. It is usually inexpensive.

Plastic Resin Glue (Urea Formaldehyde). Plastic resin glues are sold in powder form, and mixed with water to the consistency of thick cream. They're recommended for laminating layers of wood and for gluing structural joints. Plastic resin glue is water-resistant but not waterproof, and isn't recommended for use on outdoor furniture; it is resistant to paint and lacquer thinner. Clamping is required for up to eight hours; curing time is 18 to 24 hours. Use plastic resin glue only at temperatures above 70° F. It is inexpensive.

Resorcinol Glue. This two-part glue, consisting of a liquid and a powder, is sold in cans. It is waterproof, and forms strong and durable bonds; it is recommended for use on outdoor furniture, kitchen counters, structural bonding, and boats and sporting gear; it can also be used on concrete, cork, fabrics, leather, and some plastics. Resorcinol glue has excellent resistance to temperature extremes, chemicals, and fungus. Clamping is required; curing time is 8 to 24 hours, depending on humidity and temperature. It is fairly expensive.

Hide Glue. Hide glue, the traditional woodworker's glue, is available in either liquid or flake form; the flake form must be soaked for about 12 hours in water heated to 150°F, and applied hot. Hide glue forms a strong bond, but it isn't moisture-resistant. Clamping is required; curing time is about 12 hours. Hide glue dries to a clear amber; it doesn't accept wood stains. It is expensive.

Casein glue. Casein glue is made from milk; it's sold in powder form and mixed with water to the consistency of thick cream. It forms strong bonds, and is recommended for laminating resinous or oily woods; it is moisture-resistant but isn't recommended for outdoor use. Clamping is required for about 4 hours; curing time is about 12 hours. Casein glue must be stored tightly sealed. It is moderately priced.

Adhesives for Glass and Ceramics

China and Glass Cement. Many cements are sold for mending china and glass, usually in tubes. Acrylic latex-based cements have good resistance to water and heat; other types are not recommended. Clamping is usually required.

Silicone Rubber Adhesives. Only silicone adhesives made specifically for glass and china are recommended. They form very strong bonds, with excellent resistance to water and temperature extremes. Clamping is usually required.

Metal Adhesives and Fillers

Steel Epoxy. Steel epoxy is a two-part compound sold in tubes, similar to regular epoxy. It forms a very strong, durable, heat- and water-resistant bond, and is recommended for patching gutters and gas tanks, sealing pipes, and filling rust holes. Drying time is about 12 hours; curing time is one to two days. Steel epoxy is expensive.

Steel Putty. This metal putty consists of two putty-consistency parts, which are kneaded together before use. It forms a strong, water-resistant bond, and is recommended for patching and for sealing pipes that aren't under pressure; it can also be used for ceramic and masonry. Curing time is about 30 minutes; when dry, it can be sanded or painted. Steel putty is expensive.

Plastic Metal Cement. Plastic metal is a one-part adhesive and filler; it is moisture-resistant but cannot withstand temperature extremes. It is recommended for use on metal, glass, concrete, and wood, where strength is not required. Curing time is about four hours; when dry, it can be sanded or painted. Plastic metal cement is moderately expensive.

Plastic Adhesives

Model Cement. Model cements are usually sold in tubes as "model maker" glues. They form a strong bond on acrylics and polystyrenes, and can be used on most plastics; don't use them on plastic foam. Clamping is usually required until the cement has set, about 10 minutes; curing time is about 24 hours. Model cement dries clear, and is inexpensive.

Vinyl Adhesive. Vinyl adhesives, sold in tubes, form a strong, waterproof bond on vinyl and on many plastics; don't use them on plastic foam. Clamping is usually not required. Vinyl adhesive dries flexible and clear; curing time is 10 to 20 minutes. Vinyl adhesive is inexpensive.

Acrylic Solvent. Solvents are not adhesives as such; they act by melting the acrylic bonding surfaces to fuse them together at the joint. They are recommended for use on acrylics and polycarbonates. Clamping is required; the bonding surfaces are clamped or taped together and the solvent is injected into the joint with a syringe. Setting time is about five minutes. Solvents are inexpensive.

Glues for Flexible Repairs

Plastic Rubber (Neoprene). Plastic rubber, a thick cream, seals and bonds rubber, leather, vinyl, and rubberized fabric; it can also be used on shoes, and on wood, metal, glass, and some plastic. Clamping is usually not required, but weighting in place is recommended; curing time is about one hour. Plastic rubber is medium-priced.

Shoe Repair (Nitrile-Phenolic) Adhesive. Nitrile-phenolics form a strong, durable bond on leather and canvas; they are recommended for heavy-duty mending jobs on shoes and boots, and can also be used on wood, metal, ceramic, and some plastics. The adhesive is applied to both surfaces and allowed to set, like contact cement; bonding is immediate and permanent when the two bonding surfaces make contact. Nitrile-phenolics are moderately expensive.

Latex Fabric Mender. Latex fabric menders are water-based, and can be used on all fabrics; they can also be used on leather and on some plastics. Fabric menders are recommended for low-strength repairs, but they can be washed and dried. No clamping or weighting is required; curing time is about 20 minutes. Fabric menders are inexpensive.

Construction and Building Adhesives

Construction Adhesive. This heavy-duty adhesive is sold in cartridges and in bulk containers. It forms a strong, fast bond, and is recommended for use on wood, drywall, paneling, flooring, rigid foam, and masonry; it can also be used on uneven surfaces. Some support is required on vertical surfaces; curing time is about 30 minutes. The adhesive dries medium-brown. Construction adhesives are moderately priced.

Synthetic Rubber Adhesives. Synthetic rubber is a thick paste, sold in cans; it is waterproof, and is recommended for heavy-duty bonding of metal, glass, masonry, fixtures, and some plastics. It can be used for bonding over uneven surfaces, and to fill gaps or horizontal or vertical surfaces. Clamping is required, especially on vertical surfaces. Setting time is about four hours; curing time is about two days. Synthetic rubber is available in black or white, and can be sanded or painted when dry. It is moderately expensive.

Floor and Wallcovering Adhesives. Floor covering adhesives are available for indoor and outdoor use; the outdoor types are water-resistant. Clamping isn't required for floor and wall adhesives; setting time is about 25 minutes. These adhesives are medium-priced.

Fixture Adhesive. This mastic-type adhesive is very similar to construction or synthetic rubber adhesives, but it is sold in small tubes. Fixture adhesives are water-resistant or waterproof, and setting time is about 20 minutes. They are fairly expensive.

Metric Conversion Tables

To Convert From	To Convert To Metric — To	Multiply By	To Convert From	To Convert From Metric — To	Multiply By
	Length			**Length**	
inches	centimeters	2.54	millimeters	inches	0.03937
inches	meters	0.0254	centimeters	inches	0.3937
feet	centimeters	30.48	meters	feet	3.2808
yards	meters	0.9144	meters	yards	1.094
miles	kilometers	1.609	kilometers	miles	0.62137
	Area			**Area**	
square inches	square centimeters	6.452	square centimeters	square inches	0.155
square feet	square meters	0.0929	square meters	square feet	10.765
square yards	square meters	0.836	square meters	square yards	1.196
square miles	square kilometers	2.589998	square kilometers	square miles	0.3861
acres	hectares	0.40468	hectares	acres	2.471
	Mass			**Mass**	
ounces	grams	28.34952	grams	ounces	0.03527
pounds	kilograms	0.453592	kilograms	pounds	2.20462
tons (short) (2000 lbs.)	metric ton (tonnes)	0.907185	metric tons (tonnes) (1000 kg.)	tons (short)	1.10231
	Volume			**Volume**	
fluid ounces	milliliters	29.57353	milliliters	fluid ounces	0.0338
pints	liters	0.47318	liters	pints	2.11338
quarts	liters	0.946333	liters	quarts	1.05669
gallons	liters	3.7853	liters	gallons	0.2642
cubic feet	cubic meters	0.028317	cubic meters	cubic feet	35.3145
cubic yards	cubic meters	0.76456	cubic meters	cubic yards	1.30795
	Temperature			**Temperature**	
Fahrenheit	Celsius (centigrade)	5/9 after subtracting 32	Celsius (centigrade)	Fahrenheit	9/5 and then add 32

Directory of Manufacturers

Abitibi-Price Corp.
3250 W. Big Beaver Rd.
Troy, MI 48084

Acme Burgess, Inc.
Rt. 83
Grayslake, IL 60030

Acme Metal Mfg. Co.
7500 State Rd.
Philadelphia, PA 19136

Adjusta-Post Mfg. Co.
P.O. Box 71
Norton, OH 44203

The AFA Corp.
14201 N.W. 60th Ave.
Miami Lakes, FL 33014

Air Care Industries, Inc.
Union, IL 60180

Air Care convertible range hoods

Alumin-Nu Nice n Easy aluminum door and window cleaner

Air Control Industries, Inc.
213 McLemore St.
Nashville, TN 37203

**Aladdin Products Div.,
Hybrinetics, Inc.**
P.O. Box 1329
225 Sutton Place
Santa Rosa, CA 95402

**ALH, Inc.
A Subsidiary of Aladdin
Industries, Inc.**
P.O. Box 100255
Nashville, TN 37210

Alliance Mfg. Co., Inc.
27290 Lake Park Blvd.
Alliance, OH 44601

Allway Tools, Inc.
1513 Olmstead Ave.
Bronx, NY 10462

Alsons Corp.
525 E. Edna Place
P.O. Box 311
Covina, CA 91723

Alumin-Nu Corp.
5141 Northfield Rd.
Bedford Heights, OH 44146

American Lock Co.
3400 W. Exchange Rd.
Crete, IL 60417

American Metal Products Co.
6100 Bandini Blvd.
Los Angeles, CA 90040

American Safety Razor Co.
Razor Blade Lane
Verona, VA 24482

Ames Lawn & Garden Tool Co.
P.O. Box 1774
Parkersburg, WV 26102

AMF/Paragon Electric Co., Inc.
606 Parkway Blvd.
P.O. Box 28
Two Rivers, WI 54241

Water heater timer from AMF/Paragon

Aminco Industries, Inc.
9811 Valley View Rd.
Eden Prairie, MN 55344

Anderson Metal Products Corp. (AMPCOR)
111 Fellowship Rd.
Taylorsville, MS 39168

Anderson-Barrows Metals Corp.
4514 Vanowen St.
Burbank, CA 91505

Armstrong World Industries, Inc.
P.O. Box 3001
Lancaster, PA 17604

Armstrong's Woodstock Random Plank vinyl floor covering

Arrow Fastener Co., Inc.
271 Mayhill
Saddle Brook, NJ 07662

Bartlett Mfg. Co.
3033 E. Grand Blvd.
Detroit, MI 48202

Bauer Corp.
1505 E. Bowman
Wooster, OH 44691

Baxt Industries, Inc.
15606 Wright Brothers Dr.
Addison, TX 75001

Bede Industries
8327 Clinton Rd.
Cleveland, OH 44144

Benson Mfg. Corp.
14700 W. Commerce Dr.
Menomonee Falls, WI 53051

Biolet Corp.
P.O. Box 645
Beatrice, NE 68310

Bissell, Inc.
2345 Walker Rd., N.W.
Grand Rapids, MI 49504

Black & Decker (U.S.), Inc.
701 E. Joppa Rd.
Towson, MD 21204

Blue Lustre Home Care Products
7950 Castleway Dr.
Indianapolis, IN 46250

Boekamp, Inc.
8221 Arjons Dr.
San Diego, CA 92126

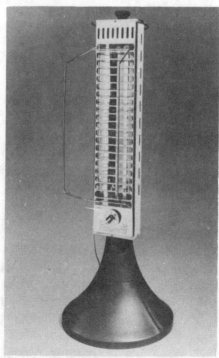

Boekamp portable quartz heater

Borden Chemical Div.
Borden, Inc.
180 E. Broad St., 16th Flr.
Columbus, OH 43215

Boss Mfg. Co.
221 W. First St.
Kewanee, IL 61443

Bostik Consumer Div.
Emhart Corp.
4408 Pottsville Pike
P.O. Box 3716
Reading, PA 19605

BQP Industries
4747 Ironton St.
Denver, CO 80239

Bradley Corp.
P.O. Box 348
Menomonee Falls, WI 53051

Brickmate Industries, Inc.
13-15 131st St.
College Point, NY 11356

Bruce Hardwood Floors Div.
Triangle Pacific Corp.
16803 Dallas Parkway
Dallas, TX 75248

BSR (USA), Ltd.
Route 303
Blauvelt, NY 10913

Cable Electric Products, Inc.
P.O. Box 6767
Providence, RI 02940

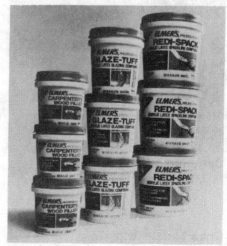

Elmer's latex-based building adhesives from Borden Chemical

Directory of Manufacturers

Calder Mfg. Co.
1322 Loop Rd.
Lancaster, PA 17601

Campbell Chain Div.
McGraw-Edison Co.
3990 E. Market St.
York, PA 17402

Carbona Products Co.
330 Calyer St.
Brooklyn, NY 11222

Carlon
An Indian Head Co.
23200 Chagrin Blvd.
Cleveland, OH 44122

Carol Cable Co.
P.O. Box 68
Pawtucket, RI 02862

The Celotex Corp.
P.O. Box 22602
Tampa, FL 33622

Celotex insulating shutters for windows
and patio doors

Certainteed Corp.
P.O. Box 860
Valley Forge, PA 19482

Chamberlain Mfg. Corp.
845 Larch Ave.
Elmhurst, IL 60126

Champ Corp.
22N159 Pepper Rd.
Barrington, IL 60010

Channellock, Inc.
1306 S. Main St.
Meadville, PA 16335

Charnas Industries, Inc.
341 Broad St.
Manchester, CT 06040

Chicago Metallic Corp.
4849 S. Austin Ave.
Chicago, IL 60638

Chicago Specialty Mfg. Co.
5700 N. Linder Ave.
Skokie, IL 60076

Clauss Cutlery Co.
223 N. Prospect
Fremont, OH 43420

Cling-Surface Co., Inc.
P.O. Box 31
Orchard Park, NY 14127

Clopay Corp.
Household Products Div.
101 E. 4th St.
Cincinnati, OH 45202

Clopay Corporation's Custom Mate
folding door

Clorox Co.
P.O. Box 24305
Oakland, CA 94623

The Colombia Moulding Co.
A Jim Walter Co.
4747 Hollins Ferry Rd.
Baltimore, MD 21227

Comfort Enterprises Co.
P.O. Box 323
Leola, PA 17540

Commodore Consumer
Products Group
761 Fifth Ave.
King of Prussia, PA 19406

Con-Serv, Inc.
7745 Reinhold Dr.
Cincinnati, OH 45237

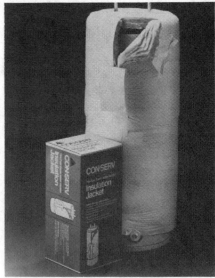

Con-Serv water heater insulation jacket

Construction Templates, Inc.
RFD 4, Nasonville
Woonsocket, RI 02895

Contractors Wardrobe, Inc.
21050 Superior St.
Chatsworth, CA 91311

The Cooper Group
P.O. Box 728
Apex, NC 27502

Cord-A-Way Industries
2401-55th Ave., N.
Minneapolis, MN 55430

CRC Chemicals, Inc.
885 Louis Dr.
Warminster, PA 18974

The Crest Co.
P.O. Box 1100
Jackson, NJ 08527

Cyclone Seeder Co., Inc.
A Div. of Jackson Mfg. Co.
P.O. Box 1649
Harrisburg, PA 17105

Ross Daniels, Inc.
1720 Fuller Rd.
West Des Moines, IA 50265

DAP, Inc.
P.O. Box 277
Dayton, OH 45401

Darworth Co.
P.O. Box K
Avon, CT 06001

Decor International
Wallcoverings, Inc.
37-39 Crescent St.
Long Island City, NY 11101

Deflect-o Corp.
7035 East 86th St.
Indianapolis, IN 46250

DeLonghi-America
350 Fifth Ave.
New York, NY 10118

W. J. Dennis & Co.
1111 Davis Rd.
Elgin, IL 60120

Desa Industries
25000 S. Western Ave.
Park Forest, IL 60466

Remington power hammer from Desa Industries

Desco Industries, Inc.
351 Oak Place
Brea, CA 92621

Design and Funding, Inc.
2500 Office Center, 1st Flr.
Maryland Rd.
Willow Road, PA 19090

Dike Div.
Gibralter Cement Products Co.
48 W. State Fair Ave.
Detroit, MI 48203

Dimplix Heating, Ltd.
1492 High Ridge Rd.
Stamford, CT 06903

Disston
1030 W. Market St.
Greensboro, NC 27401

Diversified Specialties, Inc.
Durkee-Atwood Co.
215 N.E. 7th St.
Minneapolis, MN 55413

Domino Engineering Corp.
Box 376
Taylorville, IL 62568

Douglas Products
Box 1774
Parkersburg, WV 26101

Dow Chemical U.S.A.
Styrofoam Brand Products
Midland, MI 48640

Dow Corning
Consumer Products Div.
Midland, MI 48640

Duo-Fast Corp.
Consumer Products Div.
3702 River Rd.
Franklin Park, IL 60131

Dur-A-Flex, Inc.
100 Meadow St.
Hartford, CT 06114

Dynatron/Bondo Corp.
2160 Hills Ave., N.W.
Atlanta, GA 30318

3E Corp.
401 Kennedy Blvd.
Somerdale, NJ 08083

Easco Tools, Inc.
6721 Baymeadow Dr.
Glen Burnie, MD 21061

Eastern Safety Equipment Co.
45-17 Pearson St.
Long Island City, NY 11101

Easy Heat-Wirekraft Div.
Bristol Corp.
U.S. 20 East
New Carlisle, IN 46552

Elco Industries, Inc.
1111 Samuelson Rd.
Rockford, IL 61109

Electripak, Inc.
A Subsidiary of Perfect-Line
Mfg. Corp.
175 S. Smith St.
P.O. Box 262
Lindenhurst, NY 11757

Elgar Products, Inc.
P.O. Box 22348
Beachwood, OH 44122

Embee Corp.
552 W. State St.
Springfield, OH 45506

**Emerson Environmental
Products Div.
Emerson Electric Co.**
8400 Pershall Rd.
Hazelwood, MO 63042

Emerson model HD133 console humidifier

Empire Brushes, Inc.
U.S. Highway 13 North
Greenville, NC 27834

Enderes Tool Co., Inc.
P.O. Box 691
Albert Lea, MN 56007

EnerCon, Inc.
30048 Lakeland Blvd.
Wicklitte, OH 44092

The Enterprise Companies
1191 South Wheeling Rd.
Wheeling, IL 60090

Estwing Mfg. Co., Inc.
2647 Eighth St.
Rockford, IL 61101

E-Tech, Inc.
3570 American Dr.
Atlanta, GA 30341

**Evans Paint Div.
Evans Products Co.**
1516 Cleveland Ave.
Roanoke, VA 24015

Exact Level & Tool Mfg. Co., Inc.
100 West Main St.
High Bridge, NJ 08829

**EZ Paintr Corp.
A Newell Co.**
4051 S. Iowa Ave.
Milwaukee, WI 53207

**Faultless Div.
Bliss & Laughlin Industries**
1421 N. Garvin St.
Evansville, IN 47711

Feather-Lite Mfg. Co.
P.O. Box 1159
Troy, MI 48099

Feather-Lite rolling storm door

**Fillpro Div.
JH Industries**
980 Rancheros Dr.
San Marcos, CA 92069

The Fletcher-Terry Co.
Spring Lane
Farmington, CT 06032

Fluidmaster, Inc.
1800 Via Burton
Anaheim, CA 92805

Forbo North America, Inc.
218 W. Orange St.
Lancaster, PA 17603

Franklin Chemical Industries
P.O. Box 07802
2020 Bruck St.
Columbus, OH 43207

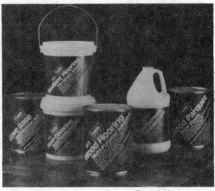

*Flooring adhesives from Franklin
Chemical Industries*

Frelen Corp.
74 Salem Rd.
North Billerica, MA 01862

**GAF Corp.
Consumer Products Group/Floor
Products**
140 West 51st St.
New York, NY 10020

*GAF's GAFSTAR floor cleaner and
floor finish*

Garelick Mfg. Co.
644 2nd St.
St. Paul Park, MN 55071

**General Electric Co.
Silicone Products Div.
RTV Products Dept.**
Waterford, NY 12188

**General Electric Co.
Wiring Device Dept.**
P.O. Box 1050
Warwick, RI 02886

General Hardware Mfg. Co., Inc.
80 White St.
New York, NY 10013

Genova, Inc.
7034 E. Court St.
Davison, MI 48423

Genova Snap-Fit roof flashing

Georgia-Pacific Corp.
900 S.W. 5th Ave.
Portland, OR 97204

Gila River Products
6615 W. Boston St.
Chandler, AZ 85224

Globe Products Co.
2000 E. Federal
Baltimore, MD 21213

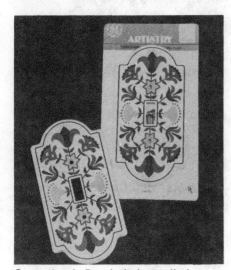

*Pennsylvania Dutch-design wall plate
from General Electric*

Glow Master Div.
TG Industries, Inc.
P.O. Box 108
Armstrong, IA 50514

Gold Bond Building Products Div.
National Gypsum Co.
2001 Rexford Rd.
Charlotte, NC 28211

Gold Bond Decorator paneling

Goldblatt Tool Co.
511 Osage
Kansas City, KS 66110

Goodyear Tire & Rubber Co.
Goodyear Adhesives &
Sealant Div.
1745 Cottage St.
Ashland, OH 44805

Grace Construction Products Div.
W. R. Grace & Co.
62 Wittemore Ave.
Cambridge, MA 02140

Great Vibrations by Interbath, Inc.
427 N. Baldwin Park Blvd.
City of Industry, CA 91746

Gries Dynacast Div.
Coats & Clark, Inc.
125 Beechwood Ave.
New Rochelle, NY 10802

G. T. Water Products, Inc.
19438 Business Center Dr.
Northridge, CA 91324

GTE Lighting Products
Sylvania Lighting Center
Danvers, MA 01923

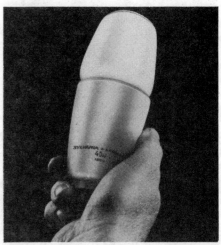

*Sylvania metal-halide lamp developed
by GTE*

Gulf Adhesives & Resins
Gulf Oil Chemicals Co.
8900 Indian Creek Pky.
P.O. Box 10911
Overland Park, KS 66210

Hamilton Beach/Dominion
Scoville Housewares Group
59 Mill St.
Waterbury, CT 06720

Hanover Wire Cloth
E. Middle St.
Hanover, PA 17331

Harrington Tools, Inc.
4316 Alger St.
Los Angeles, CA 90039

Hartco
P.O. Box A
Oneida, TN 37841

Hartline Products Co., Inc.
2186 Noble Rd.
Cleveland, OH 44112

Heath Co.
Benton Harbor, MI 49022

Vic Heath Enterprises
P.O. Box 368
Tustin, CA 92680

Hempe Mfg. Co., Inc.
2750 S. 163rd St.
New Berlin, WI 53151

Hillwood Mfg. Co.
21700 St. Clair Ave.
Cleveland, OH 44117

Hillwood masonry nails

HMS Industries, Inc.
P.O. Box E
1200 Boston Post Rd.
Guilford, CT 06437

*Lift Off paint and varnish stripper from
Homagic*

Homagic Div.
Midco Products Co., Inc.
11697 Fairgrove Industrial Blvd.
St. Louis, MO 63043

Home Equipment Mfg. Co.
Div. of Kenton Industries, Inc.
14481 Olive St.
Westminster, CA 92683

Homelite Div.
Textron, Inc.
P.O. Box 7047
Charlotte, NC 28217

Homelite ST-20 electric trimmer

Howmet Aluminum Corp.
Building Products Div.
6235 W. 73rd
Bedford Park, IL 60638

*Howmet's Weather Breaker insulated
garage door*

Hull Manufacturing Co.
P.O. Box 246
Warren, OH 44482

Hyde Mfg. Co.
54 Eastford Rd.
Southbridge, MA 01550

Illinois Bronze Paint Co.
300 E. Main St.
Lake Zurich, IL 60047

Insta-Foam Products, Inc.
Consumer Products Div.
1550 Cedar Wood Dr.
Joliet, IL 60435

Irwin Auger Bit Co.
92 Grant Ave.
Wilmington, OH 45177

ITT Holub
1701 Bethany Rd.
Sycamore, IL 60178

JAB Industries, Inc.
11 East 26th St.
New York, NY 10010

Jackes-Evans Mfg. Co.,
A Div. of GSW, Inc.
4427 Geraldine Ave.
St. Louis, MO 63115

Jade Controls
P.O. Box 271
Montclair, CA 91763

Jefco Laboratories
618 W. Jackson Blvd.
Chicago, IL 60606

Johns-Manville Corp.
P.O. Drawer 17L
Denver, CO 80217

Judsen Rubber Works, Inc.
4107 W. Kinzie St.
Chicago, IL 60624

Kelley Mfg. Co.
P.O. Box 1317
Houston, TX 77001

Kester Solder Div.
Litton Industries
4201 Wrightwood Ave.
Chicago, IL 60639

Keystone Brass & Rubber Co.
500 Maryland Dr.
Fort Washington, PA 19034

King Cotton Cordage Co.
A Div. of John H. Graham
Co., Inc.
617 Oradell Ave.
Oradell, NJ 07649

King Koal Div.
Bohanna and Pearce, Inc.
P.O. Box 576
San Leandro, CA 94577

Kirsch Co.
Sturgis, MI 49091

The Continental curtain rod from Kirsch

Klean Strip Div.
W. M. Barr Co.
P.O. Box 1879
Memphis, TN 38101

Kohler Co.
Kohler, WI 53044

Le Gran pedestal lavatory from Kohler

Kwik Mix, Inc.
Box 4, Stoney Creek
Ontario, Canada L8G 3X7

Leslie-Locke Div.
Questor Corp.
2872 W. Market St.
Akron, OH 44313

St. Moritz ceiling fan by Leslie-Locke

Leviton Mfg. Co., Inc.
59-25 Little Neck Pky.
New York, NY 11362

Levolor Lorentzen, Inc.
1280 Wall St., W.
Lyndhurst, NJ 07071

Riviera mini-slat blinds by Levolor

Liteway Corp.
1119 Beaver St.
Bristol, PA 19007

Litton Industries
New Britain Tool Div.
P.O. Box 1320
South St.
New Britain, CT 06050

Loctite Corp.
4450 Cranwood Ct.
Cleveland, OH 44128

Duro plastic aluminum from Loctite

Lomanco, Inc.
P.O. Box 519
Jacksonville, AR 72076

Lynnwood Distributing Co., Inc.
P.O. Drawer T
140 Greenwood Ave.
Midland Park, NJ 07432

Macco Adhesives
30400 Lakeland Blvd.
Wickliffe, OH 44092

Magic American Chemical Co.
23700 Mercantile Rd.
Cleveland, OH 44122

Magic plastic window cleaner from Magic American Chemical

Magic Touch Mfg. Corp.
1140 Broadway
New York, NY 10001

Magnolia Products
P.O. Box 1367
Columbus, MS 39701

Magnolia Products' wood-grain finish toilet seat

Marion Tool Corp.
P.O. Box 365
Marion, IN 46952

Marshall Brass Co.
450 Leggit Rd.
Marshall, MI 49068

Marshalltown Trowel Co.
P.O. Box 738
Marshalltown, IA 50158

Masonite Corp.
20 N. Wacker Dr.
Chicago, IL 60606

Mateflex-Mele Mfg. Co.
1712 Erie St.
Utica, NY 13503

Mayes Brothers Tool Mfg. Co.
P.O. Box 1018
Claremont Dr.
Johnson City, TN 37601

Mayhew Steel Products Co.
Shelburne Falls, MA 01370

Pilot punch set from Mayhew Steel Products

McCoy Industries, Inc.
1201 Distel Dr.
Lafayette, CO 80026

Mechanical Plastics Corp.
Castleton St.
P.O. Box 328
Pleasantville, NY 10570

Melard Mfg. Corp.
153 Linden St.
Passaic, NJ 07055

Mercer Plastics Co., Inc.
1 Jabez St.
Newark, NJ 07105

Michigan Production Grinding Co.
A Div. of Core Industries
1 Coreway Dr.
Pioneer, OH 43554

Michlin Chemical Corp.
9045 Vincent
Detroit, MI 48211

Middlefield Corp.
P.O. Box 795
Middlefield, OH 44062

The K. J. Miller Corp.
22711 County Rd. 14 E.
Elkhart, IN 46516

Millers Falls Div.
Ingersoll-Rand Co.
Deerfield Industrial Park
South Deerfield, MA 01373

Moeller Mfg. Co., Inc.
Box 1318
Greenville, MS 38701

Montgomery Ward & Co., Inc.
Montgomery Ward Plaza, 20N
Chicago, IL 60671

Mortell Co.
550 Hobbie Ave.
Kankakee, IL 60901

Moss Mfg., Inc.
7600 N.W. 69th Ave.
Miami, FL 33165

Multicore Solders
Contiague Rock Rd.
Westbury, NY 11590

MYRO, Inc.
1987 W. Purdue St.
Milwaukee, WI 53209

MYRO Window Seal self-adhesive sealer

Mystik Corp.
60 Happ Rd.
Northfield, IL 60093

Nautilus Industries
P.O. Box 159
Hartford, WI 53027

Nautilus Infinite Speed NY Series convertible range hood

Neill Tools, Inc.
417 Woodmont Rd.
Milford, CT 06460

New Britain Tool Div.
Litton Industries
P.O. Box 1320
South St.
New Britain, CT 06050

New York Bronze Co., Inc.
201 Bay Ave.
Elizabeth, NJ 07201

Nichols-Homeshield, Inc.
Neverust Div.
1000 N. Harvester Rd.
West Chicago, IL 60185

Utility shed from Nichols-Homeshield

Nomaco, Inc.
Decorative Div.
Hershey Dr.
Ansonia, CT 06401

North American Philips
Lighting Corp.
Bank St.
Hightstown, NJ 08520

Notifier Co.
A Div. of Emhart Industries, Inc.
560 Alaska Ave.
Torrance, CA 90503

NuTone Housing Group
Madison and Red Bank Rds.
Cincinnati, OH 45227

O'Malley Valve Co.
4228 8th Ave., S.
St. Petersburg, FL 33711

Omark Industries
Consumer Products Group
4909 International Way
Milwaukie, OR 97222

Omni Corp.
Box 305
South Holland, IL 60473

Omni low-flow faucet attachment

Owens-Corning Fiberglas
Fiberglas Tower
Toledo, OH 43659

Pacific Hardware Mfg. Co.
1331 Old County Rd.
Belmont, CA 94002

Padco, Inc.
2220 Elm St., S.E.
Minneapolis, MN 55414

Padco shake pad painter

Panef Mfg. Co.
5700 W. Douglas Ave.
Milwaukee, WI 53218

Parr, Inc.
A Subsidiary of Koppers
18400 Syracuse Ave.
Cleveland, OH 44110

Directory of Manufacturers

Patrician Products, Inc.
468 Union Ave.
Westbury, NY 11590

Patton Electric Co., Inc.
P.O. Box 128
15012 Edgerton Rd.
New Haven, IN 46774

Peerless Faucet Co.
A Div. of Masco Corp. of Indiana
55 E. 111th St.
Indianapolis, IN 46280

Pella/Rolscreen Co.
100 Main St.
Pella, IA 50219

Pella passthrough folding door from Rolscreen

Permabond International Corp.
480 S. Dean St.
Englewood, NJ 07631

Phifer Wire Products, Inc.
P.O. Box 1700
Tuscaloosa, AL 35403

Philstone Nail Corp.
56 Pine
Canton, MA 02021

Pioneer Energy Products, Inc.
3065 Cranberry Hwy.
Onset, MA 02558

Plaskolite, Inc.
Box 1497
1770 Joyce Ave.
Columbus, OH 43216

Plasti-kote, Inc.
1000 Lake Dr.
Medina, OH 44256

Power Controls Corp.
P.O. Box 5860
San Antonio, TX 78201

Prestolite Electronics
An Allied Co.
511 Hamilton St.
Toledo, OH 43694

Quaker City Mfg. Co.
701 Chester Pike
Sharon Hill, PA 19079

Red Devil, Inc.
2400 Vauxhall Rd.
Union, NJ 07083

Regency Electronics, Inc.
7707 Records St.
Indianapolis, IN 46226

Revere Chemical Corp.
30809 Carter St.
Solon, OH 44139

Reynolds Metals Co.
Box 27003
Richmond, VA 23261

Transluscent light panel manufactured by Plaskolite

Rich Ladder Co.
P.O. Box 120
515 Seventh St.
Carrollton, KY 41008

Riteway Mfg. Co., Inc.
100 Triangle Dr.
P.O. Box 99
Weyers Cave, VA 24486

Roberts Consolidated Industries
600 N. Baldwin Park Blvd.
City of Industry, CA 91749

Rockford Products Corp.
A Subsidiary of Rexnord Corp.
Box 6306
Rockford, IL 61125

Frank T. Ross & Sons, Inc., U.S.A.
P.O. Box 248
West Hill, Ontario Canada
M1E 4R5

Rubberset Co. Div.
Sherwin-Williams
P.O. Box 231
Crisfield, MD 21817

W. J. Ruscoe Co.
483 Kenmore Blvd.
Akron, OH 44301

Ryan Lawn-Care Products
McClure St.
Galesburg, IL 61401

Sandstrom Products Co.
224 Main St.
Port Byron, IL 61275

Scandy Rubber Corp.
2067 Broadway, Suite 63
New York, NY 10023

Schaefer Brush Mfg. Co., Inc.
117 W. Walker St.
Milwaukee, WI 53204

Schalk Chemicals Div.
Red Devil, Inc.
2400 Vauxhall Rd.
Union, NJ 07083

Scotch Mfg. Co., Inc.
P.O. Box 4466
Dallas, TX 75208

Scovill Security Products Div.
P.O. Box 25288
Charlotte, NC 28212

Screen Patch Co.
1012 James Blvd.
Signal Mountain, TN 37377

Screws to Go
P.O. Box 1143
Kent, WA 98031

Sealeze Corp.
8011 Whitebark Ter.
Richmond, VA 23234

Sears, Roebuck and Co.
Sears Tower
Chicago, IL 60684

Seatek Co.
392 Pacific St.
Stamford, CT 06902

Sell-Even, Inc.
P.O. Box 247
Reedsville, WI 54230

Sem-Torq, Inc.
P.O. Box 46406
Bedford, OH 44146

Seymour of Sycamore, Inc.
917 Crosby Ave.
Sycamore, IL 60178

Shepherd Products U.S., Inc.
203 Kerth St.
St. Joseph, MI 49085

Shop-Vac Corp.
2323 Reach Rd.
Williamsport, PA 17701

Sinkmaster, Anaheim Mfg.,
A Div. of Tappan
4240 E. LaPalma Ave.
Anaheim, CA 92803

S-K Hand Tool Div.
Dresser Industries
3201 N. Wolf Rd.
Franklin Park, IL 60131

Slide-Co.
P.O. Box 2428
Montclair, CA 91763

Seymour Smith & Sons
900 Main St.
Oakville, CT 06779

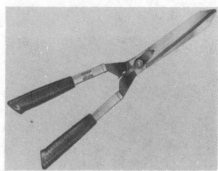

Snap-Cut hedge shears from Seymour Smith & Sons

Sparkle Plenty, Inc.
233 E. Erie St., Suite 304
Chicago, IL 60611

Stanley Hardware Div./Door Systems Div./Tools Div.
The Stanley Works
Box 1800
New Britain, CT 06050

Star Expansion Co.
Mountainville, NY 10953

Sterling Div.
Avnet, Inc.
249 Roosevelt Ave.
Pawtucket, RI 02862

Sunnyside Corp.
Consumer Products Div.
225 Carpenter Ave.
Wheeling, IL 60090

Supplex Div.
Amerace Corp.
P.O. Box 509
Worthington, OH 43085

Swivelier Co., Inc.
33 Route 304
Nanuet, NY 10954

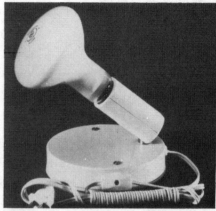

Lite-Flex adjustable lampholder by Swivelier

Symonds & Co.
333 N. Michigan Ave.
Chicago, IL 60601

The Synkoloid Co.
P.O. Box 60937
Los Angeles, CA 90060

Teco
5530 Washington Ave.
Chevy Chase, MD 20815

Stanley Surform tool

Directory of Manufacturers

Thermal-Chem, Inc.
1400 Louis Ave.
Elk Grove Village, IL 60007

**Thermo Energy
Amalgamated Mfg. Corp.**
175 W. Stratford Ave.
Salt Lake City, UT 84115

Thermwell Products Co., Inc.
150 E. 7th St.
Paterson, NJ 07524

Thoro System Products
7800 N.W. 38th St.
Miami, FL 33166

3E Corp.
401 Kennedy Blvd.
P.O. Box 177
Somerdale, NJ 08083

**3M Co. Household &
Hardware Div.**
223-1N
St. Paul, MN 55144

3M Wall Repair Compound

Tjernlund Products, Inc.
1620 Terrace Dr.
St. Paul, MN 55113

Triangle Importing, Inc.
51 Fernwood Ln.
Roslyn, NY 11576

**Trine Consumer Products Div.
Square D Co.**
1430 Ferris Pl.
Bronx, NY 10461

**True Temper
Hardware Div.**
1623 Euclid Ave.
Cleveland, OH 44115

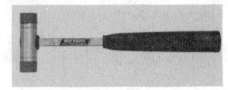

Soft-Tip hammer from True Temper

Twinoak Products, Inc.
RR 2, Box 56
Plano, IL 60546

Union Fork & Hoe Co.
500 Dublin Ave.
Columbus, OH 43216

United Gilsonite Laboratories
P.O. Box 70
Scranton, PA 18501

UGL AC-88 all-purpose acrylic caulk

United States Gypsum Co.
101 S. Wacker Dr.
Chicago, IL 60606

United Steel Products
P.O. Box 80
Montgomery, MN 56069

Universal Fastenings Corp.
45 Gilpin Ave.
Hauppauge, NY 11788

U.S. Brass
901 Tenth St.
Plano, TX 75074

U.S.E. Diamond, Inc.
P.O. Box 1589
York, PA 17405

Vaco Products Co.
1510 Skokie Blvd.
Northbrook, IL 60062

**Van Leer Plastics
Valvac Products Div.**
64 Industrial Pky.
Woburn, MA 01888

Velsicol Chemical Corp.
341 E. Ohio St.
Chicago, IL 60611

Vermont Weatherboard, Inc.
15 W. Church St.
Hardwick, VT 05843

Vydel Corp. of America
1660 Old Deerfield Rd.
Highland Park, IL 60635

*Durabond wallboard compound from
U.S. Gypsum*

Wahl Clipper Corp.
2902 N. Locust St.
Sterling, IL 61081

Warner Mfg. Co.
13435 Industrial Park Blvd.
Minneapolis, MN 55441

Wartian Lock Co.
20525 E. Nine Mile Rd.
St. Clair Shores, MI 48080

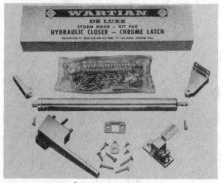

Wartian Lock's storm door parts kit

Waxman Industries, Inc.
24460 Aurora Rd.
Cleveland, OH 44146

Weather Shield Mfg., Inc.
531 N. 8th St.
Medford, WI 54451

Weber-Stephen Products Co.
100 N. Hickory
Arlington Heights, IL 60004

Wen Products, Inc.
5810 Northwest Hwy.
Chicago, IL 60631

R. D. Werner Co., Inc.
P.O. Box 580
Greenville, PA 16125

R.D. Werner's extension ladder

Wing Industries
P.O. Box 38347
Dallas, TX 75238

Wingaersheek Div.
Victor Equipment Co.
18 Cherry Hill Dr.
Danvers, MA 01923

Wolverine Fan Co.
P.O. Box 1171
Jackson, MI 49204

Wrightway Mfg. Co.
1050 Central Ave.
Park Forest South, IL 60466

Z-Brick Co.
A Div. of V.M.C. Corp.
13929 N.E. 190 St.
Woodinville, WA 98072

Z-Brick facing brick and Ruff-It acrylic sculpture coat

William Zinsser & Co., Inc.
39 Belmont Dr.
Somerset, NJ 08873

Index

Index